Author's Acknowledgements

It is almost twenty five years since I first walked into a sixth-form histo
ought to be there for I had only squeaked through 'O' level history wit
That lesson was my first real introduction to the Tudors and, in the process of writing this book, I have
been very aware of how much I owe to those who taught me then and helped me since, both in teaching
in general and with this book in particular. This page gives me the chance to say thank you.

Four people gave confidence to that nervous ex-fifth former – J.A. Shields and E.R. Shears made history
both challenging and interesting without recourse to decision-making games, role-plays or, dare I say it,
sources; Dr. N. Russell made the study of Shakespeare, Chaucer and Milton such a delight that I almost
abandoned history there and then and Arthur Emmott kept my priorities in order by insisting I play cricket
even during the exam period. All provided a model of caring and rigorous teaching that I was most
fortunate to encounter.

As a student I benefited from Nicholas Pronay's demands for precision and critical evaluation and Bob
Unwin's belief that history teaching should be exciting. Maurice Smith, Doris Brooks and Jack Thompson
demonstrated that teaching is a profession and turned a student into a teacher. More recently, Frances
Blow, Tony Boddington, Joe Scott and Denis Shemilt helped me understand far more about teaching and
learning history than I was aware I didn't know. Perhaps most importantly of all I have been lucky in the
people I have taught, from the fondly-remembered C3/IGD to the cast of Snow White and the Wars of the
Roses and beyond. The best bits of this book are a product of what I learned from my pupils and students.

As the latecomer to the challenge of Challenging History I owe a great deal to the team who built up the
idea and structure of the series. The other authors, John Traynor, Eric Wilmot, Howard Martin and Neil
Tonge shared their ideas and early drafts with great generosity. Michael Jones had provided constructive
praise whenever it was most needed. John Jones has encouraged, advised, suggested and given me the
chance to "develop" the series style. The job of Series Editor is a difficult one. John has been superb.

Besides John and Michael I am most grateful to two others who had the stamina to read the whole book
in draft. Dr. Steven Gunn of Merton College, Oxford, provided impeccable academic advice, matched
only by the tact with which he suggested amendments. Barbara Mervyn of Pensby High School for Girls
gave me the advice of a skilled and perceptive teacher and did much to maintain my confidence in the
project. Finally I must thank Dorothy Barbour for entertaining my family on cold, wet Scottish beaches
while I scribbled away and Pam Bishop who typed nearly all of this book with great speed and accuracy
and made my task indescribably easier.

To the reader I would like to say that I see this book as a bridge, helping students to gain a grasp of
issues and arguments before tackling the more demanding works of research historians. If it succeeds in
helping students both to use and enjoy such work it will have achieved its goal. In terms of content, even a
book this size has to omit something. There is little here on intellectual movements and plenty on
personality politics. I could blame the syllabus – but I won't. The balance of content and the mistakes that
are doubtless here somewhere are solely the responsibility of the subjectivity and limitations of the author.

The greatest debt of all is the one I have left until last for without their encouragement, forebearance and
support I would neither have started nor completed this book.

For Pat and Matthew, with my love and thanks for sharing the fun and enjoyment of history despite the
unaccountable absence of equations.

Ian Dawson

Contents

The People and their Rulers

The Tudor Century?

The room was already half-full of men, some seated around the table in conversation with their neighbours, others standing, talking in groups of two or three. Despite the busy sound of their voices, most were only half-listening to their colleagues, their glances checking the other figures in the room and noting new arrivals. Occasionally, individuals broke off to greet friends and draw them into the security of a group. From the sounds of the conversations an eavesdropper would have been aware of an atmosphere of caution and uncertainty mixed, in different quarters, with sparkles of confidence and self-congratulation.

Such may have been the atmosphere in early September 1485 at the first meetings of Henry VII's council. Henry had been king for no more than two weeks, having been suddenly transformed from Henry Tudor, exiled Earl of Richmond, into Henry, by the Grace of God, King of England and of France and Lord of Ireland. The confident ones amongst his councillors were those who had shared his dangerous exile in Brittany and France. The cautious and uncertain were those who had served Richard III and would still be doing so had Richard not been killed on the battlefield near Market Bosworth.

It was scarcely a month since Henry had landed his forces, a mixed group of French, Welsh and English, in Wales. They had marched east, not knowing how large an army Richard had collected. When the two armies met, Henry had still not known whether his potentially strongest allies, the Stanleys, would fight for him or against him. When Richard and his bodyguard had ridden down Henry's standard-bearer it had looked as if Richard might seize the victory by killing Henry with his own hand. Then Sir William Stanley's men had made their move. They had charged into Richard's household knights, scattering them and beating Richard to the ground, knocking his crown from his helm. For the first time since 1066 an English king had been killed in battle.

Some of the councillors awaiting the arrival of Henry still ached with the effects of the battle – bruises that had still to disappear, scars that would stay with them for life. And they had other reasons for keeping the battle sharply in mind. Some of Richard's soldiers were in prison awaiting the new king's judgement. Most had managed to escape and some of them were doubtless planning rebellion against the new regime. One or two, including Richard's nephew and heir, the Earl of Lincoln, were actually in the council chamber, a consequence of Henry's need to win over as many former enemies as possible.

Indeed, with Henry's coronation only a few weeks away, everyone present faced a new situation. For some Henry was a new and unknown leader. For others he was their deliverer from a hunted and landless exile but they still had to grow used to him as their sovereign. As they awaited his arrival, all of them knew that their own futures depended on the new king. If Henry was successful they would, more than likely, be secure and prosperous. If he failed and was deposed their likely fate would be either death, exile or imprisonment. At best, they would be fearfully attempting to win the confidence of yet another new monarch.

THEMES AND QUESTIONS

That reconstruction of the thoughts and feelings of Henry VII's councillors in 1485 suggests just how important the personality and character of a king was at that time. This had been abundantly clear during the previous thirty years, the period we call the Wars of the Roses. Back in the 1450s the king had been Henry VI. During his reign England's lands in France were lost and peace at home was destroyed because Henry could not enforce law and order. Noblemen squabbled and fought for lands and other rewards given away by Henry VI with foolish generosity. Henry's failings led to the civil wars but, from their beginnings in 1455 to Henry VII's victory at Bosworth in 1485, people of all classes retained a desire for a strong, effective ruler who would give the country peace and security.

The major theme of this book will be the extent to which the Tudor monarchs gave the people of England peace, security and wealth. Accompanying this question are three other issues (shown in the diagram) which will be discussed in each section of the book. Given this emphasis upon monarchy the main sections of the book, sections 1 – 4, focus upon monarchs, identifying and discussing the important elements of each Tudor reign – foreign policy, religious reforms, law and order, poverty and prosperity, leading politicians and their impact. Part 1, in contrast, provides a necessary introduction, looking at how people lived in the sixteenth century, what kind of ideas and beliefs they had and how they were governed. By the end of the book you will be well versed in the details of Tudor kingship and politics but will also have considered these much broader questions which will give continuity to your studies, preventing your work on the Tudors disintegrating into a set of unrelated topics.

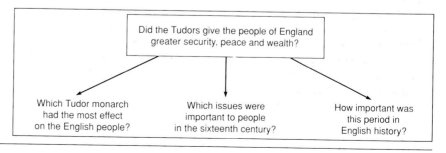

Did the Tudors give the people of England greater security, peace and wealth?

Which Tudor monarch had the most effect on the English people?

Which issues were important to people in the sixteenth century?

How important was this period in English history?

A timeline of events 1485 – 1547

1485	Battle of Bosworth. Accession of Henry VII.
1487	Invasion of England led by pretender, Lambert Simnel.
1489	Treaty of Medina del Campo with Spain. Tax riots in north.
1491	Beginning of threat from the pretender, Perkin Warbeck.
1492	Invasion of France, Henry granted pension at Treaty of Etaples.
1494	Beginning of French wars in Italy.
1495	Yorkist conspiracy discovered.
1497	Cornish Rebellion, complaining about taxation.
1499	Execution of Warbeck and Warwick, the Yorkist heir.
1501	Marriage of Prince Arthur to Catherine of Aragon.
1502	Death of Prince Arthur. Prince Henry is now the only male heir.
1509	Death of Henry VII. Accession of Henry VIII, married Catherine of Aragon.
1512	Invasion of France.
1513	Victory over Scots at Flodden.
1514	Peace with France. Wolsey emerging as Henry's chief minister.
1518	Treaty of London – European peace.
1520	Field of Cloth of Gold – meetings with Francis I of France.
1523	Invasions of France.
1525	Rioting against taxes.
1527	Beginning of Henry's quest for divorce from Catherine of Aragon. Poor harvests 1527–9.
1529	Fall of Wolsey. Calling of the 'Reformation' Parliament (to 1536).
1532	Thomas More's resignation as Chancellor. Thomas Cromwell chief minister.
1583	Henry married Anne Boleyn. Thomas Cranmer Archbishop of Canterbury.
1534	Act of Supremacy established Henry as Head of the Church of England.
1536	Dissolution of monasteries begun. Pilgrimage of Grace, a major revolt in the north.
1537	Good harvests to mid 1540s
1539	Publication of Great Bible in English.
1540	Fall of Cromwell.
1542	War against Scotland. Coinage debased.
1544	Sack of Edinburgh. Invasion of France. Rising food prices.
1545	French invasion threat. Sinking of Mary Rose.
1547	Death of Henry VIII. Accession of Edward VI.

A timeline of events 1547 – 1603

1547	Death of Henry VIII, Accession of Edward VI. Somerset becomes Protector. Move to more radical Protestantism.
1549	Rebellions in south-west and East Anglia. Fall of Somerset. First of three poor harvests.
1550	Northumberland chief minister. Abandonment of French and Scottish wars.
1551	Epidemic disease.
1553	Death of Edward VI. Accession of Mary. Attempt to make Jane Grey queen.
1554	Wyatt's rebellion. Mary marries Philip of Spain.
1555	Papal Supremacy restored. First Protestant martyrs burned.
1556	Worst harvest of century leading to epidemic disease.
1557	War with France, leading to loss of Calais in 1559.
1558	Death of Mary. Accession of Elizabeth.
1559	Elizabeth's religious settlement establishes a moderate Protestant religion.
1562	Elizabeth nearly dies from smallpox.
1568	Mary, Queen of Scots begins captivity in England.
1569	Incidents lead to deterioration in Anglo-Spanish relationship. Rising of Northern Earls.
1571	Ridolfi plot to depose Elizabeth.
1572	Duke of Norfolk executed for involvement in plots.
1576	Peter Wentworth challenges Elizabeth's right to decide what Parliament discusses.
1577	Drake begins circumnavigation of world.
1579	Irish rebellion begins (to 83).
1580	Jesuit priests arrive secretly in England.
1583	Throckmorton plot to depose Elizabeth.
1585	Outbreak of war with Spain – English troops sent to fight Netherlands.
1586	Babington plot to depose Elizabeth.
1587	Execution of Mary Queen of Scots.
1588	Spanish Armada defeated.
1593	Beginning of major rebellion in Ireland.
1594	First of four poor harvests.
1596	Second Spanish Armada blown off course by gales.
1598	Poor Law legislation to help poor but deter vagabonds. Death of Lord Burghley.
1599	Essex's campaign in Ireland fails.
1601	Essex's revolt and execution.
1603	Death of Elizabeth. Accession of James I. Irish rebellion defeated.

THE TUDOR MONARCHS

Some of the Tudor monarchs are well-known today. Others are not. Yet as kings and queens they all had some impact on the people of their own time. In what ways did they affect the people of England and which of them had the most impact on their people? By using the information below and on pages 4 – 5 to answer these questions you can start to develop your ideas about sixteenth-century monarchy and government, a basis on which you can build in the detailed chapters that follow. Beginning with an outline answer and then extending it by adding detail is the most effective way to learn. If you start with a lot of detail you may get lost in it very quickly!

1 Using the family tree and the timelines on pages 4 – 5,

(a) What relation was each ruler to his or her predecessor?

(b) Can you identify any times when a different successor to a monarch was expected?

(c) Were there any times when the Tudor dynasty was in danger because of the lack of an heir?

2 Which events or issues do you think were of the most concern to ordinary people?

3 Which Tudor monarch do you think had the most impact on his or her people? Explain the reasons for your choice.

TALKING POINT

What criteria would you use to decide how much impact a monarch had on his or her people?

What ideas do you already have about the personalities and achievements of each of the Tudor rulers?

HENRY VII.

EDWARD VI.

HENRY VIII.

MARY TUDOR.

ELIZABETH I.

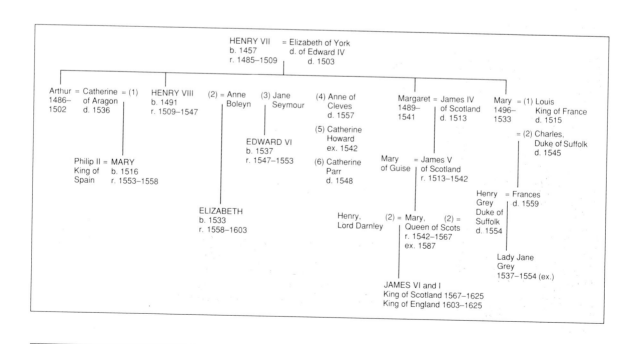

1 Tudor People – at Home and at Work

Preview

When we look back at the past, particularly the distant past, we usually feel grateful that we live now, not then. 500 years after the Tudor period, we may feel positively smug about our heating, lighting and refrigeration, ease of transport and entertainment at the press of a button. If we aren't careful we might feel sorry for those crude and simple people who lived miserable lives and had no such developments to be proud of. This, of course, is the way our descendants will feel about us in the year 2200 AD!

It is also probably the way people in the sixteenth century felt about those who lived in the 1200s and 1300s; those poor souls who didn't have the advantage of the latest Tudor technologies, fashions and comforts. This chapter allows you to investigate the people of the Tudor Century – what they were like, how they lived and the degree of change they were experiencing. But first, what had been happening to living conditions in the fifteenth century?

Source A

... The riches of England are greater than those of any other country in Europe, as I have been told by the oldest and most experienced merchants, and also as I myself can vouch, from what I have seen. This is owing, in the first place, to the great fertility of the soil. ... there is no small innkeeper, however poor and humble he may be, who does not serve his table with silver dishes and drinking cups; and no one, who has not in his house silver plate to the amount of at least £100 sterling, ... is considered by the English to be a person of any consequence, ... there is not a parish church in the kingdom so mean as not to possess crucifixes, candlesticks, censers, patens and cups of silver.

from a report on England written by a Venetian envoy to England in 1497.

Source B

... the inhabitants of [England] are rich, abounding in gold and silver and all the necessities of life. They do not drink water, except those who sometimes abstain from other drinks by way of devotional or penitential zeal. They eat every kind of flesh and fish in abundance, ... They are clothed with good woollens ... they have abundant bedding, woollen like the rest of their furnishings, in all their houses, and are rich in all household goods and agricultural equipment, and in all that is requisite for a quiet and happy life, according to their estate.

from Sir John Fortescue's *De Laudibus Legum Anglie*, written in the 1460s, for the instruction of Prince Edward, son of Henry VI.

1 What had been the pattern of population development since 1300?

2 What had happened to the value of wages in the 1400s?

3 What were the connections between population change and wages?

4 Women had more opportunities for independence in the 1400s. Can you work out why?

5 Sources A and B give descriptions of standards of living in the fifteenth century:

(a) Which of these accounts do you think is the more reliable?

(b) Do you think people did feel prosperous at the time Henry Tudor became king?

DURING THE FIFTEENTH CENTURY WOMEN HAD MORE OPPORTUNITY FOR INDEPENDENCE. THEY WERE RUNNING THEIR OWN BUSINESSES AND COULD JOIN GUILDS. IN SHEFFIELD TWO WOMEN WORKED AS BLACKSMITHS. MANY TOOK THE OPPORTUNITY TO MARRY LATER.

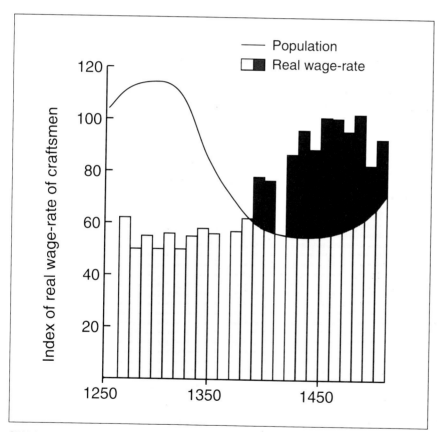

CHANGES IN THE ENGLISH POPULATION ARE SHOWN BY THE CONTINUOUS LINE. THE BAR GRAPH SHOWS THE CHANGING VALUE OF WAGES.

English Society – the Social Classes

In medieval England the great majority of people belonged to one of three classes. They were either landowners (noblemen, knights and gentry) or freemen (who might be merchants in towns or agricultural workers of varying degrees of wealth) or villeins (unfree peasants tied to their land and lord). The Black Death and the Peasants' Revolt in 1381 largely ended villeinage. By the sixteenth century people identified four classes but it was becoming harder to observe the boundaries between classes and easier for people to cross class boundaries. Thomas Wolsey, the son of a butcher, became Archbishop of York and Henry VIII's chief councillor! Here is one description of the class structure in the sixteenth century, written in 1565 by Sir Thomas Smith, a member of the royal council, in his commentary on England, De Republica Anglorum.

A TUDOR NOBLEMAN. IT HAS BEEN SUGGESTED THAT THE YOUNG MAN IS ROBERT DEVEREUX, EARL OF ESSEX, WHO WAS ONE OF ELIZABETH'S FAVOURITES.

'We in England divide our men commonly into four sorts, gentlemen, citizens or burgesses, yeomen artificers and labourers.

Of the first part of gentlemen of England called nobilitas maior: Dukes, marquises, earls, viscounts, and barons, either be created of the prince or come to that honour by being the eldest sons, or highest in succession.

Of the second sort of gentlemen which may be called nobilitas minor, and first of knights: No man is a Knight by succession ... Knights therefore be not born but made ... knights in England are most commonly made according to the yearly revenue of their lands being able to maintain that estate ...

Of esquires: ... be all those which bear arms ... a testimony of the nobility or race from which they come.

Of gentlemen: Gentlemen be those whom their blood and race doth make noble ... for that their ancestor hath been notable in riches or for his virtues. Which if the successors do keep and follow, they be 'vere nobiles' ... If they do not, the fame and riches of their ancestors serve to cover them so long as it can, as a thing once gilted though it be copper within, till the gilt be worn away ... gentlemen they be made good cheap in England. For whosoever studieth the laws of the realm, who studieth in the universities, who professeth liberal sciences, and to be short who can live idly and without manual labour, and will bear the port, charge and countenance of a gentleman, he shall be called master, ...

Of citizens and burgesses: Next to a gentlemen, be appointed citizens and burgesses, such as not only be freed and received as officers within the cities, but also be of some substance to bear the charges...

Of yeomen: ... I call him a yeoman ... which is a freeman born English, who may dispend of his own free land in yearly revenue to the sum of xl.s sterling ... This sort of people confess themselves to be no gentlemen, and yet they have certain preeminence and more estimation than labourers and artificers, and commonly live wealthily, keep good houses, do their business, and work to get riches: they be (for the most part) farmers to gentlemen, ... by these means do come to such wealth, but they are able and daily do buy the lands of unthrifty gentlemen, and after setting their sons to the schools, to the Universities, to the law of the Realm or otherwise leaving them sufficient lands wheron they may labour, do make their said sons by these means gentlemen ...

Of the fourth sort of men which do not rule: The fourth sort or class amongst us is ... day labourers, poor husbandmen, merchants or retailers which have no free land, copyholders, all artificers, as tailors, shoemakers, carpenters, brickmakers, bricklayers, masons, etc. These have no voice nor authority in our commonwealth, and no account is made of these but only to be ruled, not to rule other, and yet they be not altogether neglected. For in cities and corporate towns for default of yeomen, they make up their inquests of such manner of people. And in villages they be commonly made Church-wardens, inspectors of ale, and many times Constables ...'

1 Why do you think 'the first sort' was split into more categories?

2 What evidence is there in these extracts of class mobility?

3 What were the responsibilities of the classes?

4 Why had it become easier for people to move through the classes?

EXAMINING THE EVIDENCE
Population, Prices and Wealth

The country's population had fallen by around 30 per cent in the fourteenth century and remained low in the fifteenth century. This dramatic change helped many people, especially those lower in society. They became more prosperous as their wages bought more goods. Landowners struggled, receiving less in rents and for produce while paying out higher wages. Some towns were also hard-hit by the fall in population. The fewer the people, the less trade there was. Winchester, for example, complained of poverty, claiming that it could no longer afford to repair the town's walls, pay for burgesses to attend parliaments or pay the taxes required by the crown. Many citizens of Winchester left the town, rather than ruin themselves by paying such expenses. As a result Winchester was 'desolate of people', a place of 'decay and ruin'. Other towns, however, prospered because of their local industries. The wool and cloth towns of East Anglia and the Cotswolds boomed and the people rebuilt their churches from their profits. We can still see evidence of this today.

But what of the Tudor period? Did the population rise and prosperity increase? The sources in this section offer you the chance to decide whether the sixteenth century was a good time to be alive. What happened to the towns? What conclusion can you reach based on the evidence of the following pages?

1 Using Sources A and B describe the patterns of

(a) national and

(b) urban population growth.

2 Was England a prosperous country according to Sources C – F?

3 How important a role did London play in English life?

4 Look at Sources G – J. Which factors limited the extent of population growth?

Source A

The Population of England and Wales, 1541–1661
The population of England (estimated to the nearest 1,000) at quinquennial intervals 1541–1601

1541	2,774,000	(2,968,000)
1546	2,854,000	(3,054,000)
1551	3,011,000	(3,222,000)
1556	3,159,000	(3,380,000)
1561	2,985,000	(3,194,000)
1566	3,128,000	(3,347,000)
1571	3,271,000	(3,500,000)
1576	3,413.000	(3,652,000)
1581	3,598,000	(3,850,000)
1586	3,806,000	(4,072,000)
1591	3,899,000	(4,172,000)
1596	4,012,000	(4,293,000)
1601	4,110,000	(4,398,000)

The figures in brackets are estimates for the population of England and Wales together. They are obtained by adding a 7% allowance for the population of Wales to each of the English population figures.

Source B
Estimates of the Populations of Major Towns

City/town	1520s		c. 1600
Metropolitan London	60,000	(1582) 100,000–120,000	185,000–215,000
Norwich	8,000–12,000	(1579) 17,000–18,000	15,000
Bristol	10,000	12,000	
York	8,000	(1548) 8,000	11,500
Exeter	8,000	9,000	
Newcastle upon Tyne		(1547) 6,000–7,000	9,000
King's Lynn	4,500	8,000	
Coventry	7,500–6,000	(1563) 4,000–5,000	7,000
Salisbury	8,000	7,000	
Plymouth		(1549) 4,000 7,000–8,000	
Cambridge	2,600	(1563) 2,000–2,500	6,500
		(1587) 5,000	
Oxford	5,000	(1547) 5,500	6,500
Ipswich	3,000–4,000	5,500	
Canterbury	3,000	(1563) 2,800–3,500	5,000
Colchester	3,000–4,000	5,000	
Yarmouth	4,000		5,000–8,000
Shrewsbury		(1563) 2,700–3,400	5,000
Worcester		(1563) 4,000–5,000	5,000
Chester		(1563) 4,000–5,000	5,000

Source C

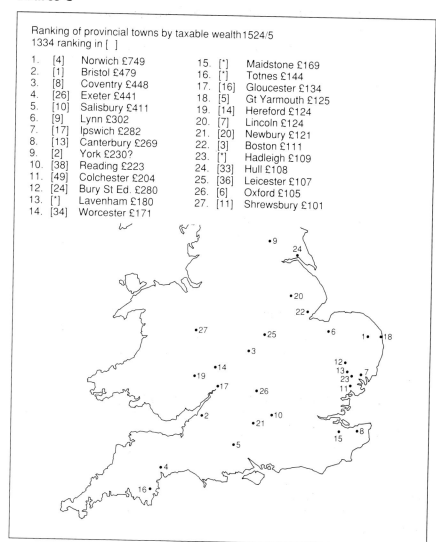

Ranking of provincial towns by taxable wealth 1524/5
1334 ranking in [ ]

1.	[4]	Norwich £749
2.	[1]	Bristol £479
3.	[8]	Coventry £448
4.	[26]	Exeter £441
5.	[10]	Salisbury £411
6.	[9]	Lynn £302
7.	[17]	Ipswich £282
8.	[13]	Canterbury £269
9.	[2]	York £230?
10.	[38]	Reading £223
11.	[49]	Colchester £204
12.	[24]	Bury St Ed. £280
13.	[*]	Lavenham £180
14.	[34]	Worcester £171
15.	[*]	Maidstone £169
16.	[*]	Totnes £144
17.	[16]	Gloucester £134
18.	[5]	Gt Yarmouth £125
19.	[14]	Hereford £124
20.	[7]	Lincoln £124
21.	[20]	Newbury £121
22.	[3]	Boston £111
23.	[*]	Hadleigh £109
24.	[33]	Hull £108
25.	[36]	Leicester £107
26.	[6]	Oxford £105
27.	[11]	Shrewsbury £101

THE MAJOR ENGLISH TOWNS IN 1524/5 ACCORDING TO TAXABLE RETURNS.

Source D

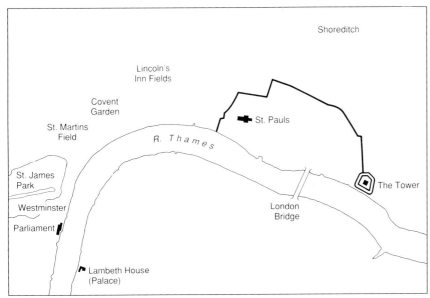

LONDON IN THE SIXTEENTH CENTURY. COMPARE THIS ILLUSTRATION WITH A MODERN MAP OF LONDON. WHICH MAJOR LANDMARKS TODAY WOULD NOT HAVE BEEN WITHIN THE WALLS OF TUDOR LONDON?

Source E

Whereas it pleased the Queen's Majesty more than two years past to command proclamation to be published for the restraining and prohibiting of new building of houses and tenements for habitation in and about the City of London, whereby as by the access of multitudes of people to inhabit the same and the 'perstering' of many families in small houses or tenements termed 'inmats and undersitters', the City has been over largely increased to the decay of other towns, boroughs and villages within the Realm.

from a letter sent to the Queen's council in 1590.

Source F

There were about 30 European cities with over 40,000 inhabitants, 11 in Italy, 7 in Spain, 6 in France, but only 1, London, in the British Isles. Their national populations were also much higher, but that was not the only reason. The Netherlands, with a combined northern and southern population less than England's, had seven cities of over 40,000 by 1600: Amsterdam, Antwerp, Ghent, Brussels, Bruges, Leiden and Haarlem. Giovanni Botero (1588) considered that 'in England, London excepted ... there is not a city ... that deserves to be called great,' while the Swiss Platter (1599) thought that whoever had visited London and the neighbouring royal palaces 'may assert without impertinence that he is properly acquainted with England'.

D M Palliser, *The Age of Elizabeth, 1547–1603*, 1983.

TALKING POINT

Societies with growing populations are often confident societies. How might confidence affect population growth? Why might a society be confident?

Source G

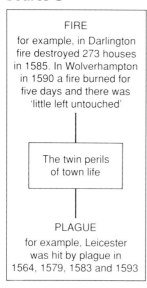

FIRE
for example, in Darlington fire destroyed 273 houses in 1585. In Wolverhampton in 1590 a fire burned for five days and there was 'little left untouched'

The twin perils of town life

PLAGUE
for example, Leicester was hit by plague in 1564, 1579, 1583 and 1593

Source H

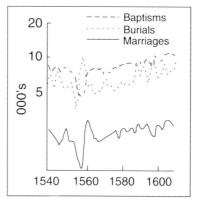

THE PATTERN OF BIRTHS, MARRIAGES AND DEATHS IN TUDOR ENGLAND.

Source I (a)

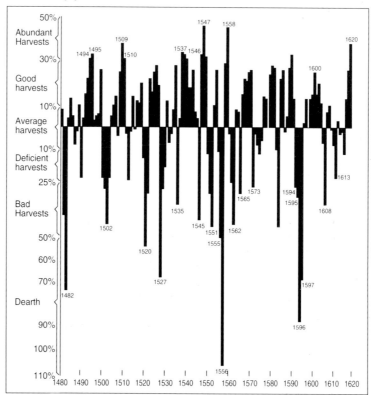

THE QUALITY OF HARVESTS DURING THE TUDOR CENTURY. HISTORIANS' ANALYSES DIFFER AS SHOWN IN THESE TABLES.

Source I (b)

Decade	Wheat (Hoskins) Abundant, & Good	Deficient, Bad, & Dearth	Average of all grains (Bowden) Abundant, & Good	Deficient, Bad, & Dearth
1470–9	–	–	6	0
1480–9	1	3	3	3
1490–9	5	1	5	0
1500–9	3	4	3	2
1510–9	5	2	6	0
1520–9	5	5	4	5
1530–9	5	1	5	3
1540–9	6	2	8	2
1550–9	4	4	1	5
1560–9	5	3	4	0
1570–9	4	2	4	1
1580–9	5	1	4	2
1590–9	4	4	5	3
1600–9	6	1	6	1
1610–9	2	2	3	3
1620–9	4	1	4	0

Source L

Indexes of (1) the price of a composite unit of foodstuffs, (2) the price of a sample of industrial products (1451–75 = 100).

	(1)	(2)
1451–60	98	99
1461–70	105	103
1471–80	93	100
1481–90	121	103
1491–1500	100	97
1501–10	106	98
1511–20	116	102
1521–30	159	110
1531–40	161	110
1541–50	217	127
1551–60	315	186
1561–70	298	218
1571–80	341	223
1581–90	389	230
1591–1600	530	238
1601–10	527	256

Source J

And albeit it has pleased God of his great goodness ... to bless this land both with peace and the fruit of peace now by the space almost of 27 years; yet let us not forget, that within those 7 years next going before, there was such a scarcity of corn within the realm of England, that the common people, in most parts of the land, were glad to make their bread of acorns.

Sir William Cecil, recalling the impact of the bad harvests in the 1550s.

Source K

Estimates of the purchasing power of the wages of agricultural labourers and building craftsmen in the south of England (1450–99 = 100).

	Agricultural labourer	Building craftsman
1450–59	105	104
1460–69	100	100
1470–79	104	103
1480–89	86	93
1490–99	104	103
1500–09	97	96
1510–19	89	88
1520–29	80	76
1530–39	80	68
1540–49	71	70
1550–59	59	51
1560–69	66	62
1570–79	69	64
1580–89	57	57
1590–99	49	47
1600–09	50	46

5 Draw a graph to show the changes in the wage rates of agricultural labourers and building craftsmen, using the figures in Source K.

6 Draw graphs to show the pattern of inflation in (a) food prices and (b) industrial prices, using the figures given in Source L.

7 The purchasing power of a building craftsman's wage in 1597 was down to 29. This was the lowest level ever between the mid-thirteenth century and mid-twentieth century. Why do you think it was so low in 1597?

8 Which group or groups in society would find life most difficult at times of inflation?

Source M

THE LEADING OCCUPATIONS IN SIX TOWNS

Chester 1558–1603		Leicester 1559–1603		Norwich 1569		Nottingham 1580–1620		Worcester 1540–89		York 1550–1600	
Shoemakers	120	Tailors	67	Worsted weavers	166	Butchers	115	Weavers	77	Tailors	309
Glovers	76	Tanners	63	Grocers	150	Cordwainers	83	Clothiers	45	Merchants	301
Tailors	76	Butchers	63	Tailors	146	Glovers	81	Mercers	28	Bakers	153
Tanners	73	Shoemakers	53	Cordwainers	59	Tanners	62	Walkers	26	Cordwainers	143
Ironmongers	68	Glovers	43	Mercers	48	Tailors	42	Drapers	16	Butchers	128
Merchants	65	Bakers	37	Dornix weavers	35	Bakers	41	Brewers	16	Tanners	127
Bakers	57	Mercers	36	Hatters	35	Blacksmiths	34	Shoemakers	15	Innholders	109
Drapers	55	Weavers	30	Tanners	34	Joiners	17	Tailors	14	Glovers	98
Weavers	55	Chandlers	20	Bakers	32	Mercers	17	Butchers	12	Carpenters	83
Butchers	52	Smiths	20	Carpenters	31	Ropers	17	Tanners	11	Drapers	78
Shearmen	51			Butchers		Fishmongers	14	Barbers	11	Tilers	71
Mercers	47			Masons	26	Yeomen	14	Smiths	11	Joiners	60

Source N

PERCENTAGE OF WORKERS IN DIFFERENT JOBS IN TOWNS

	Chester 1558–1603	Hull 1580–89	Leicester 1559–1603	Norwich 1558–80	Nottingham 1580–1620	Worcester 1540–89	York 1550–1600
Textiles	11.2	2.5	6.6	17.1	3.8	42	6.3
Clothing	10.0	9.5	16.4	16.7	6.2	4	16.0
Leather	23.9	7.5	16.9	12.2	34.2	11	15.3
Metal	11.2	4.5		5.9	9.1	7	10.6
Woodwork	4.7	–	6.2	2.5	3.2	–	–
Building	6.2	1.9	5.9	10.2	5.1	2	–
Food and drink and transport	13.3	8.9	18.6	12.3	26.7	12	8.6
Distributive	16.6	56.7	6.7	20.6	7.6	12	20.1
Professional	1.8	–		2.1	1.0		14.2
Others	1.2	8.3	22.7	0.6	3.2	9	8.9

9 What seem to have been the dominant industries in each of the towns in Sources M and N?

10 What are the chief similarities and differences among the towns in Sources M and N?

11 How does the evidence in Sources M and N show that much trade and industry in towns was closely connected with agriculture?

Source P

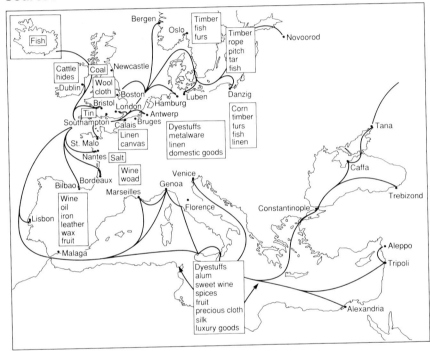

IMPORTS AND EXPORTS IN THE LATER MIDDLE AGES.

Source O

THE BASIS OF ENGLAND'S WEALTH WAS HER TRADE IN WOOL AND FINISHED CLOTH. ANTWERP AND THE LOW COUNTRIES WAS THE CENTRE OF THIS TRADE.

12 How do the imports shown in Source P suggest that English people were leading more comfortable lives in the sixteenth century?

13 What has the evidence in this section told you about the quality of daily life under the Tudors?

Examining the Evidence
Homes, Possessions and Fashions

Statistics and graphs provide a good overview of English life in the sixteenth century. However it is important to look at other kinds of evidence; at the details of individual lives and at the views and opinions of contemporaries. Does the material in this section provide further evidence to support your answer to question 13 on page 18?

Source A
Thomas Jackson of Wymondham, Gentleman

1590/1, March 21. An inventorye of all the goods and chattles which weare Thomas Jacksonns late of Wymondham in the Countye of Norffolke gent deceased taken and prysed the xxjth of Marche Anno Domini 1590 by William Burden gent Thomas Weld gent Thomas Horsnaylle gent and Robert Dey as followeth.

	£	s	d.
In apparell			
Inpr[imis] 3 hats		13	4
Item 3 cloaks	1	10	0
Item 3 doublets	2	0	0
Item 4 paier of hose	2	0	0
Item 2 freze jerkins		3	4
Item 4 paier of stockins	1	0	0
Item 2 paier of garters		1	8
Item 2 girdles		1	6
Item one purse		1	6
Item an old gowne		10	0
Item one paier of bootes and bootehose		3	4
Item 12 bandes 5 shirtes cuffs handkerchers and other smalle lynnen	1	6	8
Some	9	11	4
Item bookes	1	0	0
Item one lute	1	0	0
Item a paier of virginalls	1	6	8
Item one birdinge peece		13	4
Item a sworde		*	8
Item an old geldinge with a bridle and a sadle	2	0	0
Item a deske and other smalle things in the same		2	*
Item 2 trunckes and 2 chestes	*	*	*

A CHAIR AND A CRIB OF THE KIND USED IN A GENTLEMAN'S HOUSE.

Continued

Item	£	s	d
Item one matt a mattrice a fetherbedd a bolster 2 pillowes 3 blancketts a coverlett and a bedsted with the vallaunce and a table	*	*	*
Item 6 joynt stooles an old wainscote chaire and a needleworke chaire		9	*
Item halfe a dousen cushons a greene carpett vj curtayns and a cubborde clothe	2	0	0
Item 6 paier of sheetes 6 pillowbeeres 6 table clothes 3 cubborde clothes 4 dousen and 4 table napkins 4 towells	3	0	0
Item 2 brass potts 4 kettles 2 chafers a morter and a pestle a chafingdish with a foote a warminge pann 2 candlesticks a candle plate a brasen ladle 2 spitts a drippingepann 2 potthangers a paier of potthookes a paier of cobbirons and a paier andirons a paier of doggirons a fier shovell and tonnges a gridiron and a stone morter	2	0	0
Item a bason and an ewer a charger 6 platters a plate halfe a dousen dishes 6 sawcers 6 porrengers 6 plate trenchers 2 basons 6 window potts 4 pewter potts 3 pewter cupps a pewter pepper box a pewter salt 2 pewter candlesticks and a chamber pott	1	10	0
Item 2 dozen trenchers			8
Item 16 silver spoones whereof 9 are gilt one silver and gilt salt one silver and gilt pott one silver and gilt cupp	7	0	0
Item 3 gold ringes		10	0
Item 2 damaske cushens		2	0
Some	28	12	10

Continued

	£	s	d
Desperate debts	46	5	5
In ready monye	15	0	0
Sperate debts	82	8	7
Some	143	14	0
Some totall –	£181	18s	2d

* document unreadable

Thomas Jackson does not seem to have been a wealthy gentleman. In 1603 Thomas Crane, a draper of the same town in Norfolk, died and the inventory of his goods produced a total of £578 and 9 shillings.

Source B

John Woodfall of Wymondham, Clerk

1590/1, February 26. An inventory of all and singular the goods and cattells of John Woodfall clerk of Wymondham late deceassed seen and apprised by Thomas Lovell gent Thomas Crane and Walter Brooke yeomen xxvjth Februarie 1590.

	£	s	d.
Inprimis his coat his cassock and his goune of [?] turaned	1	0	0
Item a taffata hat and a felt hat a velvett night cap		5	0
Item a pair of knitt netherstocks			6
Item a velvett girdle and a lether girdle			4
Item a sadle and bridle		6	8
Item a chaire			8
Item four pewter platters		2	0
Item six porringers and two saucers		2	0
Item four pewter spones			2
Item four pewter dishes		1	0
Item a pewter salt seller			6
Item two tonnes of pewter and a pott and a vinegar of pewter		1	0
Item a cupp of pewter			8
Item a candlestick of latten and a chaffing dishe		2	0
Item a skillett and a kettle		1	0
Item a great kettle		3	4
Item two white candlesticks of pewter		2	0
Item a carpett of dornicks		1	0
Item a cheste		1	0

Continued

Item	£	s	d
Item a fetherbedd		10	0
Item a matteris and a boulster		5	0
Item a grene caddowe		3	4
Item a coveringe		3	4
Item iij old cushins			6
Item a brasse bott		5	0
Item a brasse posnett and a morter		5	0
Item a kettell and an old skellett		3	4
Item viij tryen dyshes and a ladell			4
Item ij pewter dyshes iij sawsers and a salt		1	4
Item a payer of bellowes			6
Item ij aundeyernes		1	0
Item ij payer of hackes		1	0
Item a gredyerne a trevet and a payer of potthookes			6
Item a payer of cobeiurnes		1	0
Item a seled beddsted	1	0	0
Item a cubard		16	0
Item j old matteris and ij old mentells		11	8
Item iiij payer of *hempinge* shettes		8	0
Item a square bord		2	0
Item an old tubb and an old lachpane			6
Item a cordinge for a bedd			4
Item iij table napkins and ij old pilowberes			6
Item a Bible or Testament		2	0
Item a booke of heminges			6
Item a booke of Martin Luther			6
Item other x small bookes and boxes			6
Summa totalis	£7	8s	6d

John Woodfall was probably amongst the poor citizens of Wymondham. Amongst his contemporaries, Thomas Woodcock, a beer brewer, left £116 16 shillings and eight pence.

1 Compare these two inventories in terms of (a) clothes (b) recreational items (c) furniture (d) bedding.

2 Which items mark out Thomas Jackson as a gentleman?

3 Do you agree that John Woodfall was living in poverty?

Source C

There are old men yet dwelling in the village where I remain which have noted three things to be marvelously altered in England within their sound remembrance, ... One is the multitude of chimneys lately erected, whereas in their young days there were not above two or three, if so many, in most uplandish towns of the realm ... The second is the great (although not general) amendment of lodging, for (said they) our fathers, yea, and we ourselves also, have lien full oft upon straw pallets, on rough mats covered only with a sheet ... and a good round log under their heads instead of a bolster or pillow. If it were so that our father had within seven years after his marriage purchased a mattress or flock-bed, and thereto a sack of chaff to rest his head upon, he thought himself to be as well lodged as the lord of the town. Pillows (say they) were thought meet only for women in childbed. As for servants, if they had any sheet above them it was well, for seldom had they any under their bodies to keep them from the pricking straws ... The third thing they tell of is the exchange of vessel, as of treen [wooden] platters into pewter, and wooden spoons into silver or tin. For so common were all sorts of treen stuff in old time that a man should hardly find four pieces of pewter (of which one was a peradvanture a salt) in a good farmer's house, ...

The furniture of our houses also exceedeth and is grown in manner even to passing delicacy; and herein I do not speak of the nobility and gentry only but likewise of the lowest sort in most places of our South Country ...

Likewise in the houses of knights, gentlemen, merchantmen, and some other wealthy citizens, it is not geason [uncommon] to behold generally their great provision of tapestry, Turkey work, pewter, brass, fine linen, and thereto costly cupboards of plate, worth £500 or £600 or £1,000, to be deemed by estimation. In time past the costly furniture stayed there, whereas now it is descended yet lower, even unto the inferior artificers and many farmers, who have for the most part learned also to garnish their cupboards with plate, their joint beds with tapestry and silk hangings, and their tables with carpets and fine napery, whereby the wealth of our country (God be praised therefore and give us grace to employ it well) doth infinitely appear.

William Harrison, *The Description of England*, 1577.

FASHIONS OF THE EARLY SIXTEENTH CENTURY.

Source D

The greatest part of our building in the cities and good towns of England consisteth only of timber, for as yet few of the houses of the commonalty (except here and there in the West Country towns) are made of stone, ... This rude kind of building made the Spaniards in Queen Mary's days to wonder, but chiefly when they saw what large diet was used in many of these so homely cottages; insomuch that one of no small reputation amongst them said after this manner, 'These English,' quoth he, 'have their houses made of sticks and dirt, but they fare commonly so well as the king.' ... As horn in windows is now quite laid down in every place, glass is come to be so plentiful and within a very little so good cheap, if not better than the other.

William Harrison, *The Description of England*, 1577.

HARDWICK HALL, DERBYSHIRE.

4 What evidence is there in Sources C and D to suggest that living conditions were improving?

5 What evidence is there in the inventories (Sources A and B) to corroborate William Harrison's description?

Source E

White meats, as milk, butter, and cheese, which were never so dear as in my time and wont to be accounted of as one of the chief stays throughout the island, are now reputed as food appertinent only to the inferior sort, whilst such as are more wealthy do feed upon the flesh of all kinds of cattle ...

In number of dishes and change of meat, the nobility of England (whose cooks are for the most part musical-headed French-men and strangers) do most exceed, sith there is no day in manner that passeth over their heads wherein they have not only beef, mutton, veal, lamb, kid, pork, cony, capon, pig, or so many of these as the season yieldeth, but also some portion of the red or fallow deer, beside great variety of fish and wild fowl ...

The bread throughout the land is made of such grain as the soil yieldeth; nevertheless, the gentility commonly provide themselves sufficiently of wheat for their own tables, whilst their household and poor neighbours in some shires are enforced to content themselves with rye or barley, yea, and in time of dearth, many with bread made either of beans, peas or oats, or of all together and some acorns among, of which scourge the poorest do soonest taste, sith they are least able to provide themselves of better.

William Harrison, *The Description of England*, 1577.

FASHIONS OF THE LATER TUDOR PERIOD.

6 Why do you think wealthy people chose to eat red meats and had few vegetables?

7 Who had the better diet – the ordinary people (who had less meat and more vegetables) or the gentry and nobility?

Source F

There is such a confuse mingle mangle of apparel ... and such preposterous excess thereof, as everyone is permitted to flaunt it out in what apparel he lusteth himself, or can get by any kind of means. So that it is very hard to know who is noble, who is worshipfull, who is a gentleman, who is not.

Phillip Stubbs, *Anatomy of Abuses*, 1585.

A MERCHANT'S HOUSE FROM MARGATE IN KENT. THE PERIOD AFTER 1570 SAW A HOUSING REVOLUTION AS HOUSES WERE SUB-DIVIDED INTO MORE ROOMS, GIVING GREATER PRIVACY.

Source G

[since] such is our mutability that today there is none to the Spanish guise, tomorrow the French toys are most fine and delectable, ere long no such apparel as that which is after the High [German] fashion, by and by the Turkish manner is generally best liked of, otherwise the Morisco [Moorish] gowns, the Barbarian sleeves, and the short French breeches

make such a comely vesture that, except it were a dog in a doublet, you shall not see any so disguised as are my countrymen of England ... Oh, how much cost is bestowed nowadays upon our bodies and how little upon our souls!

In women also it is most to be lamented that they do now far exceed the lightness of our men (who nevertheless are transformed from the cap even to the very shoe), and such staring attire as in time past was supposed meet for none but light housewives only it is now become an habit for chaste and sober matrons.

I have met with some of these trulls in London so disguised that it hath passed my skill to discern whether they were men or women.

William Harrison, *The Description of England,* 1577.

---

8 What do the writers of Sources F and G have in common?

9 Sources F and G seem to be evidence of greater wealth and variety of wealth. Why then do you think changes in fashion were criticised?

10 In this section you have used two different kinds of sources: inventories and commentaries. What are the strengths and weaknesses of each kind of source as evidence?

12 Has the material in this section amended your opinion about the quality of daily life under the Tudors?

Changing Times

To us life in the sixteenth century seems impossibly harsh. Uncontrollable hazards, such as plagues, urban fires and poor harvests endangered life and prosperity with depressing regularity. Despite this, the population rose but this in turn meant that food and jobs were in increasingly short supply. One result was inflation. As the century wore on wages bought less and less. Poverty and vagrancy became such problems that the government had to intervene, either to help the needy poor or repress the insolent beggars.

And yet, this rising population was also a sign of confidence. Tudor society was prosperous and lively. Trade at home and abroad was increasing. By the end of the century most people lived in considerably more style than their grandparents or great-grandparents with better housing, clothing and furniture. They ate more but not necessarily better. The snobbery of the nobility cost them dear for they ate few vegetables, regarding them as the foods of the poor. Henry VIII was the most famous sufferer from too much red meat, too little fruit and too few vegetables but was far from being the only one in need of dietary advice.

Women had fewer opportunities for independence. As unemployment increased, women were squeezed out of guilds and found it harder to find work in jobs that were traditionally the territory of men. Married women could share their husbands' businesses and be full partners in marriage but independent women were not accepted as men's equals. The reigns of Mary and Elizabeth did not demonstrate that this was a Golden Age for women. Instead their marital trials and negotiations showed that even they were expected to take second place on marriage. Some things however did not change. In the eyes of foreigners England was a prosperous country but the English were rather pleased with themselves!

... the English are great lovers of themselves, and of everything belonging to them; they think that there are no other men than themselves, and no other world but England; and whenever they see a handsome foreigner, they say that 'he looks like an Englishman', and that 'it is a pity that he should not be an Englishman'; and when they partake of any delicacy with a foreigner, they ask him, 'whether such a thing is made in their country?'

A report by a Venetian envoy to England, 1497.

... they are good sailors, and better pirates, cunning, treacherous, and thievish; above three hundred are said to be hanged annually at London; beheading with them is less infamous than hanging. They are powerful in the field, successful against their enemies, impatient of anything like slavery; vastly fond of great noises that fill the ear, such as the firing of cannon, drums, and the ringing of bells, so that it is common for a number of them, that have got a glass in their heads, to go up into some belfrey, and ring the bells for hours together for the sake of the exercise. If they see a foreigner very well made, or particularly handsome, they will say, It is a pity he is not an Englishman!

Paul Hentzner, *Travels in England,* 1598.

REVIEW

1 You may choose the year of your birth. It can be 1460, 1480, 1500, 1520, 1540 or 1560. You will live to the age of fifty. Which year would you choose to be born in? Explain your choice using the evidence from pages 2 – 26.

2 Which of the Tudor monarchs do you think were likely to have the hardest task in winning popularity in the light of the economic evidence in the chapter?

3 Does it seem that monarchs and governments could play a significant part in the lives of ordinary people?

2 Monarch, Government and People

PREVIEW

This book contains a great deal about politics and government and about the groups that make up governments. You will read about monarchs, councils, courts and parliaments, but what exactly were they and what did they do? It is easy to assume you know because the words are familiar but this can be dangerous. For example, parliaments in Tudor England were quite unlike parliaments today and not just because there were no television cameras. More obviously, monarchs had a very different role then than now and, because they were so important, this chapter starts by looking at monarchy.

Source A

ELIZABETH I SURROUNDED BY HER COURTIERS.

Source B

To be short, the prince is the life, the head and the authority of all things that be done in the realm of England. And to no prince is done more honour and reverence than to the king and queen of England; no man speaketh to the prince nor serveth at the table but in adoration and kneeling, all persons of the realm be bareheaded before him; insomuch that in the chamber of presence, where the cloth of estate is set, no man dare walk, yea though the prince be not there, no man dare tarry there but bareheaded.

Sir Thomas Smith, *De Republica Anglorum*, 1565.

Source C

Who that resisteth his dread sovereign lord,
Doth damn his soul by God's own very word.
A Christian subject should with honour due
Obey his sovereign.

from The Mirror for Magistrates, a collection of stories published in 1559.

---

1 What do Sources A, B and C tell you about attitudes to the monarch?

2 Compile a list or draw a spider diagram showing what you think were the ways Tudor monarchs and governments affected their people.

Examining the evidence
The Work of the Monarch in Tudor England

The monarch was at the centre of Tudor government. That is a very commonplace statement that does not tell you very much. Yes, the monarch was important, just as much as in the Middle Ages, but what exactly did he or she do? How did the Tudor monarchs affect the lives of their subjects? The evidence in this section will help you to identify more clearly and precisely the role of the monarch.

Source A

The monarch of England, king or queen, hath absolutely in his power the authority of war and peace, to defy what prince it shall please him and to bid him war, and again to reconcile himself and enter into league or truce with him, at his pleasure or the advice only of his Privy Council. His Privy Council be chosen also at the prince's pleasure ... The prince doth participate to them all, or so many of them as he shall think good, such legations and messages as come from foreign princes, such letters or occurents as be sent to himself or his secretaries, and keepeth so many embassies and letters sent unto him secret as he will ... In war time and in the field the prince hath also absolute power, so that his word is law; he may put to death or to other bodily punishment whom he shall think so to deserve, without process of law or form of judgement ... The prince useth also absolute power in crying and decreeing the money of the realm by his proclamation only. The money is always stamped with the prince's image and title. The form, fashion, manner, weight, fineness and baseness thereof is at the discretion of the prince...

... The prince giveth all the chief and highest offices or magistracies of the realm, be it of judgement or dignity, temporal or spiritual, and hath the tenths and first fruits of all ecclesiastical promotions, ... The supreme justice is done in the king's name and by his authority only. The prince hath the wardship and first marriage of all those that hold lands of him in chief.

Sir Thomas Smith, De Republica Anglorum, 1565.

Source B

HENRY VIII PRESIDING OVER PARLIAMENT. PARLIAMENT ONLY MET WHEN SUMMONED BY THE MONARCH.

Source C

An Act concerning the King's Highness to be Supreme Head of the Church of England and to have authority to reform and redress all errors, heresies and abuses in the same (1534: 26 Henry VIII).

Albeit the King's Majesty justly and rightfully is and oweth to be the supreme head of the Church of England, and so is recognised by the clergy of this realm in their Convocations; yet nevertheless for corroboration and confirmation thereof, and for increase in virtue in Christ's religion within this realm of England, and to repress and extirp all errors, heresies and other enormities and abuses heretofore used in the same, Be it enacted by authority of this present Parliament that the King our sovereign lord, his heirs and successors kings of this realm, shall be taken, accepted and reputed the only supreme head in earth of the Church of England called Anglicana Ecclesia.

Statutes of the Realm.

Source D

An Act that proclamations made by the King shall be obeyed (1539: 31 Henry VIII, c.8)... the King for the time being, with the advice of his honourable Council, ... may set forth at all times by authority of this act his proclamations, under such penalties and pain and of such sort as to his Highness and his said honourable Council or the more part of them shall see[m] necessary and requisite; And that those same shall be obeyed, observed and kept as though they were made by act of Parliament.

Statutes of the Realm.

Source E

This day Mr Peter Wentworth and Sir Henry Bromley delivered a petition unto the lord keeper, therein desiring the lords of the Upper House to be suppliants with them of the Lower House unto her Majesty for entailing the succession of the Crown. Her Majesty was highly displeased therewith after she knew thereof, as a matter contrary to her former strait commandment, and charged the Council to call the parties before them. ... The lords intreated them favourably and with good speeches; but so highly was her Majesty offended that they must needs commit them [to prison].

From the *Journals of Sir Symonds D'Ewes*, February 1593.

---

1 Using sources A – G list the different tasks undertaken by Tudor monarchs.

2 In the Middle Ages the two basic requirements of a good king were to defend the country against foreign enemies and to ensure peace and order at home. Was this still true?

3 What evidence is there of either a rise or a fall in the power of the monarch in the Tudor period?

4 Which aspects of the monarch's role had the most impact on ordinary people?

5 Which aspects of their roles do you think that monarchs themselves thought were the most important?

Source H

[Henry VII] was a man of high qualities and great ability and he devoted himself to his duties as king with a degree of devotion and a professionalism unwonted in most of his predecessors. He displayed a far-reaching comprehension of affairs of State and remained always the essential pivot upon which government turned. No minister of his at any time overshadowed the throne.

S B Chrimes, *Henry VII*, 1972.

Source F

AN EDITION OF THE BIBLE DEDICATED TO ELIZABETH I. BOOKS AND MUSIC WERE DEDICATED TO MONARCHS, USUALLY IN THE HOPE OF GAINING PATRONAGE.

Source G

MARY WITH HER HUSBAND, KING PHILIP OF SPAIN. MARRIAGES WERE AN IMPORTANT METHOD OF CEMENTING ALLIANCES AND IT WAS OF PARAMOUNT IMPORTANCE FOR MONARCHS TO PRODUCE AN HEIR, AT LEAST UNTIL THE REIGN OF ELIZABETH.

Source I

Henry [VIII] set off with an admirable determination to take his responsibilities seriously and to keep abreast of paperwork. It did not last – in which respect he was no different from most monarchs. His passion for hunting and jousting, his interest in music and theology, to say nothing of his demanding love life, meant that documents rarely received the detailed attention Henry VII had given them. Hence, there was an opportunity for a capable minister to make himself indispensable by taking over the burden. We must be careful how to interpret this however. Henry never surrendered the reins totally, and none of his ministers ever forgot that, at any moment, the prince could give them their dismissal.

J Cannon and R Griffiths, *Oxford History of the British Monarchy,* 1988.

Source J

Even in the greatest affairs of State she [Elizabeth] did not always ask her ministers' advice. In 1586 the earl of Leicester, then in command of the English forces fighting against Spain in the Netherlands, complained that he was not receiving advice from the Privy Council. Sir Francis Walsingham, the Secretary of State, replied that the councillors well understood his complaints but, 'her Majesty retaining the whole direction of the causes of that country to herself and such advice as she receiveth underhand, they know not what to write or to advise'.

A G R Smith, *The Emergence of a Nation State, the Commonwealth of England, 1529–1660,* 1984.

---

6 Read Sources H – J. Were the three monarchs discussed here equally involved in the business of government?

7 Were all monarchs equally powerful? Explain the reasons for your answer.

8 Review and, if necessary, revise your chart showing the impact of monarch and government on the people in the light of your work in this section.

2.1 The Court and the Household

Court is a familiar word, often used in connection with royalty. *King Arthur's Court* summons up images of knights, festivities, jousting, ladies and a round table. But what exactly was the court?

Confusingly the court was not a place, other than the place that was inhabited at any one time by the monarch and his or her courtiers. The court therefore moved; at one time it might be in a royal palace and at another, at the home of a leading nobleman. It is easier and more accurate to think of the court as a collection of people surrounding the monarch – those whom the monarch chose as companions for their friendship or their ability to entertain and those lesser mortals who were needed to keep the great clothed, fed, wined and watered. All these people from the queen, dukes and duchesses to the kitchen maids, porters and spit-turners, were also members of the royal household. The two terms *court* and *household* can be used interchangeably although there were technical differences. There were members of the court who were not members of the *household* but, as people in the sixteenth century found it difficult to define the court exactly, we need not worry too much about the distinctions!

The court or household has been described as a *machine for living in*. It was a machine in the sense that it had many parts, each of which had a purpose and was linked to the other parts. If one part, the kitchens, for example, did not work, everything ground to a halt. The purpose of this machine was to support and display the monarch and to enable him or her to function effectively. One of the most important aspects of the court was display to impress both subjects and foreign visitors. All Tudor monarchs, even the supposedly miserly Henry VII, spent lavishly on their courts, determined that the splendour of the court's appearance and ceremonials should make clear their own power and that of the nation.

COURTIERS PORTRAYED BY HOLBEIN AND CLOUET.

The Privy Chamber and Faction

At the very centre of the household were the royal apartments and at their centre was the Privy Chamber, most private of all the royal apartments apart from the bedchamber. The gentlemen or ladies of the Privy Chamber were chosen by the monarch (although there was rivalry to influence those decisions) and they had the greatest opportunity to influence the king or queen. The Privy Chamber was headed by the Groom of the Stool. As stool was the medieval term for toilet this gives some indication of the degree of close contact originally enjoyed by members of the Privy Chamber!

Henry VII was responsible for developing the Privy Chamber, adding to the security of the crown by increasing its mystique. People would be more in awe of the monarch if only a handful of servants had private access to the king. Elizabeth also kept a very strict limit on the numbers admitted to the Privy Chamber but Henry VIII allowed freer entry and so more people had access to the king and the chance to influence his ideas and decisions.

As a result the Privy Chamber in the reign of Henry VIII has been interpreted as a hotbed of political intrigue and factional disputes.

Courtiers were, almost without exception, ambitious people and they wanted to influence the monarch. They wanted the monarch to agree with their plans or policies, reward them or their friends with lands, jobs or money. They might also want to influence the monarch against others, their rivals for royal favour. Frequently courtiers who had an objective in common came together in what historians called *factions*, and might also be called alliances. Factions were rarely long-lasting for, once an objective was achieved, there was often little to hold them together. As you will discover from the case-study of faction on pages 34 – 35 factions could even consist of old enemies briefly united against a third foe. At times factions were the chief focus of politics. The political futures of great men such as Wolsey and Cromwell depended upon their ability to control or manipulate factions so that they retained their influence with the king. Therefore the Privy Chamber was as important for politics as was the royal council, at least in the reign of Henry VIII. Decisions reached at council meetings could be overturned by a discreet word in the king's ear from a member of his Privy Chamber. For a chance to take part in some factional intrigue and to understand the way it worked try the exercise on the next two pages.

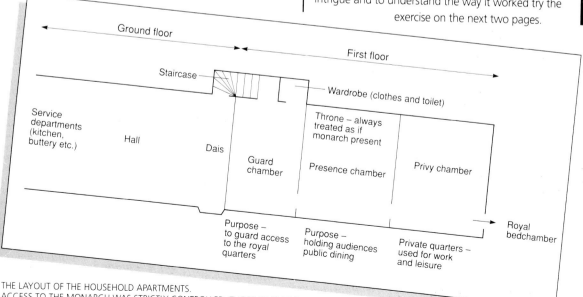

THE LAYOUT OF THE HOUSEHOLD APARTMENTS.
ACCESS TO THE MONARCH WAS STRICTLY CONTROLLED. THOSE WHO HAD
ACCESS TO THE MONARCH IN THE PRESENCE CHAMBER OR, PARTICULARLY, IN THE PRIVY
CHAMBER HAD THE GREATEST OPPORTUNITY TO INFLUENCE THE MONARCH.

2.2 Faction!

*T*hese pages are intended to introduce you to the idea of faction, using one of the most dramatic episodes in Tudor history – the fall and execution of Anne Boleyn less than three years after her marriage to Henry VIII had ended a thousand years of English loyalty to the Pope. Anne's fall allows us to see faction at work although the situations presented here have been deliberately simplified and the number of personnel reduced in order to keep the outlines clear. Understanding the changes in factions and the motives of individuals is important otherwise it would be very difficult to explain why Anne was actually executed for treason on charges of adultery and incest.

STAGE 1

The situation in January 1536

Henry's affection for Anne was cooling. She was exciting and high-spirited but also argumentative and could be critical. Henry was turning his attention to the far more placid and acquiescent temperament of Jane Seymour. Anne, however, was pregnant and if she had a son all would be well. Unfortunately Anne miscarried the baby, a boy. Henry felt betrayed. Chart A illustrates the factional relationship of those involved.

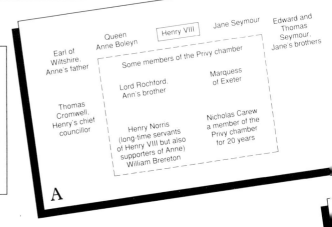

A

The objectives of those involved

- Henry VIII – to have a son and heir.
- The Seymours – to put their sister Jane on the throne and thereby gain influence with Henry.
- Exeter/Carew – to remove Anne Boleyn, whose Protestantism they disliked. They hoped to restore the Catholic Princess Mary (daughter of Catherine of Aragon) to the succession and ultimately restore Catholicism.
- Wiltshire/Rochford – to keep Anne on the throne and thereby maintain their influence with Henry.
- Cromwell – to maintain his position as the king's leading councillor. Cromwell had risen partly through his good relationship with Anne and both were committed Protestants.

Task 1

Now, if possible, share the roles amongst your group and sit in the positions shown in Chart A. Individuals should be clear on their objectives and then answer the questions addressed to them below. As you reach each stage it will help if you change positions as shown in the charts.

1 Exeter/Carew

(a) Whose help do you need to remove Anne?

(b) What opportunities do you have to influence Henry's ideas?

2 Cromwell

(a) Why do you oppose Exeter and Carew in general?

(b) If you do not stay with Anne what is the alternative and how might you achieve it?

3 Rochford/Wiltshire

(a) What opportunities do you have to influence the king?

(b) What arguments or ideas do you want to communicate to the king?

4 Henry VIII

(a) What do you want to hear from those around you?

STAGE 2

The conservative, Catholic faction headed by Exeter and Carew enlisted the help of the Seymour brothers and pushed Jane forward as a potential wife for Henry, coaching her on how best to attract the king. The Boleyn faction was losing ground steadily. Cromwell decided to change sides and persuaded Exeter and Carew that he could help them. He said he would support their wish to restore Mary to the succession! He also constructed a plot that would not just annul Henry's marriage to Anne but would lead to Anne's execution. The situation is shown in Chart B.

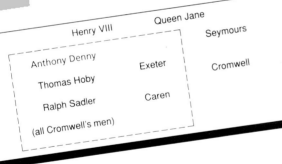

Wiltshire   Anne

Henry VIII   Jane

Rochford   Seymours

Norris   Exeter   Cromwell

Brereton   Caren

Task 2

5 Henry VIII

Why would the execution of Anne be acceptable?

6 Exeter/Carew

Why would you accept an alliance with Cromwell, a former opponent?

7 Boleyn faction

What can you do to prevent this situation developing?

8 Cromwell

(a) Are you committing yourself to a lengthy alliance with the Catholic faction?

(b) Why is the execution of Anne helpful?

Henry VIII   Queen Jane

Seymours

Anthony Denny   Exeter   Cromwell

Thomas Hoby

Ralph Sadler   Caren

(all Cromwell's men)

STAGE 3

April/May 1536

Cromwell went ahead with his plans. He prepared accusations that Anne was guilty of adultery with several courtiers, including Norris and Brereton and of incest with her brother, Rochford. These charges were untrue but they played on Henry VIII's vanity. He could not cope with either the idea of his wife's adultery or that long-time servants such as Norris had placed loyalty to Anne before himself. On 19 May, Anne was executed, two days after Norris, Brereton and two others. On 30 May Henry married Jane Seymour. Next year, in October, their son was born. The conservatives had apparently won but Cromwell also introduced his own men as members of the Privy Chamber. See Chart C.

Task 3

9 Henry VIII

(a) Are you happy with the way events have turned out?

(b) How do you feel about restoring your eldest daughter Mary to the succession, bearing in mind she is still Catholic and has refused to accept your religious changes?

10 Cromwell

(a) What have you gained from the events of 1536?

(b) How might you plan to reduce the influence of your current allies, Exeter and Carew?

11 Exeter/Carew

Is there anything you still hope to achieve?

STAGE 4

1537–38

Having saved himself by his remarkable exchange of loyalties Cromwell now attacked his new set of allies. He did not want them to have the influence that might lead Henry to reverse Protestant reforms. Using his increased influence in the Privy Chamber, Cromwell accused Exeter and Carew of working to restore Mary to the succession, knowing this was not acceptable to Henry. By the end of 1539 Exeter and Carew had been executed for treason and other supporters had lost influence. Then Cromwell packed the Privy Chamber with more of his own men.

Task 4

12 Why did people develop or belong to factions?

13 What was the main objective of any faction?

14 How important was the influence of members of the Privy Council? What evidence is there to support your answer?

15 Were factions long-lasting groupings based on principles and ideals or short-term alliances based on common needs and cynicism? Explain the reasons for your answer.

What do we mean by government?

One difficulty students of history often experience is the way historians use words like government or parliament. The trouble is that these words are familiar to us and so we do not stop to think about what exactly they mean in a different context. Yet we should stop to think because many aspects of governments in the sixteenth century were quite different from what they are today. The rest of this chapter attempts to establish what we mean by government in early Tudor England – the roles of the council and parliament, the nature of local government and taxation.

TALKING POINT

Historians' accounts of factions are often controversial and conjectural because the evidence is very limited. Why is it so limited?

1 Briefly note down what you currently think are the functions and membership of (a) the council (b) parliament (c) the justices of the peace.

2 How do you think money was raised to pay for government and the king's expenses?

3 After you have read pages 36 – 40 revise your answers to questions 1 and 2.

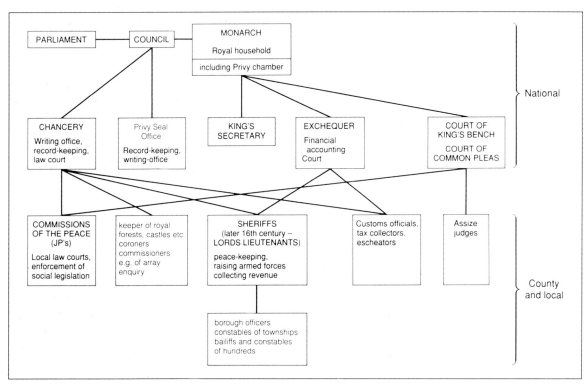

THE STRUCTURE OF THE COUNTRY'S GOVERNMENT. DESPITE THE SEEMING COMPLEXITY OF THIS DIAGRAM, THE NUMBER OF 'CIVIL SERVANTS' EMPLOYED IN NATIONAL GOVERNMENT IN THE YEAR 1600 WAS ABOUT 200.

The Council

After the monarch, the council was the most important single element of the government. It consisted of the monarch's advisers, chosen because the monarch felt that they were reliable, trustworthy and likely to be of good service. Councillors were drawn from the ranks of the nobility and the clergy (both bishops and lower ranks) and from the gentry, including gentlemen with relatively little land. One notable feature of Tudor government was the selection of councillors based on their intelligence and the quality of their work rather than because of their rank.

The council had three tasks. It gave the monarch advice on all matters as honestly as possible even if that advice differed from the monarch's view. It was also the central administrative body, detailing and ordering matters of defence and war, political negotiations, economic concerns, administrative and religious reforms. Such matters could range from the detailed planning of the invasion of France to deciding what clothes should be available for a noble prisoner in the Tower of London. Thirdly, the Council acted as a court, dealing with the issues or complaints that individuals brought direct to the king for his judgement. The king's duty to see that justice was done to all subjects was taken literally and seriously and the king and his council therefore sat in judgement.

The number of members of the council varied from reign to reign. Henry VII maintained a council of between 40 and 50 members. Not everyone attended meetings but there were often twenty or thirty present. However at the heart of this was a much smaller number (less than ten) of 'professional' councillors who attended all meetings and provided the necessary continuity. These were the most trusted of all. Henry VII was usually in attendance but later Tudor monarchs did not usually attend council meetings, receiving instead reports of its deliberations.

A major development in the history of the council came in the 1530s, probably in 1536. Thomas Cromwell reorganised the council to form the Privy council, a body of 19 or 20 members who met regularly, often daily. The members of this Privy council were the main office holders (the treasurer, the chancellor, the secretary etc.) and the leading figures in the royal household. Although the size of the council grew again under Edward and Mary it settled back to its Cromwellian size in Elizabeth's reign, falling to 13 members by 1601. The council was of central importance for the good government of England. Its members were chosen by the monarch and therefore its efficiency was, to some degree, determined by the monarch.

Parliaments

In contrast to the council or to parliaments today, Tudor parliaments were occasional events, meeting only when summoned by the monarch. The frequency of parliamentary meetings was therefore a measure of royal needs. The Reformation Parliament, for example, continued from 1529 to 1536 because Henry VIII first hoped that parliament's anti-Papalism would pressure the Pope into giving way and granting the divorce. When this failed the Parliament continued in order to enact the legislation to establish the new Church of England.

Parliament was therefore called for specific reasons. It met because the king needed to raise taxes and only parliament could sanction taxation. It met to pass laws proposed by the government and at the same time took the opportunity to pass laws put forward by its own individual members, often dealing with issues relating to one region or even one individual, such as the right to enclose land for farming that had previously been used as common land by numbers of villagers.

Parliament was a partnership. Acts of Parliament had to have the support of all three elements – the monarch, the Lords and the Commons. During the century the balance of the composition of the Lords was altered by Henry VIII's church reforms. After the monasteries were closed there were no abbots to sit in the House of Lords and so the Lords Temporal (the dukes, earls, etc.) had a clear majority over the Lords Spiritual – the bishops. The Commons changed too, growing from 296 members to 462 as a result of decisions to allow more places to gain the status of a borough and to have MPs. This was partly because towns wanted to have MPs who could be influential on the town's behalf and partly because the crown felt that it was important to have a greater number of efficient and capable members of parliament.

Elections, however, were rare. If there were potential rivals they often met to decide who would stand down. Even if there was an election the electorate in a town might consist solely of the town council. Gloucester was a rare town with as many as 400 to 500 voters. Ballots were open. There was no secrecy to safeguard the voter. Increasingly, borough MPs were country gentlemen 'recommended' by noblemen who paid the costs of the MP, saving the town money. Only a minority of borough MPs were real townsmen representing their own town but the choice of gentry did mean that parliament gained a large number of politically experienced and independent MPs. Overall, parliament's importance rose in the sixteenth century, although not as much as some Elizabethan members thought that it should. In Sir Geoffrey Elton's words 'the changes produced by the 1530s gave to Parliament a permanent place of political importance and, so to speak, finally incorporated it in the English system of government.'

Taxation

All governments need to raise money, especially if they are involved in wars or need to raise forces to resist invasions or rebellions. Throughout the sixteenth century Tudor governments were faced with the problem of finding money for these purposes as well as for the everyday expenses of the monarch and his or her household. There was no such thing as an annual income tax. Instead the crown's income came from an amalgam of sources, some consistent, some occasional, as the chart shows.

Edward IV had readily promised that he would 'live of his own', meaning that he would pay for the expenses of government out of the ordinary revenue of the crown and not resort to parliamentary taxation or other, more dubious methods of extorting money from his people. Yet by the end of his reign the Scottish wars had come close to bankrupting Edward despite the fact that he had used extraordinary revenue. The same problem faced all Tudor monarchs except that, as time wore on and inflation developed, the likelihood of the crown not requiring extraordinary revenue became minimal. Parliamentary taxation therefore became a more regular feature of English life, even if it was still far from being an annual event.

1 Explain the difference between ordinary and extraordinary revenue.

2 Which events or activities were major sources of income for the crown?

3 Which events or activities were the greatest expenses for the crown?

4 Which monarch would you expect to impose (a) the most and (b) the fewest financial burdens on his or her subjects?

(You may find it helpful also to refer to the timelines on pages 4 – 5 in answering questions 2,3 and 4)

A. Ordinary Income – monies collected regularly without the need for legislation				
CROWN LANDS	CUSTOMS DUES	FEUDAL DUES	PROFITS OF JUSTICE	CHURCH PAYMENTS (after 1534)
Lands held by inheritance or by confiscation from traitors. After 1534 Church and monastic lands were added. This was the most important element of royal income.	Long-established and often avoided. New duties were created in time of need.	Henry VII was the last king to collect a tax for the knighting of his eldest son and the marriage of his eldest daughters. Taxes on inheritance and particularly wardships could be lucrative. The crown could also buy supplies and transport at low prices it fixed itself!	Fees paid for royal writs and letters. Fines levied by the courts.	First fruits – the payment of the whole of the first year's revenue by the new holder of an appointment. Tenths – 1/10 of each year's income from each parish, bishopric etc.

B. Extraordinary Income – moneys collected as a result of parliamentary legislation

The basic tax was a fifteenth and a tenth, theoretically 1/15 of the value of moveable goods in rural areas and 1/10 in urban areas. However a fixed sum of around £30,000 was agreed but often took years to collect. Subsidies – taxes rated on incomes – were also sometimes collected.

THE SOURCES OF ROYAL INCOME.

Justices of the Peace

The council and parliaments were distant institutions to most people. The face of government that people recognised was the Justice of the Peace. Each year a Commission of the Peace was appointed for each county. The members of the Commission were the Justices. They were the local landowners, men who knew the people in their area. This knowledge and the variety and importance of their functions made the JPs the key figures in English local government.

During the Tudor period the scope of their work increased considerably and so, to some extent, did the number of JPs. In 1485 there were fewer than ten JPs per county on average. By the 1570s there were more likely to be 40 – 50 and sometimes as many as ninety in the largest counties. However this may also tell us something about the social importance of becoming a JP. Some of these higher numbers simply basked in their small glory and left the hardworking minority to do the work. For this work JPs were not paid but they did have public esteem and they did see the task as their duty to their 'country' – a term regularly used in the sixteenth century when today we would say county. This use of 'country' tells us a great deal about the close-knit nature of county communities and why good local JPs could be very effective agents of government.

There is no doubt that the workload of JPs was greatly extended by Tudor governments. In the 1590s William Lombarde, a lawyer from Kent, described the work of the JPs and identified this growth. He said that in 1485 JPs had to enforce 133 laws. A further 98 laws requiring enforcement by JPs were added between 1485 and 1558 and yet another 75 by 1597. Their work was diverse in the extreme. They supervised the maintenance of highways and bridges, licensed ale-houses, checked the fineness of pewter and brass, enforced pricing and apprenticeship regulations and fixed wages. In addition, religious reforms required them to keep a check on those who did not go to church. Increasing levels of poverty and unemployment meant that JPs were also in the forefront of the fight to prevent or punish vagabonds and to collect the poor rate that was used to pay poor relief to the deserving poor. All this was in addition to their most basic task, hearing criminal cases at quarter sessions, so-called because they were held four times a year. Sir Thomas Smith in his De Republica Anglorum said of the Justices of the Peace that there 'was never in any commonwealth deemed a more wise, a more dulce and gentle, nor a more certain way to rule the people.' Judging by the amount of work given to JPs by Tudor monarchs and councils they too had great faith in this system.

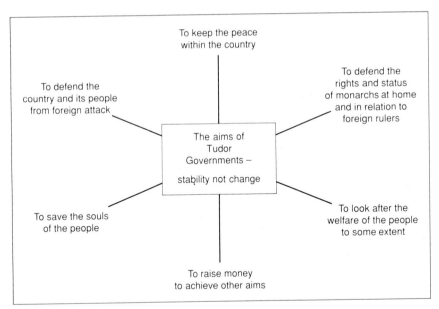

REVIEW
The Aims of Government

This chapter has endeavoured to describe what government consisted of and how it worked. These are introductory ideas that can be built on in the later chapters. It is also important to reflect on what government was for. Today governments involve themselves in our lives in many ways. Did Tudor governments have the same objectives?

Questions

1 What differences and similarities can you see between the aims of Tudor governments and those today?

2 Look back to your work on the Preview. If necessary revise your list or chart showing the impact of Tudor governments on their people.

3 The Tudors and the Wars of the Roses

PREVIEW

Put yourself in Henry VII's position in 1485. You are a new, unknown king, anxious to prevent rebellions or invasions and to unite the country. What should you do about the wars and rebellions of the past thirty years? You have a choice. Should you (a) ignore past conflicts in case people use them as an excuse or a model for attacking you, or (b) use those events as propaganda to help win support for your new regime? If you choose option b, how do you do it?

TALKING POINT

What image do you have of the Wars of the Roses? How was your image formed?

THE BATTLE OF BARNET, 1471. THE ILLUSTRATION IS FROM A CONTEMPORARY BURGUNDIAN CHRONICLE.

The Wars of the Roses

Why did the Wars of the Roses begin? The answer simply lies in the character of Henry VI, king since 1422 when he was 9 months old. While Henry was a boy the country was governed effectively by his council but Henry took over government himself in 1437. He proved to be a disaster, failing to meet the two basic requirements of a medieval king – providing security from foreign enemies and ensuring law and order at home. Between 1437 and 1453 Henry lost England's lands in France and was unable to prevent the breakdown of law and order in many parts of England. In 1450 there was a major rebellion (Cade's rebellion) in the south-east but the targets of the rebels were the king's 'evil councillors'. No-one demanded Henry's deposition, such was the respect for Henry because he was the anointed monarch, chosen by God.

HENRY VI.

The 1450 rebellion had little effect. The troubles continued and in one way grew worse because Richard, Duke of York began to appear as a rival to Henry. It is almost certain that Henry himself saw York as a rival since he consistently refused to allow York any part in the council. York, the senior nobleman in the country, had a right to a leading role in government and resented his omission but in the early 1450s he did not seek the crown itself. In his letters and propaganda he only ever said that he wanted to remove Henry's leading councillor, the Duke of Somerset, and then help Henry govern the country effectively.

The first battle took place at St Albans in 1455. York, afraid of imprisonment or execution, attacked the king's army, intent on capturing or killing Henry's advisers, notably Somerset. York was successful. As soon as Somerset was killed the battle ended. York then knelt before Henry and begged his forgiveness. For the next nine months York acted as Henry's chief adviser.

If this situation had continued there need have been no further fighting. However, York's enemies could not leave him in power. Foremost among these enemies was Margaret of Anjou, Henry's wife and queen. Henry himself seems to have become increasingly ill and unable to play any significant role in politics. Margaret therefore took the lead, clearly afraid that York would take the crown and therefore deprive her young son of his royal inheritance. By her side were the sons of the noblemen killed at St Albans in 1455. These were the Lancastrians, supporters of the house or family of King Henry of Lancaster. Their enemies were

The Battles of 1459 – 1461		
Sept 1459	Blore Heath	– the Yorkists were defeated and fled abroad.
July 1460	Northampton	– the Yorkists, led by Warwich and York's son Edward, returned and were victorious.
Dec 1460	Wakefield	– York was killed by the Lancastrian army.
Feb 1461	Mortimer's Cross	– York's son Edward defeated a small Lancastrian force.
Feb 1461	St. Albans	– a Yorkist army, led by Warwick, was heavily defeated.
March 1461	Towton	– Edward and Warwick defeated the Lancestrian army near Tadcaster.

Yorkists, followers of Richard, Duke of York. Perhaps surprisingly for us these two parties were not based in the counties of Lancashire or Yorkshire. The Lancastrian strongholds were in the Midlands, Cheshire and parts of the north. York's base was Ludlow in Shropshire, with lands on the Welsh border and Cambridgeshire as well as West Yorkshire.

Between 1459 and 1461 the two sides fought 6 battles, by far the heaviest fighting of the whole 30 year period. It began because Margaret had built up her strength to the point when she felt strong enough to attack the Yorkists. They fled and were attainted in Parliament in their absence. An Act of Attainder was the worst possible punishment. Not only did it decree execution for treason but it also meant that the family lost all its lands – neither wives nor children nor grandchildren could inherit and so the family was totally ruined. Faced with this, York had to fight or accept penniless exile. The six battles saw the advantage swing to and fro. York himself was killed at Wakefield but his eldest son, Edward, together with Richard Neville, Earl of Warwick, won the decisive battle at Towton in March 1461. Towton was the largest battle in English history with perhaps 50,000 men involved and was probably far bigger than any other battle in the Wars of the Roses.

Edward became King Edward IV. He justified deposing Henry VI by arguing that his family had really had the better claim to the throne all along. This requires close study of the family tree but really the arguments about which was 'the rightful family' are misleading. If Henry VI had been an effective monarch, York would have served him loyally and arguments about who was descended from whom would never have been voiced. These claims were only developed when conflict was certain in order to justify the Yorkists' actions against an anointed king.

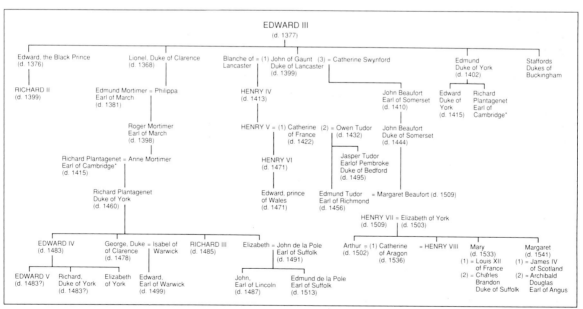

THE FAMILIES OF YORK AND LANCASTER.

Most noblemen accepted Edward as king, despite the fact that nearly all of them had wanted to keep Henry as king, however much his incompetence and sickness had increased in the 1450s. However their main objective was peace and few were so loyal as to continue the fight after Towton. There was a handful of die-hards on each side (some out of loyalty to the anointing of Henry VI, some out of self-interest) but most noblemen preferred the greater security of neutrality.

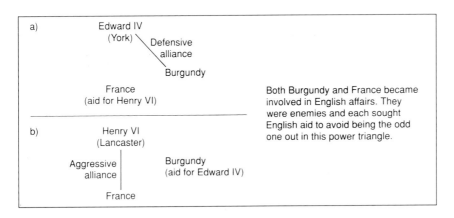

a) Edward IV (York) — Defensive alliance — Burgundy

France (aid for Henry VI)

b) Henry VI (Lancaster) — Aggressive alliance — France; Burgundy (aid for Edward IV)

Both Burgundy and France became involved in English affairs. They were enemies and each sought English aid to avoid being the odd one out in this power triangle.

For nine years Edward IV ruled England until he himself was deposed. The Earl of Warwick seems to have been disappointed with the rewards he received from Edward, although they were far greater than those given to anyone else. With the help of the King of France, Warwick constructed an amazing alliance with his old and bitter enemy, Margaret of Anjou, the remnants of the Lancastrian party and Edward's own brother, the Duke of Clarence! Warwick invaded England in 1470 and forced Edward to flee to Burgundy. Warwick re-installed the 50 year old Henry VI as king once more – by now a pitiable figure to the people of London for he was so clearly Warwick's puppet.

Henry VI's restoration was short-lived. In 1471 Edward landed in Yorkshire with only a few hundred men. As he marched south he won recruits and defeated and killed Warwick at the Battle of Barnet. He then beat Margaret's army at Tewkesbury, where Margaret's son was killed, aged seventeen. A few days later Henry VI was murdered in the Tower of London. That seemed to be the end of the House of Lancaster.

For another twelve years Edward ruled England successfully and peacefully. Then in April 1483 he died suddenly aged only 40. His heir was his twelve year old son, also called Edward. Young Edward's uncle, Richard, Duke of Gloucester, was to be Protector and rule the country for the few years until the boy came of age. This arrangement seemed logical as Richard had always been loyal to his brother but Edward V's reign lasted less than three months before his uncle Richard usurped the throne and became Richard III.

Richard's motives for seeking the crown are much debated. You can read more about this on pages 46 – 49. What we can be certain of is that his seizure of power was sudden and violent. At the beginning of June Edward's coronation was being planned. Then, on 13 June, Lord Hastings, the closest friend of Edward IV and the nobleman most likely to prevent Richard's coup, was hauled from the council chamber and beheaded without trial on Richard's orders. The shock of this political terrorism put an end to any possibility of opposition and Richard was acclaimed king on 26 June.

No-one knows for certain the fate of Edward V and his younger brother, Richard. According to Dominic Mancini, an Italian visitor to England, 'all the king's servants were taken away. He and his brother were moved into the inner rooms in the Tower. Day by day they were seen less and less behind the bars and windows, until they stopped being seen altogether. Dr Argentine was the last servant to see the king. He reported that the young king was like a victim preparing for sacrifice. He was praying every day for forgiveness because he thought that he was about to die. I have seen many men burst into tears when the young king was mentioned. Already people suspected that he had been done away with'.

Richard's usurpation caused opposition amongst many who had been loyal followers of Edward IV – men who also knew Richard well and were probably astonished by his actions. Plans for rebellions developed, intended to put Edward V back on the throne but the rebels became convinced that Edward was dead. Desperate for a new leader they turned to a most unlikely source – a young man who had been in exile since 1471 and who was the distant heir of Henry VI of Lancaster. This was Henry, Earl of Richmond – Henry Tudor. The first rising failed in the autumn of 1483 but by the summer of 1485 Henry had enough support to try again. The mix of Henry's army showed the depth of opposition to Richard. A handful of old Lancastrians mingled with many Yorkists, former followers of Edward IV, including the Woodvilles, the family of Edward IV's own queen, the mother of 'The Princes in the Tower'. On 22 August 1485 the two armies met at Bosworth in Leicestershire. Richard was killed and Henry Tudor became Henry VII but who could predict after so many dramatic changes that the civil wars were over?

The effects of the Wars of the Roses

Had the country been ruined by these wars? Certainly there were few survivors of the royal families of York and Lancaster but only a handful of other noble families died out, no more than in any generation. The Neville family, headed by Warwick 'the Kingmaker' provides a classic example of the misleading impact of the wars. Warwick and his brother were killed at the Battle of Barnet, violence seemingly ending the male Neville line and making that family a casualty of the wars. However neither man had a male heir and so the male line would have died out in any case. Historians have also calculated that fighting and manoeuvres occupied a total of only about 400 days in 30 years. Overall the fighting brought little destruction or damage because neither side wanted to create unnecessary enemies.

Questions
1 In the fourteenth century the chronicler Froissart described English noblemen as 'fickle, dangerous, arrogant and rebellious'. Does this description seem to apply to the nobles of the Wars of the Roses?

2 How might the events of 1455–1485 have helped Henry VII when he became king?

3.1 Richard III

Richard III is the most controversial king in English history. Most historians think that his seizure of the throne was motivated by ambition and not by his belief that the two princes were illegitimate, making Richard himself the rightful heir. Nor do they doubt that the princes were murdered in the early months of Richard's reign. However the fact that there is no precise and uncontestable evidence about how they died or whether Richard gave the order to kill them has led some people to doubt Richard's guilt. To them, notably many members of the 'Richard III Society', Richard was a hero, ever loyal to his brother, Edward IV, and incapable of taking the throne without good cause. Some people have suggested that the Duke of Buckingham, Richard's right-hand man during his coup, could have ordered the murder without Richard's knowledge. One contemporary jotting says that the boys died 'by the vise of the Duke of Buckingham'.

ONE OF THE EARLIEST SURVIVING PORTRAITS OF RICHARD III, PAINTED 1516–1522 AND PROBABLY BASED ON A CONTEMPORARY PAINTING.

For:

● Richard had been loyal to Edward IV in 1470–71 when Edward's other brother, George, Duke of Clarence, had been a traitor, allied with Edward's enemies.

● Richard had governed the north of England successfully for Edward after 1471 and had given no hint of treachery.

● Richard had been popular with many people in the north. After his death, the city council in York recorded on paper its sorrow at hearing of his death – a dangerous thing to do. Richard may even have intended to be buried in York.

● He showed many signs of being a good and efficient king amidst the preoccupations of rebellions.

● Elizabeth Woodville, the mother of the Princes, came out of sanctuary with her daughters to spend Christmas 1484 at Richard's court.

Against:

● Richard never produced his nephews to contradict rumours of their murders in 1483.

● By marrying Anne Neville, Warwick's daughter, Richard inherited Warwick's power and support in the north. By 1483 Richard had built on this to create for himself a huge territory, virtually making himself a sub-king in the region. However other significant northern lords, the Earl of Northumberland and Lord Stanley, may well have resented Richard's arrival and pre-eminence in the north.

● After the rebellion in 1483 Richard gave many lands in the south to his northern supporters. They filled the gaps left by gentry who had rebelled and gone into exile. These northerners were disliked by the local people.

● Richard destroyed the peace of the country with his coup and subjected England to more years of uncertainty, rebellions and danger.

● In 1483 many Yorkists rebelled against him, preferring to support the unknown Henry Tudor rather than their old king's brother.

YORK MINSTER, WHERE RICHARD APPEARS TO HAVE BEEN PLANNING TO BUILD HIS TOMB

Richard's claim to the throne

Richard claimed in June 1483 that his brother Edward's children were illegitimate. He said that he had obtained information from a bishop that Edward had been betrothed to Eleanor Boteler before he married Elizabeth Woodville in 1464. This earlier 'pre-contract' meant that the king's marriage was invalid. Edward V, his brother and sisters were bastards and could not inherit the throne. As the nearest male relative Richard was therefore the rightful heir to the crown. There is no evidence to corroborate Richard's story. It became known for the first time in mid to late June 1483. Eleanor Boteler had died years before.

Richard Plantagenet
Duke of Gloucester
1461 — afterwards
Richard III.

tant le desiere

CHARD'S BADGE, THE WHITE BOAR.

Richard's character is undoubtedly a puzzle. What conclusions can you reach about him from the material on these pages? Be warned – the material here can only touch the surface of the problem, the argument can go on and on!

Two Historians on Richard III

❝ Richard III was a man of considerable ability, energy and attractiveness. His chivalry, in particular, in an age which highly valued such martial qualities in a young nobleman, warmly commended him to his contemporaries....It was his tragedy that his ambition, and his sense of his own worth and importance, led him to disregard all law and right in the pursuit of his own interests. He did not hesitate to kill to make himself king. What he did in 1483 both surprised and horrified contemporaries not only because it was unexpected of him, but also because it went beyond the bounds of contemporary political ethics...

...he was not one-dimensional. He was neither a hateful child-murderer, nor a paragon of contemporary virtue. He was a man who lived up to several of the ideals of contemporary nobility, yet one who when tested was found wanting. It is possible that he himself came to understand this and that the realization was the cause of great anguish. ❞

A.J.Pollard, *Richard III and the Princes in the Tower,* 1991.

❝ It does not seem that Richard changed greatly when he ceased to be a subject and became a sovereign. The intellectual depth and political ability was always there. So too were the gentler qualities of piety and generosity. The charm, persuasiveness and self-advertisement are constant features. The aggression, ambition, opportunism, foresight, dissimulation, and ruthlessness of the acquisitive duke are present also in the usurpation story....Ultimately his own interests came first: above his family; above also his obligations as a subject, a knight, a guardian and as a king towards his people. ❞

M.A.Hicks, *Richard III: The Man behind the Myth,* 1991.

The Reigns of Edward V and Richard III – a Chronology

1483

April 9 — Edward IV died. Prince Edward was in Ludlow. Richard was in Yorkshire.

April 29/30 — Richard and his chief supporter, the Duke of Buckingham seized control of Edward V at Northampton. The young king's uncle, Earl Rivers, and other attendants were sent north as prisoners. Queen Elizabeth fled to sanctuary with her other children when the news reached London.

May 4 — Edward V and Richard reached London.

May 10 — The council appointed Richard as protector and fixed Edward's coronation for the end of June.

June 13 — Lord Hastings was executed without trial on Richard's orders. Hastings was likely to be young Edward's strongest supporter.

June 16 — Queen Elizabeth was persuaded to let her younger son join Edward V in the royal apartments in the Tower.

June 22 — Edward IV's children were proclaimed bastards.

June 26 — Richard was acclaimed king as Richard III. Rivers and others were executed.

July 6 — Richard III was crowned king.

October — The rebellion usually known as 'Buckingham's rebellion' failed. Buckingham, described by Richard as 'the most untrue creature living', was executed.

1484 March — Richard's son, Edward, died.

1485 March — Richard's wife, Anne, died.

August 22 — Richard was killed at the Battle of Bosworth. Key northern lords, Northumberland and Stanley, did not fight for Richard and Stanley intervened on Henry's side. One contemporary writer reported that the night before the battle Richard had seen 'a multitude of demons' in a terrible dream.

A NINETEENTH CENTURY PAINTING SHOWING THE SCENE FROM SHAKESPEARE'S "HENRY VI" WHEN THE NOBILITY CHOSE ROSES AS BADGES. THE WHITE ROSE WAS A YORKIST BADGE BUT THERE IS LITTLE EVIDENCE OF THE RED ROSE BEING USED BY THE LANCASTRIANS.

TATTERSHALL CASTLE. LIKE OTHER MID-FIFTEENTH CENTURY CASTLES IT WAS BUILT OF BRICK WITH LARGE WINDOWS FOR MAXIMUM COMFORT. ANOTHER SIGN OF PROSPERITY WAS THE RE-BUILDING OF PARISH CHURCHES IN EAST ANGLIA AND THE COTSWOLDS.

The fifteenth century was also a prosperous time for many. Ordinary people had probably never been better off because, with the population low after the Black Death, wages were high and prices were low (see pp 8 – 9). Housing, clothing and diet were all improving. Greater education and literacy led to the demand for more books and hence the development of printing.

Therefore historians now tend to suggest that England was far from being a chaotic, gloom-ridden country as a result of the Wars of the Roses. However it is interesting to reflect upon the most famous book written during this period, Sir Thomas Malory's Morte D'Arthur which retold the story of King Arthur and his knights. Malory told of an ideal king who rescued his country from chaos, helped by an aristocracy of knights who abandoned their private quarrels and ambitions for the good of their country. Perhaps Malory was motivated or influenced by the political events of his own day. The people of England who had seen war in 1455, hoped that it would be brief but then saw major conflict between 1459 and 1461. Again they hoped for peace but there were more battles in 1464 and so the pattern repeated itself in 1469 – 1471 and 1483 – 1485. Each time hopes of peace disintegrated as a few noblemen again destroyed the country's peace. Perhaps the Wars of the Roses did have an important psychological effect on the people of England even if their lives were not directly disrupted by armies or battles.

TALKING POINT

In what ways can literature provide useful evidence for historians?

Creating Propaganda

Since the 1960s there has been an enormous amount of research into the period of the Wars of the Roses. Historians have vastly increased our knowledge and have overturned many old ideas about the period. This has been far from easy because the old ideas are very strong, particularly as they were enshrined in Shakespeare's history plays. However Shakespeare was not the first to write about the events of the Wars of the Roses. This had begun immediately after Bosworth. Throughout his reign Henry VII and his councillors had to work long and hard to ensure his security. This work involved developing policies and taking decisions and it also meant persuading the country that Henry was both the rightful heir and a successful king. As his reign went on, his subjects needed to be reassured that England really was a more peaceful country since Henry had become king.

One way the people were persuaded of Henry's virtues was by propaganda which showed how the past events of history justified Henry's actions and his right to be king. This use of propaganda continued under every Tudor monarch. The second half of this chapter examines the way past events were used to give the Tudors greater security but first it may help if you try out this problem for yourself.

---

1 On the next page you can see a list of events from the period known as the Wars of the Roses. Can you use this information to retell the story of the Wars of the Roses so that you justify Henry's position as king and thereby give him greater security?

2 In doing this you are creating propaganda. What do you think are the hallmarks of effective propaganda?

EXAMINING THE EVIDENCE
The Tudors, History and Propaganda

This section examines the history written during the sixteenth century and propaganda produced more directly by governments.

Early Examples
Source A

Cadwaladr's blood lineally descending,
Long has been told of such a Prince coming.
Wherefore Friends, if that I shall not lie
This same is the fulfiller of the Prophecy.

Part of a speech prepared to welcome Henry VII to Worcester in May 1486. Worcester had been a centre for an unsuccessful rebellion earlier in 1486. Cadwaladr, according to the most popular history of Britain, had been the last true king of Britain.

In 1422 Henry VI became King aged 9 months. His father and grandfather
had been the first two Lancastrian Kings.

1437–1450
Henry VI governed England. The country's
problems increased considerably.

1450–1453
Quarrels grew between the Dukes of York
and Somerset over who should be Henry VI's
chief councillor.

1453
Henry VI fell into a coma for 18 months,
following news of final defeat in France.
York became Protector.

1455
Battle of St. Albans – York attacked the King's
forces to remove Somerset as Henry's
adviser. Henry stayed King.

1458–1460
Battles at Blore Heath, Northampton
and Wakefield.

1460
The Duke of York was named as Henry VI's
successor by parliament but he was killed
at the Battle of Wakefield.

1461
York's son, Edward, won the throne by
defeating Henry's forces at Towton.
He became Edward IV.

1470
The Earl of Warwick deposed Edward IV
and put Henry VI back on the throne.

1471
Edward IV regained the throne after killing
Warwick at Barnet and the Lancastrian
leaders at Tewkesbury. Henry VI was
murdered in the Tower of London.

1475
Edward IV invaded France and won a large
pension from France without needing to fight.

1478
Edward IV had his brother, George Duke of
Clarence, executed for treason.

1483 April
Edward IV died. His son became
Edward V aged 12. The boy's uncle,
Richard of Gloucester was Protector.

1483 June
Richard of Gloucester took the throne
from his nephew and became Richard III.

1485 Henry Tudor defeated Richard III at Bosworth

Source B

At the entry to the city shall be built a place in the manner of heaven, of great joy and angelic harmony. Under the heaven shall be a desolate world, full of trees and flowers into which shall spring up a royal rich red rose conveyed by a device. Unto this rose shall appear another rich white rose unto whom, being together, all other flowers shall bow and give sovereignty, showing the rose to be the principal of all flowers.

A description from the York Civic Records of one of the pageants devised to welcome Henry VII to York in April 1486. York had given strong support to Richard III.

---

1 Why do you think each of these sources was produced?

2 How do these sources provide support or praise for Henry VII?

3 How reliable are these extracts as evidence about either Richard III or loyalty to Henry VII?

4 What do sources C and D tell you about Richard's appearance?

Portraits of Richard III

Source C

RICHARD III WITH A BROKEN SWORD, PAINTED DURING THE SIXTEENTH CENTURY. INFRA-RED PHOTOGRAPHY HAS SHOWN THAT IT WAS ORIGINALLY PAINTED WITH 'A VERY EXAGGERATED LEFT SHOULDER AND A VERY DEFORMED LEFT ARM'.

Source D

A PORTRAIT OF RICHARD III FROM THE SIXTEENTH CENTURY. RECENT CLEANING HAS SHOWN PORTRAITS WERE RETOUCHED TO MAKE ONE OF HIS SHOULDERS HIGHER THAN THE OTHER.

The Writings of Polydore Vergil

Source E

Richard, without the assent of the common people and by the might of certain noblemen gained the realm, contrary to the law of God and man ... [but] the guilt of a wicked conscience did so frighten him that he lived in continual fear. To end this he determined to have his nephews killed, because as long as they lived he could never be out of hazard. ... When Richard heard that the Lieutenant of the Tower had not followed his orders he committed the task of slaughter to James Tyrell who, being forced to do the king's commandment, rode sorrowfully to London and murdered those royal babes. With what kind of death these innocent children were executed is not certainly known.

Source F

Inflamed with anger Richard struck his horse with his spurs and rode against [Henry]. Henry saw King Richard come upon him and, because all his hope was in valiancy of arms, he received him with great courage. King Richard at the first brunt killed William Brandon the standard bearer and fought also with John Cheney, a man of great bravery but the king with great force drove him to the ground, making way with weapon on every side. But yet Henry took the brunt longer than ever his own soldiers had expected, who were now almost out of hope of victory. Then Sir William Stanley came to the rescue and King Richard was killed fighting manfully in the thickest press of his enemies.

Source G

[Richard] was little of stature, deformed of body, one shoulder being higher than the other, a short and sour countenance which seemed to savour of mischief, craft and deceit. While he was thinking of any matter he continually bit his nether lip, as though that cruel nature of his did rage against itself in that little body. Truly he had a sharp mind, subtle but apt to dissemble. His courage was high and failed him not even at his death.

Source H

Henry took to wife Elizabeth, the daughter of Edward IV, a woman shrewd indeed above all others, and at the same time, beautiful. This must be regarded as the work of providence, for by this union all the causes of the two most deadly factions were completely destroyed, whereby the two houses of Lancaster and York became one, and from it sprang the true and established royal line which now reigns.

Vergil came to England in 1502. He already had a high reputation as a scholar when he was invited by Henry VII to write a history of England. His Anglica Historia was based on documentary research and conversations with those involved in recent events. It was completed by 1513 although it was not published until 1534. James Tyrell (Source E) was a close supporter of Richard III but then served Henry VII until 1502 when he was tried and executed for treason. After his death the story of his involvement in the murders of the Princes began to circulate but there is no documentary evidence to support this story.

5 Read Sources E – H. Vergil did not create an entirely evil picture of Richard III.

(a) What examples of this can you find in these extracts?

(b) Why might Vergil have avoided a totally evil portrayal of Richard?

6 Do these extracts have any value for historians of the period? Explain your answer.

Royal Badges and Heraldry
Source I

TUDOR BADGES ON A DOOR AT WESTMINSTER ABBEY. THESE BADGES INCLUDED THE TUDOR ROSE, THE PORTCULLIS OF THE BEAUFORT FAMILY (HENRY VII'S MOTHER WAS MARGARET BEAUFORT), AND THE CROWN IN THE THORNBUSH, WHICH SUGGESTS THAT THE STORY OF RICHARD III'S CROWN ROLLING INTO A BUSH AT BOSWORTH WAS TRUE.

7 What does Source I tell you about the nature of Tudor propaganda?

William Shakespeare

Source J

Richard

But I, that am not shap'd for sportive tricks,
Nor made to court an amorous looking-glass,
I, that am rudely stamp'd, and want love's majesty
To strut before a wanton ambling nymph;
I, that am curtail'd of this fair proportion,
Cheated of feature by dissembling nature,
Deform'd, unfinish'd, sent before my time
Into this breathing world scarce half made up,
And that so lamely and unfashionable,
That dogs bark at me as I halt by them;
Why, I, in this weak piping time of peace,
Have no delight to pass away the time,
Unless to spy my shadow in the sun,
And descant on mine own deformity:
And therefore, since I cannot prove a lover,
To entertain these fair well-spoken days,
I am determined to prove a villain, ...

King Richard III, Act I, Scene i, the opening scene of the play.

Source K

Richmond

... We will unite the white rose and the red.
Smile heaven upon this fair conjunction,
That long have frown'd upon their enmity!
What traitor hears me, and says not amen?
England hath long been mad, and scarr'd herself;
The brother blindly shed the brother's blood,
The father rashly slaughter'd his own son,
The son, compell'd, been butcher to the sire:
All this divided York and Lancaster,
Divided in their dire division.
O, now let Richmond and Elizabeth,
The true succeeders of each royal house,
By God's fair ordinance conjoin together,
And let their heirs, God, if thy will be so,
Enrich the time to come with smooth-fac'd peace,
With smiling plenty and fair prosperous days!
Abate the edge of traitors, gracious Lord,
That would reduce these bloody days again,
And make poor England weep in streams of blood!
Let them not live to taste this land's increase,
That would with treason wound this fair land's peace!
Now civil wounds are stopp'd, peace lives again:
That she may long live here, God say amen!

King Richard III, Act V, Scene iv.

KING ARTHUR PORTRAYED IN
FIFTEENTH CENTURY ARMOUR
BECAUSE THERE WAS LITTLE
UNDERSTANDING THAT LIFE IN
THE PAST HAD BEEN DIFFERENT.

8 How far does Richard's self-portrait in Source J agree with the descriptions earlier in this section?

9 How does Extract K provide support for the Tudor dynasty?

10 In what ways might Shakespeare's play be a more effective piece of propaganda than the others you have seen in this section?

11 To what extent does the evidence in this section support the argument that there was a deliberate attempt by Tudor monarchs and governments to secure the dynasty through propaganda?

12 'Tudor propaganda tells us nothing useful about Richard III and the Wars of the Roses'. Explain why you agree or disagree with this statement.

Ideas about History in the Tudor Period

Using Evidence
Most medieval and Tudor writers copied out earlier writers' words rather than looking for contemporary sources and analysing them.

Analysing change and continuity
There was little realization that people in previous eras has differed from 16th century people in ideas, speech or dress – there was no sense of anachronism.

Suggesting explanations
Explanations were usually simple rather than complex and often involved God's judgement.

TALKING POINT

The Tudor rose has been described as the royal logo! How well does the propaganda of the Tudor period compare with the work of advertisers and propagandists today?

Propaganda – an old idea

People in the fifteenth and sixteenth centuries were certainly interested in history. This interest was partly because their sense of national identity – of being English – was growing, aided by the great English victory of Agincourt. This heightened sense of Englishness in turn inspired a greater interest in the origins of the nation. The main book that people turned to was Geoffrey of Monmouth's History of the Kings of Britain, written in the early twelfth century. Geoffrey had linked Britain to the great civilisations of the past by telling how Britain had been founded by Brutus after he had fled from the destruction of Troy and how Britain had achieved greatness under the leadership of King Arthur.

A second reason why people were interested in history was the dramatic nature of recent political events. The successes in the French wars under Edward III (1327 – 1377) and Henry V (1413 – 1422) had been glorious. Now, after the civil wars of the mid-fifteenth century, people were nostalgic about those victories. In addition more and more people were learning to read; thirty per cent of the population, more in London. The result was that scriveners (men who made their living by copying books and documents by hand) were producing an ever-increasing number of English histories and adding recent events onto the end of them.

This level of interest in the past means that it is not surprising that history was used to strengthen the Tudors' position after 1485. It is also equally clear that the Tudors were only doing what others had done before. Geoffrey of Monmouth's History of the Kings of Britain ended with the defeat of the last British king, Cadwaladr, and the prophecy that his heirs would one day return to claim the throne. Edward IV had buttressed his claim to be the true king by having genealogies prepared showing his descent from Cadwaladr and therefore from the incomparable King Arthur. Edward also used government officials to write propaganda. In 1470 a detailed account called 'The Rebellion of Lincolnshire' was produced to prove Warwick and Clarence's involvement and treachery. This was a very detailed account, full of dates, movements of armies, freely given confessions and even a casket of incriminating documents.

How good was Tudor history?

Much of the story told by Hall, Shakespeare and others was factually wrong or wildly exaggerated but people believed it because it had its roots in reality. There had been intermittent civil war even if the practical effects on most people had been very limited. Richard III had taken the crown from his nephew. At the very beginning of Richard's reign Londoners had believed that Richard murdered the Princes. Therefore it was possible to believe that Richard had been plotting and murdering his way to the throne long before his brother's death. Shakespeare's picture of Richard in full murdering flow at the first Battle of St. Albans could be accepted. That he was in reality only two years old at the time was easily ignored. After all, God had given his judgement at Bosworth against Richard so he must have been an immoral, evil figure.

The second reason why these accounts were believed was that there were hardly any historical researchers to challenge or correct mistakes. The study of history based on careful examination of sources was only just beginning. The great majority of writers kept to the approaches you can see in the chart on page 57.

However developments in the writing of history were slowly taking place. By the end of the sixteenth century the old style of chronicle writing was being sneered at for providing only a list of 'Mayors and Sheriffs and the dear year and the great frosts'. The historian who had the greatest impact was Polydore Vergil. Vergil imposed an interpretation on his account and explained the reasons for events rather than just listing and describing what happened. This made his work a history rather than a chronicle. Vergil also searched out documents and oral evidence rather than simply copying another writer's words. However the very qualities of Vergil's work brought problems. He failed to find any evidence to support Geoffrey of Monmouth's account of King Arthur and so he said that Geoffrey's story was a myth. The English were outraged and Vergil was accused 'of polluting our English chronicles most shamefully with his Romish lies and other Italish beggaries'.

TALKING POINT

As Vergil's work shows, chronicle writing was being replaced by the writing of history. Perhaps the first real piece of English historical writing was the continuation of the Crowland Chronicle written by a government official in 1486. This is the most important narrative source for the Yorkist kings. Why was this development in writing happening at this time?

REVIEW

Sixteenth century people were interested in history. They were interested because of their curiosity about the origins of their country. They were also interested because past events seemed to relate to the incidents and problems of their own day.

1 What does your work on history and propaganda in the Tudor period tell you about the intelligence and sophistication of Tudor people and governments?

2 What evidence would you use either to support or challenge these statements?

(a) The Wars of the Roses had only a limited impact on the English people.

(b) Despite the activities of a few individuals the majority of the nobility were eager for peace in 1485.

(c) The Wars of the Roses had made Henry VII's task easier.

SECTION REVIEW

1485 – The King's Priorities

This section began with a reconstruction of the atmosphere at a council meeting early in Henry VII's reign. To conclude it may help to consider, in the light of your work on chapters 1–3, the issues facing that council in 1485. This will bring into play what you have learned to date about the concerns and priorities of Tudor monarchs and governments and be a final opportunity to identify some of the differences between then and now.

1 Work in pairs. Look at the range of issues identified on these pages. Draw up an agenda for action for Henry's council, putting the most urgent issues at the top. If you wish you can decide that some issues need not be discussed by the king and his council at all.

2 Compare your agenda with those of other groups and identify the reasons for similarities and differences between them..

3 Would anyone – for example yeomen, townspeople or the poor – have expected the king to establish a different order of priorities? Explain your answer.

(a) Education

Literacy was increasing. People were spending more money on educating their children. However this was not just a practical development. Many were interested in learning for its own sake. Some noblemen built up large collections of books and visited other countries to extend their own learning.

(b) People and Poverty

Years of major epidemic disease after 1400: 1400, 1413, 1433–44, 1437, 1439, 1444, 1448–50, 1452, 1454, 1464, 1471, 1479, 1485.
Prices had been rising sharply in the early 1480s with a particularly dramatic increase in 1482. The cause was a run of poor harvests between 1481 and 1483.

(c) Overseas Expansion

Ships from Portugal had recently been exploring the African coast and developing a lucrative trade. This might open up the possibility of new routes to the riches of the east.

(d) The North of England

'King Richard, late mercifully reigning over us, with many other lords and nobility of the north parts, was piteously slain and murdered to the great heavyness of this city.'

Minutes of the Corporation of the City of York, 23 August 1485.

(e) The Printing Press

In the last years of Edward IV's reign William Caxton had introduced the printing press to England. Among the earliest printed books were those on the history of Troy, Malory's Morte d'Arthur, The Game and Playe of Chesse, The Canterbury Tales and many religious texts.

(f) Public Order

'When King Edward reigned, the people looked for prosperity and peace but it came not.' This comment from Warkworth's Chronicle records the disappointment felt when Edward IV failed to meet expectations in the 1460s. Without a strong king who ensured that laws were kept, local lords' influence could increase to the extent that they might use their retinues to influence courts or take land by force, as had happened in the 1440s and 1450s.

(g) Foreign Relations

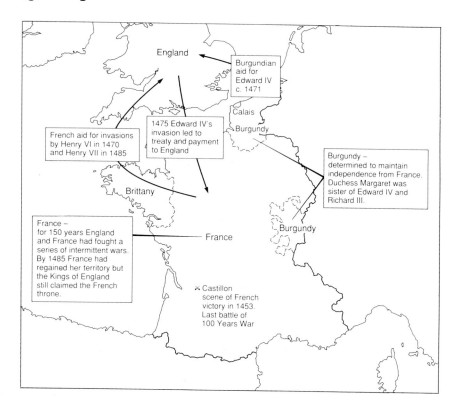

(h) Artistic Development

HENRY VI.

A PAINTING OF AN ENGLISH AMBASSADOR, EDWARD GRIMSTON. COMPARE THIS PAINTING, DONE ON THE CONTINENT, WITH THE ENGLISH PAINTINGS OF HENRY VI AND EDWARD IV.

(i) The Role of the Nobility

'The nobility, who are endowed with great honours, possessions and riches, can be compared to the firm ground while the lower people, who lack such endowments, can be likened to the unstable, running water ... the reason why the nobles need to agree and listen to each other is that the well-ordered government of every region depends on the nobility ...'

Bishop Russell, Chancellor of England, addressing Parliament in 1484.

In an age of slow communications and transport it was difficult for the king to maintain law and order in regions distant from London. Therefore, kings delegated power to their nobles to ensure good government. This could be dangerous. The Earl of Warwick had briefly deposed Edward IV. Richard, Duke of Gloucester had deposed Edward V.

(j) Religion

The English church was part of the Roman Catholic church headed by the Pope. The Venetian ambassador, writing in 1497, said that the English 'all attend Mass every day and say many Paternosters in public, they always hear Mass on Sundays in their parish church, and give liberal alms, because they may not offer less than a piece of money; nor do they omit any form of worship expected from good Christians.' The ambassador went on to say that there were Englishmen who had 'various opinions' on religion. There were dissenters, known as Lollards, who opposed the Pope's authority and demanded reforms to make religion more accessible to ordinary people. They were few but sometimes vocal.

(k) Royal Finances

'I purpose to live upon my own and not to charge my subjects but in great and urgent causes concerning the weal of themselves and also the defence of them and of this my realm.'

> Edward IV addressing the House of Commons in 1467. However Edward was almost bankrupt when he died in 1483 and Richard III used large sums in defence against rebellions.

(l) Scotland, Ireland and Wales

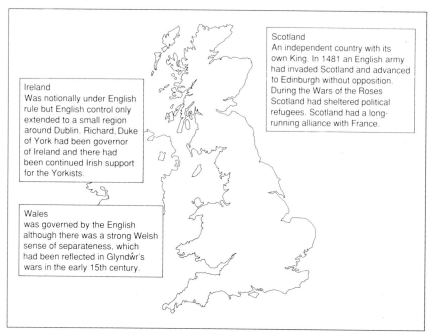

Ireland
Was notionally under English rule but English control only extended to a small region around Dublin. Richard, Duke of York had been governor of Ireland and there had been continued Irish support for the Yorkists.

Scotland
An independent country with its own King. In 1481 an English army had invaded Scotland and advanced to Edinburgh without opposition. During the Wars of the Roses Scotland had sheltered political refugees. Scotland had a long-running alliance with France.

Wales
was governed by the English although there was a strong Welsh sense of separateness, which had been reflected in Glyndŵr's wars in the early 15th century.

(m) Parliament

... the crown could not do without the cooperation of parliament for the making of laws, the legalising of its actions and the levying of taxes...

... as for taxation, parliamentary control was now firmly established in principle.

A R Myers Parliament 1422–1509 in The English Parliament in the Middle Ages
ed. RG Davies and JH Denton, 1981.

Section 1 The Reign of Henry VII

Henry VII – The Survival Game

Before studying a topic in detail it is important to have an outline understanding of events and the issues involved. Without the outline you probably won't be able to make sense of the detail and see its significance – to see the wood for the trees in other words. This game – you can compete against other individuals, groups or Henry VII! – will give you an outline of some of the key issues and events of Henry's reign and the main questions historians ask.

Your task is to work through the decisions in the game. Keep a note of your decisions, then check these decisions against the information on pp.68 – 69. You begin with 6 crowns but you will start to lose them when you make a poor decision. If you lose all six you will have lost your throne, failed your dynasty and will probably be dead! The winner will have the most crowns at the end. Good luck!

HENRY VII AS A YOUNG MAN BY JACQUES LE BOUCQ, A MID-SIXTEENTH CENTURY SKETCH.

HENRY VII, A PORTRAIT BY SITTOW PAINTED 1505.

First Decisions, August – September 1485

1 Marriage
You have already promised to marry Edward IV's daughter, Elizabeth, to win the support of Yorkists who opposed Richard III. However English kings usually marry foreign princesses to cement diplomatic links. Edward IV's marriage to an Englishwoman created rivalries and jealousies. Will you marry
(a) Elizabeth of York, uniting the families of York and Lancaster and reducing the chances of internal opposition?
(b) a French princess? France gave you aid in 1485 and might give powerful support against English rebels.
(c) a Spanish princess to warn France you will not be easily dominated?

2 Councillors
Who will be your advisers? Will you
(a) make a clean sweep of the council and leading administrators, replacing them with men who were in exile with you?
(b) replace those closest to Richard III with your men but keep the majority of councillors?
(c) make a clean sweep of the council and leading administrators, replacing them with your loyalists and give extensive lands and rewards to your supporters to ensure their loyalty?

3 Foreign Policy
The French helped you in 1485 but, as King of England, you claim to be King of France. The most successful kings have been warriors but French kings helped to de-stabilize Edward IV and Richard III to stop their aggression. What will be your policy towards France?
(a) Restate your claim to France and plan an invasion which will unite the nobility behind you?
(b) Sign a short-term truce with France, omitting any reference to your claim to France?
(c) Sign a peace treaty, giving up your claim to France in return for a French promise to support you against any rebels?

4 The Earls of Warwick and Lincoln
Both are nephews of Edward IV and Richard III. Warwick has the better claim to the throne but is still a child. Lincoln is in his 20s. Should you
(a) imprison both to prevent them becoming involved in rebellions?
(b) imprison Warwick but allow Lincoln to join the council to show that he is supporting you?
(c) free both but keep watch for their involvement in plots?

The Early Years 1485 – 1487

5 Controlling the North
Richard III had been popular in the north, especially in the city of York. Many northern lords and gentry had been well-rewarded by Richard and might join a rebellion. Should you
(a) visit York quickly to establish your presence as King and ensure that local lords know that they will be held responsible for any trouble?
(b) stay safe in the south, leaving the government of the north to the local lords as this will not provoke them to rebellion?
(c) appoint a southern lord as governor of the north, with orders to deal savagely with any trouble?

6 Rebellion, 1487
In Ireland a boy has been crowned King of England. His suporters say he is one of Edward IV's nephews. They plan to invade England with a mercenary army and take the throne. Should you
(a) imprison potential Yorkist supporters, such as Lincoln, to prevent the rebellion winning influential support?
(b) march immediately to the north-west, the most likely landing area, summoning your lords to raise troops and meet you there?
(c) await more detailed news while ordering your lords to muster their men in the Midlands?

7 France and Brittany
French forces have invaded the independent duchy of Brittany. French control would give them the whole coastline facing England. Should you
(a) ignore the French moves because it is too dangerous to act while England is still unsettled after the rebellion?
(b) use the army that put down the rebellion to invade Brittany to protect its independence?
(c) seek European allies to pressure France into withdrawing from Brittany and encourage English volunteers to fight 'unofficially' in Brittany?

8 Earl of Surrey
Thomas Howard, Earl of Surrey, fought for Richard at Bosworth. He was imprisoned but refused the chance to escape and join the 1487 rebellion. He is a capable and experienced nobleman. Should you
(a) keep him in prison to show your harshness to opponents and potential rebels?
(b) release him and make him responsible for keeping peace in the north, where he has no lands and supporters and therefore no power of his own?
(c) restore him to his family lands in East Anglia where his influence should ensure law and order?

More Problems 1487 – 1497

9 Danger from France, 1491

The King of France has married Anne of Brittany and won control of Brittany. Should you
(a) ignore this change because even an invasion cannot overturn the marriage?
(b) mount a major invasion of France? Only full control of France will end the danger from France.
(c) stage a limited invasion, designed to show that you will fight seriously if France ever threatens England?

10 Perkin Warbeck

Warbeck, who claims to be one of Edward IV's sons, has been accepted in the Netherlands as King of England. Should you
(a) ignore this because you have already beaten one pretender?
(b) ban trade with the Netherlands so that foreign merchants will put pressure on their rulers to abandon Warbeck?
(c) invade the Netherlands?

11 A Traitor, 1495

You rewarded Sir William Stanley for his vital help at Bosworth by making him Chamberlain of your Household. Now spies report that Stanley has been negotiating with Warbeck. Should you
(a) put Stanley under house arrest, sparing him because of his past record?
(b) execute Stanley for treason?
(c) imprison Stanley for life?

12 The Cornish Rebellion, 1497

Rebellion has started in the south-west while you are preparing to invade Scotland, which has been helping Warbeck. Should you
(a) continue the invasion of Scotland, relying on local lords to end the rebellion?
(b) send your army to crush the rebels, but stay well away from the trouble yourself?
(c) lead your army yourself to crush the rebels.

Peace and Quiet? 1497 – 1509

RY VII, A BUST SCULPTED
IETRO TORRIGIANO
R HENRY'S DEATH.

13 Warbeck and Warwick

Both are imprisoned in the Tower. You are seeking a marriage alliance with Spain but the king is unsure while there is still a Yorkist threat. You could end the danger by
(a) executing both on a false charge of conspiracy.
(b) executing Warwick because he does have a claim to the throne.
(c) executing Warbeck as a warning to Warwick.
(d) leave both in prison.

14 The Earl of Oxford

Oxford led your army at Bosworth. When you visit his lands he has all his men lining your route in welcome, wearing his badge and looking like his private army. This is breaking your laws. Should you
(a) ignore it because he is a loyal supporter?
(b) charge him with breaking the law?
(c) warn him but let him off this time?

15 Marriage for Prince Henry

Your eldest son, Prince Arthur, married Katherine of Spain but died young. What should you do about the marriage of your new heir, Henry? Should you
(a) marry him immediately to Katherine to preserve the alliance?
(b) send Katherine back and reconsider the possibilities?
(c) promise that Henry will marry Katherine but delay the marriage while you weigh up other possibilities?

16 A Foreign Treaty

You have the chance to make a treaty with Philip, the ruler of Burgundy. Which of these three elements of the treaty would be most important to you?
(a) a marriage agreement for you, now that your first queen is dead.
(b) a trade agreement that will please the London merchants.
(c) Philip's agreement to surrender Edmund de la Pole, a Yorkist heir and potential rebel.

Keeping your crown?

Henry VII died in April 1509 aged 52, to some extent worn-out by the dangers and decisions of his reign. He had kept his crown and passed it on to his son. Did you do as well as Henry? Check your decisions against the information below. You started with 6 crowns but unfortunately correct decisions do not add to your total – you simply don't lose one that time. How many did you have left at the end?

1 Marriage
(a) This was Henry's decision, honouring his earlier promise. This was the best way of reducing potential rebelliousness.
(b) Potentially helpful but it means going back on a promise and you might be portrayed as a French puppet. Lose 1 crown.
(c) No practical benefit while repeating the problems of (b). Lose 2 crowns.

2 Councillors
(a) You need experienced men if the administration is to work efficiently and this option would leave you very short of officials. Anyway most administrators have survived changes of dynasty. Lose 1 crown.
(b) Good choice – you keep the basis for efficient government while removing the discontented. Henry's choice.
(c) All the problems of (a) while also giving away money and land you need to build your own strength. Lose 2 crowns.

3 Foreign Policy
(a) Attractive option but very expensive – seeking heavy taxes will not win friends. France might also support Yorkist claimants against you. Lose 1 crown.
(b) Sensible option, using the link established in 1485 but not appearing to bow down to France. Not creating French enmity. Henry's action.
(c) Disastrous – will encourage French aggression against you and will provide excellent propaganda for your enemies. Lose 3 crowns.

4 The Earls of Warwick and Lincoln
(a) A harsh but sensible option, having the fewest dangers.
(b) Henry's choice, very logical but a risk in relation to Lincoln. In 1487 Lincoln joined a rebellion. Lose 1 crown.
(c) Dangerous option – Warwick might be the figurehead for a rebellion. Even someone pretending to be Warwick was a danger in 1487. Lose 2 crowns.

5 Controlling the North
(a) Henry's choice although it came close to disaster when Ricardians tried to attack him in York. At least he was demonstrating his power and position as king.
(b) Abdication by another name! People want a strong king, not another Henry VI who left everything to others. Lose 3 crowns.
(c) Half a good scheme. Several years later Henry did appoint Surrey to head the Council of the North but an over-harsh response would have stirred the revolt you want to avoid. Lose 1 crown.

6 Rebellion, 1487
(a) Good plan. Henry wasn't quick enough and Lincoln fled to head the rebellion. Weeks of worry followed. Henry's victory at the Battle of Stoke was easier than expected.
(b) What if they don't join you or move to join the rebels? You would be isolated and lacking support. Lose 2 crowns.
(c) Another sensible move. Henry did this – a pity he didn't link this to option (a)!

7 France and Brittany
(a) A signal to the King of France that he can do whatever he wishes. Not the action of a king! Lose 1 crown.
(b) A dangerous gamble, leaving the country, even if you can raise the taxes and cope with the ensuing hostility. Too much on top of the rebellion. Lose 1 crown.
(c) A reaction without risking immediate over-commitment. Henry's choice.

8 Earl of Surrey
(a) The safest route but not a good use of a capable man. His support for you would be useful.
(b) Henry's action – calculated to make the best use of Surrey with the smallest risk.
(c) Too much of a risk if Surrey doesn't prove to be loyal. Lose 1 crown.

9 Danger from France, 1491.

(a) No-one in Europe will respect you or England with this decision. It will hearten potential rebels. Lose 2 crowns.

(b) What if you lose or get caught in a long, expensive campaign that will force you to back down to France or critics of the expense at home, lose 1 crown.

(c) sensible, showing your strength without the danger of over-commitment. Henry invaded France in the autumn, indicating he was not intent on conquest. The King of France made a treaty and paid Henry a pension, allowing him to claim success.

10 Perkin Warbeck

(a) Dangerous and foolish optimism – this one has more support internationally. Lose 2 crowns.

(b) A shrewd practical move, even if some merchants at home will object. It's the only practical step possible. Henry's choice.

(c) By the time you have an army and the finance he'll have fled elsewhere. Impractical and very costly financially. Lose 2 crowns.

11 A Traitor

(a) Understandable but risky. This won't stop him plotting and may make him more desperate. Remember Richard III was depending on him and look what happened to Richard. Lose 2 crowns.

(b) The only safe course of action. Henry's choice.

(c) Will this appear weak to others as he is guilty of treason? He could continue to correspond with others or will you ban visitors and correspondence? (b) is better. Lose 1 crown.

12 The Cornish Rebellion

(a) What if they join the rebellion instead of stopping it on your behalf? Lose 3 crowns.

(b) What kind of a king are you? Your job is to lead and inspire not hide, even if this does seem the safest policy! Lose 1 crown.

(c) Good choice. Many rebels might desert if they realise they will have to face the king himself and it will ensure your men stay loyal. Henry did this successfully, remaining in clear control.

13 Warbeck and Warwick

(a) By far the safest plan. Henry chose this partly because the death of Warwick helped reassure Spain that Yorkist threats were at an end.

(b) On what charge? The plot with Warbeck is a better idea and allows you to get rid of both.

(c) But Warwick is the real danger! Lose 1 crown.

(d) Fairly safe after all these years but you have missed an opportunity. Lose 1 crown.

14 The Earl of Oxford

(a) And encourage other people to break the laws? Lose 1 crown.

(b) Quite right. Punishing Oxford will show that no-one is above the law. Henry's choice.

(c) Understandable but too weak. You seem to have favourites who are above the law. Lose 1 crown.

15 Marriage for Prince Henry

(a) Sensible in that it preserves the Spanish alliance but doesn't really take full advantage of the new situation. Loyalty isn't always the best policy amongst rulers.

(b) Insulting to Spain and liable to make any other potential ally think twice. Not a very diplomatic move. Lose 1 crown.

(c) The policy of a good diplomatist – you win all round. Henry's choice.

16 A foreign treaty.

(a) Useful if it leads to other agreements but not a top priority. It will also stop you using your marriage ability as a diplomatic weapon. Lose 1 crown.

(b) Useful but merchants will not influence your security. Lose 1 crown.

(c) The most important element. Any free Yorkists seem a danger and it is best to have them secure.

Conclusions

However well (or badly!) you did, the objective wasn't really to get the right answers or to guess what Henry did. The purpose of the game was to introduce you to some of the key issues and events of Henry's reign and the problems he had to grapple with. The game will have really been successful if you can suggest answers to these questions:

1 What were the main concerns of Henry VII as king?

2 What have you learned about Henry himself?

3 Why do you think he survived?

4 What questions do you now want to ask about his reign?

Section Preview

1485 – the beginning of a new age?

'(In 1483) all those who had begun this rebellion, realising that if they could not find someone new at their head for their conquest it would soon be all over with them, remembered Henry, Earl of Richmond, who had already spent many years in exile in Brittany.'

This comment by the well-informed Crowland Chronicler makes clear that Henry Tudor, Earl of Richmond, was not the first choice as leader of the rebellion against Richard III in 1483. This is not surprising as most of the rebels were Yorkists, supporters of Edward IV, who were outraged at Richard's treatment of Edward's sons. They had originally intended to put the elder boy, Edward V, back on the throne but had to find another leader when they became convinced that young Edward and his brother were dead. The Crowland Chronicler does make it sound as if they were rather desperate, sitting around pummelling their brains to think of a new leader with a claim to the throne, however obscure that claim might be! At last they 'remembered' Henry Tudor. Was he really such an unlikely king?

TALKING POINT

You can see three portraits of Henry VII on pages 65 and 67. Why might looking at just one portrait distort your understanding of him? What can you learn about Henry from his portraits?

Long-standing supporters of the House of Lancaster who had never been reconciled with the Yorkists, such as the Earl of Oxford.

Henry Tudor's relatives such as Jasper Tudor, Earl of Pembroke and supporters of his mother, Margaret Beaufort.

Former Yorkists – members of Edward IV's household and members of the Woodville family who had opposed Richard's usurpation. They were the majority.

Support → Henry Tudor

Henry had been born in 1457, the son of Henry VI's half-brother. Although he had royal blood no-one thought of him as a future king. This changed in 1471 when Henry VI and his son Prince Edward were killed. Henry Tudor became the Lancastrian heir and rival to the Yorkist king,

Edward IV. For safety he lived in exile in Brittany with his uncle, Jasper Tudor, Earl of Pembroke. Once Richard III became king, Henry's position became both more promising and more dangerous. In 1484 Richard reached a secret agreement with the Chancellor of Brittany. Henry fled to France from Brittany with his pursuers only an hour behind.

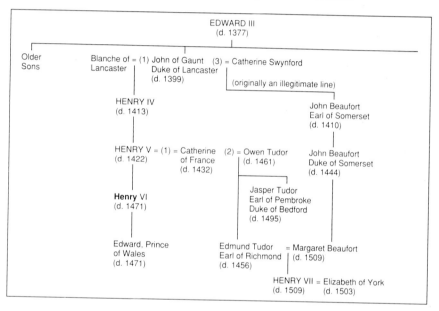

Thus, when Henry became king in 1485, aged 28, he had spent half his lifetime in exile. He had had no formal training for kingship. He hardly knew England or its governing classes, with the exception of those who had joined him in exile. Initially at least he had to rely heavily on this small group of supporters (many of whom had served Edward IV) and on the professional administrators who had stayed in office throughout changes of kings and dynasties. Nothing here promised novelty or radical change in the way the country was governed. Yet one of the most important debates about Henry VII is about change. Did he make such great changes that 1485 should be regarded as one of the most significant turning points in English history or did he rule as his medieval predecessors had done? Was he the first modern ruler or the last medieval king?

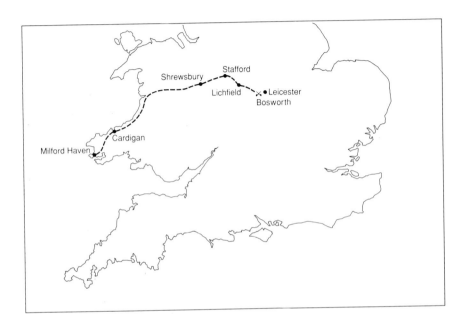

Source A

'the basic principles of his government turned out to be markedly Yorkist in character and conception, and ... his most enduring achievements were essentially a continuation of the work of the preceding quarter of a century ... There was singularly little innovation in substance in the government of Henry VII.'

S.B. Chrimes, *Lancastrians, Yorkists and Henry VII*, 2nd edition, 1966.

Source B

'(Edward IV) should not be too readily regarded as a Mark I version of Henry VII. The difference in their personalities was profound, and the differences between their policies are hardly less important than their resemblances.'

C.D. Ross, *The Reign of Edward IV* in *'Fifteenth Century England'* ed. S.B. Chrimes et al., 1972.

Source C

'The most important revolution in government of the period was surely the restoration of a high degree of peace and stability throughout most of the country, and its architect was King Henry VII. For this reason, his victory over Richard III in August 1485 deserves to be re-established as a major turning-point in English history.'

A. Grant, *Henry VII*, 1985.

Source D

'Since the monarchy's refoundation began in 1461 and was resumed by the Tudors, who at first used similar administrative methods and even many of the same councillors, it is fruitless to maintain that Bosworth marked a new dawn.'

J. Guy, *Tudor England*, 1988.

1 What similarities and differences can you find amongst the views quoted above?

2 What reasons can you suggest for the disagreements among historians?

3 Look again at the information on Henry's experience before 1485.

(a)Were there any ways in which this experience could help him as king?

(b) Would this experience be likely to make him an innovator in government?

4 Henry VII, Foreign Policy and the Security of the Realm

PREVIEW

This chapter deals with Henry VII's contacts with foreign countries. Chapter 5 describes domestic events and policies. This division of foreign from domestic policies is an artificial division and therefore can be dangerous. For Henry and his councillors the two were interwoven and this kind of separation would probably not have occurred to them. However in these chapters it is hoped that this division helps to clarify the explanations and arguments put forward by historians, the objectives and successes of Henry's foreign policies, what they tell us about Henry himself and the degree to which foreign policies changed after 1485.

Before looking at Henry's foreign policies in detail, it is important to identify the general lines of English foreign policy before 1485. Using the material in this preview can you suggest possible answers to questions 1–5?

---

1 What had been the chief elements of English foreign policy before 1485?

2 What policies could Henry VII follow that would (a) continue or (b) change the policies of his predecessors?

3 Can you suggest any factors that might lead to changes in English foreign policy?

4 Why would foreign policy be a vital issue for Henry VII?

5 What objectives do you think Henry VII should pursue in foreign policy?

France – English kings had claimed the French throne since 1330 and this had led to perpetual fear of war and to intermittent warfare. The English belief in the righteousness of their cause was reinforced by great victories, such as Crecy and Agincourt, and by the Treaty of Troyes in 1420, which said that Henry V was the heir to the French throne. The French belief in the righteousness of their cause was equally strong, confirmed by their own victories and particularly by the expulsion of the English from France by 1453. During the Wars of the Roses France had given support to Henry VI and to Henry VII in 1485 in order to reduce the chance of the Yorkist kings invading France.

Burgundy – As a result of French weakness earlier in the fifteenth century the Dukes of Burgundy had gained independence from France and also ruled the Netherlands. Until 1435 Burgundy was in alliance with England against their common enemy, France, an alliance greatly strengthened by their common trading interests. Edward IV had restored the Burgundian alliance in the 1460s and in 1471 Burgundy had helped Edward to regain the English throne but only after hearing that France, in alliance with the Lancastrian government in England, intended to invade Burgundy.

TALKING POINT

Why is it helpful to suggest answers at this stage even though you have not yet studied the topic in detail?

Scotland – Although England had recognised Scotland's independence in 1328 there had been little reduction in the tensions between the two countries. English kings still occasionally claimed overlordship of Scotland. In defence, Scotland maintained an alliance with France. The result was continued border warfare, leading sometimes to outright invasion. In the 1460s the Scots, wanting to disrupt Edward IV's government, had sheltered Henry VI. In return Edward tried to promote dissension within Scotland. In 1481, an English army had recovered the border fortress of Berwick and marched to the gates of Edinburgh.

The rest of Europe – The foreign policies of the Yorkist kings had focussed on their neighbours in north-west Europe. Despite trading links the Yorkists were not forced to pay constant attention to the activities of more distant states. Spain had only been a single country since 1479, when Ferdinand of Aragon had married Isabella of Castile, thus uniting the two kingdoms and, moreover, was preoccupied with the fight to expel Arab settlers whose devotion to Islam clashed with Spanish Christianity. The Holy Roman Empire was also more powerful in name than in reality. It consisted of many different states, whose rivalries prevented them exercising any influence in Europe as a whole.

	1340s–1360s		1370s–c.1410		1415–1435	1435–1453	1465–1485	
	Edward III's successful campaign in France		French recovery and raids on English coasts		English success in alliance with Burgundy	French recovery and reconquest, raids on England	French attempts to destabilise English politics by supporting Lancaster	
1330	1350	1370	1390	1410	1430	1450	1470	1490
Periods of heaviest campaigning 1338–1347 mid-late 1350s 1415–1430 1448–1453	1346 Battle of Crecy 1356 Battle of Poitiers		1396 Truce	1415 Battle of Agincourt		1453 Battle of Chatillon	1475 Edward IV's expedition to France	

The Beginnings of a Foreign Policy, 1485–1487

Foreign countries had played a crucial role in the Wars of the Roses. Three times English kings had been defeated and deposed by rivals supported by France or Burgundy. As the last beneficiary of foreign aid, Henry VII was well aware of the dangers that could come from abroad. He also knew the dangers of reacting aggressively to foreign interference. Warfare drained the crown's coffers, necessitated the calling of parliament to seek taxes and risked criticism once parliament had assembled. In the early years of his reign Henry tried to avoid war while still asserting his strength and capability as king – a narrow path to tread but one that avoided the greatest dangers.

The early details of Henry's foreign policy were chiefly determined by the support he had received at Bosworth. Henry had been given aid by France and, to a lesser extent, by Scotland. As king he endeavoured to maintain good relations with both countries. In October 1485 a one year truce with France was proclaimed and was later extended until January 1489. An agreement with Scotland took longer as the Scots' prime concern was to destabilise kings of England as an aid to their own security. However, Henry's active negotiations led to a three year truce signed in July 1486.

At the same time Henry was determined to ensure that the rest of Europe accepted his rights and presence as king of England. A commercial treaty was agreed with Brittany in 1486. Negotiations began for a marriage treaty with Spain which eventually led to the Treaty of Medina del Campo in March 1489. The major omission was any agreement with Burgundy, although historians disagree on where the fault lay. Negotiations did not begin for treaties of commerce and friendship until December 1487, by which time Burgundy had been closely involved in the first major foreign threat to Henry's position as king.

Rebellion from Abroad – the threat from Lambert Simnel

After Bosworth Henry's surviving opponents looked to Burgundy for assistance. Margaret, the Dowager-Duchess of Burgundy, was the sister of Edward IV and Richard III, and possessed influence and wealth. Ireland was another likely rebel base. The lords of Ireland hoped to distract Henry from closer involvement in Ireland by supporting rebels.

The man at the centre of the rebellion and earlier unavailing plots was Francis Viscount Lovell Richard's friend and chamberlain. After Bosworth Lovell had fled into hiding, maintaining contact with other Ricardians. John de la Pole, Earl of Lincoln was a less predictable rebel. The son of Richard III's sister Elizabeth, Lincoln had been Richard's heir in 1485 and had fought at Bosworth but initially appeared reconciled to Henry VII's kingship. He was even present at a council meeting in February 1487 which discussed ways of dealing with the new rebellion! Shortly afterwards Lincoln fled to join Lovell under the protection of Margaret of Burgundy.

Margaret's motive has usually been described as simple hatred of Henry after the death of her brother Richard – a tradition going back to the sixteenth century writers Polydore Vergil and Edward Hall, who described her as 'this diabolicall duches' who was 'Iyke a dogge revertynge to her olde vomyte'! Certainly Margaret showed no willingness to accept Henry Tudor but national interest rather than family loyalty may account for Burgundian involvement against Henry.

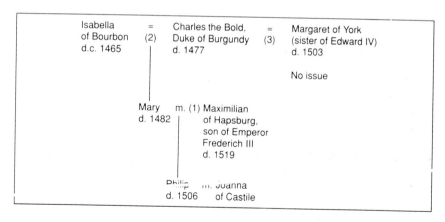

Burgundy's ruler, Maximilian feared an Anglo-French alliance against his lands, a fear exacerbated by the lack of serious negotiations between England and Burgundy. Therefore any attack on Henry which distracted or toppled him could have been advantageous to Burgundy. It is likely that in 1487 Margaret's personal and Maximilian's national needs coincided.

Margaret gave shelter to Lovell and Lincoln and raised an army of about 2000 professional infantrymen, headed by a notorious mercenary, Martin Schwarz. Margaret may also have given shelter as early as July 1486 to the boy who was the figurehead of the rebellion. The records of the city of Malines contain a reference to a gift of eight flagons of wine to 'the son of Clarence from England'. As you can see from the family tree,

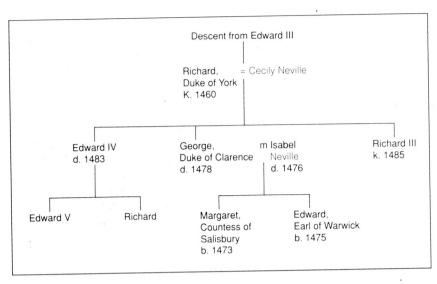

Descent from Edward III

Richard, Duke of York K. 1460 = Cecily Neville

- Edward IV d. 1483
  - Edward V
  - Richard
- George, Duke of Clarence d. 1478 — m Isabel Neville d. 1476
  - Margaret, Countess of Salisbury b. 1473
  - Edward, Earl of Warwick b. 1475
- Richard III k. 1485

Edward, Earl of Warwick, had a good claim to be king of England and it was 'Warwick' who headed the rebellion of 1487. However, the real Warwick was in custody in England and was even paraded through London early in 1487. The 'Warwick' who was crowned King Edward VI of England in Dublin in May 1487 was an imposter known as Lambert Simnel but whose real name remains a mystery.

Simnel had been trained for the part he played by an Oxford priest called Symonds, and was then taken to Ireland. Given the Anglo-Irish lords' desire for independence support for Warwick came naturally as a means of overthrowing Henry Tudor. The connection was given a further emotional twist by the fact that Warwick's father Clarence had been born in Dublin.

In June 1487, the forces of 'Edward VI' landed in Lancashire and marched through Cumbria into North Yorkshire, hoping to recruit support from local gentry. Many local men had been retainers of Richard III when, as Duke of Gloucester, he had ruled the north on behalf of his brother. North-western families such as the Broughtons and Harringtons had prospered then but now they found themselves taking second place to other local families who were supporters of the Stanleys, whose aid had helped Henry VII to the throne. Some of these northern Ricardians therefore rallied to the rebels.

To Henry the threat was a real one. Uncertain of the size, power and route of the rebel force, he had to wait while they took the initiative. Once beacons and messengers brought news he moved north rapidly but he was still unsure just how many would join his own army. Uncertainty increased when the rebels' speed took even the king's scouts by surprise. There was even rumours that the king had fled in the night.

In fact the rebels had failed to win enough support. They were heavily outnumbered by the king's army when they met at Stoke by Newark on 16 June. The battle lasted three hours but, if Henry was afraid of the outcome, that fear could only have been brief. Lincoln, Schwarz and many of his mercenaries, together with the poorly armed and unarmoured Irish were killed. Lovell's body was not found but he was never seen nor heard of again.

Lambert Simnel, treated as an innocent, was found working in the king's kitchens and lived to become king's falconer. He is last recorded in 1525 attending the funeral of one of the men who had fought against him at Stoke.

Brittany: the dangers of war 1487–1492

Success at the Battle of Stoke brought no respite from pressures. Even before he returned to London Henry heard that France was taking steps to end the independence of Brittany. This raised the prospect of dangerous involvement in European politics, perhaps even an expensive war with France. On this page you can follow the actions and reactions of the main countries involved. You can find further details on page 84.

France, Brittany, England

Objectives in 1487

France wanted to end Breton independence by bringing Brittany under the direct control of the French crown. Charles VIII was still a minor but his sister, Anne of Beaujeu, was a capable Regent. Brittany wanted to maintain its independence but its ruler, Francis II, was near death and had no male heir. His eldest daughter, Anne , was 12 and unmarried. England wanted to maintain Breton independence in order to prevent France controlling the whole Channel coast – a good base for invasion or attacks on English shipping.

Actions

1487 The Regent sought a marriage between Charles VIII & Anne of Brittany. The French marriage was unpopular – Francis sought to marry Anne to Maximilian and intrigued with the Regent's enemies in France. French forces invaded Brittany.

1488 Henry sent limited unofficial aid to Brittany, as did Maximillian and Ferdinand. French pushed for binding agreement. Breton & allied force defeated at St. Aubin du Corbier July 28. Francis agreed to Treaty of Sablé – could not seek help or marry daughters without permission of King of France. Francis II died in September. France claimed wardship of Anne of Brittany.

1489 Treaty of Redon agreed between Brittany and England. Brittany to pay for 6000 English troops to be sent to her defence. Henry made agreements with Maximilian & Ferdinand to build an anti-French alliance.

1490 –

1491 France gained effective control of Brittany. Anne decided to marry Charles VIII. Henry reasserted ancient claim to France and invaded France, besieging Boulogne.

1492 Treaty of Etaples, Nov.1492. Charles bought off Henry, agreeing to pay the costs of English intervention in Brittany, the arrears of the 1475 Treaty and not to assist rebels against Henry.

4.1 The Development of European Politics in the 1490s

BURGUNDY had been a very powerful state in the 1460s but the death of Charles the Bold in 1477 effectively ended Burgundy's hopes of independence from France. His lands were divided – those that did not pass to France became the property of Maximilian through his marriage to Mary of Burgundy and their heir, the Archduke Philip who married Joanna of Castile.

BRITTANY gave up its independence from France when the Duchess Anne married Charles VIII in 1491.

Maximilian of Hapsburg, King of the Romans was the link between Netherlands and the Empire. Eventually his grandson would rule the Hapsburg Empire comprising the Empire, Spain and the Netherlands.

FRANCE

Charles VIII succeeded Louis XI in 1483. Under Louis royal power had increased greatly at the expense of the French nobility and foreign powers. The crown was financially strong, collecting taxes annually without reference to parliament. France had claims to Naples and Milan and had gained control of the Duchy of Burgundy and other Burgundian lands in the Treaty of Arras with Maximillian in 1482. From this base France hoped to exploit weaknesses in the Netherlands.

Questions

1 Which countries were the most powerful in the early 1490s?
2 Which issues were likely to dominate Europe?
3 How might this affect England?
4 Why might England be a useful ally?

SPAIN consisted of two provinces, Castile and Aragon, which had been united in 1479 by the marriage of Isabella of Castile to Ferdinand of Aragon. At that stage the south of Spain was still under the control of the Moors but they were defeated and driven out in 1492. Spain also controlled Sicily, claimed Naples and was anxious to recover Cerdague and Rousillon from France. Ferdinand was renowned as the most devious politician in Europe.

HOLY ROMAN EMPIRE was in reality a ramshackle collection of small states. The Emperor Frederich III died in 1493 and his heir Maximilian hoped to centralise power. He was failed by the desire of individual states for independence and by the threat from Turkey in the east and his own ambitions in Italy.

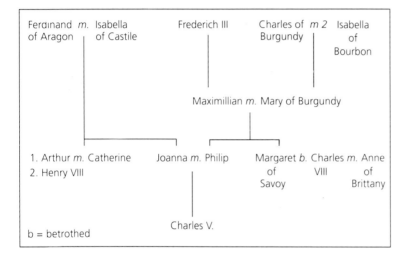

Ferdinand *m.* Isabella
of Aragon   of Castile

Frederich III

Charles of *m 2* Isabella
Burgundy   of
  Bourbon

Maximillian *m.* Mary of Burgundy

1. Arthur *m.* Catherine
2. Henry VIII

Joanna *m.* Philip

Margaret *b.* Charles *m.* Anne
of   VIII   of
Savoy   Brittany

Charles V.

b = betrothed

ITALY did not exist as a single country. It contained a number of competing states but in the 1490s the precarious balance of power amongst them collapsed. The major powers of Europe competed to gain territory in Italy.

TALKING POINT

Diplomacy

During the fifteenth century methods of communications between countries changed a great deal. Earlier kings had sent embassies abroad only when occasion demanded. These embassies consisted of large numbers of eminent councillors, armed with detailed instructions. By the reign of Henry VII permanent ambassadors were based at courts, able to respond flexibly as the need arose. They kept their own monarchs informed by sending back long reports, based on their own conversations with rulers, information supplied by influential figures to whom they paid a pension and informants of a less reputable kind. Thus diplomacy and communications became faster, more flexible and more wide-ranging in content, although the personal decisions of monarchs stayed at the centre of politics.

● How might these changes affect the course of events?

● How have these changes benefited historians researching the policies of this period?

4.2 Perkin Warbeck and the Problems of Foreign Policy, 1491–1499

A fter 1485 Henry VII faced one foreign policy problem after another but, although he dealt with them effectively, the array of new problems showed no signs of diminishing. Even as he was contemplating the dangers of an invasion of France in 1491 a new threat arose in the form of a second pretender to the throne, Perkin Warbeck.

At the beginning of the 1490s the threat of Warbeck was a considerable one given the continued weakness of Henry's position. He had no firm and committed allies to counterbalance his poor relations with Scotland and the dangers that would follow if there was a continuing war with France. As you can see in the table, Warbeck plagued Henry for much longer than Lambert Simnel and these events can tell us a great deal about Henry VII's policies.

Questions

1 What methods did Henry use to prevent support for Warbeck developing?

2 Where did the most long-lasting support for Warbeck come from? Why?

3 How did changes in European politics affect Henry's position?

4 What do you consider to be the best evidence for Henry's concern over the dangers from Warbeck?

5 Both Warbeck's landings were fiascos. Why then was Henry so concerned about his activities?

6 Does Henry's conduct of foreign policy to 1499 suggest that he was following a pre-conceived plan or that he was responding pragmatically to events?

The capture and imprisonment of Warbeck eventually allowed Henry to deal with an even older and more serious threat, the Earl of Warwick. Warwick had been kept prisoner since the beginning of the reign but he was still only 24 in 1499. As the nephew of Edward IV he was the most likely figure-head for a rebellion. Indeed, early in 1499, yet another pretender (whose real name was Ralph Wilford) claimed to be Warwick. Although Henry dealt rapidly and easily with the threat he was reported to have aged 20 years in two weeks.

Henry was not the only one aware of this threat. The Spanish ambassador dropped hints about the continued presence of Yorkist blood in England during marriage negotiations between England and Spain. In the end Henry probably felt constrained to execute Warwick in order to ensure that the marriage of Prince Arthur to Catherine of Aragon went ahead. The charge was that Warwick had been plotting with Warbeck although the 'plot' may have been set up by one of Henry's own agents. Warbeck was hanged. Warwick, who had spent every day in prison from the age of 10 to 24, was beheaded, simply because he was the nephew of the Yorkist kings. The fact that he was also the Queen's cousin made no difference to his fate.

PERKIN WARBECK WHOSE SIMILARITY TO EDWARD IV WAS REMARKABLE. THIS PICTURE MAY GIVE US A BETTER IDEA OF THE YOUTHFUL EDWARD THAN THE REMAINING POOR-QUALITY PORTRAITS.

The Travels of Perkin Warbeck

1491 Warbeck aged 17 in Cork, Ireland – undertook to impersonate Richard of York the second son of Edward IV. Limited support for Warbeck in Ireland. Henry sent small military force to Ireland.

1492 Warbeck travelled to France, where he was received as a prince by Charles VIII. France hoping to limit English intervention in Brittany. Treaty of Etaples – Charles VII agreed not to aid rebels against Henry.

1493 Warbeck travelled to Burgundy and to Vienna with Maximilian where he was received as Richard IV. Maximilian displeased by Anglo-France treaty. Henry broke off trade with Low Countries.

1494 Continued support from Maximilian hoping that Warbeck as King would aid him against France but merchants wanted to recommence trade. Henry sent administrators to Ireland to enforce control. Spies identified English plotter leading to arrest of Wm.Stanley, Chamberlain of Royal Household.

1495 Warbeck recognised Max. as heir to English throne. July – attempted invasion at Deal. Royal army routed invaders. Fled to Ireland but failed to win support.Royal forces drove PW from Ireland. Fled to Scotland.

1496 Accepted by James IV, who married Warbeck to Katherine Gordon. Scots border raid with England. Trade resumed with Low Countries. Projected Anglo-Spanish marriage threatened by uncertainties – Spain seeking alliance with England v France. Henry sought peace with Scotland through marriage of sister to James IV – Cornish rebellion made Anglo-Scottish war almost impossible.

1497 July – Warbeck to Ireland. Warbeck invaded Cornwall – little support and arrested at Beaulieu in September. Ireland remained loyal to Henry. Truce of Ayton agreed with Scotland.

1498 Attempted to escape from custody. Henry careful to treat Warbeck cautiously as he was not an English citizen.

1499 Nov. – Warbeck implicated in plot with Warwick – both executed. Spain concerned at continued presence of Yorkist blood prior to Anglo-Spanish marriage.

1487–8: France's desire to win control over Brittany was viewed with hostility by the Archduke Maximilian and Ferdinand of Aragon as well as by Henry VII. Already France was the strongest country in western Europe on account of her unrivalled political unity and economic strength. However France's opponents were distracted by domestic concerns and so their aid to Brittany was restricted to the sending of small numbers of troops. The English force, led by Lord Scales, was not given official royal support and, shortly before the Battle of St. Aubin, Henry sent envoys to mediate. On 14 July 1488 Henry also extended his truce with France until January 1490.

1 Why do you think Henry did not do more to aid Brittany in 1488, given his fears of French power?

1488–9: After Francis II's death French control of Brittany became even more likely. Accordingly Henry set about creating a diplomatic alliance with Spain and Maximilian, aimed at putting pressure on France. However neither ally was sufficiently free of problems to make a military reality of their agreements. Maximilian's chief contribution was to marry Anne of Brittany by proxy, a gesture that did nothing to aid Brittany in practice. Even Henry put strict limits on his involvement, the Treaty of Redon limiting his forces and plans so that France would not think he was initiating a war of conquest.

2 Why do you think Anne decided to capitulate in December 1491 and marry Charles?

1492: After Anne of Brittany's marriage to Charles VIII Henry faced a difficult decision. If he meekly accepted French domination of Brittany there was little likelihood of being regarded by other rulers as a significant power in Europe. This would only encourage those who wanted to take his crown. Yet if he launched an attack on the much more powerful France he was risking defeat and again the loss of his crown. Henry chose to invade France in 1492 but throughout the summer negotiations proceeded alongside was preparations. By delaying the beginning of the invasion until the autumn Henry made it clear that a serious military campaign was not intended. Charles took the hint and was quick to offer peace terms so that he could pursue his ambitions in Italy. The resulting Treaty of Etaples had advantages for both countries.

3 In what ways could the Treaty of Etaples be regarded as a considerable success for Henry's policies since 1487?

4 What do these events tell us about Henry's skills and objectives in foreign policy?

5 Did Henry's actions suggest that he was pursuing policies different from those of his predecessors?

Marriages, Deaths and Foreign Policy 1499–1509

Spanish involvement in the execution of Warwick indicates that doubts remained about Henry's position, even after 14 years as king. Other European monarchs were still aware of potential Yorkist claimants. However Henry's record of survival had won respect. A marriage treaty with Spain was finalised in July 1499, indicating Spain's acceptance of Henry's strength. Catherine of Aragon arrived in England in October 1501 and the marriage to Prince Arthur took place in the same year. Also in 1501 Henry promised his daughter Margaret to James IV of Scotland as part of the treaty of Ayton and they were duly married in August 1503. This treaty marked a general improvement in Anglo-Scots relations although the potential for problems remained, especially if Anglo-French relations deteriorated.

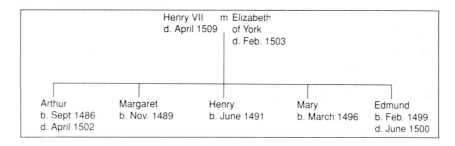

Thus developments around the turn of the century suggested that the long sought-for security had finally arrived. Instead a series of deaths from 1502 blighted this optimism and embroiled Henry in complex diplomatic manoeuvres, demonstrating the need for the king to be actively involved in European affairs in order to safeguard his and England's position.

The first of the deaths produced the greatest uncertainty. This was the death of Henry VII's heir, Prince Arthur, aged 15 in April 1502. The unexpectedness of Arthur's death underlined the fragility of life. There was suddenly real doubt about the future of the Tudor dynasty, which now depended on a single life, that of 11 year-old Prince Henry. Sources reveal speculation about Henry VII's likely successor which mentioned two Dukes but not Prince Henry.

The death of Arthur also endangered the Anglo-Spanish alliance that rested on the prince's marriage with Catherine of Aragon. Henry swiftly proposed that Catherine marry his new heir but Ferdinand of Spain was now in the stronger position. Not only was Henry much more in need of the match but Spain was now at peace with France and therefore less in need of English support. So Ferdinand demanded better terms and Henry tried to limit them until, in 1503, Franco-Spanish relations again deteriorated. Now Ferdinand had to agree to English terms, inaugurating a strong anti-France coalition of Spain, England and the Netherlands. The betrothal of Catherine of Aragon and Prince Henry took place on 25 June 1503.

This new marriage alliance ensured that England would be enmeshed in the complexities of European politics which followed the death of Isabella of Castile in November 1504. Isabella's death meant that Spain might again split into separate kingdoms. This prospect turned Henry's former allies,

Spain and the Netherlands, into rivals. One option for Henry was to support the ruler of the Netherlands, Philip of Burgundy, and his father Maximilian because they were France's enemies and indeed Henry lent Philip large sums of money. However this meant opposing Ferdinand the consequently appearing to treat his new daughter-in-law shabbily. Henry's policy was to maintain his channels of communication with both sides.

The death of Henry's queen, Elizabeth of York in 1503 was a severe personal blow to the king. However, as time went by, Henry used his own marriageability as a diplomatic response to the changes in European relationships. This was most evident in 1506 following the arrival in England of an unexpected guest, Philip of Burgundy and his wife, Joanna of Castile. Philip was driven ashore by storms. Henry responded with elaborate greetings and entertainment but also pressured Philip into the Treaty of Windsor in February 1506 – a treaty of alliance which was to be cemented by the marriage of Henry to Margaret of Savoy (see family tree on page 81). A trade agreement was also authorised, the Intercursus Malus, but this was of little and short-lived benefit to the English. Most importantly Philip surrendered the leading Yorkist pretender, Edmund Duke of Suffolk, who returned to imprisonment. The Treaty of Windsor promised Henry a strong continental ally in Philip, the more so once he and Joanna were established in Castile, but in September 1506 Philip died. The Treaty of Windsor was abandoned. The pattern of diplomacy changed again.

Philip's death meant that Ferdinand of Aragon gained control of the whole of Spain and the Emperor Maximilian took possession of Flanders. As Ferdinand had recently allied with France, Henry and Maximilian seemed natural allies, both fearful of French expansion and, as a result, a marriage was discussed between Henry's daughter Mary and Charles, the heir of Philip of Burgundy. Yet at the same time Henry offered to marry Joanna of Castile himself and to marry his son Henry (already betrothed to Catherine of Aragon) to a French princess. What was Henry up to?

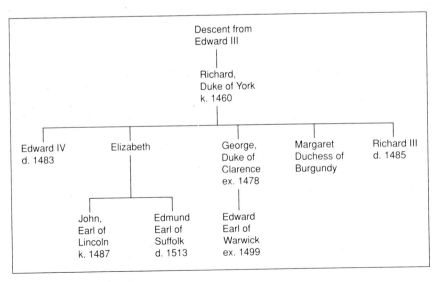

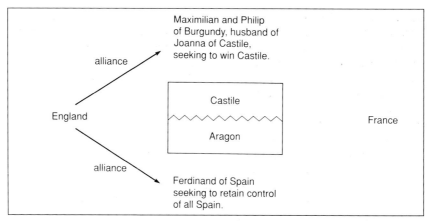

On the surface it looks as if he was doing his best to offend Ferdinand but a more logical explanation is that he was endeavouring to maintain good relations with France, a constant element in his diplomacy.

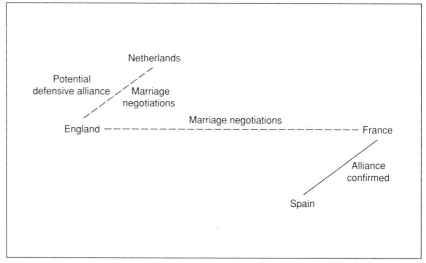

Once again events developed out of Henry's control. Ferdinand put together an alliance with France and Maximilian in 1508 (the League of Cambrai), intending to divide the state of Venice amongst themselves. Henry was excluded but this was not so important as Italy was not in his sphere of interest. More significantly, the continued possibility of a marriage between Mary Tudor and the Archduke Charles, soon to be the most powerful ruler in Europe, demonstrated that the Tudor king of England was respected as a valued ally.

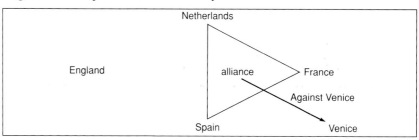

Overseas Trade

Henry VII's need for security cast its shadow over English overseas trade, just as it does over every other aspect of his reign, and here, as elsewhere, the king had to tread a narrow path between dangers. Trade was a weapon in Henry VII's battle for security. Cutting off trade could persuade a foreign ruler to change his policies in Henry's interests but, at the same time, trade needed to be encouraged. Customs revenues provided Henry with income, perhaps one-third of the total crown revenue. Wealthy merchants who believed their interests were safeguarded by the king were loyal merchants, unwilling to support potential challengers for the crown. A strong merchant fleet also provided a defence if a navy had to be assembled rapidly.

Henry certainly did use trade to serve his interests. The wool and woollen cloth trade with the Netherlands was the most financially valuable element of English overseas trade yet in 1493 he ordered the closure of this trade to bring pressure to bear on Maximilian who was providing support for Perkin Warbeck. Henry maintained the embargo until 1496, clearly identifying Warbeck as a greater danger than the discontent amongst the merchant community. The renewal of trade in 1496 with the treaty known as Magnus Intercursus gave new liberties to English traders.

One major complaint of merchants in 1485 had been that a substantial proportion of trade was in the hands of foreign carriers. Venetians carried goods to and from the Mediterranean, Englishmen were kept out of Scandinavia and the Baltic by the Hanseatic League and much of the trade with France, Spain and the Netherlands was undertaken by foreign carriers. Gradually Henry reduced foreign privileges or Englishmen gained reciprocal rights, demonstrating that Henry was aware of the need to enhance merchants' prosperity, but it was a piecemeal policy, vulnerable to changes if they were required by the flux of politics.

Henry's relations with the merchants of the Hanseatic League provided the clearest example of this. In 1486 he confirmed their trading privileges in England so as not to antagonise them immediately. He then set about steadily reducing their privileges by Act of Parliament. Pressure was also put on the Hanse to offer equal rights to English traders by turning a blind eye to attacks on their traders in London and by reaching alternative agreements with the king of Denmark. Progress was being made, albeit slowly, when in 1504 the Yorkist refugee, the Earl of Suffolk, sought shelter in Germany. Putting security before trade, Henry agreed to give back the Hanse all its old privileges as an inducement to expel Suffolk. However once Suffolk left Germany Henry found a loophole in the 1504 agreement allowing him to exclude London from the areas where the Hanse held privileges.

Elsewhere achievements were greater. To offset Venice's influence a regular trade was established with Florence designed to wring better terms from Venice. More adventurously, Henry gave support to John and Sebastian Cabot's voyages across the Atlantic, hoping to outflank Venetian and Portuguese control over trade to the east. In addition the Treaty of Medina del Campo brought major improvements for English traders in Spain. However retaliation was always likely and in 1505 Spain began to enforce its own Navigation Laws, thus allowing fewer English traders into Spain.

SEBASTIAN CABOT WHOSE VOYAGES RECEIVED SOME PATRONAGE FROM HENRY VII ALTHOUGH HENRY WAS NEVER DISTRACTED FROM THE MAIN BUSINESS OF ENSURING SECURITY IN EUROPE.

Overall overseas trade benefitted a little from Henry's policies but it remained very small-scale. The royal coffers therefore did not benefit greatly from increased trade. More predictably customs revenues increased because, under Henry VII, their collection was more efficient.

REVIEW

To help organise your conclusions about Henry VII and his foreign policies read the following sources and then answer the questions below.

Henry VII – strategist or pragmatist?

Source A

'Implores them to get the person who calls himself the son of Edward (the pretender, Perkin Warbeck) into their power. That is the most important point; that is the 'whole' thing.'

Extract from a despatch from Dr De Puebla, the Spanish ambassador in London to the King and Queen of Spain, 1496.

Source B

'It was indeed a great ambition of Henry's to be in friendship and peace with neighbouring monarchs, and specially with King James; so that his English subjects, knowing there was no refuge or place of safety for rebels in neighbouring lands would the more readily be kept in obedience.'

Polydore Vergil, *Anglica Historia*, written before 1513.

Source C

'England was … liable to be tossed about in the diplomatic cross-currents which flowed from the enmities of more powerful countries. English interests played a relatively small part in deciding the alignment of powers.'

J.A.F. Thomson, *The Transformation of Medieval England*, 1983

---

1 What do Sources A and B suggest were Henry VII's main objective or objectives in foreign policy?

2 What evidence have you met in this chapter to support this view?

3 What evidence have you read that would support an alternative view?

4 To what extent do you agree with the conclusion in source C?

5 Do you think that Henry VII had a long-term strategy for his foreign policy or that he responded pragmatically to events? Give reasons for your answer.

6 In what ways was Henry VII's foreign policy successful?

ESSAY

What were Henry VII's aims in foreign policy and how successful was he in achieving them?

Henry VII – continuity or change?

Look back to the quotations in the Preview to this section on p.72 – 73. They offer different interpretations of the nature of Henry VII's reign.

1 In what ways does the content of this chapter support the view expressed in Sources A and D?

2 In what ways does the content of this chapter support the view expressed in Sources B and C?

3 Which pair of quotations do you now think is the more correct?

4 Do you think the material in this chapter has settled the argument about whether 1485 was a watershed in English history? Give reasons for your answer.

5 'In the Sweat of his Brow' – Henry VII, Kingship and Government

PREVIEW

One of the difficulties we have when studying history is deciding whether hindsight distorts our understanding of events. Many historians, with the benefit of hindsight, say that Henry VII's reign was significant because he established order and stability. In the words of Alexander Grant, writing in 1985, 'after Henry Tudor became king the English crown ceased to be vulnerable.'

Was this the perspective of people in the late 1480s and early 1490s? If we put ourselves into the shoes of Henry VII's subjects we would hear that the king was fighting rebels, working to isolate rebels or waiting to see if rumours about rebels were true. Henry's hold on his crown might well seem precarious; his ability to pass it onto his son doubtful.

Which perspective – that of historians or contemporaries – has the more truth? We certainly need to see events from contemporaries' viewpoints as this helps us to understand their motives and actions. However they may not have understood the real causes of what was happening around them or understood its significance. Think of political events today. Do you fully understand their causes and significance? Do we need both perspectives or is one more important than the other?

This chapter attempts to provide both perspectives: the first, a contemporary view which briefly describes the major political landmarks in chronological order. The greater part of the chapter then analyses, with the benefit of hindsight, how Henry shaped his policies and actions to give himself the best chance of peace and security. Overleaf is a diagram showing the range of domestic issues facing Henry and a timeline recording the major events of his reign. Use this information to suggest some initial, tentative answers to the following questions. Note down your ideas – these questions will appear again at the end of the chapter so you will be able to reconsider your answers in the light of the detailed evidence in the chapter.

---

1 Which issues do you think would prove to be the most difficult for Henry to tackle?

2 How might solving each problem contribute to Henry's security?

3 Does the information on the timeline give you any clues about the effectiveness of Henry's actions?

---

4 What kind of personality do you think Henry had and how well suited was it to the task of governing England?

5 After your work on foreign policy do you expect Henry to introduce new ways of governing England?

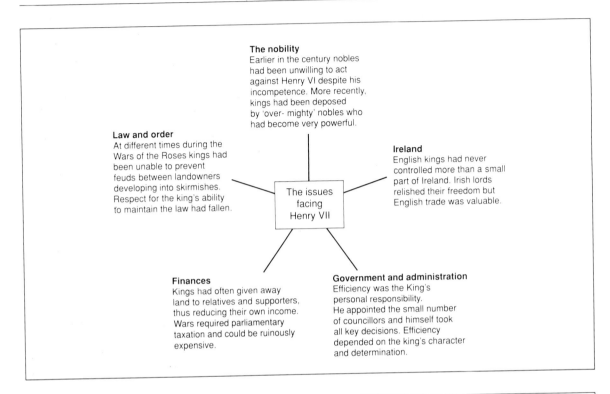

The nobility
Earlier in the century nobles had been unwilling to act against Henry VI despite his incompetence. More recently, kings had been deposed by 'over-mighty' nobles who had become very powerful.

Law and order
At different times during the Wars of the Roses kings had been unable to prevent feuds between landowners developing into skirmishes. Respect for the king's ability to maintain the law had fallen.

The issues facing Henry VII

Ireland
English kings had never controlled more than a small part of Ireland. Irish lords relished their freedom but English trade was valuable.

Finances
Kings had often given away land to relatives and supporters, thus reducing their own income. Wars required parliamentary taxation and could be ruinously expensive.

Government and administration
Efficiency was the King's personal responsibility. He appointed the small number of councillors and himself took all key decisions. Efficiency depended on the king's character and determination.

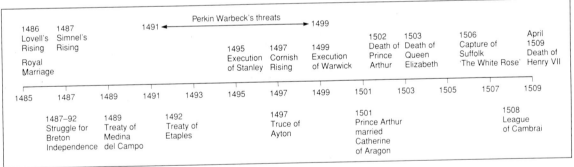

| 1486 Lovell's Rising — Royal Marriage | 1487 Simnel's Rising | | 1491 ← Perkin Warbeck's threats → 1499 | | 1495 Execution of Stanley | 1497 Cornish Rising | 1499 Execution of Warwick | 1502 Death of Prince Arthur | 1503 Death of Queen Elizabeth | | 1506 Capture of Suffolk 'The White Rose' | April 1509 Death of Henry VII |

1485 — 1487 — 1489 — 1491 — 1493 — 1495 — 1497 — 1499 — 1501 — 1503 — 1505 — 1507 — 1509

| | 1487–92 Struggle for Breton Independence | 1489 Treaty of Medina del Campo | 1492 Treaty of Etaples | | 1497 Truce of Ayton | | 1501 Prince Arthur married Catherine of Aragon | | | 1508 League of Cambrai |

Troubles Survived

Henry VII was the fourth king of England in less than three years. No-one expected him to rule unchallenged. His marriage to Elizabeth of York helped reconcile waverers but the first challenge came only eight months after Bosworth when Viscount Lovell, Sir Humphrey Stafford and his brother Thomas attempted a rising in Yorkshire and the Midlands. They failed to raise significant support but a year later Lambert Simnel's invasion aroused much greater concern. For three months the king was in real fear of a widespread, well-supported rising. However the reality of the threat was much less than Henry feared.

The longer Henry survived as king the greater should have been his security but he was constantly aware of dangers. Hence Henry's foreign policy was directed at minimising dangers and his spies were constantly active, seeking out potential traitors. The greatest and most shocking catch was Sir William Stanley whose intervention at Bosworth had turned the battle in Henry's favour and who, as Chamberlain of the King's Household, held the post usually given to the King's most reliable and trusted confidant. Stanley was discovered communicating with Warbeck in 1495, perhaps only safeguarding his own position 'just in case', and was executed for treason. If the chamberlain was disloyal, just who could be trusted by the king?

The constant pressure stemming from Warbeck's activities pushed Henry to deal with the potential dangers from Ireland and Scotland. Between 1494 and 1496 a combination of military and diplomatic actions impressed on the Irish the necessity of accepting Henry's rule. Agreement with Scotland was reached but only after the raising of taxes for an English army had helped to precipitate the so-called Cornish Rising of 1497. While Henry and his army were in the north a south-western army of 15,000 marched across England to Blackheath before being routed by the king's forces led by Lord Daubeney.

This rising has usually been described as a Cornish peasant uprising against war taxation. It 'was not dynastic' according to John Guy but his interpretation differs from that of Ian Arthurson. Dr Arthurson points out that the rebellion was far more widespread, the king's own proclamation three days after Blackheath saying that the rebels had levied war 'through the counties of Somerset, Dorset, Wiltshire, Sussex and Surrey ... so that many of the king's subjects of the same counties to them resorted'. The rebellion may have begun in Cornwall but it encompassed men and women (46 women's punishments are recorded) from the rest of the south-west.

Nor was it simply a peasant rebellion. Also recorded are the fines of numerous gentry families. In Somerset four sheriffs, three MPs and James Daubeney, brother of the commander of the king's army, were fined. The king seems to have thought it more than a peasant army! Finally the motive may have been political as well as economic. At least some rebels were former Yorkists who took their chance while Henry's loyalists in the region were absent on the Scottish campaign. This mass rising, containing peasants, townspeople, clergy and gentry, motivated by a mixture of economics and politics and adding to the dangers of Warbeck, suggests that Henry's hold on his crown was still insecure after twelve years as king. No wonder Henry rapidly pursued agreements with Scotland and Spain.

In 1499 Warbeck and Warwick were executed but in the same year Edmund, Earl of Suffolk (known as 'The White Rose') fled abroad. If Henry by now felt more confident of defeating these persistent and irritating Yorkists his mood was changed by the deaths of Prince Edmund (1500) and Prince Arthur (1502). Sometime before 1506 a conversation was reported concerning the succession – 'some of them spoke of my lord of Buckyngham ... Other ther were that spoke ... of your traytor Edmond

de la Pole, but none of them ... spoke of my lord prynce (of Wales).'
Only in 1506, therefore, when Suffolk was handed over by Philip of
Burgundy could Henry VII really feel at ease from dangers.

TALKING POINT

Changing Interpretations

The rebellion of 1497 is one example of how detailed research can question
and change long-held interpretations. The reign of Henry VII is much in need of
such research for there have been relatively few books and articles on his reign.
There may seem like a lot but compare the number with those on his son or his
granddaughter, Elizabeth or even on Richard III! To quote Dr Arthurson again
'all writers agree that Henry's relations with foreign powers are impressive,
indeed masterful. His diplomacy, we can be sure, was his finest achievement.
This, however, is a rather mysterious judgement for foreign relations is a subject
about which nothing fundamental has been written since 1932.' Or 'Henry VII's
financial policy is the only aspect of his reign which has found a degree of
description and analysis lacking everywhere else.'

● Why do you think relatively little has been written about Henry VII?

● Henry VII's reign is often included in courses beginning in 1485 and covering
the sixteenth century. Is it more important for historians studying his reign to
have an understanding of the fifteenth century or the sixteenth century?

● How might the knowledge that relatively little research has been done on
Henry VII affect your conclusions on his foreign and domestic policies?

EXAMINING THE EVIDENCE

The King in Person

To understand the way Henry VII governed England we need to try to
understand Henry himself. What kind of man was he? Before starting,
look back to your answer to question 4 on page 92. What perception of
Henry do you have to start with?

A King in Prospect?

Source A

'Henry was at Vannes (in Brittany) when he had news of the plot and,
without any delay, he sent Christopher Urswick to King Charles to ask
that he might lawfully pass into France, which he readily agreed. The Earl
Henry, realising that he needed to act swiftly, told his intentions to few of
his company. He pretended that he was sending the English nobles to the
Duke of Brittany but secretly warned the Earl of Pembroke that when
they were near the border of Brittany they should suddenly leave the
route and get themselves into France. Henry himself, accompanied by
only five servants, pretended to go to a friend and, because a huge number of English people stayed in Vannes, nobody suspected his journey.
When he had gone almost five miles he turned off the highway into a
wood and put on a serving man's clothes and, as a servant, followed one
of his own servants, riding on with such great speed that he made no stop
except to rest the horses before he had crossed into France'.

Source B

'At the time Henry stayed in France to gain assistance, many nobles were ruling France because of King Charles' youth. They did not agree amongst themselves and Earl Henry, who day and night lost no opportunity to hasten his expedition to England, was compelled to go and seek help from every man individually'.

---

1 The sources above are adapted from Polydore Vergil's *History of England*, written before 1513. What do they tell you about Henry Tudor's potential for kingship?

The King's Appearance

Source C

'His body was slender but well built and strong; his height above average. His appearance was remarkably attractive and his face was cheerful, especially when speaking; his eyes were small and blue, his teeth few, poor and blackish; his hair was thin and white; his complexion sallow.'

Polydore Vergil, *Anglica Historia*. Vergil came to England in 1502 and knew King Henry well.

---

2 In what ways does this description agree with the pictures of Henry on pp.65, 116 and above? Explain the reasons for any differences you note.

3 How important do you think appearance was to Henry VII as king?

The King's Advisers and Family

Source D

'There was present Thomas Ruthal, who was a most learned man and who for many years had been and still was Henry's private secretary, on account of his great loyalty, his experience in all types of negotiations, his steadfast attention to duty and his unremitting attention to affairs of government'.

Polydore Vergil, *Anglica Historia*.

Source E

The intensive participation of Henry's esquires of the body and gentlemen ushers in tournaments suggests that this was another way to entertain the King, who sponsored, watched and judged such exercises with enthusiasm, even though he did not participate in them. Matthew Baker and Guillaume de la Ryvers were frequent jousters, and Roland de Veleville almost obsessive ... A number of Henry's inner circle – Baker, Vaughan and Veleville – gained appalling reputations for violent and high-handed behaviour when sent to govern such outposts as Jersey and Beaumaris.

S.J.Gunn, The Courtiers of Henry VII in *English Historical Review,* 1993.

REGINALD BRAY, A PORTRAIT IN STAINED GLASS FROM GREAT MALVERN CHURCH. BRAY HAD WORKED AS AN ADMINISTRATOR FOR MARGARET BEAUFORT AND WAS CLOSELY INVOLVED IN PLOTTING HENRY'S INVASION BEFORE BECOMING HENRY'S PRINCIPAL FINANCIAL ADVISOR.

4 Using sources D, and E, what qualities do you think Henry valued in his advisers?

5 Does it appear that Henry was skilled in his choice and treatment of advisers?

Source F

.... I shall be glad to please you as your heart can desire it, and I know well, that I am as much bounden so to do, as any creature living for the great and singular motherly love and affection that it hath pleased you at all times to bear me. Wherefore, mine own most loving mother, in my most hearty manner I thank you, beseeching you of your good continuance in the same.

Madame, I have encumbered you now with this my long writing, but methinks that I can do no less, considering that it is so seldom that I do write, wherefore I beseech you to pardon me, for verily, madame, my sight is nothing so perfect as it has been, and I know well it will appear daily wherefore I trust that you will not be displeased, though I write not so often with mine own hand, for on my faith I have been three days ere I could make an end of this letter.

> A letter from Henry VII to his mother, Margaret Beaufort, probably in July 1501. Henry began by agreeing to enable her to proceed with one of her foundations at Cambridge. Quoted in S.B. Chrimes, Henry VII, 1972.

Source G

MARGARET BEAUFORT, (1443 – 1509) MOTHER OF HENRY VII. SHE GAVE BIRTH TO HENRY, HER ONLY SON, WHEN SHE WAS 13. THREE MONTHS AFTER HER HUSBAND'S DEATH. SHE REMAINED A POWERFUL INFLUENCE ON HENRY UNTIL HER DEATH.

Source H

ELIZABETH OF YORK, (1465 – 1503) ELDEST DAUGHTER OF EDWARD IV AND WIFE OF HENRY VII AND MODEL FOR THE QUEEN ON PLAYING CARDS. WHEN SHE DIED IN 1503 HENRY 'PRIVILY DEPARTED TO A SOLITARY PLACE, AND WOULD NO MAN SHOULD RESORT UNTO HIM'.

Source I

When his Grace understood that sorrowful heavy tidings, [of the death of Prince Arthur] he sent for the Queen, saying that he and his Queen would take painful sorrows together. After that she was come and saw the King her Lord, and that natural and painful sorrow, as I have heard say, she with full great and constant comfortable words besought his Grace that he would first after God remember the weale of his own noble person, the comfort of his realm and of her. She then said that my Lady his mother had never no more children but him only and that God by his Grace had ever preserved him, and brought him where he was. Over that, how that God had left him yet a fair Prince, two fair Princesses and that God is where he was and we are both young enough ... After that she departed and came to her own chamber, natural and motherly remembrance of that great loss smote her so sorrowful to the heart that those about her were fain to send for the King to comfort her. Then his Grace of true gentle and faithful love, in good haste came and relieved her ...

Quoted in S.B. Chrimes, *Henry VII*, 1972.

6 Using Sources F and G what can you learn about Henry VII?

7 What do Sources H and I tell you about Henry VII?

The King's Activities and Interests

Source J

'It must certainly not pass unremarked that this disease, hitherto unknown, only began to rage at the beginning of Henry's reign ... It was popularly supposed to presage that harshness which Henry employed in his government. But it may be that sweating sickness portended something else; that Henry should only reign in the sweat of his brow, which was certainly to be the case.'

Polydore Vergil, *Anglica Historia*.

The image of the king which is provided by this extract cannot be denied. He did work as hard or harder than any other English monarch at the business of government but is that the whole picture?

8 What do Sources K, L and M tell you about Henry VII? Do they modify any of your earlier conclusions about the king?

Source K

Privy Purse Expenses for 1495.

Jan 1.	To Scot the fole for a rewarde, 6s 8d.	**Mar 8.**	To Hugh Denes for the kinges losse at tenes 14s and for a silke girdle 6s 8d – £1 8d.
Jan 4.	To the Frenshe pleyers in rewarde, £2.		
Jan 15.	To Pratt for thirteen elles and three quarters of fyne lynnen cloth, price the elle 6s 8d – £4 11s 8d.	**Mar 13.**	To the gardiner of Shene for sedes 6s8d
		Mar 20.	Loste at the buttes to my Lorde Marques £1
Feb 4.	For offring at my lady Anne mariage 6s 8d.	**Mar 25.**	To my Lady Bray for an ymage £1 6s 8d
Feb 13.	Jaks Haute in full payment of his bille for his disguysings £13 10s 6d. To hym that pleyeth upon the bagpipe 10s.	**Mar 29.**	For the Kinges losse at the paune pley 7s 8d.
		May 3.	To nine trumpetts for ther wages £18. To four shakbusshes for ther wags £7. To three string mynstrels for ther wags £5
Feb 20.	To a Walsheman for making a ryme 10s. To the Queen of France ministrels £30.		
		May 15.	For the Kinges hatt bande of silke 4s.
Feb 27.	For Sir William Stanley buryall at Syon £15 19s.	**May 27.**	For burying of a man that was slayn in my Lady Grey chamber 6s 8d.

June 12.	Delivered by the Kinges comandment for diverse juels bought of the Lumbards £2560.	**Oct 27.**	For diverse yerds of silke bought for my Lorde of York and my Lady Margarete £7 10s.
June 14.	To Mathew Cardiff open his bille for the Kinges hosen £2 8s.	**Nov 2.**	To a woman that singeth with a fidell 2s. For a boke bought for my Lorde of York £1.
June 28.	For making the King's bonefuyr 10s.		
July 9.	To a preste that was the King's scolemaster £2.To a tumbler opon the rope in rewarde 3s 4d.July 16. To an archer of th'archeduc in rewarde £4.	**Nov 13.**	To Hugh Denes for printed bokes 13s 4d.
		Nov 15.	To Savage for rowing the King opon Monday to the Sergeants feste, 18s.
July 27.	To one that leped at Chestre 6s 8d.	**Nov 27.**	To Hampton of Wourecestre for making of balades, in rewarde, £1.
Aug 2.	To the women that songe before the King and Quene in rewarde 6s 8d.	**Dec 23.**	To Thomas Brandon for diverse castes of haukes opon a bille, £31 6s 8d.To Jakes Haute for disguysing, £10.
Sept 11.	To James Keyley for King Richard tombe £10 1s.		
		Dec 17.	To Dix the foles master for his moneths wages, 10s.
Sept 19.	For gloves and Lantony chese 4s.Sept 27. For five paire of gloves by Hugh Denes 1s 8d.	**Dec 28.**	To Raynesford that is madd, 6s 8d.

Source L

HENRY'S SIGNATURE ON DOCUMENT.

HENRY VII SPENT LAVISHLY ON BUILDING, REFLECTING THE IMPORTANCE OF DISPLAY. THIS PICTURE SHOWS HENRY VII'S CHAPEL IN WESTMINSTER ABBEY.

Source M
His famous habit of signing account books was, as K.B.McFarlane pointed out, no more than 'the ordinary practice of his magnates', and as the developing chamber administration required him to sign more often, he simplified his monogram to make the job less trouble. By 1504 his sight was failing and he found writing difficult; he gave up signing each

entry in the chamber receipt accounts and signed only once on each page ...In September 1507 he went out hunting and hawking every day, apparently unhindered by his deteriorating eyesight, though in July of that year he shot a farmyard cock by mistake with his crossbow.

S.J.Gunn, *The Courtiers of Henry VII in English Historical Review*, 1993.

Conclusion

Source N

'Henry VII wanted value for the money he expended on display – and he usually obtained it...Nowhere is Henry's practicality and dislike of unnecessary expense seen more clearly than in the field of court festivals and entertainments...they were, inevitably, instruments of prestige propaganda, and Henry Tudor was prepared to devote to them a portion of his wealth, because he was most diligent in pursuing every means, great and small, whereby his dynasty might sit more securely upon the English throne.'

S.Anglo, *Spectacle, Pageantry and Early Tudor Policy*, 1969.

---

9 Do you think this is a fair analysis of Henry VII's attitude to expenditure?

10 How would you describe the personality and character of Henry VII?

Royal Finances

By 1509 Henry VII had earned the reputation of being 'the richest lord that is now known in the world'. Edward IV had been prosperous but Henry's riches excited wonder in contemporaries. As the table (p.102) shows, Henry's income was indeed substantially higher than Edward's. Why?

Waging war was the fastest way of spending money, therefore Henry VII's wealth is primarily explained by his avoidance of foreign expeditions except in 1492 (even then he exacted a pension from France) and in 1497. However, exactly the same could be said of Edward IV, even if his pension did not run for so many years. Defence was also expensive and the cost of preparations and actions against Warbeck and the Cornish rebels cost Henry over £100,000 which he was fortunate to be able to recover in fines.

Henry's reputation for frugality and Edward's for liberality seem to suggest another possible explanation for Henry's greater prosperity but these caricatures hide interesting similarities between the two kings. Contrary to his 'image' Henry VII spent heavily on building, jewellery, gold and silver plate, clothing, banquets, gifts and loans, including £135,000 in 1505 to Philip of Burgundy. All were necessary if Henry was to look like a king, present a formidable contrast to potential rivals and perhaps, buy allies. Overall his household expenses may well have been higher than those of Edward IV. We can be certain that Henry took care to avoid undermining his own prosperity. Henry granted away fewer crown lands and their revenues to his family and supporters than Edward IV did to his supporters and, as more land came to him through death and attainder, he held this too.

5.1 Council and Councillors under Henry VII

One of the reasons for Henry VII's success was his ability to combine a very high degree of personal involvement in government with effective use of a group of excellent officials.

The basis for this efficiency was the king's council. Superficially Henry's council was very similar to Edward IV's but his use of it showed marked differences, increasing as the reign went on. The similarities lay in the number of councillors, their record of attendance and their background. Like Edward IV, Henry VII had a remarkably high number of councillors, over 240 having been identified. However, this number includes many occasional attenders and honorary title-holders. There were perhaps two dozen regular attenders with an even smaller inner group of councillors, as had been the case under the Yorkists. The most frequently recorded number of members at a council was only seven.

Such similarities are not surprising, given that many men, including some of his closest advisers, had been Yorkist councillors, although more had served Edward IV than Richard III. The balance of social rank, too, was similar in the overall proportions of noblemen, gentry, churchmen and officials. Henry did not exclude noblemen in order to reduce their power as a class. Rather he used individuals for their abilities regardless of class.

These generalisations, important as they are in showing that Henry VII had to build on the existing system, hide the degree to which Henry amended the council's organisation. One significant factor assisting this development was the long service provided by key administrators who, together with the king, increased the efficiency of the administration, establishing new bodies as offshoots of the main council, whose task was to deal with particular problems.

The most significant of these offshoots was the 'Council Learned in the Law' which came into existence by 1495. Gradually the 'Council Learned' changed from simply representing the king's interests as a landlord into an enquiry and debt-collecting agency which sought out all possible sources of royal income and supervised the fulfilment of recognizances. Given these tasks it was perhaps inevitable that the number of lawyers at the centre of government should increase.

A less clear-cut example was the tribunal set up by a Statute of 1487 which was given parliamentary authority to act as a supreme law court, dealing with significant outbreaks of disorder and law-breaking. Most importantly it could act far more quickly than the law courts, but the fact that it does not appear to have dealt with many cases creates a problem in interpreting its significance. Alexander Grant (1985) has argued that this 'was probably one of Henry's major weapons in his attempts to uphold good government'. On the other hand, R.L.Storey (1968) suggested that 'it would appear that this tribunal was no longer functioning by the end of the reign', arguing that this experiment and others 'may have been designed only as reserves, to be employed when the resources of the ordinary courts had been exhausted'. Such debates may not be resolved. The sources for the working of the council are limited in quantity and quality, sufficient to allow historians to develop hypotheses but not enough to allow them to prove their points.

John Morton (d. 1500). Trained as a lawyer, he served Henry VI as king and in exile until 1471. Reconciled to Edward IV, he became a councillor in 1473 and was rewarded with offices and the Bishopric of Ely. In 1483 he resisted Richard III's usurpation and was a key figure in the 1483 rebellion. Henry VII appointed him Chancellor and Archbishop of Canterbury in 1486. Thomas More described Morton as having 'great experience the very mother and mistress of wisdom, a deep insight in politic worldly drifts'.

Richard Fox (1448–1528). A lawyer, Fox served Edward IV, was with Henry in exile and his abilities were fully used by Henry VII. He was Keeper of the Privy Seal from 1487–1516, being constantly at council, a frequent ambassador and Henry's 'ace negotiator' in addition to holding a series of bishoprics.

Sir Reginald Bray (d. 1503). Originally in the service of Margaret Beaufort, his legal training aided his role managing her estates. Bray acted as a go-between in the 1483 plot and rapidly became Henry VII's chief financial and property administrator after 1485. He began as Chancellor of the Duchy of Lancaster but unofficially acted as general auditor for all royal lands.

Giles Daubeney (1451–1508). A member of Edward IV's household, his military career included the 1475 expedition to France. He was sheriff of Somerset and Dorset in 1480 but he rebelled against Richard III in 1483. Henry appointed him to offices which required trust – Lieutenant of Calais in 1486 and Chamberlain of the Household in 1495 after Stanley's execution. Created Lord Daubeney in 1486 he commanded forces against the Scots and the Cornish rebels.

Sir Thomas Lovell (1453–1524). A lawyer, he risked his career by joining the 1483 rebellion and after Bosworth was rapidly appointed Chancellor of the Exchequer, Treasurer of the Household and was Speaker of the Commons in 1485. He attended more council meetings than anyone except Morton.

John Heron. In 1492 Heron, the deputy accountant in the King's Chamber, succeeded Thomas Lovell as Treasurer of the Chamber and held the office until 1521. As Treasurer Heron was a key figure in the country's financial administration and was frequently called into council to give advice. His Chamber accounts were audited personally and only by the King.

Edmund Dudley (d. 1510). Trained as a lawyer, he was the main legal adviser to the corporation of London 1496–1502 and an MP in every parliament between 1484 and 1509, acting as Speaker in 1504. He and Sir Richard Empson became the leading figures in the Council Learned, hated for the efficiency of their exactions on behalf of the king and themselves. Dudley was appointed President of the Council in 1506.

John, Lord Dinham (d. 1501). A longstanding supporter of Edward IV, he also remained loyal to Richard III as Lieutenant of Calais. Under Henry VII he was appointed Treasurer in 1486, a post he retained until his death when he was succeeded by Thomas Howard, Earl of Surrey. Dinham was a frequent attender at council.

Henry VII's chief councillors

1 How does the information on this page support the arguments that:

(a) Henry VII chose councillors for their abilities rather than because of their rank or earlier loyalty.

(b) Lawyers became a dominant force in Henry VII's council.

2 Many of Henry VII's councillors had served the Yorkist kings. Do you think that their experience of politics up to 1485 would lead them to suggest new or amended policies or to continue existing policies?

The Comparative Incomes of Edward IV and Henry VII

	Edward IV	Henry VII
Crown lands (at end of reigns)	£10,000 p.a.	£42,000 p.a.
Customs (at end of reigns)	£34,000	£40,000
Lay taxation (total)	£180,000	£280,000
Clerical taxation (total)	£130,000	£160,000
Benevolence	£25,000 (1474–5)	£48,000 (1491)
Pension	£10,000 (1475–1482)	£10,000 (1492–1509) ·
Annual Income in later years of each reign (based on crown lands, customs, pension, plus miscellaneous income)	£60,65,000	£100,000+

Changes in Royal Income

Richard III

1483–1485	£25,000 p.a.	Chamber control

Henry VII

1486–87	£12,000 p.a.	Exchequer control
1487–89	£17,000 p.a.	Chamber control
1492–95	£27,000 p.a.	Chamber control
1502–05	£105,000 p.a.	Chamber control

Another possible explanation for Henry's greater prosperity is that he used a different financial administrative system. This is certainly true between 1485 and 1487 but, as you can see in the chart above, Henry's change was a financial disaster. At first Henry reverted to using the Exchequer as the department receiving income but its centuries-old system was slow and cumbersome. The Yorkists had set up the Chamber as an alternative finance department – directly under their control, because it was, as the name suggests, in the king's own chamber. Freed from tradition and therefore more adaptable, the Chamber dealt only in cash and also moved beyond simply accounting for and receiving money. Its officials and the king himself intervened in local administration to produce greater efficiency and profit. In 1485, Henry, who had not had the opportunity to gain administrative knowledge, might have been expected to continue to use this improved Yorkist system, especially as many officials continued in office. However, his reversion to the Yorkist system suggests that either he did not seek or he over-rode officials' advice with the result that in 1487 he confessed that 'his honours, manors, lands, tenements and possessions and inheritances be greatly fallen in decay...'

TALKING POINT

During his reign Henry VII aged from 28 to 52. Why is it important to remember this when studying and assessing Henry's reign?

Henry's excuse was that he had been too busy with defence to spare time for financial details although R.L. Storey found this 'only partially convincing: he had not been under constant threat of insurrection in the past two years, and had time enough for hunting'.

In 1487 Henry revived the Yorkists' Chamber system and by 1492 it was having a significant effect on his revenue. The dominant official was Reginald Bray who acted unofficially as the king's chief general auditor and who was primarily responsible for the early development of the Council Learned in the Law. Amongst the Council Learned's tasks was following-up problems arising from the Chamber's accounting system. The Council Learned ensured that the Chamber received what it was owed. Vigorous pursuit of debts went hand-in-hand with seeking out possible sources of income arising from the king's position as feudal overlord. Commissions were appointed to seek out all possibilities – lists were kept of children who, with their lands, might become wards of the king on the deaths of their fathers. In one year fines amounting to £1125 were levied on newly-honoured Knights of the Bath who had failed to appear at their annual ceremony. So successful and profitable did the search for opportunities to revive the king's feudal rights become that in 1508 a new office was introduced – the surveyor of the king's prerogative.

Less dramatic but equally indicative of Henry's ability to increase the efficiency of established methods was his approach to taxation. The standard tax was the tenth and fifteenth, producing a guaranteed income of £30,000, because communities provided agreed sums, but it was so long established that it was failing to tap new sources of wealth. Several attempts to develop a new tax directly assessing individuals' wealth had failed, as did Henry VII's first attempt in 1489 which produced only a quarter of its projected income. However, in 1497 he produced a successful compromise between the old and the new. As with the older system a total figure was defined (£120,000 in 1497) which was to be collected through 2 tenths and fifteenths plus an element of direct taxation. In 1504, £30,000 was raised in this way and this compromise opened the way for later directly-assessed taxes which were not limited in the amount they had to produce.

By now it should be clear that another explanation for Henry's prosperity was the king himself. His desire for prosperity was yet another manifestation of his search for security. A wealthy king was a powerful king and the greater the gulf in riches between king and nobility the harder it would be for anyone to leap the gulf to take the crown. A poor king was hardly a king at all.

5.2 Parliaments and Great Councils under Henry VII

If the council was the engine of government, parliament had rather more in common with the spare tyre – crucial when called upon but required only on occasion and then just for brief periods! Parliament met only seven times in Henry VII's reign, its deliberations taking just 72 weeks out of a reign of 24 years. It met less frequently as time went by, only 2 parliaments (totalling 17 weeks) meeting between 1497 and 1509. Parliament did not have a role in deciding policies and its place in government was therefore subsidiary. Its significance was as an instrument of government – to attaint rebels (convict them and disinherit them for treason), to enact legislation and raise taxes. Thus parliament, despite the infrequency of its meetings, was never in danger of disappearing altogether.

Parliament for the most part did the king's bidding. The Speakers of the Commons were always royal officials, including Lovell, Dudley and Empson. On occasion, however, protests were heard. The attainders for treason against Richard III and his supporters depended for their legality on Henry dating his reign from the day before Bosworth – a piece of sharp practice that raised murmurs of discontent if no outright opposition. In 1504, parliament more successfully opposed the king's request for £90,000 in taxes and an agreement was set at £40,000. Such opposition was perhaps traditional, held no major threat for Henry and so does not explain the infrequency of parliaments. Put simply, Henry did not need parliament very often. In 1485 he had been granted customs duties for life and he pursued only one foreign war campaign, the greatest expense for any king. Neither did he initiate numerous new laws.

There was, however, one way in which Henry did recognise and, perhaps, even augment the power of parliament. His first parliament ratified his right to rule and the date when Henry's reign began. This is one of several examples from this period of kings using parliament but also, at the same time, involving parliament in important decisions. Another example, of far greater importance, was to be Henry VIII's use of parliament in the establishment of the Church of England.

If he wished to consult widely Henry VII used Great Councils, summoning five between 1487 and 1502. Henry used these assemblies to seek advice but, having made his decision, he was then able to make the decisions binding on the nobles, councillors and burgesses who were present as representatives of the country. The most dramatic example of this technique came in 1492 when Henry held a meeting in France of all 'captains of his army' and after consultation, made them sign documents pleading with him to retreat. Thereafter no-one could accuse him of cowardice! The calling of Great Councils can be seen as evidence of a desire to govern 'consensually'. It could also be seen as yet another way of reducing the freedom of potential critics and opponents.

Questions

1 What does Source A say about the significance of Henry VII's parliaments in the history of parliament?

2 Read Sources B and C. How similar was the role played by parliament under Henry VII to the role it played under Edward IV?

3 How, according to Source D, did parliament change under Edward IV and Henry VII?

4 Using all the sources and other information explain how important a role parliament played during Henry VII's reign.

5 Does the history of parliament in this period suggest that 1485 was a turning point in government?

Source A

Little or nothing of much significance occurred in the history of parliament in the reign of Henry VII ... The precedents already set over the previous century or so were followed; there were no significant innovations in procedure, so far as we know; no change in composition or electoral arrangements; few legislative measures enacted were of any great importance. No change in the relations between the king's government and any part of parliament occurred.

S.B.Chrimes, *Henry VII*, 1972.

Source B

The history of parliament in Edward IV's reign is very similar to what it was in Henry's. Legislation then was more often than not initiated by official bills ... Nor was there anything novel in the commons of Henry VII's reign electing speakers who were royal ministers ... There is another common feature in the parliamentary statistics of the two reigns. As both progressed, parliaments were less frequently held ... due to the same reason in both reigns: they reflect the success of Edward and Henry in avoiding war and realising adequate incomes from ordinary sources.

R.L.Storey, *The Reign of Henry VII*, 1968.

Source C

The parliaments of Henry VII's reign, and, indeed, those of Henry VIII before 1529, were very like those of the Yorkists ... The king's control of parliament was at this period almost total. In the parliament of 1478, for example, no one had opposed Edward IV when he accused his own brother, the duke of Clarence, of treason ... Henry VII never found it necessary to veto a bill, because no measure of which he disapproved could reach the stage of presentation....

Although some important pieces of social and economic legislation were implemented ... Henry VII's

parliaments were much more concerned with the needs of the monarch and his greater subjects than they were with the good of the country as a whole.

J. Loach, *Parliament under the Tudors*, 1991.

Source D

...early Tudor Parliaments were examples of an institution which had only occasional value to the Crown ... This poverty of Parliaments contrasts dramatically with previous centuries when, for example, Edward III had called forty-eight in a reign lasting half a century. Parliaments had continued to meet, more or less annually, until, and during, the Wars of the Roses. However, under strong Yorkist kingship the incidence fell and continued to do so under the early Tudors....

Parliament was not just an occasion for the king to extract money and laws. It was, as always, a 'coming-together' of Crown and governing class and each had its expectations. Chrimes might dismiss the legislative record of Henry VII's parliaments because few of the 192 Acts were of major importance to the Crown. Yet their intrinsic significance should not be denied. Over twenty Acts restored attainted persons or (more usually) their heirs. The lawyers' hands were writ large in legal reforms concerning murder, abduction, bail, fraud and counterfeit ...Manufacturers and merchants, supplying small domestic markets, were shielded by protectionist measures against imports of foreign bowstaves, silk, lace, ribbons and wine conveyed in 'forrayne bottomes'. ... London always loomed large, with two Acts on its mayor and others on its exports ... So did England's staple industry, cloth ... Every aspect of England's economy was grist to the parliamentary mill: cordwainers, tanners, and itinerant pewterers, hats and caps, weights and measures (three), the sale of salmon, servants' wages ...

M.A.R.Graves, *The Tudor Parliaments: Crown, Lords and Commons, 1485 – 1603*, 1985.

Henry VII and the nobility

One problematical development in fifteenth century England had been the appearance of men whom historians have called 'over-mighty subjects' or, more recently, 'super-nobles', men who had influence over a whole region and over lower ranking noblemen. Such men were valuable to kings because their strength ensured stability and good order in a region (Richard of Gloucester's work in the north on behalf of Edward IV, is a classic example) but they could also be dangerous if their ambitions and the king's interests did not coincide and the king was not a strong enough personality to exercise control.

These 'super-nobles' achieved their wealth and lands through their close blood-ties with the king or through inheritance and marriage. Richard Neville, already heir to lands worthy of two peers, gained two more inheritances when he married Anne Beauchamp. With this power behind him it is not surprising that he was able to make and depose kings. Henry VII was well aware of the danger of powerful noblemen joining conspiracies against him. That he did not have to face a new 'Warwick the Kingmaker' was the product of his own policies and of chance, the accidents of birth and death.

Chance was evident in the absence of alternative centres of power within the royal family after 1485. Unlike Edward IV, Henry VII was not festooned in male relatives whose egos and ambitions needed massaging as much as their pockets needed filling. Henry had no brothers and neither of his sons grew old enough to form an alternative power source during the reign. He did have two uncles but one, Lord Welles, seems to have been content to stay quietly on his estates and the other, Jasper Tudor, Earl of Pembroke and (from 1485) Duke of Bedford, was the man who had fostered and guided Henry since his youth.

These accidents of birth were aided by policy. None of Henry's few relatives were given large rewards of land. Policy also determined Henry's choice of husbands for his sisters-in-law. One was married to Lord Welles, his uncle. The other two remained unmarried until 1495 when they were given to noble husbands of whose loyalty Henry was sure. Henry also controlled the marriages of noble heiresses so that a nobleman could not hugely increase his power by marrying the heiress to extensive estates.

History joined chance and policy in strengthening Henry's position in relation to the rest of the nobility. The political conflicts of 1483–85 had virtually killed off the 'super-nobles', even if they had not reduced the number of noble families overall. The lands of the House of York were now royal property. The Duchy of Buckingham was in the hands of a minor, whose lands were therefore controlled by the king. The Earl of Northumberland's failure to commit himself to one side or the other in 1485 seems to have reduced his political influence and, after his murder in 1489, that title too was held by a minor.

More generally, many noblemen believed that the safest policy was to avoid political commitment. Less than three weeks after Bosworth, Lord Mountjoy wrote to his sons, begging them to 'live righteously and never to take the estate of baron upon them if they may lay it from them, nor to desire to be great about princes'. In retrospect this advice was probably

TALKING POINT

Medieval kings nearly always married foreign brides. Why? Why did Henry VII not follow suit?

unnecessary as Henry VII was notably unwilling to give anyone 'the estate of baron' as the table shows.

Nobles created by Edward IV and Henry VII				
	Edward IV		Henry VII	
Total Number of Nobles	1461	42	1485	50
	1483	46	1509	35
Number of Dukes, Marquises, Lords (Higher Nobility)	1461	7	1485	16
	1483	12	1509	10

Although Henry reduced the number of nobles he was not 'anti-noble'. He could not afford to be for he depended on them as a class for effective local government. He did give responsibility to individuals, such as Bedford, Oxford and Shrewsbury. All three had given Henry notable support before 1485 but Henry did not give responsibility for past service, only for present skills. The career of Thomas Howard demonstrates the king's hard-headed attitudes. Howard had fought for Richard at Bosworth, where his father, the Duke of Norfolk had been killed. Howard was imprisoned and attainted but in 1487 took his first steps to rehabilitation. The Lieutenant of the Tower offered to release him during Simnel's rebellion but he refused, saying that he would accept release only from the king. In 1489 he was released and restored to his earldom but received only some of his inheritance. Gradually, through loyal and effective service, he regained the Duchy of Norfolk lands but Henry never gave him the title nor other lands his father had gained from Richard III. The title only came after he had led the victorious English army against the Scots at Flodden in 1513.

This policy of limited reward and trust must have been confirmed by Henry's experience of the Stanley family, who had guaranteed him victory at Bosworth. For this they were well rewarded in land and titles. Thomas, Lord Stanley (Henry's step-father) became Earl of Derby and his brother Sir William became Chamberlain of the King's Household. However following Sir William's execution for treason in 1495 all his lands were returned to royal hands. Later, when Henry felt the Stanley family was using its power in the north-west to its own rather than royal advantage, he used recognizances for massive sums to ensure good behaviour. Royal favour only lasted as long as it was merited.

A recognizance or bond was an agreement to pay the king a specified sum of money if a person did not keep set conditions. The system had been used before 1485 and Henry used it efficiently in his early years but after 1502 recognizances became central to government, not as a means of raising money but of ensuring the loyalty and good behaviour of his nobility. Over half the nobility had to give recognizances at some stage, even such staunch Lancastrians as the Earl of Shrewsbury. Nobles required to act as tax collectors had to give recognizances against the sums they were expected to collect. This did not aid the nobles' local popularity but made sure they did not shirk their duty.

TALKING POINT

Why do you think 1502 was a turning point? Was it a turning point in any other aspect of the reign?

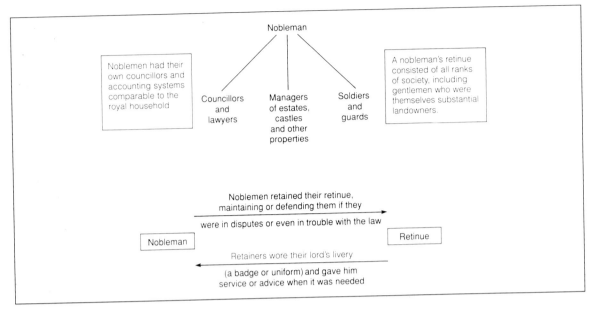

Politically unreliable figures had to pledge huge sums should they transgress. The Marquis of Dorset pledged all his lands (bar two manors) and £11,000 as early as 1492, to be forfeit if he acted against the king's interests. Such a threat of ruin was the purpose of a recognizance. Henry did not gain much financially but he ensured good behaviour. Less happily, the system created, in J.R. Lander's words, 'an atmosphere of chronic watchfulness, suspicion and fear'. Henry's recognizances completed the work of the civil wars in ensuring that noblemen were very hesitant about opposing the king or his policies. Recognizances did not make him popular but Henry did not court popularity. He sought security.

One further example of Henry VII's drive to reduce instability was his policy towards retaining. All late medieval kings knew the problems that could result from nobles' recruitment of retainers. Edward IV's 1468 Act appeared to be a severe attack on retaining but lords, not the king, decided what was 'lawful service' and so the Earl of Warwick, for example, was able to continue taking 'to hyme in fee as many knyghtys, squyers, and gentylmenne as he myght, to be stronge'.

Henry VII's Acts of 1485, 1487 and 1504 produced different results. Now it was the king, not the lords, who decided if exceptions from the law were valid. The king's personal involvement was even clearer when the 1504 Act said that lords could receive licences to retain but these had to list the whole retinue and be signed by the king. Failure to comply was treated seriously. In 1506 James Stanley was fined £245,610 (calculated at £5 per month per retainer) – an impossible sum which was therefore replaced by a heavy recognizance. One calculation suggests that Stanley's fine would be 50 million pounds at today's prices. Another miscreant, Lord Burgavenny, was fined over £70,000 for retaining 471 men. This impossible sum was reduced but he still paid a reduced fine of £5,000 in instalments over 10 years, found 26 people who collectively took on a recognizance of over £3,200 that he would remain loyal and law-abiding and himself held another recognizance that he would not enter Kent, Surrey, Sussex or Hampshire without royal permission. Recognizances were thus commonly used by the king to limit the likelihood of illegal retaining and the results were significant. Records suggest that nobles, aware of the king's strictures and efficiency, did have smaller retinues whose composition complied with the law. Policy, enforcement and the spirit of the age ensured that retainers and their masters were once again a force for stability not instability in the reign of Henry VII.

Local Government: Justices of the Peace and Law and Order

One of the two chief tasks of a medieval king was to give his people security at home by ensuring that the laws were kept and justice was administered fairly. Edward IV had tackled the problem of law and order energetically but did not reign for long enough to counteract the feeling that lawlessness was very close to the surface of society and that the nobility and gentry, who should have been ensuring good justice, were themselves abusing the courts and the laws to their own advantage. Henry VII explicitly recognised the problem in an introduction to a statute of 1489 'against the negligence of the Justice of the Peace'.

'ITEM, The Kyng our Sovereyn Lord considereth that by the neclicence mysdemeanyng favour and other inordinat causes of the Justices of peas in every Shire of his Reame, the lawes and ordenaunces made for the politique wele peas and good rule of the same, And for the profit suerte and restfull lyvyng of his subgettes of the same, be not duely executed accordyng to the tenour and effecte that they were made and ordeyned for; Wherefore his subgettes ben grevously hurt and out of suretie of their bodies and goodes, to his grete dyspleisure; for to hym is noo thyng is more joyous thenne to knowe his subgettes to live peasible under his lawes and to encrease in welthe and prosperite.'

Although Henry did enact new legislation the main need was for efficient implementation of the existing laws, through the system of local government and law enforcement. The people principally responsible for ensuring law and order were the Justices of the Peace. Henry VII had to create the conditions in which JPs could and would fulfil their duties properly. Perhaps the first task was to reduce the likelihood of JPs being over-awed by mightier lords. Edward IV had played with fire by giving regional responsibility to several great magnates, the 'super-nobles'. Henry VII made sure that there were no 'super-nobles' who might pervert justice. The supervision of JPs was in the hands of the king not the regional lords.

The second task was to ensure that JPs kept the law themselves because disputes between gentry were perhaps the most general cause of disrespect for the law. Here the king turned to personal intervention and recognizances to deter political law-breakers. Rather than pursue cases slowly through the courts Henry summoned those involved in disputes to appear before him in council. Those found guilty were bound under recognizance to the king and it has been estimated that 'thousands' of gentry had heavy fines hanging over them. In such circumstances the sensible course of action was to keep the law!

More positively, Henry VII ensured that JPs fulfilled their duties by building up his own power in the counties intending that he should be

5.3 Ireland – the best chance of all?

❛ *In all Ireland there are only two sorts of men ... of which one is gentle and cultured. To these wealthier and more civilised inhabitants many of the merchants of neighbouring peoples come on business; and the English in particular often journeying there, these Irish easily acquire their manner of life and the greater part understood the language as a result of this constant commerce. Such Irish all obey the English king. The other type of islander is savage, rude and uncouth. From their indifference to all refinement and their primitive habits they are known as 'wild men of the woods'; but for all that they are good Christians. They have various rulers to whom they are subjected and who constantly fight among themselves. It is for this reason that these Irishmen excel the others in ferocity, and – being more eager for revolutions – are found readier to support any type of upheaval.* ❜

Polydore Vergil, *Anglica Historia*

Events and policies

Even if Henry VII agreed with the second half of Vergil's description of the Irish, he certainly would have doubted the statement that 'Such Irish all obey the English king'. As the timeline shows, Ireland caused Henry great concern and he used two different strategies for maintaining control over Ireland. Between 1485 and 1494 and then again between 1496 and 1509 Henry relied upon a local nobleman to act as Lord Deputy, to rule Ireland on the king's behalf. This had long been the approach taken by kings of England, largely because it produced the maximum benefit (Ireland did not threaten the peace or security of England) for the minimum cost.

This approach was also favoured by the Anglo-Irish nobility as it gave them freedom from undue English intervention. The Earl of Kildare was re-appointed Lord Deputy by Henry in 1485. However, Kildare's preference for his own rather than the king's interests created serious problems. In 1496 Henry changed his strategy and appointed an Englishman, Sir Edward Poynings, as Lord Deputy, whose task was to prevent the Irish adding to the king's insecurity. Poynings' expedition has been described as a major turning point in Anglo-Irish relations but Henry VII's objectives were not grandiose or far-sighted. He wanted to protect himself against rebellion.

The major limitations on Poynings' expedition were imposed by money. Eventually Henry decided that enough had been achieved – more would increase the costs dramatically, and they were already high. Happily the years between 1492 and 1496 convinced Kildare that acting as Henry's deputy was a better prospect that trying to oppose him. Therefore after 1496 the king could revert to the traditional policy of ruling through an Anglo-Irish nobleman with renewed confidence and security.

Poynings' Law

'...no parliament be holden hereafter in the said land, but as such season as the Kings Lieutenant and Counsaile there first doe certifie the king under the great seale of that land the causes and considereations, and all such acts as them seemeth should passe in the same Parliament, and such causes, considerations, and acts affirmed by the King and his Counsaile to be good and expedient for that land, and his licence thereupon, as well as in affirmation of the said causes and acts, as to summon the said parliament vnder his great seale of England had and obtained, that done, a Parliament to be had and holden after the forme and effect afore rehearsed: and if any Parliament bee holded in that land hereafter, contrary to the forme and prouision aforesaid, it be deemed voyd and of none effect in law.'

Questions

1 Why was Henry VII so consistently concerned about events in Ireland?

2 What limitations were there upon the king's freedom of action in Ireland?

3 In what ways did Poynings' law show the dominance of the King of England?

4 What are the similarities and differences between the conclusions of Ellis and Elton?

5 Is Elton's conclusion that Henry VII missed the best opportunity to solve 'the Irish Problem' a fair one?

Interpretations

‘The king's reaction to the crisis strikingly confirmed ... that unless a threat to his security should arise there, the king was basically uninterested in the lordship. Though he might talk about reducing the country, he was unwilling to provide the necessary resources for this task, and once the crisis passed, he was content with the Yorkist policy of maintaining and strengthening a bridgehead in the country at no cost to himself, by governing the Pale and its borders through Kildare and exercising a more tenuous oversight of the other Anglo-Irish districts. ... Poynings' expedition was generally a success. Henry achieved his principal object, the security of the lordship against disloyalty and the threat from a pretender; ...’

S.G.Ellis, 'Henry VII and Ireland' in *England and Ireland in the Later Middle Ages*, 1981.

‘The problem of Ireland had turned out to be too big for solution; the return of Kildare meant the end of effective English control, despite the operation of Poynings' laws; and Henry VIII, Elizabeth, and Oliver Cromwell had to face a problem grown ever bigger in the interval. Henry VII had the best chance of all to win success, before the Reformation came to complicate matters; but parsimony (however necessary) and opportunism triumphed. There were no claimants about to disturb the peace from Ireland; why, then, waste good money on a probably futile policy of direct rule? Henry VII was lucky to die before the Irish problem revived, but revive it did – and largely because he gave up the fight.’

G.R.Elton, *England under the Tudors*, 1955.

Anglo-Irish Events

1485	Kildare continued as Lord Deputy.
1487	Kildare gave support to Lambert Simnel, albeit only after the arrival of the mercenary army.
1488	Sir Richard Edgecombe sent to Ireland to re-assert authority. Kildare and Irish lords took oath of loyalty but refused to enter into bonds.
1491–4	Kildare failed to take action for the king against Perkin Warbeck and was dismissed in mid-1492. New leaders were appointed from amongst the Anglo-Irish nobility but failed to provide strong leadership or maintain peace. Anglo-Irish lords advised Henry to intervene directly, at least partly because it was in their interest to eliminate the problem of Gaelic Ireland by conquest.
1494 Sept.	Sir Edward Poynings appointed Deputy.
Oct.	Poynings landed in Ireland with 700 soldiers. His objectives were to assert loyal authority, establish peace and justice and bring a larger area under royal control.
Dec.	Parliament opened in Drogheda and passed 49 Acts, the most famous of which became known as 'Poynings' Law'.
1495 Feb.	Kildare arrested for conspiring against Poynings, probably wrongly. This ended the chances of a successful military conquest, for which Poynings needed Kildare's assistance.
Dec.	Poynings returned to England, having secured English rule.
1496 Aug.	Kildare re-appointed as Deputy, a post he held until the end of the reign. In England, Kildare had married the king's second cousin.
1497	Warbeck received no support in Ireland.
1498	Kildare sought permission from Henry VII to hold a parliament in Ireland.

seen as the chief local lord. In general, gentry had regarded the local nobleman as their lord and had been retained by them, which could be dangerous for the king if loyalty to the lord and king clashed. To counteract this Henry passed an Act in 1487 saying that men who held royal land, tenancies or offices could only be retained by the king. Thus gentlemen regarded the king as their immediate and only lord rather than as a distant figure to whom they owed service only at second hand.

Overall, justice was exercised more diligently. If it had not been, Henry VII would not have heaped more and more responsibility onto JPs. They acquired new powers, both legal and administrative. JPs now had to check the choice (empanelling) of juries by sheriffs, enforce vagrancy laws, assess taxes, check weights and measures, supervise enquiries into unlawful retainers. By the end of the reign 'they had superseded the sheriff and the feudal lord as administrative agents' and their direct relationship with the king therefore enhanced royal power.

Local Government: Securing the Borders

In an age when communications were slow, problems far from London could develop dangerously before the king was able to act. The distant parts of the kingdom therefore needed particularly careful supervision, especially Wales and the north of England, where responsibility for justice in some areas lay in the hands of the local lords and royal officials were excluded.

Henry VII's dealings with Wales and the north show a similar pattern to other areas of his administration. There was an initial continuity of method which then gave way to distinctively different developments. In both regions Henry ultimately relied on councils responsible to the crown which by-passed the local 'super-nobles' on whom Edward IV had depended.

In the north there was particular need for strong and sensitive government after Richard III's dominance of the region. Initially Henry was assisted by the local influence of the Earl of Northumberland but, after his murder in 1489, his chief representative in the north was the Earl of Surrey. Surrey had no lands in the north and was dependent on the king's favour for further restoration of his family lands. He was very definitely the king's man, heading the Council of the North which, perhaps strangely, confined its activities to Yorkshire and probably Northumberland. Cumberland and Westmoreland were mostly left to run riot – literally. So isolated was the region that Henry's government seems to have neglected to enforce justice as it did elsewhere. It appears that Henry's major demand of the border regions was that they should not challenge his security. If they did not, then he avoided expensive and time-consuming attempts to bring them as closely under his supervision as other areas. The clearest example of this was his policy towards Ireland.

REVIEW

At the beginning of this chapter you were asked a set of questions about Henry VII and his domestic policies. Your answers were expectations or just plain guesses. Now that you have studied the topic in more depth what are your answers to these questions now? Question 5 from page 92 is dealt with in the Section Review.

1 Which of the issues on the diagram on p.92 proved to be the most difficult for Henry VII to tackle?

2 How did tackling each one contribute to Henry's security?

3 How effective do you think Henry's domestic policies were?

4 What kind of personality do you think Henry had and how well suited was he to the task of governing England?

Essays

Choose one essay title from the list below. Working with one or two others prepare a brief and direct answer to the question, amounting to no more than one side of writing. Add a list of any questions or uncertainties you have that would need further reading before writing an essay.

Present your answer to another or other groups (either on paper, orally or both) and take note of their comments, criticisms and disagreements. Then write a full essay based on these discussions.

1 To what extent was the monarchy stronger in 1509 than in 1485?

2 At no time in his reign could Henry VII have felt secure on his throne. Discuss this statement.

3 To what extent was Henry VII's success attributable to the war-weariness of the English aristocracy?

4 Account for the success of Henry VII's financial and administrative policies.

5 Henry VII's success in domestic affairs was due to his own abilities and to the effectiveness of his ministers. Comment on this statement.

Chapters 4 and 5 concentrated on the events of the reign and the policies and activities of the king, his ministers and of a handful of rebellious subjects. However, as the Section Preview (pp. 70 – 73) indicated, historians also discuss the broader significance of Henry's reign. The first such debate revolves around the phrase 'New Monarchy' and began in the late nineteenth century. The period of the New Monarchy was identified as 1471 – 1509, years when the monarchy achieved a new level of power, crushing the power and privileges of the nobility. At this time the monarchy was despotic, which has been defined as 'tyrannical but legal'.

This idea of a 'New Monarchy' was attacked and largely destroyed in the 1950s and 1960s when Sir Geoffrey Elton and K.B.McFarlane argued that there was nothing new in the methods of Edward IV and Henry VII. Instead these two 'new monarchs' were seen as using medieval methods to achieve the same objectives as their predecessors. If there was a difference after 1471 it lay in their vigorous and determined pursuit of their objectives.

This argument over the New Monarchy led into a second debate, highlighted in the Section Preview, about the similarities and differences between Edward IV and Henry VII. The New Monarchy theory assumed a similarity that was challenged by historians who saw the two kings as being significantly different from each other. The Focus section on the next two pages examines this issue more closely. It might seem odd to look more closely at Edward IV now – after you have studied his successor Henry VII – but your study of Henry VII should provide an effective context for the comparison.

5.4 Edward IV and Henry VII

D uring this chapter you have met several questions inviting comparisons of Henry VII's government with that of Edward IV. These questions have dealt with finances, administration, parliament and the nobility. The sources here re-cap a little on these issues but also offer a wider perspective on the question of whether Henry VII inaugurated a new era of English kingship.

Source A

Edward was of a gentle nature and cheerful aspect: nevertheless should he assume an angry countenance he could appear very terrible to beholders. He was easy of access to his friends and to others, even the least notable ... he seized any opportunity that the occasion offered of revealing his fine stature more protractedly and more evidently to on-lookers. He was so genial in his greeting, that if he saw a newcomer bewildered at his appearance and royal magnificence, he would give him courage to speak by laying a kindly hand upon his shoulder....Though not rapacious for other men's goods, he was yet so eager for money, that in pursuing it he acquired a reputation for avarice ... it was his habit, so I have learned, to take an emetic for the delight of gorging his stomach once more. ... He was licentious in the extreme: moreover it was said that he had been most insolent to numerous women after he had seduced them, for, as soon as he grew weary of dalliance, he gave up the ladies much against their will to the other courtiers.

Dominic Mancini, *The Usurpation of Richard III*, written in 1483.

Source B

As sovereign, Edward expected allegiance and obedience without prevarication. Neither devious nor cunning, but direct and straightforward, Edward was a king with whom one knew where one stood. ... He was a dashing and daring general, whose seizure of the strategic and tactical initiative was too much for his over-cautious rivals. His splendid clothes, jewels and buildings, his jousting, hunting, hawking, feasting, and wenching were tastes that almost all aristocrats shared. ...he foreshadowed Henry VII rather than sharing his achievement. Chamber finance gave him control over his finances, but his estate administration was not systematically improved and the quantity of land kept in hand was very small. ... Edward valued lands primarily as a source of political support, Henry VII as a source of income. ...impressive though Edward appeared and conscientious though he was, he could be managed. ... His awesome powers to review his patronage were exploited by his favourites to their own benefit.

M.A.Hicks, *Who's Who in Late Medieval England*, 1991.

Source C

There is ample evidence amongst the records of his reign that Edward took his kingly duties very seriously. Beyond all doubt the business of state was his main preoccupation. A very large number of warrants, letters and petitions bear the royal sign-manual, in the form of the monogram 'R.E.'. Occasionally the king added further instructions written in his own hand to an official mandate ...

Immunity from an 'Irish problem' was bought at the price of virtual surrender of effective royal control. The rare occasions when Edward tried to assert his authority produced trouble, from which he hastily retreated. In effect, Yorkist policy in Ireland amounted to little more than a sell-out to the interests of the Anglo-Irish aristocracy.

...Edward does not emerge with any distinction in his direction of foreign affairs. The entanglement with Scotland was a major misjudgement which greatly weakened his position in relation to continental powers. ... He was irresolute in that he would neither take the steps necessary to put real pressure on King Louis nor exploit the alternative advantages of a definitely anti-French policy. From his own standpoint his foreign and dynastic policies had been ruined by the time he died ... Yet it would be unfair to overlook his difficulties. In the Machiavellian phase in European power-politics which marks his lifetime he was dealing with opponents who were notably unprincipled, self-interested and shifty, above all with Louis XI, who was too clever for all his own opponents (and sometimes too clever for his own good). Edward had neither the financial and military resources nor the backing of popular enthusiasm to enable him to indulge freely in ambitious schemes on the Continent. ... Finally, it is worth noticing that, if for rather different reasons, Henry VII chose to follow the essential principles of Edward's foreign policy towards France and the Low Countries. He pursued them, however, with a cleverness, a consistency, and a grasp of reality notably absent from Edward's later years.

C.D.Ross, *Edward IV*, 1974.

Source D

Edward IV chose to delegate power to others, some would argue with fatal consequences for his sons and his dynasty ... He was the lord of lords of a family of allied retinues. His regime therefore was both backward looking and centrifugal. The logical end of his policy was not to centralise his kingdom, but to reinforce its divisions ... Henry VII, on the other hand, followed a determinedly opposite course. He ruled through his own men in every corner of his kingdom. He refused to allow his servants to be retained by any of his subjects. He kept strict control of the independent retaining of the peers, even if they were his own committed supporters. He indeed did maintain central control. Whereas Edward IV's household was a looseknit fellowship under the king's leadership, Henry VII's was a tightknit team under the king's control.

Not only is it misleading to see Henry VII's household rule as a continuation of Edward IV's; it is also myopic to see the aims, methods and doctrines of either Yorkists or Henry VII in isolation from the longer course of English political history since 1377. The problem facing late fifteenth-century kings in endeavouring to assert their own personal power and to recover authority was similar to that faced by Richard II ... what Richard tried and failed to do has been condemned by historians as tyranny, whereas what Henry VII succeeded in doing has been praised by them as statesmanship ...

...not only were the differences between Edward IV and Henry VII greater than the similarities, but ... also the strategy being pursued by the early Tudors to restore royal authority had its roots in the late-fourteenth century.

A.J. Pollard, New Monarchy Renovated?, 1461 – 1509, *Medieval History, vol.2*, 1992.

Source E

'It is fair to say that Henry VII's approach to government was strongly traditional, and that parallels to it, notably in his reliance on professional administrators, can be traced in the fourteenth century. It was the reign of Henry VI, when magnate influence was excessive, which in fact deviated from customary practice. The search of historians for a 'New Monarchy' or a 'more modern' form of kingship, whether of the Yorkists or the Tudors, is in that sense the pursuit of a myth. In political terms, however, there is some justification in regarding Henry VII's accession as the start of a new epoch, because the dynastic change brought with it in the long run a more securely based royal authority than had previously existed.'

J.A.F. Thomson, 'The Transformation of Medieval England, 1370–1529', 1983.

Questions

1 For each source identify the strengths and weaknesses it reveals in Edward's kingship.

2 In what ways does each source suggest either similarities or differences between Edward IV and Henry VII?

3 Using the material in this Focus section and in chapters 4 and 5 as a whole, do you agree with the statement that 1485 was a major turning-point in English history?

SECTION REVIEW

Henry VII

If the last two chapters have seemed complex at times you can take comfort from the words of the author of what has been described as 'the best modern survey of the reign'. Margaret Condon began her article with a reference to 'this difficult and still largely obscure reign'. Perhaps one of the more comprehensible aspects is the personality of the king and it is certainly fitting to conclude with the king himself. Here are some contemporary assessments. To what extent do you agree with them?

Source A

Bacon has a story of how, to the great rejoicing of the whole court, Henry's pet monkey tore up the notebook in which the king had recorded the characters and demeanours of those about him. This trivial incident, whether or not it actually occurred, encapsulates the essence and the fragility of Henry's rule. It perhaps suggests, too, a certain superficiality of achievement despite all the auguries of change: an impermanence, a fragility caused in part by the tensions which Henry VII himself caused in binding and dividing the ruling elites themselves.

M. Condon, Ruling Elites in the Reign of Henry VII in C.D. Ross (ed.) Patronage, Pedigree and Power in the late Medieval England, 1979.

THE BUST OF HENRY VII BY TORRIGIANO, MADE C.1512 – 1519.

Source B

'His politic wisdom in governance was singular, his wit always quick and ready, his reason pithy and substantial, his memory fresh and holding, his experience notable, his counsels fortunate and taken by wise deliberation, his speech gracious in diverse languages, his person goodly and amiable, his natural complexion of the purest mixture, his issue fair and in good number; leagues and confederacies he had with all Christian princes, his mighty power was dreaded everywhere, not only within his realm but without also; his people were to him in as humble subjection as ever they were to king; his land many a day in peace and tranquility; his prosperity in battle against his enemies was marvellous; his dealing in times of perils and dangers was cold and sober with great hardiness. If any treason was conspired against him it came out wonderfully; his treasure and riches incomparable; his buildings most goodly and after the newest cast of all pleasure.'

The Funeral Oration made by John Fisher, Bishop of Rochester, 1509.

Source C

'His spirit was distinguished, wise and prudent; his mind was brave and resolute and never, even at the moments of greatest danger, deserted him. He had a most pertinacious memory. Withal he was not devoid of

TALKING POINT

Does this suggestion of avarice detract from Henry VII's achievements?

TALKING POINT

If Henry had lived longer or his successor had been a different character historians might well be more critical of Henry VII. Does the sense of achievement about Henry VII's kingship owe a good deal to the fact that he was succeeded by a reasonably competent monarch who provided continuity and a contrast?

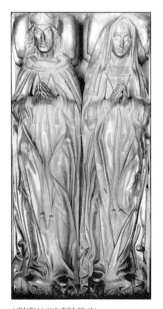

HENRY VII'S TOMB IN WESTMINSTER ABBEY. HENRY CHOSE A DESIGN THAT WAS UNLIKE ANYTHING PREVIOUSLY BUILT IN ENGLAND, REFLECTING RENAISSANCE DEVELOPMENTS. THE SCULPTOR WAS A FLORENTINE, PIETRO TORRIGIANO. WAS HENRY A RENAISSANCE PRINCE OR A MEDIEVAL RULER?

scholarship. In government he was shrewd and prudent so that no one dared to get the better of him through deceit or guile. He was gracious and kind and was as attentive to his visitors as he was easy of access. His hospitality was splendidly generous; he was fond of having foreigners at his court and he freely conferred favours on them. But those of his subjects who were indebted to him and who did not pay him due honour or who were generous only with promises, he treated with harsh severity. He well knew how to maintain his royal majesty and all which appertains to kingship at every time and in every place. He was most fortunate in war, although he was constitutionally more inclined to peace than to war. He cherished justice above all things; as a result he vigorously punished violence, manslaughter and every other kind of wickedness whatsoever. Consequently he was greatly regretted on that account by all his subjects, who had been able to conduct their lives peaceably, far removed from the assaults and evil doings of scoundrels...

[After 1502] he began to treat his people with more harshness and severity than had been his custom, in order (as he himself asserted) to ensure they remained more thoroughly and entirely in obedience to him. The people themselves had another explanation for his action, for they considered they were suffering not on account of their own sins but on account of the greed of their monarch. It is not indeed clear whether at the start it was greed; but afterwards greed did indeed become apparent, so irresolute, vacillating and corrupted are all human purposes.'

Polydore Vergil, Anglica Historia.

Source D

'I have perused the books touching all such matters as I was privy to and have written down such persons as I think were hardly treated and more sorely than the causes required ... the king's grace, whose soul God pardon, was much set to have many persons in his danger at his pleasure ...The Abbot of Furness had a hard end for his pardon for he paid and is deemed to have paid 500 marks for a little matter. The Lord Abergavenny had a very sore end, for any proof that was against him to my knowledge. The King's Grace dealt sore in the matter of my lady Strange for her lands. The executors of Master Bray were hardly dealt with at divers times.

Extracts from the petition of Edmund Dudley,
written in August 1509 before his execution.

The Reign of Henry VIII

'Heaven smiles, earth rejoices'

[Henry VIII is] a prince whose exceptional and almost more than human talents you know so well ... by virtue of the fact that he has written to you under his own hand, as he has not done to many others. And if you knew how courageously and wisely he is now acting, and what a passion he has for justice and honesty, and how warmly he is attached to men of letters ... Oh, Erasmus, if you could only see how happily excited everyone is here, and how all are congratulating themselves on this prince's greatness, and how they pray above all for his long life you would be bound to weep for joy! Heaven smiles, earth rejoices; all is milk and honey and nectar. Tight-fistedness is well and truly banished. Generosity scatters wealth with unstinting hand. Our King's heart is set not upon gold or jewels or mines of ore, but upon virtue, reputation, and eternal renown.

From a letter by William, Lord Mountjoy to Erasmus, 27 May 1509, advising Erasmus to travel to England to seek patronage.

HENRY VIII PAINTED BY AN UNKNOWN ARTIST C. 1520 WHEN HE WAS 29.

Henry VII died on 21 April 1509 and, to some people at least, a new age seemed to be beginning. Mountjoy, who had been Henry VIII's tutor, might be expected to rejoice in the new king. Less predictably (but far more ironically) Sir Thomas More wrote in a poem for the coronation, 'This day is the end of our slavery, the fount of our liberty; the end of sadness, the beginning of joy.'

However not all reactions were so straightforward. With the benefit of a little hindsight, Edward Hall provided a more realistic description of reactions in 1509.

Wonder it were to write, of the lamentation that was made, for this Prince amongst his servants and other of the wisest sort, and no joy that was made for his death by such as were troubled by rigour of his law. Yet the toward hope, which in all points appeared in the young king, did both repair and comfort the heavy hearts of them which had lost so wise and sage a prince: and also did put out of the minds such as were relieved by the said King's death, all their old grudge and rancour and confirmed their new joy by the new grant of his pardon.

From Edward Hall. *The Union of the Two Noble and Illustre Families of Lancaster and York*, 1548.

In even greater contrast to the reactions of Mountjoy and More was the letter sent by Ferdinand of Spain to Henry VIII, congratulating the new king on his accession but also hoping that he had ascended the throne unopposed. Should Henry VIII need aid, Ferdinand promised that 'a powerful army will be sent without delay from Spain.'

Questions

1 Why do you think there was such celebration of the accession of Henry VIII?

2 Do you think that many of the people of England would react so joyfully to Henry VIII's accession?

3 Security had been the continuing theme of Henry VII's reign. What can be learned from Ferdinand's letter to Henry?

Henry VIII – the Glory Trail?

When Henry VIII became king of England in April 1509 he was 17 years old. Nowadays he would have been trying on his new crown while beginning the final countdown to his A levels. What would a 17 year old monarch want to achieve? What would you have aimed to achieve if you had become king in 1509? Write down your objectives for your reign. Below is a series of issues that faced Henry VIII during his reign. What would you have done in each situation given the objectives you have identified? Keep a record of your decisions and then compare them with those of others. Assess each other's success in achieving your objectives.

TALKING POINT

If you are the same age as Henry was in 1509 are you better equipped to understand his early decisions and first years as king than much older historians?

1 Your father died with a reputation for avarice. Some of his advisers are highly unpopular for their part in his 'extortions'. Should you

(a) make a clean start with a new council?

(b) keep most of your father's councillors but punish (perhaps even execute) the most unpopular individuals?

(c) keep all your father's councillors for you need their experience and, despite criticisms, your father was very successful?

2 France is your country's oldest ancient enemy. You have been brought up to enjoy tournaments and jousting. Will you

(a) continue your father's policy of defensive isolation?

(b) lead a war of conquest immediately?

(c) lay plans for war when you have secured the right alliances?

3 1516 – your chief minister, Thomas Wolsey, is the subject of much gossip and some opposition. Men say he is too powerful and that he diminishes your status in the eyes of your subjects and foreign rulers. Should you

(a) dismiss Wolsey to show who is truly king?

(b) ignore such talk because you know you are in control?

4 1518 – Wolsey proposes that you act as intermediary between France and the Empire to produce a European peace treaty. Should you

(a) agree with this plan because it will enable you to pose as the key figure in Europe?

(b) dismiss the plan because there is nothing glorious in peace? An alliance with one or the other could lead to a glorious war.

5 1527 – you have been married to Queen Catherine for 18 years. You have one daughter but no son. Should you

(a) accept the will of God and make plans for Princess Mary's marriage to secure the dynasty?

(b) change the succession to enable your illegitimate son, the Duke of Richmond, to inherit the crown?

(c) seek an annulment of your marriage from the Pope?

6 1529 – attempts to persuade the Pope have failed. Wolsey has enemies who say that he has not been working hard enough in your cause. Should you

(a) dismiss Wolsey as a warning to the Pope that you are still determined on a divorce?

(b) ignore the talk? Wolsey has been your leading minister for 15 years.

(c) demote Wolsey from his leading position?

7 1532 – Thomas Cromwell has emerged as a man with the talent and drive to take on Wolsey's former role. Should you

(a) refuse to accept Cromwell as chief minister as another such minister will diminish your status?

(b) refuse to accept Cromwell because he supported Wolsey to the last?

(c) use Cromwell as chief minister for it will free you of the tedium of detail but leave you in charge of overall strategies?

8 1533 – Anne Boleyn is pregnant with your child. Should you

(a) make further representations to the Pope for a divorce?

(b) cut England off from the Roman Catholic church, declare yourself head of a new church and free to marry Anne? England has been part of the Roman church for nearly 1000 years.

9 1536 – the dissolution of some monasteries has helped to spark a major rising in the north. Should you

(a) march north at once at the head of your army?

(b) send your leading general, the Duke of Norfolk, to command your forces although he has some sympathies with the Catholic religion?

(c) negotiate with the rebels and put an end to religious reform?

10 1539 – you feel uncomfortable with the degree of religious reform. People, even women, are even said to be discussing religion at home and in taverns. Should you

(a) ignore your qualms and proceed with further reforms because it will allow you to act as leader of the Protestant cause in Europe?

(b) stop reform here but go no further back towards Catholicism in case it prejudices your role as supreme head of the church?

(c) return to the Catholic church you were brought up in now that you have a male heir and both Catherine and Anne are dead?

11 1540 – you have married Anne of Cleves despite your dislike of the lady. Cromwell urged the match because of the dangers of a foreign crusade against England. Now the foreign policy situation has changed and the match is no longer needed. Should you

(a) retain the marriage in case the situation changes once more?

(b) end the marriage and dismiss Cromwell as his enemies are urging you to do? He has humiliated you.

(c) end the marriage but keep Cromwell in office?

12 1542 – the prospect of war with France arises. Should you

(a) attack Scotland immediately as a forerunner for a lengthier campaign against France?

(b) attack France immediately?

(c) ignore war at your age? It is costly and will cause suffering at home.

HENRY VIII PAINTED C. 1542 WHEN HE WAS 51 ALTHOUGH, IF COMPARED WITH THE MATSYS PORTRAIT, THIS MAY WELL BE FLATTERING!

TALKING POINT

When Henry died he did leave a male heir. Was this the fulfilment of his most important objective?

TALKING POINT

Which options do you think Henry took? What does this tell you about his personality?

HENRY VIII PAINTED BY CORNELIS MATSYS SHOWING THE CHANGES IN THE KING'S APPEARANCE IN THE 1540s.

Faction at the court of Henry VIII

One of perhaps the major problems in understanding Henry VIII's reign lies in deciding on the role of faction. Faction has been defined by Professor Ives as 'an alliance whose target was an individual, which operated by seeking to put pressure on the ruler, and which sought to exploit the mechanisms of the court.' This in turn raises questions about Henry VIII himself. Was he fully in control of ministers and courtiers or was he the victim of their manipulations? Pages 32 – 35 have introduced you to one possible example of the workings of faction but there is no doubt that historians differ about its significance.

1 What differences are there in the views contained in the two extracts below?

2 Why do you think it is so difficult for historians to reach agreement on the role of the king himself?

Source A

Henry VII's style of management left no room for faction; Henry VIII, on the other hand, with his fluctuations, enthusiasms, and irregular handling of business, gave it an open invitation to flourish ...Indeed it seems clear that it was the mounting dispute over religion, and the King's failure to come down firmly on either side, that screwed faction to such a pitch of intensity by the later years of Henry VIII's reign.

D.Starkey, *The Reign of Henry VIII: Politics and Personalities*, 1985.

Source B

[Was] Henry VIII ... a weak man, often the plaything of factions, whose arena was the court? Should the fall of Wolsey, the fall of Anne Boleyn, the fall of Cromwell be seen as the work of a court faction? But Wolsey was very much the king's servant who fell not because of any politicking against him but because he had let the king down over the divorce and because his dismissal in 1529 was a skilful way of threatening both the Pope and the church in England. Cromwell fell because the king was horrified by his dangerous dabbling with heresy. It may be rather that Henry VIII was far more in control than factional explanations would suggest.

G.W.Bernard, *The Power of the Early Tudor Nobility: A Study of the Fourth and Fifth Earls of Shrewsbury*, 1985.

6 The King and the Cardinal

PREVIEW

Despite the welcome given to the new king it often appears that the first half of Henry VIII's reign was dominated by the King's minister, Thomas Wolsey, Cardinal Archbishop of York. Wolsey's political and administrative skills became apparent to the King during his French campaigns between 1513 and 1514 and thereafter Wolsey was so powerful that some observers believed that it was the Cardinal who really ruled England.

In this chapter the dominant issue will be the extent to which Henry VIII controlled his own government and its decisions. What do these sources suggest about the balance of power between the King and the Cardinal?

THOMAS WOLSEY. WHAT IMAGE IS CREATED BY THIS PORTRAIT?

Source A

'the Cardinal of York ... ruled both the king and the entire kingdom. On Giustinian's first arrival he used to say to him 'His majesty will do so and so'. Subsequently, by degrees, he went forgetting himself and commenced saying 'We shall do so and so'. He had then reached such a pitch that he used to say 'I shall do so and so'.

He (Wolsey) was about 46 years old, very handsome, learned, extremely eloquent, of vast ability and indefatigable. He transacted alone the same business as that which occupied all the magistrates, offices and councils of Venice, both civil and criminal; and all state affairs were managed by him.'

Report by the Venetian Ambassador to England, May 1519.

Source B

'Mine own good Cardinal ... thank you for the great pain and labour that you do daily take in my business and matters, desiring you (that when you have well established them) to take some pastime and comfort to the intent you may the longer endure to serve us, for always pain cannot be endured. Surely you have so substantially ordered our matters, both of this side of the sea and beyond, that in mine opinion little or nothing can be added.'

Letter from Henry VIII to Wolsey, 1521.

Source C

'I thank our Lord, son,' quoth he, 'I find his grace my very good lord indeed, and I believe he doth as singularly favour me as any subject within this realm. Howbeit, son Roper, I may tell thee I have no cause to be proud thereof, for if my head could win him a castle in France (for then there was a war between us) it should not fail to go.'

From *A Life of Sir Thomas More* by William Roper, written in 1535. Roper was More's son-in-law.

The Enthusiasms of Youth, 1509 – 1514

The accession of Henry VIII created a great atmosphere of change. Many men felt glad to be free of Henry VII's intrusive watchfulness. This sense of breaking free from imprisonment was encouraged by the new king's early actions. On the second day of his reign Henry VIII ordered the arrests of Empson and Dudley, men who symbolised his father's policy of security through financial threats and extortion. Recognizances were eased or abandoned and commissions of enquiry appointed to seek out breaches of the law. In effect this was inviting criticisms of the previous regime. The heart and muscles of Henry VII's government – Chamber finance and the Council Learned – were regulated by parliamentary statute. And yet these actions have the appearance of being gestures, winning support by meeting the contemporary mood half-way. It was sixteen months before Empson and Dudley were executed as it had proved impossible to pass an Act of Attainder through parliament. Neither did the commissions of enquiry lead to charges and prosecutions.

Major changes in the methods and machinery of government were, in reality, unlikely. Most of Henry VII's councillors and officials remained in office. More importantly, Henry VIII did not have the experience to make changes. Not quite eighteen, he had never been given responsibility in state affairs. Now it was necessary for him 'to have some time an intercourse into the Council, there to hear what was done in weighty matters.' Sooner or later, however, Henry VIII would have to establish his own style – and policies – as king.

There were two possible routes to successful kingship for the young Henry. One was to model himself on his father, to become an administrator-king. The other lay in the forms of warrior-kings such as Edward III and Henry V, whose militarism had united the nobility behind them. The two routes may also reflect competing groups who jostled for influence over Henry VIII. His father's councillors wanted, for the most part, to continue the policies that had achieved security. Many young (and not so young) noblemen, on the other hand, saw this as their time of opportunity. The mark of success would be the nature of foreign policy. The determining factor would be the new king's personality.

With hindsight it was a foregone conclusion that Henry VIII would play the part of a warrior-hero. Even before 1509 the signs were there for all to see. Henry VII had taken great pains to protect his sole male heir but it seems to have been impossible to stop young Henry practising his favourite sport – jousting. Once king, Henry did not trouble to hide his intentions. A Venetian merchant reported that Henry had sworn 'immediately after his coronation to make war on the King of France. Soon we shall hear that he has invaded France'. The King's rapid marriage to Catherine of Aragon cemented the Anglo-Spanish alliance which could only have one target. Henry's boon companions were young men of high birth, men who would only encourage his impatience with past caution.

Henry was set on war but it took some time for the young man's gestures to become effective actions. The king walked out of an audience with the French ambassador and then denied any knowledge of a letter of friendship sent to Louis XII. Even so, a peace treaty was signed with France in March 1510. The anti-war group, led by Henry VII's old

AN ILLUSTRATION FROM JOHN, LORD BERNER'S TRANSLATION OF FROISSART'S CHRONICLES WHICH TOLD THE STORY OF THE HUNDRED YEARS WAR AND WAS HIGHLY POPULAR WITH HENRY AND HIS COURTIERS.

TALKING POINT

When studying Henry VIII's early years as king what problems are created by our knowledge of later events or our images of Henry in his later years?

councillors, retained their dominance when a Great Council discussed war in 1511. They argued that foreign involvement wasted money and threatened security. When the change did come it owed something to Henry's maturing ability to assert himself but it was fundamentally the product of changes in European politics. The League of Cambrai (1508) had united France with the rest of Europe against Venice but by 1511 France was outsider once more. The Pope headed the Holy League to drive France out of Italy and this made Henry confident of having allies for an attack on France. The possibility that Louis XII intended to depose the Pope strengthened the case for English involvement against France, as it would be in defence of the Church.

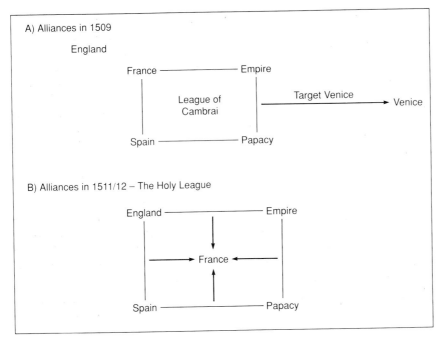

A) Alliances in 1509

B) Alliances in 1511/12 – The Holy League

While the Holy League was forming Henry took his first steps towards war. A small force of archers was sent successfully to help the Emperor Maximilian against a local rival and, more importantly, to encourage Maximilian to join the Holy League. For a similar reason, Lord Darcy led 1000 men to Cadiz to aid Ferdinand of Spain in an expedition against the Moors in North Africa. On arrival Darcy was informed that the expedition had been cancelled. Darcy set sail sixteen days later, leaving a trail of devastation after his drunken soldiers had vandalised farms and killed locals.

Real war began in June 1512 when an English army of 12,000 set sail for Gascony. It was intended to join the Spanish forces for a combined assault on France but again Ferdinand failed to keep to the plan. He used the English presence as a threat to aid his seizure of Navarre and then sat back. The English waited in vain for Spanish troops to assemble for the attack on France. Heavy rain, sickness, inadequate supplies and divided leadership turned the English army into a near-mutinous mob.

The blame for this fiasco was placed on the Marquis of Dorset and other leaders. Henry himself, certain that he was above such incompetence,

1 To what extent does Henry VIII appear to have decided English foreign policies between 1509 and 1514?

2 Is there any evidence to support or refute the view that Henry VIII was more interested in the image than the reality of war?

3 How might the outcome of the French expeditions have been regarded by

(a) Henry VIII and

(b) senior councillors who had served his father?

set about preparing a direct invasion of northern France. Exhaustive diplomacy promised a four pronged attack by Henry, Ferdinand, Maximilian and the Pope but, even before it was agreed, it was being undermined by Ferdinand's agreement to a separate truce with France! Two unsuccessful naval engagements followed before Henry's moment arrived. In June 1513 Henry VIII landed in France at the head of his army. Pageantry was at its height as the English moved forward a full three miles per day, seeking someone to attack. The campaign that followed was high in prestige but low in achievement. A hectic chase after the French cavalry produced a galaxy of prisoners but scarcely merited the name of 'Battle of the Spurs'. The towns of Therouanne and Tournai were captured but were of significance to Maximilian, not Henry, although the English held Tournai at great cost until 1518. The one clear gain from the campaign was that it brought Thomas Wolsey right to the fore. The organisation and administration of the campaign lay in his hands and was a great success.

The English had been led astray from their own objectives. At best Henry had created a base for a more successful campaign in the next year but again the course of events proved to be beyond his control. Pope Julius II died and his successor reached an agreement with France. Ferdinand and Maximilian lost interest in attacking France, leaving Henry alone with his dreams of military glory. Within a year financial realities and his lack of allies had led to an Anglo-French Treaty surprisingly beneficial to England. Henry's sister, Mary, married the French King and Henry recovered his French pension. The English emerged secure from the king's adventures, albeit without any real military success, except for the one won behind Henry's back.

In September 1513, while Henry was in France the Battle of Flodden had been fought. The Scots had invaded England but, led by the Earl of Surrey, the English defenders routed the Scots, killing most the Scottish nobility and James IV himself. The contrast between this success and the incompetent strategies pursued in France was profound.

1513	English Policy and Actions	European Policies and Actions
Leo X became Pope Battle of the Spurs Capture of Therouanne and Tournai Battle of Flodden	English successes in France were limited but Henry intended to continue the war. He intended a triple attack on France in 1514 with the Empire and Spain, despite Ferdinand's past record of breaking agreements. Two of Henry's leading generals, Thomas Howard and Charles Brandon were promoted to the Dukedoms of Norfolk and Suffolk.	The Emperor and Ferdinand of Spain agreed to join Henry in a further attack on France, provided that England paid for their armies. Maximilian's heir, the Archduke Charles, was bethrothed to Henry VIII's sister, Mary, to cement the agreement.
	1 In what ways does this suggest that Henry was determined to continue the war against France?	
1514 Anglo-French peace treaty	Henry's preparations for war continued and he reached an agreement with the Swiss, requiring them to attack France at Henry's request. In June the English raided Cherbourg but soon two of Henry's leading councillors, Fox and Wolsey, were arguing for peace with France. In August a peace was agreed. The French were to pay the arrears of the English pension and Mary Tudor was married to King Louis.	Early in the year Ferdinand left the alliance, followed shortly afterwards by Maximilian. The new Pope, who favoured peace with France, put pressure on Henry to make peace and the French themselves proposed peace. Once the Anglo-French treaty was agreed France's attentions returned to Italy and she was not interested in an English proposal for a joint attack on Spain.
	2 Why did Henry reverse his policy and agree to an Anglo-French peace treaty?	

EXAMINING THE EVIDENCE
Henry VIII – 'A Perfect Model'?

More people can probably conjure up an image of Henry than of any other king – an image usually dependent on films, television or historical novels. The trouble with a picture or an image is just that – it is singular. How can one picture capture a person's character when people change and develop as they grow older? Henry VIII was not quite eighteen when he became king, fifty-five when he died – during the thirty eight years of his reign his appearance changed dramatically. Compare for example the portraits in the decision making activity in the Section Preview on pages 118 and 120. His activities and pastimes also changed but is the same true of his attitudes and personality? Our task is not to settle for one image of Henry VIII but to understand his development, to identify what changed and what stayed the same.

The sources in this section provide evidence of Henry in the first half of his reign. In addition to answering the specific questions on the sources think about whether this king would allow Wolsey to dominate government and whether Henry was the kind of king who would revolutionise life in England?

TALKING POINT

How useful are the portraits of this period for enhancing our understanding of the personalities we are studying? Are portraits more or less useful than photographs as evidence?

'The King Excelled'

Source A
8 July came 3 ambassadors ... to the king, who was practising archery in a garden with the archers of his guard. He cleft the mark in the middle, and surpassed them all, as he surpasses them in stature and personal graces. ...'

From John Taylor's diary of the expedition to France in 1513.

Source B
The King is the handsomest potentate I ever set eyes on, above the usual height, with an extremely fine calf to his leg, his complexion very fair and bright, with auburn hair combed straight and short, in the French fashion, and a round face so very beautiful that it would become a pretty woman, his throat being rather long and thick ... He speaks French, English, and Latin, and a little Italian; plays well on the lute and harpsichord, sings from a book at sight, draws the bow with greater strength than any man in England and jousts marvellously.

Pasqualigo, a Venetian Ambassador, April 1515.

Source C
His Majesty came into our arbour, and addressing me in French, said 'Talk with me awhile. The King of France, is he as tall as I am?' I told him there was but little difference. He continued 'Is he as stout?' I said he was not; and he then enquired 'What sort of legs has he?' I replied 'Spare'. Whereupon he opened the front of his doublet, and placing his hand on his thigh, said 'Look here, and I have also a good calf to my leg.

Pasqualigo, a Venetian Ambassador, May 1515.

IN 1513 JOHN TAYLOR RECORDED HOW THE 'KING AND LORD LISLE CHALLENGED ALL COMERS – THE KING EXCELLED EVERY ONE AS MUCH IN AGILITY AND IN BREAKING SPEARS'. THE EYEWITNESS RECORD IS SUPPORTED BY SURVIVING SCORE CHEQUES WHICH SHOW THE KING'S VICTORIES IN THE TILTYARD.

Source D

He was very religious; heard three masses daily when he hunted and sometimes five on other days besides having the office daily in the Queen's Chamber. He was extremely fond of hunting and never took that diversion without tiring 8 or 10 horses .. he was also fond of tennis, at which game it was the prettiest thing in the world to see him play; his fair skin glowing through a shirt of the finest texture ... He was affable and gracious ...

Giustinian, a Venetian Ambassador, writing in 1519 on his return to Venice after a long period in England.

Source E

Nature in producing this prince did her utmost to create a perfect model of manly beauty in these times.

The Secretary to the Venetian ambassador, January 1529.

---

1 Mountjoy described Henry VIII as having 'almost more than human talents'. What evidence is there of Henry's talents in Sources A–E?

2 Is there any evidence in sources A–E that detracts from the view that Henry VIII was an ideal king?

The King and the Court

Source F

[in 1510] ... one morning His Grace, the Earls of Essex, Wiltshire and twelve other noblemen came suddenly into the Queen's Chamber, all apparelled in short coats and hose of Kentish Kendal, with hoods on their heads, every one of them with bows and arrows, a sword and a buckler like outlaws or Robin Hood's men, whereof the Queen, the Ladies and all other there were abashed, as well for the strange sight as for the suddenness and after certain dances and pastime made they departed.

Edward Hall, *The Union of the Two Noble and Illustre Families of Lancastre and Yorks,* 1548.

Source G

May Day – The Queen was richly attired with 25 damsels on white palfreys – they went into a wood, where they found the King and his guard in green liveries, with bows in their hands, and in the wood were bowers filled with singing birds. ... Then followed the jousts, where in truth his majesty looked like St George on horseback. They jousted for three hours to the constant sound of trumpets and drums. The King excelled all others, shivering many lances and unhorsing one of his opponents.

N.Sagudino, a Venetian visitor to London, May 1515.

Source H

There entered two ladies on palfreys, in robes of purple damask, leading two ancient knights with beards of silver and when they came before the Queen they put up a bill saying that, although their youth had left them and age

CATHERINE OF ARAGON.

had come, yet courage, desire and good will abode with them and bade them to break spears, which they would gladly do if it pleased her to give them licence. The Queen and her ladies praised their skill and give them licence.

Then the knights threw away their robes and it was known that it was the King and the Duke of Suffolk. ... after supper the King came into the Queen's Chamber – where the Lords and Ladies danced.

> Edward Hall 'The Union of the Two Noble and illustre Families of Lancastre and York, 1548. A description of events at Christmas, 1524.

---

4 In what ways did life at court reflect Henry VIII's interests?

5 What kind of men did Henry choose as his companions?

6 What can you learn from these sources about Henry's relationship with Queen Catherine?

7 What do sources F – H suggest about Henry's view of the ideals of kingship?

The King at Work

Source I
King Francis next asked what sort of statesman [Henry] made. Avoided giving any answer, for to bestow praise on this score was impossible but being repeatedly questioned on this subject at length said that King Henry devoted himself to pleasure and ease and left the cares of State to the Cardinal.

> Report by S Giustinian, Venetian Ambassador to London in September 1519.
> Giustinian visited France on his way home.

Source J
Your Highness has the said letter with yourself either to be copied or else to be written with your own hand as shall stand with your pleasure. I beseech Your Grace, though it shall be to your pain, to do somewhat herein.

And for as it should be painful to Your Grace to sit and over read the whole treaty I shall therefore summarily note and take out the substantial effect and points thereof ...

> Extracts from two letters from Wolsey to Henry VIII, 1521 and 1523.

Source K
... used the King upon holy-days, when he has done his devotions, to send for him into his travers, and there sometime in matters of astronomy, geometry, divinity and such other faculties, and sometimes of his wordly affairs, to sit and confer with him. And other whiles would he, in the night, have him up into his leads, there for to consider with him the diversities, courses, motions and operations of the stars and planets.

> From A Life of Sir Thomas More by William Roper,
> written in 1535. Roper was More's son-in-law.

In the 1530s Henry VIII made decisions that brought great changes in England. Has there been any evidence in this section to suggest that Henry was likely to revolutionise life in England?

PART OF THE MANUSCRIPT OF PASTIME WITH GOOD COMPANY, A SONG WRITTEN BY HENRY HIMSELF WHICH SUMS UP SO MUCH ABOUT THE KING.

8 What evidence is there in Source I that Giustinian did not exaggerate his description of Henry to please King Francis?

9 What evidence is there in Source J to support Guistinian's view of Henry VIII?

10 Why do you think Henry VIII was reluctant to deal with the administrative duties of a king?

11 Do you think that Henry VIII was likely to allow Wolsey

(a) complete control over the government?

(b) control over detail but shaped policies himself?

(c) to do only what he ordered?

Give reasons to support your answer.

EXAMINING THE EVIDENCE
The rise and reputation of Thomas Wolsey

Thomas Wolsey was a remarkable man. He headed England's administration, keeping a firm grasp on the details of foreign policies and domestic matters, for a decade and a half. That task alone required enormous stamina and outstanding intelligence but Wolsey was also the leading figure in the English church, a Cardinal who aspired to the Papacy. He was also, as a result of his position and his sense of grandeur, the head of a household comparable with that of the king himself for its scale and magnificence. He was a patron of musicians and artists, a builder on a scale normally associated with royalty and a scholar.

Perhaps none of this is surprising for Henry VIII was a remarkable man who needed equally remarkable servants, especially if they were to last the pace of fifteen years in his service. What is surprising is the torrent of criticism that has been unleashed on Wolsey, even from historians. Professor Garret Mattingley pictured Wolsey as an 'unwieldy hulk of corrupted flesh bearing perilously the supple, powerful brain, a demoniac incandescence of ambition and pride driving and lighting from within the bloated, rotting body.' Such judgements are rooted firmly in contemporary opinion for no sixteenth century politician was so vilified as Wolsey.

Source A

Wolsey, with his arrogance and ambition, raised against himself the hatred of the whole people and, in his hostility towards nobles and common folk, procured their great irritation at his vainglory. His own odiousness was truly complete, because he claimed he could undertake himself almost all public duties...

Every time he wished to obtain something from Henry he introduced the matter casually in top his conversation; then he brought out some small present or other, a beautifully fashioned dish, for example, or a jewel or ring or gifts of that sort, and while the king was admiring the gift intently, Wolsey would adroitly bring forward the project on which his mind was fixed.

> Polydore Vergil, *Anglica Historia*, published in 1555 but probably 'first assembled from Vergil's contemporary jottings about 1532–3' and revised about 1546.

Source B

So rygorous revelyng,
in a prelate specially;
So bold and so bragging,
and was so baselye borne;
So lordlye of hys lokes,
and so dysdayneslye;
So fatte a magott,
bred of a flesshe-flye...

> John Skelton, *'Speke, Parott'*, 1521.

The Career of Thomas Wolsey

c. 1473	born in Ipswich
c. 1488	took his degree at Oxford
1498	ordained priest
1507	appointed chaplain to Henry VII following periods as chaplain to the Archbishop of Canterbury and then Sir Richard Nanfan, Deputy of Calais.
1509	Dean of Lincoln, Royal Almoner and 'informal royal secretary'.
1513	Bishop of Tournai
1514	Bishop of Lincoln and then Archbishop of York
1515	Cardinal; Lord Chancellor of England
1518	Legatus a Latere; Bishop of Bath and Wells
1524	Bishop of Durham (exchanged for Bath and Wells)
1529	Bishop of Winchester (exchanged for Durham) October – resigned as Chancellor
1530	November – death at Leicester

TALKING POINT

Good propaganda has to be based on some semblance of truth. Does this affect your view of Sources A, B and C?

Source C

Ye are so puffed with pride
That no man nay abyde
Your high and lordely lokes.
Ye caste up then your bokes
And vertu is forgotten...
Ye boost, ye face, ye crake,
And upon you take
To rule Kynge and Kayser.
And yf ye may have layser,
Ye wyll brynge all to nought.
And that is all your thought.

John Skelton, *Collyn Clout*, 1522.

Source D

Early in 1514 [Vergil] visited Italy, where his principal task seems to have been the furthering in Rome of Wolsey's schemes to become a cardinal. ... Vergil was back in England by February 1515. By the end of April he was imprisoned in the Tower on Wolsey's orders. ... As soon as the news of Vergil's arrest reached Rome a steady stream of letters was addressed to Wolsey and the king. The most effective argument on Vergil's behalf was the elevation of Wolsey to the cardinalate in September 1515, and he was set at liberty the following Christmas.

D.Hay (ed.), *The Anglica Historia of Polydore Vergil*, 1950.

Source E

In 'Speke Parott' the poet's aim was to attract royal patronage by criticizing Wolsey at a time when he seemed to have aroused Henry's distrust. Thereafter, in 'Collyn Clout' and 'Why come ye nat to courte?', his object was to secure patronage from the wealthier citizens of the city of London. Hence he forged his satires to appeal to their current concerns, most notably their objection to the forced loans of 1522 imposed by Wolsey ... Conventional jibes at worldly prelates were added to the satires in order to give them greater substance and to widen their appeal. They should not be mistaken for the object of the attacks, nor for personal criticisms of Wolsey the man.

G.Walker, Wolsey and the satirists in S.J.Gunn and P.G.Lindley (eds.), *Cardinal Wolsey, Church, state and art*, 1991.

Source F

[Wolsey's] sentences and witty persuasions in the council chamber were always so pithy that the councillors, always as occasion moved them, assigned him for his filed (persuasive) tongue and ornate eloquence to be their mouth-piece unto the King's Majesty in all their proceedings. The King conceived a most loving disposition towards him, especially as he was most earnest and readiest among all the council to advance the King's mere will and pleasure. The King ... called him more near unto him, and esteemed him so highly that his estimation and favour put all other ancient councillors out of the accustomed favour ...

[He] took upon him therefore to disburden the King of so weighty a charge and troublesome business, putting the King in comfort that he should not need to spare any time from his pleasure for any business that should necessarily happen in the council.

George Cavendish, *Thomas Wolsey, late Cardinal, his Life and Death,* written c.1554 – 1558.

Source G

Cavendish is describing what he actually saw ... [his] view is, of course, a partial one. As a gentleman-usher he was concerned above all with external appearances. he was never an intimate friend of Wolsey, and knew little or nothing about the intricate political manoeuvres in which the Cardinal was engaged. ... Cavendish is not always a reliable witness. Sometimes out of loyalty to his master he professes ignorance where it is likely that he knew the truth ... Cavendish entered Wolsey's service in the early 1520s ... and served his master faithfully as gentleman-usher until the end came at Leicester Abbey.

R.Lockyer (ed.), *Thomas Wolsey, late cardinal, his Life and Death* written by George Cavendish, 1962.

Source I

In the controversies of the English Reformation both sides vilified him, the Protestants as the symbol of all that was worst in the unreformed church, and the Catholics as the man who might have saved Catherine of Aragon and stopped the Reformation, but did not. For a while in the heyday of empire he enjoyed some celebrity as the early flexer of England's international muscle ...

S.J.Gunn, *Cardinal Wolsey in Context,* History Sixth, volume 9, 1991.

1 How do Sources A, B and C portray Wolsey?

2 How might the information in the Table (Wolsey's career) help to explain these opinions?

3 In the light of the evidence in Sources D and E should we place any value on Sources A, B and C?

4 In what ways does Source F support or contradict Sources A,B and C?

5 Given the evidence in Source G should we place more faith in Cavendish than in Skelton or Vergil?

6 Compare the portrait (Source H) with the portrait on page 122. What similarities and differences are there between the two portraits? How might each affect your view of Wolsey?

7 Using Source I and your own ideas explain why historians today may differ in their views of Wolsey.

8 What does the evidence in this section tell us about the nature of politics at the time of Wolsey?

9 Wolsey succeeded in this political world. What does this suggest about Wolsey?

Source H

A PORTRAIT OF WOLSEY BY LE BOUCQ. DOES THIS PORTRAIT CONFIRM OR CONTRADICT THE IMAGE CREATED BY THE PORTRAIT ON PAGE 122 ?

TALKING POINT

Do you think that the ways of politics and politicians have changed a great deal across the centuries?

Wolsey and English Foreign Policy: 1514 – 1529

It was ironic that Wolsey proved his administrative skills in the preparation of Henry's French campaigns for he was more naturally disposed towards a policy of peace. His early government service under Henry VII and Bishop Fox had impressed upon him the advantages of a peaceful, non-interventionist policy. The prevailing humanist sentiment was also against nationalistic pride and war-mongering and, as a man of high intellect, Wolsey was in sympathy with these ideas.

Yet there were other sides of Wolsey's personality that did not favour quiet and cautious isolation. His desire for power, influence and recognition could not be met except by intervention in Europe and here he was very much in tune with the king. Henry VIII's grandiose dreams demanded English involvement in Europe for how else could he demonstrate his superiority over other monarchs? Therefore England aspired to determine the course of European affairs in order to glorify both its king and its Cardinal.

Was England likely to wield influence in Europe? There was no recent evidence of England having done so. Henry VII had probably welcomed the focus of diplomacy moving to Italy in the 1490s. Nor had Henry VIII's early foreign adventures suggested that England had been a sleeping lion awakening 'to fright the souls of fearful adversaries'.

Both physically and in terms of significance England was on the fringe of European affairs. Therefore Henry VIII and Wolsey had to propel England into the centre of events, a policy that carried risks, especially as the king was temperamentally disposed to fight his way to fame and the Cardinal preferred to negotiate his way to glory. France was still the national enemy but she was also the greatest power in Europe. Would England overcome her by force or hamstring her with treaties?

A summary of the main features of English foreign policy between 1514 and 1529 is on page 134. Use this information to suggest answers to the questions below and then check your answers against the more detailed analysis that follows.

---

1 When does England appear to have been successful in playing a leading role in European politics?

2(a) Was this success achieved by war or negotiation or both?

(b) What might this suggest about the relative influences of the king and Wolsey?

3 How significant a part did England play in European politics in this period as a whole?

4 Why was England's role at the level you described in your answer to question 3?

TALKING POINT

Historians have sometimes disagreed in their interpretations of Wolsey's motives. How might these disagreements be explained by the complexities of Wolsey's personality?

English Foreign Policy 1514–1529

Major Events	Aims of English Policy	Effects of English Policy
1. 1514–1518 Accession of Francis I of France – 1515. France won control of Milan after victory at Marignano – 1515. Ferdinand of Spain died and was succeeded by Charles – 1516.	The death of Louis XII ended the Anglo-French truce. England's ancient distrust of France reasserted itself, aided by Henry VIII's sense of personal rivalry with Francis I and Papal fears of France. Therefore England tried to limit the power of France.	England failed to achieve any substantial results. She made her presence felt through constant diplomacy, the construction of alliances and plans for war but, even when campaigns began, they achieved nothing.
2. 1518–1521 Treaty of London – 1518. Death of Maximilian in 1519 resulting in Charles V's control of Empire and Spain. Field of Cloth of Gold (Henry and Francis) – 1520 Meetings of Henry and Charles V – 1520	Faced by the continuing power of France and the new power of Charles V, Henry and Wolsey had the chance to achieve power by acting as the peace-makers of Europe. Hence the diplomatic onslaught from England, aimed at establishing peace in Europe.	The Treaty of London, a non-aggression pact which aimed to guarantee peace in Europe, appeared to achieve England's aims and represented the peak of English influence. However England did not have the power to restrain Francis or Charles if they really did want war. If war came England was faced with a choice between choosing sides and choosing inglorious neutrality.
3. 1521–1525 England declared war on France – 1522. Charles V defeated and captured Francis I at Pavia – 1525. Amicable Grant Risings – 1525.	While Wolsey still worked for peace, Henry's ambitions turned again to war against France, given France's weakness in comparison with the Empire. The likelihood of real English commitment waxed and waned and Wolsey was still seeking peace with France when France was defeated at Pavia. The natural response was then to propose alliance with Charles to take advantage of France's weakness.	With Wolsey striving to delay a major English commitment the main achievement was the saving of money. English forces almost invaded France in 1523 to join French rebels but the revolt petered out before the English could arrive. After Pavia, England was rebuffed by Charles who had no intention of using his strength to aid England. Neither Henry's desire for war nor Wolsey's desire for European peace had been satisfied.
4. 1525–1529 League of Cognac formed against Emperor – 1526. Anglo-French treaty – 1527. Sack of Rome; Pope surrendered to Charles – 1527. Peace of Cambrai between France, Empire and Pope – 1529.	Snubbed by Charles V, England aimed to reduce the power of the Emperor and re-establish peace. This would show England's significance and support for the Pope. After 1527 these remained English aims and Wolsey strove for the Pope's release – a need made more urgent by Henry's wish to get Papal approval for a divorce from Queen Catherine.	England helped to negotiate and finance the League of Cognac but did not join it. An Anglo-French treaty was equally ineffective in reducing the Emperor's strength. In reality England lacked the power and reputation to have a decisive influence on events, hence she was disregarded in 1529 when a peace was reached. England had not been accepted as a first-class power, let alone the dominant state in Europe.

1514–1518: Henry began 1514 keen to return to war against France but, deserted by his allies, was quickly compelled to agree to a peace treaty. His anguish at yet another betrayal by Ferdinand briefly led him to contemplate attacking Spain in concert with France but he soon returned to an anti-French stance. A combination of circumstances ensured France remained in her role as national enemy – the accession of Francis I to the French throne and Henry's feeling that Francis challenged his self-image as the young buccaneer of Europe, Papal pleas for help against the renewed French threat in Italy and the accumulated history of wars with France. Francis, determined on action in Italy, also provoked Henry by stirring unrest in Scotland, where Henry's sister Margaret was acting as Regent for her son.

Henry's response to Francis's ambitions in Italy was confident and direct, 'If I choose he will cross the Alps and if I choose he will not'. A less realistic assessment would be hard to imagine. By the end of September 1515 Francis had forced a treaty on the Pope, crushed the Swiss at the Battle of Marignano, won control of Milan and forced Margaret to flee from Scotland. And yet, so great was the degree of French success, that it paradoxically raised English hopes of a league against the new champion of Europe and Wolsey reported that he expected Henry to invade France once again. Wolsey's great energies were directed towards constructing alliances or simply buying allies although Wolsey probably hoped to avoid the expense of a full-scale English invasion. He need not have worried. The alliances fell apart (even without the help of Ferdinand who had died in 1516). So, after much activity and expense, Europe was well aware of England but not in the ways that Henry and Wolsey had hoped. Instead of imposing England's will they had been increasingly desperate in their efforts to match France's power and influence until, deserted yet again by Maximilian, Henry was left, according to Scarisbrick, 'the laughing stock of Europe'.

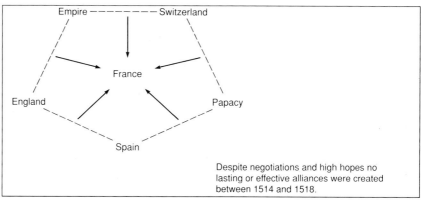

Despite negotiations and high hopes no lasting or effective alliances were created between 1514 and 1518.

ALLIANCES 1514 – 18.

1518 – 1521: With one bound England and her King were free, the 'laughing stock' converted into the 'arbiter of the affairs of Christendom'. This miraculous conversion proved the highpoint of England's reputation in this period and its architect was Wolsey, with Henry enthusiastically working to the Cardinal's plan. The centrepiece was the Treaty of London of 1518 – a treaty of 'universal peace'. At its heart was an Anglo-French peace treaty, guaranteed by a non-aggression pact embracing all the major powers and twenty minor ones. Any aggressor would be corrected by the might of the majority and so no-one would dare breach the peace of Europe. At least, that was the theory.

In origin the idea had been the Pope's, inspired by Moslem attacks on Italy. He called for a Crusade but the proposal was hi-jacked by Wolsey and translated into The Treaty of London, a more credible option because it matched the immediate possibilities. However the papal plea, coupled with humanist calls for peace amongst Christian states, did help to win support for the idea of a universal peace. More practically, no-one was able to challenge France's power so a treaty which left France supreme but offered security to everyone else was the most that could be expected. Wolsey, since the deaths of Ferdinand and Maximilian, had shown himself the most devious as well as the most astute politician in Europe and he had seized the moment triumphantly, bringing glory to his king and more power to himself.

But the moment was brief. The inheritances of the Emperor Charles V had created the Hapsburg empire, a new power bloc strong enough to challenge the pre-eminence of France and thus inaugurating a new phase of European politics built around these two 'super-powers'. Between 1519 and 1521 Henry and Wolsey strove to maintain European peace and with it England's role as 'peacemaker of Europe'. 1520 saw two conferences between Charles and Henry and the 'eighth wonder of the world', the Field of Cloth of Gold, where Henry met Francis. The greatest testament to Henry VIII's enthusiasm for his role as peacemaker was his refusal in 1520 to accept Charles's invitation to join an alliance against France.

However England's position gradually changed. Incidents between France and the Empire increased and England tried to warn each of the aggressors away from war by threatening to join the other side. In all likelihood there was only one choice. Old enmities, France's meddling in Scotland and papal pressure pushed England into alliance with Charles V. The alternative was isolation but the inevitable consequence – a fall in England's prestige – was unthinkable to Wolsey and his master after the triumphs of the Treaty of London and the Field of Cloth of Gold.

TALKING POINT

Marriage alliances seem to have been at the heart of Tudor diplomacy. Do you think they were likely to have been as effective as the participants hoped?

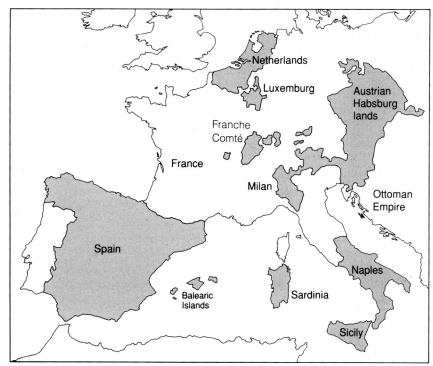

CHARLES V'S EMPIRE IN EUROPE. CHARLES WAS MUCH CONCERNED WITH THE THREAT FROM THE OTTOMAN EMPIRE, AN IMPORTANT REMINDER THAT ENGLAND WAS NOT THE FOCUS OF EUROPEAN DIPLOMACY.

1521 – 1525: Now English foreign policy reached its peak of complexity under Wolsey. Events abroad required the English constantly to reconsider strategy and detail but differences in style and method between the King and Wolsey also made it seem that two policies were being conducted. Overall England moved towards an alliance with the Emperor and war with France. Henry was the more enthusiastic, hoping to marry his young daughter, Mary, to the Emperor. It is possible that even in the early 1520s Henry's lack of a legitimate male heir was influencing his foreign policy. Wolsey still sought peace, because peace was important in itself and because war was expensive and risky. Even when the Anglo-Imperial treaty was signed in August 1521 Wolsey negotiated the delay of England's entry to the war until May 1523 and in the interim worked himself to illness and exhaustion in the pursuit of peace through negotiation.

In addition there was no popular demand for war, quite the opposite in fact as parliament vigorously criticised war taxation in 1523. However English forces did invade France in 1522 and 1523, their chance of success apparently increased by rebellion in France which promised a divided and vulnerable France. In 1523 an English force of 10,000 men led by Suffolk took such advantage of these divisions that a rapid advance brought them within 50 miles of Paris. Then the alliance with the Emperor collapsed and the weather turned foul. The retreat was miserable, Henry lost interest in joining his army and Wolsey returned to peace negotiations.

The Battle of Pavia in February 1525 appeared to turn affairs upside down once more. Imperial forces routed the French army and captured Francis I. France had never seemed more open to invasion. English ideas of peace disappeared and Henry VIII rejoiced. When he heard the news he told the messenger 'You are like Saint Gabriel who announced the coming of Christ'. He talked of planning with the Emperor 'the means of getting full satisfaction from France. Not an hour is to be lost'. But even now Henry's dreams came to nothing. Charles V had no intention of invading France, especially not to help Henry VIII to a success when England had consistently put off aiding the Empire. At home attempts to raise war taxes – the Amicable Grant – brought reaction that ranged from flat refusal to pay to full rebellion in Suffolk (see pp 142). Wolsey returned to the negotiating table and in August 1525 an Anglo-French peace treaty was agreed, ending three years of largely theoretical war. The years since 1521 had been profoundly disappointing.

1525 – 1529: The most realistic English policy would have been to withdraw from involvement in Europe but this was temperamentally impossible for Henry and Wolsey. Although prepared to fight either France or the Empire if the circumstances were right their most consistent efforts went into recreating the 1518 Treaty of London – another universal peace shedding glory on the peacemakers of England. Wolsey helped to construct the League of Cognac (made up of France and the Italian states), financed it but did not actually join because he intended to act as peacemaker once the League had forced Charles to terms. Unfortunately Charles's strength was too great and, in 1527 after his troops sacked Rome, even the Pope became the Emperor's prisoner.

Working to free the Pope became the greatest test of Wolsey and of English influence. If he could not be freed, Wolsey even constructed a breath-taking plan to act as a substitute Pope. As well as establishing Wolsey truly at the centre of affairs, this plan would have solved the problem of the king's divorce. By 1527 Henry was seeking a divorce from Catherine and, for a time, Charles's capture of the Pope seemed to advance Henry's prospects as the Pope looked kindly on those who might save him from the Emperor and disgrace. However intensive diplomatic manoeuvres by Henry and Wolsey failed to win the Pope's agreement to the divorce.

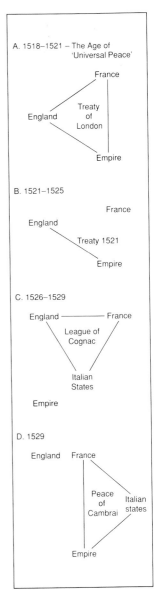

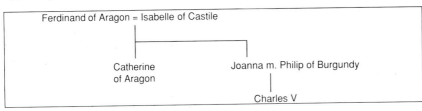

THE RELATIONSHIP BETWEEN CHARLES V AND CATHERINE OF ARAGON.

Wolsey also tried to bring pressure to bear on the Netherlands, the trading centre of Charles's empire. He forbade English cloth traders to use the key Dutch markets and also considered an assault by the garrison at Calais. However these efforts failed as English merchants were held hostage in retaliation. Even worse, there was unrest and hostile gatherings in English towns as clothworkers, already hard-hit by the poor harvest of 1527, gave vent to their protests.

When, in 1529, the Peace of Cambrai brought a settlement between France, the Empire and the Pope, England played no part. Henry preferred Wolsey to remain in England dealing with the trial of the divorce issue. Wolsey, probably rightly, thought he could have done more to advance Henry's cause if he had taken part in the international negotiations. England's ambitions in Europe had been shown to be a delusion. She could not compete with or act as a broker between France and the Empire unless they wanted her to do so. More immediately, the Pope's amity with the Emperor left no hope of a divorce for Henry. In 1529, for all his past energies and undoubted successes, Wolsey's foreign policy had little to offer his king.

Conclusions

Between 1514 and 1529 England maintained a constant involvement in European politics. Her influence peaked in 1518, but at other times the degree of activity masked her lack of influence over stronger powers. Wolsey's awareness of the folly of expensive forays into war co-incided with his natural instinct towards peace but he was able to maintain the drive for peace largely because his vast appetite for work enabled him to control the details of policy-making. However, he was prepared to fight if necessary, as in 1523 when war offered the cheapest and simplest way to realise his objectives. On such occasions the Cardinal was most in tune with his king, although Henry did genuinely relish his role as peacemaker in 1518 – better to be the arbiter of Europe than merely one of the combatants!

When Henry did exert himself there was no doubt that he made the key decisions. In the 1520s Henry may have insisted on a Hapsburg alliance because he was influenced by the need for a male heir. If that was the case then Wolsey had in fact little hope of achieving a reprise of the universal peace of the Treaty of London. However Henry's attention frequently waned and then 'Le Cardinal pacyfike' could regain some initiative through his devotion to detail. Certainly Henry could not have kept England so constantly involved at the centre of European policies. Only Wolsey's 'high-flown, almost megalomaniac optimism', in Professor Scarisbrick's words, achieved this, together with his great energy and his ability to keep the king's confidence. However at the end of the 1520's Wolsey was increasingly under pressure. The king needed success, as he saw it, to preserve the dynasty. Wolsey had never failed him before but now the situation seemed to have moved beyond the Cardinal's control or even influence. In 1529 the memory of past success only made the appearance of current failure greater.

Wolsey and English Domestic Policies, 1509 – 1529

The domestic objectives of English governments in the sixteenth century were often less clear-cut than foreign objectives. A monarch was expected to maintain law and order, organise an efficient but not over-bearing administration and raise taxes but not too much and not too often. Domestic failure did bring criticism but success could never be dramatic and so did not win praise. Domestic success therefore could not boost the king's status and so there was little stimulus to pursue extreme efficiency and even less to do so by innovation. This was never more true than in those years when Henry's VIII's desire for 'pastime with good company' and dreams of foreign glory squeezed out any vestige of interest he may have had in domestic government. He was content to leave detailed matters to Wolsey, who pursued administrative efficiency with enthusiasm but few of his plans were followed through to success, thus acquiring descriptions such as 'promising but barren'. Even Thomas Cromwell, the most loyal of Wolsey's servants, commented on 'many words without deeds'.

Administration and Finance

Although Henry VII's death removed the driving force, administration did not grind to a halt. Experienced officials continued the business of government. In such circumstances major changes were unlikely and what was achieved arose out of the experience of officials (such as Sir John Heron who remained Treasurer of the Chamber until 1524) or the need to solve problems created by the king's death. For example, the general surveyors (who controlled and audited the revenues from royal lands) were unofficial appointments, dependent previously on Henry VII's approval. A series of Acts of Parliament established their formal powers.

If anyone took on Henry VII's centralising role as England's 'business manager' it was Wolsey by virtue of his dominance of the council and his presiding over Star Chamber. However no major reform of government administration took place. On two occasions he prepared plans but neither was carried through, simply because their prime objective was not greater efficiency. In both cases, in 1519 and again in 1526 with the Ordinance of Eltham, Wolsey proposed reform of the royal household as a means of defeating political rivals and thereby ensuring his own political supremacy. When he achieved his victory without reform there was no reason to proceed with the changes.

In local government Wolsey pursued his centralising drive with some success. Local officials responded more rapidly and efficiently to royal instructions. To achieve this Wolsey appointed the king's servants or his own to key county positions, built up the king's affinity in each locality and placed outsiders on commissions to break up complacent local gentry groupings. There was nothing new in this. Henry VII had used these methods but they certainly did contribute to the overall stability of Henry VIII's first two decades.

Legal Reforms

The law aroused Wolsey's intellectual interest and this goes a long way towards explaining why, domestically, his greatest impact was in legal reform. In 1516 he put forward a reforming plan intending to end corruption in the legal system and provide cheap and impartial justice. His success lay in the exposure and punishment of many individual examples of corruption but was limited by the inability of the legal system to cope with the overall demands placed upon it without major reform.

The centre of Wolsey's work was the Court of the Star Chamber, where he sat in judgement several times a week. Star Chamber's work increased dramatically. Compared with the previous reign it dealt with ten times as many cases, rooting out cases of perjury, contempt of court, intimidation of juries and other examples of legal corruption. Wolsey publicly asked for cases to be brought before him, promising that social status would be no protection. In 1516 the Earl of Northumberland was committed to prison for contempt of court. The following year Sir Robert

Sheffield, a royal councillor, was sent to the Tower as an acce͟
crime. Such activities may have increased respect for Wolsey but ͟
made enemies.

Wolsey also increased the work of the Court of Chancery, which handled cases to do with property, wills and contracts. Here Wolsey's decisions created precedents and through them he has been credited with making a major contribution to English law. He also established a permanent judicial committee dealing with cases brought by the poor – for Wolsey the law was not solely available to those who could pay 'a fat fee'. What did limit justice was the number of courts available. Those that did exist were swamped by demand and the reforms that might have produced improvement were not forthcoming as Wolsey became more and more distracted by the needs of foreign affairs.

Enclosures

Wolsey's policy on enclosures also showed a willingness to challenge the interests of landowners. Unfortunately Wolsey, in common with nearly all contemporaries, failed to see enclosures as a symptom of the longer-term economic change that was producing inflation. Enclosure seemed to be merely the product of landowners' greed and therefore Wolsey acted against landowners. Following a national enquiry in 1517 to identify enclosed land and the demolition of buildings legal proceedings were begun against over 260 landowners. 222 actually came to court, a remarkably high figure indicating both Wolsey's involvement and concern. Such efficiency however had little practical effect. Enclosing continued to take place and, if it did lead to vagrancy, this was not reduced. Again Wolsey had shown himself to be energetic and well-intentioned but the most practical result was further opposition to the Cardinal from the landowning class.

CHRIST CHURCH COLLEGE, OXFORD, WHICH WAS FOUNDED BY WOLSEY AS CARDINAL COLLEGE. WOLSEY SHOWED CONSIDERABLE INTEREST IN EDUCATIONAL PROJECTS, ALSO FOUNDING A SCHOOL IN HIS HOME TOWN, IPSWICH.

Finance and Parliament

If the constructive elements of Wolsey's domestic policies created enemies, those which were mishandled were much more likely to create a climate of hostility. Wolsey's handling of economic matters can be at best described as a mixed success. Wolsey's major financial achievement was the development of the tax known as the subsidy. He replaced the inadequate fixed tax rates and yields with a flexible system based on accurate valuations of taxpayers' wealth. Taxation was therefore realistic in terms of the ability to pay and the crown's needs. Wolsey also sought to increase the revenue from the crown's own lands but never achieved the level reached by Henry VII because royal land had been granted away. Royal income was indeed hopelessly inadequate for the demands placed on it by war, hence Wolsey's need to seek grants from parliament and, in 1515, to introduce an Act of Resumption returning lands to the crown which had earlier been granted away.

Wolsey's inability to manage parliament in the early 1520s seems to have been a combination of his own temperament and the near-impossibility of winning taxation for wars that had already happened. In 1515 parliament was dismissed before it granted taxation because Wolsey wanted to stop it criticising the church. His lack of humility, blustering persuasion and even lies led to confrontations, little economic benefit for the crown and increased hostility. The forced loan of 1522 had not been repaid and the subsidy of 1523 was still being collected when, in 1525, Wolsey demanded a non-parliamentary tax, the 'Amicable Grant', to meet the needs of war. The result was rebellion in East Anglia and clear refusal to pay elsewhere – and the rebels won. The Amicable Grant was abandoned and the leaders of the rebellion were pardoned.

The Church

Wolsey was the most powerful churchman in England by virtue of his appointment as the Pope's Legate, which gave him precedence over Archbishop Warham of Canterbury. However it is difficult to detect the extent of Wolsey's personal piety. Was he simply a civil servant in bishop's raiments in spite of Cavendish's claims that he usually heard two masses a day and that, even after twelve hours work, he went to Mass before he ate? Perhaps the best guide lies in Wolsey's own words, also recorded by Cavendish, 'If I had served God as diligently as I have done the King ...'.

Did Wolsey weaken the church? At first glance it might appear so, for shortly after Wolsey's death Henry was able to become head of the church. However Wolsey had not allowed Henry to interfere excessively in church life before 1529 – and, in truth, Henry had no wish to. There was nothing radical about the king's approach to religion. Where Wolsey did pave the way for the events of the 1530s was in his own centralising involvement in all aspects of church affairs. Churchmen became used to orders and enquiries from the crown – Wolsey was clearly the king's agent before he was their ecclesiastical superior – and their sense of independence was reduced, and therefore became harder to re-assert in time of crisis. Nor did Wolsey's own personal record do anything to bolster the church against its critics. He did not visit his dioceses and his public displays of wealth appeared a direct contradiction of the way of Christ. In this Wolsey was creating propaganda for his enemies and those of his church.

Conclusions

Any conclusion on Wolsey seems to carry an air of disappointment. His capacity for detailed hard work together with his creativity promised more than was delivered. Indeed he himself, with his own golden, orator's tongue promised more than could possibly be fulfilled. By twentieth century standards his achievements seem limited but there is a danger of judging by anachronistic standards. We expect change and improvement where the sixteenth century sought stability and security – objectives that are not necessarily achieved by change. It is also easy to forget that ultimate responsibility lay with the king and to criticise Wolsey's domestic policies is also to criticise Henry for his lack of involvement.

For contemporaries Wolsey's years were a continuation of the latter part of Henry VII's reign. Domestic peace was little disturbed by civil conflicts or riots. Parliament met rarely. There is little or no exaggeration in Cavendish's judgement that 'I neuer sawe thys realme in better order quyotnes and obedyence than it was in the tyme of his auctoryte and Rule ne Iustice better mynestred with indifferencye'. Wolsey deserves credit for this and yet he created enemies, chiefly through his 'indifferencye' to rank. Contemporaries respected him or admired and feared his ability but

Meetings of Parliament 1509–1529	
1510	21 January–23 February 1510
1512–14	
(1)	4 February–30 March 1512
(2)	4 November–20 December 1512
(3)	23 January–4 March 1514
1515	
(1)	5 February–5 April 1515
(2)	12 November–22 December 1515
1523	15 April–29 July 1523

few were close to him. Only the king needed him and therefore Wolsey was safe – as long as he proved a reliable and successful chief minister.

THOMAS HOWARD, DUKE OF NORFOLK, A CENTRAL FIGURE IN POLITICS FROM THE MID 1520s.

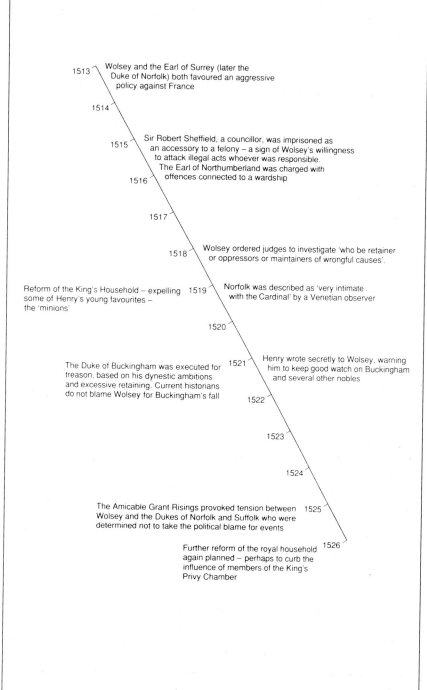

1513 — Wolsey and the Earl of Surrey (later the Duke of Norfolk) both favoured an aggressive policy against France

1514

1515 — Sir Robert Sheffield, a councillor, was imprisoned as an accessory to a felony – a sign of Wolsey's willingness to attack illegal acts whoever was responsible.

1516 — The Earl of Northumberland was charged with offences connected to a wardship

1517

1518 — Wolsey ordered judges to investigate 'who be retainer or oppressors or maintainers of wrongful causes'.

Reform of the King's Household – expelling some of Henry's young favourites – the 'minions' **1519** — Norfolk was described as 'very intimate with the Cardinal' by a Venetian observer

1520

The Duke of Buckingham was executed for treason, based on his dynastic ambitions and excessive retaining. Current historians do not blame Wolsey for Buckingham's fall **1521** — Henry wrote secretly to Wolsey, warning him to keep good watch on Buckingham and several other nobles

1522

1523

1524

The Amicable Grant Risings provoked tension between Wolsey and the Dukes of Norfolk and Suffolk who were determined not to take the political blame for events **1525**

Further reform of the royal household again planned – perhaps to curb the influence of members of the King's Privy Chamber **1526**

WOLSEY'S RELATIONSHIP WITH NOBLEMEN AND COURTIERS WAS SOMETIMES STORMY. HE DID NOT HESITATE TO ATTACK INDIVIDUALS WHO BROKE THE LAW. HOWEVER HE DID NOT HAVE AN 'ANTI-NOBLE' POLICY WHICH LED TO NOBLEMEN AS A GROUP BRINGING ABOUT HIS DOWNFALL.

Examining the Evidence
Thomas Wolsey: King's Minister or Country's Ruler?

Why come ye not to court?
To which court
To the King's Court
Or to Hampton Court?
The King's Court
Should have the excellence
But Hampton Court
Hath the pre-eminence.

This extract from John Skelton's poem 'Why come ye nat to courte?' is a very attractive source. Its attack on Wolsey begs to be quoted and nearly every book on this period does quote it. It's such an ideal source that you actually want to believe it, especially if there is corroborative evidence, such as Sebastian Giustinian's report in May 1515: 'we had a private audience with the King and exhorted him to continue in alliance with Francis, and help Venice to recover her territory. Were answered by Wolsey, who enlarged on the union of England, France and Venice ...'

Yet are such accounts of Wolsey's pre-eminence accurate? Foreign envoys could be deceived by Henry allowing Wolsey to speak on his behalf. Others, like Skelton, had their own political reasons for attacking Wolsey. Was Wolsey really the country's ruler?

Source A

He is set so hye,
In his ierarchy
Of frantycke frenesy
And folysshe fantasy
That in the Chambre of Sterres
All maters there he marres,
Clappynge his rod on the borde.
No man dare speke a worde,
For he hath all the sayenge
Without any renayenge....

Set up a wretch on hye,
In a trone triumphantlye,
Make him a great astate,
And he wyll play checke mate
With ryall majeste
Counte himselfe as good as he.

Extracts from John Skelton's *Why come ye nat to courte?* 1522.

Source B

'And after mass he would return into his private chamber again, and being advised of the noblemen and gentlemen and other persons attending in his chambers outside, he would issue out into them, apparelled all in red, in the habit of a cardinal ...

And as soon as he was entered into his presence-chamber, he found there – attending his coming, to await upon him to Westminster Hall – as well noblemen and other worthy gentlemen as noblemen and gentlemen of his own household. Thus he passed forth, with two great crosses of silver borne before him; with also two great pillars of silver, and his sergeant-at-arms with a great mace of silver gilt. Then his gentlemen-ushers cried, and said: 'On, my lords and masters! Make way for my Lord's Grace!'

From *Thomas Wolsey, late Cardinal, his Life and Death* by George Cavendish.

Source C

[Wolsey] took upon him therefore to disburden the King of so weighty a charge and troublesome business, putting the king in comfort that he should not need to spare any time from his pleasure for any business that should necessarily happen in the council. So long as [Wolsey] was there, and had the King's authority and commandment, he doubted not to see all things sufficiently provided for and perfected. He would first make the King aware of all such matters as should pass through the councillor's hands, before he would proceed to the finishing or determining of the same. And he would fulfil and follow the King's mind and pleasure to the uttermost, wherewith the King was wonderfully pleased ...

... Thus the Almoner [Wolsey] ruled all those that before ruled him; such did his policy and wit bring to pass. Who was now in high favour but Master Almoner? Who had all the suit but Master Almoner? And who ruled all under the King but Master Almoner?

From *Thomas Wolsey, late Cardinal, his Life and Death* by George Cavendish.

Source D

HAMPTON COURT, BEGUN BY WOLSEY AND INDICATIVE OF HIS GREAT LOVE OF DISPLAY.

'Well, well, Master Kingston,' quoth he, 'I see the matter against me how it framed. But if I had served God as diligently as I have done the King, He would not have given me over in my grey hairs. Howbeit, this is the just reward that I must receive for my worldly diligence and the pains that I have taken to do the King service and to satisfy his vain pleasures, not regarding my godly duty. ... I have often kneeled before him in his privy chamber on my knees the space of an hour or two, to persuade him from his will and appetite; but I could never bring to pass to dissuade him therefrom. Therefore, Master Kingston, if it chance you hereafter to be one of his privy council, as for your wisdom and other qualities ye be fit so to be, I warn you be well advised and assured what matter ye put in his head, for ye shall never pull it out again.'

From *Thomas Wolsey, late Cardinal, his Life and Death* by George Cavendish.

Source E

If you will follow my poor advice, you shall, in your counsel giving unto his grace, ever tell him what he ought to do, but never what he is able to do. So shall you show yourself a true faithful servant and a right worthy Councillor. For if a lion knew his own strength, hard were it for any man to rule him."

From *A Life of Sir Thomas More* by William Roper, written in 1535. Roper was More's son-in-law.

1 Which sources or parts of sources could be used as evidence to support the hypothesis that Wolsey was more powerful than the king?

2 Which sources or parts of sources could be used as evidence to support the hypothesis that Wolsey was never more than the king's minister?

3 Why might contemporary observers have been misled or wrong about the extent of Wolsey's power?

4 Do you agree that Wolsey had served his king more diligently than his God?

5 In your opinion was Wolsey the country's ruler or the king's minister?

The Downfall and Death of the Cardinal

The section you have just read has emphasised one of the central debates about this period – 'was Wolsey more than the King's Minister?' This debate is more the product of disagreements about Henry's personality than about Wolsey's. Recent writers tend to agree on Wolsey's role as the extremely able, ferociously hard-working minister who also notably enjoyed the pomp and splendour of his many offices. But there is far more disagreement about Henry. Was he 'a bit of a booby and a bit of a baby' who was manipulated by faction? Or was he the director of overall policy, confidently delegating detail while retaining real and final power? The last few years of Wolsey's life have been a particular focus for this debate.

Cardinal Thomas Wolsey, Chancellor of England, was ordered to hand over his seal of office on 22 September 1529 and to retire from public life. His retirement was at first far from honourable. The Cardinal and his household lived without 'beds, sheet, tablecloths, cups and dishes'. Wolsey's bishopric of Winchester and abbacy of St. Albans were taken from him. The school he had founded at Ipswich was closed and a new gallery at Esher – the very home where Wolsey was staying – was taken apart and carried away for the King's use.

And yet Wolsey had hope, for in between these acts reeking of cruelty and malice, the king sent him tokens of friendship, suggesting that his restoration was possible. Unfortunately for Wolsey, this restoration never took place. In April 1530 Wolsey was despatched by royal orders to his diocese of York. Far from settling for retirement Wolsey still hoped to return to the centre of political events but on 4 November 1530 he was arrested, charged with intriguing 'both in and out of the kingdom' and with 'presumptuous sinister practices made to the court of Rome'. This was treason. Faced with the prospect of trial, shame and execution the Cardinal plodded south but, instead, he died a natural death at Leicester Abbey on 29 November.

Why did Wolsey fall from power? The simple answer is that Wolsey failed to obtain the Pope's agreement to the divorce. He failed but there can be no suggestion that Wolsey did not try to secure the divorce. He simply lacked the power to do so. Charles V at the vital stage, controlled the Pope. Charles had no wish to provide any favours for Henry since England had spent several years organising leagues against the Empire. England's foreign policy, so publicly associated with Wolsey, turned out to be responsible for the Pope's refusal to accommodate Henry's wishes for a divorce.

Therefore Wolsey failed to win the divorce and he was dismissed from power. Unfortunately this splendidly simple cause and effect is too simple. For historians, Wolsey's failure to win a divorce for Henry is the starting point for competing arguments of greater depth. These arguments disagree about the significance of faction and the character of the King. On the one hand it is argued that Wolsey's dismissal was the work of his enemies, a faction centred on Anne Boleyn, her father (Lord Rochford) and the Duke of Norfolk. Once Wolsey's early attempts to secure the divorce had failed they took their chance to influence and manipulate the King until he dismissed the Cardinal. The contrary view, advanced by Peter Gwyn, is that there was no such faction and that Henry himself was the prime mover. Gwyn's interpretation of Henry is therefore that of a much stronger figure, driving forward his own policy completely independently and sacrificing his old servant in the process.

Events of 1529–1530

1529 June 18	Opening of the Commission headed by Wolsey and Campeggio
21	Battle of Landriano. Imperial forces defeated the French, confirming Hapsburg control in Italy and leading to the Peace of Cambrai.
July	A factional plot led by conservative nobles failed to topple Wolsey. Campeggio adjourned the Commission
October 9	A charge of praemunire was laid against Wolsey
18	Wolsey lost the post of Chancellor
(late)	Wolsey received a message from Henry 'to be of good cheer'
December	A petition of complaints against Wolsey was presented in parliament
1530 February	Wolsey received a royal pardon and was restored to the Archbishopric of York
April	Wolsey set out to visit York for the first time
	By Easter he had opened correspondence with the King of France, the Emperor, the Pope and Catherine of Aragon
November 4	Wolsey was ordered to return to London
24	Wolsey died at Leicester

The issues of the King's character and the existence of faction are inextricably inter-twined. The first argument outlined above suggests that faction was the hub of political life at Henry's court at the end of the 1520s. Most vibrantly portrayed by David Starkey in *The Reign of Henry VIII, Personality and Politics*, the story is of Wolsey recreating Henry VII's style of government and moving 'ruthlessly' to prevent the development of faction. which threatened his own hold on power. However even Wolsey could not compete with Anne Boleyn's influence over the King! In Dr.Starkey's words, 'She broke Wolsey's monopoly of power... The result was to unleash the forces which only Wolsey's power and personality had held in check. The Council and the Privy Council alike split into factions; alliances changed swiftly and bewilderingly; and the allegiance of even some leading figures was equally mutable.' The main reason why factions emerged was that Henry VIII 'with his fluctuations, enthusiasms and irregular handling of business, gave it an open invitation to flourish'. Thus, in 1529, Henry was influenced to dismiss Wolsey by the Boleyns aided by the pre-eminent nobles Norfolk and Suffolk. But was Henry so changeable and malleable? It is hard to deny Starkey's description of the King as 'prone to lightning enthusiasms, about people and things'. But does it therefore follow that the following judgement is accurate?

'Henry was Wolsey's "loving master"; Henry Norris was "the best beloved of the King"; Anne Boleyn "mine own darling". Here again the enthusiasm burned out, but destructively. Like a child grown tired of a toy, the King broke each sometime beloved in pieces: Wolsey was hounded to his death; Norris and Anne were executed. And they were but three of many.'

D.Starkey, *The Reign of Henry VIII: Personality and Politics,* 1985.

THE FALCON AND THE POMEGRANATE, AN ILLUSTRATION FROM A SHEET OF MUSIC. THE FALCON WAS ANNE BOLEYN'S BADGE. THE POMEGRANATE WAS CATHERINE OF ARAGON'S.

Peter Gwyn's Henry is very different.

'It was Henry who had made Wolsey, and it was Henry who destroyed him, just as he was to make and destroy Thomas Cromwell. He made all the important decisions and appointments. In every sense he ruled.'

Peter Gwyn, *The King's Cardinal: The Rise and Fall of Thomas Wolsey,* 1990.

According to Gwyn, this decisive Henry did not dismiss Wolsey out of boredom. The dismissal of Wolsey was 'a calculated act of policy on Henry's part to further the divorce negotiations'. As a result dismissal was not at first accompanied by charges or punishment because Henry could see further uses for Wolsey in the campaign for a divorce. Unfortunately for Wolsey these uses turned out to his disadvantage. Eventually Henry charged him with treason because

'what was important for Henry was to create a climate of opinion which would make it more difficult for the Church as a whole to resist his wishes; and it would not have helped to have the man most guilty of the crime of praemunire swanning around the diocese of York, while his so-called accomplices stood trial. Very much more to Henry's purpose would have been the spectacle of that man standing trial for treason, for there could hardly have been a more effective way of demonstrating that the Church was a thoroughly untrustworthy institution'

Peter Gwyn, *The King's Cardinal: The Rise and Fall of Thomas Wolsey,* 1990.

With Henry dominant and creating his own policy there is little scope in Gwyn's account for the idea of a noble faction destroying Wolsey. Not only was Henry the puppeteer rather than the puppet but

'the evidence for Wolsey being destroyed by an aristocratic faction is slight, ... Wolsey got on perfectly well with individual nobles such as Norfolk and Suffolk, but also with the nobility as a group. This was not particularly because Wolsey was a 'nice guy', but because he was a good politician, who could see no advantage in antagonizing people upon whom the good government of the kingdom depended, and who, if he got on the wrong side of them, could have made things very difficult for him.'

Peter Gwyn, *The King's Cardinal: The Rise and Fall of Thomas Wolsey,* 1990.

TALKING POINT

Peter Gwyn's biography of Wolsey was published in 1990. It has 639 pages plus an introduction. In 1991 a collection of essays on Wolsey was edited by S.J.Gunn and P.J.Lindley, contributing a further 315 pages of discussion of the cardinal. Is it likely that the last word had been said on Wolsey?

More recently Professor Ives has re-asserted the importance of faction in a detailed article tracing the politics of the last two years of Wolsey's life. Text books often skim over this period, particularly that encompassing Campeggio's revocation of the divorce question to Rome, Wolsey's dismissal and, finally, his death. The result is that Wolsey's fall seems inevitable as soon as Campeggio reached his decision. In contrast, Professor Ives has shown that Wolsey survived one attack by his political enemies in the summer of 1529 and, although dismissed, had very good grounds for expecting a recall. Twice, royal messengers brought him a ring of the king's as a token of esteem. One of them told Wolsey that the king had acted 'for no displeasure that he beryth you, but oonly to satysffie more the myndes of some whiche he knowyth be not your frendes.' Thus Wolsey's enemies feared his return and re-doubled their efforts. They centred on Anne Boleyn who believed that Wolsey was not willing to pursue the divorce vigorously. At the same time Wolsey was showering gifts on courtiers, including Anne herself, but Anne won. Wolsey was ordered north to his Archdiocese and there, losing hope in a recall from the king, entered into correspondence with France, the Emperor, Catherine of Aragon and the Pope, intent on creating the conditions in which Henry would be forced to call back his old servant. Such correspondence was treason and led to the final charges. The resounding lesson of this account is the changing nature of politics, of uncertainty as individuals and factions struggled to win the king to their view of events, of Henry's reluctance to act against Wolsey until there was no alternative option at all.

REVIEW
The King and the Cardinal

One of the problems of studying history is that sooner or later you have to make up your mind about an issue. This is particularly difficult if historians, instead of agreeing with each other and thereby making your decision easy, insist on disagreeing. How can you choose between the arguments of historians who have spent many years working on a topic? They have read the sources and you haven't. It is so tempting to sit on the fence – but also uncomfortable!

This is decision time. How good a minister was Wolsey and did he, not the King, really rule England? To help you, here are those irritating historians disagreeing with each other, although their disagreements are often subtle. Answering the questions below may help you move beyond repeating their ideas to forming your own.

---

1 Construct a table (such as that shown overleaf) summarising the views in Sources A to D together with those in any other books you are using under two headings.

(a) How effective was Wolsey as a minister?

(b) Was Henry or Wolsey the real ruler of England?

2 What are the similarities and differences in extracts A to D?

3 What are your own prejudices about Wolsey and Henry VIII? How are they likely to affect your judgement?

4 Write your own answers to each of questions 1a and 1b.

	Wolsey's effectiveness as a minister	Henry or Wolsey? The Country's Ruler
A. G.R. Elton (1968)		
B. J.J. Scarisbrick (1968)		
C. P.J. Gwyn (1990)		
D. S.J. Gunn and P.J. Lindley (1991)		

Source A

'Anyone with eyes in his head could see that Wolsey had tried to do the impossible, to rule as king when he was not king, to ignore the legal and constitutional traditions of England and substitute for them his own self-confident judgment, to do a highly professional job in a very amateur manner. He had lasted so long because in two things he was not amateur at all: he knew how to promote himself, and for most of the time he knew how to keep Henry satisfied.

... Wolsey's long period of ascendancy proved essentially sterile, nor do the many links between the before and the after alter this verdict at all. And why should this surprise? Wolsey was not a creative or reflective man, but an uncomplicated activist, a magnificent if often extravagant manipulator of what was available. And here lies some measure of redemption. To recognise that Wolsey contributed virtually nothing to the future is not to discard his present. For fifteen years he impressed England and Europe with his grandeur, his hard work, his skill and intelligence, and his very positive action in the affairs of this world. He often achieved what he set out to do, even if subsequent events showed his aims to have been mistaken and his solutions to have been patchwork. He made a great and deserved name, and his age would have been very different without him. And surely, this is something; surely it is enough.'

G.R.Elton, Introduction in A.F.Pollard, 'Wolsey' 1965.

Source B

For all his faults, there had been something lofty and great about him – as a judge, as a patron of education, as a builder, as an international figure. For all his faults, he deserved more generous treatment from his king, and has, perhaps, deserved more generous treatment from some historians. Furthermore, though it is true that he failed to use his large legatine and authority for any but rather desultory and tentative ecclesiastical reform, and was himself seriously ill-equipped to promote the renewal which the

Church in England so manifestly required, it is not just to accuse him (as he has been accused) of having left that Church brow-beaten and dispirited – easy prey, in other words, to the king – and, to compound his guilt, of having clearly pointed the way to the Royal Supremacy by his own union of high spiritual and temporal authority. Wolsey as 'author of the schism' is scarcely more convincing than Wolsey as 'author of the divorce'. ... English churchmen showed little sign of having been broken by the legate and, in the months that followed the latter's fall, met the king's advances firmly.

J.J. Scarisbrick, *Henry VIII*, 1968.

Source C

... if one turns to the documents that went out under Wolsey's name, what immediately impresses is not only their quantity and length – each one frequently over five thousand words – but the range of business they cover. It might be the formation of an alliance with a foreign power, or a 'universal peace treaty'; an enclosure commission or a new constitution for the Augustinian canons; the founding of a college at Oxford or the settling of a dispute in chancery – and often all these things at much the same time! The multiplicity is endless and the workload is staggering; but Wolsey was evidently able, both physically and mentally, to take it in his stride.

... that he had these qualities should come as no surprise. Why it might is because there has been a tendency to hide Giustinian's man 'of vast ability' under the glitz and razzmatazz of Renaissance politics, in the process turning Wolsey into some kind of strutting peacock devoted only to self-glorification and self-indulgence. The truth is much more sober, which is not to deny a glamorous side to politics. It is also true that ability and hard work can combine very happily with intense ambition – and even worse! It is right to start with the fact that Wolsey was a man of enormous ability, for it provides the simple answers to the question why he became the king's leading minister.

P.Gwyn, *The King's Cardinal: The Rise and Fall of Thomas Wolsey,* 1990.

Source D

The cardinal's contemporary reputation must also have suffered from his ready identification with the policies of Henry VIII ... In his determination to enforce the king's laws and augment the king's revenues, his confrontations with noblemen, Londoners, reluctant taxpayers and even defenders of clerical privilege – all victims of Henry VIII – stirred up widespread enmity ... The completeness of his executive control over the king's affairs opened Wolsey to more general hostility, not only from those who felt themselves excluded from power, but also from all those who conveniently failed to recognize the royal will behind the cardinal's often painful imposition of the crown's authority ...

In ecclesiastical affairs Wolsey perhaps lacked the vision displayed in so many of his initiatives in government and diplomacy, from the enclosure commissions and the treaty of London to the general proscription and his sponsorship of an expedition to find the North-West Passage. Yet the sheer scale of his enterprises, and the vigour, skill and personal attention to detail with which he pursued them, were common to Wolsey's activities in the church, the state and the arts. They made him a leading promoter of the English Renaissance in education and in a number of decorative arts, an important architect of England's re-emergence as a European power, and a significant agent of the strengthening of English royal government initiated by Edward IV and Henry VII and continued by the cardinal's servant, Thomas Cromwell. These qualities were tempered by a realism which made him compromise when faced with insoluble difficulties like the Kildare ascendancy in Ireland or the foreign policy crises of 1525 and 1528, while the execution of his schemes was facilitated by the exercise of a political skill so great that William Tyndale thought his fall from power was just a clever trick to escape from a tight corner.

S.J.Gunn and P.G.Lindley, 'Introduction' in S.J.Gunn and P.G.Lindley, Cardinal Wolsey, Church, state and art, 1991.

7 Henry VIII's Revolution – The English Reformation

PREVIEW

In 1535 there were 9,000 monks and nuns living in about 800 monasteries and convents. In 1536 the king founded a new monastery at Bisham. By 1540 all these religious houses, the old and the new, had been closed. Their lands had been taken over, their goods sold or stolen, the monks and nuns scattered. This Dissolution of the Monasteries ended 1,000 years of monastic history in England. There had been monks in England ever since 597 A.D. when St. Augustine arrived to preach Christianity and brought England into the Church of Rome, headed by the Pope. That link too was cut in the 1530s. The Pope was no longer the head of the church in England: rather the king was the head of the Church of England.

These changes were not just theories that affected only kings and popes. Monks and nuns had provided care, charity and shelter for the poor. They had educated thousands of children. They had sung masses to speed the souls of the dead to heaven. Would the gates of heaven now be closed because of the silence on earth?

This was the English Reformation – the name we give to the religious changes that were started by Henry VIII in the 1530s. The Reformation was certainly one of the most important periods in English history but the label 'Reformation' can be misleading. It suggests that from the very beginning people knew that something earth-shattering was taking place. It also suggests that the events were all clearly linked together as part of a pattern of religious reform, initiated by someone who knew just what would happen next. And yet, according to C.S.L.Davies, 'most of those involved in bringing about the Reformation, including the King himself, had little understanding of the implications of what they were doing.'

This chapter will explore the events of the Reformation of the 1530s. Was there a religious revolution in England? Why did these events happen? Was there a guiding hand or was it just an extremely complicated accident?

TALKING POINT

Do you think that labels, like 'The Reformation', are useful or do they package past events into too neat and tidy a pattern? Which other labels can you identify and how might they be misleading?

FOUNTAINS ABBEY IN YORKSHIRE, ONE OF THE MANY MONASTERIES DESTROYED BY HENRY VIII.

7.1 The Church before the Reformation

Source A

Long before Henry VIII broke with Rome numerous developments were preparing Englishmen for some sort of religious and ecclesiastical change or crisis. Anticlericalism ... had reached a new virulence by the early years of the sixteenth century ... monasticism was lukewarm and insular, commanding little veneration outside the cloister ... Altogether, the English Church during the period 1500 – 1530 stood poorly equipped to weather the storms of the new age. It was a grandiose but unseaworthy hulk, its timbers rotted and barnacled, its superstructure riddled by the fire of its enemies, its crew grudging, divided, in some case mutinous ...

A.G.Dickens, 'The Reformation in England' in The Reformation Crisis, ed. J.Hurstfield, 1965.

Source B

There were those who despaired of the spiritual state of the nation and more particularly of its Church. The English people had a reputation for formal piety. They offered freely to saints and went on pilgrimages; ... Masses for souls in purgatory remained a very popular item in testaments. Though the monastic ideal was ceasing to attract recruits – with the exception of the stricter orders like the Carthusians or the Observant Franciscans – chantries were still being founded in large numbers ...

Yet all was not well with the Church in England. ... the clergy themselves attracted more dislike than love. The state of the Church was widely believed to be rotten. Popular anticlericalism thrived on tales of gluttonous monks, lecherous friars, ignorant and dishonest parish priests. ... Satirists unquestionably exaggerated the evils in the Church, but they had enough reality to draw on to carry widespread conviction. The Church was showing all the signs of an institution in danger but unaware of its peril.

G.R.Elton, Reform and Reformation, 1977.

Source C

We have hitherto been content with the image of the Tudor regime unleashing and then riding the back of the tiger of popular anticlericalism, anti-papalism, patriotism and so on. If that is now suspect, this is because one can no longer find much of a tiger.

...up to the very moment when the traditional medieval religious institutions and practices were swept away, English layfolk were pouring money and gifts in kind into them. Wills are a source which, quite rightly, has attracted plenty of attention recently – because so many survive and because ... quite humble folk as well as those at the top wrote them ... they show a society committed to the old religion until the moment when it was supplanted.

J.J.Scarisbrick, The Reformation and the English People, 1984.

Source D

Generations of historians tracing the origins of the Reformation have cited examples of negligence and immorality among the clergy. There were scandals, it is true – but they were very rare. The inmates of a few of the religious houses could live in opulent idleness, but most monasteries were workaday communities offering charity, education, employment, and prayers for departed souls. Some parish priests were neglectful, but many more were thoughtful ministers to the needs of their people. It would be difficult to explain the high levels of lay benefactions to the Church and of lay recruitment to the priesthood if the clergy had really been as slothful and self-seeking as Protestant historians have suggested. We should not isolate the evidence of deficiencies in the Church, and ignore the evidence of efficiency. On balance, the Church was a lively and relevant social institution, and the Reformation was not the product of a long-term decay of medieval religion. ... Henry VIII did not challenge a moribund Church and a declining religion: he attacked institutions and forms of piety which were growing and vigorous.

C.Haigh, The English Reformation Revised, 1987.

WESTERN ZOYLAND CHURCH IN SOMERSET, ONE OF MANY PARISH CHURCHES WHICH UNDERWENT EXTENSIVE REFURBISHMENT AND REBUILDING IN THE FIFTY YEARS BEFORE THE REFORMATION.

Source E

The clergy, for their part, seem to have afforded no deep spiritual or meditative wells from which the people – of any class – might draw personal illumination or inspiration. The parish clergy were too simply educated ... and many were remarkably transient.

Most of our testators were doubtless sincere in their faith, but they reveal few traces of misgivings or of introspection or of independent thoughts or even of independent emotions: their faith was remarkably insular, inert, and shallow, untouched by the new devotions, perfunctory almost in the old ones, uninterested in, and showing no deep acquaintance with, doctrine.

P.Heath *'Urban Piety In The Later Middle Ages: the Evidence Of Hull Wills'* in B.Dobson (ed.) The Church, Politics and Patronage in the Fifteenth Century, 1984.

Source F

...pre-Reformation Catholicism was still strong in (Lancashire), so that the early sixteenth century found the old Church not at its nadir but at its high point. There is little sign, it is true, of a deep spiritual life, but there was certainly a real enthusiasm for traditional practices.

C.Haigh, *Reformation and Resistance in Tudor Lancashire*, 1975.

Source G

... most (historians) tend to assume that the late medieval Church was a kind of monolithic whole, either wholly for or wholly against the Reformation. But when we unpack the late medieval Church we find that ... different pieces of it point in different directions as regards the Reformation; some for it, some against it. Certainly the evidence from Norwich supports this. For example, support for masses and prayers for the dead and for devotions to the saints seem to point against the Reformation; but on the other hand there is little evidence of enthusiasm for the papacy or of opposition to vernacular Bibles, which points in favour of the Reformation. ...

N.P.Tanner, *'The Reformation and Regionalism: Further Reflections on the Church in Late Medieval Norwich'* in Towns and Townspeople in the Fifteenth Century, (ed.) J.A.F.Thomson, 1988.

Source H

In the South-East, it is true, there are signs of a partial weakening of Catholic enthusiasm before the Reformation; here the Dickens/Elton model has a measure of validity. Outside this region, however, devotion generally remained strong: in most parts of England it is the Haigh/Scarisbrick model that seems the more applicable.

R.Whiting, The Blind Devotion of the People: Popular Religion in the Engish Reformation, 1989.

Questions

1 In what ways do Sources A and B agree about the condition of the English Church before the Reformation?

How do Sources C and D disagree with Sources A and B?

2 Read Sources E and F. What conclusions can you reach from them about the English Church?

3 Read Sources G and H. Why might general conclusions about the English Church before the Reformation be misleading?

The Pre-Reformation Church in Norwich

a) Between 1370 and 1524
   over 90% of wills contain bequests to parish churches
   over 60% of wills contain specific bequests for masses and prayers for the dead

b) Percentage of university graduates amongst beneficed clergy:
   1370–1449 8%
   1450–1499 32%
   1500–1532 42%

Henry, Defender of the Faith

Fidei Defensor – our coins still tell us that Henry VIII was a convinced and loyal Catholic. In 1521 Henry was awarded that title by the Pope, partly as a reward for his defence of the church in his book Assertio Septem Sacramentorum, written to answer Luther's criticisms. The other reason for the award was that Henry had been lobbying for a grand title for years. The king of France was 'The Most Christian King'. The king of Spain was 'The Catholic King'. Henry's book finally persuaded the Pope to give way to Henry's competitiveness and vanity. Henry was certainly a loyal Catholic but this did not mean he was obedient in all things to the Pope.

'By the ordinance and sufferance of God we are King of England, and the kings of England in time past have never had any superior but God alone.'

Those were Henry's words in 1515. On numerous other occasions he showed himself determined that the Pope's power would not undermine his own in England. There was therefore always the possibility of a clash because their power overlapped. Clergy could still opt to be tried in church courts where punishments were milder than in the king's courts. Some clerics still paid taxes, called annates, (the revenue from their first year as, for example, a bishop) to the Pope. However neither side wanted a quarrel and, while Wolsey was in power, they had the ideal go-between to maintain harmony. If a clash did come it would be about power, not theology.

At the same time there were radical views coming into England in the 1520s. Protestantism established itself in Oxford, Cambridge, London and some of the ports. It emphasised people's freedom to interpret the Bible for themselves and so English Protestantism's first achievement was a new English translation of the Bible by William Tyndale. Possession and reading of this Bible had to be in secret. Therefore there was some basis for a challenge to the Catholic church but there was no mass demand for change.

In 1527 Henry initiated an enquiry into the validity of his marriage to Catherine of Aragon. He would not have taken that step if he had not already decided that he wanted a new wife. There were two major motives for his decision. After 18 years of marriage Henry did not have a legitimate male heir. Catherine was now over 40 and had not been pregnant since 1518. In the masculine world of the Tudor court there was no doubt that this was Catherine's fault and that she had failed not just Henry but the Tudor dynasty.

Henry's second motive was Anne Boleyn. Henry was in love and determined that Anne should be his queen. Unlike her elder sister, Anne had steadfastly refused the inevitably short-lived consolation prize of being the king's mistress. Henry therefore needed to make her his queen or give her up.

Which of these motives was the more important is difficult to determine. To some extent it depends on the subjectivity of the observer. Perhaps Anne was the more important. Henry certainly did not countenance any other possible brides but only Henry knew the true origins of

TALKING POINT

Historians have to produce generalisations to help readers make sense of a mass of evidence. Can generalisations be more problematical than useful?

One of the major tasks of
historians is to identify the
motives of people. Is
identifying the motives of
someone like Henry VIII
the same as explaining
why an event happened?
How certain should we be
when describing
someone's motives?

his need for a divorce. Yet given Henry's 'infinitely flexible conscience' perhaps even he was not sure of the precise balance of motives.

Henry based his argument for a divorce on a passage from the Bible:
'If a man shall take his brother's wife, it is an impurity; ... they shall be childless.'

(Leviticus xx 21)

He argued that, as Catherine had been married to his elder brother, Arthur, Pope Julius II should not have given Catherine and himself permission to marry. Henry said that even the Pope had no power to set aside Biblical law. Therefore he asked Pope Clement VII to declare that Julius had exceeded his powers and that therefore Henry and Catherine had never been legally married.

Asking the Pope to criticise his predecessor was not a happy start. Henry compounded this by making clear his intention to marry Anne. Marrying the sister of one of your mistresses was equally against Biblical law. Henry was casting off one 'sister-in-law' only to marry another! Worse, there was another Biblical passage that positively approved his marriage to Catherine. 'When brethren dwell together, and one of them dieth without children, the wife of the deceased shall not marry to another, but his brother shall take her, and raise up seed for his brother.'

(Deuteronomy xxv 5)

Despite all these scriptural arguments the Pope might well, in normal circumstances, have given Henry what he wanted – an annulment of his marriage. Popes often granted the wishes of kings as part of the give and take of politics. However the twists and turns of foreign policy caught up with Henry. He had failed to give Charles V his promised support against France. Then, alarmed by Charles's victories he had abandoned their alliance. It was little wonder that Charles wrote 'the king of England does not help me as a good friend should; he does not even help me to the extent of his obligations.'

To Charles, Henry's divorce from Catherine would have added insult to injury, even if, for Henry, it was probably the logical result of the breakdown of the alliance. Charles's position was far stronger. He had won control of northern Italy, so that for the Pope it was more important to appease Charles than please Henry.

In 1528 Pope Clement offered some hope by sending Cardinal Campeggio to England. This allowed the Pope to appease Henry without doing anything definite to offend Charles. Beginning in May 1529, Wolsey and Campeggio heard the king's case but Campeggio adjourned it in July. A final victory over France had confirmed Charles's stranglehold on Italy.

Soon afterwards Wolsey was dismissed from office but what would Henry do next? Only the Pope could annul his marriage and sanction his anticipated life of happiness with Anne. Henry had to continue negotiating. What he needed was a negotiating lever that might outweigh Charles's influence.

Anne Boleyn was clearly a
central figure in the events
of this period. In many
accounts her character
has been simplified and
distorted. Why might our
task of understanding of
Anne be made more
difficult by (a) sixteenth
century attitudes to
women and (b) the depth
of religious conflict
resulting from Henry's
divorce?

What happened next?

There were many twists and turns in religious politics in the 1530s. It can be very difficult to follow the sequence of events so the exercise on these pages has been devised as an introduction. It is usually easier to remember what happened when – the chronology of the subject – if you have to work out the order of events for yourself.

1 Each of the boxes contains the events of a year between 1529 and 1539. Which box goes with which year?

2 Which years might be described as key turning points and why?

3 Was the speed of change consistent throughout the decade?

4 Was the government certain of the religious path it wished to take after 1534?

5 What evidence is there of opposition to these changes?

Box 1
- Thomas Cranmer, already one of Henry's advisers, became Archbishop of Canterbury.
- The Act in Conditional Restraint of Annates was confirmed.
- The Act in Restraint of Appeals abolished appeals to Rome in matrimonial and other cases.
- Henry married Anne; Princess Elizabeth was born.

Box 2
- Some of the great northern monasteries surrendered to the king after their abbots had been involved in the Pilgrimage of Grace.

Box 3
- The clergy bought a pardon from the charge of praemunire for £118,000.
- Henry demanded that the clergy recognise him as 'protector and only supreme head of the English church'. They agree after adding 'as far as the law of Christ allows.'

Box 4
- Campeggio revoked Henry's case to Rome and Wolsey was dismissed.
- A parliament began in November that historians call the 'Reformation Parliament'. The members criticised the church for such abuses as pluralism.

Religious Glossary

Annates
Payments made to the Pope by bishops and other holders of large benefices. They consisted of the first year's revenue from the benefice.

Chantry
Effectively a small church or chapel built at the expense of an individual or group who also paid for clergy to sing masses there for the souls of the founders and others they named.

Consubstantiation
The doctrine that the bread and wine used during the service represented (but were not transformed into) the body and blood of Christ. This was the Protestant belief.

First Fruits and Tenths
First Fruits were the first year's revenues from all benefices. Tenths were one-tenth of the annual revenue. These were paid to the Crown after the Reformation.

Pluralism
The practice of one clergyman holding a number of offices at the same time. This was a

problem if he could not fulfil the duties and paid another, usually less able cleric to act as his substitute.

Praemunire

Anyone accused of praemunire was accused of giving their allegiance to someone from outside England e.g. the Pope. More accurately it refers to a writ of praemunire designed to prevent infringements of royal rights.

Reformation Parliament

The very lengthy parliament called in 1529 which was not dissolved until 1536 and enacted all the legislation relating to the Reformation. Within that period there were seven distinct sessions of parliament and long periods when parliament did not meet. For example, it did not meet at all in 1530 or 1535.

Transubstantiation

The doctrine that the bread and wine used during the mass were transformed into the body and blood of Christ. This was the Catholic belief.

Box 5
- The larger monasteries were dissolved.
- The Act of Six Articles was a revised statement of doctrine, re-affirming a variety of Catholic practices and saying that anyone denying transubstantiation was committing treason.

Box 6
- Bishop Fisher, Thomas More and a group of Carthusian monks were executed.
- The king's commissioners began to visit religious houses, detailing their wealth.

Box 7
- The Act of Supremacy said that the king was 'supreme head of the Church of England'. Denial of the royal supremacy became a treasonable act.
- The submission of the clergy was confirmed by law and therefore deprived the Pope of any legal authority in England.
- Elizabeth Barton, the 'Nun of Kent' was executed.

Box 8
- Smaller monasteries were dissolved.
- The Pilgrimage of Grace – a widespread revolt in the north – was put down but only after some alarm.
- The Ten Articles were published – an official statement of doctrine for the new church which showed clear signs of Lutheran leanings.
- Anne Boleyn was executed and Henry married Jane Seymour.

Box 9
- Henry appealed to universities in Europe for support for his case.
- The clergy were accused of praemunire as the king began to put pressure on the church

Box 10
- In 1538 royal injunctions were issued, ordering the purchase of the Great Bible in English so that it could be read and understood in public. Shrines and other places of pilgrimage were to be removed or closed.

Box 11
- The Commons drew up the 'Supplication against the Ordinaries' (i.e. bishops) complaining that the church had its own laws and courts independent of the king. In the 'Submission of the Clergy' the church accepted that the king could veto any future laws and the present laws were to be reviewed.
- The Act in Conditional Restraint of Annates threatened to reduce payments by the English church to Rome to a merely nominal sum.
- Thomas More resigned as Chancellor.
- Ann Boleyn became pregnant.

Issues and Questions

In 1529 Henry's situation was desperate but not hopeless. His actions – seeking support from European universities and pressurising the English clergy – suggest that he still hoped to make the Pope change his mind. At the same time his actions were preparing the way for an alternative course of action which would take the marriage decision and much else out of the hands of the Pope. This situation continued for three years or more – a long time in politics and love affairs. We need to ask why it took so long for 'the king's great matter' to reach its crucial turning point.

One possible solution lies in the personnel and individuals involved. It has been suggested that Henry dithered until, in 1532, along came Thomas Cromwell to supply the new ideas and political acumen that produced the break with Rome. There were also other influential people around Henry, notably Thomas Cranmer and Anne Boleyn, who were pressing for reform. This necessarily raises questions about Henry himself. Just who was in charge of policy during this decade?

The turning point came late in 1532 and early 1533. Anne Boleyn became pregnant. Cranmer became Archbishop, taking a private oath not to let other oaths come between him and his duty to his king. He married Henry and Anne having declared Henry's marriage to Catherine invalid and that to Anne legal. All this paved the way for the legitimate birth of Henry's heir.

1534 saw the central legislation of the Reformation. The Act of Supremacy established Henry as the Head of the Church of England. The authority of the Pope was banished from Henry's realm. So, a new church had been established and the king had his divorce. Matters would end there – or would they?

The Reformation turned out to be about more than a change in the name and head of the church. Events in England were influenced by events in Europe and there were powerful voices around the king advocating reforms of doctrine – the beliefs and ideas of the church. Hence the Ten Articles and the use of the English Bible suggested the strong advance of Protestantism until, in 1539, there was a volte-face with the Act of Six Articles moving back in the direction of Catholic theology. There was no straightforward and continuous religious policy. Why not? Was this the product of changing influences about the king, his changing ideas or of external factors?

Amidst these reforms came the two stages of the Dissolution of the Monasteries. It is easy to assume that the Dissolution was a necessary part of religious reform, removing the Pope's most loyal supporters – or were there other reasons why the monasteries were dissolved? Certainly the Dissolution and the other reforms created opposition. The stand of Bishop Fisher, More and the Carthusian monks in defence of their religion was one of the great acts of principle but does this suggest that there was a great surge of opposition or do the actions of a few, brave individuals mislead us into over-estimating the opposition? Similarly the Pilgrimage of Grace, a rising involving thousands of people, suggests widespread discontent. What were the motives of those involved?

TALKING POINT

Do you think the assessment of Henry VIII in this section is a fair one? Why might historians disagree on the nature of Henry's character?

1529 – 1532: A time of drift or policy?

With hindsight, the impossibility of the Pope granting Henry his divorce makes these four years seem long, wasted years which could have been avoided by more decisive and clear-headed leadership. Is that a fair comment on Henry's actions in these years?

Overall it seems unduly harsh. Certainly Henry rarely rushed into war or other decisive encounters. This seems another example of his tendency to undergo intensive training before merely jogging on the spot while making aggressive noises of intent. However it can be argued that, on this occasion at least, Henry's habitual hesitancy (carefulness?) when on the brink went hand in hand with an effective policy.

These years saw Henry applying and maintaining pressure on the English clergy. This could bring him success via one of two routes. Either it would persuade the Pope to grant the divorce or it would browbeat the clergy into submission so that they would not resist Henry's claim if he had to make his own rules. In pressurising the church Henry had a willing ally in the members of the parliament that met in November 1529. It quickly earned its name of the 'Reformation Parliament' by seeking to reform such church abuses as pluralism – an interference that immediately worried the most astute of Henry's opponents. This anticlericalism seems to have been spontaneous but it encouraged Henry to move ahead, knowing that his own initiatives would win support.

Over the next few years king and parliament bullied the clergy into submission. This bullying was short on violence but long on menace. Symptomatic of this was the vague charge of Praemunire, in effect warning the clergy of the dangers of appearing to serve two masters at such a time. The clergy bought an expensive pardon for £118,000 but Henry quickly followed up with a demand that he be recognised as 'sole Protector and supreme head of the English church and clergy'. Led by Fisher, Convocation dodged the issue by adding the phrase 'as far as the law of Christ allows'. Doubtless some bishops felt relieved but in reality this had only succeeded in limiting the pace of Henry's advance. He had moved one step forward even if they had rebuffed the second.

Another step was taken when parliament passed the Act in Conditional Restraint of Annates in February 1532. Originally intended by the Commons to end clerical payments to Rome, it was turned into a final test of the Pope's resolution (or a piece of blackmail, depending on your viewpoint) with the insertion of the word 'Conditional' by a conservative group in the Lords who feared matters were moving too fast. They hoped that the mere threat of the Act would make the Pope reach agreement and that therefore the Act would never pass into law. The Act also said that England would ignore any punishment imposed in it by the Pope – a very clear warning that his authority was in jeopardy.

The king's growing dominance turned into outright control with the Submission of the Clergy in May 1532. Convocation agreed to assemble only with royal permission; all church laws needed the king's approval. With such royal control there seemed little hope for what remained of the Pope's claim to power. Thus, by mid-1532, the time was ripe for a more dramatic initiative.

Decisions and decision makers

It is clearly possible to argue that the time between 1529 and 1532 was well spent, testing out the ground so that most potential opposition was broken before battle was joined. However that should not lead us into assuming that this 'preparation' was a carefully devised master-plan of cumulative pressure, thought through in advance. Instead there was a series of separate decisions, each taken in response to the developing situation.

At each decision point the king himself was under pressure from different directions. Within his own mind there were competing and conflicting thoughts – desire for Anne, the need for an heir, uncertainty (perhaps fear) of rejecting the Pope and the faith he had believed in all his life and had defended only a dozen years before. From outside he was also receiving competing and conflicting advice – perhaps the dominant part of it until 1532 being those loyal but conservative voices who nagged away at Henry's determination to go forward each time he nerved himself to do so.

Perhaps the most surprising single element in these factions was the continued presence of Thomas More as Henry's Chancellor until 1532. This may well reflect Henry's desire to keep his options open and avoid confrontation for as long as possible. Until 1532 the most powerful group was that led by old established councillors such as the Duke of Norfolk. They hoped to avoid having to decide between their faith and their king but, when it came to the crunch, nearly all of them put their king before their faith.

It may have been inevitable that the conservatives' influence diminished with time. The coming force was the radical group because they offered solutions to Henry's dilemma while the conservatives only offered an even more prolonged stalemate. Cranmer had shown himself capable of original religious ideas and Cromwell, Henry's chief minister from 1532, provided political and administrative tactics. At least as important as either was Anne Boleyn, an intelligent, forceful and progressive woman who had the best opportunities of all to influence the king.

The existence of these factions raises the question of whether the reformers finally won control of Henry's mind and then pushed through their programme or whether Henry himself finally chose their solutions and initiated the vital changes. Put another way, was a 'supremely manipulable' Henry the victim of faction or was he the 'supreme manipulator', controlling the factions, perhaps without their being aware of his control?

Here again there are signs that Henry was in control and took the decision himself to break from Rome. Long before Cromwell became chief minister and when other leading figures were opposed to such moves, we have seen Henry extend his power over the church, based upon his own reading of the historical and legal evidence.

Since 1530 Henry had possessed a copy of a manuscript called the *Collectanea satis copiosa*, compiled by Foxe and Cranmer. This was a collection of legal and historical precedents which claimed to deny papal jurisdiction in England and supported Henry's position. It could be used to argue that there was a positive responsibility on the king to reclaim his spiritual power and leadership. Henry's own notes on the manuscript

TALKING POINT

The absence of a 'master-plan' suggests that the break with Rome was far from inevitable, even in 1530 and 1531. Can you suggest any events that might have prevented the English Reformation or made the break unnecessary?

indicate that he was thoroughly aware of this content and he was certainly intelligent enough to appreciate its implications. For example, it suggested that while the king of England was not a priest like the Pope he did have authority over the church – he could summon bishops to convocation, define the church's laws and even, though the event was surely unlikely, pronounce his own divorce.

A second indicator of Henry's control is the way that the options were kept open until the last moment. If one or other group had really controlled the king the options would have been closed down as a sign of their dominance. In fact Henry gave hope to all, including his greatest opponents, who drew comfort from More's presence as Chancellor. More himself would surely not have stayed in office if he had thought that the King was the prisoner of another faction. The king does seem to have been in charge - the factions were jockeying for influence.

By mid-1532 Henry was moving more quickly to a decision. The clergy had submitted, Thomas Cromwell had risen to execute Henry's orders and add the details to the king's generalisations, Archbishop Warham had died, leaving the way open for a more amenable successor. Even then foreign policy seemed to slow the momentum. A new Anglo-French alliance conjured up the prospect of over-awing the Pope but then came the truly decisive moment. Anne Boleyn became pregnant. Action was needed to guarantee the legitimacy of the new Tudor heir.

Here we can see the limits of Henry's decisions. While he had decided to break with Rome it was Anne's pregnancy that decided the timing of the break. After years of refusing to sleep with Henry it seems that Anne now gave way, most likely because Henry had committed himself privately to the break with Rome. Inevitably there are alternative scenarios. Perhaps Henry would still not agree to the break and Anne's pregnancy was the means to force the king's decision? The accidents of fertility (and particularly Tudor fertility) seem to suggest that such a plan could only have been conceived by an incorrigible optimist. Perhaps their joint visit to France, the food and the wine were responsible, with no thought of politics and church affairs?

The Reformation established

Events now moved very rapidly. They had to. There was less than the nine months of Anne's pregnancy to ensure the legitimacy of the heir. This may have influenced the choice of Cranmer as the new Archbishop. He was the man most likely to produce the necessary changes.

In January 1533 Henry secretly married Anne at a ceremony performed by Cranmer. Next, the crucial Act in Restraint of Appeals was passed, declaring that England was 'an empire' governed by 'one supreme head and king'. The Act forbade appeals to the Pope. Instead any matter relating to the king was to be decided by the bishops in convocation. When put to the test the bishops did their duty to their king. They declared his marriage to Catherine invalid and that to Anne valid. Anne was crowned Queen on 1 June 1533.

The bishops' support for the king was unsurprising. Not only had they been browbeaten into submission but a worse enemy than Henry had arisen. Thomas Cromwell and others regarded the Act in Restraint of

TALKING POINTS

Can chance play a significant part in the development of events? Can you think of any examples of the impact of chance? When you are trying to develop an explanation in an essay do you look out for the workings of chance?

Appeals as a mere compromise. They wished to see the clergy subject not just to the king but to the king-in-parliament. The clergy did not want to be liable to interference from a parliament that had already shown signs of anti-clericalism. Therefore a majority of bishops actually supported Henry's actions in the 1530s because they promised to be less sweeping and threatening than those parliament might produce. They also felt that Henry's slow and reluctant progress meant that he was unlikely to revolutionise the doctrine of the church. In this they reflected the attitude of the population as a whole, which was able to cope with these changes because they developed at such a slow pace. Even now it took eighteen months for the Act of Supremacy to follow on from the Act in Restraint of Appeals.

The Act of Supremacy, in accordance with Henry's argument, said that it was simply recognising what had been the real situation all the time but had been hidden by the Pope's usurpation of power – the 'King's Majesty justly and rightfully is and oweth to be the supreme head of the Church of England'. However the exact nature of the king's role in relation to the church was not clear. This was to be defined by actions in the years ahead.

The Reformation did not end with the Act of Supremacy, as it might have done. Henry, happy with his new wife, could have left the bishops to define doctrine and therefore maintain Catholicism without the Pope. However the king did choose to exert direct influence over spiritual matters himself, playing a large part in defining the teachings of the church. Henry's intense interest in theology was not the only factor. His interest created change because it combined with the influence of the new faces around him – Cromwell, Cranmer and Anne – and the influence of unfolding events, including those in Europe. Once again those involved moved forward a decision at a time, deciding and creating as they went, with little ability to predict what lay ahead.

A Licence to Experiment: Religious Reform 1534 – 1536

Although the key decision had been Henry's there continues to be scope for debate about the roles of the king and his advisers in the development of religious reform. As Henry's Vicegerent or Deputy, Cromwell, together with Cranmer, developed the detail of the changes, fuelled by their personal commitment to Protestantism. Were they forging ahead while the king slept or even against his wishes? The answer is almost certainly 'No'. While Henry had no coherent plan of religious reform in his own mind and was later to go back somewhat on Protestant advances there are sufficient examples of his willingness to abandon Catholic orthodoxy to make clear that policy was not hijacked by the reformers without his knowledge. Most telling is the education of Prince Edward by Protestant tutors in the 1540s. There was also no shortage of conservative voices (notably Norfolk and Gardiner, the Bishop of Winchester) who would have grasped at any sign of the king's discontent with Cromwell and Cranmer to swing the Church of England back towards Catholic doctrines. It seems that Henry's interest in theological debates led him to give Cromwell and Cranmer a licence to experiment – one that they took advantage of while being careful not to alarm Henry. Only when significant opposition developed did Henry move to curtail their innovations.

Cromwell's was the inventive and disciplined mind behind the move towards Protestantism. As Vicegerent, Cromwell's task was to ensure loyalty to Henry as head of the Church. He ordained that all adult males swore an oath agreeing to the Act of Succession (declaring Mary illegitimate and establishing the rights of future heirs to the crown); all religious and lay officials also swore an oath repudiating Papal authority and supporting the king's supremacy. At the same time Cromwell embarked on a campaign of persuasion to reduce the need for enforcement. He used the new technological marvel, the printing press, to circulate treatises arguing the case for the king's supremacy in a style that would be understood by the majority. Preachers were licensed – provided they were 'reliable'. They gave sermons against Papal authority and in defence of the king's marriage and supremacy.

Even more redolent of propaganda techniques that we assume are twentieth century devices were Cromwell's personal letters. The recipients were 'specially elected and chosen', their letters handwritten rather than printed to give them a spurious individuality. However the content of each was the same. Bishops and JPs were asked to enforce legislation, make arrests and provide information against dissidents. Unlike the junk mail of today Cromwell's missives were unlikely to end in a rubbish bin.

The clearest indication of the direction of the changes is in the Ten Articles of 1536, which omitted four of the seven Catholic sacraments and denied the full doctrine of purgatory. At this stage the emphasis was more on omitting elements clearly associated with Catholicism than underlining the new Protestant theology. The Ten Articles reflect the balancing act being performed by the reformers. The Dissolution of the Monasteries gives a clearer indication of the direction they wished to follow.

The Dissolution of the Monasteries

To convinced Protestants the monasteries were a clear reminder of the survival of Catholic ideals. One of their main functions was to pray for the souls of the dead – an intercession thought unnecessary by Protestants. The monasteries were also members of international organisations, owing obedience to their mother houses as well as the Pope. They might well find it more difficult than others to accept the king's supremacy. Therefore the abolition of monasteries would be a real measure of the triumph of Protestantism. However the Dissolution was not simply a matter of religion – money, foreign policy and the need to ensure the loyalty of the landed classes to the new church all helped to close the monasteries.

Throughout the 1530s the king needed money to meet the expenses of government. Inflation meant that money was losing its value. His own lands were providing less but the new church promised the possibility of more than making good the shortfall. In 1534 the Act for First Fruits and Tenths annexed the whole of the first year's revenue from bishoprics and also broadened the tax to include all benefices. In addition all clerics had to pay one tenth of their income to the crown annually. Together these measures raised over £40,000 per year.

This was just the beginning. In 1534 Henry and Cromwell also considered the possibility of confiscating all episcopal lands. Although this was abandoned they set in train the Valor Ecclesiasticus of 1535, a valuation of all church lands and wealth. The results made tempting reading. The regular clergy – members of monasteries and convents – had an income of around £136,000 per annum. Even a proportion of this total would be immensely valuable to the crown and acquiring that proportion was not unthinkable. Monasteries had been suppressed before (most recently by Wolsey in the 1520s) and their reform had long been seen as a sign of religious renewal. Closing the smaller monasteries, where abuses were said to be more common, might even re-invigorate the larger establishments. And so, in 1536, those monasteries worth less than £200 a year were closed following visitations by the king's men, whose reports provided the justifications for the closures.

In fact Cromwell always intended to close the rest of the monasteries, despite the statement in 1536 that in them 'thanks be to God, religion is right well kept and observed.' By 1540 all the monasteries had been dissolved, at least in part because of the threat of a Crusade against the heretic King Henry VIII. The Pope, when formally excommunicating Henry, had called upon Francis I and Charles V to attack England in the name of the Catholic Church. When their ambassadors were recalled English fears of invasion were widespread. An orgy of building took place, erecting castles and other defences around the south coast in perhaps the greatest concerted piece of fortification in English history. Such building needed money and the greater monasteries provided it.

Another factor in their closure was the hunger for land among those who had benefited from the 1536 Dissolution. Many amongst the political classes were only too eager to support the final suppression if they could benefit further. For the government this was good news for, in the longer term, such people were unlikely to support a return to Catholicism and the papal supremacy if it meant giving up newly acquired land. Conservatives such as Norfolk were particularly important catches.

The Dissolution was perhaps the greatest sign of the religious changes of the 1530s. It did not in itself make England more Protestant but it did remove a gigantic symbol of Catholicism, making the development and acceptance of Protestantism more likely. This symbolism was important to convinced Protestants and Catholics alike, which was why the Dissolution was an important factor in the opposition that developed in 1536, opposition that briefly appeared so widespread and threatening that some feared and others hoped that it would topple Henry from his throne.

Examining the Evidence
The Pilgrimage of Grace

In the last months of 1536 over 30,000 men joined a mass rising in the north of England. They included commoners, clergy, gentry and nobility although they were led by a commoner, Robert Aske. Nearly all the main towns east of the Pennines surrendered to them, including York and Hull. When the royal force faced them it was so heavily outnumbered that its leader, the Duke of Norfolk, had to seek a truce. However this rising was

TALKING POINT

Another very important symbol was the English Bible. Why was this so important? What kind of effects was it likely to have on society in general as well as on religion?

THE BADGE OF THE PILGRIMS, SHOWING THE FIVE WOUNDS OF CHRIST.

not a simple political rebellion – its name 'The Pilgrimage of Grace' tells us that – and the reasons for the rising are complex.

There were really three risings. The first, in Lincolnshire, was over within a fortnight but it had triggered the much larger and more widespread Pilgrimage, which must in any case have been about to start. The Pilgrimage was ended by its leaders' agreements with the king in late December. Then came the third stage when new revolts broke out in the East Riding of Yorkshire and the north-west of England in January and February 1537. This time the rebels were ruthlessly suppressed immediately.

The risings had begun in Lincolnshire at a time when there were three different sets of commissioners busy in the area. One was suppressing the smaller monasteries, the second was collecting a subsidy or tax, the third was enforcing the new religious laws (including the Ten Articles) and investigating the quality and morals of the clergy. Fear of the outcomes of their activities sparked and motivated the rebels.

Trouble broke out in Louth on 1 October and by the 5th 10,000 people were marching on Lincoln, raised and rallied by the local priests and gentry. The fury and fear of the rebels was shown when the Chancellor of the Bishop of Lincoln was beaten to death but then the rising fell apart. As the Duke of Suffolk approached with an army the gentry leaders took fright and sought pardons. Without their leadership the rest simply ghosted back to their villages and towns.

By then the Pilgrimage itself was already under way. The size and geographical spread of the movement made it a severe threat even if the rebels protested their loyalty and criticised councillors, not the king. Henry's new 'Supremacy' had to be defended by the defeat of the Pilgrims for again no attitude other than complete support for the king was deemed suitable. The trouble was that there were too many to be defeated.

On 8 December the Duke of Norfolk, commanding the King's force, bought time. A pardon was read. He promised that suppressed abbeys would be restored and a free parliament held where the rebels' grievances could be discussed. The Pilgrims, particularly many gentry, were only too eager for conciliation, not knowing Norfolk's words to Henry 'I beseech you to take in gode part what so ever promes I shall make unto the rebells for sewerly I shall observe no part thereoff.' The Pilgrims dispersed, many thinking they had been victorious.

The outbreak of the third set of risings played into the king's hands. They were partly caused by the fear of the commoners that the gentry had or would desert them. This division allowed the king to crush the new risings, hanging 74 of the rebels immediately as a warning to others. Now he also had a pretext for arresting the leaders of the Pilgrimage. After trials the list of those executed included Lords Darcy and Hussey, Robert Aske and the Abbots of Jervaulx and Fountains Abbeys as well as other gentlemen and clergy.

The Pilgrimage has been described as 'the crisis of the reign'. In a brief description like this it is easy to forget that it lasted many months, the pilgrims heavily outnumbered the royal army and the king and government were genuinely afraid of what might happen. Difficult as it was it could have been far worse. The Pilgrims had high hopes that more senior noblemen of Catholic sympathies, perhaps even Norfolk himself, Derby or Shrewsbury, would join them. That they didn't was not entirely due to their loyalty to Henry. They also felt that they could use their influence at court to halt or turn back the advances of Protestantism.

Source A

Ye shall not enter into this our Pilgrimage of Grace for the Commonwealth, but only for the love that ye do bear unto Almighty God his faith, and the Holy Church militant and the maintenance thereof, to the preservation of the King's person and his issue, to the purifying of the nobility, and to expulse all villein blood and evil councillors against the Commonwealth from his Grace and his Privy Council of the same. And that ye shall not enter into our said Pilgrimage for no particular profit to yourself, nor to do any displeasure to any private person, but by counsel of the commonwealth, nor slay nor murder for no envy, but in your hearts put away fear and dread, and take afore you the Cross of Christ, and in your hearts His Faith, The Restitution of the Church, the suppression of heretics and their opinions, by all the holy contents of this book.

This oath was devised by Robert Aske and it was first taken by the gentry and then the rest of the pilgrims in October 1536.

Source B

Alacke! Alacke!
For the church sake
Pore comons wake,
And no marvell!
For clere it is
The decay of this
How the pore shall mys
No tong can tell

For ther they hadde
Boith ale and breyde
At tyme of nede,
And succer grete
In alle distresse
And hevyness
And wel intrete.

Crim, crame, and riche
With thre ell and the liche
As sum men teache
God theym amend!
And that Aske may,
Without delay,
Here make a stay
And well to end.

Extracts from a ballad probably composed at Sawley Abbey. Other similar ballads were composed at the time of the Pilgrimage.

Source C
To the Kyng our Soveraign lorde.

1 The suppression of so many religiouse howses as are at this instant tyme suppressed, whereby the service of our God is not wel (maintained) but also the (commons) of yor realme by unrelieved, the which as we think is a gret hurt to the common welthe and many sisters be (put) from theyr levyings and left at large.

2 ...we humbly beseache your grace that the acte of use may be suppressed because we think by the sayd act we your true subjects be clearly restrayned of yor liberties in the declaration of our wylles concernying our landes ...

3 ...weyr your grace hath a taxe or a quindeyne granted unto you by act of parliament payable the next year, the which is and hath been ever leveable of shepe and catals, and the shepe and catals of yor subjects within the sayde shire are now at this instant tyme in manner utterly decayed...whereby your grace to take the sayde tax or quindeyn yor sayde subjects shalbe distrayned to paye iiiid for every beast and xiid for xxtie shepe, the which wolde be an importunate charge to them considering the poverty that they be in all redye and losse which they have sutayned these ii years by past.

4 ....we wor yor true subjects thinke that yor grace takes of yor counsell and being a boute you suche persons as be of low byrth andd small reputation which hath procuryed the proffits most especially for theyr own advantage, the which we suspect to be the lord cromwell and Sir Richard Riche Chanceler of the augmentations.

5 ....we your true subjects fynd us grevyd that there be diverse bisshopes of England of yor Graces late promosion that hath (not) the faith of Christ, as we thinke, which are the bisshops of Canterbury, ..Rochester..Worcester..Salisbury..St.Davids and Dublin, and in especiall we thynk the begynyngs of all the trouble .. and the vexation ..of yor subjects the bisshop of Lincoln.

> Extracts from the articles written by Aske and sent to the Mayor of York when the city submitted to the pilgrims on 15 October.

Source D
They called this, their seditious and traitorous voyage, a holy and blessed pilgrimage; they also had certain banners in the field whereon was painted Christ hanging on the cross on one side, and a chalice with a painted cake in it on the other side, with various other banners of similar hypocrisy and feigned sanctity ... only to delude and deceive the simple and ignorant folk.

> From Edward Hall's *The Union of the Two Noble and Illustre Families of Lancastre and Yorke*, written during Henry VIII's reign.

Source E
... the abbeys in the north partes gaf great almons to pour men and laudable servyd God; in which partes of lait dais they had but smal comfort by gostly teching. And by occasion of the said suppression the devyn service of almightie God is much minished, greate nombre of messes unsaid,

and the blissed consecracion of the sacrement now not used ... And the profites of thies abbeys yerley goith out of the contrey to the Kinges highnes, so that in short space little money, by occasion of the said yerly rentes, tentes and furst frutes, should be left in the said countrey ... Also diverse and many of the said abbeys wer in the montaignes and desert places, wher the people be rud of condyccions and not well taught the law of God, and when the said abbeys stud, the said peuple not only had worldly refreshing in their bodies but also sperituall refuge ... not only theis tenauntes and servauntes wantes refresshing ther, both of meat, cloth and wages, and knowith not now wher to have any liffing, but also strangers ... for non was in thes partes denyed, nether horsemeat nor manesmeat, so that the people was greatlie refresshyed by the said abbeys ... Also the abbeys was on of the bewties of this realme to al men and strangers passing threw the same; also al gentilmen much socored in ther nedes with money, their yong sons ther socored, and in nonries ther doughters brought up in vertuee ...

Taken from the interrogation and answers of Robert Aske in 1537.

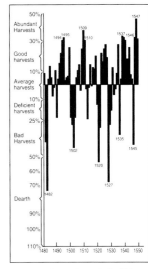

HARVEST QUALITY IN THE 1530s.

The Causes of the Pilgrimage

Source F

Recent taxation was much disliked and the new subsidy, unusually, had come in peacetime. ... When Holland rose to support the rest of Lincolnshire, the articles there stated that the king should demand no more money of his subjects except for the defence of the realm. Coming after two years of dearth, following bad weather and poor harvests, resentment at the new subsidy may have been particularly important in prompting support for the rising in the Yorkshire dales and in Marshland: the evidence of the tax assessments in the early Tudor period has shown that these were the poorest areas of the West Riding. Yet taxation can hardly be accounted a major element in the rebellion.

A. Fletcher, *Tudor Rebellions,* (third edition), 1983.

Source G

'...the vast majority of clergy did not regard the divorce and supremacy as important issues in themselves; protests were delayed until it became clear to what purposes the supremacy would be turned. It was Cromwell's vicegerency, his injunctions, statutes and proclamations aimed at the duties, incomes, and, finally, the beliefs of the Catholic clergy, that roused a surge of opposition. It was the dissolution of the monasteries that fuelled outright rebellion in Lincolnshire and the northern counties, though in London and the south-east the scale of resistance was small.

...Was the Pilgrimage spontaneously begun by people and clergy after whom the nobles and gentry were swept along against their will, or planned in advance by nobles and gentry who used their territorial power to raise the country? Although this question has been disputed, compelling signs exist that the noble and gentry supporters of Princess Mary joined forces with Catholic lawyers from the inns of court in revolt against Cromwell's administration. This connection links Lords Darcy and Hussey, Sir Robert Constable, Robert Aske ... and others. In particular,

Darcy and Hussey had assured Chapuys in September 1534 that, if Charles V were to declare war, English politics would be transformed 'by the insurrection of the people, who would be joined immediately by the nobility and the clergy'. ... Yet, although Darcy, Hussey and Aske encouraged pre-planning and the northern parochial clergy incited the people to revolt, the actual sequence of events differed from their schemes. In fact, the 'conspirators' were taken by surprise when revolt broke out in Lincolnshire. The speed with which the protest movement spread suggests, furthermore, that 'the quantity of explosive material was such that it needed very little to set it off'. While Catholic factionalism divided some members of the governing elite, the mobilization and solidarity of so many northerners cannot be taken for granted. Also there were lesser disturbances in southern counties: East Anglia, Somerset, and Cornwall. So, while Court plotting shaped the form of the Pilgrimage to some degree, it does not sufficiently explain its force and extent.'

John Guy, *Tudor England,* 1988.

---

1 What causes of the Pilgrimage can be identified in Sources A – E?

2 Which of the primary sources provide the most reliable indicators of the motives of the Pilgrims?

3 What other causes are identified in Guy's analysis (Source G)?

4 How might motives for joining the Pilgrimage have differed amongst the Pilgrims?

5 Is it possible to identify one cause as the most important cause of the Pilgrimage? Explain your answer.

6 What evidence have you found to justify the statement that this 'was the greatest challenge Henry ever faced from his English subjects'?

8 Was Henry saved by the rebels' loyalty rather than by his own actions?

BISHOP JOHN FISHER

FOCUS

7.2 Opposition from Individuals

'This day the Nun of Kent, with ii Friars Observants, ii monks, and one secular priest, were drawn from the Tower to Tyburn, and there hanged and headed. God, if it be his pleasure, have mercy on their souls. Also this day the most part of this City are sworn to the King and his legitimate issue by the Queen's Grace now had and hereafter to come, and so shall all the realm over be sworn in like manner. The bishops of Durham, Winchester, and York are now sent for, to what intent God knoweth. Some thinketh they shall to the Tower.'

An extract from a letter from John Husee in London to Lord Lisle in Calais, 20 April, 1534.

THOMAS MORE.

'Be it therefore enacted...that if any person or persons, after the first day of February next coming, do maliciously wish, will, or desire by words or writing, or by craft imagine invent, practise, or attempt any bodily harm to be done or committed to the King's most royal person, the Queen's or their heirs apparent...or slanderously and maliciously publish and pronounce, by express writing or words that the King our sovereign lord should be heretic, schismatic, tyrant, infidel or usurper of the Crown...and...being lawfully convict...shall have and suffer such pains of death and other penalties as is limited and accustomed in cases of high treason.'

Extract from the Treason Act of 1534.

These two sources give us some idea of the atmosphere in England in 1534. Opposition to the king's policies had come into the open. Measures were being taken to deal with such 'traitors'. The Treason Act was extended to cover treason by words as well as by deeds. However nobody knew how much opposition there would be. In the end was there more or less than the king and his ministers feared? This section and the Examining the Evidence section on the Pilgrimage of Grace look at the extent of opposition. These pages and the questions below focus on the opposition of individuals in the early years of the reformation.

Questions

1 What atmosphere do you think is conveyed in the two sources on this page?

2 Why did individuals oppose Henry's reforms?

3 Why could the government not tolerate such opposition?

4 Why did so few bishops oppose the changes?

5 Why do you think mass opposition, such as the Pilgrimage of Grace, did not happen earlier?

6 The papal connection, in spite of the extreme caution with which Henry had approached the matter, was cut away amidst general indifference.' (C.S.L.Davies) Explain why you agree or disagree with this statement.

Opponents and Survivors

ELIZABETH BARTON was known as the Nun or Holy Maid of Kent. When she was 16 in 1525 she had visions of the Virgin Mary, which helped her recover from illness. After that many people, including Archbishop Warham regarded her as a true prophetess and holy messenger. However she also began to speak about political matters and Henry's wish for a divorce. She prophesied that he would die if he married Anne Boleyn. She was probably manipulated by others but the government decided to make an example of her. She and five supporters were attainted of treason and executed in April 1534.

CATHERINE OF ARAGON was continually popular throughout her husband's quest for a divorce. She refused to accept his wishes and fought for her rights and those of her daughter, Mary, although Mary was barred from her company for several years. With the Act of Succession Mary was officially declared a bastard. When she went out in public Catherine was greeted enthusiastically, unlike her rival Anne, who was once referred to in Suffolk as a 'goggle-eyed whore'. When Catherine died in January 1536 Henry celebrated, dressed all in yellow. To any neutral observer her brave defiance had been far more admirable than his rejection of the woman who had been his unquestioned wife for 20 years.

THE BISHOPS OF ENGLAND originally stood against Henry's wishes. However by 1534 only one of them still sustained his opposition. Others had been intimidated; those who had died had been replaced by more 'reliable' men. Even so such a readiness to compromise may seem surprising until their background is taken into account. Most had gained their bishoprics because of their talents as administrators – the majority had degrees in law not theology. They were therefore the king's servants and would have agreed with Bishop Gardiner's view that no man's private views should stand 'against the determination of the whole realm'. Besides, they were well aware of the abuses of the Catholic Church and many of them had tried to bring about reforms before 1530. They were too practical a group not to see that religious renewal might well be more likely under the new regime.

JOHN FISHER, BISHOP OF ROCHESTER was the senior and most respected of the English bishops by 1529. Many years before he had preached at Henry VII's funeral and was now renowned for the simplicity of his life and his learning. Both sides therefore sought his support but he was staunch in support of Catherine, writing and speaking constantly on behalf of her and their church. Despite threats and a stay in prison he refused to be silenced and even appealed secretly to Charles V for armed intervention. He was arrested for refusing to swear the oath accompanying the Act of Succession and was executed in 1535. Shortly before this he was made a Cardinal by the Pope, an act that enraged Henry. Of all the events of this decade Fisher's execution aroused the greatest outrage in Europe.

SIR THOMAS MORE had been extremely critical of the state of the Catholic Church and had expressed doubts about the absolute power of the Pope. However he had far more doubts about the right of the king and particularly of parliament to legislate 'against the union of Christendom'. While Chancellor, More was spared involvement with the 'King's Great Matter' and even after he resigned he remained silent in public. Then he fell foul of the oath of succession for, although he avoided denying Henry's supremacy he did not support it by taking the oath. He was found guilty of treason, on the unsupported and possibly perjured testimony of the Solicitor General, Richard Rich, and possibly with the aid of a rigged jury. Clearly by then those who did not declare that they were for Henry were deemed to be against him. After his trial More spoke out freely, describing the changes in the church as 'a second betrayal of Christ'. He was executed in July 1535.

The winding road of religious reform, 1536 – 1540

The Dissolution loomed so large in the Pilgrims' complaints because it was the greatest symbol of the state's renunciation of Catholicism. However the Dissolution was not merely a symbol – it had immediate, practical effects for many people.

Monks and nuns were the most obvious people affected. Many were lucky in the pensions they received. The pensions were very generous for many abbots and priors, even 'reasonably generous' for ordinary monks at £5 a year, especially if they could add the income from a parish. Nuns fared far worse. £2 a year left them in severe financial plight, dependent on the support of families because they were still forbidden to marry. Fortunately most nuns came from comfortably-off families. The worst-off were the 1800 monks from the monasteries dissolved in 1536 who did not transfer to larger monasteries. They were said to have voluntarily given up monasticism and received no pension.

Just as hard hit were the people who had worked as indoor servants in the monasteries. They simply lost their jobs and faced poverty. Fellow sufferers were those who had depended on monasteries for alms. Although monasteries only used two per cent of their income for alms this had been a very significant sum, meaning survival and freedom from hunger for the individuals who received help.

Some people argued that such benefactions should be continued by the state, with some of the money gained from the Dissolution being channelled to help the poor, schools and universities. Money did go to colleges at Oxford and Cambridge or to help found new bishoprics. However most of the projected down-to-earth schemes – help for schools, hospitals, the poor, road improvement – were simply abandoned.

Less damaging to individuals but just as much a result of the Dissolution was the widespread destruction of buildings, libraries of books and church ornaments, such as jewellery, plate and candlesticks. Valuable items were melted down or sold to help swell the king's income. The rest was simply vandalism. It is little wonder that many people who witnessed such actions found it hard to believe that the reforms were inspired by spirituality or concern for the religious well-being of the nation.

As we have seen, such actions inspired wild rumours about other possible changes. Even if the very wildest did not come true there were changes in everyday religion that would have been unthinkable ten years earlier. The late 1530s saw the removal of images from churches, the destruction of shrines and of the relics of saints. These had been the touchstones of the beliefs of ordinary people. In their place came dangerous literature intended to reach every man, woman and child and subvert any remaining Catholic ideals. This was the Bible, written in English. Only a few years earlier possession of an English Bible led to prosecution and even death. In 1538 all churches were ordered to have an English Bible for public reading. The next year an official translation, largely by Miles Coverdale, was published.

The English Bible was the most important element in the establishment of Protestant ideas. Its style, which seems difficult and even impenetrable today, was to contemporaries direct and hard-hitting compared with the totally incomprehensible Latin Bible. Hearing or reading first-hand the

A PAGE FROM THE BIBLE.

words of the Bible encouraged people to talk about religion, so much so that Henry VIII complained that 'the word of God is disputed, rhymed, sung and jangled in every alehouse.' In 1543 Parliament actually tried to stop most women and the lower-classes reading the Bible, such was its subversive nature.

The development of the English Bible was the most positive statement of Protestantism. Other measures were concerned with removing the most obvious manifestations of Catholicism. Cromwell and Cranmer had to proceed slowly and only when confident of Henry's support. If they moved too quickly they risked losing everything. If that seems unlikely it is worth noting that, in the aftermath of Anne Boleyn's fall in 1536, the Pope held hopes of a reconciliation with Henry and the readmission of England into the Catholic fold.

The need for caution was also emphasised by the back-tracking that took place when necessary. In 1537 the Bishop's Book restored the four sacraments omitted by the Ten Articles, although they were regarded as less important than the first three. In 1539 the Act of Six Articles reaffirmed basic Catholic theology to the extent that two Protestant bishops – Latimer and Shaxton – resigned. This Act said that the denial of transubstantiation was heresy and confirmed the importance of oral confession, celibacy for the clergy, private masses and the permanent nature of monastic vows.

This Act continued to define official doctrines for the rest of the reign. The pendulum had stopped swinging towards Protestantism but now it simply stopped. It did not swing back towards Catholicism. Even after Cromwell's fall in 1540 the conservative faction at court could not undermine the progress of Protestantism. Perhaps it was already impossible because any attempt to restore Catholicism might be seen by the king as a challenge to his supremacy.

REVIEW
How could it happen with so little opposition?

The changes of the 1530s were such that it is hard for us, in a less religious society, to understand their significance. One modern equivalent might be the fall of the Berlin wall and the ending of single-party government in many eastern European states in 1990 but that was a change forced by pressure from below. The Reformation was largely imposed from above, by the king and his ministers. Given this, it is surprising that there was not more and prolonged opposition. How do the following quotations help to explain the lack of opposition?

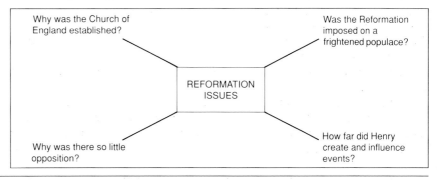

A	The condition of the English church	
B	Henry's love for Anne Boleyn	
C	The growth of protestantism in Europe	
D	The effects of foreign policy and the wars in Italy	
E	Henry's lack of a male heir	
F	Support for protestant ideas at Henry's court	
G	The impact of humanism	
H	Others?	

1 What order of significance would you put these causes in? Explain your reason.

2 Why is it difficult for historians to agree on one cause as the main reason?

3 In the nineteenth century most historians thought cause A was by far the most significant. Today far fewer historians think so. Why do you think cause A is now thought to be less important?

CAUSES OF THE REFORMATION.

Source A

'Be you of good comfort, and be steadfast in your faith and be not wavering, and God shall reward us the more. For these things will not last long, I warrant you; you shall see the world change shortly.'

A London priest in 1536.

Source B

'If it fortune the king to die, you shall see this world turned up-so down or clear changed.'

A priest in St. Albans in 1535.

Source C

'Remember how often in times past these ways hath been attempted, and what end the authors thereof hath come unto. Remember this world will not continue long. For although the king hath now conceived a little malice against the bishop of Rome because he would not agree to this marriage, yet I trust that the blessed king will wear harness on his own back to fight against...heretics.'

Dr John London in 1534.

Source D

Because the Reformation came piecemeal, the significance of the pieces was not recognized, and this was the key to its success. The conservative people of England would find a wholesale Reformation distasteful – indeed, they gagged in 1536 when they were asked to swallow, in rapid succession, the suppression of the monasteries, reformist Injunctions, and the abrogation of saints' days. But the meal was more manageable when fed in tiny morsels, and the English ate their Reformation as a recalcitrant child is fed its supper, little by little...

C. Haigh, *The English Reformation Revised*, 1987.

Was the Reformation imposed on a frightened populace?

	Treason by words	Treason by writing	Conspiracy	Others	Totals	Court politics	Pilgrimage of Grace	Total
Executions	52	1	38	19	110	20	178	308
Prob. Executions	11	0	1	5	17	4	1	22
Acquitted	11	0	2	4	17	0	15	32
Prob. Acquitted	3	0	0	2	5	0	0	5
Case Quashed	7	0	0	0	7	0	0	7
Prob. Quashed	6	0	0	0	6	0	0	6
Pardoned	9	1	23	5	38	2	56	96
Prob. Pardoned	3	0	0	0	3	0	9	12
Not Indicted	16	0	9	4	29	0	8	37
Reprieved	9	0	1	0	10	1	3	14
Prob. Reprieved	0	0	0	1	1	1	0	2
Fled	6	0	2	3	11	4	14	29
Died in prison	10	0	2	0	12	0	3	15
Prob. died	0	0	1	0	1	0	0	1
Dropped	89	2	9	13	113	1	0	114
Prob. Dropped	95	5	7	2	109	0	0	109
Unknown	68	1	2	2	73	1	0	74
Totals	395	10	97	60	562	34	287	883

Taken from G.R. Elton, 'Policy and Police' C.U.P., 1972.

The period 1532–1540 has been described as a 'reign of terror'. These figures provide evidence for the number of executions and cases in that period.
Do you think that the description 'Reign of Terror' is justified? Explain your reasons.

The future?

Amidst the uncertainties one thing is certain. The Reformation was not complete nor even its nature decided by 1540. The Church of England had been established but its doctrines might still change and a return to Catholicism was possible. The beliefs of ordinary people had, perhaps, changed least of all. The future directions of religious reform would, like the events of the 1530s themselves, unfold as the result of factors and incidents unthought of by those who set them in train. Monarchs would be central in choosing directions for the church but even he – or she – could be far from certain that the church would reach the chosen destination.

HENRY VIII IN 1530s.

Essay

'The English Reformation came about because Henry VIII needed a divorce and for no other reason'. Explain why you agree or disagree with this statement.

8 A Second Revolution? – Government 1530–1540

PREVIEW

'The plain fact is that Henry VII ascended the throne of a medievally governed kingdom, while Elizabeth handed to her successor a country administered on modern lines. Much had gone, much been freshly invented, much profoundly changed, in the intervening century, even though a great deal had been simply preserved. We are familiar with the notion that the sixteenth century saw the creation of the modern sovereign state: the duality of state and church was destroyed by the victory of the state, the crown triumphed over its rivals, parliamentary statute triumphed over the abstract law of Christendom, and a self-contained national unit came to be, not the tacitly accepted necessity it had been for some time, but the consciously desired goal.

In the course of this transformation there was created a revised machinery of government whose principle was bureaucratic organisation in the place of the personal control of the King's estate. The reformed state was based on the rejection of the medieval conception of the kingdom and the King's estate, his private concern, properly administered by his private organisation; it conceived its task to be national, its support and scope to be nation-wide, and its administrative needs, therefore, divorced from the King's household...

It would, of course, be wrong either to see no signs of such changes before 1530 or to believe that the work was all done by the end of that momentous decade. Yet the rapidity and volume of change, the clearly deliberate application of one principle to all the different sections of the central government, and the pronounced success obtained in applying that principle, justify one in seeing in those years a veritable administrative revolution. Its unity is further demonstrated and indeed caused by the personality which appears in every aspect of it. Thomas Cromwell, whose own career displayed the bureaucrat, was behind this deliberate and profound reforming activity.'

G R Elton, *The Tudor Revolution in Government,* 1953.

TALKING POINT

Choosing one extract to introduce this argument was not easy. What dangers are there in using such a brief extract from a book of well over 400 pages?

This lengthy quotation is taken from the most influential and controversial book to be written on Tudor England. Since its publication in 1953 historians have debated, supported, contradicted its conclusions, not just in terms of the 1530s or indeed the reign of Henry VIII but in relation to the whole Tudor century and even beyond. What arguments did Elton put forward? Re-read the extract above. It is not an easy passage to interpret at first so the the questions below seek only general answers. More detailed analysis follows in the next section.

---

1 What, according to Elton, was the difference between the governments of Henry VII and Elizabeth?

2 Why, according to this extract, was the decade of the 1530s so important?

3 Who was responsible for this 'revolution'?

THOMAS CROMWELL.

A Tudor Revolution in Government?

The Preview introduced the concept of the 'Tudor Revolution in Government' in the 1530s. Here is a summary of the 'revolution' thesis which will help you to identify more precisely what Elton believes was happening at that time.

Source A

'According to Professor Elton, Thomas Cromwell, whom he has elsewhere described as 'the most remarkable revolutionary in English history', seized the unique opportunity presented by Henry VIII's marital problems to turn England into a unified, independent sovereign state, ruled by a constitutional monarch through national and bureaucratic institutions. By using statute – the law made by parliament – to solve a variety of complicated legal and constitutional problems, and by exploiting the powers devolved upon him by the monarch, Cromwell was able to shift the burden of government from the personal servants of the royal household to properly organised departments of state. Thanks to his work, the King was recognised as the (divinely appointed) supreme head of an independent, but still Catholic, Church of England, with the power not only to regulate its laws and courts, but also to determine its doctrine and ritual. Royal authority was extended into the dark corners of the realm, by the abolition of the liberties and franchises, the provision of royal justice and shire administration for all England and Wales, and the strengthening of the Councils in the North and the Marches. Government and administration – very much Professor Elton's central concerns – were transformed in a number of ways: by the creation of a complex bureaucratic system (eventually comprising six separate revenue courts) to manage the royal finances; by the reorganisation of the haphazard medieval Council into a more formally constituted board of government; and by the promotion of the principal secretary (Cromwell himself) to the position of chief executive and co-ordinating minister. Moreover, Parliament's share in these dramatic events had, as Cromwell intended, important consequences for its own institutional development. The Lords and the Commons now clearly established their identity as Houses of Parliament, separate institutions within one body, and as necessary partners, albeit subordinate and occasional ones, in the business of government; statute law was shown to be universally binding, all-embracing, and free of the restrictions of natural and divine law; and a new concept of sovereignty – the sovereignty of King-in-Parliament – was established by Parliament's provision of the laws which alone made the Henrician Reformation enforceable.

'C.Coleman, 'Professor Elton's 'Revolution" in C Coleman and D R Starkey (eds), *Revolution Re-assessed: Revisions in the History of Tudor Government and Administration*, 1986.

TALKING POINT

Elton has described the administrative changes of the 1530s as a revolution. What is a revolution?

---

1 Explain in your own words what is meant by these terms

(a) household government

(b) national bureaucratic methods

(c) modern sovereign state

(d) administrative revolution

2 What was the revolution taking place in the 1530s? Again explain this in your own choice of words.

3 Copy the diagram, explaining briefly under each heading what happened to (i) parliament (ii) council (iii) finances (iv) royal control over the whole kingdom (v) the royal household.

4 Does it appear that royal power increased or decreased at this time?

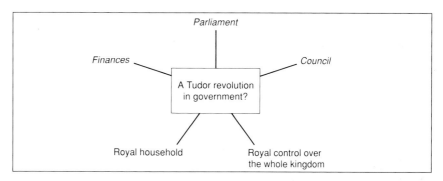

Thomas Cromwell: The man and his abilities

Thomas Cromwell, like Wolsey, came from a humble family. His father was variously a clothworker, smith and brewer who at times had been on the brink of prosperity but at others fell foul of the law. Thomas, born around 1485, left home by his late teens, exploring Europe as a soldier and merchant. He did not return to England until about 1512, by then brimful of experience and fluent in Italian and French. Once home he married and found work in Wolsey's household by 1516 – a choice of master that scarcely seems accidental. The Cardinal had plenty of intelligent servants so it is a sign of Cromwell's high qualities that he became Wolsey's leading councillor in the 1520s. He gained a wider experience in Parliament as an MP in 1523. Why was Cromwell so successful?

The answer is many-sided, like the man himself, who was far from solely interested in the details of laws and administration. Certainly he was highly intelligent. At some time he gained a legal training and was recognised as a very skilled and knowledgeable lawyer. From his work he was also well-acquainted with merchants and their trades, recognised their value and the importance of their support. He was a gifted, eloquent speaker who could persuade, encourage and flatter by his choice of words but he was also gifted with a more down-to-earth ability to get on well with people. He didn't forget old friends and he always appeared to have time to listen to the problems of the poor or unfortunate. He had enormous stamina, being able to work longer and harder than anyone else and scarcely ever taking a holiday. His memory was prodigious – he once learned the New Testament by heart while travelling to Italy!

However, these skills would not have been enough to make Cromwell Henry VIII's chief minister if he had not also been blessed with exceptional political skills and the ability to make difficult political decisions swiftly and decisively. Cromwell realised the advantages of caution and patience in politics and the need to adjust policies to circumstances. The one area where he perhaps took risks was in religion, where his beliefs were more radical and principled than those of the king, even though he said in 1538 that 'as the world stood' he believed 'even as his master, the King believed'.

Cromwell's political drive brought him power and influence. Once there he used his interest to tackle problems facing the government. Professor Elton identified in Cromwell's approach 'the recurrence of certain striking features'.

THOMAS CROMWELL. DOES THIS PORTRAIT CREATE A DIFFERENT IMPRESSION OF CROMWELL THAN THAT ON PAGE 180?

'Once Cromwell identified the existence of a problem requiring solution he formulated it precisely (often, of course, with the aid of others), devised a solution which went to the root of the issue, converted this solution into practical politics by framing a specific measure of reform (usually distinguished by its thorough exploration of the details), and lastly endeavoured to apply it with tireless persistence. These are the familiar hallmarks of successful action, and one expects statesmen to possess such qualities. Few, however, in that age or any other, have evinced them at all consistently, and fewer still with the regularity of insight, speed of execution and relentless follow through which distinguished Cromwell. Not without reason was he, who performed his promises, compared favourably with Wolsey who was forever promising without hope or intention of performing.

G R Elton, *'Thomas Cromwell Redivivus'* in
Studies in Tudor and Stuart Politics and Government, Vol III, 1983.

Cromwell possessed another quality that is less often associated with successful politicians but may well have appealed to Henry as much as the other skills – this was Cromwell's sense of loyalty. His loyalty was shown most obviously in Wolsey's final days when ambitious men might have been expected to be deserting the sinking Cardinal. Instead, according to George Cavendish, servant and biographer of Wolsey, 'there could nothing be spoken against my Lord in the Parliament House, but he [Cromwell] would answer it incontinent, or else take unto the next day, against which time he would resort to my Lord to know what answer he should make on his behalf. He was ever ready furnished with a sufficient answer, so that at length, for his honest behaviour in his master's cause, he grew into such estimation in every man's opinion, that he was esteemed to be the most faithful servant of his master, or all the others, wherein he was of all men greatly commended.'

This loyalty was also shown throughout Cromwell's service to the king. It is described by Thomas Cranmer in a letter to the king in 1540 after Cromwell had been arrested and charged with treason. Cranmer's intercession was dangerous but the danger enhances the value of his view of

Cromwell. 'Who cannot be sorrowful and amazed that he should be a traitor against Your Majesty – he whose surety was only by Your Majesty – he who loved Your Majesty, (as I ever thought), no less than God – he who studied always to set forward whatsoever was Your Majesty's will and pleasure – he that cared for no man's displeasure to serve Your Majesty – he that was such a servant (in my judgement) in wisdom, diligence, faithfulness and experience as no prince in this realm ever had ... I loved him as my friend, for so I took him to be; but I chiefly loved him for the love which I thought I saw him bear ever towards Your Grace, singularly above all other.'

Thomas Cromwell: survival, crises and execution

Such a recital of Cromwell's abilities and virtues goes a long way towards explaining his achievement but it does not present the whole picture. One crucial missing element is the atmosphere in which Cromwell had to work and this was one of perpetual uncertainty and frequent crisis. The King's quest for a divorce, the establishment of the Church of England, the Pilgrimage of Grace, the King's marriages and remarriages and struggles for influence at court all required Cromwell's energies. Amidst these events he set about improving, reforming and perhaps revolutionising the country's administration.

The mainspring of events was religion. Cromwell's reforms were a product of personal conviction as much as, if not more than, the desire to serve the King. To protect his reforms he had to fight off the influence of others, notably Norfolk and Gardiner, the Bishop of Winchester. Thus, later in this chapter, you should not picture Cromwell as an isolated civil servant, working objectively and calmly on his plans for administrative reform. Instead you need to see his administrative work against a backdrop of constant struggle for influence until his political skills, Henry's wilfulness and the unpredictability of events brought his downfall.

The first crisis, 1536

Cromwell became the King's chief minister because he could, together with Cranmer, solve Henry's problems. Even better, he could then tackle the resulting reforms with a detailed application worthy of Wolsey or Henry VII. In 1534 the triumvirate of Cromwell, Cranmer and Anne Boleyn, united by religion and mutual need, seemed unassailable. A son for Anne would be the clinching factor.

Unfortunately Anne miscarried in January 1536. Henry, already growing tired of Anne, declared that this was evidence of God's wrath. Soon it was said that Henry had been bewitched by Anne and the altogether quieter, and more submissive and less challenging Jane Seymour was being prepared for the role of Queen.

8.1 The Fall of Anne Boleyn

*A*midst the theoretical complexities of administrative revolutions, privy chambers and religious doctrines it may be a relief to turn to something as straightforward as Henry VIII's marital life. Henry tired of Anne Boleyn and married Jane Seymour. Anne was executed, on trumped-up charges of incest and adultery that meant she could be disposed of quickly so that Henry could continue his quest for a male heir. Or was it so simple?

Hypothesis A

This study of her life takes seriously the claims ... that many of her contemporaries actually viewed her as a witch. ...information from a wide range of sources will be used to support the argument that she miscarried a defective fetus in 1536. It was because Henry viewed this mishap as an evil omen, both for his lineage and his kingdom, that he had her accused of engaging in illicit sexual acts with five men and fostered rumors that she had afflicted him with impotence and had conspired to poison both his daughter Mary and his illegitimate son, Henry, Duke of Richmond. All of these are activities his contemporaries associated with witchcraft.

Since theologians and clergymen charged that god visited deformed babies upon parents who were guilty of gross sexual conduct, her husband's ministers began to search for Anne's lovers among his courtiers. The candidates chosen were those reputed to be libertines ...

R.M.Warnicke, *The Rise and Fall of Anne Boleyn*, 1989.

Hypothesis B

The plot against Anne Boleyn was most carefully calculated. Jane Seymour deliberately tantalised the king, at the same time poisoning his mind against Anne. The rest of the queen's enemies joined in the chorus when and how they could, the Imperial ambassador included. When the king agreed to a commission of enquiry into Anne's conduct, they had their chance. Jane kept the king occupied while Cromwell duly produced evidence enabling him to assure Henry that the suspicions voiced to him were indeed justified.

E.W.Ives, *Faction in Tudor England*, 1979.

Hypothesis C

It thus becomes possible to suggest what happened in spring 1536. The Countess of Worcester became pregnant. Sir Anthony Browne, her brother, berated her on her misconduct. The Countess defended her name by saying she was not the worst, and accused the Queen. Browne told two of the king's closest friends – might these have been his half-brother Sir William Fitzwilliam and Thomas Cromwell? They in turn told the King. ... What happened then, was no monstrous casting off of an unwanted wife by an utterly selfish king, no cynical and ingenious manipulation of a weak king by a conservative faction or a calculating minister, but a quarrel between one of the Queen's ladies and her brother, provoked by chance ...Perhaps the safest guess for a modern historian is that Anne had indeed committed adultery with Norris, and briefly with Mark Smeaton; and that there was enough circumstantial evidence to cast reasonable doubt on the denials of the others.

G.W.Bernard, 'The Fall of Anne Boleyn,' in English Historical Review, 1991.

EVENTS OF 1536

January **27** Anne miscarried a child.

April **24** Henry established a commission to investigate Anne's behaviour.

30 Arrest and confession of Mark Smeaton (a court musician) to adultery with Anne.

May **1** Anne attended May Day joust. Arrest of Henry Norris.

2 Arrest of Anne and Lord Rochford, her brother.

3 Arrest of Sir Francis Weston.

4 Arrest of William Brereton.

12 Trial of Norris, Weston, Brereton.

15 Trial of Anne and Rochford.

17 Execution of Rochford, Norris, Weston, Brereton and Smeaton.
Henry's marriage to Anne declared void because her sister Mary had been his mistress.

19 Anne's execution. A decree of dispensation was issued, allowing Henry to marry Jane Seymour.

30 Henry married Jane Seymour.

ANNE BOLEYN.

Source D

Unfortunately for connoisseurs of ingenious theories, there is not a shred of evidence that the foetus was deformed. The most that Warnicke can adduce is a remark of the Catholic historian Nicholas Sander, writing in 1585, that Anne gave birth to 'a shapeless mass of flesh', too vague a comment, even if it were well-informed, to prove any deformity. Apart from that, Warnicke's case rests entirely on supposition. Moreover, there is strong contemporary evidence that the foetus was not deformed. According to Chapuys, it looked like a male child which she had carried for only three and a half months....

G.W.Bernard, 'The Fall of Anne Boleyn' in English Historical Review, 1991.

Source E

Thus much for the data of Anne Boleyn's fall: powerful indications of innocence; inescapable evidence of a deliberate intention to destroy her and others; a miscellany of court and popular story with little substance, but with the potential to be manufactured into a case against them; and apparent corroboration of the Crown's case which, on examination, turns out to be an elaborated repetition of it. This is palpably no justification for suggesting that 'Anne and at least some of her friends were guilty'. The hypothesis which does satisfy the evidence is that Anne's fall was the consequence of a political coup and a classic example of Tudor faction in operation. What in the event of guilt would be unnecessary chicanery then becomes the means to an end, the immorality charges merely a weapon and the evidence of innocence irrelevant.

E.W.Ives, 'The Fall of Anne Boleyn Reconsidered', English Historical Review, 1992.

uestions

Summarise in your own words hypotheses A,B and C.

What conclusions can you reach on the validity of these hypotheses after reading Sources D,E, F and G?

Why do you think historians disagree about the causes of Anne's fall?

Why is the fall of Anne worth studying?

Source F

The fall of Anne Boleyn is not just a salacious whodunnit: it has implications for our understanding of early Tudor politics. Perhaps Henry's reactions were harsh by our standards but they were not irrational. Nor should we assume in advance of a critical scrutiny of the evidence that people who did unusual things must have been manipulated. The explanation offered here thus casts further doubt on the validity of the influential notion of faction as an explanation of political crisis in early Tudor England and raises the possibility that, on this and other occasions, Henry VIII was more in control and less the victim of factional manipulation than some recent accounts claim.

G.W.Bernard, 'The Fall of Anne Boleyn' in English Historical Review, 1991.

Source G

I do not say that I have always borne towards the king the humility which I owed him, considering his kindness and the great honour he showed me and the great respect he always paid me; I admit, too, that often I have taken it into my head to be jealous of him ... But may God be my witness if I have done him any other wrong.

An extract from Anne Boleyn's speech at her trial.

The Charges against Anne Boleyn

I Adultery with Norris, Weston, Brereton, Smeaton and her brother, Lord Rochford.

2 Imagining the king's death in words.

3 Taking the allegiance of the king's servants.

4 Conspiracy with her alleged lovers to procure the king's death.

A modern description

To us she appears inconsistent – religious yet aggressive, calculating yet emotional, with the light touch of the courtier yet the strong grip of the politician – but is this what she was, or merely what we strain to see through the opacity of the evidence? As for her inner life, short of a miraculous cache of new material, we shall never know. Yet what does come to us across the centuries is the impression of a person who is strangely appealing to the later twentieth century. A woman in her own right – taken on her own terms in a man's world; a woman who mobilized her education, her style and her presence to outweigh the disadvantages of her sex; of only moderate good looks, but taking a court and a king by storm. Perhaps, in the end, it is Thomas Cromwell's assessment that comes nearest: intelligence, spirit and courage.

E.W.Ives, Anne Boleyn, 1986.

The attack on Queen Anne was motivated by both personal dislike and religious beliefs. Those who had grudgingly to accept the establishment of the new church blamed Anne. Now they hoped to turn the religious clock back and restore the Catholic Princess Mary to the succession. Cromwell was in danger of falling together with Anne, until he took the initiative and emerged as the leader of those opposing the Queen.

Cromwell may well have saved himself by finding the way to condemn Anne, procuring evidence of her adultery with several courtiers and incest with her brother, Lord Rochford. These accusations are highly unlikely to have been true but they did play on Henry VIII's jealousy if anyone showed the slightest tendency to put loyalty to friends before loyalty to him.

Anne was executed on 19 May 1536. Cranmer wept for her but also declared her marriage to Henry invalid on the grounds of the King's earlier affair with Anne's sister. Cromwell, meanwhile, consolidated his power by turning on his allies. He accused Princess Mary's supporters, headed by the Marquess of Exeter, of planning to restore her to the succession. They lost their influence at court and Cromwell became Lord Privy Seal and Lord Cromwell of Wimbledon. His quick-footed manoeuvres had allowed him to emerge more powerful from the strife at court, his followers now surrounding the King in the privy chamber.

JANE SEYMOUR C.1509 – 1537

The second crisis, 1540

Although some of Cromwell's Catholic and noble opponents were executed in 1538 in the wake of the Pilgrimage of Grace (Lord Montague, the Marquess of Exeter, Sir Edward Neville and Sir Nicholas Carew – part of a discontented Catholic group in the south-west) there were still senior figures who opposed his influence. The powerful combination of foreign policy and religion enabled them to achieve their coup.

The projected Franco-Spanish crusade against England in 1539 did not take place. However, the threat remained and Cromwell sought a new marriage for Henry as a means of winning allies abroad. The Duke of Cleves – a Catholic already allied to Protestants – was an ideal compromise and so his daughter Anne became Henry's fourth bride, in January 1540. Unfortunately Cromwell's diplomacy faltered on Henry's distaste for Anne. 'I liked her before not well, but now I like her much worse'. With Henry now also showing his intention to put a stop to religious innovation Cromwell's enemies, Norfolk and Gardiner saw their chance.

For a time the battle for influence was inconclusive. In April 1540 Cromwell appeared to have survived when he was made Earl of Essex and Lord Great Chamberlain but in reality he was poorly placed to resolve Henry's latest marital dilemma. After all he had created it and it was Norfolk who possessed the answer – his young niece, Catherine Howard. As the marriage to Anne of Cleves had never been consummated, divorce would be straightforward.

ANNE OF CLEVES.

In the end Henry became convinced that Cromwell had failed him, the ultimate, unforgiveable, disloyalty. As the Franco-Spanish alliance fell apart it appeared that Henry need not have undergone the 'humiliation' of the Cleves' marriage. Finally Cromwell's religious convictions brought his political fall. He was accused of protecting Protestants who had been denounced as heretics and thus of failing to enforce the Act of Six

Articles. On 10 June 1540 Cromwell was arrested and on 28 July he was executed. In between he had supplied the evidence that enabled Henry to divorce Anne of Cleves. He was loyal to the last.

Few would have joined Cranmer in pleading for Cromwell's life. By 1540 his work on the king's behalf had unsettled or attacked too many individuals and groups. Those who had influence with the king were mostly only too glad to see the last of the omniscient minister. Despite this the attractive side of Cromwell was not entirely forgotten, as these words by Sir Thomas Wyatt show.

Was there a 'revolution in government'?

Having reviewed political events it is time to return to Professor Elton's hypothesis. The sources below present commentaries on his arguments.

1 For each extract identify

(a) the main points it is making.

(b) how these relate to Elton's argument using your version of the chart on page 181.

2 Which arguments do you find most convincing?

TALKING POINT

Elton has described Thomas Cromwell as 'the most remarkable revolutionary in English history' yet few people have heard of him. Why is this? Should you have studied him in history lessons when you were younger?

TALKING POINT

One issue amongst historians is transition from medieval to modern government. How would you describe the difference between the medieval and modern worlds? Can you think of other possible turning points between the two eras?

Source A

The story of transition from medieval to modern forms of government is the story of how control of policy was taken out of the sovereign's hands and given instead to ministers. That was a long process – the change was not complete until the nineteenth cenury – and the Tudor period did not represent a vital stage in the development. During the years 1500 to 1600 control of policy remained indubitably in the hands of the Crown.

Moreover when we turn from government to administration it appears that the Elizabethan system combined elements of bureaucracy with informal arrangements on a fairly large scale. ... Elizabethan administrative practice combined 'household' and 'bureaucratic' methods....

A.G.R.Smith, *The Government of Elizabethan England*, 1967.

Source B

'Cromwell's treatment of the administration did not amount to a preparation for bureaucratic government. He did not reorganise the bureaucracy. He was an improver and exploiter of what existed. His new institutions, the Court of Augmentations and the Council of the West, were based on existing models and neither survived as institutions for long. It may be claimed that in the Secretaryship and the Privy Council he produced what were virtually new institutions and that he altered the centre of gravity in the administration. Yet these changes appear to be more nearly related to the principal needs of his personal ascendancy and the position, allowed to him by the King, than to any plan for a national bureaucratic government. They were to the advantage of royal rather than bureaucratic rule.'

B W Beckinsale, *Thomas Cromwell*, 1978.

Source C

'A review of the administrative machine and its resources does not suggest that the Tudors had created a new and powerful state. The roles of Privy Council and Secretary of State were certainly extended to meet the fresh demands upon government and to assist the encroachments of the Crown into new areas of activity. Printing and literacy provided the state with important means of control, multiplied the volume of paper, and increased the amount of desk-work. But the men at the top were supported by only the most rudimentary bureaucratic apparatus. Councillors and Secretaries were inextricably involved in the minutiae of daily administration; and the Secretaries depended on their personal servants rather than a permanent corps of royal bureaucrats. Intervention by government in the social and economic life of the nation was seldom accompanied by the creation of new executive posts and enforcement was generally left to the existing officials, to local commissions, or to private enterprise. Nor was the bureaucracy well suited for the conduct of effective administration. Offices were held in plurality; meagre salaries tempted men to take gratuities and bribes; and payment by fees sparked off fierce demarcation disputes which often absorbed the energies of officials.'

P Williams, *The Tudor Regime*, 1979.

TALKING POINT

When you read a history book you should always check when the book was written. Why?

Source D

Government in the sixteenth century, unlike government in the fifteenth, did not need and did not get radical overhaul. Within its limits it worked very well; some modifications were of course required, and they took place. But they happened ad hoc and without great drama. It is always a pity to drive a great idea, Coriolanus-like, off the stage, but it must be done: Tudor readjustment in government indeed, but no revolution.

D.Starkey, 'After the 'Revolution'' in C Coleman and D R Starkey, *Revolution Reassessed: Revisions in the History of Tudor Government and Administration*, 1986.

Source E

Elton's emphasis on institutional history appears fully justified. But institutions, the institutional historian too easily forgets, are not self-sufficient entities. They are only one side of the story; the other is personality...

Just as much business was done, no doubt, when the Council dined together as when they sat in proper session, and more and more important affairs were transacted when, late at night and alone, the king and his Secretary were closeted together ...

[Henry VIII] remodelled both Council and Chamber. And all at more or less the same time, between 1526 and 1540. This is the true 'Tudor revolution in government'. It did not depersonalise government, as Elton thought. Instead it focused it more directly than before on the king's person and his palace...

There was no 'revolution in government', nor even an evolution in politics.

D Starkey, The English Court: from the Wars of the Roses to the Civil War, 1987.

In 1988 Elton re-stated 'In the running of the government of England, there was after all a major break – a Tudor revolution initiated in the days of Thomas Cromwell's ascendancy.' This clearly contradicts some of the views above. Is Elton justified in upholding his thesis? Now turn to the detail on pages 189 – 197. Your task is to decide whether, in each section, there is sufficient evidence to uphold the idea of a revolution or whether, in Dr. Starkey's words 'There was no revolution in government.'

Administrative Reforms

A. Royal power throughout the kingdom

Cromwell was well aware that in everyday matters of law and administration the king's power was not what it seemed. The most general problem was the existence of sanctuaries – churches or other recognised places which could not be entered by law officers. Such places were well known to criminals who could readily escape to them or even use them as a base for operations. In 1540 an Act of Parliament abolished the rights of most sanctuaries to shield criminals and completely abolished the right of sanctuary for serious crimes, such as murder, rape, arson and burglary.

Other areas of the country, known as franchises or liberties, offered more general freedoms from the king's officers and laws. Theoretically the king's officers could not enter or carry out justice although these freedoms were in sharp decline by 1530. Even so it was clear that the king was not treated as a King ought to be. Therefore, an Act of Parliament abolished such liberties and franchises in 1536.

The abolition of sanctuaries and liberties bears the hallmark of Cromwell. Sweeping measures were used to remove problems that might have been tackled piecemeal by others. Both saw the virtual end of medieval practices that clashed with the notion of the king's national power. In the same grand manner Cromwell tried to improve the medieval patterns of government in Wales, Calais and Ireland, but there he had more mixed success.

In Wales a council existed for governing the country and the border regions but its recent record was one of ineffectiveness. Serious law-breaking was widespread. As a first stage of reform Cromwell appointed Rowland Lee, Bishop of Coventry and Lichfield, as President of the Council of Wales in 1534. Lee has been described as a 'man totally devoid of all the human graces which could reasonably be expected in a

Christian bishop' but this was presumably why Cromwell gave him the job. Lee restored a good measure of order, allowing Cromwell to turn to a longer term solution, incorporating Wales into the English legal and administrative system. The Act of Union of 1536 established the principles. In 1543 a further Act detailed the new administrative structure. Wales was divided into shires, each with its JPs and other officers appointed by the king. Wales sent 24 MPs to Parliament and English common law replaced local customary law. English became the language of documentation and local officials.

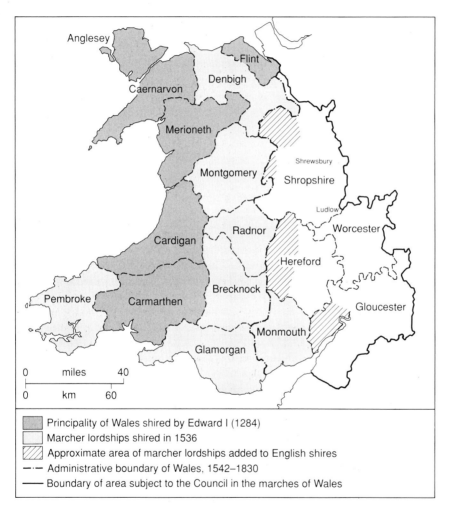

Anglesey
Flint
Denbigh
Caernarvon
Merioneth
Shrewsbury
Montgomery
Shropshire
Ludlow
Radnor
Worcester
Cardigan
Hereford
Brecknock
Pembroke
Carmarthen
Gloucester
Monmouth
Glamorgan

| 0 | miles | 40 |
| 0 | km | 60 |

Principality of Wales shired by Edward I (1284)
Marcher lordships shired in 1536
Approximate area of marcher lordships added to English shires
—·— Administrative boundary of Wales, 1542–1830
—— Boundary of area subject to the Council in the marches of Wales

Calais, England's last European possession, posed different problems. As a front-line defence and an important trading link good administration was essential but that was exactly what it was not receiving from the king's deputy, Lord Lisle. For reasons that are obscure, Lisle, an illegitimate son of Edward IV, retained his post while the administration was reorganised beneath him by a parliamentary act of 1536. Calais became part of the English system, sending two representatives to Parliament. However, it was not within Cromwell's power to remove the incompetent Lisle and, even if he had, Calais would always be an expensive burden for England to carry.

The Yorkist kings had introduced a Council of the North but Cromwell reorganised the council after the Pilgrimage of Grace and rebuilt its authority. After this the council had responsibility for law and order north of the River Trent, nominating and overseeing JPs, dealing with serious crimes including treason and also having responsibility for trade and food supplies. Through the new Council of the North the king's authority was to be more direct and rapidly felt.

Cromwell may have intended a similar role for the Council of the West, set up in 1539 after the execution of the region's leading nobleman, the Marquess of Exeter. However this council did not outlive Cromwell. Its only real impact was to establish its president, John Russell, later Earl of Bedford, as the dominant landowner and power in the region.

Overall these reforms strengthened the power of the crown and the nation became far more of a single entity with few exceptions from central control. The remaining weakness was the reliance on the voluntary aid of local landowners who, as JPs, enforced the laws. They expected to share in government and to be given some independence. This independence created the risk of failure but it could be limited by the use of trusted nobles to oversee local government in the regions. Not even Cromwell could conduct a thorough purge of incompetent or corrupt JPs without provoking hostility and a complete vacuum in local government. King and minister had of necessity to rely on the goodwill and fluctuating efficiency of local volunteers.

B. The Council

The creation of a Privy Council of about 20 members has been described as the 'crux' or the 'cornerstone' of the 'Revolution' debate. Henry VIII, like earlier kings, had a large council of over 70 even if there was an inner-core of administrator councillors who did the real work. Sometime in 1536 a Privy Council appeared, comprising about twenty leading figures, all more or less involved in the daily workings of central government. Such a body made for more efficiency, security and confidentiality and therefore it seems natural to credit Cromwell with the planning that produced the Privy Council, even more so given a note in Cromwell's handwriting on the back of a letter of 1534 'To remember the King for the establishment of the Council'.

However plans are not necessarily the same as intentions. An alternative argument, put forward by John Guy, is that the Privy Council was the product of the crisis of the Pilgrimage of Grace. Then it appeared as an emergency council with each member's signature at the foot of its orders and letters. The curious point is that the Privy Council which emerged in 1537 contained a majority of members who, as religious conservatives, were Cromwell's opponents. If he had created the Privy Council would he have filled it with so many men out of sympathy with his religious direction? Thus Cromwell, between 1537 and 1540, did not allow the Privy Council to exercise authority but instead built up his own office as King's secretary, a relatively minor post in 1534.

8.2 Ireland under Henry VIII

England had never controlled the whole of Ireland, asserting influence only over the Pale and the Anglo-Irish Earldoms. The costs of defending English territory were high but the costs of gaining complete control were impossible. Even so, Ireland, like Calais, was a financial burden that could not be given up for strategic, dynastic and nationalist reasons and, in Henry VIII's reign, England's commitment to control of Ireland increased significantly. Was this commitment part of Cromwell's revolution in government? How successful was the English policy?

STAGE 1: 1509 – 1530

Henry VIII continued the policy inherited from his father of ruling through the leading Anglo-Irish nobleman, the Earl of Kildare. This policy assumed that the interests of Crown and Kildare were compatible but, above all, it was cheap. The disadvantages of a different policy were shown in 1520–22 when the earl of Surrey was appointed Deputy but without sufficient men or money to assert his influence over Kildare's supporters. Thereafter Kildare resumed as Deputy but the English government also gave support to Kildare's rival, the Earl of Butler and suspicion and mistrust developed between Kildare and Henry.

STAGE 2: 1530 – 1540

In 1534 Kildare's son, known as Silken Thomas, rebelled against reforms implemented by Cromwell, including his father's replacement by an Englishman. Thomas was captured and executed. Kildare himself died in prison but the suppression of the rebellion had cost £40,000 and fourteen months of effort. Cromwell thus ended the policy of delegating responsibility to the Earls and established direct rule through a Lord Deputy who was, henceforward, to be English. Cromwell intended to keep much tighter control over Deputies than previously. This change also necessitated the placing of a permanent military garrison in the Pale and the revival of the Irish Parliament. Thus, Cromwell tried to realise English claims to rule non-Gaelic Ireland but, sensibly, did not attempt to extend English political rule into Gaelic Ireland. His policy towards Ireland mirrored his work in Wales and Calais. In 1536 the Irish parliament's legislation introduced the Reformation, mirroring the laws passed in England including the dissolution of the monasteries.

STAGE 3: 1540 – 1547

In 1540 the new Deputy, Sir Anthony St. Leger embarked on a new policy, aiming to bring Gaelic Ireland under English control in a single national state. The methods echoed Henry VIII's own desire in 1520 that Ireland should be brought under control by 'sober ways, politic drifts and amiable persuasions founded in law and reason'. Indeed Henry was declared King of Ireland in 1541, replacing the previous title of 'Lord'. St. Leger developed a policy of 'surrender and regrant' whereby Gaelic chiefs agreed to surrender their lands, which were then regranted to them by the king in return for their becoming vassals of the English crown and introducing English laws to their lands. The Irish chiefs gained the security of the king's support against any rival claimants. This was an ambitious but potentially successful plan that ground to a halt in 1543 because of the expense required.

Source A

Between 1520 and 1547 the nature of Tudor government in Ireland had been fundamentally altered and its claims over the inhabitants vastly extended. ... In political terms the transition from aristocratic delegation to direct rule was successfully effected by Cromwell, but militarily the position remained unstable until Gaelic opposition to an English governor and garrison was exorcised by St. Leger, and despite the king's best efforts the lordship's financial self-sufficiency was never restored. ... Where Cromwell had envisaged governing outlying English districts like the Pale, St. Leger's anglicisation programme also committed the crown to the reduction and anglicisation of the whole island. Again, the extension of the Henrician Reformation to Ireland created problems of enforcement in the lordship in the 1530s and throughout the island thereafter, although ... St. Leger's own conciliatory approach on matters ecclesiastical minimised the government's difficulties in this sphere in Henry VIII's last years. In sum, the Tudor regime was by 1541 embarked on what was administratively a highly ambitious policy, even though governmental resources there were notoriously inadequate and had not been substantially increased after 1534. Indeed, perhaps the main reason why the policy did not immediately break down, but on the contrary began rather well, was the emphasis on economy rather than rapid progress: in particular the king unwittingly assisted in this by vetoing on financial grounds all attempts to force the pace.

S.G.Ellis, *Tudor Ireland 1470–1603*, 1985.

Source B

... under Henry VIII the government had made substantial progress. The appearance of religious continuity had been largely maintained, general conformity had been imposed throughout the English districts, and even Gaelic chiefs and bishops had displayed some willingness to conform. St. Leger's strategy had dissolved the threatened combination of political and religious malcontents in the Geraldine League and disarmed a vigorous papal riposte to government policy. The papacy's failure was spelt out by the reception accorded to the first Jesuit mission to Ireland in 1542: O'Neill and O'Donnell ignored two Jesuits bearing papal letters and they departed after a fruitless four months. The government's general success is strikingly illustrated by the absence in the lordship of any general movement of popular protest akin to the Pilgrimage of Grace.

S.G.Ellis, *Tudor Ireland 1470–1603*, 1985.

Source C

... down to mid-1534 Cromwell had rather a series of ideas about what he wanted to do than any clear idea as to how to bring this about. Thereafter something more akin to a coherent policy emerges. ... In the case of Ireland the gap between intention and achievement is quite apparent, as also the extent to which Cromwell was forced to modify his policy in important respects in 1534–5, 1537 and 1539 in order to take account of financial and military realities, the views of the Palesmen, and above all those of the king. But perhaps again the lordship may not be all that untypical. Can we really be so sure that in general Cromwell envisaged, say in 1532, so much of the change which had been accomplished in England by the death of Henry VIII?

S.G.Ellis, *'Thomas Cromwell and Ireland'* in *The Historical Journal*, 1980.

Questions

1. In what ways was Cromwell's approach to Ireland similar to his approach to Wales and Calais?

2. What were the strengths and weaknesses of St. Leger's policies after 1540?

3. Most people today would expect English plans to founder because of religious differences. Was this the case by 1547?

4. What does the example of Ireland tell us about Cromwell's 'administrative revolution'?

8.3 Parliament

Simple arithmetic tells us that something important was happening to parliament in Henry VIII's reign. The 'Statutes of the Realm' containing all the laws enacted from Magna Carta in 1215 to Henry VII's death in 1509 amounts to 1092 printed pages. The statutes for Henry VIII's reign alone cover 1032 printed pages. Clearly the role and the work demanded of Parliament had changed. Did this change begin when the Reformation Parliament was called in 1529? And what exactly did happen to parliament under Henry VIII?

Source A

... it is necessary to see the pre-Reformation Parliaments in their proper perspective. They remained important occasions in the vital continuing relationship between the king and his governing class – a collaborative exercise in taxation and legislation and a sounding-board to test the acceptability of his policies. So it was a clear warning to the king when, in 1523, a member of Parliament bluntly told him that his acquisition of Therouanne, a meagre return for so much treasure and blood, had cost the Crown and the kingdom 'more than twenty such ungracious dogholes could be worth'. ... Nevertheless early Tudor Parliaments were examples of an institution which had only occasional value to the Crown and which, moreover, was notably acquiescent when it met.

M.A.R.Graves,
The Tudor Parliaments,
Crown, Lords and Commons,
1485 – 1603, 1985.

Source B

... few of Henry's subjects, including those in parliament, saw the statutes passed in this parliament as the beginning of 'the Reformation'. They could be viewed either as long-overdue rationalization of church organization, or as another round in the centuries-long dispute between popes and monarchs over control of the church, but they did not mark any substantial shift away from orthodox doctrine.

J.Loach, *Parliament under the Tudors,* 1991.

Source C

The Reformation Parliament was crucial to the development of the institution... The Cromwellian achievement had three important consequences for Parliament:

Changes in the membership of the House of Lords

1529	Summons to Parliament were issued to
	51 lay peers
	49 spiritual peers
	(20 bishops, 29 abbots and priors)
1540	Approximate membership (numbers of lay peers necessarily fluctuated a little because of deaths)
	50 lay peers
	20 bishops
1540–42	Henry created 6 new bishoprics (Bristol, Westminster, Oxford, Chester, Peterborough, Gloucester)

Meetings of the Reformation Parliament, 1529–1536

(1) 3 November–17 December 1529
(2) 16 January–31 March 1531
(3) 15 January–14 May 1532
(4) 4 February–7 April 1533
(5) 15 January–30 March 1534
(6) 3 November–18 December 1534
(7) 4 February–14 April 1536

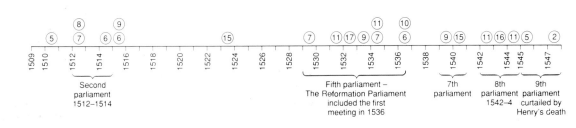

Numbers in circles = no. of weeks parliament met for
In some years there were two sittings of parliament

Second parliament 1512–1514

Fifth parliament – The Reformation Parliament included the first meeting in 1536

7th parliament

8th parliament 1542–4

9th parliament curtailed by Henry's death

Procedures
In 1532 the Commons divided (voted) for the first time on Henry's orders. Few would be publicly seen to go against the King.

Government

Influence over membership
In 1533 Cromwell ensured that vacancies e.g. for knights of the shire for Essex were filled. These were perhaps the first by-elections. This continued in other sessions.

Propaganda
Books and pamphlets were prepared, specifically to influence members of parliament.

Influence over attendance
Members of the Lords who disagreed with royal policy were told that 'they need not attend'. Abbots may have been forbidden attendance in 1536.

Questions

1 What was unusual about the pattern of parliamentary meetings under Henry VIII?

2 'The characteristic of the Reformation Parliament was consensus politics and it displayed a remarkable degree of agreement and co-operation in a period of acute crisis.' (M.A.R.Graves) How does the information in Sources A and B help to explain these characteristics of the Reformation Parliament?

3 Why might the phrase 'Reformation Parliament' confuse understandings of its original purpose and intentions?

4 What was Thomas Cromwell's contribution to the development of parliament?

5 What evidence from these pages would you use to support the statement that 'the Reformation Parliament was crucial to the development of the institution'?

1 It destroyed the limitations on statute ... Statute thereby proved its capacity to deal in matters spiritual. It also overrode the sanctity of property rights on a massive scale ... Acts of Parliament became supreme and omnicompetent law.

2 It may be that the Crown's resort to Parliament and statute for solutions to matters great and small encouraged the governing class to follow suit. Cromwell certainly set an example with his commonweal legislation on such matters as trade, industry, the control of food prices, and above all, rural depopulation and poverty...

3 ...The Crown had become an integral part of Parliament and the important distinction now was between the limited power of rex solus (the king alone) and the sovereign authority of king-in-parliament. Henry himself acknowledged both of these points when, in 1542, he informed members of the Commons 'that we at no time stand so highly in our estate royal, as in the time of parliament, wherein we as head, and you as members, are conjoined and knit together into one body politic'

M.A.R.Graves,
The Tudor Parliaments,
Crown, Lords and Commons,
1485 – 1603, 1985.

Source D

[Cromwell] devoted far more attention to parliament and its management than any minister had done before him, worrying about attendance and by-elections, drawing up lists of members for various purposes, bullying, threatening, and doubtless also praising. That this meeting is so significant in the history of parliament as well as that of the church is undeniably due in large measure to these efforts.

J.Loach, *Parliament under*
the Tudors, 1991.

Source E

Parliaments which met in war-time automatically enhanced the Commons' role as the initiator of subsidies, as was shown in 1510–15, 1523, 1542–5, 1547–50 and 1558. On the other hand ... the Lords could exert a formidable influence even on sensitive matters of the purse. More important triggers of change were the placement of the monarch's chief minister and parliamentary manager, and above all, the conduct of the two Houses. If, for example, opposition to a particular official policy or bill was likely to occur in the Lords, then it was a sound parliamentary tactic for the government to ally with the other House and place its bills there first. Henry VIII did this in the Reformation Parliament, at first because he feared the opposition of the spiritual lords and then, increasingly, because Thomas Cromwell, who sat in the Commons, managed his parliamentary affairs. However, in 1539–40 the newly-ennobled Cromwell took his seat in the Lords, and immediately the upper chamber became the more important one, where most official business was initiated.

M.A.R.Graves, *Early Tudor*
Parliaments, 1485 – 1558, 1990.

Only after Cromwell was executed did the Privy Council develop as a body, gaining its own register and secretariat. Thus Guy argues the 'Privy Council was 'created' less because [Cromwell] lived than because he died'.

Why is the role of the Council so important? The answer is that it was the body that was to give 'drive and continuity to royal government'. No longer was the drive and continuity dependent on the personality of the monarch or even on a chief minister. The Privy Council could manage the day-to-day business of governing England, leaving the monarch to take the major policy decisions. This situation had certainly developed by Elizabeth's reign – but whether it developed in the 1530s as a product of Cromwell's reforming drive is open to doubt.

C. Finance

The Dissolution of the Monasteries brought vast revenues and land to the crown, doubling the crown's income from £150,000 to £300,000. This new wealth needed to be handled efficiently and so new courts (we might say ministries) were established. The Court of Augmentations was established by Cromwell in 1536 to deal with the former monastic lands. It had a central staff and also receivers in the regions who dealt directly with each estate. The Court of Wards looked after lands that were temporarily in the king's hands because the owner had died with the heir still a child. Two similar courts appeared after Cromwell's death. The Court of First Fruits and Tenths (in 1540) dealt with revenues received from clergymen and the Court of General Surveyors (1542) looked after revenues from the older crown lands. As a group these Courts were intended to collect money more efficiently for the crown. What Cromwell did not do was sweep away the notoriously slow Exchequer and build from scratch. Nor did his system necessarily simplify matters as there was no single agency bringing together the revenue from the courts. Cromwell developed a series of ad hoc solutions to particular problems, efficient but not a master plan embodying a new start. By the 1550s Cromwell's courts were regarded as inefficient because of the lack of a centralising body and so the Exchequer was reformed and restored to its central position in financial administration.

D. The King's Household

The king's household consisted of his personal rooms and staff. Here government was carried out, centred around the king himself. Edward IV and Henry VII used the king's chamber as the royal treasury, taking in and paying out from money literally within the king's grasp. The 'revolution' thesis is that these close, personal methods were replaced by a more independent set of departments, acting in the king's interests rather than with his individual authority on every issue.

Historians' research has altered this picture too. Medieval historians have suggested that medieval government was more bureaucratic and less concentrated on the household than suggested by Elton. Others have argued that the king's Privy Chamber at the heart of the household continued to play a central role in politics and government in the 1530s and beyond. If not, why did Cromwell seek to influence the choice of personnel in the Privy Chamber? Finally Elton himself showed that

TALKING POINT

Had parliament been transformed from a medieval to a modern institution in the reign of Henry VIII?

Cromwell did not always use bureaucratic methods. He employed a treasurer rather than establish a Court to administer the First Fruits and Tenths to ensure straightforward, informal access to its funds in times of need. Overall the administration continued a mixture of household and bureaucratic styles.

Conclusions

While Cromwell was the king's chief minister current events created new difficulties to set alongside older established problems. This meant looking at existing methods of government and either increasing their efficiency or replacing them with new methods and bodies. In assessing these needs Cromwell was more clear sighted than his predecessors, more capable of producing results. However, many historians have remained doubtful whether Cromwell approached these issues with a grand plan, a blueprint for bureaucratic government. He seems to have been more pragmatic than purist, using old or new methods according to needs, engaged as he often was in fighting for his political life and, in the end, for life itself. Such distractions make a grand plan seem less likely but, conversely, they do add to Cromwell's achievement.

TALKING POINT

Do you think that Cromwell's reforms merit the description of 'medieval' or 'modern'?

Does Cromwell's work amount to a revolution?

EXAMINING THE EVIDENCE
The Role of a Historian

This chapter has explored the debate about Professor Elton's 'Tudor Revolution in Government'. This section examines some of the issues raised by the arguments. Is debate valuable? How can one historian alter or affect the work of others? Should historians only study brief periods in depth or should they study much longer periods and so develop a broader perspective over time?

The Value of Debate

Source A

... what reflections should a review in which much has been praised but perhaps more has been criticised provoke on the state of our discipline? Such disagreements, both about the conclusions presented and, in some cases, the ways in which they have been developed, should emphatically not be seen as supporting the case of those critics of the study of history who would dismiss it as worthless because historians so rarely agree and so often and so bitterly seem to disagree. First, and basically, it should be stressed that even the most contentious history contains information and ideas that add to anyone's knowledge: few, if any, works of history are totally worthless. Virtually all those noticed here are full of details that will inform their readers, whether undergraduates or specialists. Secondly, that historians disagree does not mean that they are all wrong or that it is not possible to approach the truth. No two historians are ever likely to totally agree but by their practice most historians implicitly accept that there is an historical truth, were there but sources enough to show it and human intelligence powerful enough to grasp it, and that some attempts at presenting the past are closer to that truth than others. Thirdly, it should be remembered that part of the way in which historians learn is by reflecting on how other historians have interpreted often ambiguous and scrappy evidence and how they have imposed an order on a mass of disparate information. By examining how others have interpreted their sources and deployed their arguments, they can substantially refine their own understanding. What matters here is that historians should develop a sense of historical proportion and take care to set their claims in a broad context: they should as Professor Keith Robbins has reminded us always 'stand back and ask questions, consider alternatives, probe ambiguities before expressing a view', and in that task close attention to the writings of others is immensely valuable.

G.W. Bernard, *Historical Journal*, 1988.

---

1 What, according to Source A, is the value of historical debate?

The Shoulders of a Giant

Source B

'The 'revolution' with which Professor Elton's name is usually associated is, of course, the subject of his first book, 'The Tudor Revolution in Government'. But he deserves to be associated with another. For the influence of this seminal work, and the author's continuing energy and activity within his chosen field, have revolutionized Tudor studies. Not only has he provided us with a brilliant and imaginative interpretation of the crowded events of the 1530s, but he has transformed our view of the century as a whole, and shaped our perceptions of the way in which it ought to be studied. Not satisfied with telling us what happened and why, and simplifying it all in two splendid volumes of general history, he has also taught us what history is and how to practise it. To make matters easy for us, he has taken on the tedious, but necessary, chore of providing an annual bibliography of historical literature, which has included even works not related to the sixteenth century. And when we have published our own views, he has corrected them, in over two hundred and fifty trenchant reviews. It is thus hardly surprising that so much of the published work of recent years bears the unmistakable imprint of his mind and personality.'

C.Coleman, *'Professor Elton's 'Revolution''* in C Coleman and D Starkey, *Revolution Reassessed: Revisions in the History of Tudor Government and Administration*, 1986.

---

2 Use Source B and your conclusions from this chapter. Why has Elton's work dominated the study of Tudor history?

3 'If, as the editors think, they now see some aspects of the sixteenth century a little more clearly than Professor Elton did thirty years ago, it is only because they have the advantage of standing on the shoulders of a giant.'
(C Coleman and D Starkey). Do you agree that Professor Elton is 'a giant'?

TALKING POINT

When a historian has had such a great impact is it important to learn something of his or her background and personality?

Surveys and Revolutions

Source C

'It is only when the state itself is being refashioned fundamentally that revolutions take place in the methods of government. The Anglo-Norman creation of a centralized feudal state governed by the King in his household was one such revolution. It produced a system which endured until a new kind of polity arose. ... the true driving force of government continued to be with the King in person and the men who immediately surround him. The restoration of good government by the Yorkists, Henry VII, and Wolsey, employing as they did the old methods of an elastic household system, proved that point. But the reforms of the 1530s did more than improve details of old practice. They cast off the central principle of centuries and introduced a new one. When an administration relying on the household was replaced by one based exclusively on bureaucratic departments and officers of state, a revolution took place in government. The principle then adopted was not in turn discarded until the much greater administrative revolution of the nineteenth century, which not only destroyed survivals of the medieval system allowed to continue a meaningless existence for some 300 years, but also created an administration based on departments responsible to parliament – an administration in which the crown for the first time ceased to hold the ultimate control.

G R Elton, *The Tudor Revolution in Government*, 1953.

TALKING POINT

If historians cannot agree, especially on such a central idea as the 'Tudor Revolution in Government', is the continued study and writing of history pointless?

TALKING POINT

Sir Geoffrey Elton is internationally famous amongst historians for his re-interpretations of Tudor history and his influence on other historians. To the general public he is unknown and you are unlikely to see one of his books in a popular bookshop. By contrast, queues formed to read the latest works of the most famous nineteenth century historians. Does it matter that historians such as Elton are unknown to the public?

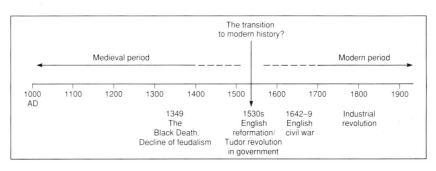

4 How does this brief survey of 900 years help to establish the significance of the 1530s as a turning point in English history?

5 Here Elton has provided a panorama of 1000 years of administrative history. What are the advantages and dangers of historians ranging widely over the centuries rather than just writing studies of clearly-defined short periods?

REVIEW

This is probably the most difficult chapter in this book. Certainly it has been the most difficult to write. There are at least two reasons for this. Firstly the subtleties of historians' debates about the 'Tudor Revolution in Government' are difficult to understand unless you have taken part in them yourself. Outsiders like this writer and nearly all readers will naturally struggle to come to terms with details and concepts that are second nature to the participants in the debate. The second reason is the absence of personalities – apart from the ever present and intriguing Cromwell – and this absence may well lead to administrative reform being, how shall I put it, less than exciting! So if it is difficult, why should we bother to study Cromwell and governmental change?

The answer lies in the thesis of the Tudor Revolution in Government. However much it has been amended and developed it is clear that something very important was happening in the 1530s that helped to shape the future of England. This 'something' included religious change, an enhanced role for parliament, the extension of effective royal power in the regions and, related to all these, the developing idea of England as a sovereign state reflected in the Act of Appeals declaration that 'this land of England is an Empire'. These developments in themselves raise the question of whether the 1530s mark a borderline between the medieval and modern worlds. The changes that took place in administration add to that argument even if they do not, in themselves, now have the same appearance of being revolutionary as when Professor Elton first put forward his hypothesis. Historians now speak about readjustment rather than revolution but, dealing more broadly than just administration, perhaps the decade still deserves to be seen as revolutionary? Elton's revolution was in government not just in administration. The establishment of the Church of England might well be seen as revolutionary.

TALKING POINT

Did the 1530s mark the transition of the medieval into the modern world?

Essay

'Revolution' or 'Readjustment'? How would you describe Thomas Cromwell's administrative and governmental reforms of the 1530s?

The idea of the age or period usually demands a consistency of interpretation so that what is regarded as characteristic of the age is seen to be manifest in all its aspects. If the distinguishing characteristic of the 1530s is that it was a revolutionary age then the tendency is to view all its aspects in terms of its essentially revolutionary character.

B.W.Beckingsale, *Thomas Cromwell*, 1978.

Essay

'The 1530s was truly a revolutionary decade for the people of England.' To what extent do you agree with this statement?

9 A Return to Tradition? 1540–1547

PREVIEW

In 1540 Henry was 49 years old. His father had died aged 52. His grand-father, Edward IV, had lived only to 40. Therefore Henry was well-advanced in years, especially as the routine of a king was gruelling, involving frequent travel and the stress of decision taking. Of course, there was always someone else to work out the details and Henry did his best to avoid work and stress with a constant round of exercise and merry-making but even these distractions had their dangers. In 1524 he had been nearly killed while jousting. In 1536 he was unconscious for two hours after his armoured horse rolled on top of him after a jousting fall. By 1540 such exercise was beyond him as his weight increased and debili-tating leg ulcers caused great pain.

With hindsight it is easy to interpret Henry VIII's last years as a time of inevitable decline and little significance. The execution of Cromwell seems to be a clear turning point. Such a pattern was not obvious to peo-ple in 1540. They might have discerned two possible routes ahead rather than one single road leading downhill to the king's death.

One route was similar to the path Henry had ambled along in the first twenty years of his reign. Then he had been indistinguishable from his medieval predecessors, seeking foreign glory while maintaining the coun-try as it was. Reform was not initiated unless it was to enhance the royal treasury. The other route was the highway of reform and revolution which Henry sped along in the 1530s.

What would be the character of the years that lay head after 1540? Would they see a return to traditional, conservative government or would the reforming movement of the 1530s continue? Would these years be important in themselves or would politicians be preoccupied by preparing for the next monarch? What would you have predicted, taking into account the issues listed below?

- The security of the Tudor dynasty
- The possibility of attack by either France or Spain
- The religious trends of the later 1530s
- Henry's character and enthusiasms
- Henry's age and health
- The ideas and attitudes of the king's advisers
- The possibility of the unexpected – in 1530 a break from Rome could not have been predicted.

	Evidence for Henry being in control of government	Evidence of this period being one of a) decline b) conservation c) change	Evidence of actual or impending crisis
Foreign Policies			
Standards of living and the economy			
Religious policies			
Faction and the succession			

Two other questions need to be borne in mind while working on this chapter. One has been a constant theme – the degree to which Henry was master of his own destiny. The other will come to the fore in the next section on Edward VI and Mary. Was there a crisis in mid-Tudor government? Some historians have dated this 'crisis' from 1540, identifying clear evidence of its causes and beginnings under Henry VII. Noting evidence on a grid like the one above will help keep track of these main themes.

The King's health

The young Henry had been a great athlete until, in the mid-1520s, he began to be troubled with pains in his foot. In May 1527 he briefly wore a velvet slipper for comfort in daytime. These pains continued sporadically but the major change in his health came in the spring of 1537 when he was first reported to have ulcerated legs. These ulcers – infected, open sores that do not heal or scab over – threatened the king's life. In April 1538 Henry's doctors decided to bandage them up. The king rapidly became speechless and black in the face. Fortunately the doctors changed their treatment. The bandages were removed and Henry rapidly recovered but not before there had been arguments over the succession, as courtiers and councillors stood anticipating the king's death.

Swollen, ulcerated legs were not the only symptom of the king's declining health. He suffered frequently from colds, constipation and bad breath. His moods were unpredictable and he became more and more lethargic. Most dramatically, his whole body became swollen as the por-

A WOODCUT OF HENRY VIII FROM THE 1540s.

HENRY VIII PAINTED BY MATSYS IN THE 1540s.

TALKING POINT

Do you think that an understanding of a politician's health and fitness is vital to understanding his or her decisions and actions?

traits from the 1540s and the size of his armour show. These symptoms have been much analysed by modern doctors, who have disappointed the gossip mongers by ruling out syphilis. The most coherent diagnosis is that Henry suffered from the rather mundane but intensely painful and damaging illness of scurvy, which is usually associated with sailors deprived of fresh fruit and vegetables on long voyages.

Scurvy can however just as easily affect people on land if their diet is inadequate and it can be protracted, lasting over 30 years if there are periods of remission when the sufferer's diet improved. Henry's diet explains why he was vulnerable to scurvy. The king and his nobles ate meat, meat and more meat, being prejudiced against earthly things such as fruit and vegetables because they formed the main diet of the ordinary people. This seasonal nature of Henry's symptoms is the final clue to Henry's sufferings. Many, if not most, of the references to his illnesses occur in the winter or early part of the year from January to April. These were the months when fresh food was least available (exacerbated by refusing to eat certain foods during Lent) and Henry's recoveries coincided with the availability of fresh food and presents of fruits from abroad as spring and summer developed.

Thus Henry was increasingly preoccupied by discomfort and pain and appeared more unpredictable to others as he fluctuated between bouts of energy and lethargy. How do you think the king's health was likely to affect the way England was governed and on the character of the years after 1540?

EXAMINING THE EVIDENCE
Portraits and Pictures

The details of Henry's health enhance the image of decline which is all too readily created simply because we know these were Henry's last years. However there is other important evidence that paints a different picture – quite literally! This section allows you to see and assess it. What does this visual evidence tell you about Henry and his ambitions in the 1540s?

Portraits of the King
Sources A – F

1 Compare Sources A, B and C. How does the presentation of the king differ in Source C from that in Sources A and B?

2 Compare the different representations of the kings in Source D. How does the presentation of the king change?

3 Why do you think the later portraits of Henry VIII in sources B – D differ from those earlier in his reign?

4 Look at Sources E and F. What messages are these portraits projecting about Henry VIII?

5 Why do you think Henry was projected in this way?

6 'With Henry's health deteriorating the king's influence was also in decline.' Do Sources A – F support this statement?

Source A

HENRY VII PAINTED BY AN UNKNOWN ARTIST IN THE 1490s.

Source B

HENRY VIII PAINTED C.1520.

Source C

HOLBEIN'S PORTRAIT OF HENRY VIII PAINTED C.1536. HOLBEIN (1497 – 1543) SETTLED IN ENGLAND IN 1532 AFTER A BRIEF EARLIER VISIT. THE HIGH QUALITY OF HIS ARTISTRY PLAYED A CRUCIAL PART IN TRANSFORMING THE IMAGERY OF THE KING.

Source D

COINS OF HENRY VIII (LEFT) AND HENRY VII.

Source F

HENRY VIII FROM WHITEHALL MURAL. THE SURVIVING PAINTING IS A SEVENTEENTH CENTURY COPY OF A MURAL BEGUN BY HOLBEIN IN 1539. IT WAS PAINTED AT WHITEHALL, HENRY'S PRINCIPAL PALACE AND CREATED A NEW, FULL-LENGTH IMAGE OF THE KING. THE MURAL WAS IN THE PRIVY CHAMBER, A DOMINATING BACKDROP TO HENRY'S OWN PRESENCE FOR THOSE WHO HAD AN AUDIENCE WITH THE KING.

Source E

HENRY VIII AND THE BARBER-SURGEONS PAINTED BY HOLBEIN IN 1540 TO COMMEMORATE THE MERGER OF THE COMPANY OF BARBERS AND GUILD OF SURGEONS.

EDWARD VI PAINTED C. 1550. WHY WAS THE YOUNG KING PAINTED IN THIS POSE?

Source G

MEDIEVAL ILLUSTRATION OF A FOURTEENTH CENTURY CORONATION.

The King and the Church
Sources G – J

7 Compare Sources G and H.

(a) What relationship is shown between the king and the church in these pictures?

(b) How do they support the view that Henry's early years were little different from those of his medieval predecessors?

8 How do Sources I and J project the power of the king?

9 What do Sources G – J and the pictures on pages 204 and 205 tell you about Henry's attitude to his supremacy in the 1530s and 1540s?

Source H

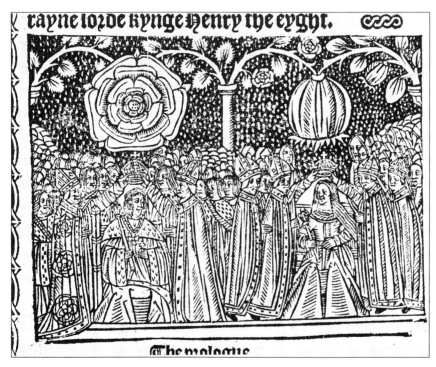

A WOODCUT OF 1510 SHOWING THE CORONATION OF HENRY VIII AND CATHERINE OF ARAGON.

Source I

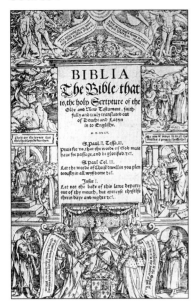

THE TITLE PAGE OF THE COVERDALE BIBLE, DRAWN BY HOLBEIN IN 1535. NOTE THE POSITIONING OF THE KING IN RELATION TO THE BISHOPS AND LORDS, AND IN RELATION TO CHRIST AND OTHER BIBLICAL FIGURES.

Source J

THE TITLE PAGE OF THE GREAT BIBLE, 1539. HENRY PRESENTS THE WORD OF GOD TO CRANMER AND CROMWELL. THE GREAT BIBLE BROUGHT THE KING'S IMAGE INTO EVERY PARISH CHURCH.

Source K

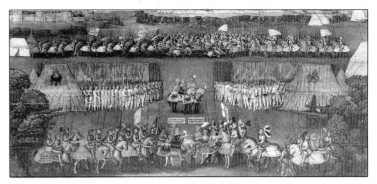

HENRY VIII MEETING MAXIMILIAN. THE PAINTING SHOWS THREE KEY EVENTS IN THE CAMPAIGN AGAINST FRANCE IN 1513. HOWEVER IT WAS PAINTED C.1545.

Source L

THE FIELD OF THE CLOTH OF GOLD, ALSO PAINTED C.1545, SHOWING THE MEETING AND RIVALRY OF HENRY AND FRANCIS I IN 1520.

The King as a soldier
Sources K – L

10 Why do you think Sources K and L were painted?

11 These pictures, together with those on page208, could all be seen by visitors to Henry's court. What image were these pictures projecting of Henry?

12 Do these pictures suggest that Henry's days as a soldier were over?

The Tudor Dynasty

Sources M – N

13 What was the propaganda message of Sources M and N for those who saw them?

14 Do these paintings suggest that Henry was feeling secure or insecure about the future of the Tudor dynasty?

15 Does the evidence in this section as a whole support the idea that the 1540s were years of decline?

Source M

THE WHITEHALL MURAL. THE FULL VERSION OF SOURCE F, SHOWING HENRY VII AND ELIZABETH OF YORK, HENRY VIII AND JANE SEYMOUR.

Source N

THE FAMILY OF HENRY VIII, PAINTED C.1545. HENRY IS FLANKED BY PRINCE EDWARD AND JANE SEYMOUR WITH PRINCESS MARY ON THE LEFT AND PRINCESS ELIZABETH ON THE RIGHT. THIS PAINTING WAS HUNG IN THE PRESENCE CHAMBER AT WHITEHALL AND WAS SEEN BY MANY MORE PEOPLE THAN THE WHITEHALL MURAL.

Foreign Policies to 1547

As you have seen, there is a good argument that the 1530s was a vital decade in the modernisation of English government, effectively forming the border between the medieval and modern eras. It is ironic that such a change came about in Henry VIII's reign for Henry was undoubtedly a medieval king in his attitudes to foreign affairs. His dreams of military glory had had to be postponed in the 1530s. Now he revived them but the consequences of his wars added greatly to the problems of his subjects.

In the 1540s Henry had twin foreign concerns, Scotland and France. Historians have debated over which concern came first. The older view is that his interest in Scotland was part of a broad plan to rule the whole of Britain and that his war with France was a separate issue, simply a product of martial ambition. More recently historians have argued that Henry's policies towards Scotland and France were intertwined as he initially became involved in Scotland in order to secure his back door prior to an attack on France. However his army in Scotland achieved early, unexpected and dramatic success and Henry was drawn much further into Scottish affairs than he had intended.

Foreign Policies in the 1530s

Before examining the validity of this view of the 1540s we need to look at foreign relations in the 1530s. Overall it was a decade when Henry was forced into a defensive role, uncongenial to him because he was unable to play a significant role in European affairs. Until the question of the king's divorce had come between them, England's natural ally had been Charles V. The one positive reason for this was the flourishing trade between England and the Netherlands. The two negative reasons were that the English claim to the French throne and the Franco-Scottish alliance naturally pushed England towards an alliance with France's enemies, who were led by Charles V.

The 'King's Great Matter' had turned this natural alliance into undeclared enmity, based on the new religious divide and Henry's treatment of Charles's aunt, Catherine of Aragon. Therefore, that diplomatic rarity, an Anglo-French alliance, became more likely but was not achieved because an uneasy peace existed between Francis and Charles between 1529 and 1536. The French did not need the help of England – especially not the help of a heretical England. However the peace had to end and war flared again between the two great powers in 1536 over their competing claims to Milan. By now the prospect of an Anglo-Hapsburg alliance had re-emerged, aided by the death of Catherine of Aragon and the execution of the 'cause' of the original division, Anne Boleyn. However the year of the Pilgrimage of Grace was not one in which Henry could have sensibly contemplated military involvement. English activity was confined to a flurry of diplomacy intended to show that European politics could not be continued without the involvement of England and her king. Europe does not seem to have agreed!

1538 saw the declaration of a ten-year truce between Charles and Francis. Urged on by the Pope, the two great powers considered a Crusade against England in the cause of the true Catholic religion. With

DEAL CASTLE IN KENT. ONE OF THE FORTRESSES BUILT IN THE EXPECTATION OF A FRANCO-SPANISH ASSAULT IN THE LATE 1530s.

TALKING POINT

Did Henry's position as Head of the Church do more to alter the style of royal portraiture than the arrival of Holbein at court?

Scotland a willing third ally, the English felt remarkably vulnerable, 'a morsel amongst these choppers' according to Thomas Wriothesley. In the south-east ditches and ramparts were dug, beacons were built and there was extensive building of castles and ships.

There were other signs of the real difficulty of England's position. This was the time when Henry showed signs of religious moderation and maybe hinted at an about-face with the Act of Six Articles. Diplomatically he made overtures to the Protestant German princes, leading to the unfortunate Cleves marriage. Finally this threat from abroad brought echoes from Henry VII's reign. Fifty years after Bosworth there were still heirs of the Yorkist kings who were regarded with suspicion, partly because of their blood-line but now also because of their adherence to the Catholic cause. The two families concerned were the Poles and the Courtenays. In November 1538 Henry Pole, Henry Courtenay, Marquis of Exeter and Sir Edward Neville were arrested and executed in the following month. Margaret, Countess of Salisbury was imprisoned. The immediate cause was the involvement of Cardinal Reginald Pole in the Catholic Crusade against England. His brother, Geoffrey, was forced to confess family involvement in treasonable activities. The Countess of Salisbury was spared execution until 1541, when another plot was uncovered in Yorkshire, involving a junior branch of the Neville family. Thus she died, forty-two years after her brother, Warwick, had been beheaded on Henry VII's order. Another echo, of an earlier reign still, was the imprisonment and disappearance of Henry Pole's small son.

Thus, if in 1540 Henry VIII looked back on his thirty years of involvement in European politics, the last decade must have made a sad and inglorious contrast with his first ten years. What was needed was action. After the religious reforms and administrative changes that had preoccupied the 1530s he could get back to his real purpose in life and the natural target for his warrior-spirit was France.

Anglo-Scottish relations

By 1540 the Franco-Hapsburg alliance was expected to break down in the near-future. Then Henry hoped to reconstitute the Anglo-Hapsburg alliance. In the meantime he could turn to Scotland because a subdued and frightened Scotland would be less likely to interfere with his attack on France and because he wanted to impose himself upon his nephew, James V of Scotland, who had, in Henry's eyes, failed to show the desired level of respect for his uncle's status as the senior monarch in Europe. Both in 1540 and early in 1541 Henry had written to James advising him how to deal with the church. These letters were, from Henry's viewpoint, sincerely helpful. To James they were intolerably patronising.

Henry's clumsy diplomacy can have done nothing to reduce James's own anti-English feelings nor the flourishing anti-English and anti-Protestant sentiments generally held at his court, led by Scotland's leading churchman, Cardinal-Archbishop David Beaton. These sentiments were reflected in James's two marriages, both to French princesses, the second of which, to Mary of Guise, may even have exacerbated the poor state of Anglo-Scottish relations. At one stage Henry had himself seriously considered Mary as a bride, only to discover that Scottish negotiations had been speedier and successful. While Europe in 1540 was littered with ladies whom Henry had briefly intended to marry, Mary's presence as Queen of Scots cannot have made Henry more tolerant of James's independent outlook.

Accordingly, Henry set out to impress his personality and views on James in person. A meeting was arranged at York, a clear sign of Henry's determination for this was to be his first visit to the north of England, a region he had regarded with great distrust and hostility since the Pilgrimage of Grace. Henry reached Yorkshire – the bedrock of these 'evil people' – in August 1541, accompanied by a huge and colourful court to impress his magnificence and power on the locals. He arrived in York on 18 September to await James's arrival. He waited and waited. James did not arrive, his council probably refusing to let him go for fear of kidnapping. This was a great and very public insult to Henry, to be repaid with force. Revenge took the form of an English attack on Scotland.

1541 also saw the end of good relations between Francis and Charles V. By the summer of 1542 Charles and Henry had reached an understanding that they would both invade France in 1543. Thus Henry launched his attack on Scotland in October 1542, his forces led by the Duke of Norfolk. The attack amounted to a large-scale piece of vandalism, Norfolk's men spending six days burning, wrecking and looting before they returned to Berwick. Scottish unwillingness to risk a war was changed by Norfolk's savagery. On 23 November a Scottish force of perhaps 20,000 men advanced on a smaller English army at Solway Moss but fled after little more than a skirmish. This was not a massive military defeat like the Battle of Flodden but Henry did gather many important prisoners. Two weeks later, James V died, of shame so it was said. He was succeeded by his week-old daughter, Mary Stuart. This unexpected and undeserved success changed the intended pattern of events. Henry had simply wanted to frighten the Scots into passivity before he proceeded with the important business of invading France. Suddenly, a different prospect had opened up – of establishing clear and permanent control over Scotland, ending the nuisance value of a kingdom which had

TALKING POINT

Allowing for your own regional prejudice, why do you think Henry VIII was so loathe to visit the north? What would his northern subjects know of him?

not had the good sense to acknowledge his overlordship. It was a sufficiently promising situation for Henry to postpone his intended invasion of France for a year. Unfortunately for Henry, a combination of Scots' determination on independence and his own ability to say or do the wrong thing at the wrong time was to prevent him from achieving anything further.

Nevertheless early in 1543 Henry had high hopes. The new Regent of Scotland, the Earl of Arran, seemed ready to co-operate with Henry and had arrested Beaton, the pillar of the Franco-Scottish alliance. The Scots parliament showed signs of following Henry's religious policies by sanctioning a translation of the Bible. Most importantly, negotiations began for the marriage of the infant Queen Mary to Prince Edward and this was enshrined in the Treaty of Greenwich in July 1543.

However all these signs were misleading. Arran was, in fact, the heir presumptive to Mary. As he had reasonable hopes of becoming King of Scotland himself one day Arran was playing Henry along while trying to consolidate his own position. When Henry tried to reassert his overlordship and demanded the end of the French alliance, Arran and the Scots parliament repudiated the Treaty of Greenwich, Beaton came back to power and the 'Auld Alliance' of France and Scotland was firmly re-established.

In reality only armed conquest could have won control of Scotland for Henry but he was not temperamentally suited to the long drawn out and determined campaign this entailed. Henry had tried to win through politics, diplomacy and trickery but had been completely outmanoeuvred. He then punished the Scots for what he saw as their treachery by sending the Earl of Hertford to burn Edinburgh and the Lowlands. This 'rough wooing' was carried out with vicious efficiency but there was nobody who would surrender to this kind of wooing. The English had lost their chance although this English terrorism was repeated in 1545. Henry had only succeeded in confirming the solidity of the alliance between his oldest enemies, Scotland and France.

England and France

In July 1544 Henry finally launched the invasion of France that he had agreed with Charles V. The plan was clear and direct. A two-pronged attack on Paris would quickly bring France to its knees, just the sort of plan that Henry would have delighted in thirty years earlier but even then he had never summoned up the strategic courage to commit himself fully to a major attack. In 1544 he was still temperamentally weighed down with caution, inclined to move his army at the same speed he himself could muster, which varied between very slow and desperately slow as he usually had to be carried in a litter. Nor could Henry's commanders, the ageing Dukes Norfolk and Suffolk, promise greater speed. Although the scale of the army (48,000 men, the largest army to leave England before the 1690s) promised much it seems inevitable that Henry's dream of a glorious defeat of the French would not be realised. Indeed, in C.S.L. Davies' words 'Probably neither Henry nor Charles ever intended to keep their bargain; it was a question of who would double-cross the other first'. Henry had 30 years' experience of being let down by allies. The result was that neither ally followed the plan through and each blamed the other.

Henry's contribution was to ignore Paris altogether. He divided his forces, Norfolk unsuccessfully besieging Montreuil but Suffolk and Henry capturing Boulogne on 18 September. On the very same day Charles V made peace with France, leaving himself free to deal with his Protestant enemies in Germany. Boulogne was therefore the only prize to emerge from the expedition and Henry determined to hold onto this evidence of his military might. This proved to be a remarkably short-sighted and subjective decision which flattered Henry's ego at the expense of the country's welfare.

THE MARY ROSE. CONFIDENT ATTEMPTS WERE MADE TO SALVAGE HER IN 1545 BUT WERE FOILED BY THE FACT THAT THE MAINMAST HAD BROKEN.

Boulogne was virtually indefensible but Henry had it garrisoned and rebuilt to withstand French attacks. The cost in the year after its capture was over £130,000, swelling the cost of the campaign to over one million pounds. While Boulogne was under siege by the French an attempt by an English fleet to support the defenders failed. The French mounted a counter-invasion in July 1545, raiding a number of south coast towns although the key French objective, the capture of the Isle of Wight, was not achieved. The English defence was, however, far from heroic. Henry had to watch his Mary Rose sink with the loss of 500 men.

These disappointments came to a close when Henry agreed to the Treaty of Camp with France in June 1546. This allowed Henry to keep

Boulogne for eight years. France also agreed to recommence paying the pension won by Edward IV in 1475, although this came nowhere near meeting the costs of the upkeep of Boulogne. Henry's last foreign adventure had been a futile disaster.

The foreign policies of the 1540s were the King's own work, pursued as a result of his own dreams and ambitions. The King himself directed policy. Even in 1546, when his councillors were urging peace upon him, he ordered different groups of councillors to negotiate with France and the Emperor, each group unaware of the other's instructions. But Henry, without a Wolsey, was not up to the task of playing a major role in European affairs. English resources did not match his ambitions and neither, by the 1540s (if they ever had), did his own diplomatic and military skills. It is difficult to improve upon Bishop Gardiner's contemporary verdict:

'We are at war with France and Scotland, we have enmity with the Bishop of Rome; we have no assured friendship here with the emperor and we have received from the landgrave, chief captain of the Protestants, such displeasure that he has cause to think us angry with him ... Our war is noisome to our realm and to all our merchants that traffic through the Narrow Seas.'

Economic Policies

Henry VIII saw war as the natural pastime of kings, reflecting his kinship with his medieval predecessors. The costs of war had, however, risen beyond the worst nightmares of Edward III and Henry V. The economic planning of Henry VIII's council was defeated by the huge cost of defences (at Berwick, Calais, Boulogne and south-coast ports), of mercenaries (more reliable but more expensive than noblemen's levies), the size of the armies and the unexpected length of the wars against both France and Scotland. The impact of Henry VIII's wars on the English economy proved to be disastrous. Prices of all goods had been rising well before the 1540s but they rose dramatically between 1540 and 1560. The major causes of this surge were the measures taken to pay for Henry's wars which, therefore, affected everyone in England in the most practical and harmful way, increasing the prices of the food they ate and devaluing the wages they received.

The financial equation was relatively simple. In a normal year the ordinary revenue received by the king from his lands, customs duties etc. just covered his normal expenses. The result was harmony because no taxation was required. However the wars of the 1540s required an annual extraordinary expenditure twice as large as the king's normal revenue. Even taxation granted by Parliament could not make up this amount. Therefore the council needed to consider and implement new options, even though inflation kept defeating their calculations.

War demonstrated the value and limitations of parliamentary taxation. Parliament granted subsidies in 1543 and 1545 but, as their instalments were spread out, taxes were being collected in 1544 and 1546 as well. The total yield was £430,000, an unprecedented sum in such a short span of years. One sign of this undesirable novelty was the growth in the gap between the expected and the actual yield, which increased from around one per cent to six per cent. In 1542 and 1545 the King also

TALKING POINT

Henry VIII had far more impact on his subjects through his wars and the resulting inflation than through his church reforms. Do you agree with this statement?

TALKING POINT

If the harvests had been poor do you think that rebellions would have been likely in the 1540s?

raised forced loans of over £110,000, bringing his income from his traditional extraordinary sources to £650,000. As this was still only a quarter of what was needed he had to turn to more desperate expedients, the sale of royal lands and the debasement of the coinage.

The sale of royal lands or, in fact, ex-monastic lands now in royal hands, was the more predictable way of finding money. Neither Henry nor Cromwell had ever intended to keep all the monastic wealth but it is hard to believe that Cromwell would have approved of such a rapid disposal of, perhaps, half the lands gained in the 1530s. One million pounds was raised but in the long-term these sales (and those that were to follow in the reigns of Henry's children) seriously diminished the freedom of the crown, for it had fewer of its own resources to fall back on and therefore needed to seek the help of Parliament and others sooner rather than later.

The debasement of the coinage had far more serious short-term results. The theory behind debasement was fairly straightforward. The government collected existing coins, melted them down and then produced new coins. The new coins were theoretically of the same value but they had less precious metal – usually silver – in them. The intensive debasement that continued from 1544 to 1551 has been described as 'a fraud instigated by the English government purely for fiscal purposes'. It was a fraud that worked, for the government gained around 1.3 million pounds in these years, a sum vital for meeting war expenses. Unfortunately the debasement also gave a sharp boost to the developing inflation. If it had not been for the good fortune of a series of good harvests between 1538 and 1547, the dissent that developed in his son's reign might well have developed under Henry VIII.

Religion

The mid-1530s ended in an atmosphere of reaction, embodied by the Act of Six Articles of 1539. The cause of this reaction was political and social rather than religious and doctrinal for the dangers of rapid change had been demonstrated by the Pilgrimage of Grace and threats from abroad. These dangers suggested that religious policy should be more cautious and Henry VIII was fundamentally a cautious man. Thus during the 1540s, he defended what he had won (notably his own supremacy) against further Protestant reforms which might provoke a conservative rebellion and against Catholic reaction that might ultimately seek a return to Rome.

STEPHEN GARDINER.

Henry involved himself in religious policy, determining both the broad directions and the detail. Thus it is hard to believe in a Catholic reaction that forced Henry to retreat from Protestantism in the 1540s. Indeed the signs are that he continued to promote his own version of doctrine, one that undoubtedly disappointed the extremists of both sides but allowed the moderate majority to accommodate themselves to the Church of England. The Act of Six Articles remained the basis of that doctrine, more Catholic in nature than the Ten Articles of 1536, but Henry urged the teaching of the Creed, the Lord's Prayer and the Ten Commandments in English. Henry's own closest involvement was in the production of the King's Book, which was a statement of the doctrines of the Church of England. This may have been written and was certainly heavily amended by the king himself. He was also insistent on restricting access to the English Bible. It was one thing for it to be read in churches and expounded in sermons but it was not to be read by 'women or artificers, apprentices, journeymen, serving men of the degrees of yeoman or under, husbandmen nor labourers'. Transgressors received a month in prison for the aim was to stop the spread of 'erroneous opinions' and dissent which might challenge the social hierarchy. Noble and gentle women were excepted and allowed to read the Bible privately, presumably because they were unlikely to challenge or question the order of society.

This social and political purpose behind religious policy in the 1540s was apparent in other incidents, which showed the king aware of the factions around him and putting social order before religious extremism. In 1543 Cranmer was attacked by his conservative enemies, headed by Gardiner. They hoped that their accusations of heresy would lead to the Archbishop's downfall but Henry defended Cranmer from the charges. This was not simply a matter of Henry's loyalty to Cranmer. The incident came in 1543, with the Scottish war in progress and the French war on the horizon. Punishment of Cranmer could have stirred major unrest, particularly in Kent where many Protestants were already feeling pressured by the conservative reaction of the late 1530s. The defence of Cranmer maintained a balance between factions divided by religion and avoided the danger of unrest in Kent.

The final piece of evidence that Henry was not being controlled by a Catholic conservative faction lies in the fate of Henry's last queen, Catherine Parr. Anne Askew, a Lincolnshire gentlewoman, was accused of heresy and under torture betrayed connections at Court which might have involved the queen, whose interest in religious reform and patronage of radical thinkers was well-known. However, the ensuing investigation did not lead to charges against the queen. In an interview with the king, which may have been stage managed, she accepted Henry's directions in religion. Again Henry had warned the radical Protestants but had also shown Catholic sympathisers that there was a clear limit to reaction.

Faction, Politics and the Succession

Henry VIII did not create another chief minister after the fall of Cromwell in 1540. According to the king, Cromwell had over-reached himself in religious reform and in negotiating the Cleves marriage. Henry did not wish to grant that degree of responsibility to anyone in future. Neither did Cromwell's enemies in the conservative faction wish to raise an individual to replace him. Their model of good government was conciliar, based on a broad council of predominantly noble origins. More decisive still, there was no one with the combination of ambition, drive and intellect which had propelled Wolsey and Cromwell to eminence. Henry had to make do with a group of lesser advisers and, in the 1540s, this suited him very well.

Henry's role in government continued to be as significant and as spasmodic as it had been ever since 1509. The detail of foreign affairs, war and religion sometimes enticed him. More mundane matters were left to the Privy Council, which at first seemed likely to be dominated by the conservative faction, led by Norfolk and Bishop Gardiner. The conservatives had dual objectives – personal power and a counter-reformation in

CATHERINE HOWARD C.1523 – 1542.

CATHERINE PARR C.1512 – 1545.

MARY TUDOR, (1496 – 1533) HENRY VIII'S SISTER, AND HER HUSBAND, CHARLES BRANDON, DUKE OF SUFFOLK. MARY'S FIRST HUSBAND WAS LOUIS XII OF FRANCE AND WHEN HE DIED MARY WAS INTENDED FOR ANOTHER DIPLOMATIC MATCH. INSTEAD SHE SECRETLY MARRIED SUFFOLK. HENRY'S ANGER WAS IMMENSE BUT SHORT-LIVED.

religion, moving back towards Catholicism, further indeed than Henry had gone in 1539. When the succession issue arose in the mid-1540s these twin aims were united in a drive to control the minority of Henry's heir. However they did not succeed and, by 1547, had been decisively outmanoeuvred by a faction that had not existed in 1540, comprising an amalgam of courtiers, noblemen and civil servants, held together by a combination of ambition, self-preservation and general support for the cause of religious reform.

Why did the conservatives fail to secure and hold onto power? The answer lies in the king's attitude and the membership of the faction. Henry himself appears to have been unwilling to allow one faction to dominate, seeming to encourage Gardiner at one moment and then, when Gardiner hoped to bring about the fall of Cranmer in 1543, supporting Cranmer. Certainly Henry had no wish to reverse his religious changes as this might detract from his supremacy as Head of the Church.

Important too were the individuals concerned. By the 1540s the Duke of Norfolk was an ageing figure who should have been handing over his influence to the younger generation but his son, the Earl of Surrey, was too irresponsible to be seen as a political leader by seriously ambitious men. Bishop Gardiner was very able and an effective politician but he spent nearly all of 1541 as ambassador to Charles V and therefore his influence was lost at a crucial time. Others, like Sir Thomas Wriothesley and Lord Russell, were, essentially, supporters rather than leaders. Most dramatically, the conservatives' trump-card was thrown away, when Norfolk's niece and Henry's fifth queen, Catherine Howard, was convicted of treasonable adultery and executed.

Henry's marriage to Catherine had been a triumph for the conservatives. Their enemy, Cromwell, had given Henry a wife he detested on sight. They had given him a young and pretty girl, apparently intoxicated with love for the king. Unfortunately Catherine's delight was short-lived. She had had lovers before she met the king. Now she committed adultery, an act of treason for which she was arrested and executed. Like Anne Boleyn, she was a victim of politics. Catherine had been dangled in front of the king by her uncle, Norfolk, the bait in their political trap despite the fact that she was temperamentally wholly unsuited for the role of queen. If Henry had destroyed the Howards he might well have been forgiven by a twentieth century mind for destruction seems a just reward for their manipulation of Catherine. The short-term imprisonment of Norfolk's mother, brother and sister-in-law seems to fall short of justice. Even more so was the way Norfolk and Gardiner escaped any formal punishment although they were, doubtless, very frightened by events. They owed their escape to the presence of supporters in the Privy Council.

The king's preoccupation with war and diplomacy in the mid-1540s appears to hide the domestic political rivalries but, in reality, they were sharpened by war. Norfolk had not emerged from the French campaign with credit. Suffolk had been more successful but died in 1545. As a result new commanders won fame, notably Edward Seymour, Earl of Hertford (Jane Seymour's brother and therefore Prince Edward's uncle) who commanded the army against the Scots and John Dudley, Viscount Lisle who was Lord Admiral. Both men were also very ambitious and inclined to Protestant reform.

Therefore, in the middle 1540s a new grouping was developing, with Hertford as its natural leader, in view of his closeness to Prince Edward, his office of Chamberlain of the Royal Household and his military prestige. Also central to this grouping was Catherine Parr, whom Henry married in July 1543. Catherine was a widow aged 31, as different from Catherine Howard as was possible. She too was a Protestant reformer. Her brother William Parr, Earl of Essex, was a rising courtier and her brother-in-law, Sir William Herbert, was to become chief gentleman of the Privy Chamber.

Indeed the Privy Chamber was the vital source of this group's influence. The senior figure there was Sir Anthony Denny, who controlled access to the king. As, by 1546, Henry emerged less and less from his private apartments this power became increasingly important. The gentlemen of the Privy Chamber in the 1540s were very different from the young, athletic and sometimes frivolous characters who had surrounded Henry in his early years as king. Denny himself was over 40, serious and interested in books and learning, well able to meet the older Henry's needs for discussion and consolation in matters religious and philosophical. Politically astute, Denny allied himself with the rising Hertford group. So too did Sir William Paget, the ablest administrator of the period, the king's secretary and a key member of the Privy Council.

EDWARD SEYMOUR, EARL OF HERTFORD. UNDER EDWARD VI HE BECAME LORD PROTECTOR AND DUKE OF SOMERSET.

1546 was the crucial year. The prize was control of the government after Henry's death, for it was clear that he would not live to see his nine year old son reach adulthood. The Hertford faction's immediate objective was to consolidate and confirm their position during the rest of Henry's lifetime. For their conservative opponents there was a pressing need to regain influence over the king or power and their religious ideals would disappear during the minority.

The intensity of this struggle is most clearly seen in the attempts made by the conservatives to link Anne Askew, who was executed for heresy, to the queen's circle of religious reformers. If evidence of heresy had been found then the whole of the Parr-Hertford group might have fallen, once again leaving the field clear for the conservatives. Hence the belief that two of the Privy Council, Wriothesley and Rich, personally turned the rack to torture Anne Askew in their desperation to extort the names of their rivals.

The late summer of 1546 saw the Hertford faction tightening its control. A key change came in August when Denny was given control over the 'dry stamp'. This apparently boring administrative item was political dynamite. The dry stamp was a mirror-image of Henry's signature. To save him the immense effort of signing his name, an official pressed this stamp onto the document so that it left an impression. Then the official inked in Henry's signature. At first Henry had retained the stamp and given permission for its use. Now Denny kept it and decided when it should be used. This created the opportunity to act independently of the King.

At the turn of the year the conservative faction was dismembered. Gardiner was removed from the Privy Council and barred by Denny from personally interceding with the king. Wriothesley and Rich were enticed into Hertford's camp by offers of a share in the patronage and prizes that would come during the minority. That left only Norfolk and Surrey and Surrey's careless ambition played into their opponents' hands. He was accused of treason, of aiming for the crown himself, on the basis

A PAGE FROM HENRY VIII'S WILL. SINCE THE TEXT OF THIS BOOK WAS WRITTEN (1992), PROFESSOR IVES HAS CHALLENGED THE VIEW THAT HENRY'S WILL WAS TAMPERED WITH BY THE SOMERSET FACTION. HE ARGUES THAT THE FINAL WILL WAS HENRY'S OWN WORK AND REFLECTS HIS WISHES TO PREVENT DISPUTES DURING HIS SON'S MINORITY. HOWEVER, SOMERSET EXPLOITED A LOOPHOLE IN THE WILL TO SEIZE POWER AS PROTECTOR.

TALKING POINT

This introductory paragraph is critical of Henry VIII. Is such criticism anachronistic because Henry and his nobility would have regarded war quite differently from the way we do?

of his remarks about his ancestry and his choice of decorative coats of arms for his window glass. Both Surrey and his father were convicted of treason. Surrey was executed on 21 January 1547 and Norfolk was scheduled for execution on the 28th. Norfolk was saved by the king's own death only hours before he was due to face the axe.

Henry's will has caused historians immense problems, probably almost as many as it caused the politicians who awaited the king's death with some impatience. For the king's will was not signed until after he died! For a month Henry seemed close to death. He altered his will to exclude Norfolk and Gardiner from the regency council after the arrest of the Howards in mid-December. His major revisions, on 26 December, left the Crown to Edward, Mary and Elizabeth successively and created a regency council of 16 named members to govern until Edward was eighteen, but the will was not signed before Henry died at 2 am on 28 January. Using the dry stamp to its fullest potential, his signature was added after his death, together with a clause giving the council 'full power and authority' to take any action it thought necessary for the welfare of the country during Edward's minority. Another clause was added or rewritten, empowering the Council to award any gifts that Henry had intended to make but had not made officially. Both these clauses were rapidly used by Hertford to establish his position as Protector.

So died Henry VIII, amidst scenes that typify much of his reign. Cranmer, whom the king trusted far above all others in religious affairs, held the dying man's hands. His son was entrusted to a council dominated by Protestant reformers. This was almost certainly what Henry intended (why else had he allowed Edward to taste the atmosphere of reform amidst the reformers patronised by Catherine Parr?) but somehow he had not quite got round to signing his will. In so much else he had hesitated and delayed until pushed into action by circumstances or by more decisive minds. At the last he was no different.

REVIEW

In many ways the 1540s saw a return to traditional kingship. Henry was pre-occupied with war, diplomacy and his status abroad. Images of the king betray his belated attempts to realise the dreams of his youth. However he was far less successful than he had been thirty years earlier and his foreign wars plunged the country into economic crisis. French wars had always affected the people of England – positively by boosting morale, creating a sense of nationality and bringing captured wealth, negatively through deaths, taxation and French attacks on the south coast. However no earlier French war had come near the practical impact of Henry's wars in the 1540s, given the way they boosted steadily growing inflation. For the second time in his reign Henry had affected the lives of every man, woman and child in his kingdom.

1 The paragraph above makes a number of judgements about the 1540s. How far do you agree that

(a) the 1540s saw a return to traditional kingship?

(b) Henry's foreign adventures were unsuccessful?

(c) Henry's wars created a crisis by damaging the lives of his people?

2 Do you think that his wars had more or less effect on the people than his religious changes?

3 Read the quotations below.

(a) What similarities and differences are there amongst the views quoted?

(b) Which view or views of Henry's role in the 1540s do you find convincing?

4 Would 'Years of Decline' have been a more appropriate title for this chapter than 'A Return to Tradition'? Explain the reasons for your choice or the reasons for another title that you think would be better.

Source A

'Cromwell had no successor. No one minister would ever again monopolize the conduct of affairs in Henry's reign. ... Henry can be seen – as he could be seen in 1530 and 1531 – as the dominant policy maker. The Council suggests, discusses, pleads; problems are tossed between it and the king; ambassadors are sent to and fro between them. But the policy which it executes is essentially the king's.'

J.J.Scarisbrick, *Henry VIII*, 1968.

Source B

'The King probably thought (after all, he had good reason to) that he was in charge; his ministers and courtiers equally seem to have thought and behaved as though they could manipulate the King. Perspective is all. ... There was in fact no novelty in the outstanding features of Henry's behaviour in the 1540s – like his tendency to postpone decisions till the last possible moment and then take them in a rush, often late at night; or his fondness for secret messages, rings, tokens and the whole apparatus of cloak-and-dagger. They are present throughout the reign ... The difference lay not so much in Henry as in circumstance. In the earlier crises overwhelming pressure finally forced a decision out of him. In the 1540s, on the other hand, the pressures were so finely balanced that his natural indecisiveness was never overcome.'

D.Starkey, *The Reign of Henry VIII: Personalities and Politics*, 1985.

Source C

'It is often argued that the Privy Council contained no one of Cromwell's talent in 1541–7, therefore Henry VIII consciously decided upon 'personal rule'. This is misleading. Cromwell's fall marked the triumph of adversaries who justified his overthrow as a victory for 'conciliarist' over 'ministerial' government. It is clear from the Privy Council's own registers that nine privy councillors best described as loyal 'Henricians' or politiques ran the country (and the wars) until the king's death. Although Henry intervened, he did so spasmodically and in matters that had always concerned him: diplomacy, military strategy, theology, and his wives.'

J.Guy, *Tudor England*, 1988.

SECTION REVIEW

Questions

1 Would you make any changes or additions to the description of Henry's personality in Source A?

2 Portraits of Henry tell us more about the man, his nature and his development than do any number of written sources. Do you agree with this statement?

3 Henry VII had been a most successful king. To what extent was Henry VIII's personality well-suited to sixteenth century kingship?

Henry VIII in perspective

Heaven smiled and the earth rejoiced when Henry VIII became king, or so the flatterers said. The 'courageous and wise' young monarch was praised for his 'exceptional and almost more than human talents'. Despite the exaggerations Henry was a talented man. How did he develop as a king? This review offers the chance to come to some overall conclusions.

Henry the man

Source A

He was a formidable captivating man who wore regality with splendid conviction. But easily and unpredictably his great charm could turn into anger and shouting. When (as was alleged) he hit Thomas Cromwell round the head and swore at him, or addressed a lord chancellor (Wriothesley) as 'my pig', his mood may have been amiable enough, but More knew that the master who put his arm lovingly round his neck would have his head if it 'could win him a castle in France'. He was highly strung and unstable; hypochondriac and possessed of a strong streak of cruelty.

... for all his power to dazzle, for all the charm and bonhomie which he could undoubtedly sometimes show, and for all the affection which he could certainly give and receive, it is difficult to think of any truly generous or selfless action performed by him and difficult not to suppose that, even those who enjoyed his apparently secure esteem, like Jane Seymour or Thomas Cranmer, would not have been thrown aside if it had been expedient to do so...

J.J.Scarisbrick, *Henry VIII*, 1968.

Source B

From first to last he was a dangerous and appalling animal, and the physical decline from splendid adolescence to bloated and sick old age did not signify a similar decline in his character, which was deplorable from the first. Complete selfishness and the ruthless pursuit of private advantage always marked a man who invariably discovered that God and his conscience conveniently backed his desires... Only Henry VIII solved all his problems by killing – killing innocent wives and loyal servants – on the principle that the best way out of difficulties was to sacrifice scapegoats. The fact that he was handsome in his youth and intelligent all his life should not disguise a horribleness which piled up corpses in his day and problems for a century after.

Henry and Faction

Source C

That Henry was central is beyond question, his will was law, but one has to ask how his attitudes and decisions were formed and by whom. There is no contradiction between a dominant Henry and a Henry dependent on others for information and advice, whose courtiers staked a lifetime and sometimes life on the conviction that he was vulnerable to pressure.

E.W.Ives, *'Stress, Faction and Ideology in Early-Tudor England* in
The Historical Journal, 1991.

Source D

Revisionist voices have of late been raised against the suggestion that 'faction' is a helpful concept for the understanding of Tudor society and Tudor politics. At a human level the objection is understandable – historians, like everyone else, are tempted to react against something which threatens to become a new orthodoxy, ... But historians are, nevertheless, obliged to take evidence seriously. Hypotheses which do not may be more interesting, but only those which grapple with the record as it actually exists are entitled to consideration. Thus, if Thomas Wyatt writes about the pressures and choices implicit in the life of a courtier, he must be taken seriously. When all the ambassadors in London report to their governments in 1529 that powerful groups were plotting against Wolsey, that must be taken seriously. 'Faction' is a phenomenon which cannot be ignored by historians of the sixteenth century, because at the time, both Englishmen and strangers alike took it for granted...

THE MOST FAMOUS IMAGE OF HENRY VIII PAINTED BY HANS HOLBEIN C.1536. IT IS ONLY 28 X 20 CMs.

It is equally important, however, not to go to the other extreme. 'Faction' is not a universal and all-sufficient explanation for every problem in Tudor history. Suggestions that Wolsey's fall was 'nothing but faction' would be puerile. The events of 1529 were shaped by a variety of factors ranging from Italian ecclesiastical politics and the interplay of European diplomacy, through the niceties of canon law and theology, to the personalities and relationships of the leading protagonists. To argue for a role for faction is not to deny all this. It is, rather, to suggest that the interplay of these factors was significantly affected by political alignments in the court and beyond.

E.W.Ives, *The fall of Wolsey* in *Cardinal Wolsey, Church, state and art,* (eds.)
S.J.Gunn and P.G.Lindley, 1991.

Source E

In other periods and in other countries, the role of factions and ministers, so strongly emphasized in much historical research undertaken in the late 1960s and early 1970s, has subsequently been questioned or diminished, and the part played by kings and queens seen as much greater. ... Close scrutiny of politics tends to undermine the impression of ministerial dominance or factional manipulation, impressions so often based on a single remark drawn out of context, or on crudely mechanistic models of the operation of politics: but perhaps it should not be so surprising that in an age of personal monarchy kings and queens ruled as well as reigned.

G.W.Bernard, *'The Fall of Anne Boleyn: A Rejoinder'* in
English Historical Review, 1992.

4 Read Sources C, D and E. How do the authors differ about faction?

TALKING POINT

Source D suggests that
faction was at one time a
fashionable interpretation
of events. Why might
such a view of Tudor
politics be fashionable?

Source F

Empson and Dudley fell at the beginning of Henry's reign, not 'by the
malice of them that with their authority in the late king's days were
offended', but because Henry himself thought it politically expedient that
they should go. ... Wolsey's long period of office rested upon his favour
with the King. He did not purge the Privy Chamber of young courtiers
who were supposedly a threat to his influence with the King: the King
himself, reacting to their boisterous and idle behaviour, sent them away
from Court to do a proper job of work and acquire greater maturity.

G.W.Bernard, '*The Fall of Anne Boleyn: A Rejoinder'* in
English Historical Review, 1992.

5 The extracts in Source F come from a longer passage describing key events of
Henry VIII's reign. In this passage Henry himself is seen as the initiator of political developments.

(a) Choose other incidents and describe them from the same standpoint.

(b) Now adopt the interpretation that Henry was much influenced by factions.
Rewrite the two incidents in Source E and your choice of incidents using the
factional interpretation.

6 Why, despite the extent of historians' knowledge, does this debate about faction continue?

7 What is your view of Henry VIII and faction? What evidence would you use to
support your conclusion?

The significance of Henry's reign

Source G

The compilation of the Valor Ecclesiasticus (a work cast on the scale of Domesday Book), the imposition of the oaths of Succession and Supremacy, the immense operation of dissolving the religious houses and distributing their property, the heavy taxation of the lay and clerical estates, the marshalling of large forces by sea and land, all this over and above the achievement of an ecclesiastical and doctrinal revolution, was a concentrated display of the power and ubiquity of central authority the like of which had not been seen hitherto ... never before had Parliament been called upon to carry out so vast and consequential a programme of legislation as that which came onto the statute book between 1529 and 1545 ... Henry's reign in many ways left a deeper mark on the mind, heart and face of England than did any event in English history between the coming of the Normans and the coming of the factory.

J.J.Scarisbrick, *Henry VIII*, 1968.

Source H

... early phases of the Reformation were indecisive, ... major Protestant advance took place mainly in the Elizabethan period. It was only in the latter part of the sixteenth century, when a Protestant regime remodelled commissions of the peace and diocesan administrations to give power to supporters of reform, when the redistribution of clerical patronage weakened conservative interests and when the universities produced a supply of committed preachers of the new religion, that Protestantism had a real and widespread impact.

C.Haigh, *'The Recent Historiography of the English Reformation'* in C.Haigh (ed.)
The English Reformation Revised, 1987.

Source I

... change, although considerable, was not total; Parliament in the sixteenth century was still recognizably the same body as its medieval predecessors. ... Parliament, at least until the 1580s, and probably beyond, was a medieval institution. It met only when summoned by the sovereign, who could prorogue or dismiss it at will. ... The House of Lords still played an important, and perhaps dominant, role in many areas of legislation...

J.Loach, *'Parliament: A 'New Air'?'* in C.Coleman and D.Starkey (eds.) *Revolution Reassessed, Revisions in the History of Tudor Government and Administration*, 1986.

---

8 Do you think that the people of England experienced greater security, peace and wealth during the reign of Henry VII or of Henry VIII? What evidence would you use to support your argument?

Henry VIII – A Balance Sheet

Henry had great charm and the ability to win and keep the affection of people of all ranks.	Henry was ruthless, willing to kill others for his own benefit – 'it is difficult to think of any truly generous or selfless act performed by him'.
He led England into wars, reviving old glories and winning short-lived prestige.	Wars brought no lasting gains and helped to cause great economic problems, including inflation, following the debasement of the coinage.
Henry left a son to succeed him and there was no succession crisis.	He created the crisis himself by seeking to annul his marriage to Catherine. If Henry had died between 1529 and 1537 there would have been a far graver crisis than if he had accepted Mary as his heir.
Henry left England politically more centralised and integrated and the crown richer because of wealth from the monasteries.	Henry created deep and long-lasting religious divisions that were, in the future, to play a large part in deposing kings and causing hatred between communities.
He was a great patron of building, building more than any other Tudor monarch, notably at Whitehall and Nonsuch and St. James's Palace.	Henry's religious change destroyed the beauties of monastic architecture and works of art in glass, wood, plate and vestments. They also destroyed people of integrity and courage, including Fisher, Aske and Catherine of Aragon.
Henry raised hopes that monastic wealth would be spent on schools, hospitals and the poor – providing for the common weal.	The great bulk of monastic money went to landowners or to finance wars. Little social improvement resulted.

BASED ON J.J. SCARISBRICK, *HENRY VIII*, 1968, CHAPTER XV.

TALKING POINT

Do you agree with the contents of this balance sheet? What evidence would you use to support or challenge it?

9 Were Henry VII and his son chiefly responsible for their subjects' security, peace and wealth or were these largely the product of other factors such as harvest successes and failures?

10 Do you agree with Professor Scarisbrick (Source F) about the significance of Henry VIII's reign?

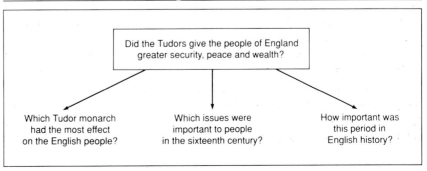

Did the Tudors give the people of England greater security, peace and wealth?

Which Tudor monarch had the most effect on the English people?

Which issues were important to people in the sixteenth century?

How important was this period in English history?

SECTION 3 PREVIEW

Edward VI and Mary: Crises, Consolidation or Achievement?

Forgettable Tudors?

Henry VIII and Elizabeth have a good claim to being the most well-known monarchs in British history. Certainly theirs are the faces that spring to mind when the word 'Tudor' is mentioned. The other Tudors – Henry VII, Edward VI and Mary – are overshadowed by the long reigns and dramatic deeds of Henry VIII and Elizabeth. Who would make a film or write a novel about the first three when you could focus on the glamour of either of the other two? Around 1970 BBC TV did make two highly popular series – on Henry VIII and Elizabeth. A similar series on Henry VII flopped!

TALKING POINT

Many novels and films have been written and made about the Tudors. Are they a valuable resource for students of the period?

EDWARD VI.

MARY I.

There is a danger for students that these popular attitudes can be transferred into historical studies of Edward and Mary. You may be ready to move on from Henry VIII but you're probably not as naturally inquisitive about Edward and Mary as you were when starting work on Henry or you will be when trembling on the brink of Elizabeth. If you have low expectations you probably won't be surprised to discover that some historians have seen the years from 1547 to 1558 as years of low achievement, even failure, and of crisis. Your low expectations may pre-condition you to accepting such interpretations. Worse, you may assume that these were two reigns of little importance and that you will have to get through them as best you can, gritting your teeth against the boredom. To start you thinking about the reigns of

TALKING POINT

How have your preconceptions of the Tudors been changed by your studies so far?

Edward and Mary, suggest answers to the questions below, perhaps after talking them over with others. You can reconsider them at the end of this section.

1 Look at the portraits of Edward and Mary.

(a) What words would you use to describe the characters portrayed?

(b) Why might problems develop because of the monarchs themselves?

2 Complete the boxes in the grid below, basing your answers on your knowledge and your expectations of Edward and Mary.

3 Do you expect either Edward VI or Mary to affect the lives of English people to the same extent as Henry VII or Henry VIII?

ASPECTS OF CRISIS

	What signs of crisis were evident 1540–1547?	How might Edward and Mary affect policies?	Were problems likely to get better or worse?	Is the idea of crisis justified?
Religious policies				
Foreign policies				
Economies/ Standards of Living				
Faction, peace and law and order				

Political and Religious Change 1547 – 1558

These dozen years saw three different political regimes. Under Edward VI, England was ruled first by the Duke of Somerset and then by the Duke of Northumberland. Then came the reign of Mary. Each of these three phases saw different political and religious policies being implemented and this required adjustment and decisions by those involved in government. This decision-making activity is based on the early career of a young man called William Cecil. Later in life he was to become Elizabeth's chief adviser and the man she trusted above any other. Yet events before her reign began could have brought Cecil's career to an end. What would you have done in the situations that faced him?

Cecil's early life

The family fortune had been begun by William's grandfather, an obscure Welsh gentleman called David Syssil or Sitsilt. David had joined Henry Tudor in 1485 on his way to Bosworth and, presumably, fought in the battle. Afterwards he became a member of the Yeomen of the Guard, Henry's private bodyguard, became an MP and was given lands in Stamford in Lincolnshire. David's son served Henry VIII as a page at the Field of Cloth of Gold and gained more land for the family after the dissolution of the monasteries. Clearly, loyalty to the Tudors was bred in young William.

William was born in 1520 and was educated at Grantham Grammar School and Cambridge University, where he studied law. In 1541 he married his first wife, Mary, but she died only two years later, leaving him with a young son. His second wife, Mildred, was the daughter of Sir Anthony Cooke, Prince Edward's governor, suggesting that William was winning support at court. Mildred was a formidable and alarming character, speaking fluent classical Greek, and she was a good match for William. He entered the king's service, reputedly because he was overheard defending the king's supremacy against two visiting Irish priests. As he had been only 14 at the time of the Act of Supremacy William had grown up accepting the Church of England and had no experience of lengthy loyalty to Rome.

Decision 1

In the first part of Edward VI's reign William Cecil established himself as a talented and able young man. He became private secretary to the Protector, Edward Seymour, Duke of Somerset (formerly Earl of Hertford). Being closely associated with Somerset he must have been concerned when Somerset's position began to crumble in 1549. Widespread risings in the

WILLIAM CECIL, LATER LORD BURGHLEY.

summer then gave Somerset's opponents the chance to force him from office. Somerset and then Cecil himself were imprisoned but then released. The new leader of the Council, the Duke of Northumberland, readmitted Somerset to the Council but their rivalry had not ended. What should Cecil do?

(a) accept the opportunity to work for Northumberland?

(b) refuse the offer and continue to work for Somerset in the hope that his plotting will recover power?

(c) stay out of governmental office and try to reconcile the two men privately?

Decision 2

Cecil's efforts to reconcile Somerset and Northumberland were to no avail. Somerset's scheming only led to his own rearrest in 1551 and execution. After this, Northumberland's government continued efficiently and Cecil became the junior of the king's two secretaries, putting into practice the orders of the council. Early in 1553 the previously healthy Edward fell ill and it rapidly became clear that he was dying. His heir was his sister, Mary, a devout Catholic, and neither Edward nor Northumberland wanted a Catholic ruler. There was no time to call parliament to alter the succession so Edward and Northumberland launched a scheme to change the succession in favour of Lady Jane Grey, who did have a claim to the throne and was the Duke's daughter-in-law. Cecil was asked to sign the document agreeing to change the succession. Should he

(a) sign the document, obeying Northumberland, who was also expected to imprison or even execute opponents?

(b) refuse to sign because the process was unlawful and it meant disinheriting the rightful Tudor heir?

(c) flee to join Mary and hope she would be successful?

Decision 3

Cecil was therefore embroiled in the attempt to prevent Mary gaining the throne. However Northumberland had little real support and, when Mary began to gather support, the half-hearted councillors abandoned the Duke. He was arrested but the future was still worrying for Cecil and the members of the council. Mary was known to be intent on restoring Catholicism and did not trust her brother's councillors, who were tainted by their pro-Protestant policy and their involvement in Northumberland's scheme. Once Mary appeared to have triumphed the council decided to send its secretary, Cecil, to the Queen to proclaim their loyalty. Should he

(a) escape into exile abroad just in case Mary took vengeance?

(b) go to meet Mary, declare his loyalty and beg for mercy?

(c) refuse and return to his estates and live quietly in retirement?

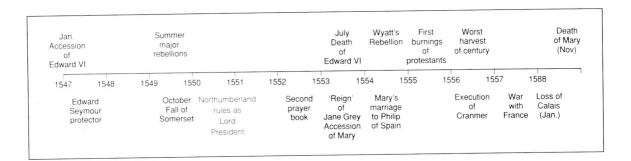

| 1547 | 1548 | 1549 | 1550 | 1551 | 1552 | 1553 | 1554 | 1555 | 1556 | 1557 | 1588 |

Above the timeline:

Jan. Accession of Edward VI — Summer major rebellions — July Death of Edward VI — Wyatt's Rebellion — First burnings of protestants — Worst harvest of century — Death of Mary (Nov)

Below the timeline:

Edward Seymour protector — October Fall of Somerset — Northumberland rules as Lord President — Second prayer book — 'Reign' of Jane Grey Accession of Mary — Mary's marriage to Philip of Spain — Execution of Cranmer — War with France — Loss of Calais (Jan.)

Cecil's Choices

Decision 1
Cecil, as a Tudor servant, would have had no difficulty in deciding to work for the new regime as he was still serving Edward VI. Refusal might have created suspicions and he had little to gain personally by supporting Somerset. Out of office he would have had little chance of acting as a go-between but, while serving Northumberland, he did his best to reconcile the two men.

Decision 2
Although Mary was Catholic, Cecil and nearly all the other councillors found it impossible to ignore their duty to the Tudor dynasty. Therefore he refused, although a letter to his wife reveals that he expected execution. Then the decision was taken out of his hands for he was ordered by the king to sign. Again, as a good Tudor servant, Cecil had no choice but to sign.

Decision 3
Cecil prepared two hide-outs, one near the Thames, and used his influence in his home area to prevent Northumberland raising troops. He did travel to meet Mary on behalf of the council and was forgiven after he told the queen his story. He may have stressed that as an official he had even less choice in obeying Edward VI than had the councillors. However he did not hold government office under Mary, even though she used most of Edward's councillors because she needed their experience and skill. Cecil was too loyal to the Tudors to oppose Mary directly. He lived on his estates until Mary's death. Since 1550 Cecil had also been surveyor of Princess Elizabeth's lands. He continued to serve her during Mary's reign and returned to government when she became queen.

TALKING POINT

What have you learned about
(a) attitudes to the Tudor dynasty?
(b) the nature of political life in the sixteenth century?
(c) the qualities needed by successful politicians?

10 Edward VI: 'Woe to thee, O land, where the king is a child'

PREVIEW

Boy Kings

HENRY III aged 9 in 1216. Henry inherited the throne in the midst of a civil war fought by his father, John, and rebellious barons aided by King Louis of France. Fortunately Henry's supporters quickly defeated their own opponents, whose chief complaints had been directed at John himself. Henry's minority saw many quarrels in council but no return to civil war. These were years of comparative stability compared with John's reign or Henry's own later years.

RICHARD II aged 10 in 1377. Richard also inherited the throne in a time of crisis. His grandfather, Edward III, had relinquished control in his last years to councillors who were in turn unsuccessful and unpopular. Plagues, defeats by France and heavy taxes added to discontent and caused the Peasants' Revolt in 1381. 14 year old Richard was the hero of the hour, riding out to confront and disperse the rebels. Once in control, Richard exacerbated rather than healed divisions amongst his nobles, creating enemies who, in self-preservation, forced his deposition in 1399, aged 32.

HENRY VI aged 9 months in 1422. Henry's father was the great soldier-king, Henry V, victor of Agincourt. Henry's minority lasted 15 years until 1437, a time of rivalries amongst factions in council but the French empire was retained and England was relatively peaceful. England declined into disorder and civil war, losing her French territories, once Henry VI became King and supported one faction, pushing other powerful noblemen into the political wilderness.

EDWARD V aged 12 in 1483. Edward was king for only 3 months, the victim of a power struggle between his paternal uncle, Richard, Duke of Gloucester, and his mother's family. Richard usurped the throne, deposing Edward, and shortly afterwards Edward and his younger brother disappeared. Contemporaries assumed that they had been murdered. This overshadowed Richard's reign, for the murder of children was beyond any moral code. Revolt followed quickly and Richard was overthrown in 1485, having failed to win much support despite his efficiency.

EDWARD VI aged 9 in 1547. Henry VIII's will had established a governing council but Henry's last years had seen a harsh struggle for power between factions. The more radical religious group had emerged victorious.

1 What problems arose during minorities?

2 Was Edward VI likely to be deposed?

3 Would any problems during his minority necessarily end when Edward VI came of age, probably at 16?

4 Do you think the quotation in this chapter title was justified by the events of medieval minorities?

Edward VI – The Boy King

Edward's boyish interests can be glimpsed occasionally – stopping the coronation procession to watch an acrobat, complaining that the Duke of Somerset restricted his 'pocket money', being beaten for lack of attention to his lessons. However, this boy-king had to cope with powerful lords kneeling before him, crowds cheering his appearance, simply being regarded as more important than anyone else. This may sound attractive but for a youngster who must often have had only a limited understanding of events, politics and people it would frequently have seemed frightening and intimidating. The natural reaction was to become reserved and aloof and, gradually, to assume that he was always right and should be obeyed.

It is difficult to assess young Edward's qualities accurately, given the natural tendency of contemporaries to praise him whenever there was an opportunity. Roger Ascham wrote 'The ability of our Prince equals his fortune, and his virtue surpasses both ... he is wonderfully in advance of his years', but then the quality of his education was far in advance of anyone other than a handful of other royal and noble children. He was trained in Latin and Greek, modern languages and astronomy, history and geography, archery, music, hunting and other courtly pastimes.

Did young Edward influence the events of his reign? One vital point is that his early death was not expected, given that he was a healthy child until his last six months. Therefore, although still a child, his ideas and beliefs did have an important impact on politicians. In religion, Edward was a convinced Protestant and the increasingly radical policies of Somerset and Northumberland were in part a reflection of the young king's wishes. Neither could have expected to continue in Edward's favour when he assumed power if their actions had not been in tune with Edward's wishes.

Edward's influence was even felt in the last months of his reign. Seeking to safeguard his religion, he worked with Northumberland to exclude his Catholic sister, Mary, from succession, naming Jane Grey as his heir. Edward thus created a situation which could have led to civil war. Edward may not have wielded the full powers of a king but his influence should not be assumed to be insignificant.

Issues and Questions

The dominant personalities of the reign were the Dukes of Somerset and Northumberland. Somerset held power as Lord Protector from the earliest days of the reign until he was removed from office in October 1549.

TALKING POINT

Do you think that the political events of his childhood affected Edward? Is it useful for historians to consider the childhoods of rulers and politicians?

Northumberland did not use the title of Protector but retained power until toppled by Mary Tudor. The achievements of these two men have been thoroughly reassessed by historians in recent years. Earlier praise of Somerset has been replaced by criticism whereas Northumberland's reputation has risen, at least in part because Somerset's has fallen. Comparison is made easier because they faced the same range of problems – religion, foreign war, social and economic discontent – but tackled them differently.

EDWARD SEYMOUR, DUKE OF SOMERSET.

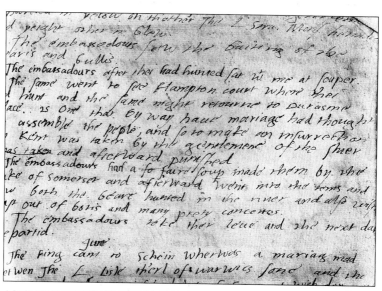

A PAGE FROM EDWARD VI'S JOURNAL, PROBABLY KEPT AS A PIECE OF 'HOMEWORK'. IT LACKS SPONTANEITY, RARELY REVEALING THE YOUNG KING'S PERSONALITY.

Somerset's rise to power

At the time of Henry VIII's death (27 January 1547) Edward Seymour was still Earl of Hertford and merely one of the 16 councillors appointed in Henry's will to govern on behalf of Edward VI. However Seymour seized power with great efficiency. The way had been charted by the loopholes in Henry's will. The governing 16 had been named but were able to dispose of power as they thought fit. Hertford acted immediately, personally fetching his nephew Edward VI to London and presenting him to the council. On 31 January the council named him Protector and governor of the young king. Key assistance came from the leading administrator, Sir William Paget. Later, near the end of Somerset's protectorate, Paget wrote to Somerset: 'Remember what you promised me in the gallery at Westminster before the breath was out of the body of the King that dead is. Remember what you promised me immediately after, devising with me concerning the place which you now occupy ...'

So far, so good for Hertford but, even as Protector, he was theoretically one of the councillors, not their master. The next stage was to implement another vague clause in Henry's will, concerning gifts which Henry had, perhaps, intended to give if he had been spared. Councillors were raised in the peerage, Lord Lisle, for example, becoming Earl of Warwick. The Earl of Hertford himself became Duke of Somerset.

All naturally needed gifts of land to suit and justify their new status. The potential opposition of Lord Chancellor Wriothesley was bought off with the Earldom of Southampton. In March Somerset achieved sole power. He was given the power to appoint the king's councillors – no longer was he simply one of them. They were dependent on him for their offices. He was in practice a substitute king during his nephew's minority.

Foreign Affairs – Scotland and France

Somerset's political career had been initiated by his sister Jane's short-lived marriage to Henry VIII but it had been consolidated by his successes in Scotland in the mid-1540s. It is not therefore surprising that Scotland was at the centre of Somerset's interests and ambitions while Protector. Unfortunately for Somerset, initial success quickly disintegrated amidst vast expenditure of money with the result that, by the autumn of 1549, his failure in Scotland had done much to undermine his position as Protector.

Somerset wanted to see the 1543 Treaty of Greenwich implemented, with Edward VI's marriage to Mary, Queen of Scots leading to a union of the two crowns. His strategy was to wear Scotland down by the imposition of a series of forts and garrisons in the south and east of Scotland, expecting (or hoping) that their presence would eventually persuade the Scots that resistance was useless. He got off to a good start, winning a smashing victory at the Battle of Pinkie (only nine miles from Edinburgh) in September 1547. Somerset then set about building up his garrisons but the policy was not a practical success, partly because of strategic mistakes, partly because it only increased Scottish hostility and partly because of influences beyond his control.

Somerset's mistakes were to give the Scots breathing space, failing to capture either Edinburgh or Dunbar and to enforce the naval blockade of the Firth of Forth. This allowed Scottish resistance to stay alive and to receive aid from France, now led by the youthful, aggressive Henry II. Henry had succeeded Francis I in March 1547 and was determined to assert his superiority over the English. Somerset was unlucky in this timing as Francis would have been more cautious but it is equally true that Somerset did not combat French influence in Scotland. He failed to work with the 'Assured Scots' – Anglophiles opposed to French influence.

In June 1548 6,000 French troops landed in Scotland. They established their own forts, captured some of the English ones and, far worse, covered the departure of Mary, Queen of Scots to France, where she was intended to marry the Dauphin, the heir to the French throne. Mary was now out of reach of an English marriage, thus removing the central feature of Somerset's policy. This might have been the moment to admit defeat and withdraw but this was not a real possibility when Somerset had invested so much, financially and psychologically, in Scotland.

To defend England's weakening position, Somerset sent three more armies to Scotland, in August 1548 and in January and July 1549. These were now defensive measures, designed to safeguard what had been won earlier, but economically the cost was very damaging. Somerset spent over half a million pounds on war in Scotland, 50 per cent more than Henry VIII's expenditure in only half the time.

On top of this Somerset faced humiliation from France. He did his best to avoid war but Henry II declared war in August 1549, taking advantage of the deterioration in Somerset's position in Scotland. Faced by war Somerset offered to return Boulogne immediately (rather than in 1554 as agreed by treaty) but Henry confidently demanded Calais as well. The loss of both and therefore all English lands in France was impossible to accept but this only led to more fortifications and more expense. The French attack on Boulogne was beaten off – just.

In September 1549 Somerset withdrew his forces from Haddington, his chief fortress in Scotland. The Scottish war had been an expensive failure, seriously damaging Somerset's reputation, making his removal from power easier. His achievement had been to unite the Scots and the French even more strongly against England.

Could Somerset have been successful? The answer is no, for conquest or domination of Scotland was virtually impossible for reasons of geography and costs. However, it was also virtually impossible for him not to make the attempt, given the background in the 1540s. To back away from war, apparently leaving Scotland open to French influence would not have appeared an auspicious or even honourable opening to Edward VI's reign. Perhaps Somerset need not have thrown good money after bad once Mary, Queen of Scots was in France but again such a view would only have been possible for an outstanding politician and ruler like Henry VII. Somerset simply followed in his master, Henry VIII's, footsteps. In due course Northumberland did adopt a different policy towards Scotland and France, but that was in 1549, not 1547, with the full knowledge of the problems and errors of Somerset's policy.

TALKING POINT

The Scottish war has been described as 'A war that could not be won'. Was it also 'a war that could not be avoided'?

Religious Reform – a balancing act

Radical Protestant reformers must have been optimistic in the spring of 1547. The Catholic party had been routed by Somerset and the new Protector was sympathetic to reform. King Edward was avowedly Protestant. Radicals who had fled England in the wake of the Act of Six Articles therefore returned, some to places in Somerset's own household. Reform did take place but not on the scale such people wanted, for the reforms were such that they still allowed the veteran traditionalist, Bishop Gardiner, to accommodate himself to the new regime. By the time of Somerset's fall in October 1549 the religious situation was still confused, some have said chaotic. Radical Protestants and some historians might well be displeased by this 'chaos'. More moderate commentators might discern a sane compromise that attempted to follow William Paget's advocacy of reforms 'as God be pleased and the world little offended.' Unfortunately enough people were offended and the religious reforms played a part in causing the rebellions of 1549.

Why was there compromise instead of a clear cut Protestantism? The answer lies both abroad and at home. To give himself a chance of success against the Scots and the French Somerset had to prevent Charles V joining forces against him. The cost of the Catholic Charles's neutrality was a cautious approach to reform. England was also a divided country. Protestantism had made little or no headway in the south-west, the midlands or the north. In these regions the danger was that further reform would push people into rebellion. There was, however, a very vocal Protestant minority in the south east, East Anglia, Bristol and London. Only 20 per cent of Londoners were committed Protestants but after Henry VIII's death they anticipated change by abandoning the mass, using English for services and stripping images from the churches. Minority though they were, Somerset could not risk disappointing them either. He also needed to pursue reform policies desired by the king. Hence the religious policy of Somerset's protectorate was to reform to appease the reformers but to do so in such a way as to avoid pushing traditionalists – from Bishops to peasants – into revolt. Somerset was well-suited to this as a moderate supporter of reform who was not sufficiently interested in theology to worry about doctrinal niceties. He would not persecute people if they chose to interpret a word or phrase differently. The policy almost succeeded.

For most people the most dramatic changes were visual, thanks to the sweeping away of the 'superstitions' so hated by radicals. Images were demolished, pictures of saints in stained glass windows were destroyed, wall-paintings were covered. Candles, ashes and palms no longer appeared at Candlemas, Ash Wednesday or Palm Sunday. Chantries (where masses had been sung for souls of the dead) were finally dissolved. The appearance of churches changed profoundly, which may have led some of those who rebelled in 1549 to over-estimate the changes that had taken place in doctrines.

The government's resolution of doctrinal debate came with the Book of Common Prayer, enforced by the Act of Uniformity in 1549. The Book of Common Prayer was initiated by the council, which ordered Cranmer to draft 'one convenient and meet order, rite and fashion of Common Prayer.' Approved by the Bishops, its emphasis on 'Common Prayer', that is on the participation of the congregation in prayer, was clearly Protestant. Previously congregations had devoutly witnessed the priest communicating with God on their behalf. The new book also set out to affirm that the communion service commemorated rather than re-enacted Christ's sacrifice. But the wording was ambiguous, allowing even Gardiner to interpret the service in a Catholic manner. Conservatives also took comfort from the retention of altars and priests' continued use of their traditional vestments.

To some contemporaries – radicals who hoped for clear, direct and far reaching Protestant reform – Somerset's religious policies were a failure. They excused the compromises 'lest the people, not having yet learned Christ' should be deterred by too extensive innovations from embracing his religion' but they could not have been happy. However there is much more to be said for compromise. Protestant refugees were welcomed to England at the same time as Princess Mary's Catholicism was tolerated; the Act of Six Articles was repealed; Somerset allowed many Protestant texts that had been banned by Henry VIII to be printed; priests were permitted to marry; Bishop Bonner of London was imprisoned for opposition but there were no executions, a far cry from the events of other reigns.

In downgrading Somerset's achievement, historians may have gone too far, in the religious sphere at least. A.G.R. Smith's assessment redresses the balance – the Book of Common Prayer was a 'shrewd, statesmanlike

TALKING POINT

Why were some areas of the country usually the first to embrace new ideas while other regions resisted them?

TALKING POINT

C.S.L. Davies has described the Prayer Book as 'a remarkable achievement'. John Guy has said 'it failed because it was ambiguous: neither Catholics nor Protestants accepted it'. Which of these views would you agree with?

The Population of England	
1541	2,774,000
1546	2,854,000
1551	3,011,000
1556	3,159,000
1561	2,985,000
1566	3,128,000

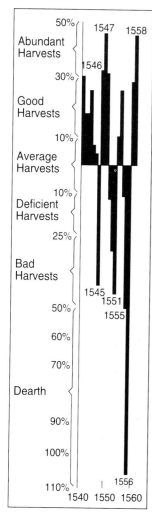

HARVEST QUALITY 1540 – 1560. THE GRAPH SHOWS PROFESSOR HOSKIN'S ESTIMATE OF WHEAT HARVEST QUALITY. THE GRID ON p238 PROVIDES A DIFFERENT INTERPRETATION BASED UPON OTHER CROPS.

measure' and his religious policy overall was 'the best possible for the country in circumstances when it was dangerous to go either too slowly or too far'. Even so, religion played a significant part in the rebellions of 1549.

Economic Difficulties

The economic legacies from Henry VIII's reign were just as problematical as those in religious and foreign affairs. Inflation was rapidly increasing prices (especially of all staple foods except for grain, whose prices stayed low from 1547 until the harvest of 1549) and thus reducing the value of wages. The long-term cause of these price rises was population growth but war and the debasement of the coinage had been very significant short-term boosts to the problem. One councillor, Sir Thomas Smith, did identify the problem correctly and argued that the only solution was recoinage to reverse the effects of debasement. This was economically wise but politically impossible, given that the Scottish war required more ready cash, not less.

The general view was that rising prices were the product of greed on the part of self-interested landlords, who were enclosing land, thus depriving agricultural labourers of land and work and therefore reducing the quantity of food available for sale. The prevailing atmosphere demanded that 'something must be done' and Somerset was prepared to support those who said they could provide a solution.

In 1548 and 1549 commissioners were appointed to investigate enclosures, but only one, headed by John Hales in the Midlands, proceeded. Hales did find evidence of illegal enclosures but, apart from ploughing a symbolic furrow across the Earl of Warwick's parkland, could do nothing practical to reverse enclosures. Landowners objected to interference with their right to do as they wished with their land. Parliamentary legislation was blocked. Somerset issued a proclamation to coerce landowners into reversing enclosures – an act that could not have endeared him to many other members of his class.

Another notable critic was Hugh Latimer, Bishop of Worcester until he had resigned in protest against the Act of Six Articles. Latimer denounced the greed of 'lording loiterers' and 'unpreaching prelates'. He was certainly not preaching social equality but those who heard him (or heard reports of his words) might have been forgiven for assuming he was attacking the nobility as a whole.

'For ever since the prelates were made lords and nobles the plough standeth; there is no work done, the people starve. They hawk, they hunt, they card, they dice; they pastime in the prelacies with gallant gentlemen ... if the ploughman of the country were as negligent in their office, as prelates be, we should not live long, for lack of sustenance.'

Latimer's fellow Protestant, Nicholas Ridley, Bishop of London, was another agitator, seeking workhouses and hospitals for the poor of London. They and others like them stirred the hopes of the people, suggesting that salvation from economic and social problems was at hand. It wasn't. Enclosure was the wrong target. The Protector was preoccupied with Scotland and, for all his support for Hales, as opposed as any of his class to challenges to the social order. All in all, the years 1547–1549 were a thoroughly confusing time. It seems that the death of Henry VIII released all kinds of hopes and tensions, encouraging people to talk, to offer ideas on religion, economics and society. Somerset encouraged this atmosphere and, in religious matters, controlled developments with some skill. In economic and social affairs he was much less successful. He raised the hopes of the poor with proclamations on social justice but failed to meet them. He raised the fears of the landowners without then calming them. The result was riot, rebellion and his downfall.

1549 – the Year of Rebellions

Revolts
- May in Somerset, Wiltshire, Hampshire, Kent, Sussex, Essex
- June in Devon and Cornwall (The Western Rising)
- July in Oxfordshire, Suffolk, Yorkshire, Cambridgeshire and Norfolk (Ket's Rebellion)
- August in Leicestershire, Rutland

As this list shows, disturbances were widespread. In most places the local gentry dealt with the troubles. Troops intended for Scotland were used in Oxford and Suffolk. However, forces had to be raised to deal with the major outbreaks of revolt in the south-west and in Norfolk and they ended with battles. 2,500 rebels were killed by Lord Russell's army in Devon. The Earl of Warwick's men killed 3,000 in Norfolk.

The Western Rising began at Sampford Courtenay in Devon on 10 June and spread quickly through Devon and Cornwall. The rebels besieged Exeter but the Protector, busy with other risings, at first responded by offering a pardon on condition the rebels dispersed. The rebels refused and drew up their demands while the siege continued. Not until early August did government troops arrive to raise the siege and defeat the rebels, again at Sampford Courtenay on 16 August.

Ket's rising in Norfolk began in early July. Robert Ket, a prosperous tanner, was not the instigator but quickly assumed the leadership and led 16,000 men to Norwich. There the authorities cooperated, fearing that the high unemployment in the town allied to the rebels' arrival could lead to widespread destruction. However the rebels maintained good order and petitioned the Protector, again receiving an offer of pardon if they dispersed, together with a sympathetic hearing of their complaints. Dissatisfied, the rebels took control of Norwich and then beat off a small royal army. A large army, led by Warwick, only arrived on 23 August. This led to many rebels taking the re-offered pardon but many others fought and died. Ket and other leaders were executed.

These two major risings each lasted two months. Why did they take place? How effective was the Protector's handling of the situation?

Decade		1540 to 1549	1550 to 1559
Wheat (Hoskins)	Abundant and Good	6	4
	Deficient Bad and Dearth	2	4
Average of all Grains (Bowden)	Abundant and Good	8	1
	Deficient, Bad and Dearth	2	5

EXAMINING THE EVIDENCE
The Rebellions of 1549
Source A

1 Fyrst we wyll have the general counsall and holy decrees of our forefathers observed, kept and performed, and who so ever shal agayne saye them, we hold them as Heretikes.

2 Item we will have the Lawes of our Soverayne Lord Kyng Henry the viii concernynge the syxe articles, to be in use again, as in hys time they were.

4 Item we wyll have the Sacrement hange over the hyeyhe aulter, and there to be worshypped as it was wount to be, and they whiche will not thereto consent, we wyl have them dye lyke heretykes against the holy Catholyque fayth.

7 Item we wyl have holy bread and holy water made every sondaye, Palmes and asshes at the tymes accustomed, Images to be set up again in every church, and all other auncient olde Ceremonyes used heretofore, by our mother the holy Church.

8 Item we wil not receyve the newe servyce because it is but lyke a Christmas game, but we wyll have oure olde service of Mattens, masse, Evensong and procession in Latten not in English, masse, as it was before. And so we the Cornyshe men (whereof certen of us understande no Englysh) utterly refuse thys newe Englysh.

9 Item we wyll have everye preacher in hys sermon, and every Pryest at hys masse, praye specially by name for the soules in purgatory, as oure forefathers dyd.

> Extracts from the final manifesto of the south-west rebels, drawn up outside Exeter.

Source B

... Where ye declare that thoocasyon of being able to levie so fewe in Somersetshire is the evil inclynation of the people, and that there are amongs them that do not styck openly to speak such traterous words agaynst the kyng and in favour of the trayterous rebells. Ye shall hang two or three of them, and cause them to be executed lyke traytors ... sharpe justice must be executed upon those sondrie traytors which will learne by nothing but by the sword.

> The Lord Protector and Council to Lord Russell, army commander in the south-west, 27 July 1549.

Source C

1 We pray your grace that were it is enacted for inclosyng that it be not hurtfull to such as have enclosed saffren grounds for they be gretly chargeablye to them, and that from hensforth noman shall enclose any more.

2 We certifie your grace that where as the lords of the manours hath byn charged with certe fre rent, the same lords hath sought meanes to charge the freholders to pay the same rent, contrarye to right.

3 We pray your grace that no lord of no mannor shall comon uppon the Comons.

4 We pray that prests from hensforth shall purchase no londs neyther ffre nor Bondy, and the lands that they have in possession may be letten to temporall men, as they wer in the fyrst yere of the reign of Kyng henry the vii.

5 We pray that Redeground and medowe grounde may be at suche price as they wer in the first yere of Kyng henry the vii.

8 We pray that prests or vicars that be not able to preche and sett forth the woorde of god to hys parisheners may be thereby putt from hys benyfice...

16 We pray thatt all bonde men may be made ffre for god made all ffre with his precious blode sheddyng.

17 We pray that Ryvers may be ffre and comon to all men for fyshyng and passage.

20 We pray that evry propriatorie parson or vicar havyng a benefice of £10 or more by yere shall eyther by themselves or by some other persone teche pore mens chyldren of ther paryshe the boke called the cathakysme and the prymer.

> The articles listed by Ket's rebels in East Anglia – the articles omitted here were on the same themes as those included.

Source D

I told your Grace the trouthe, and was not believed: well, now your Grace seithe yt what seythe your Grace? Mary, the King's subjects owt of all discipline, owt of obedience, caryng neither for Protectour nor King, and much lesse for any other meane officer. And what is the cause? Your own levytie, your softnes, your opinion to be good to the pore. I knowe, I saye, your good meaning and honest nature. ... societie in a realme dothe consiste and ys maynteyned by meane of religion and lawe ... Loke well whether youe have either lawe or religion at home, and I feare youe shall fynde nether. The use of the old religion is forbydden by a lawe, and the use of the newe ys not yet prynted in the stomaches of the eleven of twelve partes in the realme, what countenance soever men make outwardly to please them in whom they see the power restethe. Now, Syr, for the lawe: where ys it used in England at libertie? Almost no where. The fote taketh upon him the parte of the head, and comyns ys become a kinge ... I know in this matter of the commons every man of the Counsayle hath myslyked your procedings, and wyshed it otherways.

> Letter from William Paget to Somerset, 7 July 1549.

---

1 Read Sources A and C. What were the similarities and differences between the motives of the two groups of rebels?

2 What weaknesses did Paget (Source D) observe in Somerset's handling of the rebellions?

3 Does Somerset's letter (Source B) contradict Paget's criticisms?

Source E

The 1549 revolts were the closest thing Tudor England saw to a class war. No single cause was responsible: agrarian, fiscal, religious and social grievances fused. It was a hot summer and the crops failed; prices rose and the Protector compounded the problem by fixing maximum prices at terrifyingly high metropolitan levels ...

Somerset mishandled the revolts. He vacillated in the spring of 1549, not wishing to disrupt his Scottish campaign. He relied on pardons and proclamations and was criticized by Paget, Russell and Smith for ignoring the Council's advice. In July he ordered military reprisals without scruple and cancelled his Scottish project, but the charge of procrastination levelled against him turned into an accusation of unwarranted leniency, even sympathy with the rebels.

J Guy, Tudor England, 1988.

Source F

In quelling disorder, the government's policy towards the rebellions of 1549 was eminently successful. Most of the risings were dispersed as the government intended, with minimal effort and expense. This was true both of the spring risings and the summer ones. Plenty of evidence continued to justify the government's initial policy of delaying direct military action, and the year demonstrated that the traditional offer of a royal pardon and promises of remedy was the most effective way to subdue peasant rebels. Furthermore, in the exceptional cases where the government applied the sword, it easily accomplished its objective without heavy losses of capital and men ...

... Because of the aristocracy's extreme conception of rebellion, sympathy for it implied support for revolution. The final step was, in the light of this leniency, to re-assess Somerset's social programme as an attack on the traditional order. In July Paget reported to Somerset the rumour that 'you have some greater enterprise in your head that lean so much to the multitude'...

There was no question of Somerset deserving the reputation [of a radical]. While sympathetic towards certain of the grievances which the rebels professed, his attitude towards rebellion was one of conventional antipathy. His policy towards rebellion stemmed not from radical sentiments but form his urgent need to wage war in Scotland and to withstand the French, as well as to demonstrate the efficacy of redressing social ills as a means of quelling disorder. When conciliation failed, he proceeded to use force.

M L Bush, The Government Policy of Protector Somerset, 1975.

---

7 To what extent do Guy (Source E) and Bush (Source F) agree on Somerset's handling of the revolts?

8 Bush implies that Paget (Source D) was over critical of Somerset. Do you think Bush or Paget provides the better assessment of Somerset's handling of the crisis?

9 How would you assess Somerset's responsibility for and handling of the rebellions?

The Fall of Somerset

By October 1549 the build up of resentment amongst other political leaders combined with the problems caused by Somerset's policies to ensure his downfall. The rebellions gave Somerset's opponents their opportunity. Credit for suppressing the rebels went to Warwick and Russell who had led the armies and therefore appeared to represent the short, sharp, shock tactics that everyone agreed, in hindsight, had been needed all along.

In London Warwick's army helped to influence the city to turn against the Protector. Russell's army, arriving from Devon, stood between Somerset and any soldiers of his own on his south-west estates. Somerset was arrested on 11 October 1549 and imprisoned. It seems surprising, after the judicial bloodshed of Henry VIII's reign, to discover that he survived to return to the council in 1550.

Somerset's government had failed in war and stimulated rebellion at home. His policies are easily described as disastrous, a word less often applied to Henry VIII who produced not dissimilar results. Certainly Somerset did fail. He did not stay in power nor achieve success against Scotland – his own prime objectives. He did not ease economic and social tensions and he pursued policies long after they had been shown to be mistaken. The religious questions remained unresolved – although it could well be argued that leaving them unresolved was less harmful to individual people than forcing a destructive solution in favour of one extreme. Somerset lost power because of these failures and because they played into the hands of opponents, alienated by his personality and emphasis on his own right to rule.

Having said that Somerset failed, it is also worth saying that he had not pursued his policies against the wishes of other councillors. Overall they agreed and supported him until events showed them to be mistaken. They could only use the events of 1549 against him by misrepresenting his motives. In another sense too Somerset was not alone. In the atmosphere that followed Henry VIII's death, many men were determined to take action, to float ideas, to remedy problems, virtually regardless of the wisdom of their ideals and ideas. Somerset certainly represented this, determined to be a ruler who achieved success. He also refused to quell the enthusiasms of others, such as Hales, whose ideas caused opposition. Thus a more tranquil and cautious policy would have been difficult given the spirit of the years 1547–1549. Policies could be changed by Somerset's successors because they had learned from Somerset's failures.

TALKING POINT

Was Somerset's handling of the 1549 rebellions very different from Henry VIII's handling of the Pilgrimage of Grace?

The Struggle for Control, 1549–1550

Somerset was not immediately succeeded by another, single, dominant figure. The reason is that he was brought down by a coalition of men whose first priority was to end Somerset's dominance. Other than that, they had no coherent programme of action. Once Somerset had been removed the artificiality of this coalition became obvious and the next few months were a time of desperate, factional politics amongst these erstwhile allies until the Earl of Warwick emerged as triumphant. Warwick had played a leading role in 1549 but his own dominance was not inevitable. He had to survive the rivalry of others (particularly Thomas Wriothesley, Earl of Southampton and the Earl of Arundel), initiating and developing his own plans in response to the manoeuvres of others and the unfolding of events. Warwick's rise was a defensive campaign, his political skills proving to be the most sophisticated of the competitors. Warwick succeeded in winning control of the two centres of power – the royal household and the council. Without a Protector, Warwick dominated the composition, business and decision-making of the council, having won the support of key figures such as Paget and Russell.

Warwick, Northumberland and Historical Interpretations

TALKING POINT

Why do you think Warwick did not take the title of Protector?

Aside from the complexities of his rise to power and his policies, Warwick creates difficulties for students of history because of his bewildering number of names. He started life as John Dudley, the son of one of Henry VII's leading councillors who was then executed in 1510 by Henry VIII. Like Somerset, he rose to real influence as a military leader in the 1540s as Viscount Lisle and then gained the Earldom of Warwick in 1547 in the handout of honours that accompanied Somerset's arrival as Protector. We have seen him, as Warwick, suppress Ket's rebels and achieve power himself but then, in 1551, he took the title of Duke of Northumberland. It is as Northumberland that he is best known to historians when summing up his years in power and hence he will be referred to as Northumberland throughout the rest of this chapter, even though some events mentioned took place while he was still known to contemporaries as Warwick. Should any readers achieve political eminence remember the goodwill you will create amongst historians by not changing your name!

Northumberland's reputation has risen as Somerset's has fallen. When Somerset was 'The Good Duke' Northumberland was, of necessity, devious, ambitious, self-seeking and tyrannical. His sheer awfulness was 'proved' by his plot to place his daughter-in-law, Jane Grey, on the throne instead of Mary Tudor, thus sacrificing young Jane for his own ambitions. His reputation as a father-in-law almost matched Richard III's legendary role as an uncle. Recent reassessments have changed much of this image, Professor Hoak going so far as to describe Northumberland as 'one of the most remarkably able governors of any European state during the sixteenth century'.

JOHN DUDLEY, DUKE OF NORTHUMBERLAND 1504 – 1553.

Foreign Policy under Northumberland

Somerset's war fixation had ruined his government. It did not take a political genius to recognise this but we should not underestimate the bravery required to negotiate peace with France and Scotland, no less a humiliating experience because it was realistic. Carrying through a peace policy was a measure of the strength of Warwick's determination in 1550 and the realism of most of his fellow councillors. Somerset, after all, was still on the council and other bellicose voices must have shouted 'shame' and 'betrayal'. Northumberland rapidly agreed the Treaty of Boulogne with France on 29 March 1550. England surrendered Boulogne four years ahead of schedule, receiving £130,000, only half of the compensation agreed in 1546. Northumberland also withdrew English troops from

10.1 Edward Seymour, Duke of Somerset

'Rude, harsh and arrogant', 'personally obnoxious', 'an aloof man who found it difficult to take advice', 'domineering, tactless and rude'. These are some of the ways historians have described Somerset in recent years, a far cry from the image of 'the Good Duke' that held sway for most of this century. In 1975 M L Bush's 'The Government Policy of Protector Somerset' demolished Somerset's reputation and historians have been heaping damning adjectives upon the Protector ever since, reinforced by further research revealing Somerset's shortcomings.

As you have seen, Somerset's policies were an overall failure. However these failures of policies do not necessarily explain his fall. Here his personality and style of government are important too and may be crucial.

Somerset's style of government

- His was an intensely personal style of government. He undermined and ignored the council, using his own household officials as the country's administrators. Even allowing for the competence of men such as his personal secretary, William Cecil, his style was too 'kingly' for councillors who felt ill-treated.

- Councillors complained that only Wolsey amongst commoners had produced letter 'so princely written'. Paget's letters to Somerset spoke of 'your foreign affairs', 'your navy', 'your order for religion'.

- Somerset frequently used proclamations to announce decisions and changes in the law, doing so far more frequently than any other early Tudor ruler.

- In October 1549, as he was fighting for survival, Somerset wrote of 'the poor commons being injured by the extortions of gentlemen, had our pardon this year by the mercy of the king and the goodness of the protector' and said of his fellow councillors that they had 'come up of late from the dung hill ... more meet to keep service than to occupy ... offices'.

- In the same month a proclamation signed by 19 of the 29 councillors accused Somerset of 'malice and evil government ... pride, covetousness and extreme ambition'.

Questions

1 What does the evidence in this section tell you about Somerset's personality?

2 What part do you think Somerset's personality played in his downfall?

3 Do you think that Somerset deserves to keep the title 'the Good Duke' or can you suggest a suitable alternative?

The evidence of Sir William Paget

(a) 'Remember what you promised ... and that was to follow mine advice in all your proceedings more than any other man's. Which promise I wish your grace had kept.'

(b) 'And put no more so many irons in the fire at once as you have had within this twelve month war with Scotland, with France ... commissions out for that matter, new laws for this, proclamation for another, one in another's neck.'

(c) 'Is victuals and other things so dear in England and nowhere else? ... What is the matter then ...? By my faith, Sir ... liberty, liberty!'

A Historian's Verdict

Underlying the policy of the Somerset regime was the Scottish war. Because of the war, the course it took and the pressures it exerted, the government's policy as a whole acquired much of its character. The war determined the nature of the regime's domestic as well as its foreign concerns...

His personality rather than his political thinking produced a policy which was distinct from that of other Tudor governments. Somerset's basic aims – the garrisoning of Scotland, religious reform, the control of inflation and maintaining the security of the state – were far from strange to his contemporaries. His political and social beliefs and assumptions were, for the most part, shared by the rest of the government. In fact, much of the regime's policy was a joint responsibility, not something attributable to Somerset alone....

Essentially, Somerset struggled to uphold conventional values, principles and aims, handicapped by a difficult personality and by critical circumstances, some of which like the Scottish war and the peasant risings were largely his responsibility, while others, such as the minority, inflation, religious schism and the exhaustion of the country after the wars of Henry VIII, were not. The specific character of the regime's policy sprang from the difficulties in which the government was placed both because of Somerset's inflexible personality, and because of these circumstances.

M L Bush, *The Government Policy of Protector Somerset,* 1975 .

The Protector's Brother

Thomas Seymour was the Protector's younger brother. He also married Queen Catherine Parr, three months after Henry VIII's death, a marriage intended in 1543 but abandoned when Henry VIII declared his interest in Catherine. In the early days of Edward VI's reign Thomas was at odds with his brother when he sought the post of the young king's governor. Somerset wanted to retain the role himself and bought his brother off with a place on the council, the post of Lord Admiral, and a barony.

After Catherine Parr's death in 1548, rumours spread that Thomas would marry Princess Elizabeth, then that she was pregnant by him. Thomas apparently encouraged the rumours, presumably to strengthen his chances of marrying one of the heirs to the throne. At the same time he was probably involved in defrauding the royal mint and dabbling in obscure plots against his brother.

In January 1549 Thomas was arrested on the orders of the Council and charged with 33 articles of treason. He was attainted in parliament without trial. Effectively he had been set up by men, led by Warwick and Wriothesley, who hoped to end Somerset's rule. They left Somerset with a choice. Pardon Thomas and appear to connive with his treason or be accused of inhumanity for executing his own brother. Thomas was executed.

Scotland, abandoning Somerset's dream of uniting the crowns through the marriage of Edward to Mary, Queen of Scots. In fact the Treaty of Angers in 1551 saw Edward betrothed to a French princess. The objective throughout was to cut costs to improve the country's finances.

Government, Economy and Social Order

Administrative efficiency and economic prudence were the goals of Northumberland's regime. Ending the wars was a vital step but did not ensure success. Northumberland had to work hard on improving the country's administration and financial efficiency and one measure of his success is that, despite bad harvests from 1549 to 1551, which doubled the price of grain, there was no repetition of the risings of 1549. However, Northumberland ran out of time in 1553 and we cannot be sure whether incomplete reform programmes would really have produced further benefits. Historians are nowadays more inclined to suggest that Northumberland would have achieved more given time, based on analysis of his methods which, according to Professor Hoak, 'reveal the man's innate and very considerable executive abilities: he clearly defined a realistic policy; he delegated responsibilities to others more experienced or capable than he; he insisted that his colleagues produce the desired results on time.'

Can we substantiate this praise? Northumberland certainly used the Privy Council efficiently, restoring it to its rightful authority under his leadership as Lord President. This was good politics for it showed respect for colleagues – doing the opposite to Somerset was again a good rule of thumb. Efficiency came with the acceptance of Paget's advice on the routine of the council. A fixed pattern of business was initiated with a small working group at the heart of the larger council membership of 33. Northumberland did not use proclamations half so much as Somerset, recognition of his desire to work with others.

The most pressing need was to improve the country's finances: 'To have His Majesty out of debt' as Northumberland put it. Some success was achieved but many problems remained. Sensibly, Northumberland turned to experts for guidance, admitting that 'my capacity be not able to reach so far in this matter [of finance] as some of your lords doth'. He gave responsibility to William Cecil, used the experienced Sir Walter Mildmay to advise on reform of the revenue courts (or ministries) and allowed Sir Thomas Gresham to raise new loans at lower rates of interest to pay off old debts incurring higher rates.

Northumberland's achievements were to collect crown revenues more efficiently, reduce corruption, institute a recoinage (the opposite of debasement) in 1551 and to drive down the prices of some basic foods, despite the poor harvests. He also instituted Mildmay's review of the administration of crown revenues which had been discussed since 1545 without progress. The review took only nine months, another testimony to the political will of those involved, but proved too radical for immediate implementation and was then shelved because of Edward VI's final illness. The limitations of what was possible are shown by the fact that some crown lands had to be sold to raise money and by the further debasement of the coinage that took place early in the administration. To the end Northumberland was desperate to save money. He had established a force

TALKING POINT

Twentieth century governments, with the aid of batteries of experts, computers and forecasts, cannot guarantee economic improvements. Should this affect our view of the economic policies of Tudor governments?

of 900 cavalry, raised by councillors but paid for by the crown, for use in political emergency – a response to the events of 1549. In 1552 he disbanded this force to save money. If he had kept it, it might have given him victory over Mary Tudor.

Given the continued fear of risings it is not surprising that Northumberland's administration also produced social reforms. It is likely that the poor benefitted more in these years than from Somerset's wordier efforts. There were more prosecutions of landowners for depopulation of the land under Northumberland than under Somerset. An Act of 1552 sought to protect arable land from enclosure and a new Poor Law was introduced, making contributions to poor relief well nigh compulsory. Those who had not paid were to be on the receiving end of admonitions and implicit demands for payment from their village parson or, if that did not work, their bishop!

Overall the country's administration and the English people themselves were better off in 1553 than they had been in 1549. This is not to say that all was well but much had been done, even in the face of unpredictable problems such as harvest failures and outbreaks of disease. Government was again undertaken responsibly, more so than at any stage since Cromwell's death.

Religion – the triumph of Protestantism?

Whereas Somerset's religious policy had been a compromise, Northumberland's regime produced far greater advances towards Protestantism, culminating in the Second Prayer Book and Second Act of Uniformity of 1552. These marked a clear victory for Protestantism. Just as notable was the lack of violent reaction to this dramatic step – a mark of the firmness of Northumberland's government as well as of memories of the fate of rebels in 1536 and 1549.

Why did this Protestant advance take place? This simple question does not have a simple answer. Undoubtedly the end of the French war helped because the English government no longer needed to pay heed to Charles V's wishes. More importantly Edward VI was a crucial influence as the end of his minority grew nearer. He was 15 in 1552 and would become king in deed in three years at the most. Northumberland must have been anxious to obey Edward's wishes so as to ensure his own future and, if that meant a Protestant revolution, then a Protestant revolution he would have.

This raises the issue of Northumberland's own commitment to Protestantism. The simple interpretation is that he acted out of self-interest in giving Edward the religious change he wanted. Allied to this was the belief of most Tudor ministers that they did not have the right to a religious conscience of their own. Their monarch's religion was their religion, without question. Thus Northumberland, moderate under Henry VIII, radical under Edward VI, actually rejected Protestantism and accepted Catholicism on the eve of his execution. What else would a nobleman do now that the monarch was Catholic?

So far, so simple and this tale of Northumberland dutifully following the monarch's line also fits in with his avowed lack of deep philosophical interest in religion. Northumberland was not a man to argue over the tedious details beloved of extremists on both sides. However other things muddy the waters. If Northumberland was so uncommitted to one religious view why was Mass not said in house at any time after Henry VIII's death? Why did he promote the extreme Protestant, John Hooper, to the Bishopric of Gloucester and side with him in his ensuing arguments over consecration with Thomas Cranmer? Cranmer above all men would seem to have been the man an uncommitted Northumberland would have agreed with. During his years in power Northumberland does seem to have been influenced by radicals like Hooper and John Knox so there may well have been a personal element to his promotion of Protestantism – but we cannot be sure. The precise combination of reasons for the advance of Protestantism are not known. Fortunately the details of what took place are clearer.

The signs of change came with the replacement of conservative bishops by reformers. Those who were deposed included Stephen Gardiner of Winchester who had been imprisoned since 1548. In February 1550 Nicholas Ridley became Bishop of London. He replaced altars with communion tables, sited in the centre of the church not the east end. More radical still was John Hooper, appointed to the bishopric of Gloucester, who refused to be consecrated if he had to wear the traditional vestments of a bishop.

The Prayer Book of 1552 was the final monument to Thomas Cranmer's slow search for truth. This moderate, honest man, notable for his willingness to admit his own uncertainty, now laid down the basis for the Church of England. Catholicism was finally swept away. The Prayer Book abolished the word mass, changing the structure of the service that was now to be known as the communion service. Communion tables replaced altars. Surplices were to be worn by priests instead of vestments. The words of the service were clearly Protestant, intended to end the compromise of Catholics who felt they could infer the real presence of Christ's body in the sacrament. The emphasis was on remembrance. 'Take and eat this in remembrance that Christ died for thee, and feed on him in thy heart by faith with thanksgiving.' Kneeling at communion significantly did not imply 'any adoration ... either with the Sacramental bread or wine ... or unto any real and essential presence there being of Christ's natural flesh and blood.'

The Prayer Book was followed by the Articles of Religion, establishing doctrine, and the Second Act of Uniformity. The Act required every person to attend church on Sunday and to use the Second Book of Common Prayer. Judges and JP's were empowered to enforce its use. Third-time offenders were to suffer life imprisonment.

The lack of direct opposition is perhaps surprising. The severe punishments of rebels in 1549 doubtless deterred some. Most people had probably become used to the idea of slow change over the previous 20 years. It is also clear that Protestantism had made considerable progress amongst the literate classes, especially in the Midlands and south-east. Doubtless there was considerable resentment as parishioners once more had to get used to different sights in their churches but resentment was all there was.

Thus Protestantism triumphed but within a year it was clear that Edward VI was dying of tuberculosis. He had been fit and well at the end of 1552. On 6 July 1553 the king died. The personal fate of many individuals and the religion of the country were determined by what happened next. The accession of Mary was neither certain nor trouble-free. There could well have been a Protestant queen on the throne instead of Mary.

EXAMINING THE EVIDENCE
Could Jane Grey have become Queen?

The story of Jane Grey is a very brief one. Made Queen by her father-in-law, the Duke of Northumberland, she won little other support and was speedily imprisoned by Mary Tudor's supporters. It is a sad and forlorn story but not necessarily one that had to end in despair. It is easy to assume, simply because Mary won so quickly, that Northumberland's plan had no chance of success – but was that really the case?

1 Historians disagree about whether Northumberland or Edward was responsible for the plan to make Jane Queen. Why do they disagree?

2 Was there a real chance of Jane continuing as Queen instead of Mary?

LADY JANE GREY 1537 – 1554.

Timetable of Events

1553

May 21 Jane Grey married Northumberland's son, Guildford

May A draft will was drawn up, the 'Devise for the Succession'. Edward VI's sisters were disinherited and the crown left to Jane Grey and her male heirs. The surviving copy is in Edward's handwriting.

June 11 Judges were ordered to prepare the formal document containing Edward's wishes about the succession.

July 3 Mary, travelling to see Edward, was warned that the King was close to death. She fled to East Anglia, where she had lived during Edward's reign and where many of her household officers were influential.

July 6 Edward VI died, sooner than expected. His death was kept secret for several days.

July 10 Jane Grey was proclaimed Queen by the Council. Mary proclaimed herself Queen.

July 19 The Councillors left London and declared Jane deposed.

July 20 Northumberland surrendered to Mary

August 3 Mary entered London as Queen.

August 22 Northumberland was executed.

1554

February Wyatt's rebellion against Mary involved Jane Grey's father amongst the plotters. They were motivated by religion and opposition to Mary's Spanish marriage. After the rebellion failed Jane and her husband were executed although they had no involvement in the planning or events of the rebellion.

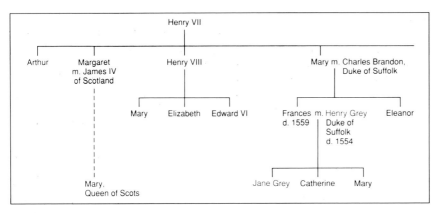

Source A

In the country there was widespread confusion, and in many places a reluctance to do anything decisive until it became clear which way the wind was blowing, though it seems fair to say that there was a good deal of sympathy for Mary, and none at all for Jane. Northumberland remained at first in London, rather than challenging Mary in the field, evidently because he did not trust his fellow councillors...

... eventually, on 14 July, he set out, ominously reminding the council before he went that they were as much involved as he was. As he rode out of London he noticed that 'no one sayeth 'God speed''. News poured in from the country at large of gathering support for Mary. The resolution of the councillors in London began to crack. The Earl of Arundel (who had spent most of the last three years in prison for sympathising with Somerset), lectured them at length on the principle of hereditary succession, a powerful argument among the landed class. The Earl of Pembroke, who had no axe to grind (Northumberland had got him his earldom, and his son was married to Queen Jane's sister, Catherine), was briefer. 'If my lord of Arundel's persuasion cannot prevail with you, either this sword shall make Mary queen, or I'll lose my life.' With relief or reluctance, the council agreed....

Yet the triumph of Mary was not inevitable. ... If the council had managed to prevent Mary's flight into East Anglia, and had imprisoned her, her cause would not have had any credibility ... and her bandwagon would never have started to roll. All this underlines the fact that there was no long-term plot on Northumberland's part. Had there been, he could have done more to prepare the ground. Whatever the financial difficulties, the core of professional soldiers would not have been dismissed in 1552. A propaganda campaign could have been mounted, stressing Mary's Catholicism, bastardy and dependence upon the Habsburgs (the imperial ambassadors had been her advisers and protectors throughout Edward's reign) and preparing the people for the possibility of a Queen Jane.

C S L Davies, *Peace, Print and Protestantism*, 1976.

Source B

Contrary to what had been thought, the scheme to alter the succession originated in Northumberland's camp and not in King Edward's brain, but, although Northumberland rightly accepted responsibility for it ...

... barring Mary from the succession was a cause in which the young King believed. The chronology of the whole episode leaves one with the impression that the original object of the 'Devise' was not to make Northumberland the manipulator of a puppet queen, but simply to ensure the rule of any one of a number of Protestants, all of whom were to be male. Indeed, it was not originally apparent (by the terms of the first draft) that either Northumberland or his family would benefit by the 'Devise', for at the time of his son's marriage Lady Jane Grey had not been named an heir to the throne. Only when it was realised that Edward VI really was dying and had not willed the throne to anyone alive did Gates persuade the boy to revise the draft in favour of Jane ...

D Hoak, *'Rehabilitating the Duke of Northumberland: Politics and Political Control, 1549–1553' in 'The Mid-Tudor Polity c.1540–1560'* ed R Tittler and J Loach.

THE DEVISE FOR THE SUCCESSION. DOUBT STILL EXISTS AS TO THE EXTENT TO WHICH PLANS FOR THE SUCCESSION WERE THE WORK OF EDWARD OR NORTHUMBERLAND. IT IS WORTH REMEMBERING THAT EDWARD WAS 15 AND LIKELY TO WANT TO DICTATE HIS SUCCESSOR.

REVIEW
The Problem of a Minority?

Whoever ruled England from 1547 to 1553 faced great problems – inflation, poor harvests and the 'sweating sickness' that killed many thousands in 1551. As a result 'perhaps no Tudor government ever stood in greater fear of rebellious commons than did that of the duke of Northumberland'

(D E Hoak).

Did the fact that the king was a minor make this situation worse?

1 Below are two arguments. Which do you agree with or would you put forward another argument about the minority?

2 'If there was a crisis in England it was not because of the minority but because of inflation and poor harvests.' Explain why you agree or disagree with this statement.

Inflation – the price of a composite unit of foodstuffs	
1491–1500	100
1501–1510	106
1511–1520	116
1521–1530	159
1531–1540	161
1541–1550	217
1551–1560	315
1561–1570	298
100 = the base price for comparison	

Argument A

An adult king would have prevented trouble developing amongst his councillors. There would have been no rivalries over power. Clear policies would also have been established, whereas the changes and compromises of Somerset and Northumberland only antagonised people. An adult king could only have improved the government.

Argument B

If Edward had ruled as an adult his policies, notably on religion, would have been too extreme too quickly and might well have prompted widespread rebellion. Edward has been called a 'boy-tyrant' which scarcely suggests he would have provided fair and good government. What was needed was a good ruler, not simply an adult ruler. Northumberland was more successful than Edward could have been.

10.2 Northumberland – Villain or Statesman?

N orthumberland's career ended in the worst possible way for his reputation. He was caught, apparently using his innocent son and daughter-in-law to ensure his own political power and deposing the rightful heir. Selfish, greedy, power-mad and prepared to cause civil war if it served his own interest – it would be easy to condemn Northumberland on the evidence of the last two months of his life.

Questions

1 What are the similarities and differences between the views in Sources A and B?

2 How might Professor Hoak (Source C) respond to the views in Sources A and B?

3 How should historians view Northumberland's treatment of the Duke of Somerset?

4 Do you think that Northumberland deserves an improved reputation?

The Death of the Duke of Somerset

The coalition of Somerset and Northumberland in 1550 was one of history's unlikelier alliances – the deposed Protector making common cause with the man who had led the opposition. However, the coalition did not outlast the defeat of their common enemy, the Earl of Southampton. In October 1551 Somerset was arrested for treason, tried and executed in January 1552. Later, according to a French eyewitness, Northumberland confessed that 'nothing had pressed so injuriously upon his conscience as the fraudulent scheme against the Duke of Somerset'. What does Somerset's death tell us about Northumberland?

Somerset spent 1551 in plotting against his rival and had some success in building up support. It is likely that Northumberland only just acted in time to prevent himself being the victim of Somerset's coup. However, Northumberland had little hard evidence against Somerset, hence the chicanery required to convict him. The arrest and trial were stage-managed, the jury hand-picked, execution this time a foregone conclusion. Along with Somerset fell William Paget. Arrested but never tried, Paget went into retirement. He was suspected of supporting Somerset and probably also opposed the religious measures of 1551–2.

'Northumberland's calculated action probably saved England the spectacle of a bloody counter-coup and the administrative chaos of a revived Protectorate.'

(D Hoak)

The assault on Paget, whose only real crime was independence of mind, lends weight to the contention that by now Northumberland's 'preoccupation with plots and counter-plots, and the very act of clinging to power, were to absorb almost the whole of the energy and resources of his government'.

(WRD Jones)

Source A

... despite his concern with consolidation of his own position, with his pursuit to its tragic end of his vendetta with Somerset, with his suppression of all evidence of popular discontent, and finally with his efforts to change the order of succession to the throne, Northumberland's regime was not barren of constructive achievement. For his ministers included men such as Cecil and Mildmay, whose prudent, perhaps time-serving, moderation in political loyalties should not detract from their undoubted administrative skill.

W R D Jones, 'The Mid-Tudor Crisis, 1539–1563', 1973.

Source B

The most notable administrative reforms undertaken touched the Crown's finances, ruined by war, debasement, extravagance and corruption. The new regime had to deal with the consequences of ten years of mismanagement and did not, in the less than four years at its disposal, succeed in remedying them all, but it made an impressive start. Though the earl himself clearly understood little of the complex issues involved, other members of the administration did ... this was a genuine reform administration, the first since Cromwell's fall and the first to follow up the initiatives started by Cromwell. It really took hold of England's government and tackled the crying needs of the day, and it did so with a thoroughness and competence that approached (at a distance) those customary in the 1530s. This judgement is also borne out by the larger policies of the day and by the gradual reappearance of government-sponsored reform legislation in Parliament ... his own health was clearly breaking down; in 1552 he was repeatedly incapacitated by illness and losing a dominance which had stemmed from determined ambition rather than great abilities or bold policies.

G R Elton, 'Reform and Reformation', 1977.

Source C

Northumberland's methods once again reveal the man's innate and very considerable executive abilities: he clearly defined a realistic policy; he delegated responsibilities to others more experienced or capable than he; he insisted that his colleagues produce the desired results on time ... Northumberland disarmed with his 'liberality', a noble courtesy difficult to resist or surpass. Affable and unusually graceful for a soldier, he commanded a 'great presence' and knew it. Perhaps his consciousness of this quality made him appear to be acting a part at times, but even his detractors spoke respectfully of his 'great courage', a force of character that suggested superior political nerves ... Allegations of avarice are irrelevant here. Was there anyone at court in Edward's last hour who had not benefited materially by the Reformation? If Northumberland is to be judged on this count, a whole generation of courtiers and Crown servants must be condemned ... On 9 December 1552 he openly admonished the members of the Council to be ready to spend not only 'our goods' but our lands and our lives for our master and our country and to despise this flattering of ourselves with heaping riches upon riches, honours upon honours, building upon building', and by 'ourselves' he did not by this time mean to include himself. It was only in men's 'evil imaginations', he said, that he had neglected the government of the King's realms ...

In sum, Northumberland's behaviour after December 1549 exhibits not the treachery of an inherently evil man, but the realistic calculations of a sixteenth-century soldier who had risen to the pinnacle of political leadership at a court already noted for its factious politics and rough justice. Because he inherited Somerset's wasteful disorder and misrule, he was determined to put right the administration of royal affairs ... Northumberland should be viewed as the architect of some of Elizabeth I's methods of government: he taught Sir William Cecil, the future Lord Burghley, how a prince should properly employ his councillors. ... given the circumstances which he inherited in 1549, the Duke of Northumberland appears to have been one of the most remarkably able governors of any European state during the sixteenth century.

(D Hoak, 'Rehabilitating the Duke of Northumberland: Politics and Political Control, 1549–53' in 'The Mid-Tudor Polity c.1540–1560' ed R Tittler and J Loach).

Evaluating Somerset and Northumberland

How would you assess the achievements of the two men who governed England under Edward VI? Draw your own version of this grid and summarise your views in each box, adding short references to the evidence that would support your view. Then develop your own argument in answer to the question 'Do either Somerset or Northumberland deserve to be remembered for their achievements rather than their failures?'

Achievement or Failure?	Somerset	Northumberland
Religious Policy		
Foreign Policy		
Economics/ Standard of Living		
Faction, Peace and Law and Order		

11 Mary Tudor – The Ill-Fortuned Queen

PREVIEW

Among the many decisions that faced Mary when she became Queen two were particularly important. These are the choices that faced her:

Religion

(a) Should Mary accept the Protestant religion as established in 1552 and maintain her own Catholic beliefs in private?

(b) Should Mary return to the religious compromise of Henry VIII's last years?

(c) Should Mary make England a Catholic country once again, revoking all changes made since 1530?

Marriage

(a) Should Mary marry an English nobleman? (This might create jealousies amongst the nobility but would avoid the complications of a foreign marriage.)

(b) Should Mary marry Philip of Spain, the Catholic heir to the Emperor Charles V?
(Philip rules the Netherlands, England's most important trading partner, but this marriage might make England's needs take second place to Philip's continental policies.)

(c) Should Mary stay unmarried? (Thus keeping her sister Elizabeth, a Protestant, as her heir?)

---

1 What would you have advised Mary to do if you had been one of her councillors? Explain the reason for your advice.

2 What do you, in the twentieth century, think she should have done?

3 Explain any differences between the answers to questions 1 and 2.

The Presence of a Queen

'to promote a woman to bear rule, superiority, dominion or empire above any realm, nation or city is repugnant to nature; contumely to God, a thing most contrary to his revealed will and approved ordinance; and finally, it is the subversion of good order, or all equity and justice'

From John Knox, *First Blast of the Trumpet Against the Monstrous Regiment of Women.*

Knox, a radical Protestant, was far from being the only voice to doubt that a woman could rule a country although, as the developer of the theory of the 'natural imbecility' of women, he was the most incorrigible. English society as a whole was uncomfortable with the idea of having a queen as ruling monarch. The established convention was that women took second place to men.

With this background it is not surprising that Parliament felt obliged to pass an Act 'declaring that the Royal power of this realm is in the Queen's Majesty as fully and absolutely as ever as it was in any of her most noble progenitors, kings of this Realm'. The fact that Mary Tudor was the first woman to rule England as queen should make us careful when making judgements about her reign. Not only did she face problems as difficult as those facing other rulers but she also had to cope with attitudes and assumptions – hers and others – that were unique in 1553.

Examining the Evidence
Mary Tudor

Mary in person

Source A

She is of low stature, with a red and white complexion, and very thin; her eyes are white and large, and her hair reddish; her face is round, with a nose rather low and wide; and were not her age on the decline, she might be called handsome rather than the contrary. She is not of a strong constitution, and of late she suffers from headaches and serious affection of the heart, so that she is often obliged to take medicine, and also to be blooded. She is of very spare diet, and never eats until 1 or 2 pm, although she rises at daybreak, when, after saying her prayers and hearing mass in private, she transacts business incessantly, until after midnight, when she retires to rest; for she chooses to give audience not only to all the members of her Privy Council, and to hear from them every detail of public business, but also to all other persons who ask it of her. Her Majesty's countenance indicates great benignity and clemency .. She is endowed with excellent ability, and more than moderately read in Latin literature, especially with regard to Holy Writ; and besides her native tongue she speaks Latin, French and Spanish, and understands Italian perfectly, but does not speak it.

... Her Majesty takes great pleasure in playing on the lute and spinet, and is a very good performer on both instruments; and indeed before her accession she taught many of her maids of honour. But she seems to delight above all in arraying herself elegantly and magnificently ...

Giacomo Soranzo, the Venetian Ambassador to England in 1554 when Mary was 38.

TALKING POINT

Why did such attitudes to women exist?

TALKING POINT

The later sixteenth century saw other women rulers – Elizabeth and Catherine de Medici amongst them. Does this contradict the idea that women were regarded as inferior?

MARY TUDOR AGED 28.

TALKING POINT

What are the strengths and weaknesses of ambassadorial reports as evidence?

MARY TUDOR IN LATER LIFE.

TALKING POINT

Compare Mary's speech with Elizabeth's Tilbury speech on page 383. Why is Elizabeth's speech famous while Mary's is not?

TALKING POINT

What do Sources A – C tell us about attitudes to women?

Source B

... not only is she brave and valiant, unlike other timid and spiritless women, but so courageous and resolute that neither in adversity nor peril did she ever even display or commit any act of cowardice or pusillanimity, maintaining always, on the contrary, a wonderful grandeur and dignity, knowing what became the dignity of a sovereign ...it may be said of her, as Cardinal Pole says with truth, that in the darkness and obscurity of that kingdom she remained precisely like a feeble light buffeted by raging winds for its utter extinction, but always kept burning and defended by her innocence and lively faith, that it might shine in the world as it now does shine.

Giovanni Michiel, Venetian Ambassador to England in 1557, when Mary was 43.

Source C

I am come to you in mine own person to tell you that which already you see and know; that is how traitorously and rebelliously a number of Kentish men have assembled themselves against both us and you. Their pretence (as they said at the first) was for a marriage determined for... and it appeared then unto our said Council that the matter of the marriage seemed to be but a Spanish cloak to cover their pretended purpose against our religion ...

Now, loving subjects, what I am ye right well know. I am your Queen, to whom at my coronation when I was wedded to the realm and laws of the same ... you promised your allegiance and obedience unto me ... And I say to you, on the word of a prince, I cannot tell how naturally the mother loveth the child, for I was never the mother of any, but certainly if a prince and governor may as naturally and earnestly love her subjects as the mother doth love the child, then assure yourselves that I, being your lady and mistress, do as earnestly and tenderly love and favour you...

... And on the word of a Queen, I promise you, that if it shall not probably appear to all the nobility and commons ... that this marriage shall be for the high benefit and commodity of the realm, then I will abstain from marriage while I live. And now, good subjects, pluck up your hearts, and like true men, stand fast against these rebels ... and fear them not, for, I assure you, I fear them nothing at all.'

Mary's speech at the Guildhall in London in January 1554
at the time of Wyatt's Rebellion.

1 What do sources A and B tell you about:

(a) Mary's appearance?

(b) her character and personality?

(c) her skills and interests?

(d) her suitability to rule England?

2 What can be deduced about Mary from source C?

Historians on Mary's character and personality

Source D

It has become something of a commonplace to assert that Mary Tudor was the most attractive member of her family – kind, long-suffering, gentle, considerate. The evidence of her recorded words and actions hardly bears this out; it shows her rather to have been arrogant, assertive, bigoted, stubborn, suspicious, and (not to put too fine a point on it) rather stupid. Her portraits show a bitter and narrow-minded woman, curiously unlike her father, brother and sister. Thirty-seven years old, she seized a power rightfully hers for the exercise of which she was utterly unsuited.

G R Elton, *Reform and Reformation,* 1977.

Source E

… there was an iron streak in her personality, in power no less than in affliction. Not only does she personally bear the responsibility for the burning of nearly 300 heretics, she also executed traitors more ruthlessly than either her father or her sister and used martial law with exceptional freedom. Mary did not earn her reputation for clemency.

D Loades, *The Reign of Mary Tudor, 2nd edition,* 1991.

Source F

On the eve of her succession, therefore, Mary Tudor was in many ways old at thirty-seven, certainly embittered and otherwise fatally shaped by her peculiar apprenticeship. Not surprisingly, she would prove a distrustful Queen. Having been either rejected by or separated from those to whom she might normally have felt closest, she came to place her faith in ideals rather than in people. Chief among such ideals was her intense, non-intellectual, and wholly uncompromising devotion to Catholicism. Also considerably important was her desire to marry, and perhaps to know as a wife and mother that domestic felicity of which she had been deprived in her own adolescence. Finally, and obviously linked to these other considerations, came her preference for and trust in Spaniards, who had ever been her aid and comfort, rather than Englishmen.

R Tittler, *The Reign of Mary I,* 1983.

4 In what ways do sources D and E agree or disagree about Mary's character and suitability to rule?

5 According to Source F, how was Mary's reign affected by her earlier experiences?

6 How far do the views of Mary in sources D – F reflect the contemporary views in sources A – C?

7 Using the sources in this section write your own assessment of Mary's character, personality and her fitness to rule.

(At the end of this chapter you will have the chance to review these assessments and make amendments in the light of further work.)

TALKING POINT

Why do you think historians' assessments of Mary have differed?

MARY TUDOR AS A PRINCESS,
PAINTED AROUND 1525 – 1527.

TALKING POINT

It is easy to assume that
Mary's early life influenced
her actions as Queen.
Should historians simply
rely on their common-
sense to make such
interpretations or do they
need to make a serious
study of psychology?

Mary's path to the throne

Mary was born in February 1516, the daughter of Catherine of Aragon and Henry VIII. She was therefore half-Spanish and the events of the 1530s were to ensure that her 'Spanish-half' was never lost. The rapid changes of the 1530s also disguise the fact that until she was 11 Mary lived a normal and happy life – for a princess! She was highly educated, the regular subject of marriage diplomacy, a devout daughter of the Catholic church. According to Professor Loades, Mary's most authoritative biographer, Henry 'was genuinely fond of her, and Mary probably had more attention and affection from both her parents than was common with royal or aristocratic children of the period'. Nevertheless Mary had relatively little 'childhood' as we would recognise it. She had her own household, away from her parents and saw them irregularly. She was treated as an adult rather than as a child and had few, if any, playmates of her own age.

When Mary was 12 Henry decided on separation from Catherine. Throughout her teens Mary lived in limbo, separated by necessity from both her parents. To Henry she was illegitimate, the daughter of an invalid marriage, The whole purpose of Henry's politics was to replace Mary with a legitimate male heir. After 1531 she was banned from visiting her mother, although the two communicated frequently by letter. The early 1530s were a humiliating time for Mary. She lost most of her household and her title and place in the succession. In these years she developed a simple sense of right and wrong. Right was adherence to her mother and the Catholic religion. Wrong was her father's conduct, his marriage to Anne Boleyn and his new church. For the most part Mary lived up to Cromwell's description of her as 'the most obstinate woman that ever was'. However in 1536 she buckled under pressure. The deaths of her mother and Anne Boleyn had raised hopes of reconciliation with Henry, but Henry wanted Mary to recognise both the invalidity of his marriage to her mother and his position as head of the Church. Mary refused point-blank but, amidst threats of charges of treason and the arrest of her servants, she had to capitulate. For the rest of Henry's reign she was restored to relative favour and in 1544 was reinstated as second-in-line to the throne, her rightful place ahead of Elizabeth.

The pressure on her in 1536 demonstrated two things. Firstly Mary was always an important figurehead for conservatives and Catholics. The strong conservative faction, some of whom in desperation sparked the Pilgrimage of Grace, perhaps saw Mary as an alternative ruler. Secondly her sense of religious right and wrong was paramount and much stronger than her political sense, which was always to remain rather naive. Although she submitted in 1536, this only strengthened her determination to put right the religious errors of the 1530s.

Under Edward she retained most of her privileges – her estate and her household and was treated as a princess. Sensibly she stayed away from court to avoid Edward's relentless Protestantism and this also saved her from the acute danger of being embroiled in plots. Even so she was deprived by Northumberland's government of the right to celebrate mass in her own household. Again this was a political decision intended to reduce the chances of her drawing supporters and heading an opposition faction.

However Mary did succeed in winning the throne. Why was Mary successful? Initially her own decisiveness in asserting her claim was crucial in fostering confidence amongst potential supporters. Then the leaders of her household quickly and very efficiently raised support amongst the gentry and the towns, although only one major nobleman (Sussex) joined her party at an early stage. The weakness of Northumberland's case was also important for there were few he could depend on, particularly after he left London. This, in part, was the result of poor planning, the product of Edward VI dying sooner than expected and Northumberland's own persistent illness. What had not happened was a widespread rising in favour of Catholicism. Certainly religion had motivated many of those who joined Mary, but so had concern for legitimacy and legality, opposition to or dislike of Northumberland and also local feuds where one family supported Northumberland and Jane Grey, and their local rivals out of opposition rather than conviction supported Mary.

When Mary became queen she brought with her important legacies from her past. She found great difficulty in trusting people. She believed in ideals, especially her religion. Englishmen, including the politicians who served her during her reign, were in her experience, the men who had excluded her from public life and had sent instructions and orders intended to stamp out Catholicism. The Spanish on the other hand represented a safe haven where the true religion was maintained and she had always been assured of support, albeit support that had never been tested. Now she was free to import Spanish integrity and revive the Catholic religion.

Mary's task

First and foremost Mary intended to restore the Catholic religion. She also intended to marry and have children to ensure the Catholic succession. Her chosen husband was Philip of Spain, heir to the Hapsburg Empire. To win support for and carry through both these projects to success would require great determination and political skills. Mary possessed the former but not the latter. She had not been trained to rule and, more importantly, did not have the incisive intelligence to make up for the loss. Sensibly she realised the need to use experienced councillors but, in doing so, created for herself a dilemma. The experienced politicians were men who had served her father and brother and therefore the Protestant reformation. She could never fully trust them but the men she did trust, who had been in her household before 1553, lacked administrative experience. Their Catholicism had debarred them from administrative work under her predecessors. Mary's solution was the dangerous and difficult one of using both groups. The Privy Council was therefore composed of experienced and able men – Paget, Petre, Winchester (formerly William Paulet) amongst them – and Mary's Chancellor was Stephen Gardiner, once again Bishop of Winchester. The Queen's Household, providing her with daily support and advice, consisted of the loyalists. The other key figure close to Mary in the first year of her reign was Simon Renard, the Imperial ambassador. Renard has been described as 'for all practical purposes ... Mary's chief adviser from August 1553 until the arrival of Philip in July 1554'.

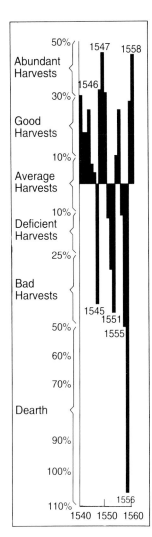

That this division between Council and Household did not lead to major problems is a tribute most of all to the politicians who served the queen. After their initial hesitancy in July 1553 they used the administrative machinery of government effectively in the service of a queen whose policies they sometimes disagreed with. In doing so they ensured that chaos or crisis was avoided. Apart from the repercussions of religious change these were very difficult years. As the chart shows prices rose sharply in 1555–7 as a result of very poor harvests, producing problems even worse than those of 1543–6 and 1550–2. In Suffolk it was recorded that 'the scarcity of bread ... was so great, in so much that the plain poor people did make much of acorns and a sickness of strong fever did sore molest them'. People died of famine and then influenza hit the greatly weakened population. As many as 20 per cent of the population may have died between 1555 and 1560. Such conditions, combined with the stresses of religious change and Mary's marriage to Philip of Spain, could have caused major disturbances, even widespread rebellion. That they did not must represent some measure of successful government.

The Marriage Treaty and Wyatt's Rebellion

On the surface the first months of Mary's reign were tranquil, suggesting a greater willingness to compromise than some had feared. The signs of this included the continuity amongst courtiers in the council and, on the public's part, acceptance of the restoration of the mass in parish churches, even before parliamentary legislation made this legal. There was one major riot in London but little other disturbance. When parliament did legislate it reversed all the ecclesiastical laws of Edward's reign (except the Chantries Act as the properties were now in the hands of many in government), thus restoring matters to the last days of Henry VIII, not to the Catholicism of the 1520s.

If she was not moving as quickly as anticipated in religion, the queen was determined to marry as soon as possible. She was 37, with few child-bearing years ahead of her. For a time there appeared to be a debate over whom she should marry. Many councillors, especially Gardiner, championed Edward Courtenay, Earl of Devon. He had several advantages – he was English, he was a great-grandson of Edward IV, his father had been executed in 1538 for his loyalty to Mary and Catholicism (see page 210). Courtenay had been in prison ever since. Unfortunately Courtenay had one major disadvantage – the queen did not want to marry him. She had already promised to marry Philip, the son of Charles V.

Given the strong and growing nationalism (or xenophobia) in Tudor England, Mary's choice of husband seemed designed to create hostility, but there was some logic. Marriage to Philip cemented the alliance with the Netherlands, England's chief trading partner, and avoided the creation of dissension amongst the nobility by raising the Courtenay family to royal status. Philip was also very experienced politically. To Mary he was Catholic and Spanish, associations that she had found reassuring and supportive during the previous 25 years.

Mary had decided on marriage to Philip by late October 1553 but did not inform her councillors until 8 November. Led by Paget (who had earlier realised Mary's determination and supported her out of ambition), the council slowly came round to supporting her plans. Several however joined a delegation from parliament who tried to dissuade her, a fruitless task which Mary cut short with the words 'Parliaments were not accustomed to use such language to the Kings of England'.

The marriage agreement was the work of Mary herself, Paget, Gardiner and Renard. Philip was given the title of King and he was to rule with Mary as joint-sovereign. However, English laws were not to be changed, nor were foreigners to be allowed to hold any offices. The eldest child of the marriage would inherit but, if there were no children, the crown would go to Elizabeth. In addition England would not be involved in Philip's wars against her will. The terms were proclaimed in January 1554 and they sparked rebellion.

Plans were already developing for co-ordinated risings in Kent, Devon, Leicestershire and the Welsh borders, timed for the spring of 1554. The proclamation of the marriage treaty and the leaking of information forced the plotters to act in January, with the result that only Kent of the centres of rebellion raised more than a handful of troops, the Duke of Suffolk, (Lady Jane Grey's father), managing a meagre 150 supporters in the midlands.

In Kent Sir Thomas Wyatt, a wealthy landowner and former sheriff of the county, raised 3000 supporters. They marched on London and at first their initiative seemed to catch the government out as they defeated a force sent from London, headed by the octogenarian Duke of Norfolk. London, fearing destruction, wavered in its support for Mary but Wyatt delayed his assault and Londoners decided to stand firm, perhaps inspired by Mary's speech (page 257). Wyatt's final assault was not strong enough. Forty of his men were killed. The rest surrendered. In the aftermath 90 people were executed, including Wyatt, Suffolk and Jane Grey and her husband, innocent though the latter two were. The vast majority of rebels were pardoned. This relative leniency may have been the result of wishing to avoid provoking further trouble in the months before the Queen's marriage. Princess Elizabeth was also spared, protected by Wyatt's refusal to implicate her and by the influence of Paget. Elizabeth had not been party to Wyatt's plans, but like Mary herself in previous years, was now the focus for opposition groups.

Why did Wyatt's rebellion take place? Wyatt said that he sought 'no harm to the Queen, but better counsel and Councillors' – but that was what rebels always said before, during and after rebellions. It is likely that nationalism was at the centre of the complaints of most rebels. The

TALKING POINT

What does the number of executions suggest about Mary? Compare the number with those executed after the Pilgrimage of Grace and other rebellions.

TALKING POINT

Why was there an upsurge of English nationalism in the fifteenth and sixteenth centuries?

author of 'The Chronicle of Queen Jane and Queen Mary' recorded how 'the people, nothing rejoicing, held down their heads sorrowfully' when the Spanish negotiators arrived and that news of the treaty 'although before not unknown to many and very much misliked, yet being now pronounced was not only credited but taken heavily by sundry men and almost each man was abashed'. After the marriage he recorded that 'there were so many Spaniards in London that a man should meet in the streets one Englishman for every four Spaniards to the great discomfort of the English nation' and also noted rumours of 12,000 Spaniards coming to England to fetch the crown and that the Archbishopric of Canterbury and other offices would be given to Spaniards. Wyatt himself was treated as a martyr, people dipping handkerchiefs in his blood after his execution.

For all this, nationalism was not the only motive. Religion was certainly the dominant motive for some rebels although it suited both Wyatt and the Queen to claim that religion was not the issue. Wyatt feared that the proclamation of an anti-Catholic rising would cause opposition amongst those who might otherwise be neutral. The queen, determined to restore Catholicism, could not believe there was such opposition to her religion. Other rebels were involved because of purely local grievances – gentry who had lost office and yeomen and lower ranks protesting about economic conditions. Like all risings Wyatt's rebellions contained a mix of motives and prompts mixed conclusions. Such an outburst of nationalism did not bode well for the queen's marriage but support for the rebels had been very limited, sufficiently limited to suggest that people would accept the queen's religion.

Philip and Mary

The royal marriage took place on 25 July 1554. It was not a marriage of equal commitment. For Mary marriage to Philip was her dearest wish. Although they had never met, Philip represented Spain and Catholicism, right and reassurance. She believed the marriage would give her happiness and an heir. For Philip, aged 26 and already a widower with a child, the marriage was a standard royal diplomatic marriage. Already heir to Spain and the Netherlands he hoped his marriage would create a three-sided alliance which would overawe France. His intentions as regards the government of England were limited to those areas linked to this policy. He wanted to build up the navy and ensure the borders and coasts were well-defended. If Mary became pregnant all well and good but Philip had no long-term ambitions to make England part of his empire.

The inequality in this marriage was there from the very beginning. Philip, expected since February, arrived in July. The queen had been waiting, humiliatingly, near the coast for a month. Philip brought his own extensive retinue, so the English household prepared for him was surplus to requirements. The couple met for the first time on 23 July and married two days later. Philip spoke no English but could understand French. Mary's Spanish had not been used for nearly 20 years but she did speak French well.

In the autumn of 1554 Mary's doctors confirmed that she was pregnant. Her baby was expected in early May, then later in the month, then in June. In July all the paraphernalia of infancy were packed away, including the specially decorated cradle. Mary had never been pregnant even if the symptoms had fooled everyone around her. A tumour or cyst was perhaps the cause. Philip left England in August 1555 and did not return until May 1557, intending to win English support for his war against France. Having succeeded he left in July. Again Mary believed she was pregnant and again she was wrong. They did not meet again.

Religious Change

Mary's religious policy has often been seen as doomed to failure, a vain attempt to stem the advance of English Protestantism before it reached its full glories under Elizabeth. But if Mary had lived longer and had had a child, Elizabeth might never have become queen and Catholicism would have had longer to establish itself. The five years of Mary's reign was a very short period in which to push against the momentum of events over the preceding two decades. As you read this section, consider which of these interpretations is supported by the evidence:

A By 1553 England was so securely Protestant that Mary had very little chance of restoring Catholicism, a chance further reduced by the opposition to the burning of heretics.

B By 1558 Mary had made good progress in her task and, if she had lived for another ten years, Catholicism would have become once again the natural religion of the English.

C By 1558 Mary had made some progress but had been hindered by her own and her advisers' over-optimistic assessments of the religious affiliation of the English. They assumed there was a general latent Catholicism and therefore failed to praise and enthuse the people. Therefore another 20 years at least would have been needed to outlast the effects of the 20 Protestant years.

Mary's main helper was Cardinal Reginald Pole, one of the leading figures of Catholic Europe. He had lived in exile since 1532, surviving English assassination attempts. As soon as Mary became queen, Pole was destined to return to use his formidable organisational skills to restore Catholicism. As Papal Legate he was also needed to absolve the country from its sins and officially welcome it back into the Pope's protection. However Pole did not arrive for nearly 18 months, in November 1554. Charles V, not wanting Pole to detract from Philip's arrival, used him in diplomatic negotiations with France. Mary, fearing Pole's hard-line over the return of chantry lands now in the hands of influential nobles and gentry, did not recall him. With hindsight, the delay of Pole lost a significant proportion of the available time.

Mary did make some early progress, although she first had to be disabused of the notion that she could simply, as queen, declare the end of the legislation she detested. She must also have been taken aback that the people did not instantly revert to Catholic doctrines and traditions, after the support she had received in 1553. Instead she had to work through parliament. Her first parliament repealed the religious legislation of Edward VI's reign, except for the Chantries Act. There was opposition to this (the voting figures in the Commons were 270–80 and debate lasted five days) and the revival of the heresy laws was defeated in the Lords. It was not until Mary's third parliament in November 1554 that the Second Statute of Repeals restored the religious legislation that had operated in 1529. This still only took place once it had been agreed that monastic lands would not be restored to the church but would stay with their lay owners. Ironically more former church lands was in the hands of Catholic families, such as the Howards, than belonged to Protestant families. Then on 30 November 1554 Pole absolved the whole realm of its sin and welcomed it back into the Papal fold.

This absolution did not extend to those individuals who, in the minds of Mary and Pole, had seduced the god-fearing multitude. Leading Protestants like Cranmer and Ridley had already been deprived of their bishoprics. Married clergy were forced to resign or renounce their wives. Most, out of economic necessity, renounced their wives but there were soon complaints about the frequency of their visits to their former spouses! Set-piece disputations also took place in Oxford, pitting Cranmer, Ridley and Latimer against the cream of Catholic thinkers. This was designed to show the poverty of the Protestant heresies in the face of 'true' argument but failed to produce the right result as the Protestants, particularly Ridley, argued their case very effectively.

Much worse was in store. Once the heresy laws had been restored, also at the end of 1554, the trials and executions began. The first burning, of John Rogers, took place in February 1555, to be followed by nearly 300 others by the end of the reign. Many more people, almost 800, went into exile in Europe. Many were gentry and other lay leaders, including several future bishops under Elizabeth. The story of the exiles seems to point both ways for assessing Mary's chances of success. They show the strength of Protestantism by their status and their energy in exile, sending back books to inspire those unable to flee. On the other hand they did leave, gloomily expecting a long, possibly unending, exile, for Mary was only 37 in 1553. Their numbers too are perplexing – was 800 a large or small number? At home, especially in London, those who could not escape ran their own 'underground' church, meeting in their own houses and inns, with congregations numbering up to 200.

Protestants, exiles or not, may well have been surprised at the brevity of their persecution, but does brevity alone explain the failure to recreate the Catholic loyalties of the 1520s? Some measures taken by Pole and Mary might well have led to success. Persecutions could be successful in ending Protestant resistance, as had been shown in parts of Europe. More directly, Pole had established the basis for an effective, new Catholic church. He planned to establish seminaries to train priests who were committed to their church. The bishops, re-appointed (like Gardiner, Bonner in London and Tunstall in Durham) or new-appointees (Goldwell at St Asaph, Pate at Worcester and White at Winchester after Gardiner's death in 1555) were very clearly a formidable group. In 1559 only one of the Catholic bishops accepted the Elizabethan settlement, a stark contrast to the response of their predecessors in 1532. Goldwell rejected a bishopric in Italy and a Cardinal's hat and planned, before stopped by illness, to return to England as an underground missionary priest.

A table defcribing the burning of Bifhop Ridley and Father Latimer at Oxford, D.Smith there preaching at the time of their martirdome.

EXECUTION OF LATIMER AND RIDLEY.

These measures showed Pole's organisational skills and educational awareness. However they were measures tuned to the belief that there was a population just waiting to return to Catholicism. As there was not, such measures could only succeed in the long term. What was needed, and what was not recognised as necessary by Mary and Pole, was preaching, designed to enthuse and capture the imaginations, spirits and minds of the people. After all, many – all those under 30 – had no memory of Catholic England. But in A G Dickens's phrase, Mary and Pole 'failed to discover the Counter-Reformation'. They were concerned that preaching would stimulate controversy and thus frighten people. Belatedly Books of Homilies, directed at the laity, were prepared to counter-balance the impact of the English Bible, but little use was made of the great new weapon, printing, and Pole also refused Ignatius Loyola's offer to send Jesuits to England. Ironically the first Jesuits arrived in November 1558, the month both Mary and Pole died.

Another problem was the Spanish connection. One of the reasons for the success of Henry VIII's revolution had been that it associated his church with nationalist feeling. For many people, a return to Catholicism meant, above all, subordination to the Pope, a foreigner. Worse, the foreign connection was made obvious by the queen's new husband and his entourage. Wyatt's rebellion and street brawls between English and Spaniards were the product of an amalgam of religious and nationalist feeling. Philip also brought priests to England and two of them became Professors of Divinity at Oxford. Quite what the real impact of these men was is unknown but their presence could only have added to the fear and resentment caused by the persecutions.

Above all, Mary and Pole failed because of the confusion and neutrality of the English people. If Catholicism was to establish a hold sufficient to survive Mary's death, even if she had died as late as 1570, the government needed to overcome the Protestant faithful and energise the rest. Unfortunately the people refused to be enthused, energised or otherwise made partisan – but this is not altogether surprising. To date the people had acquiesced in the revolution of the 1530s, the step-back in 1539, the Protestant success in 1550–53 and now in Mary's Catholicism revisited. With such a record no-one should be surprised that a return to Protestantism was accepted under Elizabeth in 1558–9 and would have been accepted ten or even twenty years later. If such as Gardiner and Northumberland argued that loyalty to the crown and state came before personal conviction who were the ordinary people to argue? Especially when their intellectual grasp on even their own personal convictions was probably very shaky after all the changes. Nor could they be guided by their priests, who in 1555, were by and large the same men who had preached a different set of beliefs to them in 1552, albeit then they had been with wives and without vestments. As the Venetian ambassador observed, Englishmen 'discharge their duty as subject to their prince by living as he lives, believing what he believes, and in short, doing whatever he commands, making use of it for external show ... rather than from any internal zeal ... (they) make this show of recantations, yet do not effectually resume their Catholic faith'. If this visitor could correctly identify both this natural trait and that there were very few pious Catholics why did not Mary, Pole and their advisers realise and act on the same attitude?

How can we sum up the progress made by Mary? She had returned England to Roman Catholicism in theory. In practice this allowed Catholics – a minority – to worship in the way that they wished and determined the way the majority of the uncommitted worshipped. Some Protestants fled or were executed but most of this other minority simply went underground or kept their beliefs to themselves. Even so some opposition was in the open, especially in London, where priests and the services were ridiculed and a cat, dressed as a priest, was hung from a gallows. London may have been atypical but it was important because of its size and influence. Nationally the re-appearance of Catholic rites suggested a real renaissance – altars, images, vestments and all the ornamentation of the mass made a revival seem clear. However there were significant gaps, particularly in those elements that Protestants had criticised as superstitious. There was no revival of the cult of saints, pilgrimages or the belief in purgatory. Few wills left money for masses for the souls of the dead. It is even unlikely that church attendances increased. There does not seem to have been a real religious revival, only the appearance of one – but could more have been done in the time available?

It seems that from the beginning Mary misunderstood her task. There were good reasons for this – her own political isolation before 1553, the spontaneous support in 1553, Northumberland's recantation of Protestantism before his execution. The latter two events simply confirmed Mary's expectation that, once the evil minority of bishops and other leaders had been removed, the majority would joyously re-embrace Catholicism. Pole, thanks to his exile, was even less well-informed about the religious state of England.

Charitably, some historians have argued that Pole deserves credit for building a good base for a Catholic revival. Certainly in 1555, when the Queen was believed to be pregnant, the future looked rosy for Catholicism and its prospects were not blighted for another two years at least. Whether this was enough seems doubtful, given the mistaken assumptions about the religious views of the people. Perhaps, like R M Pogson, we should conclude that 'in a longer and luckier reign they would still have missed important opportunities to win back England to Rome.' Another well-rehearsed argument is that the persecutions and burnings played an important part in the failure of Mary's religious policy. Next you have a chance to examine this issue for yourself.

EXAMINING THE EVIDENCE
Bloody Mary?

[Religious persecution] now became, not a principle taken for granted and rarely applied, but a fact in the experience of gentle and simple alike. Women at their marketing, men at their daily trade, the cobbler at his bench, the ploughman trudging the furrow – all learnt to know the smell of burning human flesh, the flesh of a neighbour, or a man or woman as familiar as the parish pump. Mingling with the steam of washing day, or with the reek of autumn bonfires, or polluting the sweetness of June, that stench of human burning became a matter of everyday experience. Such an experience, even in a cruel age, left behind it a memory and a disgust ...

H.F.M.Prescott, *Mary Tudor,* 1940.

Is this description by a writer markedly sympathetic to Mary a true reflection of the experience of the people of Marian England or is it an evocative exaggeration? The primary and secondary sources below will help you reach a conclusion.

Source A

... and so [Rogers] was brought ... toward Smithfield, saying the psalm 'Miserere' by the way, all the people wonderfully rejoicing at his constancy, with great praises and thanks to God for the same. And there, in the presence of ... a wonderful number of people, the fire was put unto him; and when it had taken hold both upon his legs and shoulders, he, as one feeling no smart, washed his hands in the flame, as thought it had been in cold water. And, after lifting up his hands unto heaven, not removing the same until such time as the devouring fire had consumed them – most mildly this happy martyr yielded up his spirit into the hands of his heavenly Father. A little before his burning at the stake, his pardon was brought, if he would have recanted, but he utterly refused.

From John Foxe's Acts and Monuments.

Source B

The fourth day of February the bishop of London went into Newgate prison with other doctors to degrade Hooper and Rogers, sometime vicar of St Paul's. The same day was Rogers carried, between 10 and 11 o'clock, into Smithfield and burned for erroneous opinions, with a great company of the guard. The fifth day of February between 5 and 6 in the morning departed master Hooper to Gloucester and Saunders to Coventry, both to be burned.

Extracts from the diary of Henry Machyn for 1555.
Machyn welcomed Mary and the return of Catholicism.

Source C

The people of this town of London are murmuring about the cruel enforcement of the recent acts of Parliament on heresy which has now begun, as shown publicly when a certain Rogers was burnt yesterday. Some of the onlookers wept, others prayed God to give them strength, perseverance, and patience to bear the pain and not to recant, others gathered the ashes and bones and wrapped them up in paper to preserve them, yet others threatening the bishops. The haste with which the bishops have proceeded in this matter may well cause a revolt...

Letter from Simon Renard, the Spanish Ambassador in London,
to Philip II, 5 February 1555.

---

1 Read Source A. How might such events have affected attitudes to Mary?

2 Read Sources B and C. What do they tell you about the people's response to the executions?

Source D

Touching punishments of heretics, we thinketh it ought to be done without rashness, not leaving in the meanwhile to do justice to such as by learning would seem to deceive the simple. And the rest so to be used that the people might well perceive them not to be condemned without just oration, whereby they shall both understand the truth and beware to do the like. And especially within London I would wish none to be burnt without some of the Council's presence and – both there and everywhere – good sermons at the same.

Part of the Queen Mary's instructions to her Council.

---

3 What does Source D suggest about Mary's attitude to executions?

Source E

As the bloody rage of this persecution spread neither man, woman nor child, wife nor maid, lame, blind nor cripple ... but whosoever he were, that held not as they did on the pope, and sacrament of the altar, were he learned or unlearned, wise or simple innocent, all went to the fire ...

John Foxe's verdict on Mary's reign.

Source F

(i) Ages

The ages of 52 of those executed are known:

14 were born before 1520, aged 35 and over

27 were born 1520–1532, aged 23–35

9 were born after 1532, aged 22 and under.

(ii) Men and Women

222 men

51 women

(iv) Occupations

Men (222)	Women (51)
114 unknown	19 unknown
21 priests	6 widows
13 weavers	25 wives
9 gentlemen	5 unmarried
7 husbandmen	1 gentlewoman
6 labourers	5 wives of husbandmen
4 fullers, shearmen	2 servant maids
3 tanners, sawyers, brewers, painters	2 wives of millers
2 tailors, butchers, smiths, bricklayers carpenters, tallow chandlers, servants	2 wives of weavers
	1 wife of a brewer, a pewterer, a shoemaker, an upholsterer
1 apothecary, schoolmaster, merchant, linen-draper, constable, cook, barber upholsterer, pewterer, glazier, artificer, wheelwright, glover, shoemaker, miller, merchant tailor	1 blind daughter of a rope-maker

Statistics of martyrs, taken from P Hughes,
The Reformation in England 1950.

Source G

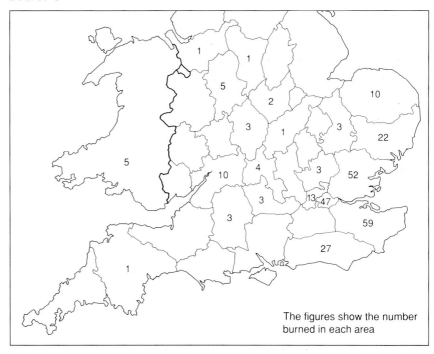

The figures show the number burned in each area

---

4 Do Sources F and G support Foxe's statement in Source E?

5 Using Sources A – G do you agree that 'all learnt to know the smell of burning flesh'?

Source H

The Book of Martyrs has all the qualities that will delight the partisan, and that must torment the historian. There is, for example, Foxe's purpose. Why did he write the lives of Queen Mary's victims? Very simply, as a mighty piece of anti-Catholic propaganda. ... the liveliest parts of the narrative, the interchanges between the judges and the prisoners, for example – in which the prisoners are invariably victorious – are presented as being the prisoner's own accounts: it is the trial, and the judge, described from the condemned cell.

P Hughes, *The Reformation in England*, 1950.

Source I

As far as his sources and the historical conventions of his day allowed, Foxe wrote good history; and for recent history, a checking of his account by such official records as survive, shows him to be substantially accurate about facts. Foxe's account was successful precisely because it invoked known truths ... one can read back from Foxe that persecution was unpopular; one cannot deduce that it was so unpopular as to be necessarily self-defeating. One of the more unpalatable lessons of history is that persecution often works.

C S L Davies, *Peace, Print and Protestantism*, 1976.

6 What conclusions can you reach, on the basis of Sources H and I about the value of Foxe's work for historians?

Source J

Burnings were not peculiar to Mary's reign, though their scale was. Protestant theologians did not, for the most part, disapprove of burning heretics, they merely disagreed about the definition of heresy, and many [like Cranmer] were themselves involved in persecution. More generally, capital punishment was common. After the northern rebellion of 1569, some seven hundred people were 'appointed for hanging'; while anything between 17 and 54 people were hanged each year in Elizabethan Essex, generally for small-scale theft ...

The burnings impinged very little, therefore, on the majority of the population; but disproportionately on those who could best make their hostility felt, and whose adhesion was likely to be decisive in a crisis. The burnings caused a good deal of local popular resentment. The London authorities were told to prevent demonstrations of sympathy at executions and specifically to see that apprentices and servants were kept at home on execution days; and there is plenty of similar evidence for other places.

C S L Davies, *Peace, Print and Protestantism, 1450–1558*, 1976.

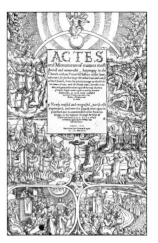

FOXE'S BOOK OF MARTYRS.

7 What evidence might support the view in Source J that 'the burnings impinged very little ... on the majority of the population'?

8 How might the spread of executions be explained by (a) the spread of Protestantism before 1553 and (b) by problems of government control and communication?

Source K

Mary ... was not pursuing a policy but fulfilling a duty. She was also, although she would probably not have admitted it, exacting a personal revenge; and the same was true of Pole. Not only had heretics and schismatics destroyed the peaceful and pious old England which they both imagined that they remembered; they had also destroyed Mary's personal happiness, and slaughtered the cardinal's family ... the momentum of persecution did not slacken. It was maintained primarily by the privy council, who harried the front line bishops, particularly Bonner of London, and constantly admonished justices of the peace to do their duty in support of the church. This insistence reflected the personal wishes of the queen. Few individual councillors were zealous persecutors in any of their other capacities, as local magnates or justices. Nor were most of the bishops, who took endless pains to argue with and cajole their victims before resorting to the extreme penalty.

D M Loades, *Mary Tudor, A Life*, 1989.

Source L

Gardiner had pressed for [the burnings] but it was Mary who obstinately backed the continuing campaign when both he and the Queen's Spanish advisers saw that they were counter-productive and urged her to stop ..

TALKING POINT

A historian's religion might affect his or her interpretations of the past. What other influences might affect a historian's objectivity? In the context of this section on Mary Tudor is it important for you to know a historian's religion?

Within dioceses heavily affected, there were concentrations in particular counties or specific areas of dioceses ... an indication, which is confirmed by detailed investigation, that initiatives in executions came primarily not from church officials but from lay magistrates, particularly those who subsequently demonstrated their adherence to Catholicism under Elizabeth.

D MacCulloch, *The Later Reformation in England, 1547–1603*, 1990.

9 Who was responsible for the executions?

The Loss of Calais

Mary's marriage to Philip created the prospect of England being involved in a war that was not in her interests. However the marriage treaty said that Philip could not of his own accord take England into war and this agreement triumphed when, on his first visit, he failed to persuade Mary and her council to enter his war against France. However his second attempt succeeded, even though the great majority of the council at first objected. The result was the loss of Calais, the last English possession in France. Critics of the Spanish marriage had been justified – or had they?

Late in 1556 Philip was at war with France. However Spain was bankrupt and Philip needed more men and resources. As king of England surely he could bring England into the war? If not, his reputation in Europe would suffer. The council's opposition to his request for aid in March 1557 (only Paget definitely supported Philip) was however logical. War was expensive; there had been famine in England and France was a valued supplier of grain. Then the unexpected overthrew logic. Thomas Stafford, a Protestant in exile, seized Scarborough Castle and proclaimed himself 'Protector of England'. Stafford had sailed from France with French weapons, albeit not very many as he only had two ships. Despite the fact that his demonstration – it hardly counts as a rising or rebellion – was immediately squashed there was now an English motive for war. Other arguments then came into play. France had been sheltering Protestants, better weather promised a good harvest, prices were falling. War would also unite a divided ruling class. Philip got what he wanted.

The Anglo-French war of 1557–8 saw English forces take part in four operations. The navy successfully cleared the Channel of French shipping and protected the English fishing fleet and the Spanish bullion fleet. A force of 5,000 soldiers helped to capture the town of St Quentin. Another force defended the border against the inevitable Scottish attack during a French war. The fourth operation involved the loss of Calais. When the 1600 men garrisoning Calais were faced by 27,000 French troops they sent for reinforcements but Philip, not anticipating winter campaigning, had none to send. The English surrendered in January 1558, not knowing that in another couple of days the French would have been forced to withdraw through lack of supplies. Worse, the French troops had only been able to make progress because the normally impenetrable marshland they had to cross was frozen. The blame for the loss of Calais can be equally distributed. The English council, Philip and the commanders at Calais underestimated the threat in winter. The commanders gave in very readily.

Historians now argue that the war was neither foolish nor against English interests. It was simply unsuccessful and unlucky. However this is less important than the effects of the loss. There were threats of a French invasion of England in the summer of 1558. The loss of Calais marked the end of what to English people was a glorious military record. Add to this the problems and fears caused by poor harvests, famine and thousands of deaths through influenza it is easy to see why Mary's reign ended with a doom-laden reputation. Before 1553 people had commented that prices had been rising ever since the break with Rome and some had superstitiously hoped for improvement once the old religion was restored. They and nearly everyone else were disappointed by the events of Mary's reign.

Worthwhile Reforms?

We started with Mary's religious policy and marriage but they, whatever the arguments for and against, do not conjure a positive picture of her reign. Less popular is administrative history – the good works of the council which did produce positive achievements but which are easily forgotten amidst more dramatic events. Both the Privy Council and parliament continued to operate effectively and produced the reforms described below.

Theoretically the council was too large, its fifty members being a product of Mary's inclusion of her favourites, the old conservatives and the necessary politician/administrators. In reality its working membership was small and made up of the experienced administrators. Its weakness, especially early on, was that it was divided by factions led by Paget and Gardiner (who died in 1555) that Mary could not control. Despite this its cohesion developed, its central figures being Paget, William Petre and William Paulet, Marquis of Winchester, who was Lord Treasurer from 1550–1572.

Revenue Reform – the report of the 1552 commission was followed up to streamline the financial administration by reducing the number of individual, money-receiving departments. The Exchequer regained its pre-eminence, handling 75 per cent rather than 30 per cent of the crown's income and doing so more efficiently. More could have been done but the Treasurer, Winchester, wanted efficiency without radicalism. The system he established lasted well into the next century and raised the status of Lord Treasurer very significantly.

Royal Finances – two measures augmented the queen's revenues. A survey of crown lands led to a revaluation and the raising of rents and entry fines, producing, at the highest estimate an extra £40,000 per annum. Customs rates were also increased for the first time since 1507, taking inflation into account. Implementation in 1558 saw income rise from £29,000 to £58,000 in Elizabeth's first year. Both measures came too late to help Mary but benefitted Elizabeth greatly.

The Navy – built up by Henry VIII, it had suffered wear and tear under Somerset and financial cut-backs under Northumberland. Aided by Philip's self-interested encouragement, six new ships were built and others repaired. In 1557 regular peacetime allocation of funds was begun, thus securing the financial administration which was supervised by Winchester with Benjamin Gonson as naval treasurer. Again Mary's bequest to Elizabeth of an efficient navy was most valuable.

The Militia – the French war revealed the inadequacies of recruitment and defence which were still dependent on nobles supplying men and equipment. The new Act for the Taking of Musters required every section of society to provide men, horses and equipment for the shire levies. Penalties for absence or desertion became harsher. A Weapons Act decreed the weaponry required by each rank in society, providing for the modernisation of weapons. These measures laid the foundation for recruitment for the rest of the century.

The Coinage – in 1553 both good and debased coins were back in circulation. By 1556 the Council initiated discussions on a wholesale reform, intending a full recoinage. However nothing was done amidst the severe economic hardships of 1556–7. A 'failure of nerve' seems understandable in such circumstances. The plans however did not disappear and were the basis for the recoinage of 1560–61.

Towns – under pressure from economic and social changes towns faced many new problems in the mid-sixteenth century. From the 1530s governments responded to individual issues and then developed broader policies. Mary's government was particularly strong in its support for towns through Acts protecting the rights of towns involved in retail trading and clothmaking against rural rivals.

---

1 List the strengths and weaknesses of these various measures. Does any pattern of action or inaction appear?

2 Tackle the material in the Focus sections on Parliament and Ireland. Do they support your conclusions in question 1?

3 How do these measures support the view that Mary's reign was not a side-issue in Tudor history?

11.1 Parliament under Edward and Mary

> This discussion of Mary's administration necessarily includes an assessment of her parliaments but this also provides an opportunity to review the parliaments of Edward VI's reign. What do the meetings of parliament between 1547 and 1558 tell us about the theory that this was a decade of crisis?

SOURCE A

The consequences of the Reformation Parliaments were immense for parliament as well as for the religious history of England. Because Henry VIII had used parliament in his fight with the pope, his son was to use it to carry through a Protestant reformation: because the Reformation had been sanctioned by parliament the Counter-Reformation of Mary's reign had also to be carried through parliament ...

However, the resurgence in parliament's importance was not confined to matters of religion. The 1530s and 1540s witnessed attempts by both theorists and men of affairs to analyse the ills of England and suggest ways in which they might be remedied, and the way in which many of them sought to improve things was by statute. ... The late 1540s and 1550s, for example, saw a crop of statutes that were a response to rising food prices. .. One consequence of all this activity was to make it more and more desirable to sit in parliament and keep an eye on what was going on. By so doing, men could protect or even advance their businesses, trades, or localities. ... Trades and industries began to organize themselves, not only to put forward certain proposals in parliament, but also to resist those that they did not care for.

J.Loach, *Parliament under the Tudors*, 1991.

SOURCE B

... general indifference in doctrinal matters on the part of the Commons can be further illustrated from the reign of Edward, a reign in which the doctrine of the English church was dramatically changed through statute. Only twice did the House of Commons raise any substantial protest against government policy. ... The picture that emerges in Edward's reign is of a malleable House of Commons, anxious about threats to material interests – for instance, in the chantries bill – but less concerned, and less interested, in dogma. The House of Lords was , of course, a different matter, for there conservative bishops and lay peers fought every change...

J.Loach, *Parliament under the Tudors*, 1991.

Questions

1 How does the pattern of parliamentary meetings compare with those of earlier reigns?

2 Why was parliament called during this period?

3 Was this a significant period in parliament's history?

4 Were parliaments a focal point of opposition to royal administrations?

5 What do parliaments tell us about the quality of Mary's government?

SOURCE C

(Mary's) reign was marked and marred by parliaments which were more disturbed than at any other time during the English Reformation. More often than not (apart from 1555) the Lords proved to be Mary's stumbling block. And, though the evidence is largely circumstantial, it is sufficient to suggest that some of the Commons' hostile actions were stage-managed, or at least prompted, by patrons in the Upper House.

M.A.R.Graves, *Early Tudor Parliaments 1485–1558,* 1990.

SOURCE D

... it seems as if the notion that the House of Commons in Mary's reign grew in organizational skills under the direction of Protestant-minded gentlemen has to be abandoned. The evidence for opposition to the queen's policies on doctrinal grounds is very slight and that for anxiety about property rights very considerable. This is not surprising when we remember that the Marian government had tacitly permitted Protestants in a position to do so to leave the country ...

Although some of those in parliament had gradually come to believe that they could interpret the wishes of the Almighty without the advice of convocation and bishops, many of the Commons clearly remained hesitant and uncertain, willing to follow the lead of the monarch and his advisers ...

J.Loach, *Parliament under the Tudors,* 1991.

SOURCE E

(Mary's parliaments seem) to have co-operated on most of the Crown's policies, especially on matters of religion, and served as a willing partner in the passage of some important social and economic legislation. It must be said for Mary herself that she recognized in their number a majority of parliamentarians who remained open to compromise on most issues, and she was prepared to meet them halfway. She thus did not press for Philip's coronation, despite his ardent desire to have it. She bowed to their desire to protect Elizabeth ... (Parliaments) exhibited more of a spirit of compromise and cooperation than has been recognised. Surely in the eyes of the government they must have seemed as a success.

R.Tittler, *The Reign of Mary I,* 1991 (2nd. ed.)

FOCUS

11.2 Ireland under Edward VI and Mary

D eveloping and carrying through an effective policy in Ireland was never easy for Tudor governments. Assumptions about the relative insignificance of the mid-Tudor years might suggest that policy in Ireland stood still. What does the material on these pages tell you about governments' policies towards Ireland?

SOURCE A

(Before 1547 St. Leger) aimed at creating by friendship and conciliation a united national state for Ireland. The essential aspect of their policy was the idea of 'surrender and regrant'. ... Between 1547 and 1558 the whole policy collapsed in ruins with first of all forcible attempts to export the Edwardian Reformation wholesale to Ireland and then, under Mary, the occupation of Irish lands by English settlers. St. Leger did have two further periods of office as Lord Deputy after his recall in 1548, but neither Edward's nor Mary's governments trusted him fully, and the decision, in 1557 during the lord deputyship of the earl of Sussex to seize and confiscate the territories of Leix and Offaly to the west of the Pale and 'plant' them with English settlers was a very clear sign that conciliation had been replaced by aggression.

A.G.R.Smith, *The Emergence of a Nation State, The Commonwealth of England 1529 – 1660*, 1984.

SOURCE B

The danger of France intervening in Ireland and using it as a base from which to attack England was very real during the reigns of Edward VI and Mary, and there was consequently a greater willingness to spend money on Ireland's defence. Furthermore, Sir Edward Bellingham, Somerset's deputy in Ireland, argued that the garrisons would be self-financing if the soldiers were granted lands in the vicinity of the forts

instead of wages. It was to procure such lands that Bellingham launched a succession of attacks upon the Gaelic areas of Leinster as a prelude to the construction of forts.

... The intentions were a) to confiscate the lands in the immediate vicinity of these forts and populate it with soldiers ... b) to drive the indigenous cultivators towards the River Shannon; ... this would have left the Pale surrounded by a secure belt of soldier – cultivators, and all Gaelic areas within striking distance of Dublin would have been under constant surveillance...

N.P.Canny, *The Elizabethan Conquest of Ireland*, 1976.

SOURCE C

Somerset's government had discussed in 1550 the concept of plantation, whereby settlers of proven loyalty would be sold confiscated lands and would move in to stabilise the area of settlement. Mary's government picked up this idea and set about establishing such a colony. ... (Sir Thomas Ratcliffe) largely succeeded in establishing the plantations of Leix and Offaly, renamed Queen's and King's Counties, between 1556 and 1563. ... we may still rightly consider this as England's first experience with several elements of colonial rule, from town planning to the administration of justice, which would be applied in the Empire of the future.

R.Tittler, *The Reign of Mary I*, 1991 (2nd. ed.)

Events in Ireland 1547–1558

1548 Sir Edward Bellingham replaced St. Leger as Deputy.

1549 Order for the enforcement of the First Book of Common Prayer

1550 French envoys agreed treaties with O'Neill and other Irish leaders. St. Leger returned as Lord Deputy with instructions for the resumption, survey and leasing of Leix-Offaly.

1551-2 Sir James Croft Lord Deputy.

1556 Thomas Radcliffe, lord Fitzwalter (created Earl of Sussex 1557) sworn in as Lord Deputy.

1557 Parliament met at Dublin and passed Acts for the settlement of Leix-Offaly and the establishment of Queen's and King's Countries. Repeal of Henrician and Edwardian religious statutes.

Source D

Protector Somerset's garrison strategy for Gaelic Ireland – an adaptation of his Scottish policy to what superficially appeared a similar problem – was an expensive mistake; and neither Northumberland nor Mary, apparently, were able for long to resist similar demands for ambitious but ill-conceived experiments

S.G.Ellis, *Tudor Ireland*, 1985.

Questions

1 Why was this period important in the history of Anglo-Irish relations?

2 Which reign – that of Edward or Mary – saw the more significant developments?

3 Why was the plantation policy introduced?

4 What does this section tell you about the quality of Mary's government?

Leix-Offaly plantation, 1556–57

O'Donnells

ULSTER

O'Neills (Tyrone)

Burkes

CONNAUGHT

The Pale

Dublin

Geraldines (Kildare)

LEINSTER

Butlers (Ormonde)

Geraldines (Desmond)

Waterford

MUNSTER

Cork

Mary, Elizabeth and the succession

Mary died on 17 November 1558, aged 42. Her last illness was brief. Although her health had deteriorated in May, there was no alarm until late September. As recently as the beginning of 1558 Mary had hopes of being pregnant and thus avoiding the succession of her sister, Elizabeth. Not until early November 1558 did Mary explicitly recognise that Elizabeth would succeed her.

In Mary's eyes, Elizabeth was a Protestant bastard. She was the illegitimate daughter of Henry VIII and Anne Boleyn, the woman who had illegally and immorally supplanted her own mother. The events of Mary's youth had led her to hate Elizabeth, a feeling that was not diluted by suspicion of her involvement in Wyatt's rebellion and other Protestant plots, by Elizabeth's youth and beauty and the assumption that she would have children. Michieli, the Venetian ambassador, commented that this hatred 'although it is dissembled, it cannot be denied that she displays in many ways the scorn and ill-will she bears her.'

However Mary could do nothing about the succession. She had come to the throne on a wave of loyalty to the Tudor dynasty. She could not therefore repeat Northumberland's attempt to alter the line of inheritance. One possibility, urged by Philip, was for Elizabeth to be married off to a European Catholic ruler but Elizabeth refused all possibilities. Thus, although Elizabeth was legally Mary's heir, she was kept in comfortable imprisonment for eleven months in 1554 and at later periods. Such treatment and Mary's refusal to recognise Elizabeth's status only made Elizabeth, in turn, hostile to Mary.

When Mary died the focus of attention had already shifted to Elizabeth, around whom a new court was assembling. Just hours after Mary died Elizabeth's accession was proclaimed in London and in the afternoon 'all the churches in London did ring, and at night did make bonfires and set tables in the street and did eat and drink and made merry for the new queen, Elizabeth'. Were the Londoners simply welcoming Elizabeth or also expressing relief at the end of Mary's reign? Someone else who may have felt relieved was Philip, who expressed his 'reasonable regret' for Mary's death, a fitting epitaph for their one-sided marriage.

All this makes Mary's death all the more pitiful but there were alternative views. The contemporary author of these lines is unknown.

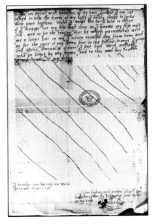

AFTER WYATT'S REBELLION ELIZABETH WAS SENT TO THE TOWER, WHERE SHE WROTE THIS LETTER BEGGING THAT SHE MIGHT SEE MARY TO DECLARE HER LOYALTY. ELIZABETH CLEARLY FEARED FOR HER LIFE IN 1554.

> She never closed her ear to hear
> The righteous man distressed
> Nor never spared her hand to help
> Where wrong or power oppressed
>
> Her perfect life in all extremes
> Her patient heart did show
> For in this world she never found
> But doleful days and woe.

REVIEW

'Mary's reign was doomed to failure by the queen's own attitudes and principles'

Stage 1

Review your assessments of Mary's character and fitness to rule written in answer to question 7 on page 258. Prepare a second version if necessary in the light of your work on Mary's reign.

Stage 2

Write a review of Mary's achievements as they might have been seen by contemporaries early in 1555.

Stage 3

Consider the validity of these statements:

(a) The Spanish marriage was a mistake that should have been avoided and which seriously reduced Mary's chances of success in her religious policy.

(b) Considerable progress was made towards Catholicism and the deferential attitudes of the English would have ensured the success of Mary's religious mission in only a few more years.

(c) Mary was an effective ruler. She got her way on the issues that mattered to her – religion and her marriage. Sensibly she left her administrators to develop reforms that were important and show the significance of her reign.

(d) Mary's reign appeared to be a time of gloom and failure because of poor harvests and epidemics rather than because of her policies.

Stage 4

Write an essay discussing the statement at the top of this Review section.

The Views of Historians

Source A

Normal people live in a world of compromise. It is not that they lack a sense of right and wrong, but their actions are normally determined by their judgement of what is feasible. Mary was innocent of that kind of reaction. Her best intentions could be frustrated by circumstances, and occasionally her moral sense disorientated, but she was incapable of assessing the needs of her subjects except in terms of the imperatives which governed her own life. Had she restored religion as her father had left it, and married some lesser prince ... both her life and her achievement might have lasted longer. Above all, if she had honoured Elizabeth and cajoled her into a suitable match, her work might not have been destroyed overnight by a vengeful successor with a grievance to indulge. However the story of her life had made such options impossible, and left England with a piece of history which has the ingredients of pure tragedy.

D M Loades, *Mary Tudor, A Life*, 1989.

Source B

The short duration of the reign is important in the process of evaluation because so many of Mary's policies lay unfinished or unfulfilled at her death. Even in the opening months of her successor's regime her two greatest achievements – the alliance with Spain and the restoration of Roman Catholicism – were abandoned altogether. On the other hand, the search for new trade routes, the reform of coinage, the increase in government support for measures of economic and social control and the revival of the navy were continued and brought to fruition only in Elizabeth's long reign. Ironically, many of these Marian legacies have been held up as unique accomplishments of Elizabethan rule, and have been used as points of contrast with the 'sterile' government of Mary ...

R Tittler, *The Reign of Mary I,* 1983.

Source C

Moreover, in spite of arousing considerable opposition and in spite of having to endure the misfortunes of harvest failure and exceptional mortality, Mary survived. She succeeded in enforcing her will over three major matters: her marriage, the return to Rome and the declaration of war. The weakness of Mary's government lay in the making of decisions, not in their implementation ... the queen was often confused and lacking in self-confidence, so that unless her conscience was aroused she often failed to resolve the disagreements among her advisers. Because of her policies and sometimes because of her lack of them, Mary tested the resources of her government severely, but they always proved adequate to the task. Justice was fairly administered and opposition severely punished. In all its ordinary aspects the country was as well and as fully governed as at any other time during the century. Despite the political and religious tensions it was no distraught or ungovernable country which Elizabeth inherited ...

D Loades, *The Reign of Mary Tudor,* 2nd edition, 1991.

	Religious Policy	Economy and Public Order	Foreign Policy	Government/ Administration
Henry VIII 1540–1547				
Somerset 1547–1549				
Northumberland 1550–1553				
Mary 1553–1558				

SECTION REVIEW

How would you assess the mid-Tudor period? The grid on page 283 will help you to sum up the achievements and failures of these years. In the grid summarize your views of each ruler's handling of the four areas of policy. It may be easier to split the initial work amongst a group – each person taking responsibility for one ruler – and then reviewing the conclusions. The quotations below, the Talking Points and charts may also be of assistance.

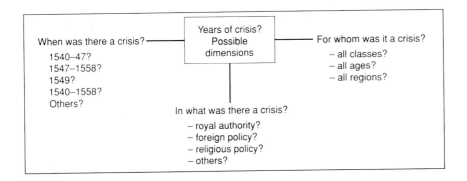

Essay

Crisis, consolidation or achievement? Which word provides the best description of the period 1547 – 1558?

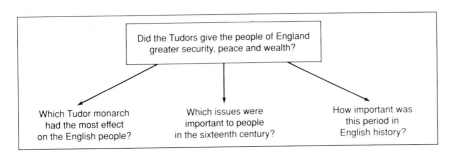

TALKING POINT

Was it likely that any problems would disperse when Elizabeth became Queen? What would you expect to be the character of her early years as Queen?

Source A

The mid-Tudor period ... now looks much more like the remainder of the sixteenth century than it did. But work done in an area not accessible to the earlier historians who shaped our gloomy view of the period has revealed that it was in one way bleaker even than they had imagined. 1558–59 saw the greatest demographic crisis not merely of the sixteenth century, but of the whole period between 1541 and 1871, and 1557–58 the second greatest. The last years of the 1550s thus experienced the worst demographic disaster in modern English history – indeed, the disaster is only surpassed in the whole of recorded English history by the Black Death. The critical issues for most mid-sixteenth century English men, women, and children were not the jockeying for position of nobles and politicians, nor the debates of theologians about precisely what happened when the Last Supper was commemorated, nor even variations in the value of coins and the price of food. Disease and the fear of death were the major preoccupations of the majority of people.

J.Loach, *A Mid-Tudor Crisis?*, 1992.

TALKING POINT

Elizabeth's reputation is very high. How does this affect opinions on the two rulers before her? Elizabeth came close to death from smallpox in 1562. The Spanish Armada could have succeeded in 1588. How might a different outcome to either event have affected her, and her predecessors' reputations?

TALKING POINT

Is 'Mid-Tudor Crisis' just a label used to fill the gap between Henry VIII and Elizabeth in books like this? Can you suggest a better label?

SECTION 4
Gloriana – The Reign of Queen Elizabeth

Elizabeth – The Survival Game

Tudor monarchs ruled as well as reigned. Their ministers advised but the monarchs decided. Therefore to begin this section with another decision-making game needs no apology because it reflects an essential feature of royal government. By examining the decisions facing Elizabeth we can also gain some understanding of the complexity of the issues she encountered. It is one thing to read that Elizabeth was faced with a problem and decided to do 'x'. If we accept that account too easily the decision may seem obvious, the situation one of no great difficulty. However, if we are presented with the same problem and several possible courses of action – each of which has arguments in its favour – the difficulty of Elizabeth's position is much clearer and we should understand more clearly why events took the course that they did. In the process of decision-making, take your time, discuss the options with your ministers – discussion and taking advice is not the sign of a weak, indecisive ruler.

The Rules of the Game

You have six crowns to begin. At each decision point you may lose one or more crowns, depending on your decision. Details of this are on pages 288 – 289. If you lose all six crowns you have been deposed, your country is in chaos! The Tudor dynasty has come to a sad and pitiful end!

---

1 A Marriage Proposal
Your brother-in-law, King Philip of Spain, offers to marry you now that he is a widower. Should you:
(a) accept his proposal because friendship and alliance with Spain will help you with the war against France?
(b) reject his proposal politely?

2 A Religious Settlement
After the religious changes of the last 25 years you have to decide the nature of the religion to be followed during your reign. Should you:
(a) postpone a decision indefinitely to avoid offending any one group?
(b) retain a Catholic church and doctrine?
(c) end Catholic doctrine and return to a moderate Protestantism, similar to that followed under Henry VIII?
(d) respond to the appeals of return Protestant exiles and establish a radical Protestant church similar to that under Edward VI?

3 France in Scotland, 1559
French influence in Scotland is considerable with a French regent, Mary of Guise. Mary, Queen of Scots was also Queen Consort of France and has claimed the English throne. A Protestant rebellion against the French has broken out. Should you:
(a) send an army to side with the rebels?
(b) send secret aid, postponing the decision to send an army?
(c) refuse to send any aid?

4 Marriage, 1560
You have developed a great affection for Robert Dudley, son of the Duke of Northumberland. His wife died recently, having fallen down stairs. She had been ill for some time. Should you:
(a) marry Dudley?
(b) stay single?
(c) stay single but become Dudley's mistress?

5 Lady Catherine Grey
Your cousin, Catherine Grey (a possible successor if you remain childless), has married without seeking your permission.
Should you:
(a) reprimand her for a breach of etiquette but allow her to retain an honourable position at court?
(b) send her a belated present?
(c) imprison her in the Tower of London?

6 Parliament, 1566
Members of the Commons ask you to marry to guarantee the succession. Some MPs introduce bills to amend the religious settlement, making the church more Protestant. Should you:
(a) agree to both demands because they will please members of parliament and vocal Puritans at court?
(b) agree to marry in order to secure the succession but refuse to amend the religious settlement?
(c) refuse both demands?

7 **Mary, Queen of Scots, 1568**
Mary has fled from Scotland after nearly a decade as ruling Queen. Her second husband, Lord Darnley, was murdered and she has provoked widespread opposition amongst her people. Mary has declared that she ought to be Queen of England and may have Catholic supporters in England. Should you:
(a) help Mary, as a fellow-monarch, to regain her throne?
(b) send her into exile abroad, perhaps to France?
(c) hand her over to the Scottish rebels for punishment?
(d) keep her in England, effectively imprisoned?

8 **War with Spain? 1568**
There have been clashes with Spain following the arrival of a Spanish army to crush a revolt in the Netherlands. Spanish bullion has been seized in an English port. An English fleet in America has been attacked. Should you:
(a) declare war on Spain, joining Dutch Protestants in a war of religion against Catholicism?
(b) apologise to Spain for the problems?
(c) wait upon events, trying to avoid war without appearing weak?

9 **The Duke of Norfolk, 1569**
Your cousin, the Duke of Norfolk, has been arrested. He is accused of plotting to marry Mary, Queen of Scots and of involvement in a Catholic rebellion. Should you:
(a) refuse to execute Norfolk despite the Council's urgings?
(b) order Norfolk's execution immediately?

10 **Marriage, 1572**
Negotiations begin for a marriage with the Duke of Alencon, brother of the French king. If the marriage produces a child this will resolve concerns about the succession. The marriage will also cement an Anglo-French alliance against the possible Spanish threat. Should you:
(a) marry Alencon?
(b) end the negotiations because you do not wish to appear to be playing second-fiddle to France?
(c) continue the negotiations in case a French alliance is needed urgently if the diplomatic situation worsens?

11 **Archbishop Grindal, 1577**
You have ordered Archbishop Grindal to take action against a group of radical Protestants who deny the need for bishops and a church hierarchy. They also seek great changes in your religious settlement. Grindal has refused, preferring a more moderate policy. Should you:
(a) dismiss Grindal from his post as Archbishop of Canterbury and appoint someone who will do your bidding?
(b) suspend Grindal which will warn Puritans that you will make no concessions
(c).Dismiss Grindal and take the necessary measures yourself as Head of the Church?

12 **Aid to the Netherlands, 1582**
Spanish troops are beginning to make effective progress in the Netherlands. Many of your councillors, including Robert Dudley, Earl of Leicester, are urging you to send support to the Dutch Protestants.
Should you:
(a) appoint Leicester to lead an army to resist Spanish progress?
(b) allow unofficial aid to reach the Dutch Protestants but refuse direct aid?
(c) refuse all aid because of the danger of provoking war with Spain?

13 **Aid to the Netherlands, 1585**
Spanish troops have made significant progress in the Netherlands. Spain has also reached agreement with Catholics in France for a Catholic League. Your councillors are once again urging you to send aid to the Netherlands. Should you:
(a) appoint Leicester to lead an army to resist Spanish progress?
(b) allow unofficial aid to reach the Dutch Protestants but refuse direct aid?
(c) refuse all aid because of the danger of provoking war with Spain?

14 **Mary, Queen of Scots, 1586**
Mary has been caught corresponding with Catholics plotting to free her and make her Queen. She has been tried and found guilty. Parliament is pressing for her execution. Should you:
(a) order her execution immediately?
(b) refuse her execution because it may precipitate an invasion by Spain?
(c) refuse to agree to Parliament's pressure?

15 **Wentworth and parliamentary privilege, 1593**
Peter Wentworth, an MP who has often complained that you have limited the topics discussed in parliament, has once again tried to open discussion of the succession. King James of Scotland is your likely successor. Should you:
(a) permit the House of Commons to discuss the issue now that you have decided against marriage and the Spanish Armada has been defeated?
(b) continue to forbid discussion and imprison Wentworth?
(c) publicly declare that James will be your heir?

16 **Your Portrait**
Paintings of you have been circulating that are not entirely flattering! They show an ageing monarch far removed from the image created by poets and courtiers. Should you:
(a) ban all such portraits and enforce a system of censorship so that only one style of portrait is produced?
(b) accept that time catches up with everyone and that your people revere you for your achievements?
(c) order that more flattering pictures are circulated in greater numbers?

17 **Starvation, 1597-8**
There have been four successive poor harvests. There is news that people are dying of starvation in the far north. Should your government:
(a) import extra food to alleviate problems?
(b) ignore the issue because such matters are not a concern of government?
(c) clamp down on vagrants to prevent the dangers of riots?

18 **The Earl of Essex, 1601**
The last of your favourites, the Earl of Essex, has led an abortive rising. It was a fiasco but treason. Should you:
(a) order his execution immediately?
(b) pardon him because his rising proved to be such a failure?
(c) postpone his execution? So many of your old servants have died in recent years that it would be hard to lose another.

ELIZABETH – THE SURVIVAL GAME

The points below suggest which decisions were better than others, although in such situations is often difficult or impossible to say with certainty which decisions were 'the best ones'. Elizabeth's choices were not necessarily the best choices, especially in the eyes of many of her subjects and even in the opinion of such loyal servants as William Cecil. How well did you do? Did you even survive?

1 A Marriage Proposal
(a) Have you learned nothing from the hostility to your sister's marriage? And why tie yourself to the shining knight of Catholicism? Lose 2 crowns.
(b) As inevitable as any decision you will take.

2 A Religious Settlement
(a) An attractive option because it seems to avoid offending anyone but in fact it will infuriate all Protestants and, if you eventually decide to introduce a form of Protestantism, the Catholics will feel tricked. Of course many people are not caught up in the detail of religious strife but, even so, lose 1 crown.
(b) After all you went through in Mary's reign? And it would grievously disappoint your most committed supporters. Lose 1 crown.
(c) A compromise that will not end criticism but makes outright revolt less likely. Only time will tell if this is the best option.
(d) And push the potentially powerful Catholic minority into outright revolt? Who can say just how powerful they are? Lose 1 crown.

3 France in Scotland
(a) Expensive and risky as it could lead to a French invasion and certainly will increase French involvement in Scotland. Lose 1 crown.
(b) Dangerous because you may appear weak and indecisive but less dangerous than the other options.
(c) The rebels will be discouraged. French influence in Scotland will increase and put pressure on your throne. Lose 1 crown.

4 Marriage, 1560
(a) Gossips will undoubtedly suggest you are involved in Lady Dudley's death, even though she died from natural causes. Other nobles may well be jealous and you will also lose the chance to use your marriage as a bargaining counter in diplomatic negotiations. Lose 1 crown.
(b) Dull, frustrating and sensible. Who would be a queen?
(c) Fun, tempting and infinitely dangerous. How will you avoid becoming pregnant? Can you keep your affair a secret? Lose 1 crown.

5 Lady Catherine Grey
(a) Quite the most appropriate action but as you can't marry Dudley this doesn't provide an adequate amount of revenge!
(b) Why should she be so lucky?
(c) Elizabeth's jealous and vindictive action but you don't lose any crowns here.

6 Parliament, 1566
(a) What right have they to discuss such matters? Next they will be trying to choose your husband and decide the details of doctrine. Lose 1 crown.
(b) As (a). Lose 1 crown.
(c) Your natural course provided you refuse in a way that flatters and pleases parliament. You intend to marry one day ... don't you?

7 Mary, Queen of Scots
(a) She is a Queen and you detest rebellion but she is a danger to you if she is a powerful influence in Scotland. Lose 2 crowns.
(b) Quite foolish! If French aid restored her in Scotland she would be even more dangerous. Lose 3 crowns.
(c) Tempting but you hate rebels. Even so, probably the safest option.
(d) How effective will her imprisonment be? This was Elizabeth's choice but a dangerous one. Lose 1 crown.

8 War with Spain
(a) War is expensive and thoroughly dangerous. You will need to call parliament and members will harry you over the succession and religion. Will English Catholics be loyal? Lose 1 crown.
(b) Why not give away your crown and learn Spanish at the same time? What a weak and pathetic monarch. Everything they said about women is clearly true. Lose 2 crowns.
(c) It's called 'masterly inactivity'. Philip does not want a war either – yet – so the dangers should die down.

9 The Duke of Norfolk
(a) Exactly what Elizabeth did and Norfolk became embroiled in further plots. Lose 1 crown.
(b) This is what your grandfather, Henry VII, would have done. Norfolk may be your cousin but, more importantly, he is dangerous.

10 Marriage, 1572
(a) And will Spain see this as a threat? You will also infuriate many at home and lose future diplomatic independence. Lose 1 crown.
(b) And offend France, potentially one half of a Catholic League against the puny Protestant powers of England and the Netherlands? Lose 1 crown.
(c) Why not, it might be fun, Alencon will bring you expensive presents and you might marry one day ... mightn't you?

11 Archbishop Grindal
(a) To do so may well provoke a good deal of opposition. Remember you are a woman and many loyal subjects are sceptical of a woman's right to head the Church. Lose 1 crown.
(b) Stern but sensible
(c) As (a) but worse. Lose 2 crowns – the Puritans (at least all but the most extreme) are your strongest supporters against the Catholic threat.

12 Aid to the Netherlands, 1582
(a) Effectively a declaration of war against Spain. As before, this will be costly, you don't know whether English Catholics will be loyal and Spain is far more powerful than you, especially as Philip has recently taken control of Portugal. Lose 1 crown.
(b) Once again the wonders of a compromise but only time will tell if this is the best option.
(c) Thus allowing Spain to win control of the Dutch coastline facing England, an ideal base for invasion. Why should Spain fear such a weak creature? Lose 2 crowns.

13 Aid to the Netherlands, 1585
(a) You don't want to but there's now no turning back. You have sought to avoid war with Spain for over 20 years but this is a declaration of war. Lose 1 crown.
(b) Probably not enough now, see 12(c). Lose 2 crowns.
(c) Probably a worse decision than last time. Lose 3 crowns.

14 Mary, Queen of Scots
(a) Yes. Wield the axe yourself if necessary. The woman is a menace even if she is Queen.
(b) Weak and pathetic – and is this your real motive? Lose 2 crowns.
(c) But what will you do in the end? You're just playing for time again. If you're not careful someone will take the initiative for you! Lose 1 crown.

The Spanish Armada
If you are still alive and reigning gain three crowns for surviving the invasion threat. You are a heroic symbol of national and religious pride for your people.

15 Wentworth and parliamentary privilege
(a) This tedious little man has been told before not to interfere in matters that do not concern him. This is not a matter for parliament. Lose 1 crown.
(b) A very queenly act. With luck he will die there!
(c) This is tantamount to abdication. All attention will shift to James and factions will compete for his favour. Lose 1 crown.

16 Your Portrait
(a) Quite right too! What else is royal power for?
(b) But they are more likely to revere you if they imagine you as a beautiful, ageless 'Fairie Queen'.
(c) Good idea – in addition to (a)!

17 Starvation
(a) Yes, it will reduce the chances of revolt.
(b) Dangerous because the problems are serious and there are mutterings that, with the war against Spain still continuing and taxes high, a new monarch would bring improvements. Lose 1 crown.
(c) In addition to (a) – valuable action against potential troublemakers.

18 The Earl of Essex
(a) Yes, you've learned at last! Your grandfather would be proud of you.
(b) The weakness of an ageing woman, not the action of a Queen. He may try again. Lose 1 crown.
(c) As (b). Lose 1 crown.

TALKING POINT
What appear to be the central issues and problems facing Elizabeth during her reign?

TALKING POINT
What have you learned from this activity about Elizabeth's personality, objectives and tactics as Queen?

TALKING POINT
Re-read these comments after you have studied chapters 12–15. Do you agree with the comments here on the decisions and on losing crowns?

12 Elizabeth, The First Ten Years 1558–1568

PREVIEW

Elizabeth Tudor became queen on 17 November 1558. She was twenty-five years old. Her youth made her popular; so too did the belief that she would not subordinate England's interests to those of the Pope. For a country exhausted by disastrous harvests and epidemic diseases, battered by defeat in France and humbled by a feeling of subservience to Spain and the Papacy, Elizabeth's accession offered a fresh start. The crowds cheered her, hoping that she would bring them a happier, prouder, calmer future.

PRINCESS ELIZABETH AGED ABOUT 13.

TALKING POINT

Can you suggest any possible consequences of the four points below?

TALKING POINT

How important is it to understand the early life of a politician or ruler if you are to understand their actions and attitudes in power?

No problems, however, were solved simply because Elizabeth and not Mary was queen. The war against France had still to be brought to a conclusion after the dismal loss of Calais. The harvest would be good, bad, satisfactory or indifferent whoever was on the throne. In addition, new problems were created by Elizabeth's accession. A new religious settlement was anticipated but what form would it take and who would support and who would oppose it? Crucially, how strongly would anyone oppose it? England's relationship with Spain would also need to be re-established but on what basis? Would Philip II contemplate marrying his sister-in-law, Elizabeth, try to overawe her with his empire's wealth or consider war if Elizabeth's religion offended his beliefs? Elizabeth's accession solved nothing. It simply created a new set of questions. Her handling of them can perhaps be explained by her experiences before she became queen.

- Elizabeth was born in September 1533. News of her mother's pregnancy had hastened the breach with Rome.
- May 1536 – Elizabeth's mother, Anne Boleyn, was executed. Elizabeth herself was proclaimed a bastard and was removed from the line of inheritance.
- Elizabeth was restored to the succession in 1544, after her brother, Edward and sister, Mary.
- During Mary's reign Elizabeth was suspected of being in league with rebels. She was held in the Tower of London for weeks, on suspicion of involvement in Wyatt's Rebellion.

A New Administration

Elizabeth's chances of solving the problems that faced her were greatly dependent on her choice of advisers. She chose wisely and, in doing so, made some of her intentions clear. By January 1559 she had re-organised the household and the Privy Council. The household was greatly changed. Only one leading household official kept his post. All of Mary's ladies in waiting were replaced, not simply because they were Catholic, but because their loyalties might well be divided between herself and the Pope and because they were closely associated with a regime that had treated her as a potential traitor. The new household officials and ladies in waiting were 'trusties' – members of her new Privy Council and her own relatives, through her mother, Anne Boleyn.

The changes in the Privy Council were central to Elizabeth's intentions. Mary's Council had grown to 39 members whereas Elizabeth considered 'a multitude doth make rather discord and confusion than good counsel'. Most of the thirty-nine were therefore dismissed. Elizabeth retained ten, seven noblemen (influential figures such as Arundel, Derby, Pembroke and Shrewsbury) and three experienced administrators, Mason, Petre and Lord Treasurer Winchester. Such men had welcomed Mary's restoration of Catholic ceremonies but did not support Papal supremacy. Thus they could serve Elizabeth but she also needed them, for their power and experience and because their inclusion in her administration clearly showed her desire to rule with the support of as wide a group as possible.

The ten Marian councillors were augmented by nine newcomers. There were two magnates, the Earl of Bedford (powerful in the west country) and the Marquis of Northampton, brother of Catherine Parr and supporter of Lady Jane Grey in 1553. The others were also experienced men who had served Edward VI. Sir Nicholas Bacon held the office of Lord Keeper of the Great Seal and William Cecil became Secretary of State. Cecil, aged 38, was the second youngest member of the council (the average age was 50) but he was the central figure, the man Elizabeth trusted above all others. The strengths of this council were its abilities, its experience, its range of religious views and, in addition, its involvement in the royal household. In Henry VIII's reign problems had arisen as council members and household men vied to win the King's support and determine policy. Under Elizabeth the same group held office in the council and in the household and influenced other members of both institutions and members of parliament. The potential for disruptive factional disputes was therefore much reduced.

The Religious Settlement 1558–1568

The problems of reaching a settlement

There was no doubt that Elizabeth's first priority was to establish a new form of religion. Catholicism or, more specifically, the Pope's authority was undeniably unpopular. Anti-Catholic rioting took place in London. Elizabeth was expected to be 'the Protestants' Queen' but the problematical question was what form or degree of Protestantism would Elizabeth introduce? The signs were not clear. She had appointed Cecil and other ardent Protestants to her council but she also retained religious conservatives. Radical Protestants were doubtless cheered by the court masque on Twelfth Night which depicted cardinals as crows and bishops as asses but they learned nothing about the specific intentions of the queen.

Elizabeth was herself a sincere Protestant and her religion was important to her. It had been her imminent birth that had triggered her father's break from Rome. She herself had suffered during her Catholic sister's reign. However in 1558 Elizabeth was even more aware of the needs of the present and the future. She saw her task as to introduce a form of religion that would minimise the risk of dissent or revolt. The methods of achieving this were much discussed and at least one document, the Device for the Alteration of Religion, was prepared, outlining the possibilities, problems and a way forward. The well-informed (but to us anonymous) author of the Device clearly identified the main danger facing Elizabeth – being misled into thinking that the voluble and influential body of radical Protestants in the south-east and East Anglia represented the country's religious views. He correctly said that they would be angry if 'their doctrine which they embrace is not allowed' and that they would describe any compromise as 'a cloaked papistry or a mingle-mangle'. However he went on to say 'better it were that they did suffer than her highness and commonwealth should shake or be in danger'. The great majority of the population was not in sympathy with radical Protestants, preferring instead the comfort of known Catholic rites of worship, even if they did not want to be subjected to the Pope.

ROBERT DUDLEY, EARL OF LEICESTER. THERE SEEMS LITTLE DOUBT THAT LEICESTER AND ELIZABETH WERE IN LOVE IN THE EARLY YEARS OF HER REIGN.

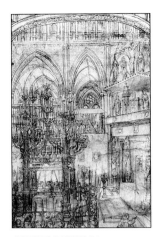

CANDLES CARRIED IN PROCESSION. ANOTHER SIGN OF CATHOLICISM THAT PURITANS WISHED TO SEE ABOLISHED.

The accuracy of this analysis was shown when Elizabeth's first attempts to establish her religious settlement were wrecked in parliament by conservative opposition. This legislation was based on the Edwardian Book of Common Prayer of 1552. It was passed by the Commons after noisy debate but was opposed and amended to the point of destruction by the Lords, where Mary's Catholic bishops found allies in a number of conservative peers. Thus instead of parliament being over by Easter 1559 it had to be recalled. When Lords and Commons reconvened they were doubtless aware that Elizabeth's private chapel on Easter Day had reflected the Edwardian rites she intended to have. Opponents also knew that two bishops had been imprisoned and some conservative peers were 'unavoidably absent'. Even so the Uniformity Bill which enacted the Prayer Book only passed by three votes, with nine lords (including two privy councillors) voting against. Elizabeth had had to compromise because of conservative opposition.

The discussion above presents one account of the development of the religious settlement. However there is another, developed by Sir John Neale. In his Elizabeth I and her Parliaments 1559–1581 (1953) Neale argued that the queen originally intended a moderate settlement and, indeed, meant to postpone some decisions but was pushed into a more radical Protestant settlement by a voluble Puritan opposition group. Later historians have continued the argument. Unfortunately the sources for the parliament of 1559 (and for early Elizabethan government in general) are relatively sparse. There are no draft bills as there are for the 1530s.

Source A

At Easter 1559 Elizabeth decided 'to try again for a parliamentary sanction of the royal supremacy and a Protestant settlement, ... The stumbling block that had tripped her drive for a religious settlement was the power of the bishops and Catholic laymen in the House of Lords'.

N L Jones, *Elizabeth's First Year* in C Haigh (Ed). *The Reign of Elizabeth I*, 1984.

Source B

Some historians, aware of ... weakness in Neale's explanation of the evolution of the 1559 church settlement have tried to demolish it entirely ... Dr Jones believes that Elizabeth always intended to have an act of uniformity as well as an act of supremacy, and that the uniformity that she wanted was that of the 1552 book.

All this is, in the final analysis, incapable of firm proof ... It seems highly improbable that this settlement was what Elizabeth had intended. Certainly her subsequent actions suggest little sympathy for the 1559 settlement ... a month after the end of parliament Elizabeth authorized a set of injunctions. They were conservative in tone ... When we add ... this to Elizabeth's insistence on the use of a crucifix in the chapel royal and her dislike of married clergy, it becomes difficult to accept the arguments of ... Jones about Elizabeth's Protestantism.

J Loach, *Parliament under the Tudors*, 1991.

1 How does N L Jones disagree with Neale over the 1559 settlement?

2 Does the extract from Jennifer Loach's book prove that either Neale or Jones is correct?

3 Why is such an event as the 1559 settlement still the cause of disagreements amongst historians?

The Legislation

Elizabeth's religious settlement of 1559 consisted of two Acts, the Act of Supremacy and the Act of Uniformity. The Act of Supremacy abolished Papal authority and established Elizabeth as Supreme Governor of the church, not Supreme Head as her father had been. This change mollified both radical Protestants and conservatives who objected to the idea of a lay person and especially a woman being described as Head of the Church. The Act of Uniformity imposed the 1552 Book of Common Prayer but again with significant amendments, framed to meet the demands of the conservative critics in parliament.

The wording for the Communion service allowed two interpretations that enabled people to emphasise simple commemoration or the reality of Christ's presence. Thus the way was opened for as many people as possible to accept the Prayer Book. During the Communion service communicants heard two statements: The body of Lord Jesus Christ, which was given for thee, preserve thy body and soul unto everlasting life (1549 Prayer Book); and Take and eat this in remembrance that Christ died for thee, and feed on him in thy heart by faith with thanksgiving (1552 Prayer Book).

Secondly the Act said that decisions on the vestments to be worn by clergy and the ornaments to be used in churches were to be made by Elizabeth. She decided that clergy should use the vestments worn in 1549, much closer to the Catholic model than to those worn by radical Protestant clergy. This was much less of a middle way and was to create problems for Elizabeth.

Overall however the settlement achieved its immediate objectives. It established a national Protestant church acceptable to as many people as possible. Only about 300 priests were expelled from their livings (there were around 9000 parishes) for refusing to accept the changes. The problem was that the settlement was only the beginning. Only time would tell whether this new church won real support or whether, in attempting to please everyone, it failed to please anyone.

Creating a radical problem

In 1558 it might reasonably have been expected that Elizabeth would face her greatest danger from Catholic-inspired dissent. Henry VIII in 1536 and Edward VI in 1549 had faced risings in which support for the old religion played a significant part. Elizabeth had clearly learned from these events. Those who wanted greater change were warned in 1559 by Lord Keeper Bacon that the laws would be enforced even-handedly, upon 'those that be too swift as those that be too slow, those, I say, that go before the law or beyond the law, as those that will not follow'.

TALKING POINT

Why did the inclusion of these statements allow different beliefs? Is this good evidence for Elizabeth's moderation?

A BISHOP'S COPE. SUCH CLOTHING WAS AT THE CENTRE OF THE ARGUMENTS OVER VESTMENTS.

Ironically, in her efforts not to push Catholics into rebellion she created a radical Protestant or Puritan opposition that caused her far more problems in her early years than did Catholics.

At first many committed Protestants probably did not heed Bacon's statement. Those who took part in the commissions of visitation in 1559 certainly translated the Royal Injunctions (supporting the Acts of Supremacy and Uniformity) with Protestant fervour. They burned statues, ornaments and even vestments. Altars were removed. And yet over the next ten years Protestants may well have whispered amongst themselves that the Queen was 'soft' on Catholicism. What evidence is there for this?

In the first place Elizabeth hoped to retain some of the Marian bishops as a sign of compromise. Unfortunately all but one refused to continue in office and so her bench of bishops was undeniably Protestant, including many who had lived in exile during Mary's reign. Elizabeth chose as her Archbishop of Canterbury Matthew Parker, a moderate, a former pupil of Thomas Cranmer and chaplain to Anne Boleyn. Many of Elizabeth's bishops undoubtedly saw the 1559 settlement as a staging post to a more complete settlement but they were disappointed. The doctrine of Elizabeth's church was defined in the Thirty Nine Articles of 1563, essentially a limited revision by Parker of the Forty Two Articles of 1552. Elizabeth had no intention of advancing along the paths taken by European Protestants since the early 1550's. In 1566 she came under pressure in parliament from a combination of radical councillors, bishops and MPs who wanted further reform. Elizabeth responded by forbidding discussion of some matters as being a breach of her prerogative and simply vetoed other bills.

TALKING POINT

In 1585 Elizabeth told the Commons 'For as she found (the Church) at her coming in, and so hath maintained it there twenty-seven years, she meant in like state, by God's grace, to continue it and leave it behind her'. Why was it dangerous for Elizabeth to make concessions to radicals at any stage after the initial settlement of 1559?

As well as preventing what the radicals saw as 'progress' Elizabeth also seemed to offer hope to Catholics. She restored a crucifix and candles to her own chapel altar. She allowed communion tables to be placed where altars had stood. She wanted to stop the clergy marrying but backed down under pressure from Cecil and other councillors. Elizabeth did not even require the letter of the law to be followed. Catholics were rarely prosecuted for failing to attend church (unless they openly supported the Pope) and she said that, if someone refused to take the Oath of Supremacy he or she should not be asked to take it a second time when a second refusal meant execution.

Most obvious of all Elizabeth's attempts at moderation was her insistence that clergy should wear the vestments used in 1549 and not the simple surplice wanted by the Puritans. To them this symbolised the absurdity of attempting a compromise. The queen had given them a Protestant Prayer Book and yet she wanted them to take services dressed as Catholic priests! In 1565 the queen ordered uniformity. The next year Edmund Grindal, the radical Bishop of London, was forced to discipline thirty-seven ministers who refused to wear the required garments. Given these events it is perhaps not surprising that some Catholics even began to hope that in time Elizabeth might be won over. In 1564–5 Catholic exiles dedicated a stream of books to Elizabeth. In 1567 the Earl of Sussex expressed what was probably a common view 'although he was a native-born Englishman and knew as well as others what was passing in the country, he was at a loss to state what was the religion that really was observed here'.

The most important element in an explanation of Elizabeth's religious policy is her determination to avoid making unnecessary enemies. If there were no Catholic martyrs it was hoped that Catholicism would dwindle and die out. Elizabeth therefore seems to have felt that time was on her side but there were also other reasons for her policies. She was determined to defend her prerogatives as queen and would not bow to pressure from radical bishops or even radical councillors to amend her settlement. Even more personally, Elizabeth enjoyed the ceremony of older-style services and so was reluctant to move further towards the 'pure' religion. In this she shared the tastes of most of her people. Most of the concessions she made affected the issues that ordinary people cared about, such as the dress and marriage of priests rather than the minute details of theology beloved by the radicals.

One final crucial element of Elizabeth's religion was its nationalism. This was not only clear in Elizabeth's position as Supreme Governor but was expanded in Bishop Jewel's 'Apology of the Church of England' in 1562. In reply to Catholic accusations that Elizabeth's Church of England was created simply for political progress, Jewel argued that 'We have come as near as we possibly could to the Church of the apostles' and that it was the Pope and the Catholic church that had turned religion away from Christ's path. Nothing could have been better calculated to unite Elizabeth and her people than such a statement of national virtue, even if, in the words of one cleric, many parishioners 'are a kind of people that love a pot of ale better than a pulpit ... who, coming to divine service more for fashion than devotion, are contented after a little capping and kneeling, coughing and spitting, to help me to sing out a psalm, and sleep at the second lesson'.

Foreign Relations

If Henry VII could have viewed the foreign situation facing Elizabeth in 1558 he would have found it strikingly familiar. He had been king of the third power of western Europe, fearful of intervention in English affairs by either France or Burgundy and also fearful of an alliance between them. Elizabeth, similarly facing two major powers, France and Spain, hoped to maintain an alliance with one of them and certainly wanted to avoid their joining together against her. However the dangers of the situation facing Elizabeth were complicated by religion as they had not been in the time of Henry VII. The prospect of maintaining an alliance with one of the great powers was more difficult because of their Catholicism and England's Protestantism. Henry VII would however have approved of his grand-daughter's defensive policy of avoiding unnecessary adventures, costs and commitments and her control of both the detail and general principles of England's relations with other countries.

England, France and Scotland, 1559–1560

Elizabeth was tested first by the oldest of foreign threats, the combination of France and Scotland. Recent history showed France to be England's principal enemy and there was no reason why this should change, especially after

TALKING POINT

Which elements of the religious settlement would have been responsible for Sussex being 'at a loss to state what was the religion'?

TALKING POINT

In the sixteenth century average life expectancy was little more than forty. How did this affect the speed with which support for Catholicism would die out?

MARY I QUEEN OF SCOTS.

the recent indignity of the fall of Calais. However the first major treaty of the reign, the treaty of Cateau-Cambrésis, offered Elizabeth a face-saving formula on Calais. The Anglo-French element of the treaty (which primarily involved France and Spain) said that France was to retain Calais for eight years and then it was to be returned to England, provided England had kept the peace. Elizabeth therefore did not have to confirm the loss of Calais and could retain hopes of regaining a foothold in France. This European peace seemed to offer Elizabeth the hope of tranquil foreign relations. Then Henry II of France was killed in a jousting accident. His successor was Francis II, husband of Mary, Queen of Scots. As a result France tried to increase its influence in Scotland, a Scottish revolt erupted and Elizabeth had to decide whether or not to intervene in Scotland.

Francis II himself was only fifteen, his wife just two years older. The real rulers of France became the Guise family, the most powerful noble family in the country. The Duke of Guise's sister, Mary, was the mother of Mary, Queen of Scots was Regent of Scotland. The Guise were strongly placed to manipulate Scottish policies for the good of France. Unfortunately for them the Regent was unpopular and the use of French troops to garrison Scottish fortresses provoked a Scottish revolt that was both nationalist and religious. A group of Protestant nobles called the Lords of the Congregation led the rising.

Clearly Elizabeth did not want France to win control over Scotland. Therefore it was probably a relatively easy decision in August 1559 to despatch secret supplies of money and weapons to the Scots. The next stage was far more complex. Should Elizabeth send an army to intervene in Scotland on the side of the rebels? If they were successful the gains would be great. The danger from France would be reduced, Scotland would be indebted to England and a pro-English party established in government. Cecil also had hopes that the Scottish Protestant lords would give aid to the English in Ulster. In all likelihood Scotland would also proclaim itself a Protestant country creating a Protestant union with England and jettisoning the French alliance. If all this was achieved the power and influence of Mary, Queen of Scots would be greatly weakened, reducing the chances of her challenging Elizabeth for the throne of England. Mary had been

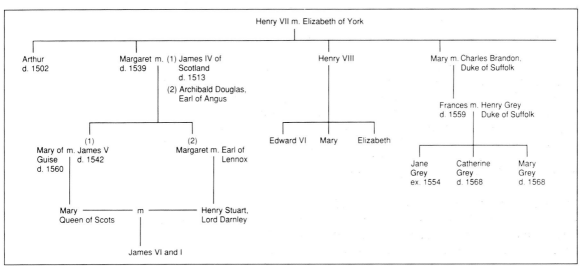

flaunting the royal arms of England, demonstrating that she saw herself and not Elizabeth as England's rightful queen.

Given such arguments it is perhaps difficult to see why Elizabeth did not despatch a strong army immediately. Yet for months Elizabeth procrastinated. She did not want to be accused of being the one who had broken the recent treaty. As a queen she did not want to aid rebels against another queen, even one who was her declared enemy. More practically, what would be the result if the rebels failed and an English army was defeated by the French on British soil? A defeat within Britain made an invasion far more likely than had the loss of Calais. Elizabeth had also to consider the attitude of Philip II, whose friendship might not last if she aided Protestants against Catholics.

Eventually the need for action overtook the potential dangers. Elizabeth sent ships to prevent the arrival of French troops and, in March 1560, having been reassured that Philip would not intervene, she sent an army to besiege the main French garrison in Leith. The decision taken, other factors worked in her favour. French Huguenots revolted. Mary of Guise died. The French fleet was destroyed in a storm. As a result France negotiated the Treaty of Edinburgh (July 1560) and agreed to evacuate her troops, leaving the Scots to establish their own government and religion. Later in 1560 Scotland did indeed complete its own Reformation, abolishing the authority of the Pope. This first foreign policy dilemma had shown Elizabeth's intentions. Her first objective was security. This was best achieved by diplomacy and inaction. Action was dangerous, being likely to antagonise other nations. Where possible she would delay committing herself, again for fear of creating unnecessary enemies. Support for Protestantism was not sufficient cause for intervention. Somehow or other she had to maintain an alliance with one of the two great powers who were both, unfortunately, Catholic.

Intervention in France, 1562–1564

Having identified such principles it appears that Elizabeth broke them when she gave aid to the Huguenots in France. Early in 1562 a massacre of Huguenots led to religious civil war. Elizabeth's favourite, Lord Robert Dudley, and another enthusiastic, radical Protestant, Nicholas Throckmorton, pleaded with Elizabeth to intervene against the Huguenots' Catholic persecutors. This Elizabeth eventually did, sending troops under the command of Dudley's brother, the Earl of Warwick, to garrison the Huguenot port of Le Havre.

Overcome by enthusiasm, radical Protestants saw this as the beginning of a campaign 'to banish idolatry out of France'. However it seems highly unlikely that Elizabeth suffered from the same lack of reality or, indeed, shared their aim. Elizabeth probably hoped to use Le Havre as a bargaining counter that she could exchange for Calais. She saw the French divisions as England's opportunity not a Protestant opportunity. Therefore she gave little aid to the Huguenots (again she would have been well aware of their status as rebels) and this was just as well. The divisions within France closed and England became the common enemy. Le Havre was taken by the French after the English garrison had been devastated by disease. In April 1564 Elizabeth had to accept the Treaty of Troyes which confirmed French control of Calais – for ever.

Intervention in France had cost Elizabeth money, men and prestige although the limits of her own ambitions had at least kept down the losses in the first two categories. A different monarch might have wasted far more. And there was another warning to Elizabeth. Spain closed the ports of Flanders to English merchants as a warning that Philip II did not approve of such aid to Protestant rebels. Trade did not resume until 1565.

Scotland: The problem of Mary, Queen of Scots

Mary's reign as queen of France was brief. Her husband, Francis II, was king for only eighteen months. When he died he was succeeded by his younger brother, Charles IX, whose mother, Catherine de Medici, became the most powerful figure in the French government. Mary was redundant and was returned (in August 1561) to Scotland, a country she had last seen when she was six. Scotland can scarcely have been home to its queen for she was a Catholic queen in a Protestant country, a product of French culture in what was now a profoundly anti-French society. Sensibly enough, Mary did not try to overturn the Scottish Reformation and the government of Scotland proceeded peacefully for several years.

After Elizabeth Mary had the strongest dynastic claim of all Henry VII's descendants although the Succession Act of 1544 had given precedence to the Greys (see family tree on page 297). Her chance of becoming queen of England was very real and was underlined by Elizabeth's serious illnesses in 1562 and 1564. Thus in the early 1560s Mary hoped to be officially recognised as Elizabeth's heir, but Elizabeth would not make such a decision. For a time some less definite understanding seemed possible and a meeting between the two was planned in 1562. However the civil war in France led to the meeting being called off (Elizabeth could not be seen to be in collaboration with a Catholic monarch) and it was not reconvened.

After that Mary became increasingly unhappy with the lack of an agreement. There was an English proposal that she should marry Robert Dudley (created Earl of Leicester) in 1564 which also came to nothing. Instead Mary married the young Lord Darnley, who was also a descendant of Henry VII, English-born and with lands in England. It seemed to be a shrewd diplomatic match, judging by the volume of protests from the English government. It seemed even shrewder when Mary's son was born in June 1566. He was christened James.

In fact the marriage to Darnley was the turning point in Mary's reign in Scotland. Until 1565 the Scots nobles had accepted her but her marriage to Darnley, heir of the Lennox family, resuscitated dormant rivalries between the Lennox and other families. Mary did not have the character to control such problems. Indeed she made them far, far worse by the chaotic and unprincipled course of her married life. Within a year of her son's birth, Mary had been taken prisoner by her own subjects and Edinburgh mobs were chanting 'burn the whore'. Within that year Darnley had been murdered and Mary had married Lord Bothwell, the man believed to be his murderer.

HENRY, LORD DARNLEY.

TALKING POINT

What would have been the attitudes of Elizabeth, Dudley and Mary to the proposed marriage between Dudley and Mary?

12.1 Marriage and the Succession

1559

There were rumours that the Earl of Arundel and Sir William Pickering hoped to marry Elizabeth. Philip II proposed marriage, as did Prince Eric of Sweden. Other possible suitors included the sons of the Holy Roman Emperor, the Archdukes Charles and Ferdinand. The Spanish ambassador reported that the court was swarming with the ambassadors of ten or twelve suitors. Parliament also pressed the Queen to marry as soon as possible for the sake of the succession. In reply Elizabeth said, 'whenever it may please God to incline my heart to another kind of life, you may well assure yourselves my meaning is not to do or determine anything wherewith the realm may or shall have just cause to be discontented ... I will never in that matter conclude anything that shall be prejudicial to the realm ... And in the end this shall be for me sufficient, that a marble stone shall declare that a Queen, having reigned such a time, lived and died a virgin'.

1560

The Archduke Charles appeared to be the most likely husband for Elizabeth. Even so gossip about the relationship between the Queen and Lord Robert Dudley hardened into the belief that they would marry. The sudden death of Dudley's wife in September (now known to be from natural causes) put paid to any real prospect of the marriage.

1561

Negotiations continued for the Swedish marriage. Lady Catherine Grey, one of Elizabeth's possible heirs, secretly married the Earl of Hertford, the son of Protector Somerset. When the Queen heard of the marriage and discovered that Catherine was pregnant the young couple were sent to the Tower. Elizabeth's relationship with Dudley continued as the Spanish ambassador reported: 'She, Robert and I being alone in the gallery, they began joking ... They went so far with their jokes that Robert told her that if she liked I could be the minister to perform the act of marriage, and she, nothing loth to hear it, said she was not sure whether I knew enough English'. Less happily, Elizabeth said about the succession 'I know the inconstancy of the people of England, how they ever mislike the present government and have their eyes fixed upon that person that is next to succeed'. The Scottish ambassador reported 'if it was certainly known in the world who would succeed her, she would never think herself in sufficient security'.

1562

Elizabeth caught smallpox and nearly died. Her doctors told Cecil they could do nothing to save her. The Privy Council was split three ways over the succession while the Queen wanted Dudley to be Protector after her death. Many echoed Bishop Jewel's words 'Oh, how wretched are we, who cannot tell under what sovereign we are to live'. 'The divisions of debate (over the succession) paled in comparison with the divisiveness of an unresolved succession when the Queen died. It is true that, in the end, her procrastination worked and the problem solved itself ... but this good fortune could not have been anticipated'.

C Haigh, *Elizabeth I*, 1988.

'Matrimonially Elizabeth was the best prize in Europe. Although the treasury was empty because of war with France, England's strategic importance, with its control of the routes from the North Sea to Europe and from Spain to the Low Countries, made her a bride worth coveting.'

(Maria Perry, The Word of a Prince, A Life of Elizabeth I, 1990)

PORTRAIT OF ELIZABETH.

Questions

Many of the quotations on these pages are from ambassadors' reports and the Queen's own words. How reliable do you think these are as evidence for Elizabeth's intentions?

What were the advantages and disadvantages of (a) a foreign marriage and (b) marriage to an Englishman?

Why did Elizabeth so vehemently refuse to name an heir?

In 1563 Elizabeth said that her 'inclination' was to be a 'beggar-woman' and single, far rather than Queen and married. Do you think she ever decided that she would not marry? If so, when?

Why was marriage such a difficult issue for Elizabeth?

1563

Parliament met. The Lords begged 'that it please your Majesty to dispose yourself to marry, where you will, with whom you will, and as shortly as you will'. The Commons similarly asked 'God to incline your Majesty's heart to marriage and that he will so bless and send such good success thereunto that we may see the fruit and child that may come thereof'. Their motives were the 'great danger and peril to all states and all sorts of men in this realm, by the factious, seditious and intensive war that would grow through want of understanding to whom they should yield their allegiances and duties'. Elizabeth avoided a direct reply, saying that she had not vowed to stay unmarried and that she would settle the succession at the appropriate time.

1564

Elizabeth told a Scots ambassador that 'I am resolved never to marry, if I be not thereto necessitated by the queen my sister's (Mary, Queen of Scots) harsh behaviour towards me'.

1565

Lady Mary Grey married one of the Queen's household without the Queen's permission. He was imprisoned. She was placed under house arrest. Negotiations for a marriage to the Archduke Charles were renewed.

1566

Parliament met and again asked Elizabeth to marry, 'to provide a known successor' and also warned that 'the Queen's Majesty, the Council and this House shall answer for all the innocent blood that shall be spilt in this cause'. Elizabeth was furious, sarcastically telling Parliament that she had already answered their questions in 1563 and that it was 'A strange order of petitioners that will make a request and cannot be otherwise assured but by the prince's word, and yet will not believe it when it is spoken'. She also accused them of worrying about the succession for their own safety and not understanding the danger she would place herself in if she named 'a second person'. 'I will never be by violence constrained to do anything ... it is monstrous that the feet should direct the head'.

1567

Negotiations with the Archduke Charles came to an end.

1568

Lady Catherine Grey died.

Elizabeth, The First Ten Years 1558–1568 **301**

Mary's own behaviour therefore caused rebellion by her people. The Scots nobles forced her to abdicate in July 1567 in favour of her son and imprisoned her for her own safety. However Mary escaped and fled to England where she appealed to Elizabeth for aid. This was certainly not a problem Elizabeth wanted for there was no satisfactory solution. Elizabeth had, perhaps, four options. She could

(a) give Mary financial and military support and use English force to restore her to her throne

(b) hand Mary back to the Scottish lords

(c) send Mary, as a guest or in exile, to France

(d) keep Mary in England under guard or with greater freedom.

In making her decision Elizabeth had to consider her duties to a fellow monarch, her distaste for rebellion, Mary's claim to the English throne, the likely policy of France, the costs of each option and Mary's religion. In the end, Mary remained in England, a captive guest.

TALKING POINT

What were the likely consequences of each of the four options? Why do you think Elizabeth chose the fourth of the options for dealing with Mary?

England's ally – Spain

In 1558 England's relationship with Spain was almost as simple as her relationship with France. France was England's enemy. Spain was her ally. Friendship with Spain and Philip II was undoubtedly a product of their mutual anti-French sentiment but it was also buttressed by trade. The bulk of England's overseas trade went through Philip II's territory of the Netherlands, principally through the port of Antwerp. Anglo-Spanish amity kept the influential merchants of both nations happy and swelled the royal coffers, for Elizabeth gained a significant proportion of her annual income from duties on the export of woollen cloths.

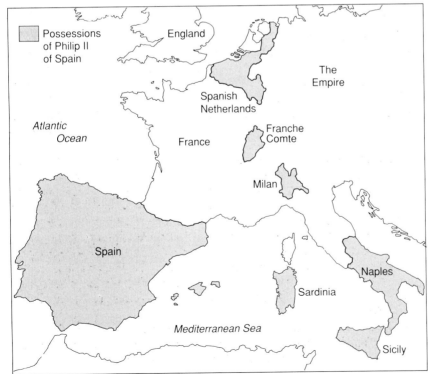

The problematical issue that lay between the two was their difference over religion but this was not enough at this time to make enemies of old allies. Neither side wanted war or even confrontation. The fact that Philip sent his Armada thirty years later does not mean that an Anglo-Spanish war had always been inevitable.

Elizabeth placed great importance on not alienating or antagonising Philip of Spain. She took a risk in 1562–4 by intervening in the French civil wars on the sides of the Huguenots but Anglo-Spanish relations were not seriously harmed. G D Ramsay has described Elizabeth as being 'rapped over the knuckles not as an enemy so much as a cheeky junior partner'. However there was one long-term result of this event. Unable to trade in the Netherlands, English merchants, in desperation, sought out alternative markets and found them in Germany and the Baltic. This was good news for the merchants and for the royal treasury but it demonstrated that English trade was not wholly dependent on the ports and towns of the Netherlands. Thus this strongest link between England and the Spanish empire began to weaken.

Philip himself had little time for the affairs of northern Europe for the most direct challenge to his territories came from Turkish fleets in the Mediterranean. In 1559 this had caused him to leave the Netherlands for Spain and he never returned. Thus, unlike Henry VIII and his rivals, Philip and Elizabeth never had the opportunity to meet as monarchs to discuss the issues that troubled them. They were dependent on the skills, or lack of them, of envoys to each other's courts. Perhaps royal meetings would have been to no purpose. In 1559 Philip had written to his ambassador in London 'It grieves me to see what is happening (in England) and to be unable to take the steps to stop it that I want, while the steps I can take seem far milder than such a great evil deserves ... But at the moment I lack the resources to do anything.'

The turning-point in Anglo-Spanish relations came in 1568. The previous year a large Spanish army under the command of the Duke of Alva had moved into the Netherlands to suppress a revolt. There was alarm in England. Cecil was afraid that this army might also be used as the spearhead of a joint Franco-Spanish attack on England. The presence of Alva's army made Anglo-Spanish relations immensely more delicate, requiring both countries to tread extremely carefully. Instead two clumsy incidents brought confrontation.

The first was far away in Mexico. An English merchant, John Hawkins, had been trading with Spanish colonies since 1562, despite Spain's claim to a monopoly of all trade in the Americas. On his third expedition in 1568 Hawkins was forced by storm damage to take shelter in the port of San Juan de Ulua. There he was caught by a Spanish fleet, whose commander regarded Hawkins as a pirate. The Spanish attacked Hawkins' ships, killing many sailors and capturing the 'Jesus' that had been provided by the Queen. Hawkins also lost much of the proceeds of his voyage. Both sides felt in the right and the news of the incident arrived in Europe just in time to add to the Anglo-Spanish hostility caused by a second confrontation.

This time it was a Spanish fleet that was driven into an English port, by storms and Huguenot pirateers in November 1568. The fleet was carrying gold to pay Alva's army. The money was seized and taken to

TALKING POINT

Does this quotation suggest an Anglo-Spanish war was inevitable? Historians often argue that no event is inevitable. Do you agree with his idea?

London. In retaliation Alva arrested all English merchants and goods in the Netherlands. Elizabeth arrested Spanish merchants in England. That old, most valued trade to the Netherlands came to a full stop. It did not recommence for five years.

In 1569 England's relations with her neighbours were perhaps more complex and more dangerous than at any stage during the first ten years of her reign. Relations with Spain had deteriorated rapidly while a potential invasion force was camped in the Netherlands. There had been no correspondingly significant improvement in Anglo-French relations although Elizabeth had not repeated her involvement in the French civil wars. Finally, as if to confirm the delicacy of her situation, Elizabeth held Mary, Queen of Scots, afraid of the dangers that Mary might create if she were free to travel abroad.

---

1 What were Elizabeth's objectives in her relations with other countries between 1558 and 1569?

2 Was Elizabeth successful in achieving her objectives?

EXAMINING THE EVIDENCE
The Queen and her Parliaments 1559–1568

For many years the most influential historian of Elizabeth and her reign was Sir John Neale. His biography of Elizabeth (published in 1934) and his detailed research and books on Elizabethan parliaments laid the basis for later historians' work. Amongst Neale's arguments were the following theses about the Queen and her first two Parliaments:

ELIZABETH SEATED IN PARLIAMENT.

---

1 The Commons contained a voluble and influential group of Puritans, including Thomas Norton and William Fleetwood, which acted as an unofficial but organised opposition to the government.

2 Parliament saw major clashes between this opposition on the one hand and the Queen and her advisers on the other hand.

3 The Commons was far more influential than the Lords, which generally supported the Queen.

Source A
What can a commonwealth desire more than peace, liberty, quietness, little taking of base money, few parliaments ...

Sir Thomas Smith, De republica anglorum, 1565.

Source B

Elizabeth's Parliaments 1558–1568

1 25 January –
8 May 1559

2 12 January –
10 April 1563

30 September 1566 –
2 January 1567

Source C

Attendance in the House of Commons

1559 24 February
54%

24 April   32%

1 May   28%

1563 attendance figures
ranged from 64%
to 31%

1566/7 attendances
averaged 33%

Source D

As she had no intention of making or allowing substantial changes to the Church created by statute in 1559, one of the most important causes of frequent Parliaments in the last thirty years had gone. Furthermore, whatever her reasons – an autocratic temper, a preference for secret politics, or a woman's defensive posture in a male-dominated world – she was not fond of Parliaments. Financial necessity and the privy council's prompting [often for other reasons ...] compelled her to call them. When she did she preferred short sessions and hustled council, Commons, and Lords on to complete official business and so make an end of it.

M A R Graves, *The Tudor Parliaments*, 1985.

---

1 Read Sources A–D. Do you think that Elizabeth and MPs shared Sir Thomas Smith's view of parliaments?

Source E

Elizabeth's Parliaments were under the influence, if not quite the control, of Elizabeth's councillors. The Council members, and especially Burghley, nominated MPs, planned business in advance, and tried to manage proceedings. Except in 1597, there were always at least five, and often eight, councillors in the Commons, and the rest sat in the Lords. In addition, the Speaker was a Council nominee, and the Council had its own business managers in the Commons. One of the most interesting developments in recent parliamentary historiography has been the recasting of Neale's leaders of the puritan opposition. By careful analysis of their correspondence, their parliamentary drafts, and especially their role in committees and debates, Michael Graves has discovered that Thomas Norton, William Fleetwood, Thomas Dannett, Thomas Digges, Robert Bell, and others were not leaders of an opposition but agents of the Council! They, and a group of aspiring lawyers, managed Commons proceedings in the interests of getting government business through in the time available. These 'men of business' led the Commons into those issues which councillors wanted discussed – which were often the issues Elizabeth wanted not to be discussed.

Christopher Haigh, Elizabeth I, 1988.

Source F

Increasingly important in Elizabeth's reign was the collective social influence of the Lords. Territorial magnates – Bedford, Huntingdon, Leicester, Norfolk and Shrewsbury – were spiders spinning webs of aristocratic patronage. Many of their clients were elected to the Commons by their good offices and they were likely to be of similar political opinion and religious persuasion to their patrons. In the campaigns to persuade Elizabeth into marriage or the choice of a successor there is evidence of collaboration, not only between the two houses but also between noble patrons and their clients in the Commons.

M A R Graves, The Tudor Parliaments, 1985.

Source G

Early was the pattern set for the rest of the reign. Councillors would use Parliament not to challenge the queen's authority – they were too loyal for that – but to 'persuade' her to their point of view which, in their male-chauvinistic fashion, they felt to be in her best interests. The session of 1566/7 exemplified this. Once again the queen required financial aid and the council persuaded her to it. This was no mere cynical political exercise on the council's part; the need was genuine enough. Nevertheless councillors had bows with more than one string. When Parliament was summoned in September 1566 Cecil chaired a council meeting at which he proposed that they press Elizabeth to marry.

M A R Graves, The Tudor Parliaments, 1985.

---

2 In what ways do Sources E, F and G show disagreements between current researchers and Sir John Neale's views?

Source H

Elizabeth adopted a tone of condescending superiority towards her Parliaments, confident that if she explained things often enough and slowly enough, the little boys would understand. For Elizabeth, parliamentarians were little boys – sometimes unruly, usually a nuisance, and always a waste of an intelligent woman's time. Queen Elizabeth did not like Parliaments, and it showed.

Christopher Haigh, Elizabeth I, 1988.

Source I

On Friday the 8th day of November (1566) ... Mr Lambert began a learned oration for iteration of the suit to the Queen's Majesty for limitation of succession ... they still discoursed of and resolved to press further that other part of their former suit touching the declaration of a successor ...

On Saturday the 9th day of November ... Sir Francis Knollys, knight, her Majesty's vice-chamberlain, declared the Queen's Majesty's express commands to this House that they should no further proceed in their suit, but to satisfy themselves with her Highness' promise of marriage ...

On Monday the 11th day of November ... Paul Wentworth, a burgess of the House, desired to know whether the Queen's command and inhibition that they should no longer dispute of the matter of succession were not against the liberties and privileges of the said House ...

On Tuesday the 12th day of November, Mr Speaker (said) that he had received a special command from her Highness to this House, notwithstanding her first commandment, that there should not be further talk of that matter in the House ...

Extracts from the journals of Sir Simonds D'Ewes.

Source J

I will never break the word of a prince spoken in a public place, for my honour's sake. And therefore I say again, I will marry as soon as I can conveniently, if God take him not away with whom I mind to marry, or myself, or else some other great let happen. I can say no more except the party were present. And I hope to have children, otherwise I would never marry. A strange order of petitioners that will make a request and cannot be otherwise assured but by the prince's word, and yet will not believe it when it is spoken ...

Your petition is to deal in the limitation of the succession. At this present it is not convenient, nor shall be without some peril unto you, and certain danger unto me. But as soon as there may be a convenient time and that it may be done with least peril unto you, although never without great danger unto me, I will deal therein for your safety and offer it unto you as your prince and head without request. For it is monstrous that the feet should direct the head.

Extracts from the Queen's speech to the representatives of parliament, November 1566. This speech was later reported to the Commons by Cecil, although Cecil redrafted it three times before doing so.

---

3 What attitudes towards Elizabeth are shown in Source I?

4 To what extent was Elizabeth's speech (Source J) likely to resolve the concerns of parliament?

5 In what ways do Sources I and J bear out Haigh's judgement in Source H?

Government and Society 1558–1568

The Council and Local Government

Elizabethan parliaments are famous for their clashes with the queen but such fireworks were not typical. Overall, parliaments did their duty, voting taxes and passing government and private bills. This reflected the general nature of Elizabethan government – efficient and smooth-running. Ministers might disagree but disagreements did not develop into disruptive feuds or faction-fighting. One criticism is that government was not innovative and missed opportunities, particularly in finance, where conservatism proved costly. Perhaps the emphasis on security and stability meant that the queen and her ministers felt that experiment was difficult and even dangerous.

Elizabeth's council worked efficiently because it was small (19 members in 1559) and its members were able. They used their power and influence as a force for stability, working for co-operation between the two houses of parliament and in their counties, where they were the senior Justices of the Peace. Such links to the regions were a powerful force for stability.

The one major newcomer to the Privy Council between 1558 and 1568 was Robert Dudley, (created Earl of Leicester in 1564). Despite (or perhaps because of) Dudley's closeness to Elizabeth he did not become a Privy Councillor until 1562. Leicester's arrival did not disrupt the Council. He certainly clashed with Cecil over his lengthy flirtation with the queen, his much briefer flirtation with a pro-Spanish policy and over other matters but the Council as a whole disagreed over the key issues of the succession and the queen's marriage. In fact Leicester's influence in the Midlands, Wales and Cheshire only added to the Council's provincial influence.

One area that the Council's influence did not readily reach was the north, the most likely area for religious revolt because loyalty to the old religion was undented by the new learning. In the far north-west the Catholic mass continued openly, regardless of London fashions and the government's laws. Northern lords remained 'in this unwonted blindness'. Therefore Elizabeth faced a difficult decision – to maintain and therefore appease these doubters and potential rebels or replace them and risk stirring them to direct opposition. She chose the latter, perhaps uncharacteristically but a clear sign of the concern over northern attitudes and particularly their potential support for the Queen of Scots. The major northern families – the Percies, Nevilles and Dacres – lost their offices, depriving them of their natural official military and political role. Southerners or northern rivals were appointed as wardens of the Scottish marches. Faced with a choice of two evils the government had chosen one but did not yet know if it was the better one.

Elsewhere local government continued almost undisturbed by the new reign. There was a handful of changes in the Commissions of the Peace. Only those who upheld the Pope's supremacy were dismissed. Similarly there was no purge of administrators or judges who had served Mary. Continuity and an influx of talent into government were the hallmarks of the new reign.

Financial and Social Continuity

Given the nature of the administration and Elizabeth's own objectives it is scarcely surprising that financial and social measures were a continuation of past policies. The outstanding financial achievement was the recoinage of 1560–1561. The new government had to receive credit for the success and rapidity of the task but it was built upon the policy initiated by Northumberland (and therefore well known to Cecil and others) and continued by Mary. The recoinage had been planned but then abandoned in 1556. The operation was extraordinarily complex, involving the collection of over £600,000 of base money that was then converted into finer coin. Paradoxically (given that debasements had been motivated by either

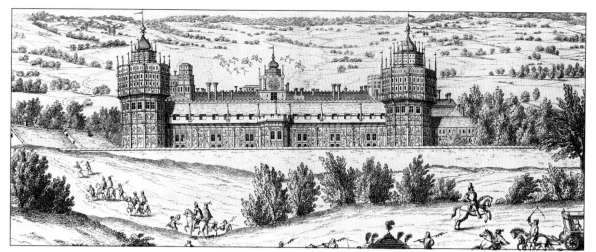

NONSUCH PALACE, ONE OF THE GREATEST TUDOR PALACES ALTHOUGH NO TRACE REMAINS TODAY. IN PURSUIT OF ECONOMY ELIZABETH SOLD OR GAVE SEVEN PALACES AS GIFTS.

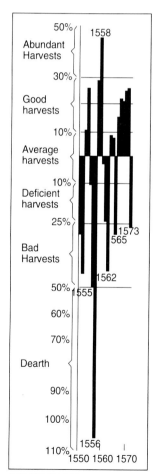

HARVEST QUALITY 1550–1572.

governments' desire for a profit) the government even made a profit of £50,000. The result of this apparently technical exercise was to restore confidence in the coinage at home and abroad and this did much to stabilise prices.

The Purchasing Power of Wage Rates

100 = value 1450–1499

	Agricultural Labourer Worker	Building Craftsman	London Building
1540–49	71	70	76
1550–59	59	51	72
1560–69	66	62	82
1570–79	69	64	81

All other aspects of financial policy were equally 'sound'. Royal expenses were saved wherever possible on non-essentials – lesser household servants now had to pay for their own breakfasts for example. Money saved could be spent on necessary royal splendour to impress foreigners and subjects. More importantly, expenditure on building projects fell to less than 10 per cent of Henry VIII's outlay. Royal lands were sold to raise income but few were given away to favourites. Renewed efforts were made to collect debts, rents and parliamentary taxation efficiently. The important omission however was any attempt to update rents and tax liability in line with inflation. The result was that fewer people paid taxes (in Suffolk 17,000 taxpayers were assessed for the subsidy in 1523, but only 7,700 in 1566) and what they paid was far less than they should.

tions of land were required on oath until 1563. Thereafter taxpayers
ot even have to swear that they had valued their land properly! The
result was that in these vital early years financial demands did not create
hostility. However this problem, a product of the conservatism of Cecil
and Elizabeth, continued throughout the reign and became much worse,
creating much trouble in the next century.

Socially the objective was also stability, if nature was prepared to coop-
erate! At first nature was not kind with two good, two bad and two
average harvests up to 1563. After that the sun and the rain co-operated
and the second half of the 1560s saw a series of good to excellent harvests. As a result prices may even have fallen and wages certainly
increased in value. The re-coinage and the fall in population (which
reduced the demand for food) also helped reduce inflation.

These developments undoubtedly helped the government, both in
reducing the likelihood of dissent (religious complaints by themselves were
not as potent as a mix of economic and religious grievances) and reducing
unemployment. The government's own wishes were reflected in two major
Acts. In 1563 an Act for the Relief of the Poor (the Beggars' Act) made
the collection of the poor-rate virtually compulsory and its collection was
overseen by churchwardens and JPs. Individuals could choose how much
to give but they went to prison if they gave nothing. In the same year the
Statute of Artificers was passed. Its aim was social stability. All men aged
12 to 60 who had not been exempted were to work in agriculture. It was
now illegal to ask for or pay more than the agreed local wage, fixed by JPs
(local wage fixing did allow for differences across the country). Other elements of the statutes attempted through apprenticeship regulations to
reduce workers' mobility and particularly migration into towns. The Act
did help some people whose wages rose. In general the gulf between the
governments' objective (of reducing the problem of vagrancy and making
the country more stable) and its ability to enforce measures was too great.
These two Acts did reveal the government's intentions but legislation was
far less effective than the benevolent impact of a full harvest.

The Role of the Queen

Elizabeth set the tone for all aspects of her reign. She was cautious but
intelligent, involved and concerned for detail. Her life, as her illness in
1562 so dramatically exemplified, seemed to stand between England and
the chaos of a disputed succession. There is no doubt that Elizabeth and
no-one else ruled England. There is the feeling of truth in the suggestion
that she was the only true Anglican in the country, for it seemed that
everyone else wanted to change the 1559 settlement in one way or
another. Nevertheless they kept to her settlement. She did not bow to
their demands for change once the settlement was in place.

Elizabeth was popular. She used her ten week summer progress to see
and, more importantly, be seen by her people. The Spanish ambassador
in 1568 told how 'she was received with great acclamations and signs of
joy, as is customary in this country'. The date of her accession, 17
November, became an annual celebration. Propaganda certainly played its
part in winning respect and love for Elizabeth as did the absence of war
and revolt and the improving economy but in addition there was the
queen herself, who reigned as she had promised the people of London in

1559: 'And whereas your request is that I should continue your good lady and queen, be ye ensured that I will be as good unto you as ever queen was to her people. No will in me can lack, neither do I trust shall there lack any power. And persuade yourselves, that for the safety and quietness of you all I will not spare, if need be, to spend my blood'.

REVIEW

Here are two descriptions of the first ten years of Elizabeth's reign.

A Elizabeth faced significant problems in 1558. She plotted her course through the next ten years with subtlety, avoiding problems whenever possible. Circumstances beyond her control meant that some problems remained and others were created but she triumphantly achieved her objective – survival – and gave England the stability it needed.

B Elizabeth faced significant problems in 1558. She stumbled through the next ten years and survived but her decisions on some issues and her indecisiveness on others created problems. In 1563 she appeared secure. By 1568 she was once again in considerable danger and the country faced yet more turmoil.

1 Draw up a table like the one on the next page and note the evidence under each heading that would support one or other of these statements.

2 Write your own description of Elizabeth's first ten years, summarising Elizabeth's effectiveness as queen.

3 Use this summary as an introduction to an essay, 'What problems faced Elizabeth on her accession and how successfully did she tackle them between 1558 and 1568?'

4 Prepare a briefing paper from the Privy Council to the queen as if for the year 1568, identifying the strengths and weaknesses of Her Majesty's policies and positions.

Problems	Problem solved	Problem postponed	Problem tackled but not solvable	Overall assessment of success
Reaching a religious settlement				
Catholic discontent				
Puritan discontent				
Marriage and the succession				
Relation with France				
Relations with Spain				
Economic issues				
Effective administration				

13 Our Golden Age? Themes in Elizabethan History

PREVIEW

TALKING POINT

What does the phrase 'Golden Age' mean? Would a period be most likely to be known as a 'Golden Age' because of political or cultural achievements or because of a high standard of living or because of any other feature?
Which other periods of history have been given or deserve this title?

Source A
This was the picture of her wondrous thought ...
And there did represent in lively show
Our glorious English court's divine image,
As it should be in this our Golden Age.

Source B
Oh! many, many years may you remain,
A happy angel to this happy land:
Long, long may you on earth our empress reign,
Ere you in heaven a glorious angel stand.

Stay long (sweet spirit) ere thou to heaven depart
Which mak'st each place a heaven wherein thou art.

Source C
Are you then travelling to the temple of Eliza?
Even to her temple are my feeble limbs travelling. some call her Pandora: some Gloriana: some Cynthia: some Belphoebe: some Astraea: all by several names to express several loves: yet all those names make but one celestial body, as all those loves meet to create one soul.
I am of her country, and we adore her by the name of Eliza.

THE PROCESSION PORTRAIT OF ELIZABETH PAINTED C. 1601.

These extracts all come from the final years of Elizabeth's reign – the first two written by John Davies, the third by Thomas Dekker. They present an image of Elizabeth and her reign which has lasted through the centuries, of an English Golden Age which was, in part, created by and, in part, a tribute to Elizabeth, 'in earth the first, in heaven the second maid'. This chapter examines some of the key elements of this image of a Golden Age, providing also a necessary backcloth to the events of Elizabeth's reign after 1568.

TALKING POINT

From your work on chapter 12 and your other knowledge of the period why do you think Elizabeth's reign was seen as a Golden Age?

EXAMINING THE EVIDENCE
When she smiled, it was a pure sunshine

How did Elizabeth achieve her popularity? Was it a product of events during her reign that were, to a greater or lesser extent, outside her control, such as the defeat of the Armada? Or did the Queen herself make a substantial contribution through the relationship with and attitude to her people?

Source A
After supper she took a boat, and was rowed up and down on the River Thames; hundreds of boats and barges rowing about her; and thousands of people thronging at the waterside, to look upon her Majesty, for the trumpets blew, flutes played, guns were discharged, squibs hurled up into the air, as the Queen moved from place to place. And thus continued till ten of the clock at night, when the Queen departed home. By these means shewing herself so freely and condescendingly unto her people, she made herself dear and acceptable to them.

An account written in April 1559.

Source B
(The Queen was greeted) with great acclamations and signs of joy as is customary in this country; whereat she was extremely pleased and told me so ... She ordered her carriage to be taken sometimes where the crowd seemed thickest and stood up and thanked the people.

De Spes, the Spanish ambassador, writing of Elizabeth's progress in 1568.

Source C
The people, being innumerable in the streets and churchyard, crying to her Majesty, 'God save your Majesty! God save your Grace!' unto whom, she rising, showed herself at both sides of her coach unto them, and often times said, 'I thank you, I thank you all'.

A contemporary account of Elizabeth's visit to Worcester, 1575.

Source D
I have laid up in my breast such good will as I shall never forget Norwich.

Elizabeth's words on leaving Norwich, 1578.

WATER PAGEANTS AND FIREWORKS MARKED ELIZABETH'S PROGRESSES. FIREWORKS COULD BE DAN-GEROUS AND ON ONE OCCASION AT KENILWORTH ELIZABETH ARRANGED A COLLECTION FROM HER COURTIERS TO COMPENSATE A FAMILY WHOSE HOUSE HAD BEEN BURNED DOWN BY A FIREBALL USED IN A MOCK-BATTLE. PAGEANTS CONTAINED STRONG ELEMENTS OF FANTASY TO ENHANCE ELIZABETH'S ENCHANTED IMAGE.

TALKING POINT

Do you think Elizabeth's Tudor predecessors had the same approach and attitude to their subjects?

ELIZABETH VISITED MANY SOUTHERN TOWNS ON HER PROGRESSES BUT NEVER TRAVELLED NORTH OF STAFFORDSHIRE OR WEST OF BRISTOL. TOWNS HOPED THAT THE QUEEN MIGHT REMIT TAXES OR RESPOND TO OTHER GRIEVANCE AND NO EXPENSE WAS SPARED TO CLEAN THE TOWN AND REPAIR ROADS. SOME THINGS DO NOT CHANGE!

Source F

I believe no prince living that was so tender of honour, and so exactly stood for the preservation of sovereignty, was so great a courtier of the people, yea of the commons, and that stooped and declined lower in presenting her person to the public view, as she passed in her progress and perambulations.

Sir Robert Naunton, *Fragment Regalia*, written in the late 1620s.
Naunton, a member of Elizabeth's court, was born in 1563.

1 What do Sources A–D suggest about

(a) Elizabeth's attitude to her people and

(b) her skills in winning support?

2 What does Source E tell us about Elizabeth?

3 What do you think were the benefits and costs for the people of entertainments, visits and progresses such as those in Sources A–E?

4 Do you agree with Source F in the light of your reading of Sources A–E?

Source G

Mr Speaker,

We have heard your declaration and perceive you care of our estate. I do assure you there is no prince that loves his subjects better, or whose love can countervail our love. There is no jewel, be it of never so rich a price, which I set before this jewel: I mean your love. For I do esteem it more than any treasure of riches; for that we know how to prize, but love and thanks I count invaluable. And, though God hath raised me high, yet this I count the glory of my Crown, that I have reigned with your loves. This makes me that I do not so much rejoice that God hath made me to be a Queen, as to be a Queen over so thankful a people. Therefore I have cause to wish nothing more than to content the subject and that is a duty which I owe. Neither do I desire to live longer days than I may see your prosperity and that is my only desire. And as I am that person that still yet, under God, hath delivered you and so I trust by the almighty power of God that I shall be his instrument to preserve you from every peril, dishonour, shame, tyranny and oppression ...

I have ever used to set the Last Judgement Day before mine eyes and so to rule as I shall be judged to answer before a higher judge, and now if my kingly bounties have been abused and my grants turned to the hurt of my people contrary to my will and meaning, and if any in authority under me have neglected or perverted what I have committed to them, I hope God will not lay their culps and offences in my charge. I know the title of a King is a glorious title, but assure yourself that the shining glory of princely authority hath not so dazzled the eyes of our understanding, but that we well know and remember that we also are to yield an account of our actions before the great judge. To be a king and wear a crown is a thing more glorious to them that see it than it is pleasant to them that bear it. For myself I was never so much enticed with the glorious name of a King or royal authority of a Queen as delighted that God hath made me his instrument to maintain his truth and glory and to defend this kingdom as I said from peril, dishonour, tyranny and oppression. There will never Queen sit in my seat with more zeal to my country, care to my subjects and that will sooner with willingness venture her life for your good and safety than myself. For it is my desire to live nor reign no longer than my life and reign shall be for your good. And though you have had, and may have, many princes more mighty and wise sitting in this seat, yet you never had nor shall have any that will be more careful and loving.

Elizabeth's 'Golden Speech' to parliament, 1601.

Source H

Sir Christopher Hatton was wont to say, 'The queen did fish for men's souls, and had so sweet a bait, that no one could escape her network'. In truth, I am sure her speech was such, as none could refuse to take delight in which forwardness did not stand in the way. I have seen her smile, sooth with great semblance of good liking to all around, and cause every one to open his most inward thought to her; when, on a sudden, she would ponder in private on what had passed, write down all their opinions, draw them out as occasion required, and sometime disprove to their faces what had been delivered a month before. Hence she knew one's

During her progresses Elizabeth travelled no further north than Staffordshire and no further west than Bristol. Why were her progresses so restricted? Does this information alter your conclusions about Elizabeth and her people?

part, and by thus fishing, as Hatton said, she caught many poor fish, who little knew what snare was laid for them ...

When she smiled, it was a pure sunshine, that every one did choose to bask in, if they could; but anon came a storm from a sudden gathering of clouds, and the thunder fell in wondrous manner on all alike. I never did find greater show of understanding and learning, than she was blessed with.

Sir John Harington, writing to Robert Markham in 1606. Harington was a courtier and god-son of the Queen.

6 What does Source G tell you about (a) Elizabeth's attitude to her people; (b) Elizabeth's attitude to her duty as Queen; (c) Elizabeth's ability as a speaker?

7 What does Source H tell you about (a) Elizabeth's skills as a ruler; (b) Elizabeth's personality; (c) attitudes towards Elizabeth?

8 Do Sources G and H suggest that Elizabeth's response to ordinary people shown in Sources B, C and D was genuine or was it a cynical attempt to win popularity?

9 Do you think Elizabeth's attitude to her subjects helped to develop the idea of an Elizabethan Golden Age?

Focus

13.1 Elizabeth and her Portraits

PAINTED BY FEDERIGO ZUCCARO IN 1575, THIS WAS THE BASIS FOR PORTRAITS UNTIL THE 1590S. A CUT-C[...] COVERED WITH PIN-PRICKS ALONG TH[...] KEY FEATURES WAS USED BY ARTISTS. THEY CREATED A TRACING BY RUBBIN[...] CHALK THROUGH THE HOLES. COMPA[...] THIS WITH EARLIER PORTRAITS OF ELIZABETH ON PAGES 290, 301.

*T*here are surprisingly few written descriptions of Elizabeth although those that exist by and large agree with each other. Happily Elizabeth did sit regularly for portraits and English people had a clearer image of her than of any previous monarch. Not only was her portrait in Bibles and other books but many people bought copies of her portrait for their walls or as miniatures to wear. Portraits of Elizabeth also circulated abroad, often sent as a component of marriage negotiations. However the Queen did not approve of all her portraits. In 1563 a proclamation was issued forbidding the production of images of the Queen until 'some special person that shall be by hir allowed shall have first fynished a portraicture thereof, after which fynished, hir Majesty will be content that all other payntors, or grauors ... Shall and maye at ther plesures follow the sayd patron on first portraictur.' Certainly pattern drawings were produced with great success, copied by a few artists with talent but many without!

Source A

In an inventory taken in 1600, she was listed as owning, among other items, 102 French gowns (which had small dipping trains), 67 round gowns (which had level hems that formed a circle round the wearer's feet), 100 loose gowns (non-waisted housecoats), 125 kirtles, 136 foreparts, 99 mantles (short-sleeved surcoats), and 99 cloaks. The materials used were invariably luxurious – cut velvets, satins, taffeta and sarcenet – and frequently slashed and pinked to reveal colourful glimpses of contrasting fabrics underneath. She owned numerous gowns and accessories encrusted with pearls, spangles and precious stones, or exquisitely embroidered, often in gold and silver thread.

A Somerset, *Elizabeth I,* 1991.

Source B

(i) For the face, I grant, I might well blush to offer, but the mind I shall never be ashamed to present.

(ii) When anyone speaks of her beauty she says that she was never beautiful, although she had that reputation thirty years ago. Nevertheless she speaks of her beauty often.

Elizabeth speaking of herself c.1547 and the comment of a French visitor to court in 1597.

Source C

The fundamental ingredients of what we now call the cult of the Virgin queen, including visual panegyric, therefore, were put together very rapidly in the years immediately before and after 1580 ... In the two and a half decades that followed, these initial statements were merely elaborated and expanded to messianic proportions, as England triumphed over the Armada and the Queen assume[...] the status of an immortal ... The[...] symbolism of her state portraits that of the virtue, peace and jus[...] of an imperial golden age ...

R Strong, *Gloriana: Portraits of Queen Elizabe[...]*

Talking point

What does the censorship of portraits tell you about Elizabethan society?
How does this affect your view of Elizabeth and her government?

THE SIEVE PORTRAIT DATING
)M C.1580–3. THE SIEVE WAS
YMBOL OF VIRGINITY DATING
M ROMAN TIMES. THE GLOBE
LSO SYMBOLISES SEA POWER
ND EMPIRE. SIR ROY STRONG
AS SAID THAT "IN THESE POR-
TRAITS OF 1579–83 WE
TUALLY SEE THE CREATION OF
HE ELIZABETH CULT WHICH IS
THING MORE THAN TENTATIVE
TIL THE CLOSE OF THE 1570s.
IT IS THESE PICTURES WHICH
TABLISH THE KEY THEMES ..".

ISAAC OLIVERS'S PORTRAIT OF 1592 WAS
INTENDED AS A PATTERN PORTRAIT BUT ONLY
ONE COPY IS KNOWN, PRESUMABLY BECAUSE
IT WAS TOO TRUTHFUL IN ITS DEPICTION OF
ELIZABETH.

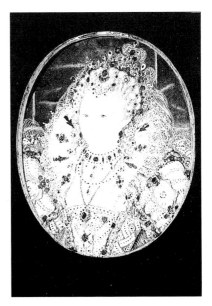

A MINIATURE BY NICHOLAS HILLIARD, PAINTED
C.1595–1600. IN 1596 "UNSEEMLY"
PORTRAITS WERE SOUGHT OUT AND
DESTROYED. INSTEAD HILLIARD CREATED THIS
IMAGE KNOWN AS THE "MASK OF YOUTH".

Questions

1 What does the evidence on these pages suggest about Elizabeth's attitude to her own appearance?

2 How did the portraits of Elizabeth change during her reign?

3 Why did the portraits change?

4 How did Elizabeth's appearance and portraits contribute to the idea of a 'Golden Age'?

THE "DITCHLEY" PORTRAIT BY
MARCUS GHEERAERTS C.1592.
EN AND COUNTRY ARE SHOWN
AS ONE AND ELIZABETH IS ALSO
HOWN BANISHING STORMS AND
SHERING IN THE SUNSHINE, THE
RLIEST EXAMPLE OF A PORTRAIT
GESTING THE QUEEN'S COSMIC
CONTROL.

CAMEO PORTRAITS OF ELIZABETH BECAME
COMMON IN THE 1580s AND WERE PARTIC-
ULARLY ASSOCIATED WITH THE BOND OF
ASSOCIATION. HERE SIR CHRISTOPHER
HATTON, ONE OF ELIZABETH'S FAVOURITES,
HOLDS A CAMEO SET WITH DIAMONDS.

13.2 William Cecil, Lord Burghley: the ideal servant?

WILLIAM C

A *lthough nearly the youngest of Elizabeth's councillors in 1558, Cecil already possessed a dozen years' experience of life and death at the centre of government (see pages 228 – 230). His relationship with the Queen had been well-established during those difficult years under Mary and they worked together until Cecil's death, despite disagreements over, for example, the treatment of Mary, Queen of Scots. Elizabeth's affection for Cecil was such that, on his deathbed, the Queen fed him from a spoon. What qualities made Cecil such a good servant of the Queen and how significant was his role at the centre of government?*

Source A

I give you this charge, that you shall be of my Privy Council and content yourself to take pains for me and my realm. This judgement I have of you, that you will not be corrupted with any manner of gift and that you will be faithful to the State, and that without respect of my private will, you will give that counsel that you think best: and, if you shall know anything necessary to be declared to me of secrecy, you shall show it to myself only and assure yourself I will not fail to keep taciturnity therein. And therefore herewith I charge you.

Elizabeth's words to Cecil,
20 November 1558.

Source B

I do hold, and will always, this course in such matters as I differ in opinion from her Majesty; as long as I may be allowed to give advice I will not change my opinion by affirming the contrary, for that were to offend God, to whom I am sworn first; but as a servant I will obey her Majesty's commandment and no wise contrary the same, presuming that she, being God's chief minister here, it shall be God's will to have her

commandments obeyed after that I have performed my duty as a councillor.

Cecil's description of his role, written in a letter to his son in 1596.

Source C

Cecil possessed 'an infinite capacity for taking pains ... (he) was so incessant and his study so great as, in cases of necessity, he cared neither for meat, sleep or rest, till his business was brought to some end ... His industry ... caused all his friends to pity him and his very servants to admire him.

From a contemporary life of Cecil, probably written by Michael Hickes, his secretary.

Source D

In William Cecil (Elizabeth) probably had the best available agent to fulfil his wishes. He was conservative, a skilful parliamentary manager and consistently loyal – even if, sometimes he also employed Parliament to bend her opinions into accord with his ... What may be mis-read as government-opposition clashes were actually co-operative exercises between the two houses, orchestrated by the council and designed to coerce Elizabeth into action; and usually one can detect the

Questions

1 Read Sources A–C. What do they tell you of the qualities that made Cecil so valuable to Elizabeth?

2 What does Source D tell you about (a.) Cecil's value to Elizabeth and (b.) his relationship with Elizabeth

(a) Read Source E. How does Elizabeth's court appear different from that of Henry VIII?

(b) How might Cecil's attitude (Sources B–D) support the conclusions i Source E?

3 Does the quarrel in Source F prove that evidence in other sources about Cecil support for Elizabeth is unreliable?

4 Using the evidence on these pages, do you agree with Source G that the roles of Elizabeth and Cecil were of equal significance

RT CECIL.

TALKING POINT

Why might historians disagree about the relative importance of the roles of Elizabeth and Cecil?

guiding hand of Burghley, combining loyalty to his queen with a determination to force her hand for her own good.

M A R Graves, *The Tudor Parliaments: Crown, Lords and Commons, 1485–1603*, 1985.

Source E

Most accounts of the Court have tended to emphasise factional strife and a vicious atmosphere of place-seeking, enmity and competition surround an alternatively goddess-like or hag-like queen ... much of the evidence for factional strife has been drawn from the 1590s and by no means reflects the reality of the previous decades. The Court was never completely free from conflict, but such conflict was less the product of faction among courtiers than of disputes between an able, charming, yet imperious and idiosyncratic queen, and councillors and intimates who generally shared a high degree of social, political and cultural homogeneity.

S Adams, *Eliza enthroned? The Court and its Politics* in C Haigh (ed), *The Reign of Elizabeth I*, 1984.

Source F

I doubt not but you understand her Majesty's great displeasure for the execution of the Scottish Queen, though justly done and most profitable for her Majesty's surety ... though her Majesty hath shown her offence to her Council that were privy to the execution, yet her offence is to me so further in some degree, as I, not having been able to appear before her with the rest, by reason of my hurt, am forbidden, or not licensed, to come to her presence to answer for myself ...

From a letter written by Cecil shortly after the Queen of Scots' execution.

Source G

... it is difficult to deny that, in a short-term context, the Queen and Burghley accomplished their main aims. They protected England's security, both at home and abroad and raised enough money to keep the country solvent. England was a stronger power, in relative terms, in 1603 than she had been in 1558 or, indeed, in 1585. Historians have differed widely in their judgements of the respective roles of the Queen and Burghley in this achievement. J A Froude ... in the later 19th century ... concluded with the belief that it was Burghley who was primarily responsible for the successes of the reign. Neale ... never wavered from his view that it was the Queen who was the driving force behind England's achievements during her reign.

Neither of these views is wholly convincing and it seems best to stress the temperamental similarities of Burghley and Elizabeth and to emphasise the co-operation during their long partnership. Their differences over issues such as the succession and Mary, Queen of Scots, which have naturally been highlighted by historians, should be seen as temporary – though very important – interludes in a fundamentally happy relationship. In the later years of the reign in particular, as two ageing conservatives, the Queen and Burghley usually found themselves in agreement on major issues. The fundamental contributions which they made to the Elizabethan age were so often made together that it is very difficult to give either one of them priority of achievement over the other.

A G R Smith, *William Cecil, Lord Burghley: Minister of Elizabeth I*, 1991.

The 'Sea Dogs': Exploration, Trade and the Navy

'The English people in full force had accepted the doctrine that their future lay upon the oceans ... the maritime traditions thus graved into the national consciousness were a factor of the utmost importance in preserving the liberties of England ... great men whose spirits blazed in such a galaxy as was never seen in England before, nor has been since.'

J A Williamson, *The Age of Drake (5th edition)*, 1965.

TALKING POINT

Williamson's book was first published in 1938. What questions does this information raise about his interpretations?

This quotation presents another important element of the Elizabethan Golden Age, those 'great men', Drake, Raleigh, Hawkins, Frobisher and the rest whose bravery and seamanship defeated the Spanish Armada, broke the Spanish and Portuguese monopoly on exploration and thus made England the world's greatest naval power. This section explores the 'sea dogs' and their achievements. How successful were the explorers? Did English overseas trade flourish? Was the navy improved to such an extent that it made possible the first British empire?

Exploration

English involvement in exploration before the 1550s had been minimal. Henry VII did sponsor voyages by the Cabots to the Americas but Henry VIII, despite his reforms of the navy, was little interested in the world beyond western Europe. The English, it seemed, were content to focus their trade and thus their voyages on western Europe and even more closely on the Netherlands and the port of Antwerp.

From 1551 this situation changed and changed drastically. Antwerp's prosperity was shaken by the devaluation of the English currency in 1551 that depressed trade. In 1557 France and Spain declared themselves bankrupt, having piled up heavy debts in the Netherlands. More dramatically, the Dutch revolt (1572) against Spain disrupted trade and finally (1585) closed the port to traders. English merchants perforce had to seek markets elsewhere. Thus the 1550s saw voyages to Morocco and the Gold Coast and, most significantly, to Russia. Here the expedition leaders, Willoughby and Chancellor, had hoped to find the north-east passage to the riches of Asia but instead opened up trade with Russia, leading to the formation of the Muscovy Company in 1555. The beginnings of exploration thus came under the governments of the Duke of Northumberland and Queen Mary. Under Elizabeth the need to diversify trade became ever more important but other motives were also present. Increasing patriotism and nationalism as a result of Protestantism and the war with Spain demanded that England should not stand back and take second place. Attacks on Spanish ships and colonies led easily onto the idea that the English had every right to establish their own colonies. Anxieties about over-population and attendant problems of disorder also led some to see colonisation as a useful way of reducing social pressures at home.

Under Elizabeth voyages of exploration thus reached a significant level for the first time (see map) and the first attempts to establish colonies were made. How successful were these ventures? In terms of their objectives they were singularly unsuccessful. Explorers hoped to find either a north-west or north-east passage to Asia and to build England's share of

1562	John Hawkins' first trading voyage to the Americas, carrying slaves from Africa
1567	Hawkins' and Drake's third voyage to Americas
1568	Spanish attack on Hawkins' ships at San Juan de Ulua
1572	Drake led expedition to attack Spanish treasure fleets
1576–8	Frobisher's three voyages to seek north-west passage
1577	Beginning of Drake's voyage of circumnavigation
1580	Drake's return from circumnavigation
1583	Humphrey Gilbert annexed Newfoundland
1584	Raleigh's fleet landed in Virginia
1585	Foundation of first colony in Virginia. Drake led assault on Spanish West Indies. Davis's voyages to seek north-west passage (and 1586, 1587)
1587	Drake's raid on Cadiz
1588	Spanish Armada
1589	Portuguese expedition led by Norris and Drake
1591	Azores expedition led by Howard and Grenville. Sinking of Grenville's 'Revenge'
1595	Expedition of Drake and Hawkins to West Indies. Death of Hawkins
1596	Death of Drake. Cadiz expedition led by Lord Howard of Effingham and Essex. Spanish Armada
1597	Essex's 'Islands Voyage' fails to capture Spanish treasure fleet. Spanish Armada

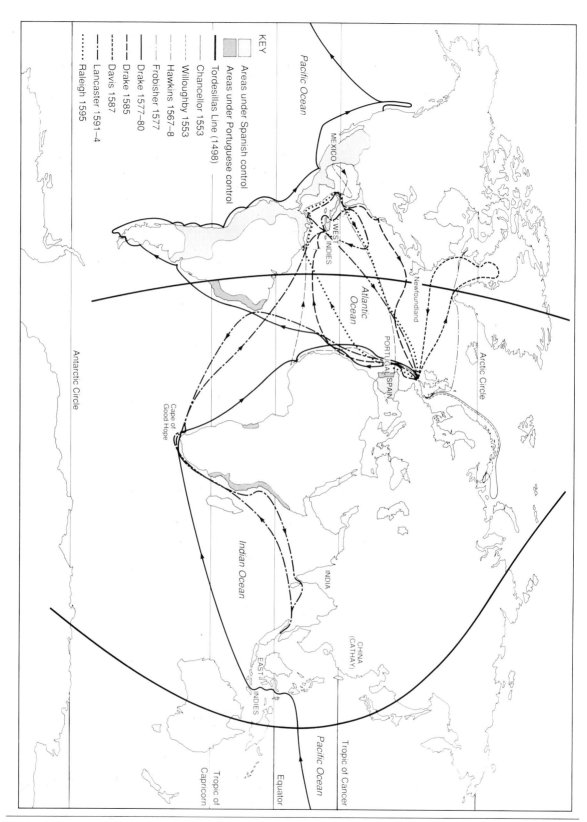

that trade that was both lucrative and mythical in its proportions. Of course no such passage was found and many lives and much money were thrown away in the attempt. Another objective was the discovery of the 'southern continent', a land believed to lie across the southern edge of the world. Discovery and exploitation would balance the Spanish dominance of America but Drake, deputed to discover this new land in 1577, followed a more traditional course, attacking Spanish ships and colonies and ultimately becoming the first Englishman to sail around the world.

The fates of the first colonies were equally dismal. In 1585 Sir Walter Raleigh settled colonists in Virginia but they swiftly returned home after suffering food shortages and failing to establish good relations with the local peoples. In 1587 Raleigh established another colony. The 150 settlers simply disappeared. Raleigh returned in 1590 to find a deserted site. Their fate has never been discovered. These failures brought a temporary end to colonising ventures, to be recommenced when the Virginia Company was established in 1606. Overall the resulting lack of enthusiasm for colonies is not surprising. Elizabeth's foreign policy was dominated by events in Europe. Her overwhelming need, right through to the end of her reign, was security and exploration and colonies made no direct contribution to security. Too great an involvement might even have

PAINTING OF A NATIVE AMERICAN BY JOHN WHITE.

THE PRINCIPALL
NAVIGATIONS, VOIA-
GES AND DISCOVERIES OF THE
English nation, made by Sea or ouer Land,
to the most remote and farthest distant Quarters of
the earth at any time within the compasse
of these 1500. yeeres : Deuided into three
seuerall parts, according to the positions of the Regions where-
to they were directed.

The first, conteining the personall trauels of the English vnto *Iudæa, Syria, Arabia,* the riuer *Euphrates, Babylon, Balsara,* the *Persian* Gulfe, *Ormuz, Chaul, Goa, India,* and many Islands adioyning to the South parts of *Asia* : together with the like vnto *Egypt,* the chiefest ports and places of *Africa* within and without the Streight of *Gibraltar,* and about the famous Promontorie of *Buona Esperança.*

The second, comprehending the worthy discoueries of the English towards the North and Northeast by Sea, as of *Lapland, Scrikfinia, Corelia,* the Baie of *S. Nicholas,* the Isles of *Colgoieue, Vaigats,* and *Noua Zembla* toward the great riuer *Ob,* with the mightie Empire of *Russia,* the *Caspian* Sea, *Georgia, Armenia, Media, Persia, Boghar* in *Bactria,* & diuers kingdoms of *Tartaria.*

The third and last, including the English valiant attempts in searching almost all the corners of the vaste and new world of *America,* from 73.degrees of Northerly latitude Southward, to *Meta Incognita, Newfoundland,* the maine of *Virginia,* the point of *Florida,* the Baie of *Mexico,* all the Inland of *Noua Hispania,* the coast of *Terra firma, Brasill,* the riuer of *Plate,* to the Streight of *Magellan:* and through it, and from it in the South Sea to *Chili, Peru, Xalisco,* the Gulfe of *California, Noua Albion* vpon the backside of *Canada,* further then euer any Christian hitherto hath pierced.

Whereunto is added the last most renowned English Nauigation,
round about the whole Globe of the Earth.

By Richard Hakluyt Master of Artes, and Student sometime
of Christ-church in Oxford.

Imprinted at London by GEORGE BISHOP
and RALPH NEWBERIE, Deputies to
CHRISTOPHER BARKER, Printer to the
Queenes most excellent Maiestie.
1589.

THE TITLE PAGE FROM RICHARD HAKLUYT'S "THE PRINCIPAL NAVIGATIONS, VOYAGES, TRAFFIQUES AND DISCOVERIES OF THE ENGLISH NATION", FIRST PUBLISHED IN 1589. HAKLUYT'S WORK SHOWS BOTH THE TECHNICAL AND POPULAR INTEREST IN EXPLORATION.

prejudiced security if royal finances had been drained by expenditure on unnecessary projects. Thus there was little practical royal backing for these ventures even if Elizabeth did perceive the propaganda value of success. Drake's circumnavigation won him a knighthood, received at the Queen's hands on board his ship in 1580. Voyages also provided experience and testing ground for ships and sailors. In the long term the importance of exploration and colonisation under Elizabeth was not what was achieved but that a start had been made that would lead to the development of much wider-ranging trade in the seventeenth century.

Trade

For the moment England's trade remained centred on Europe. The dominant export was still textiles, with lighter woollen cloths slowly taking a larger share from the long-established broadcloths. London was the dominant port, with 80 per cent to 90 per cent of exports passing through London en route to Europe. However the destinations of these goods were more diverse in the second half of the sixteenth century. Trade with the Baltic and Germany increased; there were more voyages to the Mediterranean. Companies were founded to engage in even further-flung trading activities – the Eastland Company in 1579, the Levant Company in 1581, the Barbary Company in 1585 and the East India Company in 1600. Even so, despite the exotic names and high hopes, European trade remained dominant, accounting for 95 per cent of English trade. The story of trade under Elizabeth, like that of exploration and colonisation, is thus far less dramatic than the headline events might suggest. Progress was limited but, having said that, there were signs of change. The number of merchant ships was growing and so was their size. English merchants were also taking greater control over trade, easing out other nationalities carrying goods from England. Hanseatic merchants were expelled completely in 1597. New methods also appeared. The East India Company, like the Muscovy Company, was a joint-stock enterprise wherein investors shared the profits in proportion to their investment. These developments were, with hindsight, the significant beginnings of England's future successes. To contemporaries, of course, they were nothing of the kind. They were of relatively little importance as foreign trade was far less productive than domestic trade. The later sixteenth century was also a period of trading difficulty after the boom years of earlier decades. Many Englishmen talked of religion and war with Spain. Nearly everyone discussed the harvests. Few were excited by exploration or new trading opportunities in far off lands.

The Navy and the Sea Dogs

Exploration and trade went hand in hand. To these must be added violence. As long ago as 1494 Spain and Portugal had agreed the Treaty of Tordesillas, dividing the 'New World' between themselves. Other nations were intruders, to be dealt with as enemies. Thus explorers and traders were not engaged in a neutral act, although for a time local Spanish commanders in Spanish America turned a blind eye to the trading voyages of John Hawkins. Then, in 1567, Hawkins ships were attacked by a Spanish fleet while in the Mexican port of San Juan de Ulua. Thereafter unofficial war was waged by the privateers of England and the Spanish treasure fleets and their defenders until they were overtaken by the full-blown

Anglo-Spanish war in 1585. The heroes of these events were the English sea-dogs, the most famous of whom was Francis Drake, and their greatest victory was the defeat of the Armada. The Armada itself is dealt with in detail later (see pages 376 – 385) but this is the place to examine the reality of the Elizabethan naval achievement. Drake and the Elizabethan navy are very much part of the image of the Elizabethan Golden Age. Do they deserve to be?

EXAMINING THE EVIDENCE
Drake and the English Navy
Source A

SIR FRANCIS DRAKE C.1543 – 1596.

In 1559 the Queen possessed 22 effective ships of more than 100 tons in weight and by 1603 the number had grown to 29. These royal vessels were, of course, supplemented by armed merchantmen during times of crisis and the increase in both the number and size of merchant ships which began during the 1570s enabled the Queen to assemble the

The career of Francis Drake	
1543	Born near Tavistock in Devon. His father was a yeoman farmer and former sailor.
1549	Family moved to Kent near the naval dockyard at Chatham Drake's father became a Protestant preacher to the sailors and workmen.
1566	First transatlantic voyage in an expedition financed by Hawkins.
1570–73	Voyages to Panama to capture silver. 1572 captured the town of Nombre de Dios and captured one treasure load of silver. News of the raid endangered an Anglo-Spanish reconciliation.
1577–1580	Voyage of circumnavigation.
1585–6	Attacks on Spanish West Indies. Drake failed to capture a treasure fleet but destroyed many Spanish guns and major towns.
1587	Drake attacked Cadiz destroying over twenty Spanish ships preparing for the Armarda.
1588	Drake was a senior commander against the Armada (see pages 378 – 382).
1589	The Portuguese expedition to win treasure. Formed a revolt against Spain which proved a failure. Until 1595 Drake was in disgrace.
1595	Drake and Hawkins jointly led an expedition to capture the Spanish treasure fleet. Again this was a failure and Drake died on 28 January 1596.

formidable fleet which faced the great Spanish challenge of 1588. Moreover, the reign saw very important developments in the design and striking power of new ships built for the navy. Under the auspices of Sir John Hawkins, who held the vital office of Treasurer of the Navy from 1578 until his death in 1595 and who made his influence felt behind the scenes in earlier years, ships were made longer and narrower and thus faster and more seaworthy. They were also given heavier guns than before. Many older ships were modified or rebuilt along new lines and it is clear that Hawkins was the organizer of victories in the struggle against Spain. As a result of his work the fleet became a highly efficient fighting force by the standards of the time, and it demonstrated its technical superiority against the Armada in 1588.

A G R Smith, *The Emergence of a Nation State: The Commonwealth of England, 1529–1660*, 1984.

Source B

The characteristic form of Elizabethan maritime warfare was privateering. The royal navy was not yet distinct, in functions or in personnel, from the sea-forces of the nation as a whole, and the management and conduct of the queen's ships was the responsibility of men who had grown up in the school of oceanic trade and plunder and remained promoters and leaders of the privateering war. The very strength of these interests, reinforced as they were by London's capital and the enthusiastic initiative of gentlemen-adventurers, helped to retard the growth of a powerful state navy at a time when the resources of the crown were extremely limited. In the crisis of 1585–8 it did seem that a higher level of naval organisation and operational expertise might emerge ... But with the passing of the crisis the English relapsed into privateering ... The tragic failure of Drake's last years thus epitomises the failure of English sea-power to outgrow its adolescence in the final phase of Elizabeth's reign.

K R Andrews, *Drake's Voyages*, 1967.

Source C

Although eulogised as naval commanders, strategists, and imperial pioneers, the Elizabethan 'sea dogs' were motivated by greed not altruism. If a parallel is sought, they were linked in spirit to the plunderers of religious houses in Henry VIII's reign.

J Guy, *Tudor England*, 1988.

Source D

The disorder and petty crime so prevalent among the submerged Elizabethan poor in their struggle to survive had its maritime counterpart in piracy, which the government found even more difficult to check. Indeed, the best it could do was to direct the force of this popular movement against the queen's enemies. In this it did not entirely succeed, for robbery of neutral merchantmen was an everyday occurrence in the war period. Nevertheless political and commercial circumstances and the generally Protestant feeling of the sea-going community did give these depredations a pronounced anti-Spanish bias even before the war. It was from these ranks that Drake sprang.

K R Andrews, *Drake's Voyages*, 1967.

TALKING POINT

For much of the 400 years since his death Drake has been regarded as one of the greatest British heroes. Why was this? When do you think his memory was most revered?

A WOODCUT OF THE QUEEN, 1588. ELIZABETH IS SHOWN AS THE QUEEN OF THE UNIVERSE.

Source E

... the value of prize-goods (taken by privateers) ranged from about £100,000 to about £200,000 a year.

If we bear in mind that our figures do not take into account the returns of official and semi-official ventures, this total annual haul is impressive ... Prize goods ... account for some ten to fifteen per cent of England's total imports ... the returns of privateering were worth at least as much as the Iberian trade.

K.R. Andrews, *Elizabethan Privateerings*, 1964.

Source F

It was perhaps his greatest contribution to national maritime development that he provided in his person a hero-figure upon which public imagination could focus. His remarkable achievement of 1577–80 had little practical effect apart from the immediate gain of treasure, but it did more than any other venture to publicise and stimulate English oceanic endeavour. The voyage of 1585–6, we are told, 'inflamed the whole country with a desire to adventure unto the seas', and the popularity of privateering from that date owed not a little to his example. The name of Drake was sufficient in 1589 and 1595 to attract flocks of volunteers to his flag, and after his death his memory was embroidered with legend.

K R Andrews, *Drake's Voyages*, 1967.

TALKING POINT

List the arguments for and against the Elizabethan period being a Golden Age for exploration and the navy. In your view do the achievements in these areas support the idea of an Elizabethan Golden Age?

1 According to Source A what important naval developments took place in Elizabeth's reign?

2 Read Sources A and B. What weaknesses affected the navy?

3 Drake and other Elizabeth seamen have often been pictured as heroes. Do Sources C and D justify this image?

4 Read Source F. What was Drake's contribution to the navy and warfare in this period?

WILLIAM SHAKESPEARE.

Culture: the theatre, music and education

Shakespeare! One word seems to end the argument. Shakespeare lived and wrote during the reign of Elizabeth, therefore there can be no doubt that this was a Golden Age. Although Shakespeare was to produce his most mature work under James I he wrote Richard III, Romeo and Juliet, Richard II, A Midsummer Night's Dream, The Merchant of Venice, Hamlet, Julius Caesar, many other plays and sonnets before 1603. Does the argument really stop there? At its simplest it does, for it would be strange indeed not to see an age that produced Shakespeare as having an extraordinary quality. But in other ways it is important to develop the argument to do justice to others – to other poets and musicians, to men of ideas – and to show the variations within society. The achievements suggest a rising quality of education but to what extent was there an uneducated, unreformed love of superstition, untouched by the new scientific understanding? And finally, by way of introduction, an apology. This section must fail to do justice to Elizabethan culture. The pages cannot show the colours of paintings, they certainly cannot bring you the sounds of the glorious music of Byrd and Gibbons. You cannot recapture from the written word the thrill, magic and emotion of the theatre. Discovering them for yourself is far more enjoyable than reading any book!

EXAMINING THE EVIDENCE
A Golden Age of Literature, Music and Education?

For once this section is unaccompanied by questions, although Talking Points are included. This is simply to provide variety, to allow you to explore the sources and judgements below in your own way and come to your own conclusions about the cultural achievements of Elizabethan England.

Source A
Shakespeare's greatness as a dramatist in both genres depends mainly on his poetry – poetry both of conception and execution; on his ability [as Stendhal put it] to say everything; and on the comprehensiveness of mind which makes him equally supreme in tragedy and comedy. Yet it is significant that his plays are appreciated by audiences throughout the world who have little or no knowledge of English. The quality which survives translation into other languages is his understanding of human nature revealed by his depiction of men and women in action and by his method of characterization, ... by which we are given 'conflicting impressions' of all his major characters, just as we are of people in real life.

K Muir, *'Language and Literature'* in R Blake (ed), *The English World*, 1982.

Source B
In the first twenty years of the reign of Elizabeth I (1558–1603), the poets were all small fry ... it took some time for the Elizabethan settlement to take root, for consciousness of nationhood to grow under the threat from Spain, and above all for the new grammar schools, founded after the dissolution of the monasteries, to provide a new educated middle class with literary tastes and ambitions. But the right conditions for literature are useless without men of genius ... By the example of Sidney and Spenser the general level of poetic craftmanship was immediately raised, and the poets of the last twenty years of Elizabeth's reign, however unequal in ability, could all write competent and musical verse.

K Muir, *'Language and Literature'* in R Blake (ed), *The English World*, 1982.

TALKING POINT

Do you agree with the praise of Shakespeare in Sources A and B? If not, why is your response different?

Source C
The traditional dramatic entertainments were originally performed in the open air, by occasional 'actors' to fluctuating audiences. By the 1570s the strolling players were beginning to form themselves into regular companies attached for patronage and protection to prominent noblemen: such a company, known as the Queen's men, was formed by Elizabeth's Master of the Revels in 1583. Already, James Burbage had established one of the conditions of the new drama when, as leader of the Earl of Leicester's men, he built in 1576 The Theatre, the earliest construction of its kind in England...

D Travers, *'Literature and Drama'* in B Ford (ed) *Sixteenth Century Britain: The Cambridge Cultural History of Britain*, 1988.

TALKING POINT

Several of these sources suggest reasons for the flowering of literature at the end of the sixteenth century. Do you find these reasons convincing?

Source D

It should also be noted that in the Elizabethan period there was an enormous enlargement of vocabulary by means of borrowing and coinages from French and Latin. Shakespeare, whose words totalled more than 29,000 coined many of them and used many others which had not previously appeared in print ... Shakespeare was lucky to be born into the 16th century rather than in the 18th, when propriety and good taste would have been his ruin.

K Muir, *'Language and Literature'* in R Blake (ed), *The English World*, 1982.

TALKING POINT

Sir John Cheke objected to the presence of words in the English language that were derived from foreign languages. He preferred 'hundreder' to 'centurion', 'crossd' to 'crucified' and 'moond' to 'lunatic'. Does this tell us anything about Elizabethan attitudes?

Source E

The interested and eager assimilation of new words at this time is symptomatic of the excitement generated by the new worlds which both demanded and provided more words. The unequalled power and suggestiveness of the language of this period ... derives from the way in which words and the world beyond words were felt to be connected. The first dictionaries emerged at this time. The titles of some of them – John Florio's English-Italian A Worlde of Wordes (1598) and Edward Phillips' English – English New World of English Words (1658) – suggest the felt continuity between the discoveries of language and those of the voyagers. The proliferation of words was an index of a proliferation of knowledge ...

E Cook, *'Language and Literature: Caxton to the Royal Society'* in L M Smith (ed), *The Age of Expansion*, 1986.

Source F

Look upon the common plays in London, and see the multitude that flocketh to them and followeth them. Behold the sumptuous theatre houses, a continual monument of London's prodigality and folly. But I understand they are not forbidden because of the plague. I like the policy well if it hold still, for a disease is but lodged or patched up that is not cured in the cause, and the cause of plagues is sin, if you look to it well: and the cause of sin are plays: therefore the cause of plagues are plays.

W Thomas White, *'A Sermon preached at Pawles Cross'*, 1578.

Source G

The sheer musicality of the English royal family, and its patronage of musicians throughout the sixteenth century, accounts at least in part for the extraordinary proliferation of art music during the Tudor era. It is an inescapable fact that their music-making resonated through the upper levels of English society. What the ruling monarch appreciated, the courtier could barely choose to scorn.

The musical expertise of Henry VIII and his children in turn bears witness to a social trend characteristic of the sixteenth century throughout Renaissance Europe. In an age of increasing literacy, the ability to read music itself became an accomplishment to which the educated readily aspired. Not content merely to pay others to sing and play before them, members of the nobility found pleasure in making music themselves.

J Milsom, *'Music'* in B Ford (ed), *Sixteenth Century Britain: The Cambridge Cultural History of Britain*, 1988.

Source H

Viewed as a whole, the repertoire of Tudor sacred music is astonishing for its sheer variety. In no other nation of the sixteenth century was resistance to the Reformation expressed in such emotive musical terms as in England; nowhere else did the cross-fertilisation between Renaissance humanism and nostalgia for the medieval tradition give rise to such a vigorous musical hybrid. ... Arguably, it was this very sense of national identity combined with the struggles of reformation and resistance that contributed most potently to the strength and sheer quality of so much Tudor religious music.

J Milsom, *'Music'* in B Ford (ed), *Sixteenth Century Britain: The Cambridge Cultural History of Britain,* 1988.

WILLIAM BYRD, PERHAPS THE FOREMOST COMPOSER IN ELIZABETHAN ENGLAND, WAS A CATHOLIC WHOSE RELIGION WAS WELL-KNOWN BUT TOLERATED BECAUSE OF HIS GENIUS AND BECAUSE PERSECTION MIGHT WELL HAVE CREATED MORE OVERT OPPOSITION AMONGST BYRD'S NOBLE, CATHOLIC SUPPORTERS.

Source I

Protestantism, which dominated the ideology of most Tudor patrons, brought with it a deep mistrust of images which were too life-like and pictures rivalling the creativity of God were frequently condemned as 'scandalous'. Some Tudor reactions to foreign work seen on travels seem to us very naive; the travellers got excited by rich materials, great antiquity and sheer size. Novelty was greatly admired, but composition, chiaroscuro [contrasts of light and shade] harmony and other aesthetic and theoretical qualities were usually left unnoted ...

Most of the pictures which have survived from Tudor England are portraits of one sort or another. Given the way Tudor portraits were used by their audience and by their patrons – as records of social status, of character and, to some extent, of physiognomy – there was little room for the challenge of invention within perceived traditions of art, as was expected by the very different audience accommodated by Italian painters.

M Howard and N Llewellyn, *'Painting and Imagery'* in B Ford (ed), *Sixteenth Century Britain: The Cambridge Cultural History of Britain,* 1988.

Source J

What cannot be found in any other early-modern society is a population so avid for learning of every kind. 'Every man strains his fortune to keep his children at school; the cobbler will clout it till midnight, the porter will carry burdens till his bones crack again, the plowman will pinch both back and belly to give his sone learning; and I find that this ambition reigns

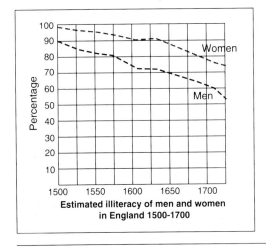

Estimated illiteracy of men and women
in England 1500-1700

nowhere so much as in this island.' There is hyperbole in James Howell's assessment but truth as well.

A Grafton 'Education and Apprenticeship' in J F Andrews (ed), William Shakespeare: His World, His Work, His Influence, Vol I, 1985.

Source K

Charters and grants of kings and great personages, letters, consultations in the council chamber, ambassadors' instructions and epistles, I carefully turned over and over. The parliamentary diaries, acts and statutes I thoroughly perused and read over every edict or proclamation ... Mine own cabinets and writings I also searched into: ... and received others from credible persons that have been before me, men who have been present at the transacting of matters, and such as have been addicted to the parties on both sides in this contrariety of religion. All which I have in the balance of mine own judgement (such as it is) weighed and examined, lest I should at any time through a beguiling credulity incline to that which is false. For the love of truth, ...

William Camden describing his methods as a historian. Camden was invited by Burghley to write a history of Queen Elizabeth.

Source L

(I) by degrees read over whatsoever printed or written discoveries and voyages I found extant either in the Greek, Latin, Italian, Spanish, Portugal, French, or English languages, and in my public lectures was the first that produced and showed both the old imperfectly composed and the new lately reformed maps, globes, spheres, and other instruments of this art for demonstration in the common schools.

From the dedication to the first edition (1589) of Richard Hakluyt's 'Principal navigations, voyages, traffics and discoveries of the English nation'.

Source M

Astrology in sixteenth- and seventeenth-century England was, therefore, an elaborate 'science' with detailed rules of procedure. Its influence penetrated to virtually all strata of the population. At the very top, Queen Elizabeth had her own astrologer John Dee ... it was Dee who chose the most auspicious day for her coronation ... Another important indication of the popularity of astrology can be seen in the number of almanacs which were sold during the sixteenth and seventeenth centuries. These little pocket-books, which contained a great deal of astrological information, were published in their thousands. They were the only books apart from the Bible to be widely distributed at almost all levels of society.

A G R Smith, The Emergence of a Nation State: The Commonwealth of England, 1529–1660, 1984.

Source N

In the 'Home Circuit' – the five counties of Essex, Kent, Hertfordshire, Surrey and Sussex – 513 people were indicted for witchcraft between 1560 and 1700. The peak period for prosecutions was Elizabeth's reign with the climax coming during the 1580s and 1590s; of the 307 prosecuted at the Essex assizes between 1560 and 1680 (Essex had far more prosecutions

JOHN DEE 1527 – 1608. DEE WAS A MATHEMATICIAN, ALCHEMIST, ASTROLOGER AND GEOGRAPHER WHO WAS CONSULTED BY ENGLAND'S LEADING SEAMEN. HE WAS RENOWNED THROUGHOUT EUROPE FOR HIS LEARNING, TRAVELLED ALL OVER THE CONTINENT AND OWNED THE LARGEST COLLECTION OF BOOKS IN ENGLAND.

than any of the other Home Counties) 163 were tried between 1560 and 1600, with 111 of the prosecutions coming in the period 1580–1600.

A G R Smith, *The Emergence of a Nation State: The Commonwealth of England, 1529–1660*, 1984.

Source O

Among the ancient novelties and new inventions that excited the minds of Elizabethan intellectuals, magic and mysticism were as influential as scientific theories and discoveries. Indeed, the boundary line between magic and science was shifting and uncertain, like a shoreline eroded and restored by the sea. Discoveries and techniques that proved in the long run to be scientific advances appeared first as aspects of magical and mystical pursuits ... The occult philosophies of John Dee and Robert Fludd subsumed mathematics and science, which they regarded as facets of natural magic; and these great magicians encouraged the advancement of mathematics, chemistry, and medicine as part of a broader quest for enlightenment.

M MacDonald, *'Science, Magic and Folklore'* in J F Andrews (ed), *William Shakespeare; His World, His Work, His Influence*, vol I, 1985.

Source P

ITEM. That no person or persons shall imprint or cause to be imprinted, or suffer by any means to his knowledge his press, letters or other instruments to be occupied in printing of any book ... and been first seen and perused by the Archbishop of Canterbury and Bishop of London for the time being, or any one of them.

An extract from a decree issued by the government in 1586.

An Architectural Revolution

'Every man almost is a builder and he hath bought any small parcel of ground, be it never so little, will not be quiet till he have pulled down the old house (if any were there standing) and set up a new after his own devise.'

William Harrison was a very perceptive and accurate observer of the Elizabethan England he lived in. You can read more of his comments on pages 22 – 25. Harrison correctly identified building as one of the wonders of the age and, in a wider context, we can see the period of 'the great rebuilding' of 1580–1620 as the most significant in English architectural history between the Roman period and the nineteenth century. In these years there was not simply an enormous quantity of building taking place but the quality of housing was revolutionised for all but the poorest. For the first time many people went upstairs to bed. The great hall, open to the rafters, became a relic of a medieval past. Downstairs the living space was divided up, with rooms having individual windows and fireplaces. People had privacy instead of sharing the communal public life of the great hall. These structural changes were accompanied by great improvements in furnishings, particularly the provision of coverings such as tapestries, and the ownership of books.

This housing revolution was possible because landowners were profiting from rising food prices. Once the building boom was underway it was further fuelled by the rivalries amongst the builders, anxious to outdo

TALKING POINT

What does the increasing number of books owned by families tell you about Elizabethan society?

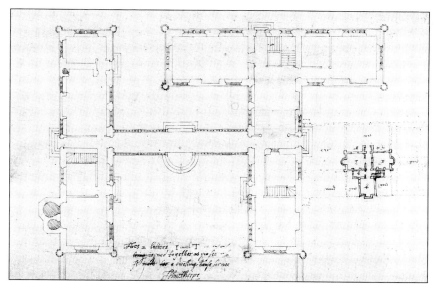

ARCHITECTURE WAS TREATED AS AN ENTERTAINMENT TO BE ENJOYED AND EXPLORED INTELLECTUALLY. SOME HOUSES WERE DESIGNED TO REPRESENT THE INITIALS OF THEIR OWNERS (IN THIS CASE JOHN THORPE) WHILE OTHERS TOOK THE FORM OF GEOMETRICAL PATTERNS.

TALKING POINT

Does this revolution in housing provide a greater justification for the term 'Golden Age' than the less practical developments in the arts and exploration?

TALKING POINT

What can you learn from the buildings shown here and on pages 23, 24 and 336 about changes and continuities in England in the Tudor period?

local or national rivalries. Houses reflected status. For the aristocracy the visits of Queen Elizabeth on progress also compelled them to build to please their monarch. The one surprising omission (largely explained by the pressures of war finance) is the absence of royal building. In stark contrast to her father, that compulsive builder Henry VIII, Elizabeth actually sold off royal palaces.

The battle for status produced far more dramatic and flamboyant buildings for the nobility than those of the first half of the century. In the heat of competition they were also continually remodelled to meet the latest fashion. Cecil's Burghley House has, for example, been described as developing from 'discreet reticence to flamboyant exuberance' and Burghley House ranked only second to Cecil's even more grandiose show palace, Theobald's.

The aristocracy built on the grandest scales and it is their houses that are best known today. However aristocrats had always lived with some degree of style and comfort. The true revolution in privacy, structure and style lay in the rebuilding and alterations to the homes of gentry and yeomen, the small landowners whose farmhouses now took on a shape and structure that would not be remodelled until the twentieth century. Inside these houses the possessions that told the same story were the tapestries and other cloth coverings that adorned every service, providing decoration, warmth and a declaration of status. The 1580 inventory of William Chappell of Exeter, a wealthy merchant, describes the 'Painted Canvas of the Storie of Joseph, and Courtanies of redd and grene saie before the windowe' and two sets of fringed bed-hangings, one of red and green, the other of blue and yellow. These and other hangings and coverings comprised over 80 per cent of the value of the contents of his first floor chamber, which was well provided with beds, table, chairs and cupboards.

Urbanisation and Poverty

The pattern of prosperity of English towns in the sixteenth century has been much debated by historians. As the population figures (Source B, page 12) show, it is difficult to identify an overall pattern but there are signs that the years after 1570 saw a recovery in many towns after the depression of the earlier part of the century. London became ever more dominant, incurring cries of wrath from ports who suffered from the capital's dominance.

Towns certainly reflected the 'great rebuilding'. When the poet, Thomas Churchyard visited Shrewsbury in 1581 he wrote of a 'world were made a newe

For building gay, and gallant finely wrought,
Had old device, through tyme supplanted cleane:
Some houses bare, that seem'd to be worth nought,
Were fat within, that outward looked leane.'

Even so, Elizabethan towns were much closer to medieval towns than the modern variety. Many were still walled, townsmen kept animals (in the 1590s almsmen in Maidstone even kept pigs in their rooms), thatching was common and fires and plagues could be devastating. Urban economics revolved around markets and fairs, religion, education, justice and royal administration. Towns were very much part of the surrounding rural economy. At the same time city authorities were seeking improvements. Plans for firefighting, street lanterns, paving, water supplies and the collection of refuse were aired in different places at different times although major improvements were not technically impossible. The poor still lived in plague ridden hovels, perhaps all the more noticeable for the improvements in housing for the wealthier classes.

London was in a different category from all other towns. Its growth caused government alarm and attempts were made to expel recent arrivals and ban buildings in the growing suburbs – to little effect. Probably to the surprise of the authorities London escaped riots and rebellion, even in the poverty-stricken years of the mid-1590s (see pages 390 – 391). In London particularly we can see the two sides of the Elizabethan Golden age. The wealth of the city attracted people anxious to share in the riches. The presence of the queen's court and government stimulated trade to such an extent that the people of Westminster complained of poverty if Elizabeth was absent on progress for long. Around this honey-pot of wealth and trade milled thousands of people, newly-arrived, many of them young and seeking work and accommodation. Some succeeded. Many suffered. Their presence frightened local and central governments into taking measures both to help the needy poor and punish vagabonds and beggars.

Individual towns acted ahead of the national government. Norwich, Ipswich, York, Exeter, Chester amongst others took measures both to protect and punish. Central government learned from this in instituting the measures shown in the table (overleaf). There was a growing concern about the poor and the vagrant in the 1580s and 1590s, particularly in the latter decade when there was a succession of atrocious harvests. One element in this concern was a genuine wish to help the poor, a concern for the common weal or welfare that harked back to the days of Thomas Cromwell. Puritanism added another strand of concern for social reform

TALKING POINT

In what ways does the experience of urbanisation support or detract from the image of the Elizabethan Golden Age?

Main provision of Poor Law Legislation 1558–1585
(for details of legislation in the 1590s see page 391)

1563   An Act for the Relief of the Poor

  (a) Re-enacted earlier legislation, including provision for whipping able-bodied beggars; the licensing of disabled beggars who were to be whipped if they left licensing areas; weekly collections of poor relief and the provision of cottages for the disabled; enslavement of sturdy beggars.

  (b) People who refused to contribute to poor-relief to be exhorted by bishops. If they still refused they were liable to imprisonment.

  (c) Fines were levied on officials for failing to carry out duties e.g. £10 for refusing to be a collector of poor relief.

1572   An Act for the Punishment of Vagabonds and for the Relief of the Poor and Impotent.

  (a) All convicted vagabonds aged 14 and over to be whipped and burned through the right ear unless given work.

  (b) Second and third offences to be treated as felonies.

  (c) Beggars' children could be put to work in household service.

  (d) Earlier measures re-enacted.

1576   An Act for the Setting of the Poor on Work, and for the Avoiding of Idlemen

  (a) Officials to gather wool and other items to provide work.

  (b) Anyone who refused to work was to be sent to a house of correction, which were to be established in all countries supported by the poor rates.

and improvement, influencing the thinking of Cecil and numerous others. At the same time the gentry and nobility feared social upheavals, a fear initiated by the upsurge in the numbers wandering the country, their mobility in itself a threat. In the Middle Ages and the earlier sixteenth century people had been much more mobile than we often think but in the late sixteenth century there seemed to be something new, aimless and threatening to the social order in the number of vagrants. The century ended with threats of risings although a worried government greatly exaggerated the dangers. Poor harvests, poverty and plague made the final decade of the Tudor century the 'iron decade' despite the golden lines of Shakespeare and the gleaming towers of Burleigh House.

Review

Royal Astraea makes our day
Eternal with her beams, nor may
Gross darkness overcome her;
I now perceive why some do write
No country hath so short a night
As English hath in summer.

John Davies, Hymns to Astraea.

'a lady shut up in a chamber from her subjects and most of her servants, and seldom seen but on holy days'

Sir John Harington, writing of Elizabeth in 1602.

Elizabeth reigned for forty-five years. During that time her accession day – 17 November – was celebrated with wild joy and gratitude for the blessings she had brought and, in other years, sceptics commented sardonically that the English would never again allow themselves to be ruled by a woman. In the 1590s particularly scandal-mongers spread rumours that Elizabeth had borne children by her lovers. In the centuries since then the cynicism of critics has been forgotten as Elizabeth's reign gained its golden image. Is this justified?

How might each of these Elizabethans respond to the question 'Was the reign of Elizabeth a Golden Age?'

(a) William Byrd
(b) Nicholas Hilliard
(c) Francis Drake
(d) Richard Hakluyt
(e) John Dee
(f) Edmund Spenser
(g) William Cecil
(h) the Mayor of London in 1596

TALKING POINT

Which Elizabethan women might be included in this list and how might they regard the reign of Elizabeth?

14 Elizabethan England 1568–1585: A Time of Threat and Plenty

PREVIEW

1568	Mary, Queen of Scots' flight to England. English seizure of Spanish gold intended for the Duke of Alva. A seminary to train English Catholic priests founded at Douai.
1569	Plot to marry Mary, Queen of Scots, to the Duke of Norfolk. The Rebellion of the Northern Earls.
1570	The excommunication of Elizabeth by the Pope. Negotiations begin for a French husband for Elizabeth.
1571	The Ridolfi plot, aiming to depose Elizabeth with Spanish help.
1572	Norfolk executed for involvement in Ridolfi plot Massacre of St Bartholomew in France.
1574	Settlement of Anglo-Spanish disputes.
1576	Demands in Parliament for freedom of speech. Archbishop Grindal refuses to obey Elizabeth's orders to suppress extreme Puritan movement.
1578	Spanish troops move into the Netherlands to suppress rebellion.
1579	Rebellion breaks out in Ireland and lasts until 1583.
1580	The first Jesuit priests arrive in England. Drake completes circumnavigation.
1583	Throckmorton plot to depose Elizabeth with foreign aid.
1584	Disputes between Queen and Parliament over the succession. Treaty of Joinville unites Spain and the French Catholic League.
1585	Spanish troops make great progress in the Netherlands. Elizabeth sends military aid, leading to the Anglo-Spanish war.

Source A

... whereas dynastic, chivalric, commercial, and personal ambitions had hitherto chiefly dominated the Renaissance stage, the polarization of rival religious creeds ... meant that politicians increasingly saw themselves as combatants engaged in a cosmic confrontation between right and wrong. The concept of the 'true church' that Catholics and Protestants promulgated in their diametrically opposed ways was pervasive; it ensured that pragmatism was overtaken by dogmatism, haggling by perpetual struggle, and compromise by persecution.

J Guy, *Tudor England*, 1988.

Source B

Stability...was one of the notable features of the Elizabethan regime during the 1570s and 1580s, the 'high Elizabethan period' to which men looked back nostalgically during more troubled times in the seventeenth century.

A.G.R.Smith, *The Emergence of a Nation State; the commonwealth of England 1529–1660*, 1984.

---

1 What change in political motivation is identified in Source A?

2 Given the political problems listed for 1568–85 why was it possible for people to look back nostalgically to this era? (It may help to refer back to Chapter 13)

3 Given the material in this preview what developments would you anticipate after 1568 in Elizabeth's

(a) religious policies?

(b) relations with other countries?

(c) attitude to the succession?

Source C

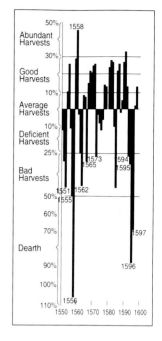

The Northern Rising 1569

The seizure of the Spanish treasure in December 1568 was not only a turning point in Anglo-Spanish relations. It also helped to create a political plot at Elizabeth's court which in turn, despite its abject failure, triggered the one serious rebellion of the reign, the Northern Rising headed by the Earls of Northumberland and Westmorland.

It was Cecil who had actually ordered the seizure of the Spanish treasure. The resulting deterioration in Anglo-Spanish relations was used by his opponents, a group of conservative nobles headed by Duke of Norfolk and the Earls of Arundel and Pembroke. They hoped to persuade Elizabeth that Cecil's actions had harmed her interests and merited dismissal. However their motives were far more ambitious than simply the removal of the Protestant upstart, Cecil. Their plan was to marry Norfolk to Mary, Queen of Scots and establish Mary as Elizabeth's declared successor. They then hoped to re-establish good relations with Spain and pave the way for a return to Catholicism.

The strange twist to this plot was that it acquired the support of those two eminent Protestants, the Earl of Leicester and Sir Nicholas Throckmorton. Their reason for involvement was not the removal of Cecil (although they probably wished to shake his confidence and security) but the amazing idea that, once married to Norfolk and restored to Scotland, Mary would become a Protestant and create an Anglo-Scottish

Protestant alliance. Whether this was extreme wishful thinking or they were misled by Norfolk publicly accepting Elizabeth's religious settlement, this made temporary allies of the most unlikely people.

Those involved discussed their plan for much of 1569 but hesitated about broaching it with the queen, especially after she had slapped down Leicester's criticism of Cecil in Parliament. By late summer the queen had discovered the details and in September Leicester confessed all to Elizabeth. Norfolk fled from court, suggestive of serious guilt, perhaps of treason. In planning to marry Mary and make her Elizabeth's successor, Norfolk had been planning to win a crown for himself.

At this stage there was no plan for rebellion. No one intended deposing Elizabeth. Norfolk may now have contemplated rebellion to save himself but, if he did, he did not do so for long. He returned to court to beg for mercy, having sent a message to his northern allies not to attempt a rising. Unfortunately that is just what they did.

THOMAS HOWARD, THE DUKE OF NORFOLK.

EXAMINING THE EVIDENCE
The Northern Rising 1569

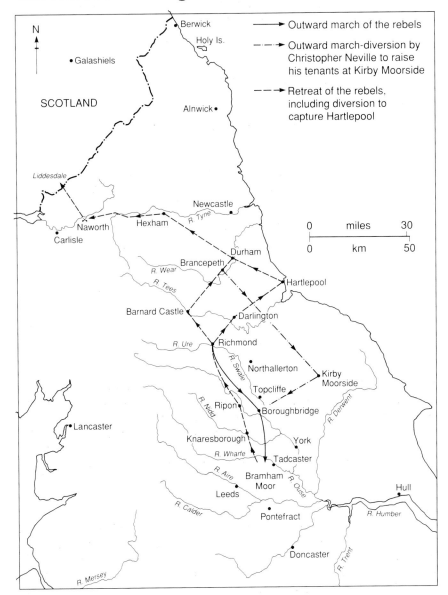

Legend:
- → Outward march of the rebels
- –·–·→ Outward march-diversion by Christopher Neville to raise his tenants at Kirby Moorside
- – – –→ Retreat of the rebels, including diversion to capture Hartlepool

Map labels: N, Berwick, Holy Is., Galashiels, SCOTLAND, Alnwick, Liddesdale, Newcastle, R. Tyne, Naworth, Hexham, Carlisle, Durham, Brancepeth, R. Wear, R. Tees, Hartlepool, Barnard Castle, Darlington, R. Ure, Richmond, R. Swale, Northallerton, Kirby Moorside, Topcliffe, R. Nidd, Ripon, Boroughbridge, R. Derwent, Lancaster, Knaresborough, York, R. Wharfe, Tadcaster, R. Aire, Bramham Moor, R. Ouse, Hull, Leeds, R. Calder, Pontefract, R. Humber, Doncaster, R. Trent, R. Mersey

Scale: 0 miles 30 / 0 km 50

The leaders of the rising were the Earls of Northumberland and Westmorland. Westmorland was Norfolk's brother in law. They had been involved on the fringes of the courtiers' plot and they seem to have taken Norfolk's flight from court as a signal to prepare a rising. This they did for 6 October, only to hear that Norfolk was seeking forgiveness. Why did they continue with the rebellion?

The Events of the Rising

Aug–Sept	Rumours of risings.
Oct 6	Date fixed by Earls for rising but abandoned after Norfolk sought mercy.
Oct 9	Earls denied knowledge of rising to Council of the North.
Oct 13	Earl of Sussex reported 'all is very quiet here and the time of year will shortly cool hot humours'.
Oct 24	Earls summoned to court by Elizabeth.
Nov 9	Church bells called people out to rising.
Nov 14	Rebels heard mass in Durham.
Nov 22–24	Rebels reached Bramham. Bowes reported 'All things are here out of order and my dealing and good will cannot amend it'. Even so, on 24th the rebels turned back north.
Nov 26	Sussex reported that his 'soldiers wax more trusty'.
Dec	Rebels captured Barnard Castle and the port of Hartlepool in case they received help from abroad.
Dec 16	The Earls disbanded their forces as the royal army reached the Tees.
Feb 1570	Lord Hunsdon's royal army defeated Lord Dacre's rebels. 500 rebels were killed or captured.

Source A

Sir I take this assembly to be more done for fear, than that there is any evil intended to be done; but assembling of themselves, for that they perhaps doubt (think) they should be suddenly suppressed.

Extract from a letter from Sir George Bowes to the Earl of Sussex, 7 November 1569. Bowes was a Yorkshire gentleman who stayed loyal. Sussex, as President of the Council of the North, had the first responsibility for preventing and suppressing trouble.

Source B

My Lady's servant declared to me that my Lord (Northumberland) had received perfect knowledge from those parts that your Majesty had commanded me to take him and send him up 'moffeled' (my Lord also told this to my secretary) and that was the cause of why my Lord was fearful ... for though he were a true man, yet he knew not how he should be used by his enemies.

Extracts from a letter from the Earl of Sussex to the Queen, 10 November 1569.

Source C

Whereas divers new set up nobles about the Queen's Majesty ... not only go about to overthrow and put down the ancient nobility of this realm, but also have misused the Queen's Majesty's own person and also have ... set up and maintained a new found religion and heresy, contrary to God's word. For the amending and redressing thereof divers foreign powers do propose shortly to invade these realms ... Wherefore we are now constrained ... to amend and redress it ourselves ... God save the Queen.

Extracts from the rebels' proclamation at Darlington, 16 November 1569.

Source D

For what cause, or intent, should the said Scottish Queen have been taken away?
The cause and intent was in the having of her, that we hoped thereby to have some reformation in religion, or at the least some sufferance for men to use their conscience as they were disposed.

At what time was it meant and intended that she should have been proclaimed Queen of England?
I do not remember I heard it opined or moved at any man's hands to proclaim her Queen of England.

When did you first enter into the conspiracy of the late rebellion?-

We did begin to talk of these matters about the time of the Duke's departure in displeasure from the court ... many gentlemen were aminded to join and take such part as the Duke did if the quarrel should be for reformation of religion or for nominating the heir apparent; for those two causes I would much danger myself. As for the marriage only I never had will nor intent to put me in hazard ...

Extracts from the Earl of Northumberland's replies in custody to Lord Hunsdon's
questions on behalf of Cecil, 1572.

Source E

Truly, my Lord, he (Northumberland) seems to be very willing to satisfy her Majesty in anything he can and, if his confessions be true, the rebellion was one of the strangest matters that has been heard of and principally procured by Old Norton and Markenfield and earnestly followed by the two wives the Countesses.

The Earl does greatly excuse my Lord of Westmorland and says plainly that they could never get any hold of him, till the last hour and that by procurement of his wife. He (Northumberland) is very timorous and, it is affirmed, has meant twice or thrice to submit himself but that his wife, being the stouter of the two does not hasten him and encourage him to persevere.

Extracts from letters from Lord Hunsdon to Cecil. Norton and Markenfield were
Catholic gentlemen. Norton had taken part in the Pilgrimage of Grace.

Source F

The ancient faith still lay like lees at the bottom of men's hearts and if the vessel was ever so little stirred came to the top.

Sir Ralph Sadler, one of the royal commanders.

Source G

Northumberland had suffered severely from Elizabeth's reassertion of the policies of her father, aimed at weakening the hold of the great magnate families on the marches. She had deprived him of his Wardenship of the Middle March and allowed him no part in the custody of Mary ... Northumberland had declined in wealth as well as status ... The Earl of Westmorland was also suffering from poverty.

A Fletcher, *Tudor Rebellions*, third edition, 1983.

Source H

Leonard Metcalf – He was servant to the Earl of Northumberland, whom he followed ...

Robert Lambert – He was at the first taken by the rebels out of his bed by force, in his father in law's house, to which place he had retired with the intent to go to Sir George Bowes ...

Robert Claxton – He was servant to the Earl of Westmorland, whom he followed ...

Extracts from a list of rebels tried in York, March 1570.

---

1 What evidence do Sources A and B provide about the rebels' motives?

2 What motives are given in Source C?

3 Do Northumberland's confessions agree more with the motives suggested by Source A or Source B?

4 What other motives are suggested in sources E to G?

5 Why did ordinary people become involved in the rising?

6 Historians have argued over whether the rising was motivated by religion or politics. What is your explanation for the rising?

TALKING POINT

Given the general pattern of loyalty since 1534 was Elizabeth's policy of conciliation towards Catholics over-optimistic?

TALKING POINT

This rebellion is sometimes called 'The Rebellion of the Northern Earls', sometimes 'The Northern Rising'. Which seems the more appropriate? Does it matter which name is used for this event?

How dangerous was the rising?

The government was frightened by the rising. For a few days in mid-November the well-armed and mounted rebel force brought normal life to a standstill around York while the Earl of Sussex struggled to raise more than a handful of trustworthy troops. However the danger was brief. The rebel army, just 6000 men, was much smaller than it might have been. Many heads of families hesitated like the Earls but, unlike them, stayed at home. Lord Dacre, the likeliest to provide strong leadership (he fought a belated battle in 1570) was in London, fighting a lawsuit against, of all people, Norfolk. Once Sussex stood firm the leaders of the rising feebly caved in. Their rising had been hastily planned and so there had been no communications with Spain seeking aid. In any case would Philip II have wanted to aid Mary, Queen of Scots at this stage, given her French connections?

In some ways the events of 1569 can be seen as a success for the centralising impetus of Tudor government. Even the far north had proved incapable of troubling the government through independent action.

14.1 Mary, Queen of Scots and Catholic plots, 1570–1585

Key events

1570	Elizabeth was excommunicated by the Pope, who also authorised her deposition and absolved Englishmen 'from all manner of duty, fealty and obedience'.
1571	The Ridolfi Plot to depose Elizabeth and make Mary Queen of England.
1572	Norfolk was executed for his role in the Ridolfi Plot. Parliament demanded Mary's execution but Elizabeth refused. She did not recognise James VI as King of Scotland and offered to send Mary back to Scotland for trial.
1574	Catholic priests arrived in England to serve Catholics in secret.
1580	The first Jesuit priests arrived in England.
1583	The Throckmorton Plot to depose Elizabeth and make Mary Queen of England.
1584	The assassination of William of Orange, the Protestant leader of resistance in the Netherlands.
1585	The outbreak of war between England and Spain.

The Ridolfi Plot 1571

Ridolfi was a Florentine banker living in London. He was the link in a plot that embraced Mary, Queen of Scots, the Duke of Norfolk, Lord Lumley, de Spes (the Spanish ambassador in London), Philip II and the Pope. The plan, uncovered by Cecil, involved the landing of 6000 Spanish troops at Harwich who would join English Catholics in deposing Elizabeth and putting Mary on the throne with Norfolk as her husband. Norfolk had only been released in August 1570 after his links to the Northern Rising. He was convicted of treason in January 1572 but the Queen could not bring herself to agree to the execution of the country's only Duke and a man who was her blood relation. She changed her mind three times before Norfolk was finally executed in June. Parliament had demanded the execution of Mary as well as Norfolk or at least Mary's removal from the succession. Instead, as Cecil disgustedly wrote, 'All that we have laboured for and had with full consent brought to fashion – I mean a law to make the Scottish Queen unable and unworthy of succession to the crown – was by her Majesty neither assented to nor rejected, but deferred.'

The Throckmorton Plot 1583

Francis Throckmorton (born in 1554) belonged to a strongly Catholic family from the Midlands. He joined a plan devised by the Duke of Guise for French armies to invade Scotland and England and help English Catholics crown Mary. The whole expedition was to be financed by Philip of Spain and the Pope. Mary knew of the plan, as did Mendoza, the Spanish ambassador in London. Francis Walsingham learned of the existence of the plan and inserted a spy into the French embassy, where he learned of Throckmorton's role as the link to Mary. Throckmorton was arrested and tortured on the rack. He confessed, providing a list of Catholic noblemen and gentry and a list of the harbours where forces would be landed. Throckmorton was executed, Mendoza was expelled but Mary was again spared.

As a result of this plot the Bond of Association was organised by the Council. It declared that if an attempt was made to assassinate the Queen 'the signatories would revenge it to the uttermost, would prevent the succession of the person in whose favour the attempt was made, and would do their best to put that person to death.' Everywhere men rushed to join the Bond, 7000 in Yorkshire alone within a month.

MARY, QUEEN OF SCOTS

WILLIAM PARRY, AT FIRST A SPY EMPLOYED
BY CECIL, THEN A CATHOLIC SYMPATHISER.
HE DISCUSSED AND, PERHAPS, PLANNED
ELIZABETH'S ASSASSINATION. ARRESTED BY
WALSINGHAM, HE WAS EXECUTED FOR
TREASON IN 1585.

Questions

1 What attitude did members of parliament take towards Mary?

2 Why do you think Elizabeth did not have Mary executed?

3 How great a danger faced Elizabeth between 1570 and 1585?

4 What else could Elizabeth's councillors do to protect her after 1585?

5 What do these events tell us about Elizabeth?

Source A

The late Queen of Scots has not only sought and wrought by all means she can to seduce the people of God in this realm from true religion, but is the only hope of all the adversaries of God throughout Europe and the instrument whereby they overthrow the gospel of Christ in all countries ... it be lawful and honourable for the Queen's Majesty to execute this woman who besides the subversion of religion has sought the life of the same our gracious Sovereign ... The late Scottish Queen has heaped up together all the sins of ... adultery, murder, conspiracy, treasons and blasphemies against God also, and if she escape with slight or no punishment her Majesty in conscience ought ... to fear that God will reserve her as an instrument to put her from the royal seat of this kingdom and to plague the unthankful and naughty subjects ...

> Extracts from a set of arguments against Mary, Queen of Scots, presented to Elizabeth by some members of both Houses of Parliament, May 1572.

Source B

Since the Queen's Majesty's will and pleasure in that we should not proceed nor deal with the first bill against the monstrous and huge dragon ... the Queen of Scots ... and although her Majesty is lulled asleep and wrapped in the mantle of her own peril, yet for my part I cannot be silent in uttering of my conscience.

> The words of Mr Saint Leger, reported in Fulk Onslow's journal of parliament, 30 May 1572.

Source C

The ways for remedy he thinks to be:
1 cutting off the heads of the Scottish Queen and Duke;
2 taking away the Scottish Queen's title;
3 by the establishment of a certain successor.

> The words of Sir Thomas Scott in parliament, 15 May 1572. From an anonymous journal.

Source D

Can I put to death the bird that, to escape the pursuit of the hawk, has fled to my feet for protection? Honour and conscience forbid!

> Elizabeth's words to her Council, 1572.

Source E

There is great expectation amongst the papists of Lancashire and Cheshire that the Earl of Derby will play as fond a part this year as the two Earls did last year. He has hitherto been loyal but has at this time many wicked counsellors. There is one Browne, a conjurer, in his house kept secretly ... if you would send some faithful and wise spy that would dissemble to come from D Alva and dissemble papery you might understand all.

> Letter from Henry, Earl of Huntingdon, to Francis Walsingham, August 1570.

FRANCIS WALSINGHAM.

Foreign Policies 1568–1585

During this period events in the Netherlands dominated European politics. Another complicating factor was the continuing religious divide in France that sometimes erupted into conflict. Use the outline of events on pages 350 – 1 to answer the questions below. The text on pages 349, 352 – 357 will allow you to develop your understanding more fully.

1 Why did Elizabeth open marriage negotiations with France and then complete the Treaty of Blois?

2 Why was the period between 1573 and 1577 one of less risk for England?

3 Why did the marriage negotiations with France reconvene in 1578–9 and why did they continue for so long?

4 'The situation for Elizabeth deteriorated in the early 1580s, slowly at first and then rapidly in 1584'. Which events provide supporting evidence for this statement?

5 Walter Raleigh said that in foreign affairs 'Her Majesty did all by halves'.

(a) What do you think he meant?

(b) Would this description fit her policies towards: (i) Spain (ii) Netherlands (iii) France?

6 In 1585 Elizabeth was under great pressure from many of her councillors to intervene in the Netherlands. What would be the arguments for and against intervention?

Scotland 1568–1585

Scotland remained a danger to Elizabeth because, as long as Mary was alive, there was the prospect of a return to Catholicism and the French alliance. Twice Elizabeth faced the decision of whether to intervene to bolster the Protestant government against Mary's supporters. On the first occasion, between 1568 and 1573, Elizabeth was forced to give limited aid. She would do no more because she did not wish to risk provoking war with France. She was also still considering the possibility of restoring Mary to her throne. By 1573 the danger was past, thanks to the determination of Scots Protestant nobles who captured Edinburgh castle from Mary's supporters with the aid of the Earl of Sussex's troops.

The Protestant Earl of Morton ruled as Regent through the 1570s until he was overthrown and executed. His opponent was the Duke of Lennox who had ingratiated himself with the adolescent James VI. Lennox's motives were purely selfish but he was also used by Spain as the focal point for a Catholic invasion of both Scotland and England. Again Elizabeth refused to intervene. Happily for her, Lennox was overthrown by a group of Protestant nobles. By the mid 1580s Scotland seemed securely Protestant, a natural ally of England because of her young king's Protestantism and his ambition to inherit Elizabeth's throne.

	SPAIN	NETHERLANDS	FRANCE	SCOTLAND	OTHER EVENTS
The situation in 1568	Anglo-Spanish relations had deteriorated after the seizure of the Spanish gold and Alva's arrival in the Netherlands.		Anglo-French relations were neither very good nor very poor.	Mary Stuart was under "protective custody" in England.	
1569					Northern Rising Revolt in Ireland (to 1573)
1570			Negotiations begin for Elizabeth's marriage to Duke of Anjou .		
1571	Spain supported the Ridolfi plot.				
1572		Protestant exiles invaded Netherlands to begin war of independence. Elizabeth allows volunteer to aid rebels.	Treaty of Blois with England – a defensive alliance. Massacre of St. Bartholomew. Alencon Elizabeth's new suitor.		
1573	Renewal of Anglo-Spanish trade after 1568 breach.	Alva recalled to Spain.		Edinburgh castle captured by Anglo-Scottish troops from Mary's supporters.	
1574	Settlement of Anglo-Spanish claims arising from 1568.		Death of Charles IX. Accession of Henry III.		First Catholic priests enter England.
1575	Spain bankrupt – unable to continue actions against rebels in Netherlands.	Elizabeth sanctions volunteer aid but refuses direct involvement.			

Year	SPAIN	NETHERLANDS	FRANCE	SCOTLAND	OTHER EVENTS
1576					
1577		William of Orange the head of a virtually independent state.			
1578	Duke of Parma sent to Netherlands to subdue revolt.		Revival of negotiations for Elizabeth's marriage to Alencon.	James VI takes control as king.	
1579		Southern Catholic provinces make peace with Spain, alarmed by extreme Protestantism of the north.	Alencon visits England.		Irish rebellion – to 1583.
1580	Philip II inherits Portugal.	Spanish operations at a standstill.	Marriage negotiations continue.		First Jesuits arrive in England.
1581		Alencon declared ruler of Netherlands by rebels.		Conspiracy to re-impose Catholicism & conquer England led by Lennox.	
1582	Parma begins reconquest of northern provinces.		End of Alencon marriage negotiations.	Lennox defeated by Protestant coup.	
1583	Spanish aid for Throckmorton plot.				
1584		Assassination of rebel leader, William of Orange.	Alencon died. New heir a Protestant. Secret Treaty of Joinville between France and Spain.		
1585	Parma makes rapid progress. English fleets seized in Spanish harbours.				

14.2 Elizabeth and the Netherlands

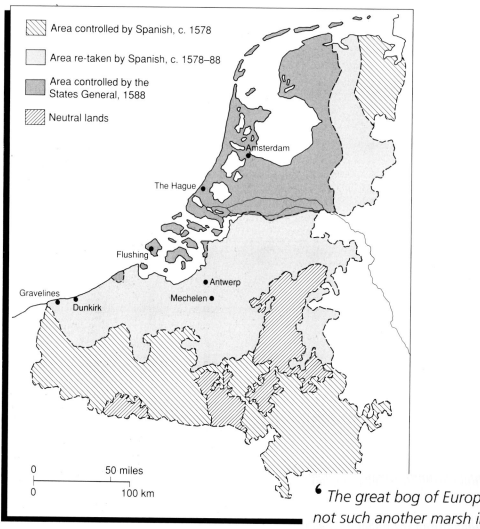

Area controlled by Spanish, c. 1578

Area re-taken by Spanish, c. 1578–88

Area controlled by the States General, 1588

Neutral lands

Amsterdam

The Hague

Flushing

Gravelines

Dunkirk

Antwerp

Mechelen

0   50 miles

0   100 km

' The great bog of Europe. There is not such another marsh in the world, that's flat. They are an universal quagmire ... Indeed it is the buttock of the world: full of veins and blood but no bones in't '.

That is what one English traveller thought of Holland and Zeeland and doubtless he was not alone in his prejudiced view of the flat, wet Low Countries. And yet 'the buttock of the world' was crucially important to England. Much of her trade went through Antwerp.

The region was also the focus for the complex and desperate diplomacy of the 1570s and 1580s. In the view of Elizabeth and her councillors events in the Netherlands might well determine the fate of England, the Protestant religion and the Tudor dynasty.

Events in the Netherlands

1548 The seventeen provinces were, for the first time, brought under a single administrative structure by Charles V despite their differences in language, customs and religion.

1556 Philip II began to act against Protestant ideas, necessitating greater Spanish involvement than in the past.

1566 A strong outbreak of Protestant iconoclasm challenged Philip's control.

1567 Alva was sent to establish Spanish control. The Protestant rebels fled abroad.

1572 Protestant exiles returned, led by William of Orange. They won control over Holland and Zeeland and continued the rebellion. Their bases were well fortified and defended, especially by waterways and their fleet of small ships stopped Spanish troops from landing.

1575 Philip II was bankrupt, his army could not be paid and so disintegrated. Catholic leaders in southern Netherlands united with William of Orange. William became the effective head of government.

1576 The Sack of Antwerp by Spanish forces cemented the unity of the Dutch provinces.

1577 William demanded that Philip recognise his government and grant freedom of worship.

1578 Alexander Farnese, Duke of Parma, arrived in the Netherlands to lead a Spanish reconquest.

1579 Parma won back the support of the Catholic provinces in the south and bribed many northern towns. His 'silver bullets' proved more effective than the real thing.

1581 Parma launched his conquest of Flanders and Brabant, the richest provinces, using his fleet to blockade trade. The Duke of Alencon arrived with 10,000 troops to become 'prince and lord' of the Netherlands.

1582 An assassination attempt on William of Orange, organised by Parma, failed.

1583 Alencon returned to France after a dismal failure to provide leadership.

1584 William of Orange was assassinated.

1585 Parma captured Antwerp, the richest town in the Netherlands.

English Intervention in 1575–76

For intervention

- The diplomatic situation was favourable. France was well-disposed towards Elizabeth while the Spanish forces in the Netherlands were making little progress.

- There was still the chance to unite the Netherlands as one strong state.

- Intervention would aid the Protestant cause and was strongly advocated by Leicester and other leading councillors.

Against intervention

- The rebels were keeping Spain at bay without official English aid.

- The cost of intervention would be considerable. Parliament would need to agree taxes and might well take the opportunity to discuss the succession issue.

- Complete defeat for Spain might open the way to French domination of the Netherlands. The pre -1566 pattern of Spanish overlordship (but not full control) was preferable.

- Intervention might be seen as provocative by Spain and raise fears in Catholic countries of a Protestant league.

English Intervention in 1585

For intervention

- The rebel cause was in danger. Spanish success would leave them in control of the coast facing England. Parma's army could be used as an invasion force.

- The Protestant cause was in danger, leaving England isolated as the sole significant Protestant power. She was no longer able to play a balancing role amongst Spain, France and the rebels.

- Since William's assassination the rebels had need of the effective leadership that England could provide.

Against intervention

- The southern provinces were already reconciled to Spain so the Netherlands could not be as great a bulwark against aggression.

- France had joined the Catholic league with Spain and intervention would lead to both countries being opposed to England.

- Since William's assassination, the rebels had had no effective leadership.

- The cost of intervention would be considerable.

Source A

Necessary for England that the State of the Low Countries should continue in their ancient government, without either subduing it to the Spanish nation or joining it to the Crown of France.

Cecil's description of the prime English objective in relation to the Netherlands.

Source B

The second (cause) is the inestimable benefit of peace during the term of ten whole years reign together and more. And what is peace? Is it not the richest and most wished for ornament that pertains to any public weal? Is not peace the mark and end that all good governments direct their actions unto?... A man that would sufficiently consider of all the commodities of peace ought to call to remembrance all the miseries of war ...

Extracts from the opening speech of Sir Nicholas Bacon, Lord Keeper of the Great Seal, to Parliament, April 1571. Bacon was arguing the case for meeting the Queen's request for financial assistance.

Source C

The foreign policy of (England) was like the navigating of a sailing dinghy across the Atlantic ... the man in the dinghy knows that his overall navigation must be correct; yet primarily he is concerned to circumvent the next mountainous wave, to ride out the force-twelve gust in the force-nine gale, to repair the frayed halyard before it snaps. In a multitude of detailed decisions, one unlucky error can sink man and boat without trace, however correct his overall navigation ... The central importance of detail in the foreign policy of little states, the fevered anxiety of every move when a little state is gambling for its survival, this is the truth about foreign policy ...

P S Crowson, *Tudor Foreign Policy,* 1973.

Questions

1. Should Elizabeth have intervened in the Netherlands in 1575–6?

2. Should Elizabeth have intervened when she did in 1585?

3. Was 1585 a better time to intervene than 1575?

4. Do you think P S Crowson's analogy (Source C) is a good one?

5. 'In 1585 Elizabeth was forced into open warfare. Therefore her policies since 1568 had failed'. Explain why you agree or disagree with this statement in the light of your whole study of Elizabeth's foreign policies since 1568.

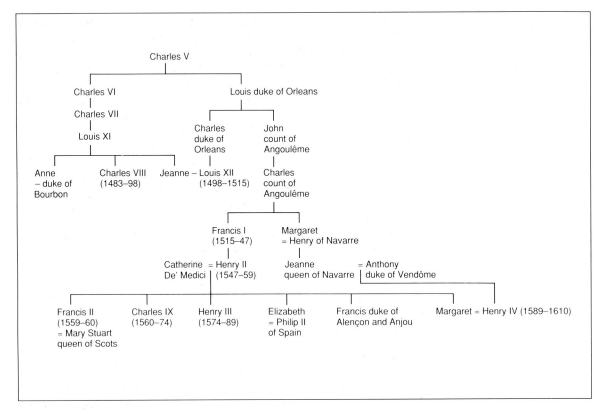

Charles V
├─ Charles VI
│   └─ Charles VII
│   └─ Louis XI
│   ├─ Anne – duke of Bourbon
│   ├─ Charles VIII (1483–98)
│   └─ Jeanne – Louis XII (1498–1515)
└─ Louis duke of Orleans
    ├─ Charles duke of Orleans
    └─ John count of Angoulême
        └─ Charles count of Angoulême
            ├─ Francis I (1515–47)
            │   └─ Catherine De' Medici = Henry II (1547–59)
            │   ├─ Francis II (1559–60) = Mary Stuart queen of Scots
            │   ├─ Charles IX (1560–74)
            │   ├─ Henry III (1574–89)
            │   ├─ Elizabeth = Philip II of Spain
            │   └─ Francis duke of Alençon and Anjou
            └─ Margaret = Henry of Navarre
                └─ Jeanne queen of Navarre = Anthony duke of Vendôme
                    └─ Margaret = Henry IV (1589–1610)

Anglo-French relations 1568–1585

The path of Anglo-French relations was extremely complex. On the one hand deteriorating relations with Spain made some kind of understanding with France desirable, if not essential, for England's security. On the other hand Elizabeth certainly did not want France's influence in Scotland or the Netherlands to increase and therefore, on occasion, had to act against the interests of her potential ally. In addition France was plagued by religious tensions between Catholics and Huguenots. Initially the Regent Catherine of Medici was threatened by the strongly Catholic Guise family and so Elizabeth tried where possible to bolster Catherine's position through diplomacy. After the fervently Catholic Henry III became king Elizabeth had little room for manoeuvre if she wanted to avoid an alliance between Spain and France.

In April 1572 circumstances combined to allow England and France to agree the Treaty of Blois, a defensive alliance intended to deter Spanish aggression. This gave England security and boosted Catherine de Medici's position in relation to the Guise. The agreement having been reached, Elizabeth abandoned negotiations for her marriage to the French heir, the Duke of Anjou.

Anglo-French relations seemed secure – until the Guise-inspired massacre of St Bartholomew (24–30 August) when 3000 Huguenots were killed in Paris. Thousands more deaths followed. It seemed impossible for Protestant England to remain close to France and yet enmity was exceedingly dangerous. Elizabeth could not afford to agree with Walsingham (then ambassador

FRANCIS, DUKE OF ALENCON, LATER DUKE OF ANJOU, WHOSE MARRIAGE NEGOTIATIONS WITH ELIZABETH WERE CLOSELY RELATED TO DEVELOPMENTS IN THE NETHERLANDS.

TALKING POINT

Review your answers to questions 1–3 on page 349.

in Paris) that 'I think less peril to live with them as enemies than as friends'. Thus Elizabeth contrived to face both ways at once. She sent secret aid to the Huguenots but began new marriage negotiations with France, this time with Anjou's younger brother. the Duke of Alencon. Both sides saw advantages in the negotiations and so they continued for nearly a decade.

However, marriage would have meant the loss of a vital diplomatic weapon. The Alencon negotiations were used at different times to reduce the influence of the Guise, threaten Philip II and intervene in the Netherlands when Alencon was accepted as their ruler by the rebels. Elizabeth played the marriage card successfully but in the end she was beaten by events outside her control. Alencon's death in 1584 meant that the heir of the childless Henry III was the Protestant Henry of Navarre. This prospect rekindled the French wars of religion and led to the one outcome that Elizabeth did not want – the Franco-Spanish Treaty of Joinville (1584) whereby Spain would help Henry III and the Guise stop Henry of Navarre becoming King of France. After 1584 she was alone.

Spain and the Netherlands 1568–1585

If Spain won control of the Netherlands it would not be long before she attempted to win control of England. Elizabeth preferred not to intervene and run the risk of precipitating war but she came under pressure from her councillors to do so, especially in 1575–6. In 1576 she also declined the offer of sovereignty of the Netherlands. She did, however, support volunteers who fought against the Spanish and, for several years after 1575, Philip's financial difficulties meant that there was little danger of war.

From 1580 however events seemed to speed beyond Elizabeth's control. Philip inherited the kingdom of Portugal with its vast territories in the New World and its huge fleet, invaluable for dominating the waters of Western Europe. In the Netherlands the Duke of Parma made great progress, threatening to put an end to the rebels once and for all. When William of Orange was assassinated in 1584 the rebels' one effective leader had been removed. For Elizabeth the assassination of a troublesome Protestant was both a political and a personal warning. If she did not act now to save the Netherlands from Spain it would be too late and then …

TALKING POINT

Now review your answers to questions 4–6 on page 349.

14.3 Ireland 1558–1585

Between 1558 and 1585 the English government took more and more action in Ireland until it was fully committed to direct intervention and conquest. This developing involvement was caused by the foreign and religious threats to Elizabeth. Ireland had to be made secure so that it could not be used as a base for an invasion of England.

Source A

It is clear that between 1565 and 1576 the English government had changed its attitude towards Ireland and had resolved to assert its authority throughout the island. Fear of foreign intervention was certainly one factor behind this about turn, but of more immediate concern to the government was the fact that Ireland was a drain on crown revenue. The programme that Sir Henry Sidney presented in 1565 was attractive to the government, because it promised to reduce the country to civility without any appreciable expense in the short-term and, with the long-term prospect that Ireland would be self-financing and, perhaps, yield a profit to the crown.

N P Canny, *The Elizabethan Conquest of Ireland*, 1976

Source B

The impact of the New World discoveries and renewed European colonization was reawakening latent colonialist attitudes in England where it was remembered that Ireland had once before been the subject of English colonization ... Certain features of Gaelic society – in particular its highly individual religious practices, transhumance (which was mistaken for nomadism), and the insubstantial dwellings even of chiefs – suggested to English colonizers that they were dealing with primitive savages in the manner of Spanish conquistadors subduing the Amerindians.

S G Ellis, *Tudor Ireland*, 1985

Source C

Here you may see the nature and disposition of this wicked, effrenated barbarous and unfaithful nation, who ... are a wicked and perverse generation ... trusty in that they be always treacherous and untrusty. They do nothing but imagine mischief and have no delight in any good thing ... the ways of peace they know not ... God is not known in their land, neither is his name called rightly upon among them ...

John Hooker's view of the Irish. Hooker was a lawyer who worked for Sir Peter Coven, one of the chief colonists.

Source D

If foreign force invade it is like to find much friendship as well for that the greatest sort are extreme papists as weary though they know not why of English government.

Sir Henry Sidney, writing in 1576 to the Council assessing the situation in Ireland.

Source E

Fitzgerald was the only rebel who sought to identify with Catholic Europe ... it appears that each rebellion in Ireland was a discrete event, and, apart from the brief liaison between Sir Edmund Butler and James Fitzmaurice Fitzgerald, there was no effort at organizing a united front against the government. The allegations of Sidney and his adherents were obviously exaggerated, and may have been consciously attuned to the ears of English privy councillors who were now terrified of Spain ...

... those who followed Sidney to Ireland and occupied themselves in the army and administration ... involved themselves in colonization. Most of these were greedy, aggressive and self-assured adventurers who saw considerable prospects for their enrichment in Ireland and ... were afraid that the English government should lose its appetite for conquest, so they prompted their patrons to persist with the programme ...

N P Canny, The Elizabethan Conquest of Ireland, 1976

Questions

1 The statement left provides an explanation for England's increasing involvement in Ireland. Look at the material on this page.

(a) Which evidence suggests there is some truth in this explanation?

(b) List the other factors that can be used to explain England's growing involvement.

(c) Rebellion in Ireland was suppressed with great savagery. Why?

(d) Explain why England became more involved in Ireland.

2 Do you think that the onset of war with Spain in 1585 was likely to affect English policy towards Ireland?

3 English policy towards Ireland has been described as 'unjustifiable by the normal tests of Elizabethan policy-making'. In what ways was it unjustifiable?

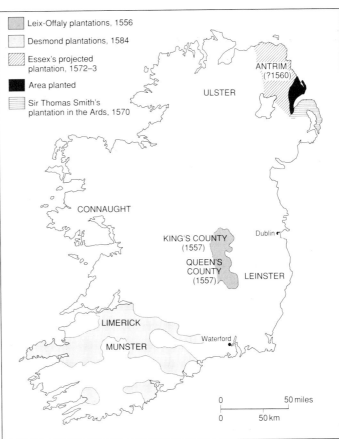

Legend:
- Leix-Offaly plantations, 1556
- Desmond plantations, 1584
- Essex's projected plantation, 1572–3
- Area planted
- Sir Thomas Smith's plantation in the Ards, 1570

SIR HENRY SIDNEY.

Chronology

1558   Shane O'Neill began his campaign to win overlordship of Ulster

1565   War between Gerald Fitzgerald, Earl of Desmond and Thomas Butler, Earl of Ormond. Sir Henry Sidney was appointed Deputy, a post he held for most of the period until 1578. He planned to assert English power but his assaults on Gaelic lordships only created resistance and alienation.

1566   O'Neill sought military aid from France.

1567   O'Neill was defeated by his local enemy, O'Donnel. He fled but was killed by Scots settlers who sent his head to Dublin pickled in a barrel.

1569   James Fitzmaurice Fitzgerald led a revolt in south-west Ireland. He appealed for foreign, Catholic aid but, according to S G Ellis, these revolts were 'very probably ... an Irish manifestation of the court intrigues which culminated in the Northern Rising of 1569–70.... another decade was to elapse before Irish dissidents would generally identify political and religious grievances and actively support the developing Counter-Reformation movement.'

1579   The rebellion of the Earl of Desmond, chiefly in Munster and Leinster. Desmond had some Spanish and Italian aid but the rising was motivated by a mixture of religion and personal needs with lesser risings in Ulster and Connaught. Suppression was chiefly in the hands of the new Deputy, Lord Grey of Wilton, but the rebellion lasted until 1583.

1580–1   Grey burned the harvest to reduce support for the rebels. Rebel leaders were executed.

1582   Famine was widespread. Edmund Spenser wrote 'In short space there were none almost left and a most populous and plentiful country suddenly left void of man or beast.' The people looked like 'anatomies of death ... they did eat the dead carrions ... yea and one another soon after, insomuch as the very carcasses they spared not to scrape out of their graves.'

1583   Fitzgerald was killed. Grey's 'pacification' paved the way for systematic colonisation.

'The dangers be so great, so evident and so imminent'
the Catholic threat 1568 – 1585

As the 1560s progressed fear of a Catholic threat dwindled. Elizabeth's refusal to persecute Catholics paid dividends because no-one was forced to put religion before sovereign. With hindsight the earliest years should have been the most dangerous but Elizabeth's moderation, a lack of leadership from the Papacy and Spain and the English people's growing association of Protestantism with their national identity ensured that the potential danger did not become a real threat. By 1568 there was only a small remnant of committed Catholics as a potential danger.

Events after 1568 seemed to create a far more dangerous situation. The quotation in the heading above comes from Sir Walter Mildmay's speech in the Commons in 1581 when he sought MPs agreement to taxes requested by the Queen. His speech was entirely concerned with the 'lewd and malicious enterprises' of the Papists. Yet historians writing in recent years have played down the danger. They argue that the great majority of the Catholic gentry would never have thought of challenging Elizabeth. Yes, they kept to their Catholic faith. Yes, they maintained priests in their households. Yes, they provided local leadership for others of the faith but the summit of their ambition was to be recognised as a minority religious group, acceptable because they did not intend to challenge Protestantism as the nation's official religion. Given this, it can be argued that Spanish ambassadors and others hopelessly over-estimated the numbers who might rise to overthrow the 'infamous, depraved, accursed, excommunicate heretic' Elizabeth. Thus Catholic plotters, however dramatic their intentions, were an isolated handful, certain to be found out by Walsingham's spies.

In addition historians have argued that the Catholic church did not help itself. Its missionaries were few in number and their impact was very limited. They converted very few English people. At the same time the Catholic church's own reforms were cutting the ground from beneath the feet of its largest potential group of supporters – the illiterate masses who did not want the plain, unvarnished Protestant truth from zealous preachers who harangued them by the hour. They wanted colour – festivals on Plough Monday, morris dancing, church ales and May games. They still believed that music kept away evil spirits and that fertility rites and astrology were a natural part of religion. Unfortunately the Catholic church was now just as keen to abolish such rituals as were Elizabeth's more Calvinist bishops.

Given these arguments it seems inevitable that there was no mass Catholic rising in 1588 to greet the Armada as a force sent by heaven. The real time of danger was past by 1568. Is that how it seemed at the time? In 1582 Leicester wrote to Walsingham, 'Nothing in the world grieveth me more than to see her Majesty believes that this increase of Papists in her realm can be no danger to her ... if she suffers this increase but one year more, as she hath done these two or three past, it will be too late to give or take counsel to help it.'

TALKING POINT

In general today's society seems less religious than Tudor society. Does this difference make it more difficult to assess the degree of the Catholic threat and to understand sixteenth century concerns?

Why did Leicester and many others regard Catholics as such a threat? There were three major reasons - the plots to depose Elizabeth, events in Europe that heightened fear of a general Catholic assault on Protestantism and the appearance of Catholic missionaries in England in 1574. The plots themselves showed the difficulty of judging the extent of the danger. Even if almost every Catholic was loyal to Elizabeth, it only needed one successful plot to bring about Elizabeth's downfall. The action of someone like John Somerville, 'a half-witted Warwickshire squire' who set out to shoot Elizabeth, might be more dangerous than the tortuous plots of the Queen of Scots' friends simply because it was unforeseeable.

Mary's availability as a Catholic heir increased the likelihood of plots, hence the frenzied calls of parliamentarians to 'cut off her head'. Another major reason for plots was the excommunication of Elizabeth in 1570. Pius V's bull 'Regnans in Excelsis' not only excommunicated Elizabeth but also declared 'her to be deprived of her pretended title to the kingdom', and charged people not to obey her. Catholics now had to make a choice and certainly those who plotted Elizabeth's fall felt that it was their duty to do so. They also did so in the knowledge that they would be absolved of all their sins. On the other hand Catholics who did not wish to make that choice could claim that the bull had never been published in England and therefore they knew nothing of its edicts.

Events abroad kept the tension bubbling. The massacre of St Bartholomew, Spanish assaults in the Netherlands and the assassination of William of Orange proved that the Pope's words were not just empty threats. There was little wonder that Mildmay in 1581 saw England as 'the chief sanctuary for the afflicted members of the church that fly hither from the tyranny of Rome'. Unfortunately, there were others who flew hither and they, missionary priests from 1574 and Jesuits after 1580, also increased the feeling that England was a fortress under assault.

In 1568 a seminary, a training college for priests, was founded at Douai in the Netherlands by William Allen, an English exile. Its purpose was to train Englishmen as priests who would return to revive Catholicism. About one hundred priests returned by 1580 and 179 in the next five years. In 1580 the first Jesuits, Edmund Campion and Robert Parsons, reached England. Mildmay called the Jesuits 'hypocrites ... a rabble of vagrant friars' but was well aware of their potential influence 'creeping into the houses and familiarities of men of behaviour and reputation, not only to corrupt the realm with false doctrine, but also under that pretence to stir sedition to the peril of her Majesty' .

The government was distinctly concerned about the Jesuits, in spite of the fact that they and other missionaries had papal orders not to interfere in politics. Campion said that his task was 'to preach the gospel, to minister the sacraments, to instruct the simple, to reform sinners, to confute errors ... I never had in mind, and am strictly forbidden by our fathers that sent me to deal in any respect with matters of state or policy of the realm'. Even so Parsons was described as 'a lurking wolf' and missionaries were hunted down and executed. It was impossible in practice to distinguish between attempts to revive the Catholic faith and efforts to overthrow the Church of England and its Supreme Governor, the queen.

How did Elizabeth and her ministers react to these differing pressures? New legislation was introduced and followed up more thoroughly, to the

TALKING POINT

At the time of their first arrival it was reported that 'three several companies of men in black marched in procession through the sky', a pack of hounds hunted in the clouds over Wiltshire and an eighty year old woman gave birth to a creature with a face like a man, a mouth like a mouse, a human body, eight legs and a tail! What does this tell you about both sixteenth century ideas and attitudes to the Jesuits?

A PRIEST'S HOLE. JESUITS AND OTHER CATHOLIC PRIESTS LIVED MISERABLE LIVES IN ENGLAND, CONSTANTLY IN FEAR OF DISCOVERY, IMPRISONMENT AND EXECUTION. THE STRAIN OF SUCH A LIFE SAYS MUCH ABOUT THE IDEALISM AND DETERMINATION OF SUCH MEN.

TALKING POINT

Which tells us more about Catholic devotion – the failure to rebel in 1588 or the daily support of refugee priests and maintenance of beliefs under pressure?

point where Catholics were excluded from public life (for example, serving as JPs) although they were still tolerated if their religious deviance remained private. In response to the bull of excommunication it became treasonable in 1571 to bring papal bulls into the country. Anyone who left the country for more than six months was to forfeit their land – a law targeted at religious exiles training as missionaries or willing to aid other countries. In 1575 the Privy Council began a carefully targeted campaign against leading Catholic laymen. Individuals were summoned to London, cross-questioned on their loyalties and subjected to dialogues with bishops, intended to persuade them of the errors of Catholicism. Those who were persuaded were allowed home. Those who were not stayed in prison or went home loaded with conditions and a financial bond. If, for example, they spoke out publicly against the Church of England or had unidentified 'guests' they would pay the fine and go to prison. The council paid particular attention to the laymen of Lancashire, Yorkshire and East Anglia but also ordered a national census of recusants.

In addition, in 1581, the Act to Return the Queen's Majesty's Subjects in their Due Obedience introduced huge increases in fines for religious misbehaviour. Anyone saying mass was fined 200 marks (£133) and imprisoned for one year. Anyone hearing mass paid half that fine but suffered the same imprisonment. The fine for non-attendance at church was increased from one shilling to £20 a month and anyone absent for a year had to guarantee a bond of £200 for future attendance. Such huge sums showed that the targets were clearly the gentry, the potential leaders of any widespread dissent. The same Act declared it treasonable to incite

WILLIAM BYRD, PERHAPS THE FOREMOST COMPOSER IN ELIZABETHAN ENGLAND, WAS A CATHOLIC WHOSE RELIGION WAS WELL-KNOWN BUT TOLERATED BECAUSE OF HIS GENIUS AND BECAUSE PERSECUTION MIGHT WELL HAVE CREATED MORE OVERT OPPOSITION AMONGST BYRD'S NOBLE, CATHOLIC SUPPORTERS.

TALKING POINT

Mildmay's speech emphasising the Catholic threat was made to request the Commons to agree to taxation. Does this undermine its value as an indication of the extent of the threat?

anyone to withdraw their allegiance from the monarch or convert them to Catholicism – the first of several Acts against missionaries. The next year a royal proclamation declared that all missionary priests were, by definition, traitors. By then the first executions had been carried out. Campion and two Douai priests had been hanged, drawn and quartered in December 1581. For Elizabeth's councillors the sense of threat did not disperse. Mildmay told parliament in 1581, 'seeing our enemies sleep not, it behoves us also not to be careless as though all (dangers) were past, but rather to think that there is but a piece of the storm over and that the greater part of tempest remains behind and is like to fall upon us'. Even if the potential for Catholic rebellion was grossly exaggerated by the Pope it was that very exaggeration that made an invasion more likely. While Mary was alive, while the Spanish made progress, while Jesuit priests arrived the danger seemed real. Elizabeth, who did not want 'to make windows into men's souls' was forced to look into some of them at least.

'wonderful presumptuous and bold'
The Puritan Challenge 1568 – 1585

TALKING POINT

If the danger of the Catholic threat seemed real in the 1580s does this mean that historians who say there was little danger in reality are wrong or that contemporaries wildly misjudged the situation?

The idea of a Catholic threat is easy to comprehend, even if there is disagreement about the degree of danger. The idea of a Puritan threat is more problematical. There was no Puritan country poised to invade England. No armed Protestant rising threatened to depose Elizabeth. During the 1570s and 1580s Puritans came to fill more places in Elizabeth's government. So how could there be a Puritan threat?

In the beginning 'Puritan' was just another insult. Presumably Puritans irritated their neighbours and fellow church-goers by behaving in a 'holier than thou' manner, convinced that they knew the true path to God. Although members of the Church of England, they believed that the Church did not yet quite follow that true path, being in their eyes a compromise or 'mingle-mangle'. Their intention was to purify the church (therefore amending the 1559 settlement), hence their nickname which developed during the 1560s.

These critics of the church did not like their 'odious name' of Puritans. They spoke of each other as 'true gospellers' or the 'godly'. Others, including Archbishop Parker, also called them 'precise folk' or 'precisians', a telling name for they would not rest content with the vagaries of Elizabeth's church. They wanted the one, true, precise way and that certainly involved expunging any vestiges of 'Romish superstition' from the church. There was no better way for a Puritan to spend his or her time than in bible-reading, listening to a rousing preacher or zealously seeking improvement in the church. Perhaps the simplest way to define Puritans is to say that what separated them from fellow-Anglicans was their willingness to challenge openly Elizabeth's settlement, criticising her church in words and by example in their own services. Unlike the acquiescent majority they agitated, sometimes desperately, for reform. Having said that, they were seeking reform from within the church in order to strengthen it. In a sense their striving for reform only became a challenge because they were so strongly resisted.

What did the Puritans want to reform? The answer comes in two parts – the liturgy (the form of worship) and the administration of the church. For Puritans the liturgy was still far too close to Roman Catholic practices. They objected to kneeling at communion, elaborate music, decorated vestments, celebration of saints' days and signs of superstition, such as making the sign of the cross on a child's head at baptism. Such things were sinful to Puritan minds, likely to lead the unwary and unlearned into error and damnation. If people were to be saved for heaven reforms were needed and urgently. Thus the vestments ordained by Elizabeth could be described as the 'rays of anti-Christ' but perhaps the worst vituperation was reserved for theatres and plays which not only 'maintain bawdry, insinuate foolery, and renew the remembrance of heathen idolatry' but, worst of all, 'call thither a thousand' whereas 'an hour's tolling of a bell brings to the sermon a hundred'.

Puritans feared that, with such temptations in view, people could not hear God's word. Hence the importance of preaching clearly and loudly, showing people the route to salvation. Here was another major frustration for Puritans. Far too few priests were zealous preachers. Many had been ordained under Mary and were only too happy to maintain the trappings of Catholicism. Others were dismissed as 'dumb dogs, unskilfully sacrificing priests, destroying drones, or rather caterpillars of the world'. Too few were 'diligent barkers against the Papish wolf' and if they did not bark, said Puritans, how could they help ordinary people join God's elect?

Thus, in Puritan eyes, the liturgical compromise of 1559 and the poor quality of the clergy threatened every individual's chance of salvation. The second grave issue of concern was the church administration which, with its hierarchy of bishops and others, seemed almost identical to the Catholic church. For Puritans their religious leaders should be enthusiastic preachers whose first duty and personal commitment was to spreading the word as laid down in the Bible. Bishops seemed to be mere administrators, little different from government officials. There was also no place in their ideal scheme for church courts and fines. Sinners should make their peace and do their penance in the heart of their own congregations. The most extreme Puritan sub-group was the Separatists (also known as Brownists after one of their leaders, Robert Brown) who rejected the idea of a national church, believing that each congregation should control its own affairs.

Elizabeth saw Puritanism as a challenge to her authority. This challenge was both indirect, implicit in Puritan distaste for church hierarchies, and direct in the demand for reform of the 1559 settlement. They demanded change. Elizabeth had no intention of changing. In Elizabeth's eyes Puritan ideals were 'dangerous to kingly rule', and through their sermons 'great numbers of our people ... otherwise occupied with honest labour for their living, are brought to idleness ... divided amongst themselves with a variety of dangerous opinion'. Puritans wanted people to think about religion for themselves. Elizabeth wanted conformity and obedience.

Given the queen's attitude it is surprising to find so many staunch Puritans at the very centre of her government. But their presence there did a great deal to maintain the momentum of Puritanism. Elizabeth's own favourite, Leicester, and his brother, the Earl of Warwick were noted

Puritans. So too were the Earls of Huntingdon and Bedford and Francis Walsingham. Other councillors and many MPs were Puritans or sympathetic to their cause. Such great figures and many gentlemen appointed puritan preachers to parishes or to university posts and protected them from investigations. Puritanism was strong in the universities and London, everywhere except amongst the poor whose illiteracy effectively excluded them. Puritan emphasis on reading and study meant that it could not be a mass movement but that it would have influence out of proportion to its numbers.

Puritanism developed as the critics realized that firstly Elizabeth would not permit change and that secondly, in her drive for conformity, she would enforce the liturgical compromises they detested. The first clash came over vestments in the 1560s. In the next decade criticism intensified as frustration grew and a new generation of Puritan leaders emerged. The new, younger men were more impatient, believing that the bishops had given in too easily to Elizabeth's demands. The most notable figure in this group was Thomas Cartwright, Professor of Divinity at Cambridge University, until deprived of the post in 1570.

Parliament was an important pressure point used by Puritans. In 1571, 1573 and 1576 MPs sought reforms in the words of Walter Strickland in 1571 'so as to have all things brought to the purity of the Primitive Church'. This was to no avail. Elizabeth declared in 1572 that 'henceforth no bills concerning religion should be received into this House unless the same should first be considered and liked by the clergy'. She anticipated that the bishops were unlikely to approve of radical demands. This was certainly true of the key issue that developed in the early 1570s – Presbyterianism. Presbyterians, led by Cartwright, argued that there was no support in the scriptures for a hierarchy of bishops acting as a church government. They said that each congregation should choose its minister, who would lead that congregation with the aid of a small group, the presbytery. Thus the whole Roman apparatus of bishops would be swept away. Thomas Wilcox, a Presbyterian, wrote 'Either must we have right ministry of God and right government of his church, according to the scriptures ... (both of which we lack) or else there can be no right religion'.

And yet briefly the heat was taken out of this clash. When Archbishop Parker died in 1575 he was succeeded by Edmund Grindal, proposed by Elizabeth's councillors because they felt he could keep the Church united. Grindal might well have brought Protestants together if he had not himself clashed with the queen over preaching. As the church was so short of trained and effective preachers, meetings were taking place where the scriptures were discussed, known as 'prophesyings'. These were training sessions but to Elizabeth they were radical and dangerous, a natural breeding ground for dissident opinions. In 1576 she ordered Grindal to suppress the prophesyings and restrict the number of preachers. Grindal refused.

In a remarkable letter to the queen, the Archbishop wrote that he marvelled 'how this strange opinion should once enter your mind, that it should be good for the Church to have a few preachers ... Public and continual preaching of God's Word is the ordinary mean and instrument of the salvation of mankind'. He refused for 'what should I win, if I gained (I will not say a bishopric but) the whole world, and lose mine soul?' Grindal was suspended for disobedience, placed in effect under house arrest. He remained in theory Archbishop until his death in 1583 but unable to carry out his duties. Elizabeth wanted to dismiss him but could not win her council's support.

The queen's treatment of Grindal foreshadowed the next stage in her dealings with those 'insolent' Puritans. However that had to wait for Grindal's death and, in the meantime, Puritanism seemed to become more dangerous. Presbyterians held more local meetings of clergy to share the scriptures and ideas. Thus after Grindal's death Elizabeth appointed as Archbishop of Canterbury, John Whitgift, the principal academic opponent of the Puritans. Whitgift clearly shared Elizabeth's belief that the religious questioning of the Puritans would, in time, lead to the questioning of Elizabeth's political authority and that would produce anarchy. Order and obedience was needed and so in 1583 Whitgift issued orders saying that no-one was to preach or hold services without first acknowledging the royal supremacy, agreeing that the Book of Common Prayer and the Thirty Nine Articles were not contrary to God's word and agreeing to use the Book of Common Prayer.

These orders forced over three hundred ministers to the brink of dismissal but they were saved by the intervention of their highly placed supporters. Leicester and others complained that the church could not afford to lose such 'diligent, learned and zealous' ministers who were, after all, the strongest opponents of the Catholic enemy. Thus a compromise was reached for the moment and only the most extreme preachers resigned.

Judging from the anxieties of the queen and Whitgift the Puritans were a threat. They would have agreed with the Bishop of Lichfield who told a Puritan in 1570 that he was worse than the papists 'for the papists are afraid to stir or say anything, but you as wonderful presumptuous and bold, fear no man and you disquiet us and the whole state more than papists.' But by 1585 there was an uneasy lull. Puritans had escaped complete suppression, knew they could expect no further concessions and yet were driven by their beliefs to seek reform.

TALKING POINT

In what ways were the Puritan and Catholic threats different from each other?

Which was the more dangerous to Elizabeth and England between 1570 and 1585?

EXAMINING THE EVIDENCE
Elizabeth and her Parliaments 1568–1585

The story of parliament in this period was one of co-operation, especially in the daily grind of business, punctuated by outbursts of dissent. There were two causes of this dissent. One was the careful orchestration of criticism of Elizabeth's policies by members of her council. They hoped that additional pressure from Parliament would force the queen to take action, whether over her marriage, the succession or the fate of the Queen of Scots. The other form of dissent came from rogue members of parliament, of whom the most famous and incorrigible was Peter Wentworth.

Meetings of Parliament

2 April to 29 May 1571	Called as a response to the Northern Rising and the Bull of Excommunication
8 May to 30 June 1572	Called to consider legal action against Mary, Queen of Scots
8 February to 15 March 1576	Called to raise revenue
16 January to 18 March 1581	Called to enact laws against Catholics following the rebellion in Ireland, the arrival of Jesuits and Philip II's accession in Portugal
23 November 1584 to 29 March 1585	Called to determine measures for the Queen's safety in the light of recent plots and the assassination of William of Orange

(The government sought revenue in addition to these aims in all parliaments except 1572)

Source A
31 January 1581

A bill from the Lords that the speaker of slanderous words against the Queen's Majesty should be set upon the pillory, lose his ears and suffer imprisonment at the Queen's pleasure ...A bill that the spreaders of slanderous words against great officers, bishops, noblemen, their wives and children ... shall make fine at the discretion of the court, be set upon the pillory and imprisoned ...A bill that all armour brought in shall be viewed by the officers of the city ... to see that the same be clean ... no stranger to bring any armour to London or within three mile thereof ...The bill against taking a second wife, living the first ...

22 February

Two bills for paving of certain streets ...A bill to enlarge a statute concerning hats and caps and requiring that no stranger use the trade of hatting nor any to keep any more than one apprentice except he has been a householder for four years ... A bill for the punishment of the family of Love, twice read and long argued whether pains of death might be inflicted to a heretic ...

23 February

A bill for the exemption of Hertfordshire from sewing of hemp and flax ...A bill concerning the preservation of wood ...A bill for the better packing of wool and for the punishment of any packer who suffers any dross, locks, sand or such like among the wool ...

Extracts from Thomas Cromwell's Journal of the Parliament of 1581.

---

1 What can you deduce about parliamentary business from the record of three days' business in Source A?

Source B
23 January 1581

This day Mr Speaker declared her Majesty's great mislike of our proceeding in agreeing to the public fast, and that we contrary to her commandment had intermeddled in causes of religion; desired the House from thenceforth to forebear to enter into such actions as were not fit for them ...

Extract from Thomas Cromwell's Journal of the Parliament of 1581.

2 What does Source B tell you about Elizabeth's attitude to parliamentary discussions on religion?

Source C

I saw (in the last parliament) the liberty of free speech, which is the only salve to heal all the sores of this commonwealth, so much and so many ways infringed ... that my mind hath not been a little aggrieved even of very conscience and love to my prince and state ...

Amongst other, Mr Speaker, two things do very great hurt in this place of which I mean to speak. One is a rumour that runs about the House and it is 'take heed what you do, the Queen's Majesty likes not such a matter; whoever prefers it, she will be much offended with him'. On the contrary, 'Her Majesty likes such a matter, whosoever speaks against it will be much offended with him. The other is sometimes a message is brought into the House either commanding or inhibiting, very injurious to the freedom of speech and consultation. I would to God, Mr Speaker, that these two were buried in Hell ...(God) did put into the Queen's Majesty's heart to refuse good and wholesome laws for her own preservation, which caused many faithful hearts for grief to burst out with sorrowful tears and moved all papists ... in their sleeves to laugh all the parliament house to scorn ... none is without fault, no, not our noble Queen. Since then her Majesty has committed great faults, dangerous to herself and the state ... these they are. It is a dangerous thing in a prince unkindly to treat and abuse his or her nobility and people as her Majesty did in the last parliament ... will not her Majesty's handling ... make cold dealing in many of her Majesty's subjects towards her?

Extracts from Peter Wentworth's speech in the House of Commons, 8 February 1576. Following this speech Wentworth was examined by the Council and then imprisoned for a month.

3 Read Source C. What were Wentworth's main complaints and arguments?

4 What does Source C tell you about the queen and Cecil's methods of managing parliament?

5 Who would have objected to Wentworth's speech?

6 Why do you think most of Wentworth's fellow MPs were shocked by his speech?

Source D

In February 1571 William Cecil was ennobled and twice within the next sixteen months he had to stage-manage Parliament's response to the crisis ... as Lord Burghley, he managed both houses from the Lords ... Parliament always remained one of his political options in time of crisis but never, however, did he lightly recommend calling one ... His attendance record in the House of Lords speaks for itself: 77 percent of sittings in 1571, 70 percent in 1572, 91 percent (1576), 68 percent (1581), 72 percent (1584) ...

M.A.R. Graves, *The Tudor Parliaments, Crown, Lords and Commons, 1485–1603,* 1985.

Source E

The great number of them of the lower house have in the proceedings in this session shown themselves modest, discreet and dutiful ... so there be certain of them, although not many in number, which ... have shown themselves audacious, arrogant and presumptuous, calling her Majesty's grants and prerogatives also into question contrary to their duty and place that they be called unto and contrary to the express admonition given in her Majesty's name in the beginning of this parliament ...

Extract from Lord Keeper Bacon's speech at the close of Parliament, May 1571.

7 It has sometimes been said that at this time the Commons became more volatile and powerful. What do Sources D and E and the fact of Cecil's ennoblement tell you about this theory?

8 'Elizabeth clashed with her parliaments because of what she did not do rather than because of what she did do'. What evidence is there to support and contradict this statement?

Review

This chapter has concentrated on the great political events of the time. However there is another story as you can see from the graphs on this page. For many people this was a time of renewed prosperity after the problems of the middle of the century. Elizabeth herself could do nothing to improve the quality of the harvest but people with full stomachs, better housing and more furniture clothes and other belongings undoubtedly thought more highly of their queen than they would have done if they had gone hungry. People who were well-fed were also far less likely to rebel. Good economic conditions did therefore help political stability.

The Purchasing Power of Wages 100 = value during 1450–1499			
	Agricultural Labourer	Building Craftsman	London Building Worker
1550–9	59	51	72
1560–9	66	62	82
1570–9	69	64	81
1580–9	57	57	78
1590–9	49	47	69

Were the years from 1568 to 1585 a political success for Elizabeth?

1 Look at the topics down the left hand side of the chart below. What do you think Elizabeth's objectives were for each topic in 1568?

2 Look at the two statements for each topic. Which statement from each pair do you agree with? What evidence would you use to support your choice?

3 Essay

'The period from 1568 to 1585 deserves to be remembered as one of great success for Elizabeth and her government.' Explain why you agree or disagree with this statement.

	Statement One	**Statement Two**
Religion	The Church of England was firmly established. Puritans were the most loyal of Elizabeth's supporters and were building support for Protestantism. The Catholic threat had been safely contained. Few Catholics joined plots, showing the wisdom of Elibabeth's policy. Effective measures had been taken against Jesuits and other missionaries.	There were many who were unhappy with the Church of England. The complaints of Puritans undermined Elizabeth's authority and showed no signs of relenting. The Catholic threat had not been extinguished and was still a danger, especially as the Queen of Scots remained as a focus for plots.
Foreign Policy	Peace had been maintained despite the pressures from within the council and the threats from abroad. France had been maintained as an ally until events beyond Elizabeth's control had led to the France-Spanish alliance.	The declaration of war with Spain was a defeat for Elizabeth's policy. Her use of marriage negotiations had failed to maintain the French alliance and she now faced the prospect of a Spanish invasion.
Parliament	Apart from sporadic outbursts from individuals parliament supported Elizabeth loyally and effectively.	Elizabeth was put under pressure by her parliaments and was forced by her council to call parliament more frequently than she wished.

15 War, Hunger and Triumph, 1585–1603

In 1585 Elizabeth was forced into a war that she had struggled for so long to avoid. Fortunately – and fortune certainly played its part- that war was successful. Elizabeth became even more popular as a symbol of pride and nationalism. In 1589 a schoolboy at Westminster, John Slye, scribbled in one of his books:

The Rose is red, the leaves are green
God save Elizabeth, our noble Queen.

Young John seems to have been a prolific doodler and the word he doodled most frequently was 'Elizabeth'. However others had different ideas. In 1592 an Essex labourer was reported as saying 'this is no good government which we now live under, and it was merry England when there was a better government, and if the queen die there will be a change'. The French ambassador in London reported that 'the English would never again submit to the rule of a woman'.

In her last years Elizabeth's popularity did seem to wane to some degree. Do you think that this was likely to have been caused by
(a) unhappiness at her opposition to religious reform?
(b) economic difficulties?
(c) boredom with a long-established ruler?
(d) unhappiness at her attitude to parliaments?

TALKING POINT

Which is the more important to a politician's success – an effective foreign policy or the country's economic well-being?

PAINTED IN THE 1620s, THIS PORTRAIT WAS INTENDED TO SYMBOLISE ELIZABETH'S MOVEMENT THROUGH DEATH TO ETERNITY. DESPITE THE DATE AND THE SYMBOLISM IT PERHAPS PROVIDES A BETTER IDEA OF THE REALITY OF ELIZABETH'S APPEARANCE IN THE LATE 1590S THAN ANY CONTEMPORARY PROTRAIT.

A Time of War

In August 1585 Elizabeth agreed to the Treaty of Nonsuch, promising to send military aid to the Dutch rebels. In December, Leicester led the English expeditionary force into the Netherlands, thus beginning the Anglo-Spanish war that was to last until 1604. Elizabeth's last years were therefore greatly affected, if not dominated, by war. English troops fought in the Netherlands, France and Portugal; English ships raided Spain, her colonies and her treasure fleets. The Armada of 1588 was not the only invasion fleet sent by Spain. Others were launched in 1596 and 1597, only to be dispersed by storms. Another was planned in 1599.

This degree of military activity caused great problems. England could not afford such a war, nor was she prepared for it. The mid-1590s also saw the worst sequence of harvests of the whole century. The strain on the English people was therefore immense. Elizabeth continued to be the centre of government although without the aid of many of her old servants.

Mildmay died in 1587, Walsingham in 1590. Sir Christopher Hatton in 1591. Leicester died in 1588 within months of the defeat of the Armada. Fortunately for Elizabeth, Burghley continued his service, old though he was, until his death in 1598. His son, Robert Cecil, took his office in practice but Burghley remained the closest of Elizabeth's advisers.

In 1585 the queen's councillors were convinced that great danger lay ahead. They organised the Bond of Association, at its worst a kind of 'lynch-law' whose purpose was vengeance against Elizabeth's murderers, and a bill for the succession. In the event of the Queen's assassination Burghley proposed that the country would be governed by a 'Great Council of the Realm' and Parliament should determine the succession. Elizabeth refused to let this bill proceed but the extent of Burghley's contingency planning reveals the fears. After all, Mary, Queen of Scots was still alive – and plotting.

Examining the Evidence
The Execution of Mary, Queen of Scots

'Let your wicked murderess know how with hearty sorrow her vile deserts compel these orders, and bid her from me, ask God forgiveness for her treacherous dealings towards the saviour of her life many a year, to the intolerable peril of my own, and yet not content with so many foreivegivenesses must fault again so horribly for passing woman's thoughts.'

So wrote Elizabeth to Sir Amyas Paulet, Mary's guardian and gaoler. The occasion was the discovery of the Babington plot in 1586. Mary knew and approved of the plan to kill Elizabeth and yet it was another five months before she was executed. After so long, why was she executed in February 1587? Was it simply that Elizabeth's patience was exhausted?

THE EXECUTION OF MARY, QUEEN OF SCOTS.

Chronology	
December 1585	Walsingham allowed Mary's 'secret' correspondence with the French ambassador to recommence. Letters went to and fro in watertight boxes inside beer casks but Walsingham intercepted, read and then sent on the letters.
mid-1586	A plot to free Mary and murder Elizabeth was discovered. The central figure was Anthony Babington, a 25 year old Derbyshire gentleman and a descendant of the Lord Darcy, executed for his involvement in the Pilgrimage of Grace. Babington was a sincere Catholic but a half-hearted plotter, used by less well-connected conspirators.
17 July 1586	Mary wrote that she approved of the plan to murder Elizabeth.
14 August 1586	Babington was arrested.
20 September 1586	Babington and other plotters were executed.
11–14 October 1586	Mary's trial began at Fotheringhay Castle.
25 October 1586	Mary was sentenced.
24 November 1586	Elizabeth refused to answer parliament's petition to execute Mary.
late December 1586	Burghley prepared Mary's death warrant but Elizabeth refused to sign it.
1 February 1587	There were rumours of Spanish landings in Wales and that Mary had escaped. Elizabeth signed the warrant but then told Davison, the Secretary of State, not to have it sealed. Nevertheless the warrant was sealed and despatched to Fotheringhay.
8 February 1587	Mary was executed.

Source A

If the matter be well handled, it will break the neck of all dangerous practices during her Majesty's reign.

From a letter from Walsingham to Leicester after he knew the details of the plot.

Source B

Mary suggested to the ambassador that, in the event of reliable means of communication failing, he should write on paper or thin white cloth in alum, soaked in a little clear water twenty-four hours beforehand: the writing was invisible, but when dipped in water it appeared ... Or he could write between the lines of books, using only every fourth page, and having green strings put on the volumes that had been treated ... letters might be stuffed into high-heeled slippers.

J E Neale, *Queen Elizabeth I*, 1934.

1 In Source A, what do you think Walsingham meant by 'if the matter be well-handled'?

2 What was Walsingham's objective?

3 Does the material in Source B suggest that Mary was likely to (a) be innocent (b) contribute to her own downfall?

Source C

In this late act of Parliament you have laid an hard hand on me, that I must give direction for her death, which cannot be but most grievous, an irksome burden to me. And lest you mistake mine absence from this Parliament, yet hath it not been the doubt of any such danger or occasion that kept me from thence, but only the great grief to hear this cause spoken of ...... accept my thankfulness, to excuse my doubtfulness and to take in good part my answer answerless.

> Extracts from Elizabeth's replies to Parliament's petition for Mary's execution.

Source D

My dearest Brother, I would to God thou knewest (but not that thou feltest) the incomparable grief my mind is perplexed with upon this lamentable accident, which is happened contrary to my meaning and intention ...

> From a letter from Elizabeth to James VI written after Mary's execution.

Source E

Most gracious and mighty Queen, although I am come to no understanding what special means to use to pacify your Majesty's heavy displeasure, so often and grievously expressed both to my friends and many others ... though I find my humble submissions to your Majesty, and most lowly requests to be heard, to be still denied ...

> From a letter from Burghley to Elizabeth, 23 February 1587. Elizabeth refused to see Burghley for a month. Davison was sent to the Tower for eighteen months and never regained his post although his salary was paid until his death.

Source F

(Davison) had sealed it (the warrant) at once, and, at a crisis meeting of eleven councillors ... it was decided to despatch the warrant and not to inform the queen 'before the execution were past'.

> J Guy, *Tudor England*, 1988.

Source G

(Elizabeth) went as far as to suggest that others might relieve her of the burden. At her request, a letter was written to Paulet asking him to do away with his prisoner without warrant according to the Bond of Association. But Paulet refused: 'God forbid', he replied, 'that I should make so foul a shipwreck of my conscience' ... Elizabeth stormed at his 'daintiness'.

> J Guy, *Tudor England*, 1988.

4 Why according to Source C was Mary's execution delayed?

5 Are Sources D and E good supporting evidence for your answer to question 4?

6 What does Source F tell you about Elizabeth's attitude to Mary's execution?

7 Does the story of Elizabeth's letter to Paulet (source G) suggest that Elizabeth was, after all, happy to see Mary die.

8 Explain why Mary's execution was first delayed and then carried out.

Foreign Policies 1585–1603

War in the Netherlands 1585–1588

War did not change Elizabeth's objectives. Her ultimate objective was still security against foreign invasion. To achieve security she had to stop both France and Spain from establishing total dominance over the Netherlands. Hence Elizabeth's preference was still for Spain to maintain a distant overlordship of the Netherlands. Elizabeth had no aspirations herself to win territory. She turned down the crown of the Netherlands in 1585 because it would have meant a long, offensive war to win back what would then have become 'her land'. What was needed was a defensive war to stop Spain controlling the European coastline and winning deep-water harbours for the use of an invasion fleet. This much was practical – just – given Elizabeth's resources.

The Treaty of Nonsuch in August 1585 laid down Elizabeth's commitment to the Netherlands. She agreed to provide 100 cavalrymen and 6400 foot soldiers plus £126,000 a year to maintain them – a sum calculated to be over 40 per cent of Elizabeth's annual income. Elizabeth also appointed Leicester as commander, a clear sign of the extent of England's commitment. At the same time a more aggressive naval policy was inaugurated. A squadron of ships under Drake's command set out to free captured English ships and sailors from Spanish ports and to attack Philip's treasure fleet.

This was clearly war and in January 1586 Philip II appointed the leader of his Armada. However the English intentions were not so clear-cut. Elizabeth's instruction to Leicester was to avoid battle. She had no wish to establish a Protestant league with other states. Unfortunately this was not in accord with Leicester's ideas, nor those of Walsingham, for both of them, as Puritans, favoured a 'godly league' and greater aggression. Leicester most clearly broke Elizabeth's guidelines when he accepted the title of Governor-General, which not only implied that, after all, Elizabeth intended to rule the Netherlands but was also the very title used by Philip II's representatives. Elizabeth was furious. Leicester had killed his own chances of persuading her to his point of view.

The English campaigns were inglorious but effective. In August 1586 Leicester captured the towns of Zutphen and Doesburg, which kept Parma to the east of the River Ijssel. Although they were recaptured Parma did not take his main target, the deep-water port of Flushing, a crucial strategic success for England. Politically Leicester was less effective, stirring factions among his Dutch allies and creating hostility by trying to control their finances and cut off their trade

SIR PHILIP SYDNEY, 1554 –1586. KILLED IN THE WAR IN THE NETHERLANDS, SIDNEY'S DEATH WAS ROMANTICISED LIKE THOSE OF SOLDIER-POETS OF LATER ERAS. INSTEAD OF DYING AT ZUTPHEN AFTER SHARING HIS LAST WATER WITH AN ORDINARY SOLDIER IT IS NOW KNOWN THAT HE DIED OF WOUNDS FOUR WEEKS AFTER THE ENGAGEMENT.

with Spain. The Dutch were also deeply suspicious of rumours that England was engaged in peace talks with Spain. This was only natural for Elizabeth who, although she had not avoided war, preferred to abbreviate it if possible. However to the Dutch it suggested that their ally was, at best, half-hearted and, at worst, treacherous. Leicester resigned his command in the autumn of 1587. He had spoken of a Protestant crusade for over a decade but it had proved a mirage. England could not finance a whole-hearted offensive in the Netherlands, even if Elizabeth believed such a policy worthwhile.

TALKING POINT

Did religious idealism or defensive strategy play the greater part in determining English policies towards the Netherlands?

EXAMINING THE EVIDENCE
Why did the Armada fail?

Source A

A MEDAL ISSUED TO CELEBRATE THE VICTORY OVER THE ARMADA.

Source B

THE ARMADA PORTRAIT OF ELIZABETH PAINTED BY GEORGE GOWER.

Source C

never was any nation blessed of Jehovah, with a more glorious and wonderful victory upon the Seas, than our vanquishing of the dreadful Spanish Armada, 1588. But why should I presume to call it our vanquishing; when as the greatest part of them escaped us, and were only by God's outstretched arm overwhelmed in the seas, dashed in pieces against the rocks ...

Richard Hakluyt, *The Principal Navigations, Voyages, Traffiques and Discoveries of the English Nation*, 1589.

---

1 How do Sources A–C agree on the reason for the Armada's failure?

2 Why might there be such a great emphasis on this one reason?

3 Do any of Sources A–C suggest any additional reason for the Armada's failure?

Source D

We found that many of the enemy's ships held great advantages over us in combat, both in their design and in their guns, gunners and crews ... in spite of all this (Medina Sidonia) managed to bring his fleet to anchor in Calais roads, just seven leagues from Dunkirk – and if, on the day that we arrived there, Parma had come out (with his forces), we should have carried out the invasion ... even our enemies will admit, although it may grieve them, that no commander in the world has done more than this one (Medina Sidonia).

Don Francisco de Bobadilla, the general in charge of the Armada's soldiers and one of Medina Sidonia's principal aides.

Source E

Drake, Drake, Drake is coming ... Chicken duke, chicken duke ...

The shouts of youths outside Medina Sedonia's lodgings after he returned to Spain.

Source F

Those who come here off the fleet and have tried to give the impression that we were not ready ... are mistaken. Everything was prepared ... nothing would have been gained by embarking things in advance, because the ships are so small that there is not even room to turn round in. Undoubtedly, the men would have sickened, the food would have rotted, and everything would have perished.

From a letter from Parma to Philip II, August 1588.

Source G

The Duke (Medina Sidonia) wished during this day (8th August) to turn and attack the enemy with the whole Armada, in order to avoid running out of the Channel, but the pilots told him it was impossible, as both wind and tide were against us, the wind blowing from the NW towards the land. They said that he would be forced either to run up into the North Sea, or wreck all the Armada on the shoals. He was therefore

FOCUS

15.1 The Armada – Planning Attack and Defence

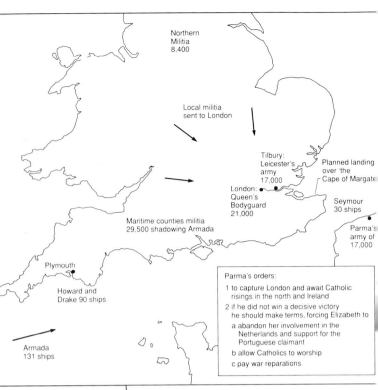

Northern Militia 8,400

Local militia sent to London

Tilbury: Leicester's army 17,000

Planned landing over 'the Cape of Margate

London: Queen's Bodyguard 21,000

Seymour 30 ships

Maritime counties militia 29,500 shadowing Armada

Parma's army of 17,000

Plymouth

Howard and Drake 90 ships

Armada 131 ships

Parma's orders:

1 to capture London and await Catholic risings in the north and Ireland

2 if he did not win a decisive victory he should make terms, forcing Elizabeth to
a abandon her involvement in the Netherlands and support for the Portuguese claimant
b allow Catholics to worship
c pay war reparations

Chronology

January 1586 — Philip II asked the Marquis of Santa Cruz to prepare a plan for an invasion of England. Another plan was prepared by Parma. Throughout 1586 preparations went ahead with the fleet being gathered in Cadiz, Lisbon and Seville.

April 1587 — Drake attacked Cadiz, sinking or burning between 24 and 37 ships.

Summer 1587 — Santa Cruz set out on a punitive expedition to hunt down and kill Drake in the West Indies. The capture of Sluys helped to determine the final plan – an invasion combining the fleet with Parma's army. The original timing was late 1587.

February 1588 — Santa Cruz died. He was replaced by the Duke of Medina Sidonia, a capable and experienced soldier and commander, well-supported by naval commanders.

30 May 1588 — The Armada left Lisbon.

19 June 1588 — The Armada was scattered off Corunna and delayed a month for repairs and revictualling.

22 July 1588 — The Armada set sail from Corunna.

(Note: the dates used here and on the following pages are those used in the new calendar, that had already been adopted in Spain in 1588. The English were still using the Julian calendar which brings dates forward by 10 days.)

Source A

Seamen	Troops	
English	16,000+	76,000
Spanish	7,000	34,000

Source B

Comparative tonnages of the English and Spanish fleets
(figures are approximate)

Tons	English ships	Spanish ships
1000–999	–	1
900–999	–	3
800–899	–	3
700–799	2	9
600–699	1	14
500–599	2	14
400–499	8	25
300–399	10	12
200–299	28	12
100–199	74	8
0–99	101	50
Total	226	151

Source C

ENGLISH SHIPS IN BATTLE WITH THE SPANISH ARMADA.

Source D

The 6,000 armed conscripts of the London trained-bands, who had been drilling twice weekly since March, were probably capable of putting up a good fight (although some doubted it), but little could be expected from the militias of the inland shires. ... they were poorly equipped ... the militia of Kent was issued with muskets, for the first time, in July 1588 ... most of the shire levies called up to resist the Armada included large contingents of archers. In any case, many units were not ordered to mobilise until 2 August and, worse still, were sent on their way without food or drink ... The fortifications at Tilbury itself were likewise unready and disorganized. Work had only begun on 3 August ... In Kent the troops at Dover (most of them raw recruits) began to desert in considerable numbers when the Armada came into sight ...

C Martin and G Parker, *The Spanish Armada,* 1988.

Source E

THE BEACON SYSTEM IN KENT FROM A CONTEMPORARY MANUSCRIPT. HOWEVER GOOD THIS SYSTEM WAS IN THEORY, ENGLAND'S DEFENCE DEPENDED ON THE QUALITY OF HER NAVY AND SOLDIERS.

Source F

Good weather ... was essential for Spanish success. It was the least of the miracles they expected from God. They needed good weather to preserve their fragile Mediterranean shipping, calm seas to maximise the effectiveness of their galleasses, clement conditions for Parma's barges, a moderate swell to compensate for the inexperience of their gunners; and above all, an easy, speedy voyage to help keep them safe despite the lack of a northern port of refuge.

F Fernandez-Armesto, *The Spanish Armada,* 1989.

Source G

If an accurate and balanced assessment of the 1588 campaign is to be made, it must take into account the strengths as well as the weaknesses, the selection of an ideal invasion area; the formidable planning and immense resources which brought the fleet from Spain and the army from the Netherlands so close together; the patient and successful diplomatic efforts which secured both the paralysis of France and the complete isolation of England throughout 1587 and 1588; the carefully-fostered divisions within the Dutch republic; the enormous benefits that the occupation of even a part of Kent – carefully exploited – could have brought to Spain.

C Martin and G Parker, *The Spanish Armada,* 1988.

Source H

Question
Did the Spanish Armada have a good chance of success?

A RECONSTRUCTION DRAWING OF SPANISH TROOPS WHO WERE USED TO FIRE THE ARMADA'S GUNS ALTHOUGH THEIR PRIME FUNCTION WAS TO BOARD THE ENGLISH SHIPS. ENGLISH GUNNERS WERE MORE EXPERIENCED AND BETTER TRAINED.

utterly unable to avoid going out of the Channel, nearly all of our trust-worthy ships being so damaged as to be unfit to resist attack, both on account of the cannon fire to which they had been exposed, and their own lack of projectiles.

From Medina Sidonia's own account of the Armada, August 1588.

Source H

For Medina Sidonia to have expected rapid and reliable communications between himself and Parma once he had put to sea reveals a profound misunderstanding of the logistical limitations of his position. It was one of his very few serious mistakes during the campaign, but it proved fatal...

... Medina Sidonia ...believed – wrongly – that Parma, being fore-warned would have his troops aboard the barges and small ships 'before' the Armada reached the Narrow Seas, and would therefore be ready to put out the instant its sails were spotted ...

Parma's vessels, stated Philip, were not of a kind 'that can put out and seek you at a distance, unless you have first cleared away all enemy ships from the straits first, because they are ships for transport and not for fighting.'

C.Martin and G.Parker, The Spanish Armada, 1988.

4 In what ways do Sources D-H support the explanation provided by Sources A-C?

5 What other reasons for the Armada's defeat are provided by Sources D – H?

6 Which Source or Sources (from A–H) would you regard as the most valuable for an investigation of the Armada's failure? Explain the reasons for your choice.

7 On the basis of Sources A-H why do you think the Armada failed?

Source I

The English knew that the troops were the Armada's greatest strength. Both sides believed that if it came to boarding, Philip's men had the advantage. The English commanders refused to take the risk and did as much damage as possible at a distance with their guns...

The fireship attack was the single most effective tactical device used by the English. It drove the Armada from its only anchorage, temporarily dispersed it and caused it to lose many irreplaceable anchors and cables. The fleet was not otherwise damaged by the action, but as the pilots had predicted, it was never able to return to Calais. The fighting now began to move northwards, away from the possibility of a link-up with Parma.

M J Rodriguez-Salgado, Armada, 1988.

Source J

So here at last is a full and sufficient explanation for the Armada's remarkable failure to inflict serious damage on the English fleet: the Spaniards simply did not fire their guns – especially their few heavy guns – often enough. But why (?)... no procedure existed for disciplined reloading as a standard battle drill. Spanish sailing-ship tactics, in line

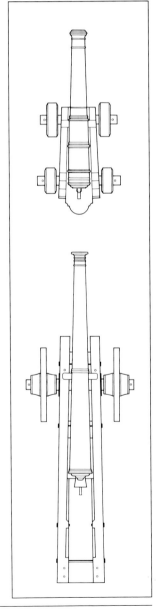

DRAWINGS OF PLANS (BOTTOM) AN 18 POUND SPANISH GUN AND (TOP) A 24 POUND GUN OF THE TYPE ON ENGLISH SHIPS, WHICH HAVE BEEN DESCRIBED AS "ENGLAND'S DECISIVE SECRET WEAPON". THE SPANISH GUNS TOOK UP FAR MORE DECK SPACE AND WERE DIFFICULT TO RELOAD. ENGLISH GUNNERS AIMED LOW, HITTING ENEMY SHIPS BELOW THE WATERLINE AS THEY HEELED OVER.

with galley experience, also envisaged the broadside as a one-off device for crippling and confusing an adversary as an immediate prelude to boarding.

The wreck of El Gran Grifon has revealed another crucial weakness ... intensive production pressures evidently caused a dramatic drop in technical standards for the 'media culebrina' recovered from El Gran Grifon is bored so far off centre that in all probability it could never have been fired ...

... the English gunners were seamen, thoroughly familiar with the guns aboard their vessels and conversant with the tasks of operating them at sea. Those detailed to work the guns were not expected, as were the Spaniards, to double as soldiers ... The English fleet's commanding position to windward of the Armada throughout all the fighting gave it a considerable advantage ... their adversaries were normally heeled away from them, presenting their vulnerable lower hulls. But it was not until Gravelines that this advantage was fully exploited by the English ... Why had the English delayed so long?

C Martin and G Parker, The Spanish Armada, 1988.

Source K

AN ENGLISH SHIP SIMILAR TO DRAKE'S "REVENGE". AS THE SPANISH SAILED UP THE CHANNEL THE ENGLISH REALISED THEY HAD LITTLE TO FEAR FROM THE SPANISH GUNS, PERHAPS AFTER DRAKE CAPTURED A SPANISH GALLEON. DRAKE'S EARLY ATTACKS MAY WELL HAVE BEEN EXPERIMENTAL TO CONFIRM THAT THE SPANISH COULD NOT FIRE FREQUENTLY OR ACCURATELY.

Source L

(The weather) was an appreciably more persistent and immeasurably more effective opponent than the English ...Howard's complaints of the storms and of the 'extreme foul' weather leave no doubt of the reality of adverse conditions. It is sometimes supposed that the weather was bad only in the eyes of the beholders and that the Spanish experienced difficulty merely because they had unweatherly ships and unseamanlike practices. Yet Howard's words to Walsingham on 22 July – 'I know not what weather you have had there, but there never was any such summer seen here on the sea.' ...

...The weather's ravages should not be seen as entirely fortuitous. Their effect depended on what was perhaps the main weakness of the Spanish tactical plan: the failure to provide a safe haven of refuge for the Armada.

F. Fernandez-Armesto, *The Spanish Armada,* 1989.

---

8 How significant a role did English tactics, skills and equipment play in the Armada's failure according to sources I – K?

9 To what extent does Source L reassert the significance of the weather as a major cause of the Armada's failure?

10 Why was there no Spanish invasion of England in 1588?

The War with Spain 1589–1603

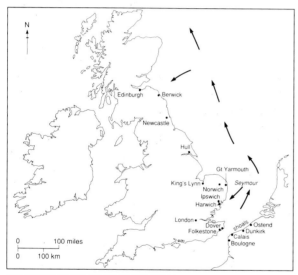

THE ARMADA'S ESCAPE ROUTE BUT FOR MANY IT LED TO WRECK AND DISASTER.

THE SITES OF ARMADA WRECKS ON THE COAST OF IRELAND.

On 12 August both sides knew that the Armada had not been defeated. It had been stopped from linking with Parma but it was still an immensely strong and threatening force. Thus far the 'Enterprise of England' had been a failure but not a disaster. However, as it headed for home, it was driven to disaster by yet more unseasonal storms and cold. At least one-third of its ships sank or were wrecked. The death toll may have been as high as fifty per cent. Many shipwrecked Spaniards were executed in Ireland on the orders of the English government in Dublin.

TALKING POINT

This speech was made after the news of the Battle of Gravelines was known. Does this timing detract from the impact of the speech or its value to historians?

In England relief spread as news of the Battle of Gravelines arrived. Elizabeth is supposed to have ridden her horse up the stairs of a hunting lodge in celebration! The flow of army recruits was halted and on 18 August Elizabeth joined Leicester's army at Tilbury where she made perhaps her most famous speech:

I am come amongst you as you see, at this time, not for my recreation and disport, but being resolved, in the midst and heat of battle, to live or die amongst you all, and to lay down for my God and for my kingdom and for my people, my honour and my blood, even in the dust. I know I have the body of a weak and feeble woman, but I have the heart and stomach of a king, and of a king of England too, and think foul scorn of Parma, or Spain, or any prince of Europe should dare to invade the borders of my realm ...

Despite the Armada's flight north, Howard and Drake were still cautious, warning of the continued danger from Parma and that the Armada might return. The English fleet too was in a poor state to repel a new attack. Howard's squadron had been struck by food-poisoning and men were dying in their hundreds in the overcrowded ships. The government did little to help and few words of thanks to sailors were even spoken in the Thanksgiving service at St Paul's. Of the £400,000 spent on combating the Armada only £180 was used for 'rewards for the injured'. It was left to the commanders to look after their men, Howard leading the way in spending his own money for their immediate needs and, in 1590, organising pensions. Burghley commented that the sailors' deaths had saved the government from having to pay them.

The events of 1588 clearly did not end the danger to England. She had defended herself but still needed to fight to save north-western Europe from the domination of the Catholic League. In 1589 Henry III of France was assassinated, leaving as his heir the Protestant Henry of Navarre. Navarre had to fight for his throne, not just against French Catholics but against Philip II's Spanish armies, which campaigned strongly in France between 1589 and 1596. The Spanish spoke of making Philip II's daughter Queen of France. If the Catholic League had succeeded then France and Spain would have been united against their Protestant enemies, the Netherlands swiftly overrun and England left to face an invasion.

Thus Elizabeth had to commit men and money to foreign intervention until the Spanish threat was defeated. However this was not a complete reversal of her earlier policy of non-involvement. Instead she saw her resources as a strategic reserve that could be committed at vital moments to aid her Dutch and French allies. This 'stingy but coherent' policy made good use of England's limited resources. Between 1589 and 1595 Elizabeth sent 20,000 troops to fight in France and 8,000 to the Netherlands plus £300,000 in aid to Henry of Navarre and £750,000 to the Dutch. This was at a time when the Queen's ordinary annual revenue amounted to no more than £250,000.

The result was a success. By 1595 Henry was securely established as king of France and ready to restore Elizabeth's ideal balance in Europe by declaring war on Spain. In the Netherlands the period since 1588 had seen consistent progress by the rebels, led by Maurice of Nassau. Parma's momentum had been destroyed by the Dutch shipping blockade

ELIZABETH AT TILBURY WITH HER TROOPS.

preventing the arrival of sea-borne supplies and then by harvest-failure and famine that caused mutiny in the starving and under-paid Spanish army. By the mid-1590s it was clear that even Philip's resources (and more silver than ever was arriving from the New World in the 1590s) had been stretched too far. In fact Dutch progress was even greater than Elizabeth wished to see. Maurice succeeded in winning independence for the northern states. Elizabeth effectively recognised the sovereignty of these United Provinces in 1596 when she entered an alliance with both France and the Provinces after Spain captured Calais. However the southern Netherlands remained under Spanish control, therefore providing the bulwark against French aggression that Elizabeth had always regarded as necessary.

Given the fame of men like Drake and of the Armada it is surprising to discover that it was the land war that was the main scene of action against Spain. The war at sea was largely confined to raiding Spanish merchant and treasure ships, a nuisance to Philip II but never a tactic that could defeat his plans. This limited policy was forced on Elizabeth because she could not finance a fleet herself and had to rely on merchants and noblemen sending their ships and recouping their expenses through the plundering of Spanish vessels. As a result she had virtually no control over leaders who paid lip-service to the queen's plans but, as soon as they were over the horizon, became intent on returning with as much loot as possible. This was never better demonstrated than by the Portuguese expedition of 1589.

This venture, led by Drake and Sir John Norris, had three official objectives – to destroy the remains of the Armada lying in harbour, to stir and support a revolt in Portugal (hence Norris's 19,000 soldiers) and to intercept the Spanish treasure ship off the Azores. In practice they ignored the Armada, attacked Lisbon but failed to stimulate the hoped-for revolt and then set off to hunt down the treasure fleet – but failed. 11,000 men died, nearly all from disease. By 1591 Philip had substantially rebuilt his navy.

A Spanish Armada was launched twice more, in 1596 and 1597, but each time was foiled by gales. Another invasion was planned but not carried out in 1599. Although none of these attempts reached the Channel there was genuine fear in England. In 1595 Hawkins and Drake, in an attempt to hit at the roots of Spanish financial strength, tried to attack Panama – a voyage that saw both men meet their deaths. Much more successful was the Cadiz expedition of 1596, led by Howard and Essex, which succeeded in capturing or destroying four Spanish ships and setting fire to the town.

Such attacks were good for morale and did some damage but they could not win the war. The only strategic naval plans were put forward by Hawkins, who envisaged a screen of ships blockading the silver convoys and thus cutting off Philip's income and by Essex in 1596. Essex advocated a total blockade of Spanish trade having first captured Cadiz and Lisbon which would be used as bases by English garrisons! The war could be prosecuted at sea and on the Spanish mainland. Elizabeth could not be persuaded to back such a venture. The war with Spain ended because Philip ran out of resources and France returned to its old role as Spain's enemy. Peace was not formally declared until 1604 but England had by then been safe for several years. The Anglo-Spanish war was a 'decisive event in the struggle of Counter-Reformation Catholicism to suppress the Reformation'. Protestantism in north-west Europe had survived the threat of the Catholic League. Elizabeth had not fought primarily to safeguard her religion but by defending her country she also did much to stem the tide of the Counter-Reformation.

The Effects of the Anglo-Spanish War, 1585 – 1604

The Anglo-Spanish war lasted for a full nineteen years, a period that can be dangerously foreshortened by the perspective of time. In real terms those aged 17 when the war began had reached a mature 36 when it ended. Such a lengthy war imposed severe strains on the country.

(The war) bred a new and more critical attitude to the central government, to the monarchy itself, even to the monarch personally. ... the Elizabethan war with Spain and the long-drawn-out burdens it imposed did play a considerable part in changing sixteenth-century Englishmen from a king-worshiping nation into a king-criticizing nation.
R.B.Wernham, *The Making of Elizabethan Foreign Policy, 1558 – 1603*, 1980.

The key phrase in that quotation is 'long-drawn-out burdens' for otherwise it seems strange that a successful war could lead to a fall in the monarch's popularity. However, as was also the case with Henry VIII's wars in the 1540s, the expenses of war could have a cataclysmic effect on everyday life, especially if they were coupled with natural disasters. The 1590s saw four successive poor harvests between 1594 and 1597, including the two worst harvests of the whole century. Plague was rampant in 1592–3 and there were further periodic, regional outbreaks. As a result food prices rose by 35 per cent during the 1590s. War was an important aid to inflation although it was secondary to the impact of harvest failures. However, for many people it was easier to blame the war. They resented the government's demands on their purses in times of hardship. They may also have felt that the queen and her councillors could have ended the war whereas they could not expect intervention to improve the harvests.

The costs of war were immense. Between 1590 and 1603 the average annual tax yield was £135,000 compared to £50,000 in the first years of the reign. People also paid for the war in their home counties because each county had to fund its own militia and raise troops for service abroad. Such costs brought complaints and protests in parliament. JPs too were unhappy because their duties were multiplying in respect of the military and financial impositions.

The war also affected trade. Those who previously had substantial trade with Spain (such as the merchants of Chester and Bristol) were devastated. If they could they looked further afield for trade, across the Atlantic or to Africa. This was an important development in the long-term but did little to feed families immediately. Some merchants turned to the new privateering 'industry', financing the adventurers who hoped to pay back loans with interest through raids on Spanish shipping.

Thus the costs of war played an important part in making the 1590s a time of hardship. People were also affected by the deaths of those on campaigns and by the burdens imposed by the return of wounded and disabled servicemen. Ironically, the focus for much discontent was the queen, the irony being that she had neither sought nor welcomed war and hoped each year to end it. It is little wonder that she too became an angry, bitter and irascible figure in her last years. She could not even reward her favourites and servants as she wished for there were more urgent calls on her income. This too caused complaint and dissent and a sense that Elizabeth's reign was in decline.

Famine and Revolt

The years between 1585 and 1603 saw peaks of real hardship as a result of plague and poor harvests. This cycle culminated in the sequence of disastrous harvests between 1594 and 1597. In 1596–7 the death rate leaped by 21 per cent and the standard of living of working men fell to its lowest point between 1216 and today. In Cumbria people simply starved to death. Nothing can detract from this horror but care must be taken to distinguish between the problems which affected different parts of the country. Harvest failures hit hardest the upland areas where marginal lands were already under cultivation or where they depended on purchases of grain from other regions. The richer agricultural regions of the south-east and East Anglia did not suffer so much and London amongst other cities was able to import grain from abroad and from the surrounding countryside. However these were the very places that were badly hit by plague, carried along the communication routes that brought the life-saving grain. While the lowlands suffered disease the uplands, scarred by starvation, escaped the worst of the plague.

Hardship manifested itself in a variety of ways. Crime increased, especially thefts and other crimes against property. However (as source D on page 390 suggests) this increase was not immediate. It was only after a sequence of poor harvests that people grew desperate. The number of marriages declined although the illegitimacy rate rose. Perhaps none of this is surprising. What may be is that there were very few protests that posed a threat to law and order. The government was certainly extremely concerned about the possibility of risings and particularly feared the return of 'camping' movements following the pattern of Ket's Rising of 1549. The extent of this fear was demonstrated by the government's over-reaction to the Oxfordshire Rising of November 1596. The planned rising seemed fearsome. The Lord Lieutenant's house was to be attacked, weapons seized and then the rebels would march on London. When the moment came, only four rebels put in an appearance at the chosen time and place and they, after waiting hopelessly for two hours, split up, only to be arrested.

Faced by this awe-inspiring demonstration of disaffection the Privy Council ordered the ringleaders to be sent to London incommunicado and with 'their hands pinioned and their legs bound'. After being tortured to reveal their plans the rebels were executed for levying war against the Queen – a remarkable exaggeration of their known acts. Their actual chance of creating a stir had been minimal, their intended associates, young artisans and servants, lacked the power, influence and experience to raise and lead a force. As elsewhere, this Oxfordshire rising showed that the yeoman middling-sort sided with the gentry against the poor and unemployed.

Although the government over-reacted this does not mean that problems were not real. Inflation received another boost (as in the 1540s) from war expenditure. Population growth, producing underemployment and therefore greater mobility of population, was another long-term factor. Enclosures, especially in the Midlands, played their part by reducing employment opportunities and periodic trade slumps hit the otherwise productive cloth trade. These long term problems were then accentuated by the plagues, harvest failures and the discharge of disabled solders and sailors.

FOCUS

15.2 Ireland 1585 – 1603

T**he outbreak of war with Spain did not lead to great unrest in Ireland. Throughout the period of the Armada the watchword of the English administration in Dublin was severity, and it ordered the deaths of many shipwrecked Spaniards. English troops even gained territory in Ulster. However a rebellion broke out in 1593 which became much more dangerous when Hugh O'Neill, Earl of Tyrone, became its leader in 1595. Ironically Tyrone had spent much time at Elizabeth's court and the council might well have hoped that such an Anglicised Irishman might have aided not threatened English control of Ireland.**

When Tyrone joined his son-in-law, Hugh Maguire, in rebellion he brought formidable skills of leadership. Most importantly he built up a disciplined force of troops, a 'professional standing army' trained by English officers with more and better-horsed cavalry than the English forces could number. They were also equipped with modern weapons. This was very different from earlier Irish risings.

Tyrone was joined by the powerful O'Donnells. Although the rebels were declared traitors Elizabeth agreed a truce in the hope that peace could be reached, saving much expense. During the truce Tyrone sought help from Spain. The Armadas of 1596 and 1597 were carrying troops to Ireland when they were scattered by gales. This did not stop Tyrone. In 1598 he inflicted a shocking defeat on the English at the battle of Yellow Ford, killing the English commander, Bagenal, and over 800 soldiers. English authority collapsed throughout Ireland.

HUGH O'NEILL, EARL OF TYRONE.

Tyrone's motives

Source A

The decline of feudalism in Ireland had begun with the overthrow of the house of Kildare in the 1530s. ... Sidney established lord presidencies in Munster and Connacht, each with a military force at their disposal with the aim of replacing the authority of the magnates with that of the crown. In 1576 the various 'countries' of Connacht were transformed into the English-style counties of Sligo, Mayo, Roscommon, and Galway. In 1583 the power of Desmond was overthrown. In 1585 ... the lords of Connacht ... agreed to pay a rent to the Crown, provide military service and introduce the common law. For a time it seemed that Ulster also would follow the example of Connacht in submitting to peaceful assimilation. In 1595, however, Hugh O'Neill who had enjoyed Crown support as Earl of Tyrone, took the great gamble of resisting the advance of the English administration into his territories...

H.Kearney, The British Isles, A History of Four Nations, 1989.

Source B

I have been informed by the bearer of this that you have written to me, but your letter has not yet reached my hands. I was confident that I should not in vain appeal to you for aid. The faith might be re-established in Ireland within one year, if the King of Spain would send only 3000 soldiers. All the heretics would disappear, and no other sovereign would be recognized than the Catholic King.

A letter from Tyrone to Spain, September 1595.

LORD MOUNTJOY.

uestions

- How valuable is Tyrone's letter for assessing his motives?

- Which factors aided Tyrone's rebellion?

- Why were the English forces able to win control in the end?

- Did events in Ireland during Elizabeth's reign make it more or less likely that future Anglo-Irish relations would be peaceful?

- Look back to the other sections on Tudor Ireland. Which events were sufficiently important to be ranked as turning points in the history of Ireland?

How great was the threat from Tyrone?
Source C

Bagenal's defeat at the Yellow Ford confronted Elizabeth with the unpalatable fact, increasingly apparent to shrewd observers ... that her Irish problem had largely transformed itself into a straight military contest against a disciplined and resourceful adversary. In this war, the geography of the confederacy's Ulster base helped to minimize the effect of vastly superior English resources. Moreover, a Spanish landing could easily have tipped the balance. In the longer term English seapower was a crucial factor, but given the prevailing winds, it was far from certain that a Spanish army operating in Ireland could not be supplied.

S.G.Ellis, *Tudor Ireland*, 1985.

Two commanders – Essex and Mountjoy

In 1599 the Earl of Essex arrived in Ireland, charged with regaining control of Ireland. Essex proved to be a disastrous leader, first heading away from Tyrone's forces and then agreeing a truce when the Queen expected him to fight. Motivated primarily by his own ambitions for power at court, Essex returned to England, deserting his post and his own soldiers. The lucky ones were only demoralized. Many were dead from disease.

Essex's replacement could not have been more different. Charles Blount, Lord Mountjoy, moved with speed (including winter campaigns that the Irish had not anticipated) and severity. He rapidly pushed Tyrone's forces back and regained territory. When 3400 Spanish troops landed at Kinsale in September 1601 Mountjoy marched rapidly to isolate them in the town and then defeated Tyrone in battle as he came to relieve the Spaniards. The Battle of Kinsale effectively ended the rebellion but Tyrone survived, free to negotiate terms at the moment of Elizabeth's death in 1603. This Compromise of Mellifont actually gave Tyrone the very power he had been seeking in 1595, recognising him as the chief lord of Ulster and thus seeming to return to the old policy of ruling through Irish feudal leaders.

England and Ireland in 1603

- England had imposed her military and political authority on Ireland

- The Gaelic Irish and old Anglo-Irish people remained loyal to the Roman Catholic church. Only the new settlers and conquerors were Protestant.

- The expense of defeating the rebellion had been huge, greater than the cost of the Anglo-Spanish war. In 1600 expenditure on Ireland was estimated at £320,000 out of the total crown expenditure at home and abroad of £437,840.

- Catholics still held most of the land in Ireland.

- The English had come to associate the Irish with the people encountered by explorers in the Americas, people they saw as uncivilised savages.

- Rebellion had been put down with great savagery and the Irish people had suffered famine.

- Some Irish lords, enemies of Tyrone and his allies, had prefered to support the crown during the rebellion.

- Many towns valued their trade with England and had opposed the rebels.

15.3 England 1585–1603: A Time of Famine and Revolt?

*I*n Somerset in 1595 rumours spread that 'before the yeare went aboute ther wold be old threshing owt of mowes and Cuttynge of throatts'. In October 1596 the Earl of Bath wrote to the Privy Council urging that gentry should be told to return to their estates 'to be at hand to stay the fury of the inferior multitude if they should happen to break out in sudden outcry for want of relief, as without good circumspection many suspect they may and will do'. These are only two of many suggestions that disorder threatened England following a series of poor harvests and outbreaks of plague. The material in this Focus section will help you to gauge the extent of the problems and the threat of disorder.

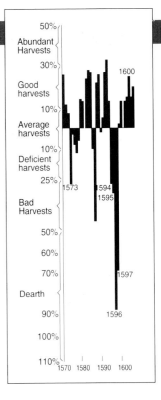

Source A

Source E

Therefore the winds, piping to us in vain,
As in revenge, have suck'd up from the sea
Contagious fogs; which, falling in the land,
Have every pelting river made so proud,
That they have overborne their continents:
The ox hath therefore stretch'd his yoke in vain,
The ploughman lost his sweat; and the green corn
Hath rotted ere his youth attain'd a beard:
The fold stands empty in the drowned field,
And crows are fatted with the murrain flock'
The nine-men's morris is fill'd up with mud;
And the quaint images in the wanton green,
For lack of tread are undistinguishable:
The human mortals want their winter here;
No night is now with moon or carol blest:
Therefore the moon, the governess of floods,
Pale in her anger, washes all the air,
That rheumatic diseases do abound:
And through this distemperature we see
The seasons alter: hoary-headed frosts
Fall in the fresh lap of the crimson rose;
And on old Hyems' thin and icy crown,
An odorous chaplet of sweet summer buds
Is, as in mockery set: the spring, the summer,
The chilling autumn, angry winter, change
Their wanton liveries: and the 'mazed world,
By their increase, now knows not which is which.

William Shakespeare, *A Midsummer Night's Dream*, Act II, scene ii, written about 1597.

Source B

The purchasing power of wages 100 = value 1450–1499			
	Agricultural Labourer	Building Craftsman	London Building Worker
1570–9	69	64	81
1580–9	57	57	78
1590–9	49	47	69
1600–9	50	46	72

Source D

Indictments for capital felonies in Middlesex				
	%	Theft	Homicide	Assault and Riot
1591	72	63	3	11
1592	126	118	5	5
1593	43	39	4	3
1594	65	57	3	6
1595	89	87	1	4
1596	69	68	1	10
1597	168	159	7	13
1598	258	239	18	43
1599	126	112	11	29

Source C

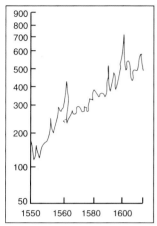

THE RATE OF INFLATION 1550 – 1605.

Source F

(i) Behold what a famine (God) hath brought into our land ... One yeare there hath been hunger; the second yeare there was a dearth, and a third, which is this yeare, there is great cleannesse of teeth ... our yeares are turned upside downe; our sommers are no sommers; our harvests are no harvest; our seed-times are no seed-times ...

Extract from a sermon by George Abbot, 1596.

(ii) Great death and famyn wherwith the country hath been punished extreamlie theis three hard yeares bypast.

A contemporary description of conditions in Gilsland, Cumbria, 1597.

(iii) a deare yeare ... manye people perished in this dearth in manye partes of Wales and other places, but not one in this Cittye.

A contemporary description of conditions in Chester, 1596–7.

Source G

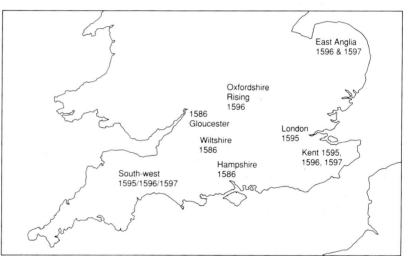

Questions

1 How does each source support or challenge the argument that this period was a time of great hardship for the people of England?

2 What does the evidence suggest about the nature of the government's response to conditions?

3 How great does the danger of rebellion appear to be?

Source H

1598 *An Act for the Relief of the Poor (summary of major provisions)*

1 Overseers of the Poor were to be nominated to employ the able poor and to administer relief in all parishes.

2 Overseers and churchwardens were given power to distrain the goods of any-one refusing to pay the poor-rate.

3 Housing was to be provided for the disabled on waste or common land.

4 County treasurers were appointed to relieve prisoners, soldiers and sailors passing through their counties.

1598 *An Act for the Punishment of Rogues, Vagabonds and Sturdy Beggars (summary of major provisions)*

1 Justices were to ensure that houses of correction be built in all counties and cities.

2 Vagrants defined as 'masterless men' and those who refused to work for statutory wages.

3 Incorrigible rogues to be sent overseas.

4 Convicted vagabonds to be whipped and returned to their parishes of birth or last residence.

Given this range of complex causes how did the government tackle the problems of poverty and social disruption? The deserving poor received aid (at least, they received as much aid as the government could organise, which was not a great deal) and vagrants and other potential threats to order were severely punished. The novelty in the government's approach lay in the direction it gave to JPs. Books of Orders dealing with dearth of food were issued in 1586, detailing measures to be taken to ease problems. These were re-issued in 1594/5. Similar Books of Orders giving instruction on how to combat plague had been printed in 1579 and were re-issued in 1592/3.

More famous than the Books of Orders were the Poor Laws of 1598 which were largely a restatement of earlier measures (see page 337) which in turn had been based on initiatives taken by individual people and towns. The Poor Laws show the two faces of government. On the one hand they reflect the genuine concern for the suffering of the poor. On the other the Vagabonds Act ordered the exile of dangerous rogues or the execution of discharged soldiers and sailors who were persistent vagrants. Here, clearly, was the fear of social disruption. The remedy was coercion – to force people to work and to maintain the balance between the population of the towns and the countryside.

The Poor Laws did give some help but probably of more use were the ad-hoc measures taken to deal with problems on the spot. In London, for example, extra corn was imported from the Baltic and the surrounding areas; increased watches were mounted to deal with vagrants and extra employment created; the wealthy provided charity independent of the Poor Law and also criticised the government for its demands for taxes and men. In building an explanation for the absence of rebellion these short-term solutions and the government's words of concern (even if the impact of the Poor Law was limited) have a significant place, alongside the unity of the middling sort with the gentry and the memory of the suppression of earlier risings.

Finance and Administration

The demands of war meant that Elizabeth had to turn her back on the successful financial policies she had pursued to 1585. She had been able to build a surplus of cash but this reserve was spent by 1588. Thereafter the government was forced to sell crown lands, borrow money and debase the Irish coinage (another sign of continuing prudence was the refusal to debase the English coinage). Royal expenses were reduced by selling or gifting away seven palaces, holding down court salaries and cutting back savagely on building work at royal properties. Tax receipts for this period (see table on right) were nearly double those for comparable earlier periods although the raw figures hide a more complex story. The yield from subsidies was falling, requiring Elizabeth to seek more subsidies, each demand in turn creating resistance that reduced the yield again. Taxation was vital but again did nothing to maintain the image of an Elizabethan 'Golden Age'.

For those close to government the gold was also tarnished by the development of corruption. As Elizabeth cut back her expenditure so the well of patronage dried up, creating fiercer competition for the offices and

Tax yields during Elizabeth's reign

	Total yield from lay taxation during period
1559–1571	£690 000
1576–1587	£660 000
1589–1601	£1 100 000

In addition the clergy paid taxes, the value of these payments particularly in the 1590s. Annual receipts of clerical taxation averaged £35 000 per year by 1598. Overall annual yields at that time were approximately £115 500 per year.

rewards that remained. Courtiers and Privy Councillors accepted payments in return for their efforts to influence Elizabeth over forthcoming wardships or government posts. When Sir George Goring died in 1594 his office as receiver-general of the court of wards became available, carrying an annual salary of £66 plus a £70 allowance. Immediately, Burghley and his son received offers of £1000 from men eager for the post. Goring in ten years, had succeeded in building two houses worth £4000 and £2000, owned several manors and had a huge cash surplus.

To contemporaries such activities were excessive but understandable. Far more criticism was directed at the monopolies handed out by Elizabeth in return for cash payments. Some monopolies were defensible and would nowadays be classed as patents whose purpose was to foster the development of new inventions. Others were justifiable because they encouraged trading companies to set up overseas bases secure from British competition. However other monopolies simply allowed courtiers complete control over the sale of certain goods, therefore allowing them to extort money from tradesmen plying their normal business. The most famous monopoly was Sir Walter Raleigh's control of playing cards but he also held monopolies of tin and the licensing of taverns. The impact of such monopolies was to raise prices at a time when inflation was already rampant. The only beneficiaries were the monopolists, 'the Bloodsuckers of the Commonwealth'. In the parliaments of 1597 and 1601 monopolies were severely attacked (see pages 398 – 399). In 1597 Elizabeth promised an investigation but the situation grew worse. In 1601, MPs' frustration was all the greater and their outrage over monopolies threatened the passage of the subsidy bill. This time Elizabeth conceded that some monopolies should be replaced or suspended and that people with a grievance against monopolies should have the right to pursue them through the law. Even so, monopolies remained to cause even greater clashes between parliament and the first two Stuart kings.

Monopolies and corruption suggest financial incompetence. In fact Elizabeth's government did remarkably well in these years, the queen dying in 1603 leaving a debt of only a little more than £350,000. Local government too had come under severe strain but had survived. Taxation had increased significantly at a local level and there was clear opposition, but the resistance was passive. JPs performed their ever-increasing tasks effectively, backed up by the influence of Privy Councillors in the counties. The dominance of councillors in their home counties was a major source of reassurance and solidity for the Elizabethan regime.

The Triumph of the Religious Settlement

By 1585 Elizabeth's religious settlement had survived for 26 years. Few people beneath the age of 35 could remember an alternative style of service or doctrine and were unlikely to agitate for something they had not known. Yet the Church of England was still under pressure. Puritan reformers were always likely to demand an end to compromise. War brought the Catholic threat to the centre of the stage. Would Catholics and Catholic sympathisers support a Spanish invasion of England? Would they rise in their thousands to acclaim Mary Queen of Scots as queen of England? These words were set to music by William Byrd, the royal composer but a staunch Catholic, and sung in at least one Tudor gentleman's house, Hengrave Hall in Sussex, on the eve of the Armada:

Look around to the East, Jerusalem,
And see the joy coming to you from God
For see, your sons are coming,
Who sent you out across the world
They are gathered in the east and are coming west
And rejoice with a holy word in honour of God.

Catholicism – Threat and Reconciliation

Government fears were based on evidence of Catholic intent. In 1588 Cardinal Allen's 'An Admonition to the Nobility and People of England' fell into Burghley's hands. Allen described Elizabeth as 'an incestuous bastard, begotten and borne in sinne of an infamous courtesan' and told English Catholics 'this is the daie no doubte of her fall, this is the lower of God's wrathe towards her and all her partakers. Forsake her therefore betune, that you be not inwrapped in her sinnes, punishment and damnation'. Allen's diatribe was never published but it would not have made any difference if it had been. Catholics did not rise because they were English first and Catholic second.

Even so the government's fear did not die away. In 1587 six priests had been executed. In 1588 21 died, together with ten lay people, all in the second half of the year as the Armada challenge mounted and then faded. Eight died on August 28 and six on August 30. The Armada, far from demonstrating England's invincibility, suggested her vulnerability. The executions continued. Between 1590 and 1603 88 Catholics were executed for defying the government, 53 of them priests. In 1589 Sir Christopher Hatton told parliament of the continued activities of 'those vile wretches, those bloody priests and false traitors, here in our bosoms, but beyond the seas especially' who 'will not cease to practise both at home and abroad ... An enemy is never so much to be feared as when he is condemned ... we have lopped off some of his boughs; but they will sooner grow again than we think of'. Hatton's words seem justified by further Armadas, the great danger of a Spanish invasion of Ireland and the uncertainties over the succession, thanks to Elizabeth's refusal to nominate her successor.

Therefore the government remained alert to the dangers of Catholic insurrection but, in reality, the danger was past and was growing ever dimmer. In the south and east the number of Catholics was falling, the result of government action, the inevitable action of mortality and Protestant preaching. It is true that in the north the number of Catholics seems to have increased but, as 1588 showed, these people were English Catholics. Their communities were headed by and, to some extent protected by, gentry – people who were most unlikely to risk their social status by attacking the government.

The willingness of English Catholics to reach an accord with the government became clearer in the 1590s. While the Jesuit missionaries and their followers retained a determination to overthrow Elizabeth others, including a number of priests, refused to follow their lead. This split became notorious after the 'Wisbech Stirs' of 1595. Many priests were imprisoned at Wisbech College. There, thirty secular priests refused to accept the Jesuit position. This division was further clarified by the 'Archpriest controversy' in 1598. Cardinal Allen had died in 1594, leaving English Catholics without a leader. The Pope appointed George Blackwell as Archpriest, a man inclined towards the Jesuits. Many English non-Jesuit priests refused to accept Blackwell's authority and some went so far as to open discussions with the government. They offered to deny the Pope's right to depose a monarch in return for the right to exercise their priestly offices without persecution.

Here was a very clear sign of nationalism triumphing and of the eventual acceptance of Catholicism as an allowable religion. However it was not yet that simple. In 1602 the government issued a proclamation declaring that Jesuits and others who maintained the Pope's authority should be exiled but that priests who denied the Pope's authority could remain. Thirteen priests did deny Papal authority, only to find that the government had no intention of actually allowing them to function as priests. Full agreement was not yet possible but Catholicism was far from being the threat it had once seemed likely to be. On the other hand it had not been destroyed and, in surviving thus far, had all but guaranteed its ultimate renewal.

Puritanism – an onslaught resisted

Catholicism survived but so too did the English Reformation and it was Protestantism that became the official religion. This simple fact and the more complex issues of doctrine were finally resolved in the last third of Elizabeth's reign. Elizabeth's reign allowed Protestantism to re-establish itself and then, over time, to work its slow way into people's minds and hearts. Elizabeth's longevity allowed her Church of England the time to settle, to improve the quality of its clergy and to resist its critics demands for change.

The appointment of John Whitgift to the see of Canterbury had underlined Elizabeth's determination to resist radical pressures on her religious settlement. In the early 1580s Whitgift attacked Presbyterianism (see pages 365 – 366) in the cause of uniformity but had not defeated it. A further clash was inevitable. Whitgift was bound to pursue uniformity until he was successful. Puritans were bound to resist because their beliefs forbade them to accept what they saw as the scandals of moderation. 1586–1587 witnessed another trial of strength. Whitgift became a member of the Privy Council, a sign of his importance in Elizabeth's policy for he was the only ecclesiastic Elizabeth appointed as a Privy Councillor other than those who had served earlier rulers. In 1586 too a decree was issued authorising the destruction of unregistered printing presses – an attack on the publicity machinery of the Puritans. No book was to be printed without the approval of the Archbishop of Canterbury or the Bishop of London.

Puritans fought back in the parliament of 1586–7, attacking the government of the church by bishops. Anthony Cope's bill would have abolished all the laws, customs and other official elements of the Church of England. Elizabeth acted swiftly. Cope and his immediate followers were imprisoned. There were complaints in parliament but no general outcry. Many MPs may have followed elements of Puritan thinking but had no truck with a Presbyterianism which so openly challenged accepted authority.

Against this background and the defeat of the Armada it is not surprising that Whitgift soon felt able to pursue his drive against the Presbyterians. Their most able leader, John Field, had also died in 1588. Before his death Field and others had set about building a national Presbyterian church in secret, a shadow alternative to the Church of England they hoped to overthrow. They had been able to hold provincial and national meetings but then Whitgift ordered the arrest of nine leaders, including Thomas Cartwright. Their papers were searched for evidence of treason and, although this was not forthcoming, the Presbyterians were destroyed as an organised force.

With the defeat of the Presbyterians, Puritanism ceased to be a 'threat' to the authority of the queen. However that does not mean that Puritanism was not an important influence on English religious affairs. Many priests had become enthused with Puritan ideals, many households read their Bibles together and followed a religion more devoted because it was based on personal conviction rather than upon ecclesiastical leadership. Moderate Puritans still hoped to 'improve' Elizabeth's religious settlement but not at the expense of destroying the national church. By 1603 Puritans had played a leading part in helping to make England a more Protestant country. Elizabeth had erected the framework in 1559 but they had done much to bring the Protestant religion to life. In the universities, Puritans were playing a key role in training a new generation of graduate clergymen. That said, England was not a deeply religious country as a whole. There were many devout Protestants and some convinced Catholics but there were probably still more confused followers who accepted the services offered to them while wishing for something more colourful. What they most clearly had in common was that they were all English.

The Earl of Essex's Rebellion of 1601

Torrential rain, famine, plague, obstreperous parliaments, a war that seemingly would not end – it cannot be surprising that there were those who believed 'we shall never have a merry world while the queen liveth' To this catalogue of problems must be added the rebellion of the Earl of Essex – perhaps the clearest sign of a decline in Elizabeth herself. Until now her favourites had been devoted to their queen. Now one dared to rebel. Robert Devereux inherited the earldom of Essex at the age of 9 in 1576. Unfortunately he inherited little else for his father, who had gambled his family's money on an unsuccessful expedition to Ireland in 1573. However, Essex although 'the poorest earl in England' was related to Elizabeth, for he was descended from her aunt, Mary Boleyn. More importantly he was Leicester's step-son and had been brought up in Burghley's household. Such advantages gave Essex a headstart over other courtiers but it was his personality that secured his pre-eminence. When he arrived at court in 1584, aged only 17, he dazzled both queen and courtiers. His 'goodly person, and a kind of urbanity and innate courtesy, combined with the recollection of his father's misfortunes, won him the hearts of both Queen and people'. Essex was indeed tall, handsome, charming, witty – although he was 'no graceful goer' on the dance floor.

ROBERT DEVEREUX, EARL OF ESSEX.

One of his servants reported that nobody accompanied Elizabeth 'but my Lord of Essex, and at night, my Lord is at cards, or one game or another with her, that he cometh not to his own lodging till birds sing in the morning.' His rise was meteoric, even by the standards of sixteenth century favourites. In 1586 he was created a knight-banneret for his courage at the Battle of Zutphen. Next year he became Master of the Horse, the post long held by Leicester. In 1588 he was made a Knight of the Garter, a sign of great personal favour from Elizabeth. Essex was still only 21.

Essex's relationship with Elizabeth was also stormy. In 1587 Essex accused Elizabeth of taking orders from Raleigh (the Queen disapproved of Essex's sister's marriage and Essex blamed Raleigh, wrongly, for her attitude). Essex and Elizabeth screamed at each other. Elizabeth insulted Essex's mother and the Earl stormed out, a grievous breach of court etiquette. Essex was also jealous of the queen's favour. When she rewarded Charles Blount with a golden chess piece for his jousting skills Essex sneered 'every fool must have a favour'. Blount challenged Essex to a duel and wounded him in the thigh. 'By God's death', said Elizabeth, 'it was fit that someone or other should take him down and teach him better manners, otherwise there would be no rule with him'.

Thus the story of Elizabeth and Essex was, from the beginning, one of quarrels, confrontations, rebukes and forgiveness. Elizabeth's forgiveness of Essex's behaviour, particularly his frequent habit of storming out of the queen's court in a high temper, shows the depth of her regard for him. It also suggests that Essex did not perhaps fully understand the queen, underrating her experience and intellect, and did not appreciate that there were limits to the behaviour of even a royal favourite. The fact that Essex was also highly popular with the public did nothing to quell his ambition. Earlier favourites, including Leicester, had been unpopular, disliked because of their presumed ambition.

Essex's public career saw him win the role of military hero. In 1588–9 Essex joined the Drake-Norreys expedition to Spain, expressly against the Queen's order. In 1591–2 he led a force in France in support of the Protestant Henry of Navarre. In 1596 he commanded the land forces which captured Cadiz and returned to wild public acclaim as a national hero. Next year he led the Islands' Voyage to capture the Spanish treasure fleet although this time he failed.

Politically too Essex appeared to be playing a key role. Elizabeth had never allowed one man or one faction to create rivalries that disrupted her court or council. Leicester and Burghley had balanced each other's influence. Now she was willing to support both Essex and Robert Cecil, Burghley's son. This should have allowed Essex to play an honourable and central role in government, if only Essex had been willing to accept it. Unfortunately he could not countenance the idea of an equal, especially the distinctly unmilitary figure of Cecil. For the first time, the court and council became deeply divided, perhaps a sign of Elizabeth's loosening grip as well as Essex's vaulting ambition.

15.4 Parliament 1585–1603

Previous chapters have shown Elizabeth reluctant to call parliaments except when financial aid was absolutely necessary. Often she was pressured to do so by councillors who hoped to use parliament as an additional lever to persuade or force the Queen into actions over issues, for example, Mary, Queen of Scots or the succession, that she preferred to avoid. There were also others who sought to use Parliament to counteract Elizabeth's policies (notably the Puritans seeking religious reforms) and the Queen also met opposition from renegades such as Wentworth over the privileges of the Commons. Overall however the story of Elizabeth and her parliaments was one of a co-operative striving for security. Did this continue?

The Parliament of 1586/7

(met 29 October 1586 to 23 March 1587)

This was a parliament of high drama, dominated by the accusations against Mary, Queen of Scots and then by the attempt of Anthony Cope and other Puritans to repeal all existing religious legislation. Once called parliament pressed for Mary's execution, orchestrated by Elizabeth's councillors, but received only Elizabeth's 'answer answerless'. Its insistence angered the Queen, as did Cope's actions, which were then supported by Wentworth who saw Elizabeth's attempts to muzzle Cope as a breach of the Commons' privilege. For his pains Wentworth went to the Tower. A subsidy was granted to help pay for the war effort but there was little by way of normal legislation. Speaker Puckering closed the session by saying 'some very few (members) have fallen and offended, rather by infirmity of judgement and through a preposterous zeal, than of any either disobedience to her Majesty or intention of disturbance to our better proceedings; yet, generally, the whole number hath from time to time no less readily assembled than quietly conferred and painfully travailed ...'

The Parliament of 1589

(met 4 February to 29 March 1589)

The principal business was the granting of a subsidy to pay for the war. To this date the normal practice had been for the subsidy bill to consist of one subsidy and two tenths and fifteenths which would yield approximately £140,000. Such was the need in 1589 that this was doubled, subject to the proviso that this would not become 'a precedent to posterity'. The Commons did challenge the crown over purveyances (purchase of necessary food and stores at low prices) but Elizabeth quashed the bill, saying that purveyance was a matter of the royal prerogative and therefore not something on which parliament could legislate. Tension rose but then Elizabeth soothed the situation by setting up discussions.

Questions

1. What do the frequency and length of parliamentary sessions tell you about Elizabeth's attitude to parliaments?

2. On which issues did Elizabeth clash with parliament?

3. Did the House of Commons increase its privileges at this time?

The Parliament of 1593

(met 19 February – 10 April 1553)

As soon as Parliament met it was told its role – 'not to make any new laws, or to spend any time about other matters, but only to treat and advise of all the good ways and means that might be invented for the safety of (the Queen)'. Thus the granting of taxation was once more the focus. The Commons magnanimously offered to repeat the double subsidy of 1589 only to find the Lords (reflecting the government's needs) offering three. The Commons, fearing that its right to decide matters of taxation was under threat reacted strongly but tempers calmed and three subsidies were granted. Once again there was Puritan agitation but by now with little support. It was swiftly quashed and the House was prepared to pass a bill against the Puritan radicals, the Separatists. Before parliament met Peter Wentworth tried to raise support for discussion of the succession. He failed and was imprisoned in the Tower, dying there a few years later. On behalf of the Queen the Lord Keeper laid out her views on the 'liberties' of parliament:'Her Majesty granteth you liberal but not licentious speech, liberty therefore but with due limitation ... It shall be meet therefore that each man of you contain his speech within the bounds of loyalty and good discretion, being assured that as the contrary is punishable in all mean, so most of all in them that take upon them to be counsellors and procurators of the commonwealth. For liberty of speech, her Majesty commandeth me to tell you that to say yea or no to bills. God forbid that any man should be restrained or afraid to answer according to his best liking, with some short declaration of his reason therein, and therein to have a free voice, which is the very liberty of the House; not, as some suppose, to speak there of all causes as him listeth and to frame a form of religion of a state of government as to their idle brains shall seem meetest. She saith no King fit for his state will suffer such absurdities ...'

The Parliament of 1597/8

(met 24 October 1597 to 9 February 1598)

Parliament once again granted a triple subsidy, even at this time of poverty. Members also introduced bills to deal with vagabonds, provide poor relief and set up hospitals which formed the foundation of the major Poor Law legislation. It was also an unsettled parliament with the first attacks on monopolies although parliament agreed to Elizabeth's decision to consider their complaints (see page 393).

The Parliament of 1601

(met 27 October – 19 December 1601)

The Monopolies debate flared again with one member suggesting that even bread would soon be a monopoly. Once more members seemed ready to breach the Queen's prerogative but her own management of parliament won the day. Despite many misgivings they once more accepted her promise of future redress. Elizabeth's 'Golden Speech' was her farewell to Parliament (page 316). Despite the opposition in some quarters parliament granted a quadruple subsidy.

Essex's great weakness was his inability to learn political lessons from experience. As a faction leader he naturally sought from Elizabeth posts and rewards for his own supporters. When he was successful he sought more. When, as was often the case, he was refused he still sought more and then exploded with resentment and anger on meeting repeated refusal. For all his intelligence he showed little understanding of the needs and policies of the queen. Essex's emphasis on chivalry and militarism was also dangerous. Despite the war Elizabeth was not a warmonger and was suspicious of those who did not see the virtue of peace. In 1596 Francis Bacon warned Essex of the dangers of his position, that he appeared to be 'a man of nature not to be ruled: that hath the advantage of [the queen's] affection, and knoweth it; of an estate not grounded to his greatness: of a popular reputation; of a military dependence ... I demand whether there can be a more dangerous image than this represented to any monarch living, much more to a lady, and of her Majesty's apprehension ...' Essex did not listen or could not understand.

FRANCIS BACON.

TALKING POINT

Why was Essex's position as described by Bacon so dangerous?

Essex's rivalry with the Cecils dominated politics from the mid-1590s. In 1598 an Irish expedition was planned. Such was the doom-laden prospect of Ireland that Essex was furious when Elizabeth proposed one of his own followers as leader. In his rage Essex turned his back on the queen. In response Elizabeth hit him across the face. Essex's hand flew to his sword, more insults flew. Perhaps, as reported, Essex told his queen that 'her conditions were as crooked as her carcass'. Howard had to throw himself between the two figures to break up the quarrel. Essex was forbidden to enter the queen's presence.

As before, the storm subsided and Essex himself led the 1599 expedition to Ireland. However his future hung on his success and everyone knew it. The crowds who went to acclaim Shakespeare's Henry V heard Chorus in Act Five predict that a successful Essex would be greeted by a delighted city. But Essex was not successful (see pages 388 – 389) and, in September 1599, returned, against explicit order, arriving in the queen's bedchamber without warning, before Elizabeth had arranged herself in the paraphernalia of her public image – make-up, jewellery and wig. He was received but was then placed under house-arrest, suspended from the Privy Council and lost his official posts.

Essex fell from grace in the autumn of 1599 but it was February 1601 before he made his chaotic attempt to win back his power. In the interim he faced the threat of treason charges (some, put together by Robert Cecil, absurdly suggesting that he had been drawn into a plot with Spain and the Pope) and his finances fell apart. Political impotence and shame seemed to be Essex's fate unless he could defeat Cecil, but that might also mean attacking the queen. In the end he headed an incredibly optimistic, short-sighted scheme (it can hardly be called a plan) to raise London as a prelude to sweeping his enemies from London.

On 8 February 1601 Essex assembled 300 supporters. When Privy Councillors arrived, bent on conciliation, they were held hostage and Essex marched his supporters – including three earls and three barons – into London. For all his popularity the citizens stood and watched. Desperately, Essex proclaimed that the queen was in danger from Spain but, instead of joining him, the city authorities raised their troops and

RICHARD II 1377 – 1399. THE STORY OF THE DEPOSITION OF RICHARD II WAS POLITICALLY NOTORIOUS IN THE 1590S. ONE PLAYWRIGHT, JOHN HAYWARD, DEDICATED HIS PLAY TO ESSEX, WITH THE IMPLICATION THAT HE WOULD SUCCEED ELIZABETH. ELIZABETH BELIEVED THAT SHE WAS BEING IDENTIFIED WITH RICHARD. ON THE NIGHT BEFORE ESSEX'S REBELLION HIS SUPPORTERS ATTENDED A PERFORMANCE OF A PLAY CALLED "RICHARD II" AND HAYWARD'S PLAY WAS USED IN EVIDENCE AGAINST ESSEX AT HIS TRIAL.

surrounded the tiny band. After a skirmish Essex and his followers retreated to Essex House where they surrendered. Even if this was not a revolt aiming at the monarch's deposition, Essex's rising was a kind of political gangsterism that could not be acceptable to Elizabeth. He was executed for treason on 25 February, aged 34. Elizabeth grieved for her favourite but had no doubt about the justice of the verdict. For once someone went to the block without royal hesitation and postponements.

EXAMINING THE EVIDENCE
Why did Essex rebel?

Source A

(Essex) shifteth from sorrow and repentance to rage and rebellion so suddenly as well proveth him devoid of good reason or right mind. In my last discourse, he uttered strange words bordering on such strange designs that made me hasten forth and leave his presence ... It resteth with me in my opinion that ambition thwarted in its career doth speedily lead onto madness. His speeches of the Queen becometh no man who hath mens sana in corpore sano.

Sir John Harington, recording a meeting with Essex in his journal.

Source B

I owe to Her Majesty the duty of an Earl and Lord Marshal of England. I have been content to do Her Majesty the service of a clerk, but can never serve her as a villain or slave ... But, say you, I must yield and submit; I can neither yield myself to be guilty or this imputation to be laid upon me to be just. I owe so much to the author of all truth, as I can never yield falsehood to be truth, nor truth falsehood ... What, cannot princes err? Cannot subjects receive wrong? Is an earthly power or authority infinite? Pardon me, my good Lord, I can never subscribe to these principles ... I have received wrong and feel it. My cause is good, I know it ...

Essex writing to Sir Thomas Egerton, 1598.

Source C

If conscience did not tell me, that, without imploring your Majesty's goodness at this time, most dear and most admired Sovereign, I should not only lose the present support of my poor estate, but the hope of any ability to do your Majesty future service, and not that alone, but the means of satisfying a great number of hungry and annoying creditors, which suffer me in my retired life to have no rest; I would appear still before your Majesty as a mute person. But since this day se'night, the lease which I hold by your Majesty's beneficence expireth, and that form is both my chiefest maintenance and mine only means of compounding with the merchants to whom I am indebted ...

Letter from Essex to Queen Elizabeth, 22 September 1600. The grant of the farm of sweet wines, his largest single source of money, ran out on 29 September.

Source D

	Land sales 1591–1600	Private Debts
Earl of Essex	£40 000	£25 000
Earl of Rutland		£5 000
Earl of Southampton	£20 000	£8 000
Earl of Sussex	£20 000	?
Earl of Bedford	£1 000	£7 000
Lord Sandys	£1 000	£3 000
Lord Cromwell	£10 000	?

Source E
When Elizabeth refused to renew his patent of sweet wines in September, his credit structure collapsed. She had effectively condemned him to a life of poverty ... creditors were pressing for payment and starting to arrest his servants who had stood surety for him. Yet Essex's motivation went beyond this. A faction leader who was denied access to the monarch was in an untenable position: the earl saw himself compelled to act because his Court opponents had exploited their 'corrupt' monopoly of power. He particularly thought himself 'called' by his lineage and rank to rehabilitate the nobility as natural political leaders. After his disgrace, his urge to oust the Cecilian 'upstarts' ... became obsessional.

J Guy, *Tudor England*, 1988.

1 What does Source A suggest about the motivation behind Essex's rebellion?

2 How did Egerton and Essex (Source B) differ in their obedience to the queen?

3 How useful is Source B in explaining Essex's revolt?

4 How do Sources C and D help to explain Essex's revolt?

5 (a) In the light of Sources A-D and pages 396 – 400 do you agree with the analysis of Essex's motives in Source E?

(b) Re-read Source A. It seems possible that by 1601 Essex was no longer thinking rationally. Are historians therefore bound to fail when they produce objective and rational explanations for Essex's rebellion?

TALKING POINT

When explaining events and motives is it possible for historians to assess how far a person acted for irrational reasons?

The Succession

Elizabeth, even in 1601, had no intention of naming her successor. In the parliament of 1601 she surveyed the state of England and her foreign involvements but said not one word about her successor. Certainly no-one dared to raise the topic. One commentator remarked that 'to determine thereof is to all English capitally forbidden, and therefore so I leave it'.

Elizabeth's motivation for her silence remained the country's security, for fear that rejected claimants might use force to overturn her decision.

Overall, this was the best policy but it was not perfect – a gap that Robert Cecil bridged by initiating in 1601 a secret correspondence with James VI. Cecil's purposes were to prepare James for his new kingdom and to secure a peaceful transition to the new regime and his own prime place within it. The correspondence between Cecil and James was based on clearly stated principles – every respect should be shown to Elizabeth, James should make no attempt to win or gain recognition of his title before his time. It was also intended to be highly secret for Cecil feared that the queen's 'age and ability, joined to the jealousy of her sex, might have moved her to think ill of that which helped to preserve her'. In this Cecil underestimated his mistress. Elizabeth may well have realised what Cecil was doing and approved of his prudent concern for the future. Her silence over the succession and his secret correspondence with James were two sides of the same coin.

Elizabeth was in good health, hunting and riding in the summer of 1602. She remained firmly in control of government until, in February 1603, she simply seemed to lose the will to live. Deeply distressed by the death of her great friend, the Countess of Nottingham, Elizabeth faded away. She could not sleep. She would not eat. This state lasted for several weeks, during which the nobility were summoned, watches doubled and Cecil sent James a draft of the proclamation of his succession. While Cecil thus ensured the security and stability she had always fought for Elizabeth slipped into unconsciousness. Between two and three o'clock in the morning of 24 March the Tudor century drifted gently to an end.

JAMES VI AND I.

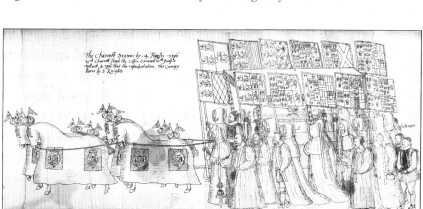

ELIZABETH'S FUNERAL PROCESSION.

REVIEW

Elizabeth reigned for over forty four years, nearly twice as long as her grandfather, Henry VII, and longer too than her father, Henry VIII. Perhaps Elizabeth lived too long. One contemporary, John Clapham, noted that there were those who watched Elizabeth's funeral cortege without sorrow, believing that they 'could not lightly be in a worse state than they were, considering that the people generally were much impoverished by continual subsidies and taxes ... that little or no equality was used in those impositions ...' Nevertheless there were plenty of people who agreed that 'the sorrow for her Majesty was so deep in many hearts, they could not so suddenly show any great joy' (at the new reign).

If Elizabeth had died in 1588 or 1590 there would not have been so mixed a reaction. The 1590s seem to cast a shadow over her achievement, but should they? Consider these two statements:

A The period from 1588 to 1603 saw continued hardship for the people of England. They had to pay the costs of war. They had to fight to survive plague and famine. There was little positive leadership from the government for the Queen was growing tired and also dispirited by the long war. Clashes with parliament, government corruption and Essex's rebellion were evidence of a regime that was living on past glories not present achievements.

B The period from 1588 to 1603 saw continued hardship for the people of England. They had to pay the costs of war. They had to fight to survive plague and famine. Once again chaos threatened England but Elizabeth led her government and people to security and calm. By 1603 Spain had been defeated, the worst economic problems had been endured, the succession issue resolved. England had not been torn apart by religious strife and parliament and the nobility co-operated with their monarch. This was certainly a troubled period but Elizabeth's achievement in dealing with its crises was just as great as in earlier decades.

---

1 Examine carefully the conclusions of each of these statements. What evidence would you use to support or attack the different elements of each statement?

2 Write your own brief assessment of Elizabeth's achievement between 1588 and 1603.

3 Using your assessment as an introduction write an essay with this title: 'After 1588 Elizabeth was faced by many problems. She outlasted them but she did little to solve them.' Explain why you agree or disagree with this statement.

SECTION REVIEW

TALKING POINT

The decision-making activity on Elizabeth's reign on pages 286 – 289 was called 'The Survival Game' echoing the earlier activity on Henry VII. Do you think that this was an appropriate title for the activity on Elizabeth? Did she have much in common with her grandfather, Henry VII?

Gloriana – The Reign of Queen Elizabeth

The noblest Queen
That ever was seen
In England doth reign this day

Now let us pray
And keep holy-day
The seventeenth day November;
For joy of her Grace,
In every place,
Let us great praise render

That ballad, composed (if that is the right word) for the queen's accession day celebrations in 1600 sums up Elizabeth's reputation as it remains for many people today. She was the 'noblest queen'. Do historians today assess Elizabeth so highly? What exactly were her achievements and what criticisms can be made of her rule?

Source A

Under Elizabeth, the nation regained its self-confidence and sense of direction. At a time when the authority of the majority of her fellow monarchs was under threat or in decline, she upheld the interests of the Crown while not encroaching on those of her subjects, restored the coinage, and created a Church which, for all its failings, came close to being truly national. While many European countries were being rent by civil war, insurrection and appalling acts of bloodshed, she presided over a realm which (with the exception of her Irish dominions) was fundamentally stable and united ... Besides this, Elizabeth was responsible for raising England's international standing, defying the most powerful nation in Christendom, and frustrating Philip II's attempts to overrun both England and France ...

Anne Somerset, *Elizabeth I*, 1991

Source B

Elizabeth's success owed much to luck – and her peculiar combination of arrogance and charm, prudence and obstinacy, intelligence and prejudice. While absolutist to a degree when pressed, she also knew how to strike a patriotic note and enjoyed playing to the crowd. Moreover, the general competence of her ministers and servants and their shared ideology gave the regime an internal coherence. On religious, social and economic issues, councillors were generally in agreement; major disputes were usually caused by foreign policy.

S Adams, Government and Politics, 1553–1625 in C Haigh (ed), The Cambridge Historical Encyclopaedia of Great Britain and Ireland, 1985.

1 Read Sources A and B. What do these authors suggest were Elizabeth's achievements and the reasons for her successes? What would you add to the achievements and reasons?

Source C

Elizabeth died unloved and almost unlamented, and it was partly her own fault. She had aimed for popularity and political security by projecting herself as the ever-young and ever-beautiful virgin mother of her people, bringing them peace and prosperity; she ended her days as an irascible old woman, presiding over war and failure abroad and poverty and factionalism at home. From 1558 to 1588, Elizabeth had successfully courted her politicians and entranced her people. She had made herself the focus of fervent devotion and earnest loyalty, the well-publicised source and guarantee of international safety and national stability. But her reign had been thirty years of illusion, followed by fifteen of disillusion. ...

   In the new and bitter world of the 1590s, Elizabeth was shown to be politically bankrupt. The only answer she and those close to her could provide seemed to be 'more of the same'. For her political style, this meant more resort to ill-temper as a tool of management, more reluctance to spend money on necessary policies, more reliance on and reward of a few trusted advisers. For her political image, this meant more extravagant praise of non-existent qualities, more far-fetched portrayals of idealised beauty, more frequent repetitions of the old slogans. The world in which Elizabeth had painstakingly built her model of female monarchy changed – but Elizabeth lived up to her motto, semper eadem, always the same. She was a ruler over-taken by events – 'a lady whom time had surprised', as Raleigh remarked.

C Haigh, Elizabeth I, 1988.

2 In what ways does the author of Source C differ in his interpretation of Elizabeth's achievement? To what extent was she the cause of problems?

Source D

The reign of Elizabeth was not one of reform but of exploitation and consolidation. After the vast but incomplete overhaul of the machinery which was part of Cromwell's amazing achievement, what was needed was a little development but in the main use; and these the great Elizabethan administrators provided ... The sorting had been done under Henry VII and Henry VIII, and in particular by the revolutionary genius of Tudor times, Thomas Cromwell; without the long labours, the years of drudgery, the high and honest endeavour of the Elizabethans no amount of revolutionary genius would have sufficed.

G R Elton, England under the Tudors, 1955.

3 Source D provides a longer-term context for Elizabeth's reign. What is the main point the author is making? Do you think his conclusion is justified?

Source E

Overall it can be argued that the traditional picture of Elizabeth's reign as a great age for the Queen and the English nation contains much truth. But it is not the whole story. There are also important elements of failure and of lost opportunities in the reign. Above all, perhaps, a more imaginative approach to the administration of the customs and the crown lands could have left the monarchy in a much happier financial position than the one which faced James I in 1603. Many of his worst troubles and those of his son, Charles I, stemmed from that unsatisfactory financial heritage ...

A G R Smith, The Reign of Queen Elizabeth I: An Assessment, in History Sixth,
vol 3.

Source F

If the breakdown of 1640–2 had a number of long-term causes, the vital dynamic was always Charles I's conduct and policies. Clarendon began his History of the Rebellion and Civil Wars by observing: 'I am not so sharp-sighted as those, who have discerned this rebellion contriving from (if not before) the death of Queen Elizabeth'. He knew that, if we read history backwards, Elizabeth's inertia and immobility in the 1590s, combined with the rise of 'venality' at Court, could be said to have established a pattern that precluded comprehensive reform ... Yet history is properly read forwards. when this is done, it is clear that a 'slide to disaster' was inconceivable in the sixteenth century.

J Guy, Tudor England, 1988

TALKING POINT

In assessing Elizabeth's achievement should we look forward to the Civil War and see if Elizabeth was in any way to blame for the conflict or should we ignore events after 1603 because Elizabeth herself could not take the future into account?

4 Read Sources E and F. Some historians have agreed that Elizabeth's reign created problems that helped to cause the Civil War of the 1640s.

(a) What are the possible links between Elizabeth and the Civil War?

(b) Do the authors of Sources E and F suggest these links are justified?

Source G

Her task could hardly have been more difficult. She had to resist the machinations of her councillors as they tried to draw her into their schemes. Her sources of intelligence were almost uniformly unreliable, and her own advisers and ambassadors, as well as foreign diplomats, fed her the information which suited them. The specific policies (or tactics) she pursued had little positive support ...And she had to achieve all this despite an appalling political handicap; she was a woman in a man's world.

... Elizabeth had a restricted conception of her role as queen. Though she spoke much of her duty to God and her care for her people, this was political rhetoric to justify her rule. After the ecclesiastical settlement of 1559, she felt no public obligation to do anything more – she did not reform administration, or purify the Church, or improve the lot of the poor, or colonise North America, because she saw no reason why she should. Elizabeth's objective as queen was to be queen; her exercise of royal power was not a means to a higher end, it was an end in itself.

C Haigh, *Elizabeth I*, 1988

---

5 Source G sums up the difficulties Elizabeth faced in ruling and her attitude to her role as Queen. Explain why you agree or disagree with the author's conclusions?

Source H

... by the late 1970s, the revisionary ferment which had brought intellectual excitement to the study of the early Tudor and early Stuart periods had changed the context of Elizabethan history, and had begun to enliven the Queen's reign itself. The implications of county and ecclesiastical studies for the general history of the period began to be recognised ...

Much new work is afoot, and some of the essays in this collection are exploratory forays and preliminary reports. Almost all the authors in the volume are now writing books on issues in Elizabethan history, and many others are engaged in work of equal (or greater) importance. It should be stressed that there is much that we do not yet know – and more that we will never know ...

C Haigh, *The Reign of Elizabeth I*, 1984

---

6 Read Source H.

(a) Why do you think interpretations of Elizabeth's reign have changed?

(b) Why do disagreements continue?

Source I

At her accession, Elizabeth's sex was looked on as a grievous disability, but she succeeded in turning even that to her advantage. Although she was sufficiently assertive to prevent her male advisers from contesting her authority, in other ways she flaunted her femininity, using it to appeal to

TALKING POINT

Elizabeth was not the only 'indecisive' sixteenth century monarch. Philip II used indecision as a 'tool of policy' and created problems when he initiated events as with his Armadas. Do you think that 'masterly inactivity' was a better overall policy in the sixteenth century than direct and decisive actions? Which other monarchs and events would you use to support your argument?

TALKING POINT

In assessing Elizabeth's achievements why is it necessary to establish Elizabeth's own objectives?

Most history has been and still is written by men. Do you think that a 'feminist perspective' on Elizabeth helps to redress the balance?

Historians writing about government and management often seem to assume that good government is decisive and strong and therefore more likely to be provided by men. Is this true or is it a clear example of sexual stereotyping?

the chivalrous instincts of the men who surrounded her, and investing her dominion over them with an aura of idealism and romance. Furthermore, Elizabeth knew that, precisely because she was a woman, her ministers were ready to make allowances for her when she behaved in a fashion that would have been deemed intolerable in a King. 'That which is natural to her sex hindereth resolution', shrugged Burghley resignedly on one occasion, and Elizabeth exploited this indulgent attitude to stave off unwelcome decisions and to avoid being hustled into commitments against her will.

Anne Somerset, *Elizabeth I,* 1991.

Source J

On the whole, and with of course a few notable exceptions, historians writing about her have been male while most novelists have been female and this has also contributed to the process of constructing a written portrait of Elizabeth, just as the political position of the writer and his or her religious standpoint have also been significant.

There is a strain running through the work of even the most eminent historians that reveals an uneasiness about Elizabeth's sex. This is manifested most obviously in the way in which Elizabeth's tactics of vacillation and her constant changes of mind have been described pejoratively as quintessentially 'feminine'. Based on the idea firstly that women are less decisive than men and secondly that decisiveness is an important quality for a person in a position of command, Elizabeth's indecisiveness has been viewed as typical of her sex. This, it seems to me, is both over-simplistic and patronising. In the early years of her life, Elizabeth learned that to hold an inflexible position could mean death; ... If she gave no direct answers, made no specific statements, kept silent on controversial issues and generalised when asked hard questions, she could keep the good will of different factions and keep her head into the bargain. This tactic worked so well in her youth that it must have become second nature. As monarch, she continued to use it ...Rather than interpreting this character trait as quintessentially feminine, it is more useful to see it for what it was – a behavioural pattern learned in childhood and carried to extremes once she was out of immediate danger. It is the clue to Elizabeth's survival.

Susan Basnett, *Elizabeth I: A Feminist Perspective,* 1988.

7 According to Source I was the fact that Elizabeth was a woman an advantage or disadvantage to her as queen? Do you agree with this conclusion?

8 Read Source J.

(a) What problems does the author suggest face a biographer of Elizabeth?

(b) Consider what you have read in this book and elsewhere about Elizabeth. Do you think that authors have taken an 'over-simplistic and patronising' attitude to Elizabeth's decision-making?

9 How might Elizabeth's achievement have been assessed by contemporaries if she had died in 1562 or 1569 or 1579 or 1586 or 1589?

10(a) What do you think Elizabeth's objectives were as queen?

(b) How would you assess the achievements and limitations of Queen Elizabeth's reign?

The Tudor Century, A Review

The introduction to this book identified a number of general questions about the Tudor century. These questions have been re-introduced at the end of each section for discussion. This conclusion offers the opportunity to re-consider these overall issues in the light of your work on the reign of Elizabeth and your overall knowledge and understanding of the period. The nature of these questions means that there are no absolute answers but they should provide a focus for sharing and debating your views and opinions about the period as a whole.

1 *Which issues were the most important to people in the sixteenth century?*

Books such as this one tend to spend most of their pages on a small range of issues – politics, diplomacy and war and, perhaps especially for this period, religion. Religion was undoubtedly important but it is worth remembering that the great majority of English people accepted the successive changes of doctrine without becoming involved in rebellions. For them religion was less, perhaps far less important than other issues.

TALKING POINTS

To what extent did the importance of issues vary according to age, sex and rank in society?

Were some issues more important at certain times than others?

In what ways were the people of the sixteenth century similar to or different from people today?

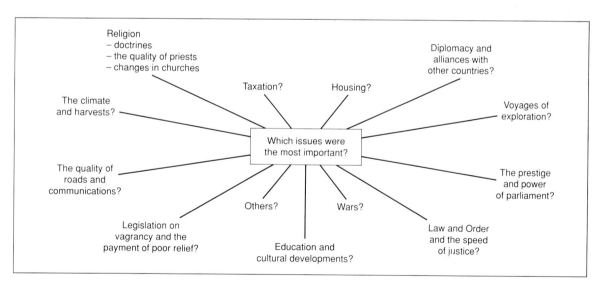

Religion
- doctrines
- the quality of priests
- changes in churches

Diplomacy and alliances with other countries?

Taxation?   Housing?

The climate and harvests?

Voyages of exploration?

Which issues were the most important?

The quality of roads and communications?

The prestige and power of parliament?

Others?   Wars?

Legislation on vagrancy and the payment of poor relief?

Education and cultural developments?

Law and Order and the speed of justice?

2 *Which Tudor monarch had the most impact on the people of England?*

The easy answer here is that it depended when you lived! If you were not born until 1560 then Elizabeth would be the only possible answer – or would it? You would still be living with, amongst others, the after-effects of Henry VII's restoration of political stability and Henry VIII's religious revolution and the inflationary impact of his wars and de-basement of coinage.

TALKING POINT

Did any other individual have more impact than the monarchs?

If you had to be one of
the Tudor monarchs for
ten minutes and had to
use that time to advertise
your achievements or
defend your actions, what
would you say?

Were the deeds of
monarchs more important
to their people than the
quality of the harvests?

TALKING POINTS

Is the division of time into
medieval and modern eras
helpful for (a) our overall
understanding of the past
and (b) helpful for our
understanding of the
Tudor period?

Can any one period be
said to be more important
than any other? Which
periods of British history
do you think were more
or less significant than the
Tudor century?

Would your answer to this
question be improved if
you had also studied a
much broader span of
English history, say from
1066 to 1900?

1 List the different ways in which each monarch affected the lives of the English
people.

2 Divide your lists into beneficial and negative effects.

3 Rank the monarchs in order of significance in terms of their impact on their
people.

3 How important was this period in English history?

The Tudor century has often been seen as the beginning of something
new, of the emergence from the Middle Ages into the modern era. Such
phrases sound grand but it can be difficult to identify any real meaning
behind them. Nowadays historians tend to identify at least as many continuities through from the fifteenth into the sixteenth century as they
identify changes although, as Chapter 8 pointed out, the greatest of
Tudor historians, Sir Geoffrey Elton, has argued that the 1530s was a
truly revolutionary decade.

The table overleaf contains a set of statements, summarising the significance of this period in terms of the themes on the left of the table. Do
you agree with these statements or do you wish to re-write them?

4 Did the Tudor monarchs give the people of England greater security, peace and wealth?

You will already have discussed most of the issues and evidence relating
to this question. These concluding sources are taken from the plays of
Shakespeare, reflecting attitudes and ideas towards the country of England
and its people.

England hath long been mad, and scarred herself;
The brother blindly shed the brother's blood;
The father rashly slaughtered his own son;
The son, compelled, been butcher to the sire;
All that divided Lancaster and York,
United in their dire division.
O now let Richmond and Elizabeth,
The true succeeders of each royal house,
By God's fair ordinance conjoin together,
And let their heirs – God, if his will be so –
Enrich the time to come with smooth-faced peace,
With smiling plenty, and fair prosperous days...

Richard III, Act 5 Scene 8.

The heavens themselves, the planets, and this centre
Observe degree, priority, and place,
Infixture, course, proportion, season, form,
Office and custom, in all line of order.
And therefore is the glorious planet Sol
In noble eminence enthroned and sphered
Amidst the other, whose medicinable eye
Corrects the ill aspects of planets evil

The Power of the Crown	The monarch's power was re-affirmed by Henry VII and extended by Henry VIII as a result of his establishment of the Church of England. The crown also gained in wealth from the monastic lands although many were sold off. Elizabeth maintained the high prestige of the monarchy although there was criticism in her later years and pressures because of the costs of war.
Parliament	The Reformation Parliament and later ecclesiastical legislation led a few parliamentarians to believe that parliament was playing a greater role in government. Parliament did deal with more significant issues but only at the Crown's behest. Royal control over parliament remained almost absolute while monarchs made clear that they valued parliaments.
The Nobility	The nobility lost much of their independent power but gained what they had been seeking in the fifteenth century – secure and, for the most part, just and stable government. Noble rebellions were few, motivated either by exclusion from power (as in the Middle Ages) or religion, Essex's failure in 1601 showed the limits of even a popular nobleman's power in the face of loyalty to the monarch.
Religion	The period was the most important since the coming of Christianity. As a result of the English Reformation there were now greater divisions and tensions within the country. Religion added a powerful element to the motives of potential rebels, some of whom would in the future claim that their consciences demanded that they put religion before monarch. As a result future challenges to the monarchy would be more dangerous.
Britain	Wales had been enveloped within the English administrative system. Scotland and England ended centuries of border warfare as a result of the joint kingdom of James VI and I. However Ireland was the subject of half-hearted involvement, mixing the desire for maximum influence with the demand for minimum expenditure. The plantations of Mary's and Elizabeth's reigns set a pattern for future English involvement while religious changes added another significant element to divisions between the two nations.
Europe and the World	English nationalism, already flourishing in the early fifteenth century in the aftermath of Agincourt, developed apace in the sixteenth century, again as a result of wars and the religious divide between England and the chief European powers. England could not rival the strength of France or Spain but lay secure behind her navy and the 'Protestant wind'. Further afield she had begun to challenge Spain's hegemony in the Americas and established her first colonies but this was far from being the beginning of an inevitable road to empire.
Standards of Living	Despite population growth many people prospered, reflected in the housing resolution at the end of the century. However there were tensions and a second sign of 'modernisation' was the development of unemployment and vagrancy. Governments mixed care for the unfortunate with punishments for the able unemployed, the Poor Laws established in Elizabeth's reign lasting until the nineteenth century.
Education and Culture	The revolution that was printing greatly encouraged enthusiasm for learning. Literacy levels increased, schools were founded, cultural entertainments proliferated. Overall however the majority still could not write or benefit from new educational opportunities. Shakespeare and a group of playwrights and musicians rivalled the standards of other nations. Artistically England remained a backwater.

And posts like the commandment of a king,
Sans check, to good and bad. But when the planets
In evil mixture to disorder wander,
What plagues and what portents, what mutiny?
What raging of the sea, shaking of the earth?
Commotion in the winds, frights, changes, horrors
Divert and crack, rend and deracinate
The unity and married calm of states
Quite from their fixture. O when degree is shaked,
Which is the ladder to all high designs,
The enterprise is sick. How could communities,
Degrees in schools, and brotherhoods in cities,
Peaceful commerce from dividable shores,
The primogenity and due of birth,
Prerogative of age, crowns, sceptres, laurels,
But by degree stand in authentic place?
Take but degree away, untune that string,
And hark what discord follows...

Troilus and Cressida, Act 1 Scene 3.

This royal throne of kings, this sceptred isle,
This earth of majesty, this seat of Mars,
This other Eden, demi paradise,
This fortress built by nature for herself
Against infection and the hand of war,
This happy breed of men, this little world,
This precious stone set in a silver sea,
Which serves it in the office of a wall,
Or as a moat defensive to a house
Against the envy of less happier lands;
This blessed plot, this earth, this realm, this England...

Richard II, Act 2 Scene 1.

TALKING POINT

How did the English regard themselves in 1603 as a result of the events of the previous century?

This England never did, nor never shall,
Lie at the proud foot of a conqueror
But when it first did help to wound itself.
Now these her princes are come home again,
Come the three corners of the world in arms
And we shall shock them. Naught shall make us rue
If England to itself do rest but true.

The last lines of *King John*, Act 5 Scene 7.

POSTSCRIPT
The Tudors – or the Beauforts?

...Queen Catherine's familiarity with the young Edmund Beaufort was already (1425) attracting attention. After the capture of his brothers at Bauge Edmund had returned to England with his mother, and between then and his departure to France in the company of Bishop Beaufort in March 1427 his activities are totally obscure. He is most likely to have lived in his uncle Exeter's household, and thus to have come into frequent contact with the court and the queen mother (Queen Catherine). By 1425 Edmund was 19 and Catherine 24. Her evident desire to marry him threatened to bring the governance of the young king more directly and permanently under the influence of the Beauforts than Gloucester, or perhaps even Bedford, was inclined to contemplate. It was this that prompted ... the passage of an act in the parliament of 1427 forbidding her to marry during her son's minority, and imposing penalties of forfeiture on any spouse...

...It is clear that in the course of 1428–31 (Catherine) had a number of meetings with Cardinal Beaufort, a period in which Edmund was apparently in his household ... Her choice of his name for her first-born may have been mere sentiment, but it must raise the suspicion that the father was Edmund Beaufort and that she contracted her disparaging marriage to Owen Tudor to save her lover the penalities of the statute of 1427. Indeed the chronicler explains her choice of Owen on the grounds that these would fall less harshly on a penniless esquire ... By its nature the evidence for Edmund Tudor's parentage is less than conclusive, but such facts as can be assembled permit the agreeable possibility that Edmund Tudor and Margaret Beaufort were first cousins and that the royal house of Tudor sprang in fact from Beauforts on both sides.

The extracts above are taken from G L Harriss, Cardinal Beaufort: A Study of Lancastrian Ascendancy and Decline, published in 1988. The first extract is taken from page 144, the second from footnote 34 on pages 178–9. Other evidence which suggests the possibility that Edmund Beaufort was the father of Queen Catherine's son Edmund has been omitted here for lack of space.

TALKING POINT

Should this book have been called the Beaufort Century?

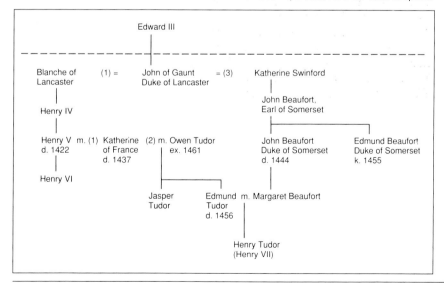

Index